Drama through Performance

WITHDRAWN

Drama through Performance

Mark S. Auburn
The Ohio State University

Katherine H. Burkman
The Ohio State University

Houghton Mifflin Company   Boston
Atlanta   Dallas   Geneva, Illinois
Hopewell, New Jersey   Palo Alto   London

For Sandy and Allan

ACKNOWLEDGMENTS
- *Oedipus the King,* translated by David Grene, copyright 1942 by The University of Chicago Press. Used with permission.
- *The Second Shepherds' Play,* translated by Clarence Griffith Child, copyright 1910, 1930 by Houghton Mifflin Company. Used with permission.
- *A Midsummer-Night's Dream,* edited by William Allan Neilson and Charles Jarvis Hill, copyright 1942, copyright renewed 1970, William Allan Neilson and Charles Jarvis Hill. All rights reserved. Used with permission of Houghton Mifflin Company.
- *Othello,* edited by William Allan Neilson and Charles Jarvis Hill, copyright 1942, copyright renewed 1970, William Allan Neilson and Charles Jarvis Hill. All rights reserved. Used with permission of Houghton Mifflin Company.
- *Phaedra.* Reprinted with the permission of Farrar, Straus & Giroux, Inc. from *Phaedra* by Jean Racine, translated by Robert Lowell. Copyright © 1960, 1961 by Robert Lowell.
- *Love for Love.* Reprinted with the permission of Hill and Wang, a division of Farrar, Straus & Giroux, Inc. from *Love for Love* by William Congreve, edited by M. M. Kelsall, © Ernest Benn Limited 1969.
- *The Wild Duck* from *Ghosts and Three Other Plays* by Henrik Ibsen, translated by Michael Meyer. Copyright © 1962, 1963, 1966 by Michael Meyer. Used with permission of Doubleday & Company, Inc.
- *The Cherry Orchard* by Anton Chekhov, translated by Stark Young. Copyright © 1939, 1941, 1947 and 1960 by Stark Young. Copyright © 1956 by Stark Young. Used with permission of Flora Roberts, Inc.
- *The Glass Menagerie* by Tennessee Williams. Copyright 1945 by Tennessee Williams and Edwina D. Williams and renewed 1973 by Tennessee Williams. Reprinted by permission of Random House, Inc.
- *The Knack* by Ann Jellicoe. Copyright © 1958, 1962 by Ann Jellicoe. Used by permission of Faber and Faber Ltd.
- *A Slight Ache* from *Three Plays* by Harold Pinter. Reprinted by permission of Grove Press, Inc. Copyright © 1961 by Harold Pinter.
- *Cinder, Tell-It: A Dance Drama for Soulful Folks* by Mary Ann Williams. Copyright © Mary Ann Williams, 1976. Used by permission of the author. For all rights apply to Mary Ann Williams, 1937 Clay Court, Columbus, Ohio 43205.

Cover: Excerpt from *The Knack* by Ann Jellicoe. Used by permission of Faber and Faber Ltd.

PN
6112
.D7

Printed in the U.S.A.
Library of Congress Catalog Card Number: 76-19458
ISBN: 0-395-24548-6

Contents

Preface

Drama through Performance is intended as a guide to the use of informal student performance in the study of dramatic literature. The text explores each play in terms of the playwright's conception of its potential performance. This emphasis leads to an inclusive approach that encompasses many traditional ways of analyzing drama. We do not wish to imply that student performance is mandatory in the study of dramatic literature or in the use of this anthology; but we do mean to argue that informal performance may be a substantial aid in understanding dramatic literature.

Our suggestions for specific ways of integrating informal student performance with the analysis of dramatic literature originate from experiments conducted over a number of years with our own students. These students, taking introductory courses in departments of literature, have had majors in such diverse fields as engineering, physics, nursing, and music, as well as English and theater. They have worked toward informal performance with teachers having little or no background in directing and with teachers experienced in the ways of the stage as well as the subtleties of the page. In virtually all cases, we have seen student motivation, understanding, and critical appreciation increase through the use of informal classroom performance.

In the Introduction, we suggest several ways of using *Drama through Performance.* As an anthology, it offers a selection of plays of enduring artistic value and substantial literary interest; as a textbook, it combines a pluralist critical method with a proven pedagogical approach. Whichever method you choose, we hope the sections and apparatus in this text help lead your students to a richer and deeper comprehension of drama as a living art.

Our approach depends heavily on the insights of Francis Fergusson discussed in *The Idea of a Theater,* which first suggested a concept of dramatic action integral with Constantin Stanislavski's theories of acting. To both the theoretician and the practicing director we owe a large critical debt. Arthur E. Adams, Dean of the College of the Humanities at The Ohio State University; John B. Gabel, former Chairman of the Department of English; and Wayne P. Lawson, former Chairman of the Division of Comparative Literature, encouraged our work in a variety of ways. So, too, did the National Endowment for the Humanities, whose grants to support the tour of a Shakespeare program and to teach a workshop on the role of dramatic performance in education were helpful in the early development of our ideas.

For their suggestions we thank Jack E. Bender, University of Michigan; Robert Blaustone, Santa Ana College; Peter Frisch, Harvard University; George W. Hendrickson, Tulane University; Maxine Klein, Boston University; Betty McCormick; and J. D. Shuchter, University of Colorado. Most particularly our gratitude and respect go to Helen Popovich, University of South Florida. To Mildred B. Munday of the Department of English at Ohio State we owe a debt of patience and understanding for her kind advice and consultation. Barbara M. Austin typed the manuscript with precision and intelligence, not once, but twice.

Mark S. Auburn
Katherine H. Burkman

Introduction

A playscript, like a musical score or choreographic notations for a ballet, is fully realized only in performance. And just as musicians who read a score may hear its effect in the mind's ear, or dancers who read notations may imagine the full ballet in the mind's eye, so a well-trained actor who reads a playscript may envision its performance. Like music or ballet, most plays are meant to be performed; hence the fullest understanding of any of these art forms includes an appreciation of both their static and dynamic forms. The goal of this anthology is to help students gain a critical understanding of dramatic literature based on an ability to grasp the performance dynamics implicit in the static playscript. Experience with performance is a means to a full critical and imaginative understanding of dramatic literature.

In *The Idea of a Theater* Francis Fergusson has coined the term *histrionic sensibility* to describe the capacity to read a play as performable. He variously defines the term as "our direct sense of the changing life of the psyche," "a direct mimetic response," or, to summarize his argument, our direct sense of a play's dramatic action. Such responsiveness in a reader can be trained, Fergusson suggests, much as the musician's ear for music or the actor's power of interpretation for the stage can be trained.

While Fergusson does not suggest that all readers should take to the stage to develop their histrionic sensibilities, he does stress the primacy of well-developed histrionic sensibilities in the criticism of dramatic art. The histrionic sensibility as he defines it involves *the direct perception of dramatic action,* and it is around the concept of dramatic action that he envisions the literary critic and the actor joining ranks in their approach to the play as performance. The playwright imitates an action, which the actor in turn identifies and "plays" in performance. One way students can develop their histrionic sensibilities, clarify and intensify their critical perception of drama, and come to understand dramatic action more deeply is to take to the stage so that they can gain some actual experience through informal performance in handling dramatic action.

Informal performance, however, does not mean attempting to turn students into polished actors or undertaking an exhaustive study of such production elements as costumes, scenery, and lighting. Much can be gained through seeing and discussing professional performances or films of plays as one studies them; such experience is always desirable. But the values of the informal performance work that we suggest are somewhat different: Informal performance not only encourages but almost demands an active relationship with the playscript. The desired result is a critical experience with dramatic literature that integrates performance and lecture/discussion. With scenes limited in length so that memorization does not become a burden and simple in conception so that rehearsal time need not be excessive, the informal student performance of scenes may contribute positively toward developing the critical and imaginative reading of plays that is our goal.

Dramatic action

To enter into the performable life of a play as reader, actor, or in this case as reader-actor, one may best work from a direct perception of a play's dramatic action. According to the fourth-century B.C. Greek philosopher, Aristotle, poetry, which includes drama, is an imitation of action. Speaking of tragedy in particular, he suggests that it "is an imitation, not of men, but of an action and of life, and life consists in action, and its end is a mode of action, not a quality" (*Aristotle's Poetics*, p. 62). All elements of a play—plot, character, thought, diction, song, and spectacle—imitate the action.

But what exactly is this dramatic action that the playwright imitates, the reader analyzes, and the reader-actor realizes in performance? Fergusson defines it as a "movement of the spirit." The activity involved is not simply physical, nor is the action the plot. Plot, as the *arrangement of the incidents*, imitates the action as do the words and the characters, but plot is not itself that action. Plot is form, action is matter. Fergusson further states that rather than being the story's events, the action is "the focus or aim of the psychic life from which the events in that situation result." One would be equally incorrect to think of language as the essence of dramatic action, for despite their importance, words imitate the action along with the play's other elements but are not themselves that action. What the playscript charts is more than physical activity and more than the exchange of words. Its movement may best be described in terms of objectives.

The acting theory of the great Russian actor-director-theorist, Constantin Stanislavski (1863–1938), is most helpful in clarifying the concept of dramatic action. Stanislavski sought to have his actors discover their characters' *actions* and then relate them to the play's major *action*, which he called a *superobjective*. Just as Aristotle sees life as an activity, so Stanislavski sees it as a series of objectives. When he instructs his actors to find and create objectives that will arouse their activity and to find the superobjective that incorporates all the actions, he is essentially asking them to identify the *central action* of the play.

Stanislavski found that the best way to indicate the central action or superobjective of a play as well as those lesser actions leading to it was through infinitive phrases. What, for example, is it that Oedipus sets out *to do* at the beginning of the first play in this anthology, Sophocles' *Oedipus the King*? Following the injunction of the oracle, he seeks to relieve the suffering of his plague-torn land by discovering the slayer of its previous king. He sets out, then, *to find the slayer of King Laius* in order *to purge the city* of the plague that is destroying its crops, its livestock, its children, and its human fertility.

A student-actor portraying Oedipus would need to investigate Oedipus's motivation as it changes during the course of the play, assigning verbs to it in order to arrive at a fuller statement of his entire action. At some point in the play Oedipus focuses on finding the answer to the question of his parentage. But how can the student-actor put together into one verbal statement of action his quest for the slayer and his quest for himself?

It would simplify things if we could use the term *motivation* for action and merely study the various motivations of the characters in order to arrive at the central action of the play. One problem here is that despite an awareness that motivation is often partly or wholly unconscious, we tend to think of it as rational. We note, for example, that Oedipus makes a conscious decision to help his people and his city by finding the culprit responsible for the city's pollution. But action and passion, though seemingly opposite, are always combined. Distinctions may be made between plays or even scenes in plays that are more rationally and ethically motivated and those that are more pathetically motivated. Passion or strong emotion also may shake the reasoned motivation of a character and lead to a new perception of what is to be sought or attained. Then, too, the seemingly opposite motivations of numerous characters should all feed into a verbal statement of the play's superobjective or central action, just as all the other elements of the play—plot, thought, diction, song, and spectacle—must be considered. Only then will one arrive at the unifying movement that is at the center.

Performance as an inclusive approach

Although this anthology focuses on the study and enactment of plays as imitations of action, it does not exclude other methods of studying dramatic art; indeed, the performance approach incorporates many of them. We have seen that the several elements of a play imitate the action, and all these elements will receive analysis. Often a close study of thought, as expressed through imagery, offers the best key to understanding the action. Analysis of the rhythms and imagery of a Shakespeare play provides an illuminating approach to its action and meaning. The spectacle, whether it be the detailed realism of an Ibsen setting or the deus ex machina (god from a machine) sometimes employed in the Greek outdoor amphitheater, also becomes a significant concern for the reader-actor in analyzing the action at the center of the play.

Then, too, since all plays are partly a product and a reflection of the particular culture in which their authors live, and since the author creates a script with the theatrical practices and possibilities of the age in mind, it follows that the imitation of action may be most fully grasped in its historical-cultural context. This anthology includes plays from most of the important periods of Western drama and from several countries so that the student can see how the imitation of action that is drama has varied through the ages. The introduction to each play deals with the physical theater of the time and country, the dramatic conventions employed (for example, the Elizabethan soliloquy, the Greek chorus, the "modern" theater's box setting), and the nature of the relationship between actor and audience.

When imitating an action, the playwright is imitating life or some aspect of life as perceived in a particular place and time. All of the time-bound local features from which playwrights consciously or unconsciously form their understanding of life influence their re-creation, their imitation of life. These features appear in a play as its particular, distinctive, characteristic form or mode of expression and contribute to its style. They are the elements that most obviously set apart a Greek tragedy from a French neoclassical imitation of ancient Greek drama or that more subtly differentiate Ibsen's naturalism from Chekhov's. In order to arrive at a play's style, then, one must give attention to form as well as content, drawing not only on analysis of how the various elements of a playscript (plot, character, thought, diction, music, spectacle) imitate an action but also on the stage conventions of a particular period: the costumes, scenic elements, and other local and period concerns that are implicit in the script. As students begin to prepare scenes from the play under consideration, some knowledge of the period and its stage conventions will necessarily accompany analysis of the play's action, always *remembering the adaptations necessary to the informal atmosphere of the classroom.* If one gives attention to period and convention as well as to speech rhythms and actions, the inevitable discovery will be that content and form are inseparable; the realization of style is actually the realization of drama as performance, the totality of the play.

The introductory material on each play will not only give details about period and convention but also will help in making the important distinctions among such generic types as tragedy, comedy, farce, and melodrama. There is no distinctive tragic as opposed to comic or melodramatic method of acting; once again, style emerges from the demands of the particular playscript itself. An understanding of generic distinctions, however, will help to keep the performance of scenes from *Oedipus* tragic or those from *Love for Love* comic.

Acting techniques

No matter what the genre, the production style, or the acting style, certain other Stanislavski acting techniques—concentration, relaxation, playing the *given circumstances,* and the magic IF—may be of fundamental help to the reader-actor. These techniques are closely related to one another and to Stanislavski's key concept of playing the action.

CONCENTRATION

Stanislavski suggests that when an actor maps out a role, it is essential that he or she grasp the superobjective, which not only includes the minor objectives and actions of a play but also enables the actor to arrive at "the thing that inspired him [the playwright] to write, and which inspires an actor to act." But concentration must focus on the actions that lead to the objective, not on the superobjective or on the result of the action. Oedipus does not act in a general way throughout "to save the city"; the actor playing Oedipus must concentrate during a specific scene—say, Oedipus's confrontation with Teiresias—on the specific demands of the moment. He might try to persuade Teiresias to help identify the culprit at one moment, but when Teiresias accuses Oedipus, he might attempt to expose Teiresias as the culprit who is conspiring for gain to misidentify Oedipus as the murderer.

RELAXATION

Concentration on a very specific goal or action is related in turn to relaxation. Stanislavski would guide the actor to avoid ham acting or clichéd acting, by asking that the performer not only play an action, but also concentrate on a very specific one. He notes that such concentration will effect the needed relaxation that helps the actor play well on stage. In *An Actor*

Prepares, Stanislavski depicts the student-actor, Kostya, studying the movement of a cat in order to master the animal's marvelous ability to relax. What he observes, in the motions both of the cat and of a visiting friend who is more relaxed swatting a fly than doing relaxation exercises, is that movement with a purpose under the unconscious guidance of nature is the best means to relaxation. Thus relaxation is best achieved by understanding the purpose of the action at every given moment and concentrating on it. Kostya's preconceived notions about acting crumble before the need to find the simple action, concentration on which will help him to relax and to arrive at the desired result.

THE MAGIC IF AND THE GIVEN CIRCUMSTANCES

If the actors are to avoid false effects by playing the action rather than the result, they may also avoid false acting by coaxing the imagination through examining the given circumstances of the play and conjecturing what it would be like IF they were in them. The given circumstances are the situation of the play, the place in which the characters live, their relationships with others, their social and economic status, the pressures that are put on them, and so forth. Actors should avoid forcing emotions by asking themselves the question: "IF I lived under these circumstances, how would I feel and behave?" Such questions will not only help student-actors arrive at a believable performance but also will enable them to get closer to the meanings of the play. The playwright, says Aristotle, is less concerned with writing about the facts of life than in communicating what is possible according to the laws of the probable or the necessary. The playwright's art is more philosophical than historical; it cuts through the details of life to arrive at the universal truths of existence. When students portray what *could* happen on stage rather than what *did* happen in life, they are entering into the spirit of creation originally undertaken by the playwright.

For instance, in *Oedipus the King,* a student involved in playing a part in the Chorus might ask, "What IF I were very old and had lost my grandchild in the plague besetting the city? What IF I felt the beginning of the illness coming on me? What is that illness like? Where do I feel it?" The more detail students can assemble from the given circumstances of the play and the more they can work their own feelings into those circumstances by imagining how they would feel if those circumstances were their own, the more convincing the performance will be, and the more the act of performance will clarify the essential nature of the tragedy they have read.

The techniques used in preparing scenes and the scene work itself in this anthology should provide avenues to a better understanding of dramatic literature. In many classes there will not be time for each student to help prepare one scene or for at least one scene to be prepared for each play. Some classes may require every student to perform at least once; others may use only volunteers. Some classes will attempt only one or two scenes during the term; others may try to prepare as many as two scenes for each play; and some classes may use little or no performance. But whatever the use of informal performance, whatever the road taken, the overlapping theories of Aristotle and Stanislavski, as first perceived by Francis Fergusson, provide a guide both for good reading and for good performance. The imaginative reader and the thoughtful reader-performer have the best chance of understanding the playwright's intentions.

According to Aristotle, the playwright should also be a performer, imagining the scene of action and even gesturing while creating. What Aristotle is suggesting for the playwright is that exercise of the histrionic sensibility that the reader in turn must exercise when studying the playwright's art. Students who augment the exercise of their histrionic sensibilities through the experience of informal performance may meet the playwright's imitation through their own imitations and so approach a rich understanding of the play.

Sophocles
Oedipus the King

OEDIPUS
> I solved the riddle by my wit alone.
>> (l. 397)

So boasts King Oedipus to the prophet Teiresias in Sophocles' *Oedipus the King*. Oedipus refers to the riddle of the Sphinx, which he had solved in the past. The answer to the riddle, "What is it that walks first on four legs, then on two legs, then on three legs?" is *man*. By answering the riddle, Oedipus saved the city of Thebes, became its king, and married Jocasta, the widowed queen of the former king.

As the play opens, Thebes is again suffering from a plague and Oedipus is asked to become its savior once more. He does so at the cost of his kingship, his wife, his home, and his eyes. According to Aristotle, this dramatic reversal of fortune is one of the essential ingredients of tragedy. Because *Oedipus the King* was Aristotle's favorite play, he used it most often in the *Poetics* to define and clarify the nature of Greek tragedy.

The tragic hero, wrote Aristotle, must be "highly renowned and prosperous" and must suffer a fall from great heights, partly because of circumstances and partly because of a flaw in character or an error of judgment. The best tragic plots employ such reversals and also contain recognitions in which the hero perceives the nature of the error and attains a new level of insight. Aristotle explains the strange pleasure we feel when viewing tragedy as *catharsis*, the purging of emotions of pity and fear that are aroused by the action. Subsequent critics suggest that such a purging of emotions liberates us from our private griefs and objectifies experience, thus helping to unify us with the community's humanity. We must inevitably feel pleasure, too, at the vision of a person spiritually undefeated in the face of the most dire events life can hold. Oedipus falls from the heights, but rises through knowledge of himself and the universe to a new sense of inner strength.

This falling and rising action is the basic pattern of Greek tragedy. The answer to the riddle is *man*, but man is not god; people are limited; they do not fully comprehend the universal order that the Greeks believed existed. And they are forced to act without full knowledge of themselves and of the circumstances that surround them. When Oedipus thinks he is most wise, the solver of the riddle, he is most blind, and the blind prophet Teiresias taunts him for his lack of insight. Yet Oedipus does achieve, at the cost of his own eyes, the kind of godlike insight that Teiresias possesses.

Fergusson suggests that the Greek theater "focused, at the center of the life of the community, the complementary insights of the whole culture" (*The Idea of a Theater*, p. 2). The Greeks were a proud people who defeated the Persian armies against amazing odds. This was accomplished, according to the historian Herodotus, because the "barbarians" were forced into battle while the Greeks fought freely for what they valued. They were a people, nevertheless, who believed in order and moderation. The gods were jealous, ready to punish the sin of *hubris*, or pride. The passions must be harmonized with reason, and after violent outbreaks, the world tends to restore itself to balance (*dike*).

Sophocles, whose life spanned the century of his city's greatest achievements (c. 496–406 B.C.), was nourished on such beliefs but did not merely reflect them in his play. The question of Oedipus's accountability for what might have been preordained is left unanswered. His pride or temper may be partly responsible for the events that led to his fall, but Oedipus has hardly been humbled in *Oedipus at Colonnus,* a play written by Sophocles in his old age that depicts the aged Oedipus as still a man of passionate outbursts though now strangely blessed and godlike in his death.

What *Oedipus the King* does reflect most fully of fifth-century Athens, however, is the spirit of inquiry, which was the life of its people. Classical Greece saw not only the birth of many of the arts and sciences but also their unparalleled development—a development that has influenced the whole fabric of Western civilization. The people of Athens gathered at religious festivals to see the dramatic poet of their triumphant years, Aeschylus (525–456 B.C.), who wrote of the Zeus-defying Prometheus giving the arts of civilization to human beings in *Prometheus Bound,* or of the integration of justice with mercy in his great trilogy, *The Oresteia.* They came to hear the understandably less popular dramatist, Euripides (c. 480–c. 406 B.C.), question them and their gods as they grew proud and imperial and hastened to their own doom at the hands of Sparta. And as Oedipus's search for the killer of Laius became the search for his own identity, this hero of the most popular of the three tragic dramatists must have held that audience, even as today Sophocles can hold audiences who still hunger for the kind of truth that brought Athens to its greatness.

Unlike today's audiences, however, the Athenians of Sophocles' time came to see his plays with what Fergusson has called a "ritual expectancy." Theater going in fifth-century Athens was a vital part of the life of the community and of its religious experience. Whether or not Greek tragedy evolved, as Aristotle claims, out of the *dithyramb,* a hymn or narrative song honoring the god Dionysus, it remained associated with his worship. Drama was first presented at one of the four festivals honoring the god of wine and fertility. By the beginning of the fifth century three playwrights were chosen to compete for first prize at the March festival, the City Dionysia, with a trilogy of tragedies often connected in subject matter and accompanied by a satyr play that burlesqued mythology, sometimes the very myths treated in the tragedies.

The City Dionysia celebrated the coming to Athens of Dionysus, a vegetation god associated in his own birth, death, and resurrection with the cycle of the seasons. His worship as a fertility god was to ensure the return of spring and the productivity of the land and its people. The only extant play that deals with Dionysus is Euripides' *Bacchae,* but Oedipus may himself be considered a scapegoat figure whose sacrifice will ensure the well-being of the city.

The festival, however, was considered a civic as well as a religious occasion. The outdoor theater could not hold the entire population but was open to all of Athens and the entire Greek world. Tickets at a minimal price were available for men, women, children, and slaves, and a fund was established to provide tickets for the poor. An *archon*, or city magistrate, was in charge and appointed wealthy citizens to bear the expense of chorus and production while the state paid the protagonists.

The physical character of the fifth-century theater is a matter of conjecture based on scanty remains of theaters, most of which were built in later periods. Essential elements seem to have been rows of temporary or permanent seats extending up a hillside and partly surrounding a circular acting area or orchestra with an altar in the center. In Athens's Theater of Dionysus, situated on the slope of the Acropolis, about 14,000 people were seated in an open, semicircular auditorium that curved around the orchestra, which was sixty-five feet in diameter. Behind the orchestra was a scene house (*skene*) for dressing, again possibly a temporary structure also serving as a façade with doors for entrances and exits. A raised stage for the actors is conjectured by some scholars, but a more certain feature of the theater was the set of entrances on each side of the orchestra called the *parodoi* through which both the chorus (and possibly the actors) and the audience entered. This combined entrance way clearly indicates the dynamic actor/audience relationship that is part of Sophocles' theatrical performance. Since the chorus usually represented a group of townspeople commenting on the action and interpreting it from the audience's point of view, it was most fitting that they should enter with that audience. The action was somewhat stylized, with three male actors taking all the main parts, dressed in tunics, cloaks, and masks, and with the chorus chanting or singing and moving to the music of a flute. And the audience was deeply involved in both the communal and religious nature of the proceedings.

Oedipus the King

Translated by David Grene

Characters
OEDIPUS, *king of Thebes*
JOCASTA, *his wife*
CREON, *his brother-in-law*
TEIRESIAS, *an old blind prophet*
A PRIEST
FIRST MESSENGER
SECOND MESSENGER
A HERDSMAN
A CHORUS OF OLD MEN OF THEBES

Scene: In front of the palace of Oedipus at Thebes. To the right of the stage near the altar stands the Priest with a crowd of children. Oedipus emerges from the central door.

OEDIPUS

Children, young sons and daughters of old Cadmus,
why do you sit here with your suppliant crowns?
The town is heavy with a mingled burden
of sounds and smells, of groans and hymns and incense;   5
I did not think it fit that I should hear
of this from messengers but came myself,—
I Oedipus whom all men call the Great.

He turns to the Priest.

You're old and they are young; come, speak for them.
What do you fear or want, that you sit here   10
suppliant? Indeed I'm willing to give all
that you may need; I would be very hard
should I not pity suppliants like these.

PRIEST

O ruler of my country, Oedipus,
you see our company around the altar;   15
you see our ages; some of us, like these,
who cannot yet fly far, and some of us
heavy with age; these children are the chosen
among the young, and I the priest of Zeus.
Within the market place sit others crowned   20
with suppliant garlands, at the double shrine
of Pallas and the temple where Ismenus
gives oracles by fire. King, you yourself
have seen our city reeling like a wreck
already; it can scarcely lift its prow
out of the depths, out of the bloody surf.
A blight is on the fruitful plants of the earth,   25
a blight is on the cattle in the fields,

a blight is on our women that no children
are born to them; a God that carries fire,
a deadly pestilence, is on our town,
strikes us and spares not, and the house of Cadmus
is emptied of its people while black Death
grows rich in groaning and in lamentation.   30
We have not come as suppliants to this altar
because we thought of you as of a God,
but rather judging you the first of men
in all the chances of this life and when
we mortals have to do with more than man.
You came and by your coming saved our city,   35
freed us from tribute which we paid of old
to the Sphinx, cruel singer. This you did
in virtue of no knowledge we could give you,
in virtue of no teaching; it was God
that aided you, men say, and you are held
with God's assistance to have saved our lives.
Now Oedipus, Greatest in all men's eyes,   40
here falling at your feet we all entreat you,
find us some strength for rescue.
Perhaps you'll hear a wise word from some God,
perhaps you will learn something from a man
(for I have seen that for the skilled of practice
the outcome of their counsels live the most).   45
Noblest of men, go, and raise up our city,
go,—and give heed. For now this land of ours
calls you its savior since you saved it once.
So, let us never speak about your reign
as of a time when first our feet were set
secure on high, but later fell to ruin.   50
Raise up our city, save it and raise it up.
Once you have brought us luck with happy omen;
be no less now in fortune.
If you will rule this land, as now you rule it,
better to rule it full of men than empty.   55
For neither tower nor ship is anything
when empty, and none live in it together.

OEDIPUS

I pity you, children. You have come full of longing,
but I have known the story before you told it
only too well. I know you are all sick,
yet there is not one of you, sick though you are,   60
that is as sick as I myself.
Your several sorrows each have single scope
and touch but one of you. My spirit groans
for city and myself and you at once.
You have not roused me like a man from sleep;   65
know that I have given many tears to this,
gone many ways wandering in thought,
but as I thought I found only one remedy
and that I took. I sent Menoeceus' son
Creon, Jocasta's brother, to Apollo,   70

to his Pythian temple,
that he might learn there by what act or word
I could save this city. As I count the days,
it vexes me what ails him; he is gone
far longer than he needed for the journey.   75
But when he comes, then, may I prove a villain,
if I shall not do all the God commands.

PRIEST

Thanks for your gracious words. Your servants here
signal that Creon is this moment coming.

OEDIPUS

His face is bright. O holy Lord Apollo,   80
grant that his news too may be bright for us
and bring us safety.

PRIEST

It is happy news,
I think, for else his head would not be crowned
with sprigs of fruitful laurel.

OEDIPUS

                              We will know soon,
he's within hail. Lord Creon, my good brother,   85
what is the word you bring us from the God?
        Creon enters.

CREON

A good word,—for things hard to bear themselves
if in the final issue all is well
I count complete good fortune.

OEDIPUS

                              What do you mean?
What you have said so far
leaves me uncertain whether to trust or fear.   90

CREON

If you will hear my news before these others
I am ready to speak, or else to go within.

OEDIPUS

Speak it to all;
the grief I bear, I bear it more for these
than for my own heart.

CREON

                              I will tell you, then,   95
what I heard from the God.
King Phoebus in plain words commanded us
to drive out a pollution from our land,
pollution grown ingrained within the land;
drive it out, said the God, not cherish it,
till it's past cure.

OEDIPUS

                    What is the rite
of purification? How shall it be done?

CREON

By banishing a man, or expiation   100
of blood by blood, since it is murder guilt
which holds our city in this destroying storm.

OEDIPUS

Who is this man whose fate the God pronounces?

CREON

My Lord, before you piloted the state
we had a king called Laius.

OEDIPUS

I know of him by hearsay. I have not seen him.   105

CREON

The God commanded clearly: let some one
punish with force this dead man's murderers.

OEDIPUS

Where are they in the world? Where would a trace
of this old crime be found? It would be hard
to guess where.

CREON

                              The clue is in this land;   110
that which is sought is found;
the unheeded thing escapes:
so said the God.

OEDIPUS

                              Was it at home,
or in the country that death came upon him,
or in another country travelling?

CREON

He went, he said himself, upon an embassy,
but never returned when he set out from home.   115

OEDIPUS

Was there no messenger, no fellow traveller
who knew what happened? Such a one might tell
something of use.

CREON

They were all killed save one. He fled in terror
and he could tell us nothing in clear terms
of what he knew, nothing, but one thing only.

OEDIPUS

What was it?   120
If we could even find a slim beginning
in which to hope, we might discover much.

CREON

This man said that the robbers they encountered
were many and the hands that did the murder
were many; it was no man's single power.

OEDIPUS

How could a robber dare a deed like this
were he not helped with money from the city,
money and treachery?   125

CREON

                              That indeed was thought.
But Laius was dead and in our trouble
there was none to help.

OEDIPUS

What trouble was so great to hinder you
inquiring out the murder of your king?

CREON

> The riddling Sphinx induced us to neglect 130
> mysterious crimes and rather seek solution
> of troubles at our feet.

OEDIPUS

> I will bring this to light again. King Phoebus
> fittingly took this care about the dead,
> and you too fittingly.
> And justly you will see in me an ally, 135
> a champion of my country and the God.
> For when I drive pollution from the land
> I will not serve a distant friend's advantage,
> but act in my own interest. Whoever
> he was that killed the king may readily
> wish to dispatch me with his murderous hand; 140
> so helping the dead king I help myself.
>
> Come, children, take your suppliant boughs and go;
> up from the altars now. Call the assembly
> and let it meet upon the understanding
> that I'll do everything. God will decide 145
> whether we prosper or remain in sorrow.

PRIEST

> Rise, children—it was this we came to seek,
> which of himself the king now offers us.
> May Phoebus who gave us the oracle
> come to our rescue and stay the plague. 150
> *Exeunt all but the Chorus.*

CHORUS

> STROPHE
>
> What is the sweet spoken word of God from the shrine of Pytho rich
> in gold
> that has come to glorious Thebes?
> I am stretched on the rack of doubt, and terror and trembling hold
> my heart, O Delian Healer, and I worship full of fears
> for what doom you will bring to pass, new or renewed in the revolv- 155
> ing years.
> Speak to me, immortal voice,
> child of golden Hope.
>
> ANTISTROPHE
>
> First I call on you, Athene, deathless daughter of Zeus,
> and Artemis, Earth Upholder, 160
> who sits in the midst of the market place in the throne which men
> call Fame,
> and Phoebus, the Far Shooter, three averters of Fate,
> come to us now, if ever before, when ruin rushed upon the state, 165
> you drove destruction's flame away
> out of our land.
>
> STROPHE
>
> Our sorrows defy number;
> all the ship's timbers are rotten;
> taking of thought is no spear for the driving away of the plague. 170
> There are no growing children in this famous land;
> there are no women bearing the pangs of childbirth.

You may see them one with another, like birds swift on the wing,   175
quicker than fire unmastered,
speeding away to the coast of the Western God.
    ANTISTROPHE
In the unnumbered deaths
of its people the city dies;
those children that are born lie dead on the naked earth
unpitied, spreading contagion of death; and grey haired mothers
    and wives
everywhere stand at the altar's edge, suppliant, moaning;   182–185
the hymn to the healing God rings out but with it the wailing voices
    are blended.
From these our sufferings grant us, O golden Daughter of Zeus,
glad-faced deliverance.
    STROPHE
There is no clash of brazen shields but our fight is with the War
    God,
a War God ringed with the cries of men, a savage God who burns   191
    us;
grant that he turn in racing course backwards out of our country's
    bounds
to the great palace of Amphitrite or where the waves of the Thra-   195
    cian sea
deny the stranger safe anchorage.
Whatsoever escapes the night
at last the light of day revisits;
so smite the War God, Father Zeus,
beneath your thunderbolt,
for you are the Lord of the lightning, the lightning that carries fire.   200
    ANTISTROPHE
And your unconquered arrow shafts, winged by the golden corded
    bow,
Lycean King, I beg to be at our side for help;   205
and the gleaming torches of Artemis with which she scours the
    Lycean hills,
and I call on the God with the turban of gold, who gave his name to
    this country of ours,   210
the Bacchic God with the wind flushed face,
Evian One, who travel
with the Maenad company,
combat the God that burns us
with your torch of pine;
for the God that is our enemy is a God unhonoured among the   215
    Gods.
    Oedipus returns.

OEDIPUS
For what you ask me—if you will hear my words,
and hearing welcome them and fight the plague,
you will find strength and lightening of your load.

Hark to me; what I say to you, I say
as one that is a stranger to the story
as stranger to the deed. For I would not   220
be far upon the track if I alone

were tracing it without a clue. But now,
since after all was finished, I became
a citizen among you, citizens—
now I proclaim to all the men of Thebes:
who so among you knows the murderer   225
by whose hand Laius, son of Labdacus,
died—I command him to tell everything
to me,—yes, though he fears himself to take the blame
on his own head; for bitter punishment
he shall have none, but leave this land unharmed.
Or if he knows the murderer, another,   230
a foreigner, still let him speak the truth.
For I will pay him and be grateful, too.
But if you shall keep silence, if perhaps
some one of you, to shield a guilty friend,
or for his own sake shall reject my words—
hear what I shall do then: 235
I forbid that man, whoever he be, my land,
my land where I hold sovereignty and throne;
and I forbid any to welcome him
or cry him greeting or make him a sharer   240
in sacrifice or offering to the Gods,
or give him water for his hands to wash.
I command all to drive him from their homes,
since he is our pollution, as the oracle
of Pytho's God proclaimed him now to me.
So I stand forth a champion of the God
and of the man who died.   245
Upon the murderer I invoke this curse—
whether he is one man and all unknown,
or one of many—may he wear out his life
in misery to miserable doom!
If with my knowledge he lives at my hearth   250
I pray that I myself may feel my curse.
On you I lay my charge to fulfill all this
for me, for the God, and for this land of ours
destroyed and blighted, by the God forsaken.

Even were this no matter of God's ordinance   255
it would not fit you so to leave it lie,
unpurified, since a good man is dead
and one that was king. Search it out.
Since I am now the holder of his office,
and have his bed and wife that once was his,   260
and had his line not been unfortunate
we would have common children—(fortune leaped
upon his head)—because of all these things,
I fight in his defence as for my father,
and I shall try all means to take the murderer   265
of Laius the son of Labdacus
the son of Polydorus and before him
of Cadmus and before him of Agenor.
Those who do not obey me, may the Gods

grant no crops springing from the ground they plough 270
nor children to their women! May a fate
like this, or one still worse than this consume them!
For you whom these words please, the other Thebans,
may Justice as your ally and all the Gods
live with you, blessing you now and for ever! 275
CHORUS
  As you have held me to my oath, I speak:
  I neither killed the king nor can declare
  the killer; but since Phoebus set the quest
  it is his part to tell who the man is.
OEDIPUS
  Right; but to put compulsion on the Gods 280
  against their will—no man can do that.
CHORUS
  May I then say what I think second best?
OEDIPUS
  If there's a third best, too, spare not to tell it.
CHORUS
  I know that what the Lord Teiresias
  sees, is most often what the Lord Apollo 285
  sees. If you should inquire of this from him
  you might find out most clearly.
OEDIPUS
  Even in this my actions have not been sluggard.
  On Creon's word I have sent two messengers
  and why the prophet is not here already
  I have been wondering.
CHORUS
                             His skill apart 290
  there is besides only an old faint story.
OEDIPUS
  What is it?
  I look at every story.
CHORUS
                   It was said
  that he was killed by certain wayfarers.
OEDIPUS
  I heard that, too, but no one saw the killer.
CHORUS
  Yet if he has a share of fear at all,
  his courage will not stand firm, hearing your curse. 295
OEDIPUS
  The man who in the doing did not shrink
  will fear no word.
CHORUS
                   Here comes his prosecutor:
  led by your men the godly prophet comes
  in whom alone of mankind truth is native.
      Enter Teiresias, led by a little boy.
OEDIPUS
  Teiresias, you are versed in everything, 300
  things teachable and things not to be spoken,

things of the heaven and earth-creeping things.
You have no eyes but in your mind you know
with what a plague our city is afflicted.
My lord, in you alone we find a champion,
in you alone one that can rescue us.
Perhaps you have not heard the messengers,   305
but Phoebus sent in answer to our sending
an oracle declaring that our freedom
from this disease would only come when we
should learn the names of those who killed King Laius,
and kill them or expel from our country.
Do not begrudge us oracles from birds,   310
or any other way of prophecy
within your skill; save yourself and the city,
save me; redeem the debt of our pollution
that lies on us because of this dead man.
We are in your hands; pains are most nobly taken
to help another when you have means and power.   315

TEIRESIAS
Alas, how terrible is wisdom when
it brings no profit to the man that's wise!
This I knew well, but had forgotten it,
else I would not have come here.

OEDIPUS
                                        What is this?
How sad you are now you have come!

TEIRESIAS
                                        Let me
go home. It will be easiest for us both   320
to bear our several destinies to the end
if you will follow my advice.

OEDIPUS
                                        You'd rob us
of this your gift of prophecy? You talk
as one who had no care for law nor love
for Thebes who reared you.

TEIRESIAS
Yes, but I see that even your own words
miss the mark; therefore I must fear for mine.   325

OEDIPUS
For God's sake if you know of anything,
do not turn from us; all of us kneel to you,
all of us here, your suppliants.

TEIRESIAS
All of you here know nothing. I will not
bring to the light of day my troubles, mine—
rather than call them yours.

OEDIPUS
                                        What do you mean?
You know of something but refuse to speak.   330
Would you betray us and destroy the city?

TEIRESIAS
I will not bring this pain upon us both,
neither on you nor on myself. Why is it

you question me and waste your labour? I
will tell you nothing.
OEDIPUS
You would provoke a stone! Tell us, you villain,   335
tell us, and do not stand there quietly
unmoved and balking at the issue.
TEIRESIAS
You blame my temper but you do not see
your own that lives within you; it is me
you chide.
OEDIPUS
Who would not feel his temper rise
at words like these with which you shame our city?   340
TEIRESIAS
Of themselves things will come, although I hide them
and breathe no word of them.
OEDIPUS
                                      Since they will come
tell them to me.
TEIRESIAS
                         I will say nothing further.
Against this answer let your temper rage
as wildly as you will.
OEDIPUS   ·
                                      Indeed I am   345
so angry I shall not hold back a jot
of what I think. For I would have you know
I think you were complotter of the deed
and doer of the deed save in so far
as for the actual killing. Had you had eyes
I would have said alone you murdered him.
TEIRESIAS
Yes? Then I warn you faithfully to keep   350
the letter of your proclamation and
from this day forth to speak no word of greeting
to these nor me; you are the land's pollution.
OEDIPUS
How shamelessly you started up this taunt!
How do you think you will escape?   355
TEIRESIAS
                                      I have.
I have escaped; the truth is what I cherish
and that's my strength.
OEDIPUS
                         And who has taught you truth?
Not your profession surely!
TEIRESIAS
                                      You have taught me,
for you have made me speak against my will.
OEDIPUS
Speak what? Tell me again that I may learn it better.
TEIRESIAS
Did you not understand before or would you
provoke me into speaking?   360

OEDIPUS

I did not grasp it,
not so to call it known. Say it again.

TEIRESIAS

I say you are the murderer of the king
whose murderer you seek.

OEDIPUS

Not twice you shall
say calumnies like this and stay unpunished.

TEIRESIAS

Shall I say more to tempt your anger more?

OEDIPUS

As much as you desire; it will be said   365
in vain.

TEIRESIAS

I say that with those you love best
you live in foulest shame unconsciously
and do not see where you are in calamity.

OEDIPUS

Do you imagine you can always talk
like this, and live to laugh at it hereafter?

TEIRESIAS

Yes, if the truth has anything of strength.

OEDIPUS

It has, but not for you; it has no strength   370
for you because you are blind in mind and ears
as well as in your eyes.

TEIRESIAS

You are a poor wretch
to taunt me with the very insults which
every one soon will heap upon yourself.

OEDIPUS

Your life is one long night so that you cannot
hurt me or any other who sees the light.   375

TEIRESIAS

It is not fate that I should be your ruin,
Apollo is enough; it is his care
to work this out.

OEDIPUS

Was this your own design
or Creon's?

TEIRESIAS

Creon is no hurt to you,
but you are to yourself.

OEDIPUS

Wealth, sovereignty and skill outmatching skill   380
for the contrivance of an envied life!
Great store of jealousy fill your treasury chests,
if my friend Creon, friend from the first and loyal,   385
thus secretly attacks me, secretly
desires to drive me out and secretly
suborns this juggling, trick devising quack,
this wily beggar who has only eyes

for his own gains, but blindness in his skill.
For, tell me, where have you seen clear, Teiresias,   390
with your prophetic eyes? When the dark singer,
the sphinx, was in your country, did you speak
word of deliverance to its citizens?
And yet the riddle's answer was not the province
of a chance comer. It was a prophet's task
and plainly you had no such gift of prophecy   395
from birds nor otherwise from any God
to glean a word of knowledge. But I came,
Oedipus, who knew nothing, and I stopped her.
I solved the riddle by my wit alone.
Mine was no knowledge got from birds. And now
you would expel me,
because you think that you will find a place   400
by Creon's throne. I think you will be sorry,
both you and your accomplice, for your plot
to drive me out. And did I not regard you
as an old man, some suffering would have taught you
that what was in your heart was treason.

CHORUS
We look at this man's words and yours, my king,
and we find both have spoken them in anger.   405
We need no angry words but only thought
how we may best hit the God's meaning for us.

TEIRESIAS
If you are king, at least I have the right
no less to speak in my defence against you.
Of that much I am master. I am no slave   410
of yours, but Loxias', and so I shall not
enroll myself with Creon for my patron.
Since you have taunted me with being blind,
here is my word for you.
You have your eyes but see not where you are
in sin, nor where you live, nor whom you live with.
Do you know who your parents are? Unknowing   415
you are an enemy to kith and kin
in death, beneath the earth, and in this life.
A deadly footed, double striking curse,
from father and mother both, shall drive you forth
out of this land, with darkness on your eyes,
that now have such straight vision. Shall there be
a place will not be harbour to your cries,   420
a corner of Cithaeron will not ring
in echo to your cries, soon, soon,—
when you shall learn the secret of your marriage,
which steered you to a haven in this house,—
haven no haven, after lucky voyage?
And of the multitude of other evils
establishing a grim equality
between you and your children, you know nothing.   425
So, muddy with contempt my words and Creon's!
Misery shall grind no man as it will you.

OEDIPUS

Is it endurable that I should hear
such words from him? Go and a curse go with you!   430
Quick, home with you! Out of my house at once!

TEIRESIAS

I would not have come either had you not called me.

OEDIPUS

I did not know then you would talk like a fool—
or it would have been long before I called you.

TEIRESIAS

I am a fool then, as it seems to you—   435
but to the parents who have bred you, wise.

OEDIPUS

What parents? Stop! Who are they of all the world?

TEIRESIAS

This day will show your birth and will destroy you.

OEDIPUS

How needlessly your riddles darken everything.

TEIRESIAS

But it's in riddle answering you are strongest.   440

OEDIPUS

Yes. Taunt me where you will find me great.

TEIRESIAS

It is this very luck that has destroyed you.

OEDIPUS

I do not care, if it has saved this city.

TEIRESIAS

Well, I will go. Come, boy, lead me away.

OEDIPUS

Yes, lead him off. So long as you are here,   445
you'll be a stumbling block and a vexation;
once gone, you will not trouble me again.

TEIRESIAS

I have said
what I came here to say not fearing your
countenance: there is no way you can hurt me.
I tell you, king, this man, this murderer
(whom you have long declared you are in search of,
indicting him in threatening proclamation   450
as murderer of Laius)—he is here.
In name he is a stranger among citizens
but soon he will be shown to be a citizen
true native Theban, and he'll have no joy
of the discovery: blindness for sight
and beggary for riches his exchange,   455
he shall go journeying to a foreign country
tapping his way before him with a stick.
He shall be proved father and brother both
to his own children in his house; to her
that gave him birth, a son and husband both;
a fellow sower in his father's bed
with that same father that he murdered.
Go within, reckon that out, and if you find me   460
mistaken, say I have no skill in prophecy.

Exeunt separately Teiresias and Oedipus.

CHORUS

STROPHE

Who is the man proclaimed
by Delphi's prophetic rock
as the bloody handed murderer,   465
the doer of deeds that none dare name?
Now is the time for him to run
with a stronger foot
than Pegasus
for the child of Zeus leaps in arms upon him   470
with fire and the lightning bolt,
and terribly close on his heels
are the Fates that never miss.

ANTISTROPHE

Lately from snowy Parnassus
clearly the voice flashed forth,
bidding each Theban track him down,   475
the unknown murderer.
In the savage forests he lurks and in
the caverns like
the mountain bull.
He is sad and lonely, and lonely his feet
that carry him far from the navel of earth;   480
but its prophecies, ever living,
flutter around his head.

STROPHE

The augur has spread confusion,
terrible confusion;
I do not approve what was said   485
nor can I deny it.
I do not know what to say;
I am in a flutter of foreboding;
I never heard in the present
nor past of a quarrel between   490
the sons of Labdacus and Polybus,
that I might bring as proof
in attacking the popular fame
of Oedipus, seeking
to take vengeance for undiscovered
death in the line of Labdacus.   495

ANTISTROPHE

Truly Zeus and Apollo are wise
and in human things all knowing;
but amongst men there is no   500
distinct judgment, between the prophet
and me—which of us is right.
One man may pass another in wisdom
but I would never agree
with those that find fault with the king
till I should see the word
proved right beyond doubt. For once
in visible form the Sphinx

came on him and all of us
saw his wisdom and in that test
he saved the city. So he will not be condemned by my mind.   512
    Enter Creon.

CREON

Citizens, I have come because I heard
deadly words spread about me, that the king
accuses me. I cannot take that from him.
If he believes that in these present troubles   515
he has been wronged by me in word or deed
I do not want to live on with the burden
of such a scandal on me. The report   520
injures me doubly and most vitally—
for I'll be called a traitor to my city
and traitor also to my friends and you.

CHORUS

Perhaps it was a sudden gust of anger
that forced that insult from him, and no judgment.

CREON

But did he say that it was in compliance   525
with schemes of mine that the seer told him lies?

CHORUS

Yes, he said that, but why, I do not know.

CREON

Were his eyes straight in his head? Was his mind right
when he accused me in this fashion?

CHORUS

I do not know; I have no eyes to see   530
what princes do. Here comes the king himself.
    Enter Oedipus.

OEDIPUS

You, sir, how is it you come here? Have you so much
brazen-faced daring that you venture in
my house although you are proved manifestly
the murderer of that man, and though you tried,
openly, highway robbery of my crown?   535
For God's sake, tell me what you saw in me,
what cowardice or what stupidity,
that made you lay a plot like this against me?
Did you imagine I should not observe
the crafty scheme that stole upon me or
seeing it, take no means to counter it?   540
Was it not stupid of you to make the attempt,
to try to hunt down royal power without
the people at your back or friends? For only
with the people at your back or money can
the hunt end in the capture of a crown.

CREON

Do you know what you're doing? Will you listen
to words to answer yours, and then pass judgment?

OEDIPUS

You're quick to speak, but I am slow to grasp you,   545
for I have found you dangerous,—and my foe.

CREON
    First of all hear what I shall say to that.
OEDIPUS
    At least don't tell me that you are not guilty.
CREON
    If you think obstinacy without wisdom
    a valuable possession, you are wrong.   550
OEDIPUS
    And you are wrong if you believe that one,
    a criminal, will not be punished only
    because he is my kinsman.
CREON
                        This is but just—
    but tell me, then, of what offense I'm guilty?
OEDIPUS
    Did you or did you not urge me to send   555
    to this prophetic mumbler?
CREON
                        I did indeed,
    and I shall stand by what I told you.
OEDIPUS
    How long ago is it since Laius. . . .
CREON
    What about Laius? I don't understand.
OEDIPUS
    Vanished—died—was murdered?   560
CREON
                        It is long,
    a long, long time to reckon.
OEDIPUS
                  Was this prophet
    in the profession then?
CREON
                He was, and honoured
    as highly as he is today.
OEDIPUS
    At that time did he say a word about me?
CREON
    Never, at least when I was near him.   565
OEDIPUS
    You never made a search for the dead man?
CREON
    We searched, indeed, but never learned of anything.
OEDIPUS
    Why did our wise old friend not say this then?
CREON
    I don't know; and when I know nothing, I
    usually hold my tongue.
OEDIPUS
                  You know this much,   570
    and can declare this much if you are loyal.
CREON
    What is it? If I know, I'll not deny it.

OEDIPUS

That he would not have said that I killed Laius
had he not met you first.

CREON

You know yourself
whether he said this, but I demand that I   575
should hear as much from you as you from me.

OEDIPUS

Then hear,—I'll not be proved a murderer.

CREON

Well, then. You're married to my sister.

OEDIPUS

Yes,
that I am not disposed to deny.

CREON

You rule
this country giving her an equal share
in the government?

OEDIPUS

Yes, everything she wants   580
she has from me.

CREON

And I, as thirdsman to you,
am rated as the equal of you two?

OEDIPUS

Yes, and it's there you've proved yourself false friend.

CREON

Not if you will reflect on it as I do.
Consider, first, if you think any one
would choose to rule and fear rather than rule   585
and sleep untroubled by a fear if power
were equal in both cases. I, at least,
I was not born with such a frantic yearning
to be a king—but to do what kings do.
And so it is with every one who has learned
wisdom and self-control. As it stands now,
the prizes are all mine—and without fear.   590
But if I were the king myself, I must
do much that went against the grain.
How should despotic rule seem sweeter to me
than painless power and an assured authority?
I am not so besotted yet that I
want other honours than those that come with profit.   595
Now every man's my pleasure; every man greets me;
now those who are your suitors fawn on me,—
success for them depends upon my favour.
Why should I let all this go to win that?
My mind would not be traitor if it's wise;   600
I am no treason lover, of my nature,
nor would I ever dare to join a plot.
Prove what I say. Go to the oracle
at Pytho and inquire about the answers,
if they are as I told you. For the rest,   605

if you discover I laid any plot
together with the seer, kill me, I say,
not only by your vote but by my own.
But do not charge me on obscure opinion
without some proof to back it. It's not just
lightly to count your knaves as honest men,   610
nor honest men as knaves. To throw away
an honest friend is, as it were, to throw
your life away, which a man loves the best.
In time you will know all with certainty;
time is the only test of honest men,
one day is space enough to know a rogue.   615

CHORUS
His words are wise, king, if one fears to fall.
Those who are quick of temper are not safe.

OEDIPUS
When he that plots against me secretly
moves quickly, I must quickly counterplot.
If I wait taking no decisive measure   620
his business will be done, and mine be spoiled.

CREON
What do you want to do then? Banish me?

OEDIPUS
No, certainly; kill you, not banish you.[1]

CREON
I do not think that you've your wits about you.   626

OEDIPUS
For my own interests, yes.

CREON
      But for mine, too,
you should think equally.

OEDIPUS
      You are a rogue.

CREON
Suppose you do not understand?

OEDIPUS
      But yet
I must be ruler.

CREON
    Not if you rule badly.

OEDIPUS
O, city, city!

CREON
    I too have some share   630
in the city; it is not yours alone.

CHORUS
Stop, my lords! Here—and in the nick of time

---

1. Two lines omitted here owing to
the confusion in the dialogue
consequent on the loss of a third
line. The lines as they stand in Jebb's
edition (1902) are:

OED.: That you may show what
manner of thing is envy.
CREON: You speak as one that will
not yield or trust.
[OED. lost line.]

I see Jocasta coming from the house;
with her help lay the quarrel that now stirs you.
        Enter Jocasta.

JOCASTA

For shame! Why have you raised this foolish squabbling
brawl? Are you not ashamed to air your private   635
griefs when the country's sick? Go in, you, Oedipus,
and you, too, Creon, into the house. Don't magnify
your nothing troubles.

CREON
                        Sister, Oedipus,
your husband, thinks he has the right to do
terrible wrongs—he has but to choose between   640
two terrors: banishing or killing me.

OEDIPUS

He's right, Jocasta; for I find him plotting
with knavish tricks against my person.

CREON

That God may never bless me! May I die
accursed, if I have been guilty of   645
one tittle of the charge you bring against me!

JOCASTA

I beg you, Oedipus, trust him in this,
spare him for the sake of this his oath to God,
for my sake, and the sake of those who stand here.

CHORUS

Be gracious, be merciful,   649
we beg of you.

OEDIPUS

In what would you have me yield?

CHORUS

He has been no silly child in the past.
He is strong in his oath now.
Spare him.

OEDIPUS

Do you know what you ask?

CHORUS

Yes.

OEDIPUS

Tell me then.

CHORUS

He has been your friend before all men's eyes; do not cast him   656
away dishonoured on an obscure conjecture.

OEDIPUS

I would have you know that this request of yours
really requests my death or banishment.

CHORUS

May the Sun God, king of Gods, forbid! May I die without God's   660
blessing, without friends' help, if I had any such thought. But my
spirit is broken by my unhappiness for my wasting country; and   665
this would but add troubles amongst ourselves to the other
troubles.

OEDIPUS

    Well, let him go then—if I must die ten times for it,   669
    or be sent out dishonoured into exile.
    It is your lips that prayed for him I pitied,
    not his; wherever he is, I shall hate him.

CREON

    I see you sulk in yielding and you're dangerous
    when you are out of temper; natures like yours
    are justly heaviest for themselves to bear.   675

OEDIPUS

    Leave me alone! Take yourself off, I tell you.

CREON

    I'll go, you have not known me, but they have,
    and they have known my innocence.
        Exit.

CHORUS

    Won't you take him inside, lady?

JOCASTA

    Yes, when I've found out what was the matter.   680

CHORUS

    There was some misconceived suspicion of a story, and on the
    other side the sting of injustice.

JOCASTA

    So, on both sides?

CHORUS

    Yes.

JOCASTA

    What was the story?

CHORUS

    I think it best, in the interests of the country, to leave it where   685
    it ended.

OEDIPUS

    You see where you have ended, straight of judgment
    although you are, by softening my anger.

CHORUS

    Sir, I have said before and I say again—be sure that I would have   689
    been proved a madman, bankrupt in sane council, if I should put
    you away, you who steered the country I love safely when she
    was crazed with troubles. God grant that now, too, you may   695
    prove a fortunate guide for us.

JOCASTA

    Tell me, my lord, I beg of you, what was it
    that roused your anger so?

OEDIPUS

                      Yes, I will tell you.   700
    I honour you more than I honour them.
    It was Creon and the plots he laid against me.

JOCASTA

    Tell me—if you can clearly tell the quarrel—

OEDIPUS

                                Creon says
    that I'm the murderer of Laius.

JOCASTA
    Of his own knowledge or on information?

OEDIPUS
    He sent this rascal prophet to me, since   705
    he keeps his own mouth clean of any guilt.

JOCASTA
    Do not concern yourself about this matter;
    listen to me and learn that human beings
    have no part in the craft of prophecy.
    Of that I'll show you a short proof.   710
    There was an oracle once that came to Laius,—
    I will not say that it was Phoebus' own,
    but it was from his servants—and it told him
    that it was fate that he should die a victim
    at the hands of his own son, a son to be born
    of Laius and me. But, see now, he,
    the king, was killed by foreign highway robbers   715
    at a place where three roads meet—so goes the story;
    and for the son—before three days were out
    after his birth King Laius pierced his ankles
    and by the hands of others cast him forth
    upon a pathless hillside. So Apollo   720
    failed to fulfill his oracle to the son,
    that he should kill his father, and to Laius
    also proved false in that the thing he feared,
    death at his son's hands, never came to pass.
    So clear in this case were the oracles,
    so clear and false. Give them no heed, I say;
    what God discovers need of, easily
    he shows to us himself.   725

OEDIPUS
                 O dear Jocasta,
    as I hear this from you, there comes upon me
    a wandering of the soul—I could run mad.

JOCASTA
    What trouble is it, that you turn again
    and speak like this?

OEDIPUS
              I thought I heard you say
    that Laius was killed at a crossroads.   730

JOCASTA
    Yes, that was how the story went and still
    that word goes round.

OEDIPUS
            Where is this place, Jocasta,
    where he was murdered?

JOCASTA
            Phocis is the country
    and the road splits there, one of two roads from Delphi,
    another comes from Daulia.

OEDIPUS
              How long ago is this?   735

JOCASTA
    The news came to the city just before
    you became king and all men's eyes looked to you.
    What is it, Oedipus, that's in your mind?
OEDIPUS
    What have you designed, O Zeus, to do with me?
JOCASTA
    What is the thought that troubles your heart?
OEDIPUS
    Don't ask me yet—tell me of Laius—   740
    How did he look? How old or young was he?
JOCASTA
    He was a tall man and his hair was grizzled
    already—nearly white—and in his form
    not unlike you.
OEDIPUS
              O God, I think I have
    called curses on myself in ignorance.   745
JOCASTA
    What do you mean? I am terrified
    when I look at you.
OEDIPUS
             I have a deadly fear
    that the old seer had eyes. You'll show me more
    if you can tell me one more thing.
JOCASTA
               I will.
    I'm frightened,—but if I can understand,
    I'll tell you all you ask.
OEDIPUS
            How was his company?   750
    Had he few with him when he went this journey,
    or many servants, as would suit a prince?
JOCASTA
    In all there were but five, and among them
    a herald; and one carriage for the king.
OEDIPUS
    It's plain—it's plain—who was it told you this?   755
JOCASTA
    The only servant that escaped safe home.
OEDIPUS
    Is he at home now?
JOCASTA
           No, when he came home again
    and saw you king and Laius was dead,
    he came to me and touched my hand and begged   760
    that I should send him to the fields to be
    my shepherd and so he might see the city
    as far off as he might. So I
    sent him away. He was an honest man,
    as slaves go, and was worthy of far more
    than what he asked of me.

OEDIPUS

O, how I wish that he could come back quickly!   765

JOCASTA

He can. Why is your heart so set on this?

OEDIPUS

O dear Jocasta, I am full of fears
that I have spoken far too much; and therefore
I wish to see this shepherd.

JOCASTA

He will come;
but, Oedipus, I think I'm worthy too
to know what it is that disquiets you.   770

OEDIPUS

It shall not be kept from you, since my mind
has gone so far with its forebodings. Whom
should I confide in rather than you, who is there
of more importance to me who have passed
through such a fortune?
Polybus was my father, king of Corinth,
and Merope, the Dorian, my mother.   775
I was held greatest of the citizens
in Corinth till a curious chance befell me
as I shall tell you—curious, indeed,
but hardly worth the store I set upon it.
There was a dinner and at it a man,
a drunken man, accused me in his drink   780
of being bastard. I was furious
but held my temper under for that day.
Next day I went and taxed my parents with it;
they took the insult very ill from him,
the drunken fellow who had uttered it.
So I was comforted for their part, but   785
still this thing rankled always, for the story
crept about widely. And I went at last
to Pytho, though my parents did not know.
But Phoebus sent me home again unhonoured
in what I came to learn, but he foretold   790
other and desperate horrors to befall me,
that I was fated to lie with my mother,
and show to daylight an accursed breed
which men would not endure, and I was doomed
to be murderer of the father that begot me.
When I heard this I fled, and in the days
that followed I would measure from the stars   795
the whereabouts of Corinth—yes, I fled
to somewhere where I should not see fulfilled
the infamies told in that dreadful oracle.
And as I journeyed I came to the place
where, as you say, this king met with his death.
Jocasta, I will tell you the whole truth.   800
When I was near the branching of the crossroads,
going on foot, I was encountered by
a herald and a carriage with a man in it,

just as you tell me. He that led the way
and the old man himself wanted to thrust me   805
out of the road by force. I became angry
and struck the coachman who was pushing me.
When the old man saw this he watched his moment,
and as I passed he struck me from his carriage,
full on the head with his two pointed goad.
But he was paid in full and presently   810
my stick had struck him backwards from the car
and he rolled out of it. And then I killed them
all. If it happened there was any tie
of kinship twixt this man and Laius,
who is then now more miserable than I,   815
what man on earth so hated by the Gods,
since neither citizen nor foreigner
may welcome me at home or even greet me,
but drive me out of doors? And it is I,
I and no other have so cursed myself.   820
And I pollute the bed of him I killed
by the hands that killed him. Was I not born evil?
Am I not utterly unclean? I had to fly
and in my banishment not even see
my kindred nor set foot in my own country,
or otherwise my fate was to be yoked   825
in marriage with my mother and kill my father,
Polybus who begot me and had reared me.
Would not one rightly judge and say that on me
these things were sent by some malignant God?
O no, no, no—O holy majesty   830
of God on high, may I not see that day!
May I be gone out of men's sight before
I see the deadly taint of this disaster
come upon me.
CHORUS
    Sir, we too fear these things. But until you see this man face to
    face and hear his story, hope.   835
OEDIPUS
    Yes, I have just this much of hope—to wait until the herdsman
    comes.
JOCASTA
    And when he comes, what do you want with him?
OEDIPUS
    I'll tell you; if I find that his story is the same as yours, I at least
    will be clear of this guilt.   840
JOCASTA
    Why what so particularly did you learn from my story?
OEDIPUS
    You said that he spoke of highway *robbers* who killed Laius. Now
    if he uses the same number, it was not I who killed him. One man
    cannot be the same as many. But if he speaks of a man travelling   845
    alone, then clearly the burden of the guilt inclines towards me.
JOCASTA
    Be sure, at least, that this was how he told the story. He cannot

unsay it now, for every one in the city heard it—not I alone. But,   850
Oedipus, even if he diverges from what he said then, he shall
never prove that the murder of Laius squares rightly with the
prophecy—for Loxias declared that the king should be killed by
his own son. And that poor creature did not kill him surely,—   855
for he died himself first. So as far as prophecy goes, henceforward
I shall not look to the right hand or the left.

OEDIPUS

Right. But yet, send some one for the peasant to bring him here;   860
do not neglect it.

JOCASTA

I will send quickly. Now let me go indoors. I will do nothing
except what pleases you.
    Exeunt.

CHORUS

STROPHE

May destiny ever find me
pious in word and deed   865
prescribed by the laws that live on high:
laws begotten in the clear air of heaven,
whose only father is Olympus;
no mortal nature brought them to birth,
no forgetfulness shall lull them to sleep;   870
for God is great in them and grows not old.

ANTISTROPHE

Insolence breeds the tyrant, insolence
if it is glutted with a surfeit, unseasonable, unprofitable,   875
climbs to the roof-top and plunges
sheer down to the ruin that must be,
and there its feet are no service.
But I pray that the God may never   880
abolish the eager ambition that profits the state.
For I shall never cease to hold the God as our protector.

STROPHE

If a man walks with haughtiness
of hand or word and gives no heed   885
to Justice and the shrines of Gods
despises—may an evil doom
smite him for his ill-starred pride of heart!—
if he reaps gains without justice
and will not hold from impiety   890
and his fingers itch for untouchable things.
When such things are done, what man shall contrive
to shield his soul from the shafts of the God?
When such deeds are held in honour,   895
why should I honour the Gods in the dance?

ANTISTROPHE

No longer to the holy place,
to the navel of earth I'll go
to worship, nor to Abae
nor to Olympia,   900
unless the oracles are proved to fit,
for all men's hands to point at.

O Zeus, if you are rightly called
the sovereign lord, all-mastering,
let this not escape you nor your ever-living power! 905
The oracles concerning Laius
are old and dim and men regard them not.
Apollo is nowhere clear in honour; God's service perishes. 910

Enter Jocasta, carrying garlands.

JOCASTA

Princes of the land, I have had the thought to go
to the Gods' temples, bringing in my hand
garlands and gifts of incense, as you see.
For Oedipus excites himself too much
at every sort of trouble, not conjecturing, 915
like a man of sense, what will be from what was,
but he is always at the speaker's mercy,
when he speaks terrors. I can do no good
by my advice, and so I came as suppliant
to you, Lycaean Apollo, who are nearest.
These are the symbols of my prayer and this 920
my prayer: grant us escape free of the curse.
Now when we look to him we are all afraid;
he's pilot of our ship and he is frightened.

Enter Messenger.

MESSENGER

Might I learn from you, sirs, where is the house of Oedipus? Or 925
best of all, if you know, where is the king himself?

CHORUS

This is his house and he is within doors. This lady is his wife and
mother of his children.

MESSENGER

God bless you, lady, and God bless your household! God bless 930
Oedipus' noble wife!

JOCASTA

God bless you, sir, for your kind greeting! What do you want
of us that you have come here? What have you to tell us?

MESSENGER

Good news, lady. Good for your house and for your husband.

JOCASTA

What is your news? Who sent you to us? 935

MESSENGER

I come from Corinth and the news I bring will give you pleasure.
Perhaps a little pain too.

JOCASTA

What is this news of double meaning?

MESSENGER

The people of the Isthmus will choose Oedipus to be their king. 940
That is the rumour there.

JOCASTA

But isn't their king still old Polybus?

MESSENGER

No. He is in his grave. Death has got him.

JOCASTA

Is that the truth? Is Oedipus' father dead?

MESSENGER
>May I die myself if it be otherwise!

JOCASTA (*To a servant.*)
>Be quick and run to the King with the news! O oracles of the 945
>Gods, where are you now? It was from this man Oedipus fled, lest
>he should be his murderer! And now he is dead, in the course of
>nature, and not killed by Oedipus.
>>*Enter Oedipus.*

OEDIPUS
>Dearest Jocasta, why have you sent for me? 950

JOCASTA
>Listen to this man and when you hear reflect what is the outcome
>of the holy oracles of the Gods.

OEDIPUS
>Who is he? What is his message for me?

JOCASTA
>He is from Corinth and he tells us that your father Polybus is 955
>dead and gone.

OEDIPUS
>What's this you say, sir? Tell me yourself.

MESSENGER
>Since this is the first matter you want clearly told: Polybus has
>gone down to death. You may be sure of it.

OEDIPUS
>By treachery or sickness? 960

MESSENGER
>A small thing will put old bodies asleep.

OEDIPUS
>So he died of sickness, it seems,—poor old man!

MESSENGER
>Yes, and of age—the long years he had measured.

OEDIPUS
>Ha! Ha! O dear Jocasta, why should one
>look to the Pythian hearth? Why should one look 965
>to the birds screaming overhead? They prophesied
>that I should kill my father! But he's dead,
>and hidden deep in earth, and I stand here
>who never laid a hand on spear against him,—
>unless perhaps he died of longing for me,
>and thus I am his murderer. But they, 970
>the oracles, as they stand—he's taken them
>away with him, they're dead as he himself is,
>and worthless.

JOCASTA
>>That I told you before now.

OEDIPUS
>You did, but I was misled by my fear.

JOCASTA
>Then lay no more of them to heart, not one. 975

OEDIPUS
>But surely I must fear my mother's bed?

JOCASTA
>Why should man fear since chance is all in all

for him, and he can clearly foreknow nothing?
Best to live lightly, as one can, unthinkingly.
As to your mother's marriage bed,—don't fear it.   980
Before this, in dreams too, as well as oracles,
many a man has lain with his own mother.
But he to whom such things are nothing bears
his life most easily.
OEDIPUS
   All that you say would be said perfectly
if she were dead; but since she lives I must   985
still fear, although you talk so well, Jocasta.
JOCASTA
   Still in your father's death there's light of comfort?
OEDIPUS
   Great light of comfort; but I fear the living.
MESSENGER
   Who is the woman that makes you afraid?
OEDIPUS
   Merope, old man, Polybus' wife.   990
MESSENGER
   What about her frightens the queen and you?
OEDIPUS
   A terrible oracle, stranger, from the Gods.
MESSENGER
   Can it be told? Or does the sacred law
forbid another to have knowledge of it?
OEDIPUS
   O no! Once on a time Loxias said
that I should lie with my own mother and   995
take on my hands the blood of my own father.
And so for these long years I've lived away
from Corinth; it has been to my great happiness;
but yet it's sweet to see the face of parents.
MESSENGER
   This was the fear which drove you out of Corinth?   1000
OEDIPUS
   Old man, I did not wish to kill my father.
MESSENGER
   Why should I not free you from this fear, sir,
since I have come to you in all goodwill?
OEDIPUS
   You would not find me thankless if you did.
MESSENGER
   Why, it was just for this I brought the news,—   1005
to earn your thanks when you had come safe home.
OEDIPUS
   No, I will never come near my parents.
MESSENGER
                              Son,
it's very plain you don't know what you're doing.
OEDIPUS
   What do you mean, old man? For God's sake, tell me.

MESSENGER
    If your homecoming is checked by fears like these.   1010
OEDIPUS
    Yes, I'm afraid that Phoebus may prove right.
MESSENGER
    The murder and the incest?
OEDIPUS
                        Yes, old man;
    that is my constant terror.
MESSENGER
                  Do you know
    that all your fears are empty?
OEDIPUS
                  How is that,   1015
    if they are father and mother and I their son?
MESSENGER
    Because Polybus was no kin to you in blood.
OEDIPUS
    What, was not Polybus my father?
MESSENGER
    No more than I but just so much.
OEDIPUS
                    How can
    my father be my father as much as one
    that's nothing to me?
MESSENGER
              Neither he nor I   1020
    begat you.
OEDIPUS
          Why then did he call me son?
MESSENGER
    A gift he took you from these hands of mine.
OEDIPUS
    Did he love so much what he took from another's hand?
MESSENGER
    His childlessness before persuaded him.
OEDIPUS
    Was I a child you bought or found when I   1025
    was given to him?
MESSENGER
             On Cithaeron's slopes
    in the twisting thickets you were found.
OEDIPUS
                      And why
    were you a traveller in those parts?
MESSENGER
                I was
    in charge of mountain flocks.
OEDIPUS
             You were a shepherd?
    A hireling vagrant?

MESSENGER

Yes, but at least at that time   1030
the man that saved your life, son.

OEDIPUS

What ailed me when you took me in your arms?

MESSENGER

In that your ankles should be witnesses.

OEDIPUS

Why do you speak of that old pain?

MESSENGER

I loosed you;
the tendons of your feet were pierced and fettered,—

OEDIPUS

My swaddling clothes brought me a rare disgrace.   1035

MESSENGER

So that from this you're called your present name.

OEDIPUS

Was this my father's doing or my mother's?
For God's sake, tell me.

MESSENGER

I don't know, but he
who gave you to me has more knowledge than I.

OEDIPUS

You yourself did not find me then? You took me
from someone else?

MESSENGER

Yes, from another shepherd.   1040

OEDIPUS

Who was he? Do you know him well enough
to tell?

MESSENGER

He was called Laius' man.

OEDIPUS

You mean the king who reigned here in the old days?

MESSENGER

Yes, he was that man's shepherd.

OEDIPUS

Is he alive   1045
still, so that I could see him?

MESSENGER

You who live here
would know that best.

OEDIPUS

Do any of you here
know of this shepherd whom he speaks about
in town or in the fields? Tell me. It's time   1050
that this was found out once for all.

CHORUS

I think he is none other than the peasant
whom you have sought to see already; but
Jocasta here can tell us best of that.

OEDIPUS

Jocasta, do you know about this man
whom we have sent for? Is he the man he mentions?   1055

JOCASTA

Why ask of whom he spoke? Don't give it heed;
nor try to keep in mind what has been said.
It will be wasted labour.

OEDIPUS

With such clues
I could not fail to bring my birth to light.

JOCASTA

I beg you—do not hunt this out—I beg you,   1060
if you have any care for your own life.
What I am suffering is enough.

OEDIPUS

Keep up
your heart, Jocasta. Though I'm proved a slave,
thrice slave, and though my mother is thrice slave,
you'll not be shown to be of lowly lineage.

JOCASTA

O be persuaded by me, I entreat you;
do not do this.

OEDIPUS

I will not be persuaded to let be   1065
the chance of finding out the whole thing clearly.

JOCASTA

It is because I wish you well that I
give you this counsel—and it's the best counsel.

OEDIPUS

Then the best counsel vexes me, and has
for some while since.

JOCASTA

O Oedipus, God help you!
God keep you from the knowledge of who you are!

OEDIPUS

Here, some one, go and fetch the shepherd for me;
and let her find her joy in her rich family!   1070

JOCASTA

O Oedipus, unhappy Oedipus!
that is all I can call you, and the last thing
that I shall ever call you.
        Exit.

CHORUS

Why has the queen gone, Oedipus, in wild
grief rushing from us? I am afraid that trouble   1075
will break out of this silence.

OEDIPUS

Break out what will! I at least shall be
willing to see my ancestry, though humble.
Perhaps she is ashamed of my low birth,
for she has all a woman's high-flown pride.
But I account myself a child of Fortune,   1080
beneficent Fortune, and I shall not be

dishonoured. She's the mother from whom I spring;
the months, my brothers, marked me, now as small,
and now again as mighty. Such is my breeding,
and I shall never prove so false to it,   1085
as not to find the secret of my birth.

CHORUS

    STROPHE

If I am a prophet and wise of heart
you shall not fail, Cithaeron,   1090
by the limitless sky, you shall not!—
to know at tomorrow's full moon
that Oedipus honours you,
as native to him and mother and nurse at once;
and that you are honoured in dancing by us, as finding favour in
      sight of our king.
Apollo, to whom we cry, find these things pleasing!

    ANTISTROPHE

Who was it bore you, child? One of   1098
the long-lived nymphs who lay with Pan—
the father who treads the hills?
Or was she a bride of Loxias, your mother? The grassy slopes
are all of them dear to him. Or perhaps Cyllene's king   1104
or the Bacchants' God that lives on the tops
of the hills received you a gift from some
one of the Helicon Nymphs, with whom he mostly plays?
    Enter an old man, led by Oedipus' servants.

OEDIPUS

If some one like myself who never met him   1110
may make a guess,—I think this is the herdsman,
whom we were seeking. His old age is consonant
with the other. And besides, the men who bring him
I recognize as my own servants. You   1115
perhaps may better me in knowledge since
you've seen the man before.

CHORUS

                   You can be sure
I recognize him. For if Laius
had ever an honest shepherd, this was he.

OEDIPUS

You, sir, from Corinth, I must ask you first,
is this the man you spoke of?   1120

MESSENGER

               This is he
before your eyes.

OEDIPUS

         Old man, look here at me
and tell me what I ask you. Were you ever
a servant of King Laius?

HERDSMAN

            I was,—
no slave he bought but reared in his own house.

OEDIPUS

What did you do as work? How did you live?

HERDSMAN
    Most of my life was spent among the flocks.   1125
OEDIPUS
    In what part of the country did you live?
HERDSMAN
    Cithaeron and the places near to it.
OEDIPUS
    And somewhere there perhaps you knew this man?
HERDSMAN
    What was his occupation? Who?
OEDIPUS
                           This man here,   1130
    have you had any dealings with him?
HERDSMAN
                           No—
    not such that I can quickly call to mind.
MESSENGER
    That is no wonder, master. But I'll make him remember what he
    does not know. For I know, that he well knows the country of
    Cithaeron, how he with two flocks, I with one kept company for   1135
    three years—each year half a year—from spring till autumn time
    and then when winter came I drove my flocks to our fold home
    again and he to Laius' steadings. Well—am I right or not in what   1140
    I said we did?
HERDSMAN
    You're right—although it's a long time ago.
MESSENGER
    Do you remember giving me a child
    to bring up as my foster child?
HERDSMAN
                     What's this?
    Why do you ask this question?
MESSENGER
                     Look old man,   1145
    here he is—here's the man who was that child!
HERDSMAN
    Death take you! Won't you hold your tongue?
OEDIPUS
                       No, no,
    do not find fault with him, old man. Your words
    are more at fault than his.
HERDSMAN
                O best of masters,
    how do I give offense?
OEDIPUS
               When you refuse   1150
    to speak about the child of whom he asks you.
HERDSMAN
    He speaks out of his ignorance, without meaning.
OEDIPUS
    If you'll not talk to gratify me, you
    will talk with pain to urge you.

HERDSMAN

O please, sir,
don't hurt an old man, sir.

OEDIPUS (*To the servants.*)

Here, one of you,
twist his hands behind him.

HERDSMAN

Why, God help me, why?   1155
What do you want to know?

OEDIPUS

You gave a child
to him,—the child he asked you of?

HERDSMAN

I did.
I wish I'd died the day I did.

OEDIPUS

You will
unless you tell me truly.

HERDSMAN

And I'll die
far worse if I should tell you.

OEDIPUS

This fellow   1160
is bent on more delays, as it would seem.

HERDSMAN

O no, no! I have told you that I gave it.

OEDIPUS

Where did you get this child from? Was it your own or did you
get it from another?

HERDSMAN

Not
my own at all; I had it from some one.

OEDIPUS

One of these citizens? or from what house?

HERDSMAN

O master, please—I beg you, master, please   1165
don't ask me more.

OEDIPUS

You're a dead man if I
ask you again.

HERDSMAN

It was one of the children
of Laius.

OEDIPUS

A slave? Or born in wedlock?

HERDSMAN

O God, I am on the brink of frightful speech.

OEDIPUS

And I of frightful hearing. But I must hear.   1170

HERDSMAN

The child was called his child; but she within,
your wife would tell you best how all this was.

OEDIPUS

She gave it to you?

HERDSMAN

Yes, she did, my lord.

OEDIPUS

To do what with it?

HERDSMAN

Make away with it.

OEDIPUS

She was so hard—its mother?   1175

HERDSMAN

Aye, through fear

of evil oracles.

OEDIPUS

Which?

HERDSMAN

They said that he

should kill his parents.

OEDIPUS

How was it that you

gave it away to this old man?

HERDSMAN

O master,

I pitied it, and thought that I could send it

off to another country and this man

was from another country. But he saved it   1180

for the most terrible troubles. If you are

the man he says you are, you're bred to misery.

OEDIPUS

O, O, O, they will all come,

all come out clearly! Light of the sun, let me

look upon you no more after today!

I who first saw the light bred of a match

accursed, and accursed in my living

with them I lived with, cursed in my killing.   1185

Exeunt all but the Chorus.

CHORUS

STROPHE

O generations of men, how I

count you as equal with those who live

not at all!

What man, what man on earth wins more   1190

of happiness than a seeming

and after that turning away?

Oedipus, you are my pattern of this,

Oedipus, you and your fate!

Luckless Oedipus, whom of all men

I envy not at all.   1196

ANTISTROPHE

In as much as he shot his bolt

beyond the others and won the prize

of happiness complete—

O Zeus—and killed and reduced to nought

the hooked taloned maid of the riddling speech,
standing a tower against death for my land:
hence he was called my king and hence
was honoured the highest of all
honours; and hence he ruled
in the great city of Thebes.
      STROPHE
But now whose tale is more miserable?   1204
Who is there lives with a savager fate?
Whose troubles so reverse his life as his?

O Oedipus, the famous prince
for whom a great haven
the same both as father and son
sufficed for generation,
how, O how, have the furrows ploughed
by your father endured to bear you, poor wretch,
and hold their peace so long?
      ANTISTROPHE
Time who sees all has found you out   1213
against your will; judges your marriage accursed,
begetter and begot at one in it.

O child of Laius,
would I had never seen you.
I weep for you and cry
a dirge of lamentation.

To speak directly, I drew my breath
from you at the first and so now I lull   1222
my mouth to sleep with your name.
      Enter a second messenger.
SECOND MESSENGER
O Princes always honoured by our country,
what deeds you'll hear of and what horrors see,
what grief you'll feel, if you as true born Thebans   1225
care for the house of Labdacus's sons.
Phasis nor Ister cannot purge this house,
I think, with all their streams, such things
it hides, such evils shortly will bring forth
into the light, whether they will or not;   1230
and troubles hurt the most
when they prove self-inflicted.
CHORUS
What we had known before did not fall short
of bitter groaning's worth; what's more to tell?
SECOND MESSENGER
Shortest to hear and tell—our glorious queen   1235
Jocasta's dead.
CHORUS
            Unhappy woman! How?
SECOND MESSENGER
By her own hand. The worst of what was done

you cannot know. You did not see the sight.
Yet in so far as I remember it
you'll hear the end of our unlucky queen.   1240
When she came raging into the house she went
straight to her marriage bed, tearing her hair
with both her hands, and crying upon Laius   1245
long dead—Do you remember, Laius,
that night long past which bred a child for us
to send you to your death and leave
a mother making children with her son?
And then she groaned and cursed the bed in which
she brought forth husband by her husband, children   1250
by her own child, an infamous double bond.
How after that she died I do not know,—
for Oedipus distracted us from seeing.
He burst upon us shouting and we looked
to him as he paced frantically around,
begging us always: Give me a sword, I say,   1255
to find this wife no wife, this mother's womb,
this field of double sowing whence I sprang
and where I sowed my children! As he raved
some god showed him the way—none of us there.
Bellowing terribly and led by some   1260
invisible guide he rushed on the two doors,—
wrenching the hollow bolts out of their sockets,
he charged inside. There, there, we saw his wife
hanging, the twisted rope around her neck.
When he saw her, he cried out fearfully   1265
and cut the dangling noose. Then, as she lay,
poor woman, on the ground, what happened after,
was terrible to see. He tore the brooches—
the gold chased brooches fastening her robe—
away from her and lifting them up high
dashed them on his own eyeballs, shrieking out   1270
such things as: they will never see the crime
I have committed or had done upon me!
Dark eyes, now in the days to come look on
forbidden faces, do not recognize
those whom you long for—with such imprecations
he struck his eyes again and yet again   1275
with the brooches. And the bleeding eyeballs gushed
and stained his beard—no sluggish oozing drops
but a black rain and bloody hail poured down.

So it has broken—and not on one head   1280
but troubles mixed for husband and for wife.
The fortune of the days gone by was true
good fortune—but today groans and destruction
and death and shame—of all ills can be named   1285
not one is missing.
CHORUS
    Is he now in any ease from pain?

SECOND MESSENGER
He shouts
for some one to unbar the doors and show him
to all the men of Thebes, his father's killer,
his mother's—no I cannot say the word,
it is unholy—for he'll cast himself,
out of the land, he says, and not remain   1290
to bring a curse upon his house, the curse
he called upon it in his proclamation. But
he wants for strength, aye, and some one to guide him;
his sickness is too great to bear. You, too,
will be shown that. The bolts are opening.   1295
Soon you will see a sight to waken pity
even in the horror of it.
  Enter the blinded Oedipus.
CHORUS
This is a terrible sight for men to see!
I never found a worse!
Poor wretch, what madness came upon you!   1300
What evil spirit leaped upon your life
to your ill-luck—a leap beyond man's strenth!
Indeed I pity you, but I cannot
look at you, though there's much I want to ask
and much to learn and much to see.   1305
I shudder at the sight of you.
OEDIPUS
O, O,
where am I going? Where is my voice   1310
borne on the wind to and fro?
Spirit, how far have you sprung?
CHORUS
To a terrible place whereof men's ears
may not hear, nor their eyes behold it.
OEDIPUS
Darkness!
Horror of darkness enfolding, resistless, unspeakable visitant sped by
  an ill wind in haste!   1315
madness and stabbing pain and memory
of evil deeds I have done!
CHORUS
In such misfortunes it's no wonder
if double weighs the burden of your grief.   1320
OEDIPUS
My friend,
you are the only one steadfast, the only one that attends on me;
you still stay nursing the blind man.
Your care is not unnoticed. I can know   1325
your voice, although this darkness is my world.
CHORUS
Doer of dreadful deeds, how did you dare
so far to do despite to your own eyes?
what spirit urged you to it?

OEDIPUS

    It was Apollo, friends, Apollo,
    that brought this bitter bitterness, my sorrows to completion.   1330
    But the hand that struck me
    was none but my own.
    Why should I see
    whose vision showed me nothing sweet to see?   1335

CHORUS

    These things are as you say.

OEDIPUS

    What can I see to love?
    What greeting can touch my ears with joy?
    Take me away, and haste—to a place out of the way!   1340
    Take me away, my friends, the greatly miserable,
    the most accursed, whom God too hates   1345
    above all men on earth!

CHORUS

    Unhappy in your mind and your misfortune,
    would I had never known you!

OEDIPUS

    Curse on the man who took
    the cruel bonds from off my legs, as I lay in the field.   1350
    He stole me from death and saved me,
    no kindly service.
    Had I died then
    I would not be so burdensome to friends.   1355

CHORUS

    I, too, could have wished it had been so.

OEDIPUS

    Then I would not have come
    to kill my father and marry my mother infamously.
    Now I am godless and child of impurity,   1360
    begetter in the same seed that created my wretched self.
    If there is any ill worse than ill,   1365
    that is the lot of Oedipus.

CHORUS

    I cannot say your remedy was good;
    you would be better dead than blind and living.

OEDIPUS

    What I have done here was best done—don't tell me   1370
    otherwise, do not give me further counsel.
    I do not know with what eyes I could look
    upon my father when I die and go
    under the earth, nor yet my wretched mother—
    those two to whom I have done things deserving
    worse punishment than hanging. Would the sight   1375
    of children, bred as mine are, gladden me?
    No, not these eyes, never. And my city,
    its towers and sacred places of the Gods,
    of these I robbed my miserable self   1380
    when I commanded all to drive *him* out,
    the criminal since proved by God impure
    and of the race of Laius.

To this guilt I bore witness against myself—
with what eyes shall I look upon my people?   1385
No. If there were a means to choke the fountain
of hearing I would not have stayed my hand
from locking up my miserable carcase,
seeing and hearing nothing; it is sweet   1390
to keep our thoughts out of the range of hurt.

Cithaeron, why did you receive me? why
having received me did you not kill me straight?
And so I had not shown to men my birth.

O Polybus and Corinth and the house,
the old house that I used to call my father's—   1395
what fairness you were nurse to, and what foulness
festered beneath! Now I am found to be
a sinner and a son of sinners. Crossroads,
and hidden glade, oak and the narrow way
at the crossroads, that drank my father's blood   1400
offered you by my hands, do you remember
still what I did as you looked on, and what
I did when I came here? O marriage, marriage!
you bred me and again when you had bred
bred children of your child and showed to men   1405
brides, wives and mothers and the foulest deeds
that can be in this world of ours.

Come—it's unfit to say what is unfit
to do.—I beg of you in God's name hide me   1410
somewhere outside your country, yes, or kill me,
or throw me into the sea, to be forever
out of your sight. Approach and deign to touch me
for all my wretchedness, and do not fear.
No man but I can bear my evil doom.   1415

CHORUS
Here Creon comes in fit time to perform
or give advice in what you ask of us.
Creon is left sole ruler in your stead.

OEDIPUS
Creon! Creon! What shall I say to him?
How can I justly hope that he will trust me?   1420
In what is past I have been proved towards him
an utter liar.
        Enter Creon.

CREON
                Oedipus, I've come
not so that I might laugh at you nor taunt you
with evil of the past. But if you still
are without shame before the face of men
reverence at least the flame that gives all life,   1425
our Lord the Sun, and do not show unveiled
to him pollution such that neither land
nor holy rain nor light of day can welcome.

To a servant
Be quick and take him in. It is most decent   1430
that only kin should see and hear the troubles
of kin.

OEDIPUS
       I beg you, since you've torn me from
my dreadful expectations and have come
in a most noble spirit to a man
that has used you vilely—do a thing for me.
I shall speak for your own good, not for my own.

CREON
What do you need that you would ask of me?   1435

OEDIPUS
Drive me from here with all the speed you can
to where I may not hear a human voice.

CREON
Be sure, I would have done this had not I
wished first of all to learn from the God the course
of action I should follow.

OEDIPUS
           But his word   1440
has been quite clear to let the parricide,
the sinner, die.

CREON
       Yes, that indeed was said.
But in the present need we had best discover
what we should do.

OEDIPUS
       And will you ask about
a man so wretched?

CREON
       Now even you will trust   1445
the God.

OEDIPUS
       So. I command you—and will beseech you—
to her that lies inside that house give burial
as you would have it; she is yours and rightly
you will perform the rites for her. For me—
never let this my father's city have me   1450
living a dweller in it. Leave me live
in the mountains where Cithaeron is, that's called
my mountain, which my mother and my father
while they were living would have made my tomb.
So I may die by their decree who sought
indeed to kill me. Yet I know this much: 1455
no sickness and no other thing will kill me.
I would not have been saved from death if not
for some strange evil fate. Well, let my fate
go where it will.
       Creon, you need not care   1460
about my sons; they're men and so wherever
they are, they will not lack a livelihood.
But my two girls—so sad and pitiful—
whose table never stood apart from mine,

and everything I touched they always shared—   1465
O Creon, have a thought for them! And most
I wish that you might suffer me to touch them
and sorrow with them.
        Enter Antigone and Ismene, Oedipus' two daughters.
O my lord! O true noble Creon! Can I   1470
really be touching them, as when I saw?
What shall I say?
Yes, I can hear them sobbing—my two darlings!
and Creon has had pity and has sent me
what I loved most?
Am I right?   1475

CREON

You're right: it was I gave you this
because I knew from old days how you loved them
as I see now.

OEDIPUS

                God bless you for it, Creon,
and may God guard you better on your road
than he did me!
                O children,   1480
where are you? Come here, come to my hands,
a brother's hands which turned your father's eyes,
those bright eyes you knew once, to what you see,
a father seeing nothing, knowing nothing,
begetting you from his own source of life.   1485
I weep for you—I cannot see your faces—
I weep when I think of the bitterness
there will be in your lives, how you must live
before the world. At what assemblages
of citizens will you make one? to what   1490
gay company will you go and not come home
in tears instead of sharing in the holiday?
And when you're ripe for marriage, who will he be;
the man who'll risk to take such infamy
as shall cling to my children, to bring hurt   1495
on them and those that marry with them? What
curse is not there? "Your father killed his father
and sowed the seed where he had sprung himself
and begot you out of the womb that held him."
These insults you will hear. Then who will marry you?   1500
No one, my children; clearly you are doomed
to waste away in barrenness unmarried.
Son of Menoeceus, since you are all the father
left these two girls, and we, their parents, both   1505
are dead to them—do not allow them wander
like beggars, poor and husbandless.
They are of your own blood.
And do not make them equal with myself
in wretchedness; for you can see them now
so young, so utterly alone, save for you only.
Touch my hand, noble Creon, and say yes.   1510
If you were older, children, and were wiser,
there's much advice I'd give you. But as it is,

let this be what you pray: give me a life
wherever there is opportunity
to live, and better life than was my father's.

CREON

Your tears have had enough of scope; now go within the house.   1515

OEDIPUS

I must obey, though bitter of heart.

CREON

In season, all is good.

OEDIPUS

Do you know on what conditions I obey?

CREON

You tell me them,
and I shall know them when I hear.

OEDIPUS

That you shall send me out
to live away from Thebes.

CREON

That gift you must ask of the God.

OEDIPUS

But I'm now hated by the Gods.

CREON

So quickly you'll obtain your prayer.

OEDIPUS

You consent then?   1520

CREON

What I do not mean, I do not use to say.

OEDIPUS

Now lead me away from here.

CREON

Let go the children, then, and come.

OEDIPUS

Do not take them from me.

CREON

Do not seek to be master in everything,
for the things you mastered did not follow you throughout your life.
    As Creon and Oedipus go out.

CHORUS

You that live in my ancestral Thebes, behold this Oedipus,—
him who knew the famous riddles and was a man most masterful;   1525
not a citizen who did not look with envy on his lot—
see him now and see the breakers of misfortune swallow him!
Look upon that last day always. Count no mortal happy till
he has passed the final limit of his life secure from pain.   1530

Action analysis and performance suggestions

The following scenes are particularly recommended for student performance: Teiresias, Oedipus, Chorus, ll. 285–512, and Jocasta, Messenger, Chorus, Oedipus, ll. 864–1109. These, particularly the second, are discussed below. Other scenes, however, can be equally effective.

As stated in the Introduction to this book, Aristotle defined tragedy as an imitation of an action. "But most important of all is the structure of the incidents [the plot]. For tragedy is an imitation, not of men, but of an action and of life, and life consists in action, and its end is a mode of action, not a quality" (*Aristotle's Poetics*, p. 62). If, as Fergusson suggests, all elements of a tragedy—plot, character, thought, diction, song, and spectacle—imitate the action, then the director and actors must try to identify that action. The actors should agree among themselves or with a student-director on an *infinitive phrase* to designate the play's main action or, as Stanislavski calls it, the superobjective. Each performer should decide on the overall objective or motive of his or her own character as well, both as it relates to the play's superobjective and as it develops from moment to moment in the scene undertaken. Here, as in all such sections throughout this book, we have stated the characters' actions in infinitive phrases.

DEFINING THE ACTIONS AND THE SUPEROBJECTIVE

Fergusson has defined the superobjective of *Oedipus the King* as a quest for the well-being of the city. To find the culprit is Oedipus's immediate action and his purpose is clearly stated in the opening lines of the play. But it is to purify the city that he seeks the culprit—that remains the objective. The Chorus also seeks the well-being of the city as do the other characters, whose very lives depend on it.

The complicating factor in *Oedipus the King*, however, is to integrate Oedipus's subsequent search for his own identity with his search for the killer. An infinitive phrase is needed to bring together all aspects of the seeking action. It may be as broad as to seek the truth in order to save the city. To arrive at a superobjective that will satisfy the participants of a scene, it may be best to start from the individual scene under preparation and explore what the characters wish to do within the scene. For example, in the scene between Jocasta, the messenger, the Chorus, and Oedipus, these kinds of questions must be answered as preparation for rehearsal.

1. *Does the Chorus have an overall action in the scene?* In its opening verses, the thought of the Chorus seems to shift so that at one moment it asserts its faith in the supernatural order: "May destiny ever find me / pious in word and deed / prescribed by the laws that live on high" (ll. 864–866). At another it calls down the wrath of God on the proud who would ignore him: "May an evil doom / smite him" (ll. 887–888). Then it seems to question the order, noting that the proud may be honored and the oracles remain uncertain: "Apollo is nowhere clear in honour; God's service perishes" (l. 910). The actors will be able to find a rich variety of presentation by shifting their concentration to the different actions, to assert faith, to call for punishment, to question the supernatural order, but the several actions need to be unified under one. A possible statement of the larger action of the Chorus in the scene is to assert faith in the face of growing doubts.

2. *How can Jocasta's shifting actions be unified under one action or objective?* At first Jocasta would seem to appeal to Apollo for escape from his oracles. At another point she wishes to allay Oedipus's fear of the oracle by asserting its falseness, and when she finally sees the truth, her action is to beg Oedipus to stop his search. In her final words she attempts to warn Oedipus or even to mourn for him as she goes to her own suicidal death. One might say that her several actions are united under the major action, to save Oedipus, whose safety she undoubtedly identifies with the well-being of both herself and the city: "These are the symbols of my

prayer and this / my prayer: grant us escape free of the curse. / Now when we look at him we are afraid; / he's pilot of our ship and he is frightened" (ll. 920–923). Hence, even when her actions seem most opposed to the saving of the city, they continually relate to her level of comprehension of its safety. Characters who know the truth before Oedipus does, such as Jocasta, Teiresias, and the herdsman, identify the well-being of the city with their king's ignorance. Thus, though their small actions may seem to thwart Oedipus in his search, they wish to shield him and the city from knowledge of a horror that only Oedipus himself has the courage finally to acknowledge and embrace as his fate.

3. *Since Oedipus speaks mostly of his fears in this episode, what action can the actor find to play?* It would be dangerous to play being fearful. A verb must be found to help the actor arrive at the fear that is part of the driving force of the scene. If you examine the text closely, you will see that fear is the condition of Oedipus's mental state and that he moves forward questioning the messenger and seeking the herdsman in order to allay his fears. Oedipus first deals with his fears by sharing them with the messenger. Then when he learns of the herdsman's probable knowledge of his birth, he asks for news of him: "It's time / that this was found out once for all" (ll. 1050–1051). The false confidence with which he continues to seek his true birth may be played as an effort to suppress his growing fears. To attack Jocasta's motives is part of that suppression.

The three major actions in this scene, the Chorus's effort to assert its faith in an order it considers necessary to the well-being of the city, Jocasta's efforts to pacify the gods or avoid an order she finally sees to be fatal to Oedipus and hence to her idea of general well-being, and Oedipus's efforts to deal with his fears and continue the search, all relate to the superobjective: to save the city. The object of Oedipus's quest, Fergusson notes, "is not clear until the end, the seeking action takes many forms, as its object appears in different lights. The object, indeed, the final perception, the 'truth,' looks so different at the end from what it did at the beginning that Oedipus's action itself may seem not a quest, but its opposite, a flight" (*The Idea of a Theater*, p. 17). Hence, for example, in the Teiresias scene, Oedipus's action at one moment is to demand the truth, but at another it is to accuse the prophet of lying for gain. This seeming flight from the truth arises from the difficulty Oedipus has in dealing with the painfulness of the accusation. Like Jocasta, Oedipus would save himself since he still identifies the well-being of the city with his own well-being and moves in passion from the truth he seeks. Here we may glimpse the temper that led Oedipus to strike down the king and his followers on the road. But one must note again that the minor actions feed into the major one of finally saving the city.

The main point for the actor is to concentrate on the verb of the moment, not on the feelings of fear, anger, and so forth, but on the action as it is expressed in infinitive phrases.

OVERCOMING OBSTACLES

Closely related to playing the action is locating the obstacles, both inner and outer, to its accomplishment. A student-director may be most helpful here. What prevents Oedipus from embracing the truth when it is first presented to him by Teiresias? The obstacle may be the lack of evidence. In Oedipus's role as detective, he must overcome the reluctance of Teire-

sias, Jocasta, and the herdsman to furnish evidence. An inner obstacle
may be simply the terrible nature of the truth and its painfulness.

THE MAGIC IF AND THE GIVEN CIRCUMSTANCES

The situation of a king who has killed his own father and married his
own mother may seem very remote to the actor. While a believable performance may result in large measure from avoiding the direct playing of
emotion and concentrating on actions and objectives, forced acting may
also be avoided by using two simple Stanislavski techniques. Do not try to
be the character. Put yourself as nearly as possible in his or her situation.
The actor playing Teiresias might think to himself, "What IF I were in a
position to destroy a man who has complete power over me and whom I
revere with knowledge that I alone possess? What IF I were blind?" Then
the circumstances of the scene must be considered. First Oedipus's words
of respect naturally make Teiresias want to protect the king, but when he
upbraids and threatens the prophet, the desire of Teiresias to expose may
arise.

The Chorus must try to imagine the major given circumstance, that
of the plague. Members of the Chorus should try to particularize for
themselves their own losses and fears in terms of the plague. The actor
playing Jocasta could imagine how the flowers might best be placed on
Apollo's altar to pacify him. What IF it were very important to pacify the
god? And exactly what are the circumstances surrounding her sacrificial
offer? The actor playing Oedipus might try to work from some unpleasant truth in his own experience, one that proved difficult to face. What IF
you were then faced with this even more terrifying truth? The main point
is not to force the imagination but to coax it through examining circumstances and conjecturing what it would be like to be in them.

CLASSROOM ADAPTATIONS TO ARRIVE AT STYLE

In order to recapture something of the communal nature of Greek drama
in performance, an effort should be made to make physical connection
with the audience. One should feel free to make adaptations, to replace
the movement of the Chorus, for example, in the circular orchestra area
of a large amphitheater with a circling of the classroom audience, or a
procession through aisles, which could be created if desks or chairs are
movable. (Note that in this case a sense of distance is being destroyed in
order to illustrate the parallel roles of the Chorus and the audience.) The
main characters can perform on a higher level, if there is any way of raising them on something stable in the classroom, while the Chorus moves
below on the floor, or all could use the floor level. Weather permitting, if
there is an area secluded from noise and passers-by, the students may elect
to perform outside, although projection problems should be taken into
consideration.

Movement and gesture should be simple, broad, and economical. Remember that in the large Greek ampitheaters such simplicity and breadth
of gesture would be essential. Costumes may be simply sheets or robes,
unless students want to research the costumes and do some designing of
their own. Masks are essential. They may be paper or cardboard, although more elaborate materials could be employed.

The movement of the Chorus should be dancelike. Much of its
movement may be discovered by playing the action. The important point

to remember here is that the movement does not illustrate the action but embodies it or imitates it. Gestures may be repeated either in unison or one by one. Small, naturalistic gestures should be avoided. The Greek plays were put on outdoors; the playwrights wrote and the actors performed with a sense of the cosmic forces at work in the surrounding landscape. Much can be done with large, repetitive movement to help give this sense of the presence of the gods in the working out of human destiny.

The Wakefield Master
The Second Shepherds' Play

COLL
>Hail, thou comely and clean one! Hail, young Child!
>Hail, Maker, as I mean, from a maiden so mild!
>Thou hast harried, I ween, the warlock so wild,—
>The false beguiler with his teen now goes beguiled.
>>Lo, he merries,
>Lo, he laughs, my sweeting!
>A happy meeting!
>Here's my promised greeting,—
>>Have a bob of cherries!
>>(ll. 710–718)

With these simple words of praise and homely amusement, the shepherd Coll addresses the baby Christ child in the manger, expressing a devotion and joy that his audience fully shared. Like *Oedipus the King, The Second Shepherds' Play* dramatizes intimately felt and collectively shared cultural and spiritual beliefs. Nineteen centuries after Sophocles, drama was still used to celebrate received religious truths. In the European Western world, however, the "good news" (gospel) of the Christian mystery had replaced the bleak heroic individualism and stubbornly endured fate of Hellenic religious philosophy. For fifteenth-century England, the Christian vision of redemption compensated for the cruel realities of life. To be sure, hardships and disasters still informed that vision: a Fall followed Creation, a Flood followed the Fall, and even though Passion led to Salvation, at the Last Judgment only the faithful would be saved. But for those faithful, from the perspective of eternity, life was a divine comedy. The image of a suffering man martyred by cruel Jews and Romans immediately brought to mind the blessed babe, wrapped in swaddling clothes, lying in a manger, before whom simple shepherds and sophisticated wise men knelt in reverence.

The celebration of this commonly held faith formed a vital part of medieval English social life. Soon before the fifteenth century, many prosperous communities in England (and on the Continent) mounted summer festivals that presented cycles of playlets dramatizing human history as seen through the Christian tradition. Thirty-two such plays about Christian mysteries—from the Creation through the Last Judgment—form the cycle presented at Wakefield, a small town in Lancashire, England. One of those mystery dramas is *The Second Shepherds' Play.* While each playlet stands by itself, together they form a dramatic unit of nearly twelve thousand lines (the equivalent of five Shakespearean plays), which would have taken about fourteen hours without intermission to present. In the 1400s the festival was held on or around Corpus Christi Day, the Catholic celebration of the mystery of the Eucharist, which occurs twelve days after Pentecost (called Whitsunday or White Sunday in England) or about nine weeks after Easter.

The Wakefield (sometimes called Towneley) cycle of mystery plays represents one extant type of medieval English drama. Other forms—the liturgical drama performed largely in Latin within the Church; Saints' plays dealing with the martyrdom of Catholic saints; morality plays often cast as allegories—were equally vital during this period. Most students, for instance, are familiar with the famous *Everyman,* a morality drama of Dutch origin. Scriptural, or mystery, drama differs from the other forms largely because of its circumscribed material—the familiar Biblical narratives of Judeo-Christian history.

Two streams fed the well of tradition from which an unknown mid-fifteenth-century playwright whom we call the Wakefield Master drew the form and materials to shape his *Second Shepherds' Play.* Throughout the Middle Ages in England there flourished a *vernacular drama,* drama written in the language of the people. Few pure examples have survived. Ephemeral, probably topical, frequently pagan, and often little more than dialogue added to minstrelsy and juggling, this vernacular drama nevertheless represented a rich and continuing theatrical art that Church authorities could not suppress. They themselves were well aware of the power of dramatization to sway minds and hearts. Instruction manuals for preaching suggest how effective oral dramatization can be in making the horrors of hell and the joys of heaven more immediate to the largely illiterate believers who formed the congregations. The Church created drama in its services in other ways as well. One of the earliest known forms of liturgical drama is a short but elaborate chant celebrating the Resurrection of Christ. Here, in the Easter Mass itself, came a dramatization of the angel asking the two Marys, *"Quem quaeritis in sepulchro?"* ("Whom do you seek in this sepulchre?") Similar tropes added dramatic color to other masses, becoming increasingly central to the celebration. The combining of vernacular, nonreligious drama first with Latin and then with vernacular liturgical drama was a natural development for a society that shared a belief in the reality of a personal God-in-Three-Persons.

The raw materials and the two traditions adopted by the Wakefield Master had already reached an advanced stage of development in the Corpus Christi cycles that were held in many different towns and cities. In some cases, the basic scriptural stories used in all the cycles provided situations whose dramatization varied very little. To a well-developed and tradition-rich group of some twenty-six or twenty-seven plays of the cycle performed in his town, the Wakefield Master added six. His special dramatic genius made its contribution in several ways. First, for his dialogue he devised a tight, nine-line stanza employing internal as well as end rhyme. His control over northern English dialect enabled him to add effective realistic details to characterization; his sense of comedy and satire led to amusing situations and blistering attacks on contemporary abuses. But most important, his conception of his plays as unique wholes related to a larger complete cycle, whose end was the communal celebration of Christian history, allowed him to forge dramas of complex power. Perhaps he was a priest in orders, for he interwove his creations with the rich symbolism, or *typology,* characteristic of much great medieval religious art. Like Chaucer, who died about twenty or thirty years before the Wakefield Master wrote, he was master of life and of scholarship.

The Wakefield Master's probable social position—that of priest in orders—made him a member of the largest single educated class in medieval times. Early fifteenth-century England was a structured, feudal society dependent on closely circumscribed, class-determined rights and responsibilities. Ruling on earth were the pope as the highest spiritual authority and the king as the highest temporal authority who de jure if not always de facto owed his fealty to the pope. The chain of authority on earth modeled itself on *the great chain of being,* the hierarchical chain of God, his angels, human beings, and beasts. Below the king and the pope in power were the nobility, who raised their eldest children to inherit political and monetary responsibility and prepared their younger children to join the Church. Farther down the chain of authority appeared the lesser gentry whose younger sons and daughters became simple monks and nuns, while the children of nobility flourished as bishops and prioresses. Below the ranks of the nobility stood the merchants, farmers, and some free citizens who owned property, but the great masses were poverty-stricken serfs and peasants little better off than slaves. In a town such as Wakefield, burgesses drawn from among the most successful merchants administered day-to-day affairs with the blessing of the Church, while the neighborhood nobility wielded much temporal influence and could behave pretty much as they wished toward those lower on the social ladder. (Coll, the first shepherd, complains bitterly of the nobles' misuse of power.) Within the social organization of a town, secular-economic and religious guilds provided both stability and a means of transcending in one's lifetime a few of the class barriers. To the trade guilds (early in the history of the cycles, and certainly by the time *The Second Shepherds' Play* was produced) fell the task of mounting the Corpus Christi festivals and the plays. Distribution of responsibility was sometimes accomplished with considerable humor. At Chester, for instance, the water-leaders and drawers (a guild responsible for maintaining the city's water supply) acted the play about Noah and the Flood, while the cooks performed the Harrowing of Hell. The Nativity plays were traditionally performed by guilds of shepherds. *The* Second *Shepherds' Play* is simply the *second* of two such Nativity plays produced in the Wakefield cycle.

Because of the paucity and malleability of the evidence that remains, any account of the production of scriptural drama can be only conjectural. Clearly associated with it, however, are *pageants* or elaborately decorated wagons (hence the often-used synonym of scriptural drama, *pageant plays*). Large four-wheeled vehicles, these pageants had *mansions* or open houses constructed above the level of the wagon beds as acting areas containing practical scenery and properties.

Each of the mystery plays was associated with its own pageant. The pageant for *The Second Shepherds' Play,* for instance, probably represented Mak's house, or perhaps Mak's house and the manger wherein lay the newborn Lamb of God. Scholars conjecture with fairly firm evidence that the ground in front of the wagons served as another acting area, perhaps the fields where Coll, Gib, and Daw tended their sheep. At some point in the presentation of the cycle—probably before any of the plays were acted—all the pageants moved in glorious procession through the town. Some scholars believe that the pageants stopped at various stations, each guild acting out its play for the benefit of an ambulatory audience in a market square or street crossing, and then moved on to a new station where another performance would be given. Others think that all the pageants were drawn up in a large natural meeting place or amphitheater where the parts of the cycle were then performed sequentially before a large audience who earlier had seen *dumb shows* (mimed tableaux and portions of the plays) on the wagons as they passed in procession.

Some of the actors were professionals; others were gifted amateurs, screened and cast by a central board drawn from the guilds who produced the plays. An important character who appeared in many different plays during the cycle—God or Jesus, for instance—might be portrayed by a single actor (if we accept the conjecture that the cycle was acted at a single site); many of the two or three hundred other characters were doubled. The actors themselves wore representational costumes: staffs and cloaks typical of Lancashire for the shepherds, symbolic halos for Mary and Jesus. The stage effects, like the costumes, were both realistic and symbolic. Thus at one moment an elaborately decorated throne might be Herod's, at another, God's; or a single soldier might represent an army, a single fight, a battle. Acting areas, on and off the pageants themselves, were fixed but fluid: Herod in his wrath is directed to "rage" in the streets according to one remaining stage direction, and devils may have pricked more than one slow-footed member of the audience toward the symbolic yet realistic "Hell's Mouth" that appeared in many sets.

Symbolic or realistic, the scenery and costumes were not theatrically unsophisticated. Traps and flying machines portrayed descent or ascent, while cloud makers and smudge pots (for fire) added realistic details. But journeys of five thousand miles, like that from Lancashire to Palestine, could be accomplished in a wish. The plays and their production balanced symbol with concretization, typology with realism. Real horses and real sheep (like Mak's new "baby boy") stood side by side with constructed camels and talking animals portrayed by humans. To these details were added songs and instrumental music, some of them comical—like Mak's attempts; some of them accomplished—like the shepherds'; and some of them ethereal—like the angel's *Gloria* announcing Jesus' birth.

The mixture of the real and the symbolic in the scriptural plays was designed to lead the festival-day audience through laughter from the concrete, the everyday, to the hidden and the true, to paraphrase Erich Auerbach's study of literature (*Mimesis*). The feast of Corpus Christi was a ritual, social occasion that has few modern counterparts in the Western world. (Homecoming Day with its floats, parades, and ritual football games is a secular American equivalent, but the massive rallies of Communist China perhaps more closely match the religious/secular fervor of a Corpus Christi festival.) Chaucer's Wife of Bath loved the gaiety, the fairlike atmosphere of the pageants, while his carpenter knew in an intimate if garbled manner the stories told in the plays. More important, although neither directly verbalizes it, both Chaucerian characters were well attuned to the religious significance of the plays themselves. When it came time for the playing of *The Second Shepherds' Play*, they would know that they were to see a drama dealing with the old familiar story of the shepherds, "abiding in the field, keeping watch over their flocks by night," that this would lead to an announcement from an angel of the birth of Christ, then to a journey to the manger, then to a scene of adoration of the Infant and his Virgin Mother. When Coll complained of the onerous burdens he faced from rapacious nobility, when Gib spoke of his discontent in marriage to a fat, prickly shrew, when Daw cursed being little more than a slave to his master, the medieval audience probably understood these immediate complaints both as contemporary, particular sorrows and as representative general woes typical of a postlapsarian world and of fallen souls whom Christ had come to redeem.

These personalized shepherds, so like their fellows in Wakefield, were both immediate contemporaries and eternal representatives, the first common men to hear the "good news." They were simultaneously both real people and characters in a well-known, symbolic story. So well known was that story that when Mak entered in his disguise, at first one might have thought he was the angel who came to announce the birth of Christ. Like the angel, he enters singing (only to earn a stinging sarcasm from Coll, who recognizes just how unheavenly his vocal ability is). However, Mak is not the angel of the Nativity story, although in his disguise he might resemble the devil (a fallen angel)—shortly he is weaving a spell around the sleeping shepherds.

Here and elsewhere the audience would see parody—comic, yet serious enough—of the birth story. Other clues to parody abound. In the stolen fat *wether* (castrated young sheep), for instance, is a lamb symbolically standing for the Lamb of God. The identification of the lamb with Christ fluctuates from low comedy to the high central mystery of the Eucharist when Gill declares:

> I vow to God so mild,
> If ever I you beguiled,
> That I will eat this child
>   That doth in this cradle lie!
> (ll. 535–538)

Later, when the shepherds give their gifts to the Christ child, the simple presents carry deep iconographic significance: The cherries are associated with the Passion, the bird with the symbolic dove of the Resurrection, the tennis ball with the orb Christ holds in glory. These and tens of other references, symbols, and metaphors indicate the interchanging surfaces of *The Second Shepherds' Play*—low rogue comedy about a wily sheep thief caught and punished, social satire of a world in which feudal inequalities sorely hurt a poor shepherd but never extinguish common human generosity, and high ritual comedy of the common citizen taking part in the central mysteries of the Christian faith.

What actor and audience participate in is something like a *trompe l'oeil* picture. On the surface is one image—realistic medieval characterization and situation—but beneath that surface are others: the common fate of human beings in the fallen world, the presence of the devil, the social and spiritual reality of sin, the promise of redemption through faith (it is charity—Daw's desire to give a present to the child—that leads to the discovery of Mak's crime), and the living reality of Christ, the Lamb of God. Actor and audience are connected by the actions and superobjective of the superficial rogue comedy.

The Second Shepherds' Play

Translated by Clarence Griffin Child
Notes by Mark S. Auburn

Characters

COLL
GIB
DAW
MAK
GILL
THE ANGEL
MARY
THE INFANT SAVIOR

COLL

Lord, but this weather is cold, and I am ill wrapped!
Nigh dazed, were the truth told, so long have I napped;
My legs under me fold; my fingers are chapped—
With such like I don't hold, for I am all lapt
　　　　In sorrow.　　　　　　　　　　　　　　　　5
In storms and tempest,
Now in the east, now in the west,
Woe is him has never rest
　　　　Midday nor morrow!

But we seely shepherds that walk on the moor,　　　　10
In faith we're nigh at hand to be put out of door.
No wonder, as it doth stand, if we be poor,
For the tilth of our land lies fallow as the floor,
　　　　As ye ken.
We're so burdened and banned,　　　　　　　　　　15
Over-taxed and unmanned,
We're made tame to the hand
　　　　Of these gentry men.

Thus they rob us of our rest, our Lady them harry!
These men bound to their lords' behest, they make the plough tarry,　　20
What men say is for the best, we find the contrary,—
Thus are husbandmen oppressed, in point to miscarry,
　　　　In life,

Stage directions enclosed in brackets
were supplied by the translator,
Clarence Griffin Child. Some of
those enclosed in parentheses
were supplied by the authors of
Drama through Performance.

10 **seely:** blameless and to be pitied;
"poor."
22 **husbandmen:** tenants, farmers.

Thus hold they us under
And from comfort sunder.   25
It were great wonder,
            If ever we should thrive.

For if a man may get an embroidered sleeve or a brooch now-a-days,
Woe is him that may him grieve, or a word in answer says!
No blame may he receive, whatever pride he displays;   30
And yet may no man believe one word that he says,
            Not a letter.
His daily needs are gained
By boasts and bragging feigned,
And in all he's maintained   35
            By men that are greater.

Proud shall come a swain as a peacock may go,
He must borrow my wain, my plough also,
Then I am full fain to grant it ere he go.
Thus live we in pain, anger, and woe   40
            By night and day!
He must have it, if he choose,
Though I should it lose,
I were better hanged than refuse,
            Or once say him nay!   45

It does me good as I walk thus alone
Of this world for to talk and to make my moan.
To my sheep will I stalk, and hearken anon,
There wait on a balk, or sit on a stone.
            Full soon,   50
For I trow, perdie,
True men if they be,
We shall have company,
            Ere it be noon.
      [*The First Shepherd, Coll, goes out (or to one side). The Second Shep-
      herd, Gib, enters.*]

GIB

Ben'cite and Dominus! What may this mean?   55
Why fares the world thus! The like often we've seen!
Lord, but it is spiteful and grievous, this weather so keen!
And the frost so hideous—it waters mine een!
            That's no lie!
Now in dry, now in wet,   60
Now in snow, now in sleet,
When my shoes freeze to my feet,
            It's not all easy!

---

28 **embroidered sleeve or a brooch:**
(emblems of noble service or
authority).
38 **wain:** wagon.
49 **balk:** ridge or hillock.

51 **trow:** think; **perdie:** (*pardieu*, by
God) surely, verily.
55 **Ben'cite:** *benedicite*, bless you;
Dominus: Lord.
58 **een:** eyes.

But so far as I ken, wherever I go,
We seely wedded men suffer mickle woe,   65
We have sorrow once and again, it befalls oft so.
Seely Capel, our hen, both to and fro
        She cackles,
But if she begins to croak,
To grumble or cluck,   70
Then woe be to our cock,
        For he is in the shackles!

These men that are wed have not all their will;
When they're full hard bestead, they sigh mighty still;
God knows the life they are led is full hard and full ill,   75
Nor thereof in bower or bed may they speak their will,
        This tide.
My share I have found,
Know my lesson all round,
Woe is him that is bound,   80
        For he must it abide!

But now late in men's lives (such a marvel to me
That I think my heart rives such wonders to see,
How that destiny drives that it should so be!)
Some men will have two wives and some men three   85
        In store.
Some are grieved that have any,
But I'll wager my penny
Woe is him that has many,
        For he feels sore!   90

But young men as to wooing, for God's sake that you bought,
Beware well of wedding, and hold well in thought,
"Had I known" is a thing that serves you nought.
Much silent sorrowing has a wedding home brought,
        And grief gives,   95
With many a sharp shower—
For thou mayest catch in an hour
What shall taste thee full sour
        As long as one lives!

For—if ever read I epistle!—I have one by my fire,   100
As sharp as a thistle, as rough as a briar,
She has brows like a bristle and a sour face by her;
If she had once wet her whistle, she might sing clearer and higher
        Her pater-noster;
She is as big as a whale,   105
She has a gallon of gall,—
By him that died for us all,
        I wish I had run till I had lost her!

65 **mickle:** much.   91 **that you bought:** who redeemed
74 **bestead:** put to it.   you.
77 **tide:** time.   100 **epistle:** Epistle, i.e., the Bible.
83 **rives:** is torn, splits.

COLL

    "God look over the row!" like a deaf man ye stand.

GIB

    Yea, sluggard, the devil thy maw burn with his brand!   110
    Didst see aught of Daw?

COLL

                   Yea, on the pasture-land
    I heard him blow just before; he comes nigh at hand
          Below there.
    Stand still.

GIB

        Why?

COLL

    For he comes, hope I.   115

GIB

    He'll catch us both with some lie
         Unless we beware.
        [*The Third Shepherd, Daw, enters, at first without seeing them.*]

DAW

    Christ's cross me speed and St. Nicholas!
    Thereof in sooth I had need, it is worse than it was.
    Whoso hath knowledge, take heed, and let the world pass,   120
    You may never trust it, indeed,—it's as brittle as glass,
         As it rangeth.
    Never before fared this world so,
    With marvels that greater grow,
    Now in weal, now in woe,   125
         And everything changeth.

    There was never since Noah's flood such floods seen,
    Winds and rains so rude and storms so keen;
    Some stammered, some stood in doubt, as I ween.—
    Now God turn all to good, I say as I mean!   130
         For ponder
    How these floods all drown
    Both in fields and in town,
    And bear all down,
         And that is a wonder!   135

    We that walk of nights our cattle to keep,

                [*Catches sight of the others.*

    We see startling sights when other men sleep.
    Yet my heart grows more light—I see shrews a-peep.
    Ye are two tall wights—I will give my sheep
         A turn, below.   140
    But my mood is ill-sent;
    As I walk on this bent,

110 **Yea . . . brand:** (i.e., for
tarrying).
112 **blow:** blow his horn.
120–126 **Whoso . . . everything
changeth:** (a typical lament on
mutability).
136 **cattle:** livestock.

138 **shrews:** rascals.
139 **Ye . . . wights:** (spoken
contemptuously).
141 **But . . . ill-sent:** (Daw reproves
his disrespect).
142 **bent:** heath, field.

I may lightly repent,
    If I stub my toe.

Ah, Sir, God you save and my master sweet!   145
A drink I crave, and somewhat to eat.

COLL

Christ's curse, my knave, thou'rt a lazy cheat!

GIB

Lo, the boy lists to rave! Wait till later for meat,
    We have eat it.
Ill thrift on thy pate!   150
Though the rogue came late,
Yet is he in state
    To eat, could he get it.

DAW

That such servants as I, that sweat and swink,
Eat our bread full dry gives me reason to think.   155
Wet and weary we sigh while our masters wink,
Yet full late we come by our dinner and drink—
    But soon thereto
Our dame and sire,
When we've run in the mire,   160
Take a nip from our hire,
    And pay slow as they care to.

But hear my oath, master, since you find fault this way,
I shall do this hereafter—work to fit my pay;
I'll do just so much, sir, and now and then play,   165
For never yet supper in my stomach lay
    In the fields.
But why dispute so?
Off with staff I can go.
"Easy bargain," men say,   170
    "But a poor return yields."

COLL

Thou wert an ill lad for work to ride wooing
From a man that had but little for spending.

GIB

Peace, boy, I bade! No more jangling,
Or I'll make thee full sad, by the Heaven's King,   175
    With thy gauds!
Where are our sheep, boy? Left lorn?

DAW

Sir, this same day at morn,

---

143 **lightly:** quickly.
148 **meat:** food, not necessarily flesh.
154 **swink:** toil.
156 **wink:** sleep.
161 **Take . . . hire:** deduct from our wages.

171 **But:** only.
172–173 **Thou . . . spending:** You would be a bad servant for a poor man to send wooing for him.
176 **gauds:** tricks, pranks.
177 **lorn:** lost.

I them left in the corn
       When they rang Lauds.   180

They have pasture good, they cannot go wrong.

COLL

That is right. By the Rood, these nights are long!
Ere we go now, I would someone gave us a song.

GIB

So I thought as I stood, to beguile us along.

DAW

        I agree.   185

COLL

The tenor I'll try.

GIB

And I the treble so high.

DAW

Then the mean shall be I.
       How ye chant now, let's see!
     [They sing (the song is not given).]
     Tunc entrat Mak, in clamide se super togam vestitus. (Then enters Mak,
     who has put on a cloak over his ordinary dress.)

MAK

Now, Lord, by thy seven names' spell, that made both moon and
     stars on high,   190
Full more than I can tell, by thy will for me, Lord, lack I.
I am all at odds, nought goes well—that oft doth my temper try.
Now would God I might in heaven dwell, for there no children cry,
       So still.

COLL

Who is that pipes so poor?   195

MAK *(Aside.)*

Would God ye knew what I endure!
(Aloud.) Lo, a man that walks on the moor,
       And has not all his will!

GIB

Mak, whither dost speed? What news do you bring?

DAW

Is he come? Then take heed each one to his thing.   200
    Et accipit clamiden ab ipso. (Daw takes Mak's cloak off him.)

MAK

What! I am a yeoman—since there's need I should tell you—of the
     King,
That self-same, indeed, messenger from a great lording,
       And the like thereby.
Fie on you! Go hence

---

180 **Lauds:** the first of the canonical
hours of daily service, midnight (as
here) or dawn.
182 **Rood:** cross.
190 **seven names' spell:** (in
Rabbinical literature, there are seven
names for God).

194 **still:** continually.
197 **Lo, etc.:** Mak disguises his voice
speaking in a southern dialect; see
line 215.

Out of my presence!   205
I must have reverence,
            And you ask "who am I!"

COLL

Why dress ye it up so quaint? Mak, ye do ill!

GIB

But, Mak, listen, ye saint, I believe what ye will!

DAW

I trow the knave can feint, by the neck the devil him kill!   210

MAK

I shall make complaint, and you'll all get your fill,
            At a word from me—
And tell your doings, forsooth!

COLL

But, Mak, is that truth?
Now take out that southern tooth   215
            And stick in a flea!

GIB

Mak, the devil be in your eye, verily! to a blow I'd fain treat you.

DAW

Mak, know you not me? By God, I could beat you!

MAK

God keep you all three! Me thought I had seen you—I greet you,
Ye are a fair company!

COLL

                        Oh, now you remember, you cheat, you!   220

GIB

            Shrew, jokes are cheap!
When thus late a man goes,
What will folk suppose?—
You've a bad name, God knows,
            For stealing of sheep!   225

MAK

And true as steel am I, all men know and say,
But a sickness I feel, verily, that grips me hard, night and day.
My belly is all awry, it is out of play—

DAW

"Seldom doth the Devil lie dead by the way—"

MAK

            Therefore   230
Full sore am I and ill,
Though I stand stone still;
I've not eat a needle
            This month and more.

COLL

How fares thy wife, by my hood, how fares she, ask I?   235

MAK

Lies asprawl, by the Rood, lo, the fire close by,

209 **But . . . will:** Listen, Mak,
you're pretending to be a saint, I
know it!
215 **Now . . . southern tooth:** leave
off speaking that southern dialect.

229 **"Seldom . . . way—":**
proverbial; i.e., the Devil is always on
the move.

And a house-full of home-brewed she drinks full nigh—
Ill may speed any good thing that she will try
      Else to do!—
Eats as fast as may be,   240
And each year there'll a day be
She brings forth a baby,
        And some years two.

But were I now kinder, d'ye hear, and far richer in purse,
Still were I eaten clear out of house and home, sirs.   245
And she's a foul-favored dear, see her close, by God's curse!
No one knows or may hear, I trow, of a worse,
      Not any!
Now will ye see what I proffer?—
To give all in my coffer,   250
To-morrow next to offer
      Her head-mass penny.

GIB

Faith, so weary and worn is there none in this shire.
I must sleep, were I shorn of a part of my hire.

DAW

I'm naked, cold, and forlorn, and would fain have a fire.   255

COLL

I'm clean spent, for, since morn, I've run in the mire.
      Watch thou, do!

GIB

Nay, I'll lie down hereby,
For I must sleep, truly.

DAW

As good a man's son was I,   260
      As any of you!

                       [*They prepare to lie down.*

But, Mak, come lie here in between, if you please.

MAK

You'll be hindered, I fear, from talking at ease,
      Indeed!

                      [*He yields and lies down.*

From my top to my toe,   265
Manus tuas commendo,
Poncio Pilato,
      Christ's cross me speed!
      Tunc surgit, pastoribus dormientibus, et dicit: (Then Mak rises, when
      the shepherds are asleep, and says:)
Now 't were time a man knew, that lacks what he'd fain hold,
To steal privily through them into a fold,   270
And then nimbly his work do—and be not too bold,
For his bargain he'd rue, if it were told
      At the ending.
Now 't were time their wrath to tell!—

237 **home-brewed:** beer.
252 **head-mass penny:** the penny
paid for a mass for her departed
spirit.

266–267 *Manus . . . Pilato:* a
garbled Latin blessing—"I commend
your hands to Pontius Pilate."
269 **that:** who.

But he needs good counsel   275
That fain would fare well,
      And has but little for spending.

But about you a circle as round as a moon,
                    [He draws the circle (casting a spell).
Till I have done what I will, till that it be noon,
That ye lie stone still, until I have done;   280
And I shall say thereto still, a few good words soon
      Of might:
Over your heads my hand I lift.
Out go your eyes! Blind be your sight!
But I must make still better shift,   285
      If it's to be right.

Lord, how hard they sleep—that may ye all hear!
I never herded sheep, but I'll learn now, that's clear.
Though the flock be scared a heap, yet shall I slip near.
                              [He captures a sheep.
Hey—hitherward creep! Now that betters our cheer   290
      From sorrow.
A fat sheep, I dare say!
A good fleece, swear I may!
When I can, then I'll pay,
      But this I will borrow!   295
      [Mak goes to his house, and knocks at the door.]
Ho, Gill, art thou in? Get us a light!

GILL

Who makes such a din at this time of night?
I am set for to spin, I think not I might
Rise a penny to win! Curses loud on them light
      Trouble cause!   300
A busy house-wife all day
To be called thus away!
No work's done, I say,
      Because of such small chores!

MAK

The door open, good Gill. See'st thou not what I bring?   305

GILL

Draw the latch, an thou will. (*Mak opens the door.*) Ah, come in, my
      sweeting!

MAK

Yea, thou need'st not care didst thou kill me with such long stand-
      ing!

GILL

By the naked neck still thou art likely to swing.

MAK

      Oh, get away!
I am worthy of my meat,   310

---

287 **that . . . hear:** (to the audience;
i.e., the shepherds are snoring).

296 **Gill:** pronounced "Jill," though
some scholars prefer "Gill."

For at a pinch I can get
More than they that swink and sweat
    All the long day.

Thus it fell to my lot, Gill! Such luck came my way!

GILL

It were a foul blot to be hanged for it some day.   315

MAK

I have often escaped, Gillot, as risky a play.

GILL

But "though long goes the pot to the water," men say,
    "At last
Comes it home broken."

MAK

Well know I the token,   320
But let it never be spoken—
    But come and help fast!

I would he were slain, I would like well to eat,
This twelvemonth was I not so fain to have some sheep's meat.

GILL

Should they come ere he's slain and hear the sheep bleat—   325

MAK

Then might I be ta'en. That were a cold sweat!
    The door—
Go close it!

GILL

      Yes, Mak,—
For if they come at thy back—

MAK

Then might I suffer from the whole pack   330
    The devil, and more!

GILL

A good trick have I spied, since thou thinkest of none,
Here shall we him hide until they be gone—
In my cradle he'll bide—just you let me alone—
And I shall lie beside in childbed and groan.   335

MAK

    Well said!
And I shall say that this night
A boy child saw the light.

GILL

Now that day was bright
    That saw me born and bred!   340

This is a good device and a far cast.
Ever a woman's advice gives help at the last!
I care not who spies! Now go thou back fast!

MAK

Save I come ere they rise, there'll blow a cold blast!

320 **token:** proverb.   341 **far cast:** far-fetched (clever)
                                                         trick.

[*Mak goes back to the moor, and prepares to lie down.*]
       I will go sleep.   345
Still sleeps all this company,
And I shall slip in privily
As it had never been I
       That carried off their sheep.

COLL

   Resurrex a mortruis! Reach me a hand!   350
Judas carnas dominus! I can hardly stand!
My foot's asleep, by Jesus, and my mouth's dry as sand.
I thought we had laid us full nigh to England!

GIB

       Yea, verily!
Lord, but I have slept well.   355
As fresh as an eel,
As light do I feel,
       As leaf on the tree.

DAW (*Disoriented.*)

Ben'cite be herein! So my body is quaking,
My heart is out of my skin with the to-do it's making.   360
Who's making all this din, so my head's set to aching.
To the doer I'll win! Hark, you fellows, be waking!
       Four we were—
See ye aught of Mak now?

COLL

We were up ere thou.   365

GIB

Man, to God I vow,
       Not once did he stir.

DAW

Methought he was lapt in a wolf's skin.

COLL

So many are wrapped now—namely within.

DAW

When we had long napped, methought with a gin   370
A fat sheep he trapped, but he made no din.

GIB

       Be still!
Thy dream makes thee mad,
It's a nightmare you've had.

COLL

God bring good out of bad,   375
       If it be his will!

GIB

Rise, Mak, for shame! Right long dost thou lie.

MAK

Now Christ's Holy Name be with us for aye!
What's this, by Saint James, I can't move when I try.

---

350 **Resurrex a mortruis:** (garbled
Latin, referring, apparently, to
Christ's resurrection).

351 **Judas carnas dominus:** Judas,
(in?)carnate lord.
370 **gin:** snare.

I suppose I'm the same. Oo-o, my neck's lain awry   380
        Enough, perdie—
Many thanks!—since yester even.
Now, by Saint Stephen,
I was plagued by a sweven,
        Knocked the heart of me.   385

I thought Gill begun to croak and travail full sad,
Well-nigh at the first cock, with a young lad
To add to our flock. Of that I am never glad,
I have "tow on my rock more than ever I had."
        Oh, my head!   390
A house full of young banes—
The devil knock out their brains!
Woe is him many gains,
        And thereto little bread.

I must go home, by your leave, to Gill, as I thought.   395
Prithee look in my sleeve that I steal naught.
I am loath you to grieve, or from you take aught.

DAW

Go forth—ill may'st thou thrive!

                              [*Mak goes.*
            Now I would that we sought
      This morn,
That we had all our store.   400

COLL

But I will go before.
Let us meet.

GIB

        Where, Daw?

DAW

        At the crooked thorn.
     [*They go out. Mak enters and knocks at his door.*]

MAK

Undo the door, see who's here! How long must I stand?

GILL

Who's making such gear? Now "walk in the wenyand."   405

MAK

Ah, Gill, what cheer? It is I, Mak, your husband.

GILL

Then may we "see here the devil in a band,"
      Sir Guile!
Lo, he comes with a note
As he were held by the throat.   410

---

384 **sweven:** dream.
389 **tow . . . had:** (proverbial) more
to look out for.
396 **sleeve:** (the full long sleeve was
used as a pocket).
403 **thorn:** (a tree of distinctive
shape used as a meeting place).

405 **walk . . . wenyand:** literally,
"walk in the waning moon," i.e., "go
where bad luck may attend you."
407 **band:** noose.

And I cannot devote
       To my work any while.

MAK

Will ye hear the pother she makes to get her a gloze—
Naught but pleasure she takes, and curls up her toes.

GILL

Why, who runs, who wakes, who comes, who goes,   415
Who brews, who bakes, what makes me hoarse, d'ye suppose!
       And also,
It is ruth to behold,
Now in hot, now in cold,
Full woeful is the household   420
       That no woman doth know!

But what end hast thou made with the shepherds, Mak?

MAK

The last word that they said when I turned my back
Was they'd see that they had of their sheep all the pack.
They'll not be pleased, I'm afraid, when they their sheep lack.   425
       Perdie.
But how so the game go,
They'll suspect me, whether or no,
And raise a great bellow,
       And cry out upon me.   430

But thou must use thy sleight.

GILL

                  Yea, I think it not ill.
I shall swaddle him aright in my cradle with skill.
Were it yet a worse plight, yet a way I'd find still.
     [*Gill meanwhile swaddles the sheep and places him in the cradle.*]
I will lie down forthright. Come tuck me up.

MAK

                      That I will.

GILL

      Behind!   435
               [*Mak tucks her in at the back.*
If Coll come and his marrow,
They will nip us full narrow.

MAK

But I may cry out "Haro,"
       The sheep if they find.

GILL

Hearken close till they call—they will come anon.   440
Come and make ready all, and sing thou alone—
Sing lullaby, thou shalt, for I must groan
And cry out by the wall on Mary and John
       Full sore.
Sing lullaby on fast,   445

413 **gloze:** excuse.
415 **wakes:** watches.
420–421 **household . . . know:**
house which does not know a woman's
care.

431 **sleight:** trick.
436 **marrow:** company.
438 **"Haro":** Woe's me! Help!
440 **anon:** soon, immediately.

When thou hear'st them at last,
And, save I play a shrewd cast,
      Trust me no more.
   [*The Shepherds enter on the moor and meet.*]

DAW

Ah, Coll, good morn! Why sleepest thou not?

COLL

Alas, that ever I was born! We have a foul blot.   450
A fat wether have we lorn.

DAW

               Marry, God forbid, say it not!

GIB

Who should do us that scorn? That were a foul spot.

COLL

     Some shrew.
I have sought with my dogs
All Horbury Shrogs,   455
And of fifteen hogs
     Found I all but one ewe.

DAW

Now trust me, if you will, by Saint Thomas of Kent,
Either Mak or Gill their aid thereto lent!

COLL

Peace, man, be still! I saw when he went.   460
Thou dost slander him ill. Thou shouldest repent
     At once, indeed!

GIB

So may I thrive, perdie,
Should I die here where I be,
I would say it was he   465
     That did that same deed!

DAW

Go we thither, quick sped, and run on our feet,
I shall never eat bread till I know all complete!

COLL

Nor drink in my head till with him I meet.

GIB

In no place will I bed until I him greet,   470
     My brother!
One vow I will plight,
Till I see him in sight,
I will ne'er sleep one night
     Where I do another!   475
   [*They go to Mak's house. Mak, hearing them coming, begins to sing a
   lullaby at the top of his voice, while Gill groans in concert.*]

DAW

Hark the row they make! List our sire there croon!

COLL

Never heard I voice break so clear out of tune.
Call to him.

---

451 **wether:** young castrated male
sheep.
452 **scorn:** evil trick.

455 **Shrogs:** thickets.
456 **hogs:** young sheep.

GIB

           Mak, wake there! Undo your door soon!

MAK

Who is that spake as if it were noon?
      Aloft?   480
Who is that, I say?

DAW [*Mocking Mak.*]
Good fellows, if it were day—

MAK

As far as ye may,
      Kindly, speak soft;

O'er a sick woman's head in such grievous throes!   485
I were liefer dead than she should suffer such woes.

GILL

Go elsewhere, well sped. Oh, how my pain grows—
Each footfall ye tread goes straight through my nose
      So loud, woe's me!

COLL

Tell us, Mak, if ye may,   490
How fare ye, I say?

MAK

But are ye in this town to-day—
      Now how fare ye?

Ye have run in the mire and are wet still a bit,
I will make you a fire, if ye will sit.   495
A nurse I would hire—can you help me in it?
Well quit is my hire—my dream the truth hit—
      In season.
I have bairns, if ye knew,
Plenty more than will do,   500
But we must drink as we brew,
      And that is but reason.

I would ye would eat ere ye go. Methinks that ye sweat.

GIB

Nay, no help could we know in what's drunken or eat.

MAK

Why, sir, ails you aught but good, though?

DAW

                               Yea, our sheep that we get 505
Are stolen as they go; our loss is great.

MAK

      Sirs, drink!
Had I been there,
Some one had bought it sore, I swear.

COLL

Marry, some men trow that ye were,   510
      And that makes us think!

478 **soon:** immediately.   499 **bairns:** babies, children.
489 **loud:** strongly.

GIB

    Mak, one and another trows it should be ye.

DAW

    Either ye or your spouse, so say we.

MAK

    Now if aught suspicion throws on Gill or me,

    Come and search our house, and then may ye see   515

          Who had her—

    If I any sheep got,

    Or cow or stot;

    And Gill, my wife, rose not,

          Here since we laid her.   520

    As I am true and leal, to God, here I pray

    That this is the first meal that I shall eat this day.

COLL

    Mak, as may I have weal, advise thee, I say—

    "He learned timely to steal that could not say nay."

GILL

          Me, my death you've dealt!   525

    Out, ye thieves, nor come again,

    Ye've come just to rob us, that's plain.

MAK

    Hear ye not how she groans amain—

          Your hearts should melt!

GILL

    From my child, thieves, begone. Go nigh him not,—there's

      the door!   530

MAK

    If ye knew all she's borne, your hearts would be sore.

    Ye do wrong, I you warn, thus to come in before

    A woman that has borne—but I say no more.

GILL

          Oh, my middle—I die!

    I vow to God so mild,   535

    If ever I you beguiled,

    That I will eat this child

          That doth in this cradle lie!

MAK

    Peace, woman, by God's pain, and cry not so.

    Thou dost hurt thy brain and fill me with woe.   540

GIB

    I trow our sheep is slain. What find ye two, though?

    Our work's all in vain. We may as well go.

          Save clothes and such matters

    I can find no flesh

    Hard or nesh,   545

    Salt nor fresh,

          Except two empty platters.

---

518 **stot:** bullock.   545 **nesh:** soft.
521 **leal:** honest, loyal.

Of any "cattle" but this, tame or wild, that we see,
None, as may I have bliss, smelled as loud as he.

GILL

No, so God joy and bliss of my child may give me!   550

COLL

We have aimed amiss; deceived, I trow, were we.

GIB

        Sir, wholly each, one.
Sir, Our Lady him save!
Is your child a knave?

MAK

        Any lord might him have,   555
           This child, for his son.

When he wakes, so he grips, it's a pleasure to see.

DAW

Good luck to his hips, and blessing, say we!
But who were his gossips, now tell who they be?

MAK

Blest be their lips—

                         [*Hesitates, at a loss.*

COLL (*Aside.*)
             Hark a lie now, trust me!   560

MAK

        So may God them thank,
Parkin and Gibbon Waller, I say,
And gentle John Horn, in good fey—
He made all the fun and play—
        With the great shank.   565

GIB

Mak, friends will we be, for we are at one.

MAK

We!—nay, count not on me, for amends get I none.
Farewell, all three! Glad 't will be when ye're gone!

                   [*The Shepherds go.*

DAW

"Fair words there may be, but love there is none
        This year."   570

COLL

Gave ye the child anything?

GIB

I trow, not one farthing.

DAW

Fast back I will fling.
        Await ye me here.
[*Daw goes back. The other Shepherds turn and follow him slowly, entering while he is talking with Mak.*]

548 **"cattle":** (with a pun on "chattel" and a gesture toward the cradle).
549 **loud:** strong (i.e., the baby smells strong).
554 **knave:** boy.
558 **hips:** (proverbial and figurative for all body).
559 **gossips:** godparents.
563 **fey:** faith.
565 **shank:** long legs.

DAW
> Mak, I trust thou'lt not grieve, if I go to thy child.   575

MAK
> Nay, great hurt I receive,—thou hast acted full wild.

DAW
> Thy bairn 't will not grieve, little day-star so mild.
> Mak, by your leave, let me give your child
>   But six-pence.
> *[Daw goes to cradle, and starts to draw away the covering.]*

MAK
> Nay, stop it—he sleeps!   580

DAW
> Methinks he peeps—

MAK
> When he wakens, he weeps;
>   I pray you go hence!
> *[The other Shepherds return.]*

DAW
> Give me leave him to kiss, and lift up the clout.
> What the devil is this?—he has a long snout!   585

COLL
> He's birth-marked amiss. We waste time hereabout.

GIB
> "A weft that ill-spun is comes ever foul out."
>
>   *[He sees the sheep.*
>   Aye—so!
> He is like to our sheep!

DAW
> Ho, Gib, may I peep?   590

COLL
> I trow "Nature will creep
>   Where it may not go."

GIB
> This was a quaint gaud and a far cast.
> It was a high fraud.

DAW
>   Yea, sirs, that was't.
> Let's burn this bawd, and bind her fast.   595
> "A false scold," by the Lord, "will hang at the last!"
>   So shalt thou!
> Will ye see how they swaddle
> His four feet in the middle!
> Saw I never in the cradle   600
>   A horned lad ere now!

MAK
> Peace, I say! Tell ye what, this to-do ye can spare!
>
>   *[Pretending anger.*
> It was I him begot and yon woman him bare.

COLL
> What the devil for name has he got? Mak?—Lo, God, Mak's heir!

---

584 **clout:** cloth.   593 **gaud:** trick.
587 **weft:** web.

GIB
> Come, joke with him not. Now, may God give him care,   605
> > I say!

GILL
> A pretty child is he
> As sits on a woman's knee,
> A dilly-down, perdie,
> > To make a man gay.   610

DAW
> I know him by the ear-mark—that is a good token.

MAK
> I tell you, sirs, hark, his nose was broken—
> Then there told me a clerk he'd been mis-spoken.

COLL
> Ye deal falsely and dark; I would fain be wroken.
> > Get a weapon,—go!   615

GILL
> He was taken by an elf,
> I saw it myself.
> When the clock struck twelve,
> > Was he mis-shapen so.

GIB
> Ye two are at one, that's plain, in all ye've done and said.   620

COLL
> Since their theft they maintain, let us leave them dead!

MAK
> If I trespass again, strike off my head!
> At your will I remain.

DAW
> > > Sirs, take my counsel instead.
> > For this trespass
> We'll neither curse nor wrangle in spite,   625
> Chide nor fight,
> But have done forthright,
> > And toss him in canvas.
> > [*They toss Mak in one of Gill's canvas sheets till they are tired. He dis-
> > appears groaning into his house. The Shepherds pass over to the
> > moor on the other side of the stage.*]

COLL
> Lord, lo! but I am sore, like to burst, in back and breast.
> In faith, I may no more, therefore will I rest.   630

GIB
> Like a sheep of seven score he weighed in my fist.
> To sleep anywhere, therefore seemeth now best.

DAW
> > Now I you pray,
> On this green let us lie.

COLL
> O'er those thieves yet chafe I.   635

609 **dilly-down:** darling.   614 **wroken:** revenged.
613 **mis-spoken:** bewitched.

DAW

    Let your anger go by,—
        Come do as I say.
      [As they are about to lie down the Angel appears.]
      Angelus cantat "Gloria in excelsis." Postea dicat: (The Angel sings
      "Gloria in excelsis," then says:)

ANGEL

    Rise, herdsmen gentle, attend ye, for now is he born
    From the fiend that shall rend what Adam had lorn,
    That warlock to shend, this night is he born,   640
    God is made your friend now on this morn.
        Lo! thus doth he command—
    Go to Bethlehem, see
    Where he lieth so free,
    In a manger full lowly   645
        'Twixt where twain beasts stand.

                      [The Angel goes.

COLL

    This was a fine voice, even as ever I heard.
    It is a marvel, by St. Stephen, thus with dread to be stirred.

GIB

    'Twas of God's Son from heaven he these tidings averred.
    All the wood with a levin, methought at his word   650
        Shone fair.

DAW

    Of a Child did he tell,
    In Bethlehem, mark ye well.

COLL

    That this star yonder doth spell—
        Let us seek him there.   655

GIB

    Say, what was his song—how it went, did ye hear?
    Three breves to a long—

DAW

            Marry, yes, to my ear
    There was no crotchet wrong, naught it lacked and full clear!

COLL

    To sing it here, us among, as he nicked it, full near,
        I know how—   660

GIB

    Let's see how you croon!
    Can you bark at the moon?

DAW

    Hold your tongues, have done!
        Hark after me now!
      [They sing (the song is not given).]

GIB

    To Bethlehem he bade that we should go.   665
    I am sore adrad that we tarry too slow.

---

639 **rend:** take back; **lorn:** lost.
640 **warlock:** devil; **shend:** spoil,
overthrow.
644 **free:** noble.

650 **levin:** lightning.
657 **breves:** short notes.
658 **crochet:** note.
666 **adrad:** adread.

DAW

> Be merry, and not sad—our song's of mirth not of woe,
> To be forever glad as our meed may we know,
>> Without noise.

COLL

> Hie we thither, then, speedily,   670
> Though we be wet and weary,
> To that Child and that Lady!—
>> We must not lose those joys!

GIB

> We find by the prophecy—let be your din!—
> David and Isaiah, and more that I mind me therein,   675
> They prophesied by clergy, that in a virgin,
> Should he alight and lie, to assuage our sin,
>> And slake it,
> Our nature, from woe,
> For it was Isaiah said so,   680
> "Ecce virgo
>> Concipiet" a child that is naked.

DAW

> Full glad may we be and await that day
> That lovesome one to see, that all mights doth sway.
> Lord, well it were with me, now and for aye,   685
> Might I kneel on my knee some word for to say
>> To that child.
> But the angel said
> In a crib was he laid,
> He was poorly arrayed,   690
>> Both gracious and mild.

COLL

> Patriarchs that have been and prophets beforne,
> They desired to have seen this child that is born.
> They are gone full clean,—that have they lorn.
> We shall see him, I ween, ere it be morn,   695
>> For token.
> When I see him and feel,
> I shall know full well,
> It is true as steel,
>> What prophets have spoken,   700

> To so poor as we are that he would appear,
> First find and declare by his messenger.

GIB

> Go we now, let us fare, the place is us near.

DAW

> I am ready and eager to be there; let us together with cheer
>> To that bright one go.   705

681–682 *Ecce virgo/Concipiet:* Behold
a virgin shall conceive (Isa. 7:14).
684 **mights:** mighty ones.
685 **aye:** ever.

692 **beforne:** before.
695 **ween:** suppose.
696 **For token:** As a token.

Lord, if thy will it be,
Untaught are we all three,
Some kind of joy grant us, that we
      Thy creatures, comfort may know!
    [*They enter the stable and adore the infant Savior.*]

COLL

Hail, thou comely and clean one! Hail, young Child!   710
Hail, Maker, as I mean, from a maiden so mild!
Thou hast harried, I ween, the warlock so wild,—
The false beguiler with his teen now goes beguiled.
      Lo, he merries,
Lo, he laughs, my sweeting!   715
A happy meeting!
Here's my promised greeting,—
      Have a bob of cherries!

GIB

Hail, sovereign Savior, for thou hast us sought!
Hail, noble nursling and flower, that all things hast wrought!   720
Hail, thou, full of gracious power, that made all from nought!
Hail, I kneel and I cower! A bird have I brought
      To my bairn from far.
Hail, little tiny mop!
Of our creed thou art the crop,   725
I fain would drink in my cup,
      Little day-star!

DAW

Hail, darling dear one, full of Godhead indeed!
I pray thee be near, when I have need.
Hail, sweet is thy cheer! My heart would bleed   730
To see thee sit here in so poor a weed,
      With no pennies.
Hail, put forth thy dall,
I bring thee but a ball,
Keep it, and play with it withal,   735
      And go to the tennis.

MARY

The Father of Heaven this night, God omnipotent,
That setteth all things aright, his Son hath he sent.
My name he named and did light on me ere that he went.
I conceived him forthright through his might as he meant,   740
      And now he is born.
May he keep you from woe!
I shall pray him do so.
Tell it, forth as ye go,
      And remember this morn.   745

COLL

Farewell, Lady, so fair to behold
With thy child on thy knee!

---

713 **teen:** injury, pain; anger,
vexation.
724 **mop:** moppet.

725 **crop:** head, topmost part.
731 **weed:** dress, covering.
733 **dall:** fist.

GIB
>   But he lies full cold!
>   Lord, 't is well with me! Now we go, behold!

DAW
>   Forsooth, already it seems to be told
>   Full oft!   750

COLL
>   What grace we have found!

GIB
>   Now are we won safe and sound.

DAW
>   Come forth, to sing are we bound.
>   Make it ring then aloft!
>   [*They depart singing.*]

Action analysis and performance suggestions

The rich comic structure of *The Second Shepherds' Play* manifests itself particularly in the long scene at Mak's cottage when he and Gill disguise the stolen sheep as their newborn son (ll. 476–628). The whole scene is rather long for informal performance (about fifteen minutes' playing time), but the exit of the shepherds (l. 569) provides a convenient break for those who lack the opportunity to perform the scene in its entirety. Another possibility is to perform the meeting on the moor of Coll, Gib, Daw, and Mak (ll. 136–268).

DEFINING THE ACTIONS AND THE SUPEROBJECTIVE

When the three shepherds arrive at the door of Mak's cottage they are greeted by an unearthly chorus of Mak's full-voiced lullaby and Gill's pretended groans: "Hark the row they make!" All three are convinced that Mak stole their sheep (a sad loss for a poor shepherd whose flock might not exceed two or three dozen animals in all) and intend to recover their sheep. Their first task is to gain entry to Mak's house, an action easily achieved since Mak intends to let them enter, for he and Gill hope to pass the stolen sheep off as their newborn son in order to retain their ill-gotten gains. Gill's groans and Mak's protestations on her behalf—"Kindly, speak soft; / O'er a sick woman's head in such grievous throes!"—do little to quiet the suspicions of the shepherds. A show of hospitality ("I would ye would eat ere ye go") is made rather nervously in light of Gib's suspicious reply, "Nay, no help could we know in what's drunken or eat," suggesting that the sheep is already butchered. While the three shepherds begin to grill Mak, he repeats his offer of a drink, still protesting his innocence. In a line that contains both irony and parody, Mak seeks to prove their innocence by swearing his child would be the first thing he would eat if he were guilty: "As I am true and leal, to God, here I pray / That this is the first meal that I shall eat this day." The shepherds continue to search the cottage while Gill adds her chorus of feigned innocence to Mak's, seeking to convince them she has just had a baby and swearing she would eat her child if she were lying. Trying to convince his fellow shepherds that they search here in vain, Gib finally admits he can find nothing. When Coll agrees, Gib and Daw question Mak about his son, attempting to make peace (however uncomfortable that action makes

Mak). However, when Daw innocently asks who the boy's godparents are, Gib's suspicions are again aroused, although he tries to hide them from his friends (but wants to share them with the audience). Mak refuses Daw's offer of friendship and thrusts them out, continuing his effort to convince them of his righteous indignation.

In the scene, all five characters try to recover what they lost. The shepherds want their sheep, while Mak and Gill want to recover the appearance of innocence, which Mak's reputation has destroyed. That this cottage is a scene of a false nativity that mirrors the true Nativity comically and ironically suggests an articulation of the superobjective of the whole play—to recover through the birth of a Child what the world has lost. The Christian vision of history marks the gift of Salvation to the world at the coming of the Messiah who is born to redeem human beings from the pain and tribulation their sins had brought on them. Mak, a most sinful man indeed, will make confession and do his penance (hence be saved) when confronted by the proof of his guilt through another man's act of charity—perhaps then he too will recover what he has lost.

OVERCOMING OBSTACLES

The comic irony of the scene is enriched when we realize that one of Mak's obstacles is internal. Not only does he have to contend with the suspicions of the shepherds; he also must subdue his own quick-witted intellect and his pride in the sham Gill and he have devised. The two oaths made over the child-sheep are dangerous, for they might raise further suspicion, but Mak and Gill delight in their wit just as Mak enjoys his ironic swipe at nobility, "Any lord might him have, / This child, for his son" (which also conveys the parody of a typological meaning, that is, the Lamb of God). Both Mak and Gill enjoy their masquerade, but they go too far. When Mak refuses to accept the shepherds' offer of pardon, he helps guarantee their return to make peace by giving a present to the child. Mak is successful in overcoming the first of his obstacles, but is unable to conquer the second. Hence he becomes the well-known figure of comedy, the rogue who overreaches himself through the very cleverness of his trick. This cleverness is the shepherds' chief obstacle; yet it is their good-natured charity, not their guile, that leads them to discover the truth.

THE MAGIC IF AND THE GIVEN CIRCUMSTANCES

The weather is cold, food is scarce, life is hard. For Coll, Gib, and Daw, shepherding is a subsistence existence; for Mak and Gill, things are hardly better. Either group would benefit from a fat wether, but the sheep does after all belong to the shepherds. Its loss is a serious economic blow to their livelihood.

What IF you had lost something quite valuable and had reason to suspect an acquaintance who was a known thief? What IF he protested his innocence, assuring you he could not be guilty since his wife had just had a baby? Would your suspicions be raised by the child's smell? By the father's hesitation in naming the godparents? How would you act IF you had no incontrovertible proof of your suspicions?

What IF you were a thief whose main recourse was your wit and intelligence, your glib tongue and clever stratagems? What IF you were confronted by your accusers but had devised a perfect alibi? What better device than moral indignation to hide your guilt? What better privileged position than motherhood?

Into these circumstances are thrust characters very well defined by their words and actions elsewhere in the play. Although each has larger symbolic significance in the play as a whole and the cycle as a whole, each also has a distinct personality that should be taken into account in arriving at the precise circumstances of the unique situation here dramatized. How do Coll's intelligence, Gib's suspiciousness and dullness, and Daw's charitable disposition affect the way they react to the circumstances of the scene?

CLASSROOM ADAPTATIONS TO ARRIVE AT STYLE

Finding the tone of boisterous low comedy will not create much difficulty for actors who concentrate on the action underlying their speeches. No characters in comedy, except wits, amuse because they try to be funny; comic characters amuse because what they do conflicts with their intentions or with the situation in an absurd way. Comic dramatic irony in this scene becomes visual when the object of a search is as large as a trussed sheep. Speeches and pokings here and there in the cottage should be carefully orchestrated with the characters' various actions. As the shepherds near the cradle, for instance, Mak's and Gill's efforts to mislead or distract them should become more intense.

The playing area should not be closed off from the audience; three-quarter-round arrangements are probably best. To imitate the pageant wagon atmosphere, the audience might stand. Actors *are* aware of the audience and may direct comments to them, as in Coll's aside, thus breaking the artificiality of the scene in favor of a community of shared responses. Costuming may be realistically suggestive: shepherd's tunics, cloaks, staffs, leggings for the men, a tattered coarse shift and headdress for Gill. Two practical properties, a bed or bench and a large cradle (perhaps a box), are the only essential furnishings, but others could be used with propriety (for instance, dishes, chairs, even a fat young wether!). No lighting or sound effects are necessary, and the playing area should be lit no differently from the audience area.

The play is part of the whole medieval Corpus Christi experience; here the distance in time and in culture may present obstacles difficult to surmount. Close knowledge of the Nativity story and of the whole *Second Shepherds' Play* will help direct the reception of the comic scene and its parody, but it is clearly not the actors' function to underline the religious symbolism to the detriment of their own various actions. That symbolism resides in the total structure of the experience shared by actor and audience and will emerge only to one attuned to the clues.

C. G. Child's translation of *The Second Shepherds' Play* retains the essential characteristics of rhyme pattern and meter of the original Middle English version. The characters are made to speak poetry, but the lines are not to be repeated in a sing-song fashion. A movement both natural and rhythmic springs from these lines, and no attempt should be made to emphasize the midline or final rhymes. The most important effect of the meter and rhyme is to identify these speeches as *made* products, hence as art. Although art is not life but an imitation of life, still, for the actor, these lines must be first and foremost life. The actor *thinks on the line* while speaking, avoids pauses at the ends of lines, and uses natural pronunciation rather than what he or she feels to be an English or Middle English accent.

William Shakespeare
A Midsummer-Night's Dream

HERMIA
    O hell! to choose love by another's eyes.
LYSANDER
    Or, if there were a sympathy in choice,
    War, death, or sickness did lay siege to it,
    Making it momentany as a sound,
    Swift as a shadow, short as any dream,
    Brief as the lightning in the collied night,
    That, in a spleen, unfolds both heaven and earth,
    And ere a man hath power to say "Behold!"
    The jaws of darkness do devour it up:
    So quick bright things come to confusion.
        (I. i. 140–149)

Near the beginning of Shakespeare's *A Midsummer-Night's Dream* (1595),
Lysander and Hermia bemoan the vulnerability of their love. Egeus, Hermia's father, insists that she marry Demetrius. Lysander and Hermia see
only confusion and "the jaws of darkness" before them. Yet we in the audience know already that things will work out to assure the lovers' happiness, whatever the chaos they now perceive. Our expectations are the reverse, however, when we hear the ominous vow of Othello, hero of
Shakespeare's great tragedy (1604): "Perdition catch my soul, / But I do
love thee! and when I love thee not, / Chaos is come again" (III. iii.
90–92). Though he swears a love for his Desdemona of truly earth-en-
compassing proportions, we know that death and destruction will be the
outcome of their relationship, that "perdition" in the form of the evil Iago
and the jealous soul of Othello has even now caught the Moor, and that
chaos has broken loose on Cyprus. Lysander's assertion that "the course
of true love never did run smooth" applies equally well to the sportive if
sometimes painful mismatches of the comedy and to the serious, destruc-
tive passions of the tragedy. In both plays, chaos is unleashed, but the restoration of order in one brings marriages and happiness, in the other a
sad calm following the devastation of five deaths. The various ways in
which order, both personal and social, is threatened and re-established, be
it in the histories, light comedies, and farces of his earlier periods or in
the tragedies, problem plays, and symbolic romances of his mature years,
is part of the fundamental action and meaning of Shakespeare's dramatic
world.

    A child of the Renaissance, Shakespeare (1564–1616) lived through a
period of relative peace marked by significant material and cultural
achievements in England. It was a time of rebirth, of *renascence*, of the rediscovery of the classical world, and of the fresh discovery of a New

World. In science, empiricism was sweeping away the faulty, scholastically supported assumptions of the past. Galileo's observations and Copernicus's discoveries about the universe revolutionized humanity's view of itself by overturning the old, earth-centered Ptolemaic system. In economics, new overseas markets and more stable currencies stimulated increased trade at home and abroad. In politics, the final sovereignty of the pope had been questioned and in England, with its home-ruled Church, overturned. In art, new standards of realism and perspective swept away much of the iconography and symbolism of the Middle Ages. And in literature, a new appreciation for the range and variety of the English language supplanted the reliance on Latin and fixed forms of literary discourse.

Such sweeping changes sound productive of chaos, as if all the time-worn verities of spiritual, cultural, and material existence were negated without the counterestablishment of new grounds of order and security. However, the Renaissance was a logical outgrowth of the Middle Ages, and its social institutions were largely developments of the ordered society Coll, Gib, and Daw knew so well. Shakespeare and his English contemporaries professed the Christian faith, even if they were no longer Roman Catholics. Government depended on a fixed hierarchy with Elizabeth the Great, Virgin Queen, ruling by the grace of God and by the old but still vital doctrine of the "divine right of kings." The "great chain of being" still implied and thereby assured the dominance of son by father, woman by man, peasant by noble, and noble by king. As head of Church and state, Queen Elizabeth tolerated much dissent but little radicalism of the left or the right. New ideas were welcome, as long as the state was not irrevocably upset. With a foreign policy that discouraged war (except in defense) and a domestic policy that encouraged both the maintenance of the status quo and the improvement of many material conditions, England was relatively peaceful, well ordered, and stable—social conditions that can inspire, as they did in the Greece of Sophocles' time (that other period of great dramatic achievement), the self-confidence needed to explore new vistas of thought and articulation.

For centuries, people have marveled that the most articulate spokesman for the English Renaissance should have been the son of a tradesman and minor village official in the obscure town of Stratford-on-Avon, Warwickshire. But such were Shakespeare's origins. With what was a meager schooling by medieval standards, Shakespeare struck out from Stratford, probably in the late 1580s, to make a career in London as an actor. (His wife and three children continued living in Stratford.) According to his contemporary Ben Jonson, he had "little Latin and less Greek" (the languages of educated men), but the evidence of his plays shows his French to be good, his Italian sufficient to lift plots from stories written in that language, and his Greek and Latin far beyond that of most college graduates today. Whether or not his learning helps explain Shakespeare's remarkable success as a dramatist, his lifelong association with the practical, working theater was certainly a factor. For three decades, Shakespeare worked as actor, manager, and playwright on the London stage. During this period he wrote thirty-seven plays, probably collaborated on several others, and when the theaters were closed by civic decree because of plague, he wrote two long narrative poems and a much-praised sonnet sequence as well. He earned enough money during this career to retire to

Stratford in his old age (about 1611), a wealthy gentleman with his own coat-of-arms, the mark of "gentle" birth.

Practical success more than literary fame probably motivated much of his work. In his nondramatic pieces Shakespeare showed full control over the literary types of his day, and in his dramas he did not ignore critical strictures when they served his purposes. However, he avoided or modified the canonized, dull scholastic forms trumpeted by the "university wits," freely used topical or currently popular dramatic material (probably writing a competing version of plays being performed by another company more than once), and molded his dramas to the capability of his company so that, viewing his work as a whole, we can chart the appearance and departure of actors who specialized in particular role-types. Yet fewer than half of his plays were published during his lifetime, and scholars have not been able to determine whether or not he personally arranged for their publication. The bulk of his plays were first printed in what is called the First Folio edition prepared by two fellow actors seven years after his death.

From the production of *The Second Shepherds' Play* in the mid-fifteenth century to the production of *A Midsummer-Night's Dream* near the end of the sixteenth century is a long jump in the history of dramatic production. Movable stages gave way to fixed theaters; the mixture of professional and amateur actors was supplanted by professional companies; and the Church-tolerated religious drama influenced by a continuing tradition of secular plays metamorphosed into fully secular plays on secular themes (kingship, rebellion, love) for a secular audience. The plays were performed not only in the courtyards of inns along the countryside but also in huge public arenas built specifically for the purpose. For the first time in Western history theater had become a large-scale, self-supporting, capitalistic venture.

With several plays a week to present throughout a good part of the year, with provincial audiences to please when they undertook a not infrequent tour, and with an educated court audience to entertain when the queen (or later the king) so chose, the acting companies had to have a wide variety of plays in their repertories. Shakespeare's company, the Lord Chamberlain's Men and later the King's Men, was perhaps the best of his time. It was organized as a corporation, and older actors who had established themselves could buy shares in the physical stock owned by the principal members. The company owned a large theater and all its properties, paid the salaries of the actors, and often maintained a resident playwright (Shakespeare was one such). Younger actors worked themselves up through the ranks. As boys whose voices had not yet changed, they were taught their initial specialization in female roles (all women on Shakespeare's stage were portrayed by men) until they grew up and took over other specialties. Each actor was probably expected to play a musical instrument, to know how to dance, fence, and tumble, and, most important, to know how to create an immediate, compelling theatrical presence. The audience, unaccustomed to reading but well practiced in listening carefully, helped them; the blank verse that makes up about 67 percent of the lines in Shakespeare's plays requires a close ear as well as an accomplished actor.

Since reading was an entertainment confined to those few lucky enough to have been schooled, the brothels and the savage sport of bear-baiting were the major competitors to the Elizabethan theater as forms of popular entertainment. Attracting perhaps twenty-five hundred spectators a performance, the theaters were built outside the London city walls, away from the civic influence of Puritans who disapproved of theatrical activity and the statutorial control of the city fathers who could close a theater on various pretexts, but within easy reach of any Londoner who could cross the Thames Bridge or pay for a ferry. The plays were presented during the day, usually in the afternoon, under minimal roofing. (Some private theaters, such as Blackfriars, were roofed and lit by candles.) Prostitutes could be found circulating freely in the theater; caught pickpockets might be seen handcuffed to the stage pillars, orange women sold their wares, and rich and noble spectators possibly sat on the stage itself.

Research indicates that the stage was a rectangular platform extending into the "round O" of Shakespeare's theater, the Globe. The name of Shakespeare's theater suggests the conscious identification in his time of the stage as a metaphor for "all the world." Although English drama of the sixteenth century was no longer overtly religious, its cultural bases remained comprehensive, its moral dilemmas spoke to all members of its society, and its stage still functioned in medieval fashion as a microcosm in which the players could, in Hamlet's words, "hold, as 'twere, the mirror up to nature."

The stage that thrust out into an audience of "groundlings" who surrounded it on three sides is one of the few attributes of Shakespeare's theater on which scholars agree. Its size is sometimes conjectured to be about three feet high, forty-three feet wide, and twenty-eight feet deep. The groundlings, members of the lower classes who paid a penny (about the price of a quart of ale) for admission and who possibly stood throughout the performance, doubtless added to the cacophony before the performance began, and perhaps during it as well. The affluent sat in two or three roofed galleries attached to the inside of the walls of the building, the few women present probably masked.

Other elements of the theater, which have been conjectured partly from a drawing of the Swan theater and partly from other bits of evidence and the plays themselves, include: a two- or three-story façade with two pillars placed midway between the façade and the front of the platform to support a *shadow*, or half roof, over the stage; at least two doors or gates on the first level for entrances and exits; a curtained enclosure between the doors that could serve as an extra playing area for discoveries; a rear stage balcony at the second-story level for action to occur "above"; a loft under the shadow called the "heavens" from which gods might descend; a space below the stage with access to it by at least one trap door through which devils and monsters might ascend; a tiring room behind the façade for storage of properties and costumes and for dressing; a hut above the roof in which musicians might reside and sound effects and machinery might be housed.

While such a reconstruction may be conjectural, without doubt the action on this very flexible stage was nearly continuous with no intermissions and at most a brief pause between episodes to indicate a change of place. Scenery was minimal, possibly with practical but nonrealistic properties for beds, thrones, torches, and so forth. The fixed façade could represent a background for numerous locations that were designated by the written word or suggested by a change of property. Costumes only occasionally suggested period; sumptuous versions of Elizabethan "modern dress" clothed most characters.

Some sense of the Elizabethan theater experience may be recaptured in today's arena theater or theater-in-the-round, where the actor must now as he did then relinquish the appearance of a person speaking in real life and project a text to the surrounding audience that sees and hears the action from different sides. The actor, however, was not the only stimulus to the imagination of the Elizabethan audience. They also enjoyed the colorful pageantry and tableaux provided by the tapestries and banners that probably decorated the stage, the ascents and descents provided by machinery, the splendid and colorful costumes (often inherited from noble persons), and the music and sound effects that could suggest atmosphere and punctuate or change the mood of the action.

The relationship between actor and audience in this theater differed from that of Sophocles' time or the Wakefield Master's. The sense of ritual and religious celebration had dwindled from primarily religious purposes to largely symbolic remains. A paying customer felt he had the right to complain or to praise as he wished. The physical conditions—distances of little more than fifty feet from actors to the most distant spectators—encouraged an intimacy unknown in the vast Greek amphitheater. When Helena spoke in soliloquy near the end of the first scene of *A Midsummer-Night's Dream*, the young boy actor probably spoke directly to the audience. Other stage conventions—the use of asides or speeches directed at the audience, which was supposed to imagine that other actors on stage could not hear; nonrepresentational disguises; invisibility, as when Puck comes into the midst of the rehearsing workmen; rapid transposition of scenic space—added to intimacy and a shared sense of social, dramatic endeavor. Shakespeare's theater was presentational, not representational. All its conventions, all its acting techniques, all its heavy dependence on language to create pictures in the mind's eye were devices designed to allow the freest play of the imagination. Curiously, the major theatrical experimentation of the twentieth century has aimed at re-establishing the intimacy lost when illusionistic modes of production triumphed and at regaining the poetic and imaginative truth that began to disappear when the fixed, if subtle, images of the cinema filled the consciousness of the audience.

Distanced though Shakespeare's professional theater might have been from the pageantry of the medieval stage, many influences of that earlier time still remained. Like the Wakefield Master, Shakespeare felt licensed to mix low comedy with high seriousness. The purity of genre preached by the university wits, who drew largely on classical models, did not prevent his adding scenes of boisterous comedy even in the most thrilling tragedy, almost always with enriching, resonating results; nor did he hesitate to break the unities of time and place that so concerned his academic contemporaries. Like the allegorizing authors of the morality plays (still popular in the mid-sixteenth century), Shakespeare could use traditional characteristics of such stock figures as the Vice to direct our moral judgment, although usually to enlarge rather than narrow that understanding.

Dependent as it was on scripture and Christian history, the subject matter of the medieval stage was rarely invented afresh, and in Shakespeare's day, the use of well-known sources was acceptable practice. Genius of invention revealed itself not in novelty but in arrangement, not in the creation of new stories but in illumination through image and motive, effect and connection. In *A Midsummer-Night's Dream,* Shakespeare turned to such diverse sources as Chaucer's "Knight's Tale," North's translation of Plutarch's *Lives,* Golding's translation of Ovid's *Metamorphoses,* and others, and molded them all together into a single, complex comedy with four distinct but mutually dependent lines of action. In *Othello,* Shakespeare turned to a simple, bloody, revenge story by Giraldi Cinthio, but he created new images—loathesome animals, the fabled uncivilized Turk, light as goodness and purity, dark as evil and destruction—and formed them all into controlling metaphors for his whole dramatic poem. By adding heroic stature to one character, virtuous innocence to another, and magnificent, nearly inexplicable evil to the villain, he wove a single, highly unified tragedy of jealousy.

In *A Midsummer-Night's Dream* the controlling metaphor concerns love and madness. Duke Theseus, a practical man of reason and authority, dismisses the young lovers' tale of their moon-drenched encounter with irrationality in the wood as being the kind of fantasy perceived by the "lunatic, the lover, and the poet." However, the daylight world of Theseus's conventionally well-ordered court encloses another kind of reality in *A Midsummer-Night's Dream.* Beyond Athens lies the wood, which the lordly Theseus enters as a hunter—a royal predator—with highly bred and highly trained hounds, but which for Lysander and Hermia, Demetrius and Helena, is a place of confusion, of shifting and unaccountable loyalties, of nightmare, and of potential madness. They become physically lost and contentious, and touched with lunacy. After all, the night is Midsummer Eve with its invitation to the supernatural, the unpredictable, the erotic, and the moon (*luna*) presides over their wandering.

This is not to suggest that *A Midsummer-Night's Dream* is gloomy. On the contrary, the play is a comedy, with the swift verbal wit, the physical vigor and resilience, and the movement from potential disaster to the happy consummation that the term implies. It is a play about the many levels and facets of love: about Theseus, who cavalierly combines authority with erotic urgency; about the young courtiers' headlong infatuation and precipitous plunge into the shadowy, moonlit wood (and into their own irrationality); about the imperious Titania and Oberon, who are native to the wood and the moonlight, but whose bickering and recrimination and final reconciliation suggest a further dimension to the marriages with which the play culminates and which these powerful supernatural creatures, all unknown to the principals, bless at the end. Even the "rude mechanicals" are in love—Bottom with himself, his companions with a pension of sixpence a day. Each of the four groups contributes unwittingly to the initial chaos, but each, in the way of comedy, is brought into harmonious relationship at the end.

Shakespeare employs here neither the personal nor the political satire practiced by the Greek comic playwright, Aristophanes (c. 448–c. 380 B.C.), in what is called Old Comedy. Instead he joins his fellow Renaissance playwrights by taking Plautus's and Terence's Roman classical renditions of Greek New Comedy as a model (the boy-meets-girl-overcomes-obstacles-and-gets-girl formula), although he retains something of an Aristophanic sense of saturnalia in his comedy. *A Midsummer-Night's Dream* fits into what Northrop Frye (*Anatomy of Criticism,* p. 182) calls Shakespeare's "drama of the green world" in which the renewal of the year is celebrated, the forces of life and love triumph over the wasteland, and those characters that have obstructed release and freedom give way and are included in the final festivities.

A Midsummer-Night's Dream

[*Dramatis personæ*
THESEUS, *duke of Athens*
EGEUS, *father to Hermia*
LYSANDER, *betrothed to Hermia*
DEMETRIUS, *in love with Hermia*
PHILOSTRATE, *master of the revels to Theseus*
HIPPOLYTA, *queen of the Amazons, betrothed to Theseus*
HERMIA, *daughter to Egeus, betrothed to Lysander*
HELENA, *in love with Demetrius*

QUINCE, *a carpenter,*			PROLOGUE
BOTTOM, *a weaver,*			PYRAMUS
FLUTE, *a bellows-mender,*	*presenting*		THISBE
SNOUT, *a tinker,*			WALL
SNUG, *a joiner,*			LION
STARVELING, *a tailor,*			MOONSHINE

OBERON, *king of the fairies*
TITANIA, *queen of the fairies*
ROBIN GOODFELLOW, *a Puck*

PEASEBLOSSOM,	
COBWEB,	*fairies*
MOTH,	
MUSTARDSEED,	

Other fairies attending their King and Queen
Attendants on Theseus and Hippolyta
        Scene: Athens, and a wood near it]

Act I

[*Scene I. Athens. The palace of Theseus.*]
Enter Theseus, Hippolyta, [*Philostrate,*] *with others.*

THESEUS
　Now, fair Hippolyta, our nuptial hour
　Draws on apace. Four happy days bring in
　Another moon; but, O, methinks, how slow
　This old moon wanes! She lingers my desires,

The explanatory notes and text of *A Midsummer-Night's Dream* were prepared by William Allan Neilson and Charles Jarvis Hill. Proper names given in parentheses (Theobald, Pope, and so forth) are those of earlier editors. According to the Preface in the Neilson-Hill edition, "Stage directions, if modern, are enclosed in [brackets]; when they are substantially those of editions not later than 1623, they are unbracketed, or are set aside by a single bracket only, or, when occurring within a line, are enclosed in (parentheses)." In the dialogue, words or phrases emended by earlier editors (or conjected, if omitted in the copy text) are also bracketed.

Like to a step-dame or a dowager   5
Long withering out a young man's revenue.

HIPPOLYTA
Four days will quickly steep themselves in night;
Four nights will quickly dream away the time;
And then the moon, like to a silver bow
New-bent in heaven, shall behold the night   10
Of our solemnities.

THESEUS
                        Go, Philostrate,
Stir up the Athenian youth to merriments;
Awake the pert and nimble spirit of mirth;
Turn melancholy forth to funerals;
The pale companion is not for our pomp.   15

                                   [*Exit Philostrate.*]

Hippolyta, I woo'd thee with my sword,
And won thy love doing thee injuries;
But I will wed thee in another key,
With pomp, with triumph, and with revelling.
         Enter Egeus, Hermia, Lysander, and Demetrius.

EGEUS
Happy be Theseus, our renowned Duke!   20

THESEUS
Thanks, good Egeus; what's the news with thee?

EGEUS
Full of vexation come I, with complaint
Against my child, my daughter Hermia.
Stand forth, Demetrius. My noble lord,
This man hath my consent to marry her.   25
Stand forth, Lysander: and, my gracious Duke,
This man hath bewitch'd the bosom of my child.
Thou, thou, Lysander, thou hast given her rhymes
And interchang'd love-tokens with my child.
Thou hast by moonlight at her window sung   30
With faining voice verses of faining love,
And stol'n the impression of her fantasy
With bracelets of thy hair, rings, gawds, conceits,
Knacks, trifles, nosegays, sweetmeats,—messengers
Of strong prevailment in unhard'ned youth.   35
With cunning hast thou filch'd my daughter's heart,
Turn'd her obedience, which is due to me,
To stubborn harshness; and, my gracious Duke,
Be it so she will not here before your Grace
Consent to marry with Demetrius,   40
I beg the ancient privilege of Athens,
As she is mine, I may dispose of her;

I.i.5 **dowager:** widow with a dowry
from an estate.
10 **New-bent** Qq. *Now bent* Ff.
13 **pert:** lively.
15 **companion:** fellow, referring to
melancholy.
19 **triumph:** public festivity.

31 **faining:** longing.
32 **stol'n . . . fantasy:** captured her
fancy (by impressing it with gifts).
33 **gawds:** trinkets; **conceits:**
devices.
34 **knacks:** knickknacks.
39 **Be it so:** if.

Which shall be either to this gentleman
Or to her death, according to our law
Immediately provided in that case.   45

THESEUS

What say you, Hermia? Be advis'd, fair maid.
To you your father should be as a god,
One that compos'd your beauties, yea, and one
To whom you are but as a form in wax
By him imprinted, and within his power   50
To leave the figure or disfigure it.
Demetrius is a worthy gentleman.

HERMIA

So is Lysander.

THESEUS

                    In himself he is;
But in this kind, wanting your father's voice,
The other must be held the worthier.   55

HERMIA

I would my father look'd but with my eyes.

THESEUS

Rather your eyes must with his judgement look.

HERMIA

I do entreat your Grace to pardon me.
I know not by what power I am made bold,
Nor how it may concern my modesty,   60
In such a presence here to plead my thoughts;
But I beseech your Grace that I may know
The worst that may befall me in this case,
If I refuse to wed Demetrius.

THESEUS

Either to die the death or to abjure   65
For ever the society of men.
Therefore, fair Hermia, question your desires,
Know of your youth, examine well your blood,
Whether, if you yield not to your father's choice,
You can endure the livery of a nun,   70
For aye to be in shady cloister mew'd,
To live a barren sister all your life,
Chanting faint hymns to the cold fruitless moon.
Thrice-blessed they that master so their blood
To undergo such maiden pilgrimage;   75
But earthlier happy is the rose distill'd
Than that which withering on the virgin thorn
Grows, lives, and dies in single blessedness.

HERMIA

So will I grow, so live, so die, my lord,
Ere I will yield my virgin patent up   80

45 **Immediately:** expressly.
51 **disfigure:** obliterate.
54 **in . . . kind:** i.e., as a husband;
voice: approval.
60 **concern:** beseem.
68 **blood:** passion.

69 **Whether.** One syllable in
pronunciation.
71 **mew'd:** shut up (a term from
falconry).
80 **patent:** privilege, liberty.

Unto his lordship, whose unwished yoke
My soul consents not to give sovereignty.

THESEUS

Take time to pause; and, by the next new moon—
The sealing-day betwixt my love and me
For everlasting bond of fellowship—   85
Upon that day either prepare to die
For disobedience to your father's will,
Or else to wed Demetrius, as he would,
Or on Diana's altar to protest
For aye austerity and single life.   90

DEMETRIUS

Relent, sweet Hermia; and, Lysander, yield
Thy crazed title to my certain right.

LYSANDER

You have her father's love, Demetrius,
Let me have Hermia's; do you marry him.

EGEUS

Scornful Lysander! true, he hath my love,   95
And what is mine my love shall render him.
And she is mine, and all my right of her
I do estate unto Demetrius.

LYSANDER

I am, my lord, as well deriv'd as he,
As well possess'd; my love is more than his;   100
My fortunes every way as fairly rank'd,
If not with vantage, as Demetrius';
And, which is more than all these boasts can be,
I am belov'd of beauteous Hermia.
Why should not I then prosecute my right?   105
Demetrius, I'll avouch it to his head,
Made love to Nedar's daughter, Helena,
And won her soul; and she, sweet lady, dotes,
Devoutly dotes, dotes in idolatry,
Upon this spotted and inconstant man.   110

THESEUS

I must confess that I have heard so much,
And with Demetrius thought to have spoke thereof;
But, being over-full of self-affairs,
My mind did lose it. But, Demetrius, come;
And come, Egeus; you shall go with me;   115
I have some private schooling for you both.
For you, fair Hermia, look you arm yourself
To fit your fancies to your father's will;
Or else the law of Athens yields you up—
Which by no means we may extenuate—   120
To death, or to a vow of single life.
Come, my Hippolyta; what cheer, my love?
Demetrius and Egeus, go along.

89 **protest:** vow.   106 **head:** face.
92 **crazed:** unsound.   120 **extenuate:** weaken.
98 **estate unto:** settle upon.

I must employ you in some business
Against our nuptial, and confer with you   125
Of something nearly that concerns yourselves.

EGEUS

With duty and desire we follow you.

                                  [Exeunt all but Lysander and Hermia.

LYSANDER

How now, my love! why is your cheek so pale?
How chance the roses there do fade so fast?

HERMIA

Belike for want of rain, which I could well   130
Beteem them from the tempest of my eyes.

LYSANDER

Ay me! for aught that I could ever read,
Could ever hear by tale or history,
The course of true love never did run smooth;
But, either it was different in blood,—   135

HERMIA

O cross! too high to be enthrall'd to [low].

LYSANDER

Or else misgraffed in respect of years,—

HERMIA

O spite! too old to be engag'd to young.

LYSANDER

Or else it stood upon the choice of friends,—

HERMIA

O hell! to choose love by another's eyes.   140

LYSANDER

Or, if there were a sympathy in choice,
War, death, or sickness did lay siege to it,
Making it momentany as a sound,
Swift as a shadow, short as any dream,
Brief as the lightning in the collied night,   145
That, in a spleen, unfolds both heaven and earth,
And ere a man hath power to say "Behold!"
The jaws of darkness do devour it up:
So quick bright things come to confusion.

HERMIA

If then true lovers have been ever cross'd,   150
It stands as an edict in destiny.
Then let us teach our trial patience,
Because it is a customary cross,
As due to love as thoughts and dreams and sighs,
Wishes and tears, poor Fancy's followers.   155

LYSANDER

A good persuasion; therefore, hear me, Hermia.
I have a widow aunt, a dowager
Of great revenue, and she hath no child.

125 **Against:** in anticipation of.	145 **collied:** blackened.
131 **Beteem:** allow	146 **spleen:** burst of passion.
136 **[low]** (Theobald). *love* Q.	150 **ever:** always.
137 **misgraffed:** mismatched.	155 **Fancy's:** love's.
143 **momentany:** momentary.	

From Athens is her house remote seven leagues;
And she respects me as her only son.   160
There, gentle Hermia, may I marry thee;
And to that place the sharp Athenian law
Cannot pursue us. If thou lov'st me then,
Steal forth thy father's house to-morrow night;
And in the wood, a league without the town,   165
Where I did meet thee once with Helena
To do observance to a morn of May,
There will I stay for thee.

HERMIA
                         My good Lysander!
I swear to thee, by Cupid's strongest bow,
By his best arrow with the golden head,   170
By the simplicity of Venus' doves,
By that which knitteth souls and prospers loves,
And by that fire which burn'd the Carthage queen
When the false Troyan under sail was seen,
By all the vows that ever men have broke,   175
In number more than ever women spoke,
In that same place thou hast appointed me
To-morrow truly will I meet with thee.

LYSANDER
Keep promise, love. Look, here comes Helena.
        Enter Helena.

HERMIA
God speed fair Helena! Whither away?   180

HELENA
Call you me fair? That fair again unsay.
Demetrius loves your fair, O happy fair!
Your eyes are lode-stars, and your tongue's sweet air
More tuneable than lark to shepherd's ear
When wheat is green, when hawthorn buds appear.   185
Sickness is catchng; O, were favour so,
[Yours would] I catch, fair Hermia, ere I go;
My ear should catch your voice, my eye your eye,
My tongue should catch your tongue's sweet melody.
Were the world mine, Demetrius being bated,   190
The rest I'll give to be to you translated.
O, teach me how you look, and with what art
You sway the motion of Demetrius' heart.

HERMIA
I frown upon him, yet he loves me still.

HELENA
O that your frowns would teach my smiles such skill!   195

HERMIA
I give him curses, yet he gives me love.

---

160 **respects:** regards.
171 **simplicity:** innocence.
173 **Carthage queen:** Dido, who
killed herself after the Trojan
Aeneas had deserted her.
182 **fair:** beauty.

186 **favour:** beauty.
187 [**Yours would**] (Hanmer). *Your
words* Q.
190 **bated:** excepted.
191 **translated:** transformed.

HELENA

    O that my prayers could such affection move!

HERMIA

    The more I hate, the more he follows me.

HELENA

    The more I love, the more he hateth me.

HERMIA

    His folly, Helena, is no fault of mine. 200

HELENA

    None, but your beauty. Would that fault were mine!

HERMIA

    Take comfort; he no more shall see my face;
    Lysander and myself will fly this place.
    Before the time I did Lysander see,
    Seem'd Athens as a paradise to me; 205
    O, then, what graces in my love do dwell,
    That he hath turn'd a heaven unto a hell!

LYSANDER

    Helen, to you our minds we will unfold.
    To-morrow night, when Phoebe doth behold
    Her silver visage in the wat'ry glass, 210
    Decking with liquid pearl the bladed grass,
    A time that lovers' flights doth still conceal,
    Through Athens' gates have we devis'd to steal.

HERMIA

    And in the wood, where often you and I
    Upon faint primrose-beds were wont to lie, 215
    Emptying our bosoms of their counsel [sweet].
    There my Lysander and myself shall meet;
    And thence from Athens turn away our eyes,
    To seek new friends and [stranger companies].
    Farewell, sweet playfellow! Pray thou for us; 220
    And good luck grant thee thy Demetrius!
    Keep word, Lysander; we must starve our sight
    From lovers' food till morrow deep midnight.

LYSANDER

    I will, my Hermia.

                                       [Exit Hermia.

                  Helena, adieu:
    As you on him, Demetrius dote on you! 225

                                    [Exit.

HELENA

    How happy some o'er other some can be!
    Through Athens I am thought as fair as she.
    But what of that? Demetrius thinks not so;
    He will not know what all but he do know;
    And as he errs, doting on Hermia's eyes, 230
    So I, admiring of his qualities.
    Things base and vile, holding no quantity,
    Love can transpose to form and dignity.

      209 **Phoebe:** Diana, the moon.   219 [**stranger companies**]
      215 **faint:** pale.   (Theobald). *strange companions* Q.
      216 [**sweet**] (Theobald). *sweld* Q.

Love looks not with the eyes but with the mind,
And therefore is wing'd Cupid painted blind.   235
Nor hath Love's mind of any judgement taste;
Wings and no eyes figure unheedy haste;
And therefore is Love said to be a child,
Because in choice he is so oft beguil'd.
As waggish boys in game themselves forswear,   240
So the boy Love is perjur'd everywhere:
For ere Demetrius look'd on Hermia's eyne,
He hail'd down oaths that he was only mine;
And when this hail some heat from Hermia felt,
So he dissolv'd, and show'rs of oaths did melt.   245
I will go tell him of fair Hermia's flight;
Then to the wood will he to-morrow night
Pursue her; and for this intelligence
If I have thanks, it is a dear expense.
But therein mean I to enrich my pain,   250
To have his sight thither and back again.

                                                           [*Exit.*

[Scene II. Athens. Quince's house.]
   Enter Quince, Snug, Bottom, Flute, Snout, and Starveling.

QUINCE

Is all our company here?

BOTTOM

You were best to call them generally, man
by man, according to the scrip.

QUINCE

Here is the scroll of every man's name, which
is thought fit, through all Athens, to play in   5
our interlude before the Duke and the Duch-
ess, on his wedding-day at night.

BOTTOM

First, good Peter Quince, say what the play
treats on, then read the names of the actors,
and so grow to a point.   10

QUINCE

Marry, our play is *The most lamentable
comedy, and most cruel death of Pyramus and
Thisby.*

BOTTOM

A very good piece of work, I assure you, and
a merry. Now, good Peter Quince, call forth   15
your actors by the scroll. Masters, spread yourselves.

QUINCE

Answer as I call you. Nick Bottom, the
weaver.

237 **figure:** symbolize.
242 **eyne:** eyes.
248 **intelligence:** news.
249 **dear expense:** costly gain.
251 **his sight:** sight of him.

ii.2 **generally:** Bottom's error for
severally.
3 **scrip:** written list.
10 **grow . . . point:** come to the
point.

BOTTOM

Ready. Name what part I am for, and   20
proceed.

QUINCE

You, Nick Bottom, are set down for Pyramus.

BOTTOM

What is Pyramus? A lover, or a tyrant?

QUINCE

A lover, that kills himself most gallant   25
for love.

BOTTOM

That will ask some tears in the true performing of it. If I do it, let the audience look to
their eyes. I will move storms, I will condole in
some measure. To the rest. Yet my chief humour   30
is for a tyrant. I could play Ercles rarely, or a
part to tear a cat in, to make all split.
              "The raging rocks
              And shivering shocks
              Shall break the locks   35
                    Of prison gates;
              And Phibbus' car
              Shall shine from far
              And make and mar
                    The foolish Fates."   40
This was lofty! Now name the rest of the players.
This is Ercles' vein, a tyrant's vein; a lover is more
condoling.

QUINCE

Francis Flute, the bellows-mender.

FLUTE

Here, Peter Quince.   45

QUINCE

Flute, you must take Thisby on you.

FLUTE

What is Thisby? A wand'ring knight?

QUINCE

It is the lady that Pyramus must love.

FLUTE

Nay, faith, let not me play a woman; I have
a beard coming.   50

QUINCE

That's all one; you shall play it in a mask,
and you may speak as small as you will.

BOTTOM

An I may hide my face, let me play Thisby
too. I'll speak in a monstrous little voice, "Thisne!
Thisne! Ah Pyramus, my lover dear! thy Thisby   55
dear, and lady dear!"

---

29 **condole:** grieve.   32 **make all split,** i.e., with passion.
31 **Ercles:** Hercules, a common   37 **Phibbus':** Phoebus'.
ranting part in early drama.   53 **An:** if.

QUINCE

No, no; you must play Pyramus; and, Flute,
you Thisby.

BOTTOM

Well, proceed.

QUINCE

Robin Starveling, the tailor.   60

STARVELING

Here, Peter Quince.

QUINCE

Robin Starveling, you must play Thisby's
mother. Tom Snout, the tinker.

SNOUT

Here, Peter Quince.

QUINCE

You, Pyramus' father; myself, Thisby's   65
father; Snug, the joiner, you, the lion's part;
and, I hope, here is a play fitted.

SNUG

Have you the lion's part written? Pray you,
if it be, give it me, for I am slow of study.

QUINCE

You may do it extempore, for it is noth-   70
ing but roaring.

BOTTOM

Let me play the lion too. I will roar, that I
will do any man's heart good to hear me. I will
roar, that I will make the Duke say, "Let him
roar again, let him roar again."   75

QUINCE

An you should do it too terribly, you would
fright the Duchess and the ladies, that they would
shriek; and that were enough to hang us all.

ALL

That would hang us, every mother's son.   80

BOTTOM

I grant you, friends, if you should fright the
ladies out of their wits, they would have no more
discretion but to hang us; but I will aggravate my
voice so that I will roar you as gently as any sucking dove; I will roar you an 'twere any night-   85
ingale.

QUINCE

You can play no part but Pyramus; for Pyramus is a sweet-fac'd man; a proper man, as one
shall see in a summer's day; a most lovely gentle-
man-like man: therefore you must needs play   90
Pyramus.

BOTTOM

Well, I will undertake it. What beard were I
best to play it in?

83 **aggravate:** Bottom's mistake for   88 **proper:** handsome.
moderate.

QUINCE
>Why, what you will.

BOTTOM
>I will discharge it in either your straw-colour   95
>beard, your orange-tawny beard, your purple-
>in-grain beard, or your French-crown-colour
>beard, your perfect yellow.

QUINCE
>Some of your French crowns have no hair
>at all, and then you will play barefac'd. But,   100
>masters, here are your parts; and I am to
>entreat you, request you, and desire you, to
>con them by tomorrow night; and meet me
>in the palace wood, a mile without the town,
>by moonlight. There will we rehearse, for if   105
>we meet in the city, we shall be dogg'd with
>company, and our devices known. In the mean-
>time I will draw a bill of properties, such as
>our play wants. I pray you, fail me not.

BOTTOM
>We will meet; and there we may rehearse   110
>most obscenely and courageously. Take pains;
>be perfect; adieu.

QUINCE
>At the Duke's oak we meet.

BOTTOM
>Enough; hold or cut bow-strings.

>>   [*Exeunt.*

Act II

>[*Scene I. A wood near Athens.*]
>*Enter a Fairy at one door and Robin Goodfellow at another.*

ROBIN GOODFELLOW
>How now, spirit! whither wander you?

FAIRY
>>Over hill, over dale,
>>>Thorough bush, thorough brier,
>>Over park, over pale,
>>>Thorough flood, thorough fire,   5
>>I do wander every where,
>>Swifter than the moon's sphere;
>>And I serve the fairy Queen,
>>To dew her orbs upon the green.

95–98 Bottom, the Weaver, refers
glibly to several familiar dyes.
111 **obscenely:** Bottom's mistake for
obscurely.
114 **hold . . . bow-strings.**
Apparently an archer's expression.
Bottom probably means, "Keep your
appointments or everything is off."

II. i, S.D. **Robin Goodfellow.** This
character is described as a Puck, a
name previously applied in English
folklore to a minor order of evil
spirits. Shakespeare recreates him as
he does the fairies.
9 **orbs:** fairy rings.

The cowslips tall her pensioners be;   10
In their gold coats spots you see;
Those be rubies, fairy favours,
In those freckles live their savours.
I must go seek some dewdrops here
And hang a pearl in every cowslip's ear.   15
Farewell, thou lob of spirits; I'll be gone.
Our Queen and all her elves come here anon.

ROBIN GOODFELLOW
The King doth keep his revels here tonight;
Take heed the Queen come not within his sight;
For Oberon is passing fell and wrath,   20
Because that she as her attendant hath
A lovely boy stolen from an Indian king.
She never had so sweet a changeling;
And jealous Oberon would have the child
Knight of his train, to trace the forests wild;   25
But she perforce withholds the loved boy,
Crowns him with flowers, and makes him all her joy;
And now they never meet in grove or green,
By fountain clear, or spangled starlight sheen,
But they do square, that all their elves for fear   30
Creep into acorn-cups and hide them there.

FAIRY
Either I mistake your shape and making quite,
Or else you are that shrewd and knavish sprite
Call'd Robin Goodfellow. Are not you he
That frights the maidens of the villagery,   35
Skim milk, and sometimes labour in the quern,
And bootless make the breathless housewife churn,
And sometime make the drink to bear no barm,
Mislead night-wanderers, laughing at their harm?
Those that Hobgoblin call you, and sweet Puck,   40
You do their work, and they shall have good luck.
Are not you he?

ROBIN GOODFELLOW
                    Thou speakest aright;
I am that merry wanderer of the night.
I jest to Oberon and make him smile
When I a fat and bean-fed horse beguile,   45
Neighing in likeness of a filly foal;
And sometime lurk I in a gossip's bowl,
In very likeness of a roasted crab,
And when she drinks, against her lips I bob
And on her withered dewlap pour the ale.   50

10 **pensioners.** Queen Elizabeth's bodyguards were called gentlemen pensioners.
13 **savours:** perfumes.
16 **lob:** lout.
20 **passing . . . wrath:** exceedingly angry and wrathful.
23 **changeling:** a child exchanged by fairies.

30 **square:** quarrel; **that:** so that.
33 **shrewd:** mischievous.
36 **quern:** handmill.
38 **barm:** yeast.
47 **gossip's bowl:** christening-cup. Gossip is used here in the original sense of godmother.
48 **crab:** crab apple.
50 **dewlap:** loose skin on the neck.

The wisest aunt, telling the saddest tale,
Sometime for three-foot stool mistaketh me.
Then slip I from her bum, down topples she,
And "tailor" cries, and falls into a cough;
And then the whole quire hold their hips and laugh,   55
And waxen in their mirth, and neeze, and swear
A merrier hour was never wasted there.
But, room, fairy! here comes Oberon.

FAIRY
And here my mistress. Would that he were gone!
        Enter the King of Fairies [Oberon] at one door with his train; and the
        Queen [Titania] at another with hers.

OBERON
Ill met by moonlight, proud Titania.   60

TITANIA
What, jealous Oberon! Fairies, skip hence:
I have forsworn his bed and company.

OBERON
Tarry, rash wanton! Am not I thy lord?

TITANIA
Then I must be thy lady; but I know
When thou hast stolen away from fairy land,   65
And in the shape of Corin sat all day,
Playing on pipes of corn and versing love
To amorous Phillida. Why art thou here,
Come from the farthest steep of India?
But that, forsooth, the bouncing Amazon,   70
Your buskin'd mistress and your warrior love,
To Theseus must be wedded, and you come
To give their bed joy and prosperity.

OBERON
How canst thou thus for shame, Titania,
Glance at my credit with Hippolyta,   75
Knowing I know thy love to Theseus?
Didst thou not lead him through the glimmering night
From Perigenia, whom he ravished?
And make him with fair AEgle break his faith,
With Ariadne, and Antiopa?   80

TITANIA
These are the forgeries of jealousy;
And never, since the middle summer's spring,
Met we on hill, in dale, forest or mead,
By paved fountain or by rushy brook,
Or in the beached margent of the sea,   85

51 **aunt:** old woman; **saddest:**
soberest.
54 **"tailor" cries:** Meaning obscure.
56 **waxen:** increase; **neeze:** sneeze.
66–68 **Corin . . . Phillida:** names
traditional in pastoral poetry.
71 **buskin'd:** wearing high boots.
75 **glance at:** cast reflections on.
79–80 **AEgle . . . Ariadne . . .**

Antiopa: These names of women
whom Theseus had loved
Shakespeare found in North's
Plutarch. Antiopa is sometimes
identified with Hippolyta, but in this
speech they are treated as two.
82 **middle summer's spring:**
beginning of midsummer.
85 **in:** on; **margent:** margin.

To dance our ringlets to the whistling wind,
But with thy brawls thou hast disturb'd our sport.
Therefore the winds, piping to us in vain,
As in revenge, have suck'd up from the sea
Contagious fogs; which, falling in the land,   90
Hath every pelting river made so proud
That they have overborne their continents.
The ox hath therefore stretch'd his yoke in vain,
The ploughman lost his sweat, and the green corn
Hath rotted ere his youth attain'd a beard.   95
The fold stands empty in the drowned field,
And crows are fatted with the murrain flock,
The nine men's morris is fill'd up with mud,
And the quaint mazes in the wanton green
For lack of tread are undistinguishable.   100
The human mortals want their winter [cheer];
No night is now with hymn or carol blest.
Therefore the moon, the governess of floods,
Pale in her anger, washes all the air,
That rheumatic diseases do abound.   105
And thorough this distemperature we see
The seasons alter: hoary-headed frosts
Fall in the fresh lap of the crimson rose,
And on old Hiems' thin and icy crown
An odorous chaplet of sweet summer buds   110
Is, as in mockery, set; the spring, the summer,
The childing autumn, angry winter, change
Their wonted liveries; and the mazed world,
By their increase, now knows not which is which.
And this same progeny of evils comes   115
From our debate, from our dissension;
We are their parents and original.

OBERON

Do you amend it then; it lies in you.
Why should Titania cross her Oberon?
I do but beg a little changeling boy   120
To be my henchman.

TITANIA

                    Set your heart at rest;
The fairy land buys not the child of me.
His mother was a vot'ress of my order,
And, in the spiced Indian air, by night,
Full often hath she gossip'd by my side,   125
And sat with me on Neptune's yellow sands,

---

86 **ringlets:** circular dances.
91 **pelting:** paltry. Ff read *petty*.
92 **continents:** banks.
97 **murrain:** diseased.
98 **nine men's morris:** a game
played in squares marked out on the
turf of the village green; something
like hopscotch.
99 **mazes:** figures; **wanton:**
luxuriant.

101 **[cheer]** (Theobald conj.). *heere*
Q.
106 **distemperature:** disturbance.
109 **Hiems:** the god of winter.
112 **childing:** fruitful
113 **mazed:** amazed.
117 **original:** origin.
121 **henchman:** page.

Marking th' embarked traders on the flood,
When we have laugh'd to see the sails conceive
And grow big-bellied with the wanton wind;
Which she with pretty and with swimming gait   130
Following, her womb then rich with my young squire,
Would imitate, and sail upon the land
To fetch me trifles, and return again,
As from a voyage, rich with merchandise.
But she, being mortal, of that boy did die;   135
And for her sake do I rear up her boy,
And for her sake I will not part with him.

OBERON

How long within this wood intend you stay?

TITANIA

Perchance till after Theseus' wedding-day.
If you will patiently dance in our round   140
And see our moonlight revels, go with us;
If not, shun me, and I will spare your haunts.

OBERON

Give me that boy, and I will go with thee.

TITANIA

Not for thy fairy kingdom. Fairies, away!
We shall chide downright, if I longer stay.   145

                    [Exit [Titania with her train].

OBERON

Well, go thy way; thou shalt not from this grove
Till I torment thee for this injury.
My gentle Puck, come hither. Thou rememb'rest
Since once I sat upon a promontory,
And heard a mermaid on a dolphin's back   150
Uttering such dulcet and harmonious breath
That the rude sea grew civil at her song,
And certain stars shot madly from their spheres,
To hear the sea-maid's music?

ROBIN GOODFELLOW

                    I remember.

OBERON

That very time I saw, but thou couldst not,   155
Flying between the cold moon and the earth,
Cupid all arm'd. A certain aim he took
At a fair vestal throned by the west,
And loos'd his love-shaft smartly from his bow,
As it should pierce a hundred thousand hearts;   160
But I might see young Cupid's fiery shaft
Quench'd in the chaste beams of the wat'ry moon,
And the imperial vot'ress passed on,
In maiden meditation, fancy-free.
Yet mark'd I where the bolt of Cupid fell.   165
It fell upon a little western flower,
Before milk-white, now purple with love's wound,

149 **Since:** when.   158 **vestal:** virgin.

And maidens call it love-in-idleness.
Fetch me that flower, the herb I shew'd thee once.
The juice of it on sleeping eye-lids laid   170
Will make or man or woman madly dote
Upon the next live creature that it sees.
Fetch me this herb; and be thou here again
Ere the leviathan can swim a league.

ROBIN GOODFELLOW
I'll put a girdle round about the earth   175
In forty minutes.

                                                          [*Exit.*]

OBERON
                    Having once this juice,
I'll watch Titania when she is asleep,
And drop the liquor of it in her eyes.
The next thing then she waking looks upon,
Be it on lion, bear, or wolf, or bull,   180
On meddling monkey, or on busy ape,
She shall pursue it with the soul of love;
And ere I take this charm from off her sight,
As I can take it with another herb,
I'll make her render up her page to me.   185
But who comes here? I am invisible;
And I will overhear their conference.
          Enter Demetrius, Helena following him.

DEMETRIUS
I love thee not, therefore pursue me not.
Where is Lysander and fair Hermia?
The one I'll stay, the other stayeth me.   190
Thou told'st me they were stol'n unto this wood;
And here am I, and wood within this wood
Because I cannot meet my Hermia.
Hence, get thee gone, and follow me no more.

HELENA
You draw me, you hard-hearted adamant;   195
But yet you draw not iron, for my heart
Is true as steel. Leave you your power to draw,
And I shall have no power to follow you.

DEMETRIUS
Do I entice you? Do I speak you fair?
Or, rather, do I not in plainest truth   200
Tell you, I do not nor I cannot love you?

HELENA
And even for that do I love you the more.
I am your spaniel, and, Demetrius,
The more you beat me, I will fawn on you.
Use me but as your spaniel, spurn me, strike me,   205

---

168 **love-in-idleness:** pansy.
190 **stay . . . stayeth:** Thirlby's
conjecture "slay . . . slayeth" has
been followed by many editors.
192 **wood:** mad.

195 **adamant:** probably with both
senses of "lode-stone" (magnet) and
"hardest metal."
197 **Leave:** give up.

Neglect me, lose me; only give me leave,
Unworthy as I am, to follow you.
What worser place can I beg in your love,—
And yet a place of high respect with me,—
Than to be used as you use your dog?   210
DEMETRIUS
Tempt not too much the hatred of my spirit,
For I am sick when I do look on thee.
HELENA
And I am sick when I look not on you.
DEMETRIUS
You do impeach your modesty too much,
To leave the city and commit yourself   215
Into the hands of one that loves you not;
To trust the opportunity of night
And the ill counsel of a desert place
With the rich worth of your virginity.
HELENA
Your virtue is my privilege. For that   220
It is not night when I do see your face,
Therefore I think I am not in the night;
Nor doth this wood lack worlds of company,
For you in my respect are all the world.
Then how can it be said I am alone,   225
When all the world is here to look on me?
DEMETRIUS
I'll run from thee and hide me in the brakes,
And leave thee to the mercy of wild beasts.
HELENA
The wildest hath not such a heart as you.
Run when you will, the story shall be chang'd: 230
Apollo flies, and Daphne holds the chase;
The dove pursues the griffin; the mild hind
Makes speed to catch the tiger: bootless speed,
When cowardice pursues and valour flies.
DEMETRIUS
I will not stay thy questions; let me go;   235
Or, if thou follow me, do not believe
But I shall do thee mischief in the wood.
HELENA
Ay, in the temple, in the town, the field,
You do me mischief. Fie, Demetrius!
Your wrongs do set a scandal on my sex.   240
We cannot fight for love, as men may do.
We should be woo'd and were not made to woo.

                                    [Exit Demetrius.]

220 **privilege:** safeguard; **For that:** because.
224 **in my respect:** to me.
231 **Apollo . . . chase:** According to the myth, Apollo pursued Daphne, but here the situation is reversed.

232 **griffin:** a monster having a lion's body and an eagle's head; **hind:** female of the red deer.
235 **questions:** arguments.

I'll follow thee and make a heaven of hell,
To die upon the hand I love so well.

        [Exit.

OBERON

Fare thee well, nymph. Ere he do leave this grove,   245
Thou shalt fly him and he shall seek thy love.
    Re-enter [Robin Goodfellow].
Hast thou the flower there? Welcome, wanderer.

ROBIN GOODFELLOW

Ay, there it is.

OBERON

              I pray thee, give it me.
I know a bank where the wild thyme blows,
Where oxlips and the nodding violet grows,   250
Quite over-canopi'd with luscious woodbine,
With sweet musk-roses and with eglantine.
There sleeps Titania sometime of the night,
Lull'd in these flowers with dances and delight;
And there the snake throws her enamell'd skin,   255
Weed wide enough to wrap a fairy in;
And with the juice of this I'll streak her eyes,
And make her full of hateful fantasies.
Take thou some of it, and seek through this grove.
A sweet Athenian lady is in love   260
With a disdainful youth. Anoint his eyes,
But do it when the next thing he espies
May be the lady. Thou shalt know the man
By the Athenian garments he hath on.
Effect it with some care, that he may prove   265
More fond on her than she upon her love;
And look thou meet me ere the first cock crow.

ROBIN GOODFELLOW

Fear not, my lord, your servant shall do so.

        [Exeunt.

    [Scene II. Another part of the wood.]
    Enter Titania, with her train.

TITANIA

Come, now a roundel and a fairy song;
Then, for the third part of a minute, hence,
Some to kill cankers in the musk-rose buds,
Some war with rere-mice for their leathern wings
To make my small elves coats, and some keep back   5
The clamorous owl that nightly hoots and wonders
At our quaint spirits. Sing me now asleep;
Then to your offices and let me rest.
    The Fairies sing.

244 **upon:** by.
254 **dances and delight:** delightful
dances.
256 **Weed:** garment.
257 **streak:** stroke.

ii.1 **roundel:** circular dance.
3 **cankers:** cankerworms.
4 **rere-mice:** bats.
7 **quaint:** dainty.

[FIRST FAIRY]

 "You spotted snakes with double tongue,
  Thorny hedgehogs, be not seen;   10
 Newts and blind-worms, do no wrong,
  Come not near our fairy queen."

[CHORUS]

 "Philomel, with melody
  Sing in our sweet lullaby;
 Lulla, lulla, lullaby; lulla, lulla, lullaby.   15
   Never harm
   Nor spell nor charm
  Come our lovely lady nigh.
 So, good night, with lullaby."

FIRST FAIRY

 "Weaving spiders, come not here;
  Hence, you long-legg'd spinners, hence!   20
 Beetles black, approach not near;
  Worm nor snail, do no offence."

[CHORUS]

 "Philomel, with melody," etc.

SECOND FAIRY

 Hence, away! now all is well.   25
  One aloof stand sentinel.

       [Exeunt Fairies.] Titania sleeps.
   Enter Oberon [and squeezes the flower on Titania's eyelids].

OBERON

 What thou seest when thou dost wake,
 Do it for thy true-love take,
 Love and languish for his sake.
 Be it ounce, or cat, or bear,   30
 Pard, or boar with bristled hair,
 In thy eye that shall appear
 When thou wak'st, it is thy dear.
 Wake when some vile thing is near.

            [Exit.]

   Enter Lysander and Hermia.

LYSANDER

 Fair love, you faint with wand'ring in the wood; 35
 And to speak troth, I have forgot our way.
 We'll rest us, Hermia, if you think it good,
 And tarry for the comfort of the day.

HERMIA

 Be it so, Lysander. Find you out a bed;
 For I upon this bank will rest my head.   40

LYSANDER

 One turf shall serve as pillow for us both;
 One heart, one bed, two bosoms and one troth.

HERMIA

 Nay, good Lysander; for my sake, my dear,
 Lie further off yet; do not lie so near.

---

11 **Newts:** water lizards.
13 **Philomel:** the nightingale.

30 **ounce:** lynx; **cat:** wildcat.
31 **Pard:** leopard.

LYSANDER

O, take the sense, sweet, of my innocence! 45
Love takes the meaning in love's conference.
I mean, that my heart unto yours is knit
So that but one heart we can make of it;
Two bosoms interchained with an oath,
So then two bosoms and a single troth. 50
Then by your side no bed-room me deny;
For lying so, Hermia, I do not lie.

HERMIA

Lysander riddles very prettily.
Now much beshrew my manners and my pride,
If Hermia meant to say Lysander lied. 55
But, gentle friend, for love and courtesy
Lie further off; in humane modesty,
Such separation as may well be said
Becomes a virtuous bachelor and a maid,
So far be distant; and, good night, sweet friend. 60
Thy love ne'er alter till thy sweet life end!

LYSANDER

Amen, amen, to that fair prayer, say I;
And then end life when I end loyalty!
Here is my bed; sleep give thee all his rest!

HERMIA

With half that wish the wisher's eyes be press'd! 65

[They sleep.

Enter [Robin Goodfellow].

ROBIN GOODFELLOW

Through the forest have I gone,
But Athenian found I none,
On whose eyes I might approve
This flower's force in stirring love.
Night and silence—Who is here? 70
Weeds of Athens he doth wear!
This is he, my master said,
Despised the Athenian maid;
And here the maiden, sleeping sound,
On the dank and dirty ground. 75
Pretty soul! she durst not lie
Near this lack-love, this kill-courtesy.
Churl, upon thy eyes I throw
All the power this charm doth owe.
When thou wak'st, let love forbid 80
Sleep his seat on thy eyelid;
So awake when I am gone,
For I must now to Oberon.

[Exit.

Enter Demetrius and Helena, running.

HELENA

Stay, though thou kill me, sweet Demetrius.

46 **Love . . . conference:** Love gives lovers true understanding.

68 **approve:** test.

79 **owe:** own.

DEMETRIUS
I charge thee, hence, and do not haunt me thus.   85
HELENA
O, wilt thou darkling leave me? Do not so.
DEMETRIUS
Stay, on thy peril; I alone will go.

[*Exit.*

HELENA
O, I am out of breath in this fond chase!
The more my prayer, the lesser is my grace.
Happy is Hermia, wheresoe'er she lies,   90
For she hath blessed and attractive eyes.
How came her eyes so bright? Not with salt tears;
If so, my eyes are oft'ner wash'd than hers.
No, no, I am as ugly as a bear,
For beasts that meet me run away for fear;   95
Therefore no marvel though Demetrius
Do, as a monster, fly my presence thus.
What wicked and dissembling glass of mine
Made me compare with Hermia's sphery eyne?
But who is here? Lysander! on the ground!   100
Dead? or asleep? I see no blood, no wound.
Lysander, if you live, good sir, awake.
LYSANDER [*Awaking.*]
And run through fire I will for thy sweet sake.
Transparent Helena! Nature shows art,
That through thy bosom makes me see thy heart.   105
Where is Demetrius? O, how fit a word
Is that vile name to perish on my sword!
HELENA
Do not say so, Lysander; say not so.
What though he love your Hermia? Lord, what though?
Yet Hermia still loves you; then be content.   110
LYSANDER
Content with Hermia! No; I do repent
The tedious minutes I with her have spent.
Not Hermia but Helena I love.
Who will not change a raven for a dove?
The will of man is by his reason sway'd;   115
And reason says you are the worthier maid.
Things growing are not ripe until their season,
So I, being young, till now ripe not to reason;
And touching now the point of human skill,
Reason becomes the marshal to my will   120
And leads me to your eyes, where I o'erlook
Love's stories written in Love's richest book.
HELENA
Wherefore was I to this keen mockery born?
When at your hands did I deserve this scorn?
Is't not enough, is't not enough, young man,   125

86 **darkling:** in the dark.   99 **sphery eyne:** starry eyes.
88 **fond:** foolish.   119 **point . . . skill:** summit of
89 **my grace:** the favor I receive.   human discernment.

That I did never, no, nor never can,
Deserve a sweet look from Demetrius' eye,
But you must flout my insufficiency?
Good troth, you do me wrong, good sooth you do,
In such disdainful manner me to woo.   130
But fare you well; perforce I must confess
I thought you lord of more true gentleness.
O, that a lady, of one man refus'd,
Should of another therefore be abus'd!

                                                        [*Exit.*

LYSANDER
She sees not Hermia. Hermia, sleep thou there;   135
And never mayst thou come Lysander near!
For as a surfeit of the sweetest things
The deepest loathing to the stomach brings,
Or as the heresies that men do leave
Are hated most of those they did deceive,   140
So thou, my surfeit and my heresy,
Of all be hated, but the most of me!
And, all my powers, address your love and might
To honour Helen and to be her knight.

                                                        [*Exit.*

HERMIA [*Awaking.*]
Help me, Lysander, help me! do thy best   145
To pluck this crawling serpent from my breast!
Ay me, for pity! what a dream was here!
Lysander, look how I do quake with fear.
Methought a serpent eat my heart away,
And you sat smiling at his cruel prey.   150
Lysander! what, remov'd? Lysander! lord!
What, out of hearing? Gone? No sound, no word?
Alack, where are you? Speak, an if you hear;
Speak, of all loves! I swoon almost with fear.
No? then I well perceive you are not nigh.   155
Either death or you I'll find immediately.

                                                        [*Exit.*

Act III

[*Scene I. The wood. Titania lying asleep.*]
Enter the Clowns [*Quince, Snug, Bottom, Flute, Snout, and
          Starveling*].

BOTTOM
Are we all met?

QUINCE
Pat, pat; and here's a marvellous convenient
place for our rehearsal. This green plot shall
be our stage, this hawthorn-brake our tiring-
house; and we will do it in action as we will   5
do it before the Duke.

---

150 **prey:** preying.   III. i.4–5 **tiring-house:** dressing room.
154 **of all loves:** for love's sake.

BOTTOM
> Peter Quince!

QUINCE
> What say'st thou, bully Bottom?

BOTTOM
> There are things in this comedy of Pyramus
> and Thisby that will never please. First, Pyra-
> mus must draw a sword to kill himself, which
> the ladies cannot abide. How answer you
> that?

SNOUT
> By'r lakin, a parlous fear.

STARVELING
> I believe we must leave the killing out,
> when all is done.

BOTTOM
> Not a whit! I have a device to make all well.
> Write me a prologue; and let the prologue
> seem to say, we will do no harm with our
> swords and that Pyramus is not kill'd indeed;
> and, for the more better assurance, tell them
> that I Pyramus am not Pyramus, but Bottom
> the weaver. This will put them out of fear.

QUINCE
> Well, we will have such a prologue; and it
> shall be written in eight and six.

BOTTOM
> No, make it two more; let it be written in
> eight and eight.

SNOUT
> Will not the ladies be afeard of the lion?

STARVELING
> I fear it, I promise you.

BOTTOM
> Masters, you ought to consider with your-
> selves. To bring in—God shield us!—a lion
> among ladies, is a most dreadful thing; for
> there is not a more fearful wild-fowl than
> your lion living; and we ought to look to't.

SNOUT
> Therefore another prologue must tell he
> is not a lion.

BOTTOM
> Nay, you must name his name, and half his
> face must be seen through the lion's neck; and he
> himself must speak through, saying thus, or to the
> same defect, "Ladies," or "Fair ladies, I would
> wish you," or "I would request you," or "I would

10

15

20

25

30

35

40

---

8 **bully:** "good old"; a term of
friendship.
14 **By'r lakin:** by our ladykin, i.e., the
Virgin Mary; **parlous:** perilous.

25 **eight and six:** alternate lines of
eight and six syllables, ballad meter.
40 **defect:** error for *effect*.

entreat you, not to fear, not to tremble: my life
for yours. If you think I come hither as a lion, it
were pity of my life. No, I am no such thing;
I am a man as other men are;" and there   45
indeed let him name his name, and tell them
plainly he is Snug the joiner.

QUINCE
Well, it shall be so. But there is two hard
things; that is, to bring the moonlight into a
chamber; for, you know, Pyramus and Thisby   50
meet by moonlight.

SNOUT
Doth the moon shine that night we play our
play?

BOTTOM
A calendar, a calendar! Look in the almanac!
Find out moonshine, find out moonshine.   55

QUINCE
Yes, it doth shine that night.

BOTTOM
Why, then may you leave a casement of the
great chamber window, where we play, open,
and the moon may shine in at the casement.

QUINCE
Ay; or else one must come in with a bush   60
of thorns and a lantern, and say he comes to
disfigure, or to present, the person of Moonshine. Then, there is another thing: we must
have a wall in the great chamber; for Pyra-
mus and Thisby, says the story, did talk through   65
the chink of a wall.

SNOUT
You can never bring in a wall. What say
you, Bottom?

BOTTOM
Some man or other must present Wall; and
let him have some plaster, or some loam, or   70
some rough-cast about him, to signify wall;
or let him hold his fingers thus, and through
that cranny shall Pyramus and Thisby whisper.

QUINCE
If that may be, then all is well. Come, sit down,
every mother's son, and rehearse your parts.   75
Pyramus, you begin. When you have spoken
your speech, enter into that brake. And so every
one according to his cue.
    Enter Robin Goodfellow [behind].

ROBIN GOODFELLOW
What hempen home-spuns have we swagg'ring here,
So near the cradle of the fairy queen?   80

---

62 **disfigure:** blunder for *prefigure.*   71 **rough-cast:** plaster mixed with
                                               pebbles.

What, a play toward! I'll be an auditor;
An actor too perhaps, if I see cause.

QUINCE

Speak, Pyramus. Thisby, stand forth.

BOTTOM

"Thisby, the flowers of odious savours sweet,"—

QUINCE

Odorous, odorous.   85

BOTTOM

—— "odours savours sweet;
  So hath thy breath, my dearest Thisby dear.
But hark, a voice! Stay thou but here awhile,
  And by and by I will to thee appear."

[*Exit.*

ROBIN GOODFELLOW

A stranger Pyramus than e'er play'd here.   90

[*Exit.*]

FLUTE

Must I speak now?

QUINCE

Ay, marry, must you; for you must understand he goes but to see a noise that he heard,
and is to come again.

FLUTE

"Most radiant Pyramus, most lily-white of hue,   95
  Of colour like the red rose on triumphant brier,
Most brisky juvenal and eke most lovely Jew,
  As true as truest horse that yet would never tire,
I'll meet thee, Pyramus, at Ninny's tomb."

QUINCE

"Ninus' tomb," man. Why, you must not   100
speak that yet; that you answer to Pyramus.
You speak all your part at once, cues and all.
Pyramus enter. Your cue is past; it is, "never tire."

FLUTE

O,—"As true as truest horse, that yet would
never tire."   105
  [*Re-enter Robin Goodfellow and Bottom with an ass's head.*]

BOTTOM

"If I were fair, Thisby, I were only thine."

QUINCE

O monstrous! O strange! we are haunted.
Pray, masters, fly, masters! Help!
  [*Exeunt [Quince, Snug, Flute, Snout, and Starveling*].

ROBIN GOODFELLOW

I'll follow you, I'll lead you about, around,
  Through bog, through bush, through brake, through brier.   110
Sometime a horse I'll be, sometime a hound,
  A hog, a headless bear, sometime a fire;

---

81 **toward:** afoot.
97 **brisky juvenal:** lively youth; **Jew:**
probably a nonsensical repetition of
the first syllable of *juvenal.*

100 **Ninus:** mythical founder of
Babylon, the setting of the tale of
Pyramus and Thisbe.

And neigh, and bark, and grunt, and roar, and burn,
Like horse, hound, hog, bear, fire, at every turn.

[*Exit.*

BOTTOM
Why do they run away? This is a knavery   115
of them to make me afeard.
  Re-enter Snout.
SNOUT
O Bottom, thou art chang'd! What do I
see on thee?
BOTTOM
What do you see? You see an ass-head of
your own, do you?   120

[*Exit Snout.*]

  Re-enter Quince.
QUINCE
Bless thee, Bottom! bless thee! thou art
translated.

[*Exit.*

BOTTOM
I see their knavery; this is to make an ass of
me, to fright me, if they could. But I will not
stir from this place, do what they can. I will   125
walk up and down here, and I will sing, that
they shall hear I am not afraid.

[*Sings.*]

   "The ousel cock so black of hue,
    With orange-tawny bill,
   The throstle with his note so true,   130
    The wren with little quill,"—
TITANIA [*Awaking.*]
What angel wakes me from my flowery bed?
BOTTOM [*Sings.*]
   "The finch, the sparrow, and the lark,
    The plain-song cuckoo gray,
   Whose note full many a man doth mark,   135
    And dares not answer nay;"—
for, indeed, who would set his wit to so foolish a
bird? Who would give a bird the lie, though he
cry "cuckoo" never so?
TITANIA
I pray thee, gentle mortal, sing again.   140
Mine ear is much enamour'd of thy note;
So is mine eye enthralled to thy shape;
And thy fair virtue's force perforce doth move me
On the first view to say, to swear, I love thee.

122 **translated:** transformed.
128 **ousel:** blackbird. Q₁ reads
woosel.
131 **quill:** pipe.
134 **plain-song:** melody without
variations.

135–136 **Whose . . . nay:** The note
of the cuckoo sounded not unlike
"cuckold," an unwelcome word to
husbands.

BOTTOM

> Methinks, mistress, you should have little 145
> reason for that; and yet, to say the truth,
> reason and love keep little company together
> now-a-days; the more the pity that some hon-
> est neighbours will not make them friends.
> Nay, I can gleek upon occasion. 150

TITANIA

> Thou art as wise as thou art beautiful.

BOTTOM

> Not so, neither; but if I had wit enough to
> get out of this wood, I have enough to serve
> mine own turn.

TITANIA

> Out of this wood do not desire to go; 155
> Thou shalt remain here, whether thou wilt or no.
> I am a spirit of no common rate;
> The summer still doth tend upon my state;
> And I do love thee; therefore, go with me.
> I'll give thee fairies to attend on thee, 160
> And they shall fetch thee jewels from the deep,
> And sing while thou on pressed flowers dost sleep.
> And I will purge thy mortal grossness so
> That thou shalt like an airy spirit go.
> Peaseblossom! Cobweb! Moth! and Mustardseed! 165
> *Enter four Fairies [Peaseblossom, Cobweb, Moth, and Mustardseed].*

PEASEBLOSSOM

> Ready.

COBWEB

> And I.

MOTH

> And I.

MUSTARDSEED

> And I.

ALL

> Where shall we go?

TITANIA

> Be kind and courteous to this gentleman.
> Hop in his walks and gambol in his eyes;
> Feed him with apricocks and dewberries,
> With purple grapes, green figs, and mulberries; 170
> The honey-bags steal from the humble-bees,
> And for night-tapers crop their waxen thighs
> And light them at the fiery glow-worm's eyes,
> To have my love to bed and to arise;
> And pluck the wings from painted butterflies 175
> To fan the moonbeams from his sleeping eyes.
> Nod to him, elves, and do him courtesies.

PEASEBLOSSOM

> Hail, mortal!

150 **gleek:** jest satirically.   158 **still:** always.

COBWEB
Hail!
MOTH
Hail! 180
MUSTARDSEED
Hail!
BOTTOM
I cry your worships mercy, heartily. I be-
seech your worship's name.
COBWEB
Cobweb.
BOTTOM
I shall desire you of more acquaintance, 185
good Master Cobweb. If I cut my finger, I
shall make bold with you. Your name, honest
gentleman?
PEASEBLOSSOM
Peaseblossom.
BOTTOM
I pray you commend me to Mistress Squash, 190
your mother, and to Master Peascod, your
father. Good Master Peaseblossom, I shall
desire you of more acquaintance too. Your
name, I beseech you, sir?
MUSTARDSEED
Mustardseed. 195
BOTTOM
Good Master Mustardseed, I know your
patience well. That same cowardly, giant-like
ox-beef hath devoured many a gentleman of
your house. I promise you your kindred hath
made my eyes water ere now. I desire you more 200
acquaintance, good Master Mustardseed.
TITANIA
          Come, wait upon him; lead him to my bower.
               The moon methinks looks with a wat'ry eye;
          And when she weeps, weeps every little flower,
               Lamenting some enforced chastity. 205
          Tie up my [love's] tongue, bring him silently.
                                        [Exeunt.

          [Scene II. Another part of the wood.]
          Enter Oberon.
OBERON
I wonder if Titania be awak'd;
Then, what it was that next came in her eye,
Which she must dote on in extremity.
          Enter Robin Goodfellow.

---

190 **Squash:** unripe pea pod.   206 [**love's**] (Pope). *lovers* Q.
197 **patience:** suffering.   ii. 2 **next:** first.
205 **enforced:** violated.   3 **in extremity:** extremely.

Here comes my messenger.
                         How now, mad spirit!
What night-rule now about this haunted grove?   5

ROBIN GOODFELLOW

My mistress with a monster is in love.
Near to her close and consecrated bower,
While she was in her dull and sleeping hour,
A crew of patches, rude mechanicals,
That work for bread upon Athenian stalls,   10
Were met together to rehearse a play
Intended for great Theseus' nuptial-day.
The shallowest thickskin of that barren sort,
Who Pyramus presented in their sport,
Forsook his scene and ent'red in a brake.   15
When I did him at this advantage take,
An ass's nole I fixed on his head.
Anon his Thisby must be answered,
And forth my mimic comes. When they him spy,
As wild geese that the creeping fowler eye,   20
Or russet-pated choughs, many in sort,
Rising and cawing at the gun's report,
Sever themselves and madly sweep the sky,
So, at his sight, away his fellows fly;
And, at our stamp, here o'er and o'er one falls;   25
He murder cries, and help from Athens calls.
Their sense thus weak, lost with their fears thus strong,
Made senseless things begin to do them wrong;
For briers and thorns at their apparel snatch;
Some sleeves, some hats, from yielders all things catch.   30
I led them on in this distracted fear,
And left sweet Pyramus translated there;
When in that moment, so it came to pass,
Titania wak'd and straightway lov'd an ass.

OBERON

This falls out better than I could devise.   35
But hast thou yet latch'd the Athenian's eyes
With the love-juice, as I did bid thee do?

ROBIN GOODFELLOW

I took him sleeping,—that is finish'd too,—
And the Athenian woman by his side;
That, when he wak'd, of force she must be ey'd.   40

    Enter Demetrius and Hermia.

OBERON

Stand close; this is the same Athenian.

ROBIN GOODFELLOW

This is the woman, but not this the man.

---

5 **night-rule:** diversion planned for the night.
9 **patches:** yokels; **mechanicals:** artisans.
13 **barren sort:** dull crew.
17 **nole:** head.

19 **mimic:** buffoon, burlesque actor.
21 **choughs:** jackdaws; **in sort:** together.
24 **his sight:** sight of him.
36 **latch'd:** anointed.
40 **of force:** perforce.

DEMETRIUS

    O, why rebuke you him that loves you so?
    Lay breath so bitter on your bitter foe.

HERMIA

    Now I but chide; but I should use thee worse,   45
    For thou, I fear, hast given me cause to curse.
    If thou hast slain Lysander in his sleep,
    Being o'er shoes in blood, plunge in knee-deep,
    And kill me too.
    The sun was not so true unto the day   50
    As he to me: would he have stolen away
    From sleeping Hermia? I'll believe as soon
    This whole earth may be bor'd and that the moon
    May through the centre creep and so displease
    Her brother's noontide with the Antipodes.   55
    It cannot be but thou hast murd'red him;
    So should a murderer look, so dread, so grim.

DEMETRIUS

    So should the murd'red look, and so should I,
    Pierc'd through the heart with your stern cruelty;
    Yet you, the murderer, look as bright, as clear,   60
    As yonder Venus in her glimmering sphere.

HERMIA

    What's this to my Lysander? Where is he?
    Ah, good Demetrius, wilt thou give him me?

DEMETRIUS

    I had rather give his carcass to my hounds.

HERMIA

    Out, dog! out, cur! thou driv'st me past the bounds   65
    Of maiden's patience. Hast thou slain him, then?
    Henceforth be never numb'red among men!
    O, once tell true, tell true, even for my sake!
    Durst thou have look'd upon him being awake,
    And hast thou kill'd him sleeping? O brave touch!   70
    Could not a worm, an adder, do so much?
    An adder did it; for with doubler tongue
    Than thine, thou serpent, never adder stung.

DEMETRIUS

    You spend your passion on a mispris'd mood.
    I am not guilty of Lysander's blood;   75
    Nor is he dead, for aught that I can tell.

HERMIA

    I pray thee, tell me then that he is well.

DEMETRIUS

    An if I could, what should I get therefore?

HERMIA

    A privilege never to see me more.
    And from thy hated presence part I so: 80
    See me no more, whether he be dead or no.

                                 [Exit.

70 **touch:** exploit.   74 **on . . . mood:** in mistaken anger.
71 **worm:** serpent.

DEMETRIUS

There is no following her in this fierce vein;
Here therefore for a while I will remain.
So sorrow's heaviness doth heavier grow
For debt that bankrupt sleep doth sorrow owe;   85
Which now in some slight measure it will pay,
If for his tender here I make some stay.

                                    [*Lies down [and sleeps*].

OBERON

What hast thou done? Thou hast mistaken quite
And laid the love-juice on some true-love's sight.
Of thy misprision must perforce ensue   90
Some true love turn'd and not a false turn'd true.

ROBIN GOODFELLOW

Then fate o'er-rules, that, one man holding troth,
A million fail, confounding oath on oath.

OBERON

About the wood go swifter than the wind,
And Helena of Athens look thou find.   95
All fancy-sick she is and pale of cheer
With sighs of love, that costs the fresh blood dear.
By some illusion see thou bring her here.
I'll charm his eyes against she do appear.

ROBIN GOODFELLOW

I go, I go; look how I go,   100
Swifter than arrow from the Tartar's bow.

                                                    [*Exit.*

OBERON

Flower of this purple dye,
Hit with Cupid's archery,
Sink in apple of his eye.
When his love he doth espy,   105
Let her shine as gloriously
As the Venus of the sky.
When thou wak'st, if she be by,
Beg of her for remedy.

Re-enter Robin Goodfellow.

ROBIN GOODFELLOW

Captain of our fairy band,   110
Helena is here at hand;
And the youth, mistook by me,
Pleading for a lover's fee.
Shall we their fond pageant see?
Lord, what fools these mortals be!   115

OBERON

Stand aside. The noise they make
Will cause Demetrius to awake.

---

87 **for his tender:** i.e., until sleep
tenders itself.
90 **misprision:** mistake.
96 **fancy-sick:** love-sick; **cheer:** face.
97 **sighs . . . blood:** It was

commonly thought that each sigh
took a drop of blood from the heart.
99 **against . . . appear:** in
anticipation of her appearance.
114 **fond pageant:** foolish exhibition.

ROBIN GOODFELLOW

    Then will two at once woo one;
    That must needs be sport alone.
    And those things do best please me   120
    That befall preposterously.
    Enter Lysander and Helena.

LYSANDER

    Why should you think that I should woo in scorn?
      Scorn and derision never come in tears.
    Look, when I vow, I weep; and vows so born,
      In their nativity all truth appears.   125
    How can these things in me seem scorn to you,
    Bearing the badge of faith, to prove them true?

HELENA

    You do advance your cunning more and more.
      When truth kills truth, O devilish-holy fray!
    These vows are Hermia's; will you give her o'er?   130
      Weigh oath with oath, and you will nothing weigh.
    Your vows to her and me, put in two scales,
    Will even weigh, and both as light as tales.

LYSANDER

    I had no judgement when to her I swore.

HELENA

    Nor none, in my mind, now you give her o'er.   135

LYSANDER

    Demetrius loves her, and he loves not you.

DEMETRIUS [*Awaking.*]

    O Helen, goddess, nymph, perfect, divine!
    To what, my love, shall I compare thine eyne?
    Crystal is muddy. O, how ripe in show
    Thy lips, those kissing cherries, tempting grow!   140
    That pure congealed white, high Taurus' snow,
    Fann'd with the eastern wind, turns to a crow
    When thou hold'st up thy hand. O, let me kiss
    This princess of pure white, this seal of bliss!

HELENA

    O spite! O hell! I see you all are bent   145
    To set against me for your merriment.
    If you were civil and knew courtesy,
    You would not do me thus much injury.
    Can you not hate me, as I know you do,
    But you must join in souls to mock me too?   150
    If you were men, as men you are in show,
    You would not use a gentle lady so;
    To vow, and swear, and superpraise my parts,
    When I am sure you hate me with your hearts.
    You both are rivals, and love Hermia;   155

119 **alone:** unique.
124–125 **vows . . . appears:** vows so born show wholly true.
141 **Taurus:** a mountain range in Asia Minor.

144 **seal:** pledge.
153 **parts:** qualities.

And now both rivals, to mock Helena.
A trim exploit, a manly enterprise,
To conjure tears up in a poor maid's eyes
With your derision! None of noble sort
Would so offend a virgin and extort   160
A poor soul's patience, all to make you sport.

LYSANDER
You are unkind, Demetrius; be not so;
For you love Hermia; this you know I know.
And here, with all good will, with all my heart,
In Hermia's love I yield you up my part;   165
And yours of Helena to me bequeath,
Whom I do love and will do till my death.

HELENA
Never did mockers waste more idle breath.

DEMETRIUS
Lysander, keep thy Hermia; I will none.
If e'er I lov'd her, all that love is gone.   170
My heart to her but as guest-wise sojourn'd,
And now to Helen is it home return'd,
There to remain.

LYSANDER
                    Helen, it is not so.

DEMETRIUS
Disparage not the faith thou dost not know,
Lest, to thy peril, thou aby it dear.   175
Look, where thy love comes; yonder is thy dear.
        Re-enter Hermia.

HERMIA
Dark night, that from the eye his function takes,
The ear more quick of apprehension makes;
Wherein it doth impair the seeing sense,
It pays the hearing double recompense.   180
Thou art not by mine eye, Lysander, found;
Mine ear, I thank it, brought me to thy sound.
But why unkindly didst thou leave me so?

LYSANDER
Why should he stay, whom love doth press to go?

HERMIA
What love could press Lysander from my side?   185

LYSANDER
Lysander's love, that would not let him bide,
Fair Helena, who more engilds the night
Than all yon fiery oes and eyes of light.
Why seek'st thou me? Could not this make thee know,
The hate I bare thee made me leave thee so?   190

HERMIA
You speak not as you think. It cannot be.

HELENA
Lo, she is one of this confederacy!

160 **extort:** wrest, torture.   177 **his:** its.
169 **will none:** i.e., of her.   188 **oes:** orbs, circles.
175 **aby:** pay for.

Now I perceive they have conjoin'd all three
To fashion this false sport, in spite of me.
Injurious Hermia! most ungrateful maid!   195
Have you conspir'd, have you with these contriv'd
To bait me with this foul derision?
Is all the counsel that we two have shar'd,
The sisters' vows, the hours that we have spent,
When we have chid the hasty-footed time   200
For parting us,—O, is all forgot?
All school-days' friendship, childhood innocence?
We, Hermia, like two artificial gods,
Have with our needles created both one flower,
Both on one sampler, sitting on one cushion,   205
Both warbling of one song, both in one key,
As if our hands, our sides, voices and minds
Had been incorporate. So we grew together,
Like to a double cherry, seeming parted,
But yet an union in partition;   210
Two lovely berries moulded on one stem;
So, with two seeming bodies but one heart;
Two of the first, [like] coats in heraldry,
Due but to one and crowned with one crest.
And will you rend our ancient love asunder,   215
To join with men in scorning your poor friend?
It is not friendly, 'tis not maidenly.
Our sex, as well as I, may chide you for it,
Though I alone do feel the injury.

HERMIA
I am amazed at your passionate words.   220
I scorn you not; it seems that you scorn me.

HELENA
Have you not set Lysander, as in scorn,
To follow me and praise my eyes and face?
And made your other love, Demetrius,
Who even but now did spurn me with his foot,   225
To call me goddess, nymph, divine and rare,
Precious, celestial? Wherefore speaks he this
To her he hates? And wherefore doth Lysander
Deny your love, so rich within his soul,
And tender me, forsooth, affection,   230
But by your setting on, by your consent?
What though I be not so in grace as you,
So hung upon with love, so fortunate,
But miserable most, to love unlov'd?
This you should pity rather than despise.   235

HERMIA
I understand not what you mean by this.

---

195 **Injurious:** insulting.
203 **artificial:** skilled in art.
208 **incorporate:** joined in one body.
213 **Two of the first:** Apparently a heraldic phrase used of two coats of arms (such as those of husband and

wife) arranged on either side of a vertical division of the shield, such division being known as "the first" of several possible divisions; [like] (Folks conj.). *life* Q.

HELENA

    Ay, do, persever, counterfeit sad looks,
    Make mouths upon me when I turn my back,
    Wink each at other, hold the sweet jest up;
    This sport, well carried, shall be chronicled.   240
    If you have any pity, grace, or manners,
    You would not make me such an argument.
    But fare ye well; 'tis partly my own fault,
    Which death or absence soon shall remedy.

LYSANDER

    Stay, gentle Helena; hear my excuse,   245
    My love, my life, my soul, fair Helena!

HELENA

    O excellent!

HERMIA

              Sweet, do not scorn her so.

DEMETRIUS

    If she cannot entreat, I can compel.

LYSANDER

    Thou canst compel no more than she entreat.
    Thy threats have no more strength than her weak [prayers].   250
    Helen, I love thee; by my life, I do!
    I swear by that which I will lose for thee,
    To prove him false that says I love thee not.

DEMETRIUS

    I say I love thee more than he can do.

LYSANDER

    If thou say so, withdraw, and prove it too.   255

DEMETRIUS

    Quick, come!

HERMIA

              Lysander, whereto tends all this?

LYSANDER

    Away, you Ethiope!

DEMETRIUS

              No, no; he'll [but]
    Seem to break loose. Take on as you would follow,
    But yet come not. You are a tame man, go!

LYSANDER

    Hang off, thou cat, thou burr! Vile thing, let loose,   260
    Or I will shake thee from me like a serpent!

HERMIA

    Why are you grown so rude? What change is this?
    Sweet love,—

LYSANDER

             Thy love! Out, tawny Tartar, out!
    Out, loathed medicine! O hated potion, hence!

HERMIA

    Do you not jest?

---

237 **sad:** grave.
242 **argument:** subject for scorn.
250 [**prayers**] (Theobald). *praise* Q.

257 **he'll [but]:** Nicolson conj. for the obviously corrupt *heele* of Q.

HELENA

                Yes, sooth; and so do you.   265

LYSANDER

  Demetrius, I will keep my word with thee.

DEMETRIUS

  I would I had your bond, for I perceive
  A weak bond holds you. I'll not trust your word.

LYSANDER

  What, should I hurt her, strike her, kill her dead?
  Although I hate her, I'll not harm her so.   270

HERMIA

  What, can you do me greater harm than hate?
  Hate me! wherefore? O me! what news, my love!
  Am not I Hermia? Are not you Lysander?
  I am as fair now as I was erewhile.
  Since night you lov'd me; yet since night you left me: 275
  Why, then you left me—O, the gods forbid!—
  In earnest, shall I say?

LYSANDER

                  Ay, by my life;
  And never did desire to see thee more.
  Therefore be out of hope, of question, doubt;
  Be certain, nothing truer; 'tis no jest   280
  That I do hate thee and love Helena.

HERMIA

  O me! you juggler! you canker-blossom!
  You thief of love! What, have you come by night
  And stolen my love's heart from him?

HELENA

                       Fine, i' faith!
  Have you no modesty, no maiden shame,   285
  No touch of bashfulness? What, will you tear
  Impatient answers from my gentle tongue?
  Fie, fie! you counterfeit, you puppet, you!

HERMIA

  "Puppet?" Why so? Ay, that way goes the game
  Now I perceive that she hath made compare   290
  Between our statures; she hath urg'd her height;
  And with her personage, her tall personage,
  Her height, forsooth, she hath prevail'd with him.
  And are you grown so high in his esteem,
  Because I am so dwarfish and so low?   295
  How low am I, thou painted maypole? Speak,
  How low am I? I am not yet so low
  But that my nails can reach unto thine eyes.

HELENA

  I pray you, though you mock me, gentlemen,
  Let her not hurt me. I was never curst;   300
  I have no gift at all in shrewishness;

---

272 **what news:** what is the matter.   300 **curst:** shrewish.
282 **canker-blossom:** worm that
destroys a blossom.

I am a right maid for my cowardice.
Let her not strike me. You perhaps may think,
Because she is something lower than myself,
That I can match her.

HERMIA

              "Lower!" hark, again.   305

HELENA

Good Hermia, do not be so bitter with me.
I evermore did love you, Hermia,
Did ever keep your counsels, never wrong'd you;
Save that, in love unto Demetrius,
I told him of your stealth unto this wood.   310
He followed you; for love I followed him;
But he hath chid me hence and threat'ned me
To strike me, spurn me, nay, to kill me too.
And now, so you will let me quiet go,
To Athens will I bear my folly back   315
And follow you no further. Let me go.
You see how simple and how fond I am.

HERMIA

Why, get you gone; who is't that hinders you?

HELENA

A foolish heart, that I leave here behind.

HERMIA

What, with Lysander?

HELENA

              With Demetrius.   320

LYSANDER

Be not afraid; she shall not harm thee, Helena.

DEMETRIUS

No, sir, she shall not, though you take her part.

HELENA

O, when she's angry, she is keen and shrewd!
She was a vixen when she went to school;
And though she be but little, she is fierce.   325

HERMIA

"Little" again! Nothing but "low" and "little"!
Why will you suffer her to flout me thus?
Let me come to her.

LYSANDER

           Get you gone, you dwarf,
You minimus, of hind'ring knot-grass made;
You bead, you acorn.

DEMETRIUS

            You are too officious   330
In her behalf that scorns your services.
Let her alone; speak not of Helena;
Take not her part; for, if thou dost intend

302 **right:** true.
310 **stealth:** stealing away.
323 **shrewd:** sharp-tongued.
329 **minimus:** dwarf; **knot-grass:** a
weed supposed capable of stunting
the growth.
333 **intend:** proffer.

Never so little show of love to her,
Thou shalt aby it.

LYSANDER

Now she holds me not.   335
Now follow, if thou dar'st, to try whose right,
Of thine or mine, is most in Helena.

DEMETRIUS

Follow! Nay, I'll go with thee, cheek by jowl.

[*Exeunt Lysander and Demetrius.*

HERMIA

You, mistress, all this coil is 'long of you.
Nay, go not back.

HELENA

I will not trust you, I,   340
Nor longer stay in your curst company.
Your hands than mine are quicker for a fray;
My legs are longer though, to run away.

[*Exit.*]

HERMIA

I am amaz'd, and know not what to say.

[*Exit.*

OBERON

This is thy negligence. Still thou mistak'st,   345
Or else committ'st thy knaveries wilfully.

ROBIN GOODFELLOW

Believe me, king of shadows, I mistook.
Did not you tell me I should know the man
By the Athenian garments he had on?
And so far blameless proves my enterprise,   350
That I have 'nointed an Athenian's eyes;
And so far am I glad it so did sort,
As this their jangling I esteem a sport.

OBERON

Thou see'st these lovers seek a place to fight;
Hie therefore, Robin, overcast the night.   355
The starry welkin cover thou anon
With drooping fog as black as Acheron,
And lead these testy rivals so astray
As one come not within another's way.
Like to Lysander sometime frame thy tongue,   360
Then stir Demetrius up with bitter wrong;
And sometime rail thou like Demetrius;
And from each other look thou lead them thus,
Till o'er their brows death-counterfeiting sleep
With leaden legs and batty wings doth creep.   365
Then crush this herb into Lysander's eye;
Whose liquor hath this virtuous property,
To take from thence all error with his might,
And makes his eyeballs roll with wonted sight.

339 **coil:** turmoil; **'long:** because.   361 **wrong:** taunts.
352 **sort:** turn out.   367 **virtuous:** powerful.
357 **Acheron:** river of Hades.   368 **his might:** its power.

When they next wake, all this derision   370
Shall seem a dream and fruitless vision;
And back to Athens shall the lovers wend
With league whose date till death shall never end.
Whiles I in this affair do thee employ,
I'll to my queen and beg her Indian boy;   375
And then I will her charmed eye release
From monster's view, and all things shall be peace.

ROBIN GOODFELLOW

My fairy lord, this must be done with haste,
For Night's swift dragons cut the clouds full fast,
And yonder shines Aurora's harbinger,   380
At whose approach, ghosts, wand'ring here and there,
Troop home to churchyards. Damned spirits all,
That in crossways and floods have burial,
Already to their wormy beds are gone.
For fear lest day should look their shames upon,   385
They wilfully themselves exile from light
And must for aye consort with black-brow'd night.

OBERON

But we are spirits of another sort.
I with the Morning's love have oft made sport,
And, like a forester, the groves may tread,   390
Even till the eastern gate, all fiery-red,
Opening on Neptune with fair blessed beams
Turns into yellow gold his salt green streams.
But, notwithstanding, haste, make no delay;
We may effect this business yet ere day.   395

                                                  [*Exit.*]

ROBIN GOODFELLOW

        Up and down, up and down,
        I will lead them up and down.
        I am fear'd in field and town.
        Goblin, lead them up and down.
Here comes one.   400
      Re-enter Lysander.

LYSANDER

Where art thou, proud Demetrius? Speak thou now.

ROBIN GOODFELLOW

Here, villain; drawn and ready. Where art thou?

LYSANDER

I will be with thee straight.

ROBIN GOODFELLOW

                Follow me, then,
To plainer ground.

                  [*Exit Lysander, as following the voice.*]

---

379 **Night's . . . dragons:** the dragons drawing the car of Night.
380 **Aurora's harbinger:** star announcing the dawn.
383 **crossways . . . burial:** Suicides were buried at crossroads, and like the ghosts of those who had drowned, having thus no proper burial, were believed condemned to cheerless wandering.
389 **Morning's love:** Cephalus, the youth loved by Aurora, or possibly Aurora herself.

Re-enter Demetrius.

DEMETRIUS

     Lysander, speak again!
Thou runaway, thou coward, art thou fled?   405
Speak! In some bush? Where dost thou hide thy head?

ROBIN GOODFELLOW

Thou coward, art thou bragging to the stars,
Telling the bushes that thou look'st for wars,
And wilt not come? Come, recreant; come, thou child,
I'll whip thee with a rod. He is defil'd   410
That draws a sword on thee.

DEMETRIUS

      Yea, art thou there?

ROBIN GOODFELLOW

Follow my voice. We'll try no manhood here.

                   [Exeunt.

  [Re-enter Lysander.]

LYSANDER

He goes before me and still dares me on.
When I come where he calls, then he is gone.
The villain is much lighter-heel'd than I;   415
I followed fast, but faster he did fly,
That fallen am I in dark uneven way,
And here will rest me. Come, thou gentle day!

                 [Lies down.

For if but once thou show me thy grey light,
I'll find Demetrius and revenge this spite.   420

                [Sleeps.]

  Re-enter Robin Goodfellow and Demetrius.

ROBIN GOODFELLOW

Ho, ho, ho! Coward, why com'st thou not?

DEMETRIUS

Abide me, if thou dar'st; for well I wot
Thou runn'st before me, shifting every place,
And dar'st not stand, nor look me in the face.
Where art thou now?

ROBIN GOODFELLOW

     Come hither; I am here.   425

DEMETRIUS

Nay, then, thou mock'st me. Thou shalt buy this dear,
If ever I thy face by daylight see.
Now, go thy way. Faintness constraineth me
To measure out my length on this cold bed.
By day's approach look to be visited.   430

           [Lies down and sleeps.

  Re-enter Helena.

HELENA

O weary night, O long and tedious night,
 Abate thy hours! Shine, comforts, from the east,
That I may back to Athens by daylight,
 From these that my poor company detest.
And sleep, that sometimes shuts up sorrow's eye,   435
Steal me awhile from mine own company.

         [Lies down and] sleeps.

ROBIN GOODFELLOW

> Yet but three? Come one more;
> Two of both kinds makes up four.
> *Re-enter Hermia.*
> Here she comes, curst and sad.
> Cupid is a knavish lad,   440
> Thus to make poor females mad.

HERMIA

Never so weary, never so in woe,
> Bedabbled with the dew and torn with briers,
I can no further crawl, no further go;
> My legs can keep no pace with my desires.   445
Here will I rest me till the break of day.
Heavens shield Lysander, if they mean a fray!

> > > > > *[Lies down and sleeps.]*

ROBIN GOODFELLOW

> > On the ground
> > Sleep sound.
> > I'll apply   450
> > To your eye,
> Gentle lover, remedy.

> > > > *[Squeezing the juice on Lysander's eyes.]*

> > When thou wak'st,
> > Thou tak'st
> > True delight   455
> > In the sight
> Of thy former lady's eye;
> And the country proverb known,
> That every man should take his own,
> In your waking shall be shown.   460
> > > Jack shall have Jill;
> > > Nought shall go ill;
> The man shall have his mare again, and all shall be well.

> > > > > > > *[Exit.]*

Act IV

> *[Scene I. The same.]*
> *[Lysander, Demetrius, Helena, and Hermia, lying asleep.]*
> *Enter Titania and Clown [Bottom; Peaseblossom, Cobweb, Moth, Mus-*
> *tardseed,] and [other] Fairies [attending]; Oberon behind [unseen].*

TITANIA

Come, sit thee down upon this flow'ry bed,
> While I thy amiable cheeks do coy;
And stick musk-roses in thy sleek smooth head,
> And kiss thy fair large ears, my gentle joy.

BOTTOM

Where's Peaseblossom?   5

PEASEBLOSSOM

Ready.

> IV.i.2 **coy:** caress.

BOTTOM
Scratch my head, Peaseblossom. Where's Mounsieur Cobweb?

COBWEB
Ready.

BOTTOM
Mounsieur Cobweb, good mounsieur, get   10
you your weapons in your hand, and kill me a
red-hipp'd humble-bee on the top of a thistle; and,
good mounsieur, bring me the honey-bag. Do not
fret yourself too much in the action, mounsieur,
and, good mounsieur, have a care the honey-bag   15
break not; I would be loath to have you over-
flown with a honey-bag, signior. Where's Mounsieur Mustardseed?

MUSTARDSEED
Ready.

BOTTOM
Give me your neaf, Mounsieur Mustardseed.   20
Pray you, leave your courtesy, good mounsieur.

MUSTARDSEED
What's your will?

BOTTOM
Nothing, good mounsieur, but to help
Cavalery Cobweb to scratch. I must to the bar-
ber's, mounsieur; for methinks I am marvellous   25
hairy about the face; and I am such a tender ass, if
my hair do but tickle me, I must scratch.

TITANIA
What, wilt thou hear some music, my sweet love?

BOTTOM
I have a reasonable good ear in music.   30
Let's have the tongs and the bones.

[*Music. Tongs. Rural music.*

TITANIA
Or say, sweet love, what thou desir'st to eat.

BOTTOM
Truly, a peck of provender; I could munch
your good dry oats. Methinks I have a great desire to a bottle of hay. Good hay, sweet hay,   35
hath no fellow.

TITANIA
I have a venturous fairy that shall seek
The squirrel's hoard, and fetch [for] thee new nuts.

BOTTOM
I had rather have a handful or two of dried
peas. But, I pray you, let none of your people   40

20 **neaf:** fist.
21 **leave your courtesy:** put on your
hat.
24 **Cavalery:** cavaliero, gentleman;
Cobweb: We should expect
Peaseblossom (cf. l. 7).

31 **tongs . . . bones:** rustic
instruments of music.
35 **bottle:** bundle.
36 **fellow:** equal.
38 [**for**] (Collier conj.). Om. Qq.

stir me; I have an exposition of sleep come upon
me.

TITANIA

Sleep thou, and I will wind thee in my arms.
Fairies, be gone, and be always away.

[*Exeunt fairies.*]

So doth the woodbine the sweet honeysuckle   45
Gently entwist; the female ivy so
Enrings the barky fingers of the elm.
O, how I love thee! how I dote on thee!

[*They sleep.*]

    Enter Robin Goodfellow.

OBERON [*Advancing.*]

Welcome, good Robin. See'st thou this sweet sight?
Her dotage now I do begin to pity;   50
For, meeting her of late behind the wood,
Seeking sweet favours for this hateful fool,
I did upbraid her and fall out with her.
For she his hairy temples then had rounded
With coronet of fresh and fragrant flowers;   55
And that same dew, which sometime on the buds
Was wont to swell like round and orient pearls,
Stood now within the pretty flowerets' eyes
Like tears that did their own disgrace bewail.
When I had at my pleasure taunted her   60
And she in mild terms begg'd my patience,
I then did ask of her her changeling child;
Which straight she gave me, and her fairy sent
To bear him to my bower in fairy land.
And, now I have the boy, I will undo   65
This hateful imperfection of her eyes;
And, gentle Puck, take this transformed scalp
From off the head of this Athenian swain,
That, he awaking when the other do,
May all to Athens back again repair,   70
And think no more of this night's accidents
But as the fierce vexation of a dream.
But first I will release the fairy queen.

[*Touching her eyes.*]

    Be as thou wast wont to be;
    See as thou wast wont to see:
    Dian's bud o'er Cupid's flower   75
    Hath such force and blessed power.
Now, my Titania; wake you, my sweet queen.

TITANIA

My Oberon! what visions have I seen!
Methought I was enamour'd of an ass.   80

---

41 **exposition of:** He means
disposition to.
52 **favours:** i.e., flowers for love-
tokens.
57 **orient:** eastern.

69 **other:** others.
76 **Dian's bud:** The flower of the
agnus castus or chaste tree was
believed to preserve chastity.

OBERON
There lies your love.

TITANIA
                    How came these things to pass?
O, how mine eyes do loathe his visage now!

OBERON
Silence awhile. Robin, take off this head.
Titania, music call; and strike more dead
Than common sleep of all these five the sense.   85

TITANIA
Music, ho! music, such as charmeth sleep!

                              [Music, still.

ROBIN GOODFELLOW
Now, when thou wak'st, with thine own fool's eyes peep.

OBERON
Sound, music! Come, my queen, take hands with me,
And rock the ground whereon these sleepers be.   90
Now thou and I are new in amity
And will to-morrow midnight solemnly
Dance in Duke Theseus' house triumphantly
And bless it to all fair prosperity.
There shall the pairs of faithful lovers be   95
Wedded, with Theseus, all in jollity.

ROBIN GOODFELLOW
        Fairy king, attend and mark;
        I do hear the morning lark.

OBERON
        Then, my queen, in silence sad
        Trip we after the night's shade.   100
        We the globe can compass soon,
        Swifter than the wand'ring moon.

TITANIA
        Come, my lord, and in our flight
        Tell me how it came this night
        That I sleeping here was found   105
        With these mortals on the ground.
                  [Exeunt. Horns winded [within].
     Enter Theseus, Hippolyta, Egeus, and all his train.

THESEUS
Go, one of you, find out the forester,
For now our observation is perform'd,
And since we have the vaward of the day,
My love shall hear the music of my hounds.   110
Uncouple in the western valley, let them go.
Despatch, I say, and find the forester.

                        [Exit an attendant.]

We will, fair queen, up to the mountain's top
And mark the musical confusion
Of hounds and echo in conjunction.   115

---

108 **observation:** observance,   109 **vaward:** vanguard.
May-day rites (cf. I.i.167).

HIPPOLYTA

I was with Hercules and Cadmus once,
When in a wood of Crete they bay'd the bear
With hounds of Sparta. Never did I hear
Such gallant chiding; for, besides the groves,
The skies, the fountains, every region near   120
Seem'd all one mutual cry. I never heard
So musical a discord, such sweet thunder.

THESEUS

My hounds are bred out of the Spartan kind,
So flew'd, so sanded, and their heads are hung
With ears that sweep away the morning dew;   125
Crook-knee'd, and dew-lapp'd like Thessalian bulls;
Slow in pursuit, but match'd in mouth like bells,
Each under each. A cry more tuneable
Was never holla'd to, nor cheer'd with horn,
In Crete, in Sparta, nor in Thessaly.   130
Judge when you hear. But, soft! what nymphs are these?

EGEUS

My lord, this is my daughter here asleep;
And this, Lysander; this Demetrius is;
This Helena, old Nedar's Helena.
I wonder of their being here together.   135

THESEUS

No doubt they rose up early to observe
The rite of May, and, hearing our intent,
Came here in grace of our solemnity.
But speak, Egeus; is not this the day
That Hermia should give answer of her choice?   140

EGEUS

It is, my lord.

THESEUS

Go, bid the huntsmen wake them with their horns.

[*Horns and shout within. Lysander, Demetrius,
Helena, and Hermina wake and start up.*]

Good morrow, friends. Saint Valentine is past;
Begin these wood-birds but to couple now?

LYSANDER

Pardon, my lord.

THESEUS

I pray you all, stand up.   145
I know you two are rival enemies;
How comes this gentle concord in the world,
That hatred is so far from jealousy
To sleep by hate and fear no enmity?

119 **chiding:** baying.
124 **flew'd:** with large chaps;
sanded: of sandy color.
128 **Each . . . each:** with varied
pitch. Elizabethan huntsmen coveted
packs of hounds whose cries would
blend; **cry:** pack.

138 **solemnity:** marriage ceremony.
143 **Saint Valentine:** Birds were
popularly supposed to choose their
mates on Valentine's day.

LYSANDER

My lord, I shall reply amazedly, 150
Half sleep, half waking; but as yet, I swear,
I cannot truly say how I came here.
But, as I think,—for truly would I speak,
And now I do bethink me, so it is,—
I came with Hermia hither. Our intent 155
Was to be gone from Athens, where we might,
Without the peril of the Athenian law—

EGEUS

Enough, enough, my lord; you have enough.
I beg the law, the law, upon his head.
They would have stol'n away; they would, Demetrius, 160
Thereby to have defeated you and me,
You of your wife, and me of my consent,
Of my consent that she should be your wife.

DEMETRIUS

My lord, fair Helen told me of their stealth,
Of this their purpose hither to this wood; 165
And I in fury hither follow'd them,
Fair Helena in fancy following me.
But, my good lord, I wot not by what power,—
But by some power it is,—my love to Hermia,
Melted as [is] the snow, seems to me now 170
As the remembrance of an idle gaud
Which in my childhood I did dote upon;
And all the faith, the virtue of my heart,
The object and the pleasure of mine eye,
Is only Helena. To her, my lord, 175
Was I betroth'd ere I saw Hermia;
But like a sickness did I loathe this food;
But, as in health, come to my natural taste,
Now I do wish it, love it, long for it,
And will for evermore be true to it. 180

THESEUS

Fair lovers, you are fortunately met;
Of this discourse we more will hear anon.
Egeus, I will overbear your will;
For in the temple, by and by, with us
These couples shall eternally be knit. 185
And, for the morning now is something worn,
Our purpos'd hunting shall be set aside.
Away with us to Athens; three and three,
We'll hold a feast in great solemnity.
Come, Hippolyta. 190

[*Exeunt Theseus, Hippolyta, Egeus, and train.*

DEMETRIUS

These things seem small and undistinguishable,
Like far-off mountains turned into clouds.

156 **where:** to a place where. 170 [**is**] (Stevens). Om. Qq. Ff.
157 **Without:** beyond.

HERMIA
Methinks I see these things with parted eye,
When every thing seems double.
HELENA
                  So methinks;
And I have found Demetrius like a jewel,   195
Mine own, and not mine own.
DEMETRIUS
               [But] are you sure
That we are [now] awake? It seems to me
That yet we sleep, we dream. Do not you think
The Duke was here, and bid us follow him?
HERMIA
Yea; and my father.
HELENA
           And Hippolyta.   200
LYSANDER
And he did bid us follow to the temple.
DEMETRIUS
Why, then, we are awake. Let's follow him;
And by the way let us recount our dreams.

                            [Exeunt lovers.

BOTTOM (*Awaking.*)
When my cue comes, call me, and I will
answer. My next is, "Most fair Pyramus."   205
Heigh-ho! Peter Quince! Flute, the bellows-
mender!
Snout, the tinker! Starveling! God's
my life, stolen hence, and left me asleep! I
have had a most rare vision. I have had a dream,   210
past the wit of man to say what dream it
was. Man is but an ass, if he go about to expound
this dream. Methought I was—there is no man
can tell what. Methought I was,—and methought
I had,—but man is but a patch'd fool, if he will   215
offer to say what methought I had. The eye of
man hath not heard, the ear of man hath not seen,
man's hand is not able to taste, his tongue to conceive, nor his heart to report, what my dream was.
I will get Peter Quince to write a ballad of this   220
dream. It shall be called "Bottom's Dream,"
because it hath no bottom; and I will sing it in the
latter end of a play, before the Duke; peradventure,
to make it the more gracious, I shall sing it at her
death.

                            [Exit.

193 **parted:** out of focus.
196–197 **[But]** . . . **awake?**
(Steevens conj.). *Are you sure that we
are awake?* Qq. Om. Ff.

211 **go about:** attempt.
214 **patch'd:** wearing motley.
223–224 **at her death,** i.e.,
Thisbe's.

[Scene II. Athens. Quince's house.]
Enter Quince, Flute, Snout, and Starveling.

QUINCE
Have you sent to Bottom's house? Is he
come home yet?

STARVELING
He cannot be heard of. Out of doubt he is
transported.

FLUTE
If he come not, then the play is marr'd. It   5
goes not forward, doth it?

QUINCE
It is not possible. You have not a man in
all Athens able to discharge Pyramus but he.

FLUTE
No, he hath simply the best wit of any
handicraft man in Athens.   10

SNOUT
Yea, and the best person too; and he is a
very paramour for a sweet voice.

FLUTE
You must say "paragon"; a paramour is, God
bless us, a thing of naught.
Enter Snug.

SNUG
Masters, the Duke is coming from the temple,   15
and there is two or three lords and ladies more
married. If our sport had gone forward, we
had all been made men.

FLUTE
O sweet bully Bottom! Thus hath he lost six-
pence a day during his life; he could not have   20
'scaped sixpence a day. An the Duke had not
given him sixpence a day for playing Pyramus,
I'll be hang'd. He would have deserved it. Sixpence a day in Pyramus, or nothing.
Enter Bottom.

BOTTOM
Where are these lads? Where are these   25
hearts?

QUINCE
Bottom! O most courageous day! O
most happy hour!

BOTTOM
Masters, I am to discourse wonders, but
ask me not what; for if I tell you, I am no true   30
Athenian. I will tell you everything, right as it
fell out.

QUINCE
Let us hear, sweet Bottom.

ii.14 **thing of naught:** naughty thing.   19–20 **sixpence a day:** i.e., as royal
pension.

BOTTOM

Not a word of me. All that I will tell you
is, that the Duke hath dined. Get your apparel   35
together, good strings to your beards, new ribbons
to your pumps; meet presently at the palace; every
man look o'er his part; for the short and the long
is, our play is preferr'd. In any case, let Thisby
have clean linen; and let not him that plays the   40
lion pare his nails, for they shall hang out for the
lion's claws. And, most dear actors, eat no onions
nor garlic, for we are to utter sweet breath; and I
do not doubt but to hear them say, it is a sweet
comedy. No more words; away! go, away!   45

[Exeunt.

Act V

[*Scene I. Athens. The palace of Theseus.*]
Enter Theseus, Hippolyta, Philostrate, Lords [and Attendants].

HIPPOLYTA

'Tis strange, my Theseus, that these lovers speak of.

THESEUS

More strange than true; I never may believe
These antique fables, nor these fairy toys.
Lovers and madmen have such seething brains,
Such shaping fantasies, that apprehend   5
More than cool reason ever comprehends.
The lunatic, the lover, and the poet
Are of imagination all compact.
One sees more devils than vast hell can hold;
That is, the madman. The lover, all as frantic,   10
Sees Helen's beauty in a brow of Egypt.
The poet's eye, in a fine frenzy rolling,
Doth glance from heaven to earth, from earth to heaven;
And as imagination bodies forth
The forms of things unknown, the poet's pen   15
Turns them to shapes and gives to airy nothing
A local habitation and a name.
Such tricks hath strong imagination,
That, if it would but apprehend some joy,
It comprehends some bringer of that joy;   20
Or in the night, imagining some fear,
How easy is a bush suppos'd a bear!

HIPPOLYTA

But all the story of the night told over,
And all their minds transfigur'd so together,
More witnesseth than fancy's images,   25
And grows to something of great constancy;
But, howsoever, strange and admirable.

39 **preferr'd:** chosen.   11 **Helen:** Helen of Troy; **brow of**
V.i.8 **compact:** composed.   **Egypt:** gypsy's face.
                                   26 **constancy:** certainty.

Enter lovers, Lysander, Demetrius, Hermia, and Helena.

THESEUS

Here come the lovers, full of joy and mirth.
Joy, gentle friends! joy and fresh days of love
Accompany your hearts!

LYSANDER

      More than to us   30
Wait in your royal walks, your board, your bed!

THESEUS

Come now; what masques, what dances shall we have,
To wear away this long age of three hours
Between our after-supper and bed-time?
Where is our usual manager of mirth?   35
What revels are in hand? Is there no play
To ease the anguish of a torturing hour?
Call Philostrate.

PHILOSTRATE

      Here, mighty Theseus.

THESEUS

Say, what abridgement have you for this evening?
What masque? what music? How shall we beguile   40
The lazy time, if not with some delight?

PHILOSTRATE

There is a brief how many sports are ripe.
Make choice of which your Highness will see first.

                 [Giving a paper.]

THESEUS *[Reads.]*

"The battle with the Centaurs, to be sung
By an Athenian eunuch to the harp."   45
We'll none of that: that have I told my love,
In glory of my kinsman Hercules.
"The riot of the tipsy Bacchanals,
Tearing the Thracian singer in their rage."
That is an old device; and it was play'd   50
When I from Thebes came last a conqueror.
"The thrice three Muses mourning for the death
Of Learning, late deceas'd in beggary."
That is some satire, keen and critical,
Not sorting with a nuptial ceremony.   55
"A tedious brief scene of young Pyramus
And his love Thisbe; very tragical mirth."
Merry and tragical! Tedious and brief!
That is, hot ice and wondrous strange snow.
How shall we find the concord of this discord?   60

PHILOSTRATE

A play there is, my lord, some ten words long,

---

39 **abridgement:** pastime.
42 **brief:** list, schedule.
44 **Centaurs:** The Centaurs and the Lapithae fought at a wedding which Theseus would remember, since he had taken part on the side of the latter.
48–49 **The riot . . . rage:** Orpheus,

the poet-musician, was killed by the frenzied women followers of Bacchus.
52 **The thrice three Muses:** A topical reference has been seen in these lines, but no explanation is satisfactory.
55 **sorting with:** befitting.

Which is as brief as I have known a play;
But by ten words, my lord, it is too long,
Which makes it tedious; for in all the play
There is not one word apt, one player fitted.   65
And tragical, my noble lord, it is;
For Pyramus therein doth kill himself.
Which, when I saw rehears'd, I must confess,
Made mine eyes water; but more merry tears
The passion of loud laughter never shed.   70
THESEUS
    What are they that do play it?
PHILOSTRATE
    Hard-handed men that work in Athens here,
    Which never labour'd in their minds till now,
    And now have toil'd their unbreath'd memories
    With this same play, against your nuptial.   75
THESEUS
    And we will hear it.
PHILOSTRATE
                    No, my noble lord;
    It is not for you. I have heard it over,
    And it is nothing, nothing in the world;
    Unless you can find sport in their intents,
    Extremely stretch'd and conn'd with cruel pain,   80
    To do you service
THESEUS
                    I will hear that play;
    For never anything can be amiss,
    When simpleness and duty tender it.
    Go, bring them in; and take your places, ladies.

                                    [Exit Philostrate.]
HIPPOLYTA
    I love not to see wretchedness o'er-charged,   85
    And duty in his service perishing.
THESEUS
    Why, gentle sweet, you shall see no such thing.
HIPPOLYTA
    He says they can do nothing in this kind.
THESEUS
    The kinder we, to give them thanks for nothing.
    Our sport shall be to take what they mistake;   90
    And what poor duty cannot do, noble respect
    Takes it in might, not merit.
    Where I have come, great clerks have purposed
    To greet me with premeditated welcomes;
    Where I have seen them shiver and look pale,   95
    Make periods in the midst of sentences,
    Throttle their practis'd accent in their fears,

---

74 **unbreath'd:** unpractised.
80 **stretch'd:** strained.
85 **wretchedness o'ercharged:**
weakness overburdened.

92 **takes . . . merit:** takes the will
for the deed.
93 **clerks:** scholars.

And in conclusion dumbly have broke off,
Not paying me a welcome. Trust me, sweet,
Out of this silence yet I pick'd a welcome;   100
And in the modesty of fearful duty
I read as much as from the rattling tongue
Of saucy and audacious eloquence.
Love, therefore, and tongue-ti'd simplicity
In least speak most, to my capacity.   105
    [Re-enter Philostrate.]

PHILOSTRATE
So please your Grace, the Prologue is address'd.

THESEUS
Let him approach.   *[Flourish of trumpets.*
    Enter [Quince for] the Prologue.

PROLOGUE
If we offend, it is with our good will.
    That you should think, we come not to offend,
But with good will. To show our simple skill,   110
    That is the true beginning of our end.
Consider then we come but in despite.
    We do not come as minding to content you,
Our true intent is. All for your delight
    We are not here. That you should here repent you,   115
The actors are at hand, and by their show
You shall know all that you are like to know.

THESEUS
This fellow doth not stand upon points.

LYSANDER
He hath rid his prologue like a rough colt; he
knows not the stop. A good moral, my lord: it is   120
not enough to speak, but to speak true.

HIPPOLYTA
Indeed he hath play'd on this prologue like
a child on a recorder; a sound, but not in
government.

THESEUS
His speech was like a tangled chain; nothing   125
impaired, but all disordered. Who is next?
    Enter with a trumpet before them, Pyramus and Thisbe, Wall,
    Moonshine, and Lion.

PROLOGUE
Gentles, perchance you wonder at this show;
    But wonder on till truth make all things plain.
This man is Pyramus, if you would know;   130
    This beauteous lady Thisby is certain.

105 **to my capacity:** in my opinion.
In the sympathetic speech of
Theseus a tribute was very likely
intended to the graciousness of
Queen Elizabeth, who may on some
occasion have witnessed this play.
106 **address'd:** ready.
108 ff. The comic device of
misconstruing punctuation had been
used some sixty years before in *Ralph
Roister Doister.*
118 **stand . . . points:** A quibble
upon (1) "to be scrupulous" and (2)
"heed punctuation."
123 **recorder:** an instrument like a
flageolet.
124 **government:** control.

This man, with lime and rough-cast, doth present
 Wall, that vile Wall which did these lovers sunder;
And through Wall's chink, poor souls, they are content
 To whisper. At the which let no man wonder.   135
This man, with lantern, dog, and bush of thorn,
 Presenteth Moonshine; for, if you will know,
By moonshine did these lovers think no scorn
 To meet at Ninus' tomb, there, there to woo.
This grisly beast, which Lion hight by name,   140
The trusty Thisby, coming first by night,
Did scare away, or rather did affright;
And, as she fled, her mantle she did fall,
 Which Lion vile with bloody mouth did stain.
Anon comes Pyramus, sweet youth and tall,   145
 And finds his trusty Thisby's mantle slain;
Whereat, with blade, with bloody blameful blade,
 He bravely broach'd his boiling bloody breast;
And Thisby, tarrying in mulberry shade,
 His dagger drew, and died. For all the rest,   150
Let Lion, Moonshine, Wall, and lovers twain
At large discourse, while here they do remain.
    [*Exeunt Prologue, Thisbe, Lion, and Moonshine.*

THESEUS
 I wonder if the lion be to speak.
DEMETRIUS
 No wonder, my lord; one lion may, when
 many asses do.   155
WALL
 In this same interlude it doth befall
 That I, one Snout by name, present a wall;
 And such a wall, as I would have you think,
 That had in it a crannied hole or chink,
 Through which the lovers, Pyramus and Thisby,   160
 Did whisper often very secretly.
 This loam, this rough-cast, and this stone doth show
 That I am that same wall; the truth is so;
 And this the cranny is, right and sinister,
 Through which the fearful lovers are to whisper.   165
THESEUS
 Would you desire lime and hair to speak
 better?
DEMETRIUS
 It is the wittiest partition that ever I heard
 discourse, my lord.
   Enter Pyramus.
THESEUS
 Pyramus draws near the wall. Silence!   170
PYRAMUS
 O grim-look'd night! O night with hue so black!
  O night, which ever art when day is not!
 O night, O night! alack, alack, alack,

---

140 **hight:** is called.   148 **broach'd:** stabbed.

  I fear my Thisby's promise is forgot!
And thou, O wall, O sweet, O lovely wall,   175
  That stand'st between her father's ground and mine!
Thou wall, O wall, O sweet and lovely wall,
  Show me thy chink, to blink through with mine eyne!
        [*Wall holds up his fingers.*]
Thanks, courteous wall; Jove shield thee well for this!
  But what see I? No Thisby do I see.   180
O wicked wall, through whom I see no bliss!
  Curs'd be thy stones for thus deceiving me!

THESEUS
  The wall, methinks, being sensible, should
  curse again.

PYRAMUS
  No, in truth, sir, he should not. "Deceiving 185
  me" is Thisby's cue. She is to enter now, and
  I am to spy her through the wall. You shall
  see it will fall pat as I told you. Yonder she
  comes.
    Enter Thisbe.

THISBE
  O wall, full often has thou heard my moans, 190
    For parting my fair Pyramus and me!
  My cherry lips have often kiss'd thy stones,
    Thy stones with lime and hair knit up in thee.

PYRAMUS
  I see a voice! Now will I to the chink,
    To spy an I can hear my Thisby's face. 195
  Thisby!

THISBE
  My love, thou art my love, I think.

PYRAMUS
  Think what thou wilt, I am thy lover's grace;
  And, like Limander, am I trusty still.

THISBE
  And I like Helen, till the Fates me kill. 200

PYRAMUS
  Not Shafalus to Procrus was so true.

THISBE
  As Shafalus to Procrus, I to you.

PYRAMUS
  O, kiss me through the hole of this vile wall!

THISBE
  I kiss the wall's hole, not your lips at all.

PYRAMUS
  Wilt thou at Ninny's tomb meet me straightway? 205

THISBE
  'Tide life, 'tide death, I come without delay.
        [*Exeunt Pyramus and Thisbe.*]

183 **sensible:** capable of feeling.
199–200 **Limander . . . Helen:**
blunders for *Hero* and *Leander.*
201 **Shafalus to Procrus:** blunder
for *Cephalus to Procris,* also famous
lovers.
206 **'Tide:** betide.

WALL

Thus have I, Wall, my part discharged so;
And, being done, thus Wall away doth go.

[*Exit.*

THESEUS

Now is the moon used between the two
neighbours.   210

DEMETRIUS

No remedy, my lord, when walls are so
wilful to hear without warning.

HIPPOLYTA

This is the silliest stuff that ever I heard.

THESEUS

The best in this kind are but shadows; and
the worst are no worse, if imagination amend   215
them.

HIPPOLYTA

It must be your imagination then, and not
theirs.

THESEUS

If we imagine no worse of them than they of
themselves, they may pass for excellent men. Here   220
come two noble beasts in, a man and a lion.

Enter Lion and Moonshine.

LION

You, ladies, you, whose gentle hearts do fear
    The smallest monstrous mouse that creeps on floor,
May now perchance both quake and tremble here,
    When lion rough in wildest rage doth roar.   225
Then know that I, as Snug the joiner, am
A lion fell, nor else no lion's dam;
For, if I should as lion come in strife
Into this place, 'twere pity on my life.

THESEUS

A very gentle beast, and of a good con-   230
science.

DEMETRIUS

The very best at a beast, my lord, that e'er
I saw.

LYSANDER

This lion is a very fox for his valor.

THESEUS

True; and a goose for his discretion.   235

DEMETRIUS

Not so, my lord; for his valour cannot carry
his discretion, and the fox carries the goose.

THESEUS

His discretion, I am sure, cannot carry his
valour; for the goose carries not the fox. It

---

209 **moon used** Qq. *morall downe* Ff.
Pope's conj. *mural down* has been
generally followed. All are
unsatisfactory.

221 **man:** Many edd. emend to *moon.*
226 **as** Qq. *one* Ff.

is well; leave it to his discretion, and let us   240
hearken to the moon.

MOONSHINE
This lantern doth the horned moon
present;—

DEMETRIUS
He should have worn the horns on his
head.   245

THESEUS
He is no crescent, and his horns are invisible
within the circumference.

MOONSHINE
This lantern doth the horned moon present;
Myself the man i' th' moon do seem to be.

THESEUS
This is the greatest error of all the rest.   250
The man should be put into the lantern.
How is it else the man i' th' moon?

DEMETRIUS
He dares not come there for the candle; for,
you see, it is already in snuff.

HIPPOLYTA
I am aweary of this moon. Would he would   255
change!

THESEUS
It appears, by his small light of discretion,
that he is in the wane; but yet, in courtesy,
in all reason, we must stay the time.

LYSANDER
Proceed, Moon.   260

MOONSHINE
All that I have to say, is, to tell you that
the lantern is the moon; I, the man i' th'
moon; this thorn-bush, my thorn-bush; and
this dog, my dog.

DEMETRIUS
Why, all these should be in the lantern; for   265
all these are in the moon. But, silence! here
comes Thisbe.
          Re-enter Thisbe.

THISBE
This is old Ninny's tomb. Where is my love?

LION (*Roaring.*)
Oh——

                                    [*Thisbe runs off.*

DEMETRIUS
Well roar'd, Lion.   270

THESEUS
Well run, Thisbe.

244–245 **horns . . . head:** The   254 **in snuff:** quibble on (1)
inescapable jest about the "horns" of   "offended" and (2) "in need of
the "cuckold."   snuffing."

HIPPOLYTA
Well shone, Moon. Truly, the moon shines
with a good grace.

[The Lion shakes Thisbe's mantle and exit.]

THESEUS
Well mous'd, Lion.
Re-enter Pyramus.
DEMETRIUS
And then came Pyramus.
LYSANDER
And so the lion vanish'd.   275
PYRAMUS
Sweet Moon, I thank thee for thy sunny beams;
I thank thee, Moon, for shining now so bright;
For, by thy gracious, golden, glittering [gleams],
I trust to take of truest Thisby sight.   280
                    But stay, O spite!
                    But mark, poor knight,
            What dreadful dole is here!
                    Eyes, do you see?
                    How can it be?   285
            O dainty duck! O dear!
                    Thy mantle good,
                    What, stain'd with blood!
            Approach, ye Furies fell!
                    O Fates, come, come,   290
                    Cut thread and thrum;
            Quail, crush, conclude, and quell!
THESEUS
This passion, and the death of a dear friend,
would go near to make a man look sad.
HIPPOLYTA
Beshrew my heart, but I pity the man.   295
PYRAMUS
O wherefore, Nature, didst thou lions frame?
        Since lion vile hath here deflow'r'd my dear;
Which is—no, no—which was the fairest dame
        That liv'd, that lov'd, that lik'd, that look'd with cheer.
                    Come, tears, confound;   300
                    Out, sword, and wound
            The pap of Pyramus;
                    Ay, that left pap,
                    Where heart doth hop.   *[Stabs himself.]*
            Thus die I, thus, thus, thus.   305
                    Now am I dead,
                    Now am I fled;
            My soul is in the sky.
                    Tongue, lose thy light;
                    Moon, take thy flight.   *[Exit Moonshine.]*   310
            Now die, die, die, die, die.   *[Dies.]*

279 **[gleams]** (Knight). *beames* Q.   291 **thrum:** the loose threads at the
283 **dole:** grief.   end of the web.
                                                292 **quail:** overpower; **quell:** kill.

DEMETRIUS
No die, but an ace, for him; for he is but
one.

LYSANDER
Less than an ace, man, for he is dead; he is
nothing.   315

THESEUS
With the help of a surgeon he might yet recover, and yet prove an ass.

HIPPOLYTA
How chance Moonshine is gone before
Thisbe comes back and finds her lover?
                    Re-enter Thisbe.

THESEUS
She will find him by starlight. Here   320
she comes; and her passion ends the play.

HIPPOLYTA
Methinks she should not use a long one for
such a Pyramus. I hope she will be brief.

DEMETRIUS
A mote will turn the balance, which Pyr-
amus, which Thisbe, is the better; he for a man,   325
God warrant us; she for a woman, God bless us.

LYSANDER
She hath spied him already with those sweet
eyes.

DEMETRIUS
And thus she moans, *videlicet:*—   330

THISBE
            Asleep, my love?
            What, dead, my dove?
        O Pyramus, arise!
            Speak, speak! Quite dumb?
            Dead, dead? A tomb   335
        Must cover thy sweet eyes.
            These lily lips,
            This cherry nose,
        These yellow cowslip cheeks,
            Are gone, are gone!   340
            Lovers, make moan.
        His eyes were green as leeks.
            O Sisters Three,
            Come, come to me,
        With hands as pale as milk;   345
            Lay them in gore,
            Since you have shore
        With shears his thread of silk.
            Tongue, now a word!
            Come, trusty sword;   350
        Come, blade, my breast imbrue!   [*Stabs herself.*]

312 **ace:** the lowest cast of the dice.   343 **Sisters Three:** the Fates.
330 **moans** Qq. Ff. *means:* laments;   351 **imbrue:** stain with blood.
videlicet: as follows.

                    And, farewell, friends;
                    Thus, Thisby ends.
                Adieu, adieu, adieu.

                                                                [*Dies.*]

THESEUS

    Moonshine and Lion are left to bury the   355
    dead.

DEMETRIUS

    Ay, and Wall too.

BOTTOM [*Starting up.*]

    No, I assure you; the wall is down that
    parted their fathers. Will it please you to see
    the epilogue, or to hear a Bergomask dance   360
    between two of our company?

THESEUS

    No epilogue, I pray you; for your play needs
    no excuse. Never excuse; for when the players are
    all dead, there need none to be blamed. Marry, if
    he that writ it had played Pyramus and hang'd   365
    himself in Thisbe's garter, it would have been a fine
    tragedy; and so it is, truly; and very notably dis-
    charg'd. But, come, your Bergomask; let your
    epilogue alone.

                                                            [*A dance.*]

    The iron tongue of midnight hath told twelve.   370
    Lovers, to bed; 'tis almost fairy time.
    I fear we shall out-sleep the coming morn
    As much as we this night have overwatch'd.
    This palpable-gross play hath well beguil'd
    The heavy gait of night. Sweet friends, to bed.   375
    A fortnight hold we this solemnity
    In nightly revels and new jollity.

                                                            [*Exeunt.*

        Enter Robin Goodfellow.

ROBIN GOODFELLOW

            Now the hungry lion roars,
                And the wolf [behowls] the moon;
            Whilst the heavy ploughman snores,   380
                All with weary task fordone.
            Now the wasted brands do glow,
                Whilst the screech-owl, screeching loud,
            Puts the wretch that lies in woe
                In remembrance of a shroud.   385
                Now it is the time of night
                That the graves, all gaping wide,
            Every one lets forth his sprite,
                In the church-way paths to glide.
            And we fairies, that do run   390
                By the triple Hecate's team

360 **Bergomask dance:** a rustic
dance named from Bergamo in Italy.
374 **palpable-gross:** palpably crude.
379 [**behowls**] (Warburton). *beholds*
Q.

381 **fordone:** worn out.
391 **triple Hecate's:** Hecate ruled in
three capacities: as Diana on earth,
as Cynthia in heaven, and as
Proserpine in hell.

From the presence of the sun,
    Following darkness like a dream,
Now are frolic. Not a mouse
Shall disturb this hallowed house.   395
I am sent with broom before,
To sweep the dust behind the door.
Enter Oberon and Titania with their train.

OBERON

Through the house give glimmering light
    By the dead and drowsy fire,
Every elf and fairy sprite   400
    Hop as light as bird from brier;
And this ditty, after me,
Sing, and dance it trippingly.

TITANIA

First, rehearse your song by rote,
To each word a warbling note.   405
Hand in hand, with fairy grace,
Will we sing, and bless this place.

                          [Song [and dance].

OBERON

Now, until the break of day,
Through this house each fairy stray.
To the best bride-bed will we,   410
Which by us shall blessed be;
And the issue there create
Ever shall be fortunate.
So shall all the couples three
Ever true in loving be;   415
And the blots of Nature's hand
Shall not in their issue stand;
Never mole, harelip, nor scar,
Nor mark prodigious, such as are
Despised in nativity,   420
Shall upon their children be.
With this field-dew consecrate,
Every fairy take his gait,
And each several chamber bless,
Through this palace, with sweet peace;   425
And the owner of it blest
Ever shall in safety rest.
Trip away; make no stay;
Meet me all by break of day.
            [Exeunt [Oberon, Titania, and train].

ROBIN GOODFELLOW

If we shadows have offended,   430
Think but this, and all is mended,
That you have but slumb'red here
While these visions did appear.
And this weak and idle theme,
No more yielding but a dream,   435

---

394 **frolic:** merry.   419 **prodigious:** unnatural.
397 **behind:** from behind.

Gentles, do not reprehend.
If you pardon, we will mend.
And, as I am an honest Puck,
If we have unearned luck
Now to 'scape the serpent's tongue,   440
We will make amends ere long;
Else the Puck a liar call.
So, good night unto you all.
Give me your hands, if we be friends,
And Robin shall restore amends.   445

[*Exit.*]

Action analysis and performance suggestions

The following scenes are particularly recommended for informal classroom
performance: act I, scene ii, the first meeting of the rude mechanicals to
make preparation for their play, and act III, scene ii, line 122, LYSANDER:
"Why should you think that I should woo in scorn?" to line 344, HERMIA: "I
am amaz'd, and know not what to say." Because Shakespeare may
profitably be approached through a close study of his poetry, students may
want to prepare individual speeches such as Helena's soliloquy, act I, scene
i, lines 226–251; Titania's speech to Oberon, act II, scene i, lines 81–117;
or Puck's broom speech, act V, scene i, lines 378–397.

DEFINING THE ACTIONS AND THE SUPEROBJECTIVE

The traditional boy-gets-girl formula of New Comedy becomes the overall
action of *A Midsummer-Night's Dream* and is clearly set forth in Puck's "Jack
shall have Jill; / Nought shall go ill; / The man shall have his mare again,
and all shall be well." Accomplishing the superobjective, to overcome the
obstacles that keep lovers apart, takes only a little fairy magic plus Theseus's relaxation of the harsh Athenian law, which Egeus would use to ob-
struct true love.

However, the play's dream world embodies the anxieties and transformations of a nightmare as well as the desires that characterize a pleasant dream. Helena's contention that "Things base and vile, holding no
quantity, / Love can transpose to form and dignity" would describe the action of the comedy well were it not for Shakespeare's exploration of the
potential destructiveness of love as well as its creative powers. Demetrius
and Lysander pursue Helena in the wood with the same intensity and lack
of scruples they showed in pursuing Hermia just moments before, and
Titania switches her affections from the young changeling boy she is with-
holding from Oberon to the metamorphosed Bottom within an instant.

Yet the blindness of passion is made to look far more ridiculous than
tragic. "What fools these mortals be" is Puck's observation as well as ours,
and the comedy is climaxed with the Pyramus play, so inappropriate for the
forthcoming nuptial festivities with its tale of tragic lovers and so unwittingly transformed from tragedy into uproarious farce by Bottom and his
troupe of rude mechanicals. In *Othello* Shakespeare explores the transformation of the noble and loving Othello into a bestial monster in tragic
terms, but in *A Midsummer-Night's Dream* the many transformations that

---

440 **serpent's tongue:** hissing.   444 **Give . . . hands:** applaud.

love undergoes remain absurd, and the obstacles both exterior and interior that keep Jill from Jack are finally overcome through the guiding charity of Oberon and Theseus.

The scene of confusion and dissension among the four lovers in the wood is at the heart of the play and provides some of its richest comic moments. Despite its apparent chaos of feelings and its battles, the actions are carefully orchestrated and must be carefully followed if the nature of the farce is to emerge.

The overall action of the scene is to win a lover. Hermia wants to win Lysander back, Lysander and Demetrius want to win Helena's love, and Helena wants to win Demetrius's love. Lysander's efforts to convince Helena of his love for her, a love mistakenly induced by Puck's ministration of the love juice to the wrong lover, include the use of tears, but Helena is inclined to dismiss his love for Hermia and her as "light as tales." When Demetrius awakes with a change of heart, induced by Oberon's magical application, and proceeds to protest his love to her, Helena thinks the men have conspired to mock her. She berates them and tries to shame them into more manly behavior. Lysander and Demetrius proceed to attack each other as faithless and offer each other Hermia as a love object.

When Hermia appears to reclaim Lysander, he is not content to humor her but tries to get rid of her by assuring her his love has turned to hate. Helena is now convinced that Hermia too has joined the others to mock her and proceeds to play the martyred maiden. In the name of their girlhood friendship and their sex she chides Hermia for joining the men in their conspiracy and attempts to gain more sympathy with threats of suicide. As Hermia continues to hang on to Lysander, and the two men continue to vie for Helena's love, Lysander tries to dislodge Hermia's hold on him in order to do battle with Demetrius. Once Hermia realizes that Lysander in fact has transferred his affections to Helena, her action is to accuse Helena of stealing Lysander's love: "What, have you come by night / And stolen my love's heart from him?"

The focus of the action now switches from the men's combat over Helena to the women's combat with each other. Hermia attempts to get at Helena's eyes while Helena hastens to taunt Hermia about her lack of height at the same time that she calls on the men for help. Lysander succeeds in disengaging himself from Hermia and exits with Demetrius "cheek by jowl" in order to fight for Helena while Helena exits with a final taunt on size and Hermia is left actionless and amazed.

OVERCOMING OBSTACLES

If Demetrius wants to win Helena and Helena wants to win Demetrius, then what prevents their union? Demetrius's obstacles are two: Lysander, whose courting of Helena sidetracks him into a fight for her, and Demetrius's own past change of heart from Helena to Hermia, which causes Helena to suspect his protestations of love. Not only is Demetrius's past faithlessness an obstacle that makes Helena doubt him but also Lysander's sudden protestations of love make Helena think Demetrius and Lysander have conspired to mock her. However, even when she begins to believe Demetrius's sincerity, Hermia, who she thinks has previously stolen Demetrius's affections, remains an obstacle in her mind; hence she attacks her friend.

Lysander is beset by even more obstacles in his efforts to win Helena. At the same time that Demetrius claims Helena and challenges him to fight, Hermia holds him physically and claims his love, while Helena continually disdains his advances. The obstacles that prevent Hermia from winning back Lysander are caused by the power of the magical juice that Puck mistakenly applies to Lysander, and by her own efforts to hold him, which cause the reverse of her desire, bringing on protestations of hate rather than of love; her very pursuit of Lysander becomes its own obstacle.

THE MAGIC IF AND THE GIVEN CIRCUMSTANCES

The given circumstances of the scene are a moonlit night, the power of the magic love juice that possesses both men, and the sense of being lost in the wood and overcome by tumultuous emotions. Although Demetrius has proved changeable in his affections at the outset of the play, the setting emphasizes an atmosphere in which everything changes in the moonlight, all is uncertain, and identity itself is in question. "Am not I Hermia? Are not you Lysander?" Hermia asks at one point, and at times it is difficult to tell the four quarreling lovers apart.

What IF, like Hermia, you risked all and fled security for a lover who for no apparent reason deserted you for another? What IF, like Lysander, you were so possessed by the attraction of a woman that you lost all sense of chivalry or even decency toward your now obstructionist former love? What IF, like Demetrius, your fickle heart was set now on one, now on another with a childlike insistence on having what you want? What IF, like Helena, you found the men who formerly despised you offering their love? Would you believe them, suspect them? Suspect even your girlhood friend whom they both previously claimed to love? What IF it were a night dimly lit by the moon and all the certainties of your life had become fluid and open to question?

CLASSROOM ADAPTATIONS TO ARRIVE AT STYLE

Although the scene of the lovers' contention in the wood lacks aside or soliloquy, the audience should be invited to share directly in the fun. No particular separation of actors and audience is necessary; the latter may surround the action on three sides or even four as in theater-in-the-round. If such an arrangement is employed, a student-director is needed to see that the action is of interest from all sides.

Weather permitting, the scene lends itself to outdoor presentation, especially if a few trees or bushes are available and distraction is at a minimum. As Bottom's troupe demonstrates in their Pyramus play, moonlight need not be presented in any illusory way whether indoors or out. Much may be achieved simply by having the actors pretend they are trying to see in dim light. Today's audience, like Shakespeare's, may be asked to use their imaginations.

Nothing is required for the scenery at all since the area could be considered a clearing in the woods. Chairs could be used for bushes, trees, or rocks, or some authentic rocks might be included. If the scene is done outdoors, plenty of running and dodging about real trees and bushes would be effective.

Elizabethan costuming may be suggested with long dresses for the ladies and capes and swords for the men, although the swords could be long sticks. In a scene with as much potential for physical action as this one, it is essential that the women as well as the men be able to move. If modern dress is preferred, the four actors could wear any comfortable fashions. Whatever the decision, partial disarray is in order to suggest the hardships of sleeping in the woods.

The most important clue to Shakespeare's style in production lies in his use of poetry. Many actors mistakenly think that they should ignore the rhythms and rhyme scheme in order to make Shakespeare sound as natural as possible to today's audiences. They break the flow of the basic iambic pentameter that he employs, inserting the pauses we so often use in daily conversation, and slurring over the rhymes in order to make "sense" of the artificial structure on the page. The result is as disastrous as the other extreme, which the mechanicals doubtless employ in presenting the jouncing rhythms of their Pyramus play, and that is to concentrate on the rhythms and rhymes for their own sake. While the rhythms and rhymes can be ignored only at the peril of losing the sense of the lines, they must not become ends in themselves delivered in sing-song fashion, but the means to expressing the content of the lines.

Look briefly at Helena's response to Lysander's protestations of love (III. ii. 128–133) and note the even flow of the iambic beat:

You do advance your cunning more and more.
When truth kills truth, O devilish-holy fray!
These vows are Hermia's; will you give her o'er?
Weigh oath with oath, and you will nothing weigh.
Your vows to her and me, put in two scales,
Will even weigh, and both as light as tales.

Literally all of Shakespeare's characters speak their thoughts as frankly, openly, and quickly as Helena does here. She is picking up the content of Lysander's declaration that his vows must be true since they are accompanied by tears. If he is true to her, then what of his vows to Hermia ("truth kills truth")? After disparaging his vows, which were formerly made to Hermia, Helena quickly brings her point home (that neither vow has meaning) with the figure of the scales and the rhyme of "scales" and "tales." The actor should move along in her attack as quickly as possible. If she waits, for example, for an answer to her question, "Will you give her o'er?" she may sound natural, but she will lose the force of her argument. The question is rhetorical, a statement, and must be immediately followed by her final dismissal of his vows.

One way of avoiding a sing-song quality in rendering the lines and still maintaining the proper emphasis is to be sure not to pause at the end of each line, that is, keep the voice moving until the sentence is finished. "Scales" would be followed immediately by "will even weigh." Another way of avoiding overemphasis on rhyme or rhythms is through varied inflection, modulations of the voice and pitch, and the tone of the voice. Helena is clearly angry in the speech and in terms of her action is trying to shame Lysander. But the actor may use many notes of her voice and many modulations to scold him, underlining the variety of the exclamatory "O devilish-holy fray!" as opposed to the rhetorical question, "Will you give her o'er?" and the final accusation in the last two lines of the speech. The pitch at which a speech begins may be greatly varied as the actor moves through the speech, and it is best to avoid returning to the starting note of that pitch until the final line. If, then, the actor keeps the verse moving, keeps the pitch and hence the verse up until the end, and avoids overemphasis of the end of lines, following the sense and the punctuation instead, then a nice balance should be achieved between the natural and the artificial, and the meaning should emerge as intended.

In Shakespeare's later plays, and even at times in *A Midsummer-Night's Dream,* the rhythms are less even and rhyme is rarely employed. Still the same general principles hold in approaching the poetry. The actors must think on the line, keep up with the fast movement of the characters' thought and expression, and vary pitch and inflection in order to keep the verse up and bring the poetry to life.

Despite the lack of explicit stage directions in the scene, its consistently physical nature is suggested by the lines themselves. Lysander's and Demetrius's protestations of love are so exaggerated that they almost demand clichéd movement such as going down on one knee or putting hands over the heart. Hermia is described as clinging to Lysander, who says, "Hang off, thou cat, thou burr! Vile thing, let loose," and she lets him go only to attack Helena, whom both men defend. The comic movement possibilities for Helena's taunting of Hermia as the men continue to block her attacks are endless.

The secret for keeping the farcical effect of the scene in movement is for the performers to keep their actions going when they stop speaking. For example, when Helena appeals at length to the men to protect her from Hermia, Hermia should never stop trying to attack her or to get loose from the hold of the men. Hermia too should find a number of ways to continue clinging to Lysander during his speeches. She may hold on to his leg, jump on his back, and so forth. The result, if the performers do not let up and keep thinking on the line, should be uproarious farce resulting not from a tongue-in-cheek awareness on the actors' part that they are being funny but from the exaggerated way they play their actions and the extremes that are suggested in the lines.

The same holds true for the even more farcical scene of rehearsal with the mechanicals. They must take their task completely seriously, with Bottom utterly convinced that he can take on any part and making sincere attempts to do so. Bottom's exaggerated sense of his powers of transformation—making him one moment want to play Thisbe in "a monstrous little voice," the next anxious to play the lion and "roar you an 'twere any nightingale" so as not to frighten the ladies—is what makes him at play's end unsure of whether he is, or has been, an ass.

William Shakespeare
Othello

OTHELLO
> Perdition catch my soul,
> But I do love thee! and when I love thee not,
> Chaos is come again.
> (III. iii. 90–92)

Othello is the most intense and compressed of Shakespeare's thirteen tragedies. Nearly two-thirds of its thirty-two hundred lines are spoken by the three principal characters, at least one of whom appears in every scene except the herald's brief proclamation (act II, scene ii). The events of the first act cover a few hours of midnight darkness, those of the next four acts little more than two days. Every character and every situation exists only to bring into sharpest focus the moral and spiritual decay of a once calm and commanding military leader jealously aroused by an incredibly skillful, utterly unredeemable villain who himself speaks more than a third of the lines in the play.

This intensity and compression separate *Othello* from Shakespeare's other tragedies, most of which cover greater lengths of time, distribute the dialogue among more major characters, create situations or characters in parallel or contrast to the tragedy of the hero, or use more and varied reversals (*peripetia*) in the course of the representation. But in common with the other three great Shakespearean tragedies (*Hamlet*, *King Lear*, and *Macbeth*), *Othello* portrays an exceptional hero of high estate who suffers extraordinarily and falls through a combination of fault and fate. Like those of the other great tragedies, the central conflict of *Othello* consists in both interior and exterior actions. Like them, it renders a piteous, fearful, and mysterious tragic world in moral rather than merely social terms; and with the complete unfolding of the drama, it brings us to a state of psychic rest neither crushed, rebellious, nor desperate but emotionally and intellectually convinced that, in spite of the grievous calamities we have seen befall characters with whom we sympathized, justice has finally been done and order finally restored.

In these respects—quality of the hero, moral determinateness of the action, cathartic effect of the whole—*Othello* and the other great Shakespearean tragedies resemble Greek tragedy as exemplified by *Oedipus the King*. In *Othello* the suffering and fall of the tragic hero is not so greatly influenced by fate, by arbitrary predestined calamity, or by some hereditary bloodguilt. Character is fate in Shakespeare, and it was his greatest achievement to explore and develop even beyond the interests of his

For additional information on Shakespeare's life, times, and art, see the introduction to *A Midsummer-Night's Dream,* pages 87–93.

forebears two areas that have subsequently become central to tragic drama and fiction: the development and/or deterioration of character, and the nature of evil in human beings.

Chance or accident usually influences some part of the action in Shakespearean tragedy, as it does in *Othello* when Desdemona carelessly drops her handkerchief. The supernatural usually plays a role, from the witches of *Macbeth,* to the stormy weather and imaginary demon of *King Lear,* to the ghost of *Hamlet,* or to the sorcery with which Brabantio taxes Othello and in which Othello later comes to believe. But looming larger than these is the character of the tragic hero, both as the cause and in its changed state as the effect of his suffering. The Othello who majestically stops a street brawl with a mature and commanding "Keep up your bright swords, for the dew will rust them" (I. ii. 59), the graceful and powerful orator who draws the whole Venetian senate to accept his miscegenation through his explanation of the only "witchcraft I have us'd" (I. iii. 169) is led through his misplaced trust in one man and his concealed jealous insecurities to release the chaotic barbarism from his own soul and to seek the hidden evil in the souls of those most dear to him. Open directness leads to low, eavesdropping stratagems. Commanding assurance degenerates into epileptic trances. Chastity and love are murdered. However, just as Shakespeare revealed the seeds of destruction in Othello's soul early in the play, so even at the ending he allows the once bright greatness of spirit and accomplishment to reassert themselves: "Speak of me as I am . . ./ . . . one that lov'd not wisely but too well; / . . . one not easily jealous, but, being wrought, / Perplex'd in the extreme" (V. ii. 342–346). Othello not only perceives and recognizes his tragic failing and his changed relationship with the universe; he further discovers that his character itself has helped cause these changes and has been changed by them.

In Shakespeare's tragic worlds, when evildoers try to evoke the baseness in human nature they usually succeed. Richard III corrupts all he touches; Macbeth (and Lady Macbeth) find willing or silent accomplices all around them; Claudius infects all Denmark. While human beings are noble creatures whose angelic triumphs of soul and spirit deserve praise, they are also creatures with the potential for evil, sharing in original sin, born with base impulses that may break out and bring chaos on the world. Even a pure, innocent, and naïve Desdemona can be led to lie, as she does when she denies that the handkerchief is lost (act III, scene iv, lines 8 ff.). This evil, disordered aspect of human nature is of constant fascination to Shakespeare in his tragedies, and there is always closely examined, psychological probing to make clear the complex causes of individual evil motivation.

Iago is the best example. Neither an ordinary man whose motives for redress deserve sympathy nor a creature of "motiveless malignity" (as the great poet-critic Samuel Taylor Coleridge argued), Iago appears to others in *Othello* as blunt, sympathetic, and honest, to us as crafty, cynical, single-minded, incredibly efficient, and boldly opportunistic in his ability to arouse and incite the worst in people's natures. He has many motives for his actions, although hardly enough. But in a sense his many motives do not matter. While he complains that a mere "arithmetician" was promoted above him because of special interests, he himself appealed to Othello through "Three great ones of the city, / In personal suit to make me his lieutenant" (I. i. 8–9). Unjustly he believes of Othello that "'twixt my sheets / He has done my office" (I. iii. 393–394) or fears "Cassio with my night-cap too" (II. i. 316), yet admits "it is my nature's plague / To spy into abuses, and [oft] my jealousy / Shapes faults that are not" (III. iii. 146–148). Motives such as these give only partial explanation to a character who never, until this point, has been detected in a crime, to a character who himself gives voice to what may be his primary motive, "to plume up my will / In double knavery" (I. iii. 399–400). The inexplicable, unknowable, chaotic evil in all people (which bursts forth only in some) identifies Iago and allows him to say with some truth, "I told him [Othello] what I thought, and told no more / Than what he found himself was apt and true" (V. ii. 176–177).

Othello, the Moor of Venice

[*Dramatis personæ*]
DUKE OF VENICE
BRABANTIO, [*a senator,*] *father to Desdemona*
[*Other*] *Senators*
GRATIANO, [*brother to Brabantio,*] ⎫ *two noble*
LODOVICO, [*kinsman to Brabantio,*] ⎭ *Venetians*
OTHELLO, *the Moor* [*in the military service of Venice*]
CASSIO, *an honourable lieutenant*
IAGO, [*an ensign,*] *a villain*
RODERIGO, *a gulled gentleman*
MONTANO, *governor of Cyprus* [*before Othello*]
CLOWN [*servant to Othello*]
DESDEMONA, [*daughter to Brabantio and*] *wife to Othello*
EMILIA, *wife to Iago*
BIANCA, *a courtezan*
Gentlemen of Cyprus, Sailors, [*Officers, Messenger, Herald,*
Musicians, and Attendants]
[*Scene: Venice; a sea-port in Cyprus*]

Act I

Scene I. [*Venice. A street.*]
Enter Roderigo and Iago.

RODERIGO
[Tush]! never tell me! I take it much unkindly
That thou, Iago, who hast had my purse
As if the strings were thine, shouldst know of this.
IAGO
['Sblood], but you'll not hear me.
If ever I did dream of such a matter,
Abhor me.   5
RODERIGO
Thou told'st me thou didst hold him in thy hate.

The explanatory notes and text of *Othello* were prepared by William Allan Neilson and Charles Jarvis Hill. According to the Preface in the Neilson-Hill edition, "Stage directions, if modern, are enclosed in [brackets]; when they are substantially those of editions not later than 1623, they are unbracketed, or are set aside by a single bracket only, or, when occurring within a line, are enclosed in (parentheses)." In the

dialogue, words or phrases emended by earlier editions (or conjectured if omitted in the copy text) are also bracketed.
I.i.1 [**Tush**]Q: Qm.F.
3 **this:** Desdemona's elopement.
4 ['**Sblood**] Q: Om. F. Profane exclamations in brackets, such as this and that in I.i.33, were omitted in F on account of the Act of 1605 against swearing. Frequently *Heaven* was substituted for *God*.

IAGO

Despise me if I do not. Three great ones of the city,
In personal suit to make me his lieutenant,
Off-capp'd to him; and, by the faith of man,   10
I know my price; I am worth no worse a place.
But he, as loving his own pride and purposes,
Evades them with a bombast circumstance
Horribly stuff'd with epithets of war,
[And, in conclusion,]   15
Nonsuits my mediators; for, "Certes," says he,
"I have already chose my officer."
And what was he?
Forsooth, a great arithmetician,
One Michael Cassio, a Florentine,   20
(A fellow almost damn'd in a fair wife)
That never set a squadron in the field,
Nor the division of a battle knows
More than a spinster, unless the bookish theoric,
Wherein the [toged] consuls can propose   25
As masterly as he. Mere prattle without practice
Is all his soldiership. But he, sir, had th' election;
And I, of whom his eyes had seen the proof
At Rhodes, at Cyprus, and on other grounds
Christen'd and heathen, must be be-lee'd and calm'd   30
By debitor and creditor; this counter-caster,
He, in good time, must his lieutenant be,
And I—[God] bless the mark!—his Moorship's ancient.

RODERIGO

By heaven, I rather would have been his hangman.

IAGO

Why, there's no remedy. 'Tis the curse of service,   35
Preferment goes by letter and affection,
And not by old gradation, where each second
Stood heir to th' first. Now, sir, be judge yourself
Whether I in any just term am affin'd
To love the Moor.

RODERIGO

                I would not follow him then.   40

IAGO

O, sir, content you;
I follow him to serve my turn upon him.
We cannot all be masters, nor all masters
Cannot be truly follow'd. You shall mark
Many a duteous and knee-crooking knave   45
That, doting on his own obsequious bondage,
Wears out his time, much like his master's ass,
For nought but provender, and when he's old, cashier'd.

13 **circumstance:** discourse.
15 [**And . . . conclusion**] Q: Om. F.
23 **division:** array.
25 [**toged**] Q: wearing a toga.
    tongued F.
31 **counter-caster:** accountant.

33 [**God**] Q: Om. F.
36 **letter:** i.e., of recommendation.
37 **old gradation:** seniority.
39 **affin'd:** bound.
48 **cashier'd:** dismissed.

Whip me such honest knaves. Others there are
Who, trimm'd in forms and visages of duty, 50
Keep yet their hearts attending on themselves,
And, throwing but shows of service on their lords,
Do well thrive by them and, when they have lin'd their coats,
Do themselves homage. These fellows have some soul;
And such a one do I profess myself. For, sir, 55
It is as sure as you are Roderigo,
Were I the Moor, I would not be Iago.
In following him, I follow but myself;
Heaven is my judge, not I for love and duty,
But seeming so, for my peculiar end; 60
For when my outward action doth demonstrate
The native act and figure of my heart
In compliment extern, 'tis not long after
But I will wear my heart upon my sleeve
For daws to peck at. I am not what I am. 65

RODERIGO
What a full fortune does the thick-lips owe,
If he can carry 't thus!

IAGO
                  Call up her father,
Rouse him. Make after him, poison his delight,
Proclaim him in the streets. Incense her kinsmen,
And, though he in a fertile climate dwell, 70
Plague him with flies. Though that his joy be joy,
Yet throw such [changes] of vexation on't,
As it may lose some colour.

RODERIGO
Here is her father's house; I'll call aloud.

IAGO
Do, with like timorous accent and dire yell 75
As when, by night and negligence, the fire
Is spied in populous cities.

RODERIGO
What, ho, Brabantio! Signior Brabantio, ho!

IAGO
Awake! what, ho, Brabantio! thieves! thieves!
Look to your house, your daughter, and your bags! 80
Thieves! thieves!
    Brabantio [appears] above, at a window.

BRABANTIO
What is the reason of this terrible summons?
What is the matter there?

RODERIGO
Signior, is all your family within?

IAGO
Are your doors lock'd?

---

50 **visages:** semblances.
60 **peculiar:** private.
63 **compliment extern:** external
show.

66 **thick-lips:** i.e., the Moor; **owe:**
own.
72 [**changes**] Q: *chances* F.
75 **timorous:** terrifying.

BRABANTIO

       Why, wherefore ask you this?   85

IAGO

['Zounds], sir, you're robb'd! For shame, put on your gown.
Your heart is burst, you have lost half your soul;
Even now, now, very now, an old black ram
Is tupping your white ewe. Arise, arise!
Awake the snorting citizens with the bell,   90
Or else the devil will make a grandsire of you.
Arise, I say!

BRABANTIO

     What, have you lost your wits?

RODERIGO

Most reverend signior, do you know my voice?

BRABANTIO

Not I. What are you?

RODERIGO

My name is Roderigo.

BRABANTIO

       The worser welcome;   95
I have charg'd thee not to haunt about my doors.
In honest plainness thou hast heard me say
My daughter is not for thee; and now, in madness,
Being full of supper and distemp'ring draughts,
Upon malicious [bravery] dost thou come   100
To start my quiet.

RODERIGO

Sir, sir, sir,—

BRABANTIO

     But thou must needs be sure
My spirits and my place have in their power
To make this bitter to thee.

RODERIGO

       Patience, good sir.

BRABANTIO

What tell'st thou me of robbing? This is Venice;   105
My house is not a grange.

RODERIGO

      Most grave Brabantio,
In simple and pure soul I come to you.

IAGO

['Zounds], sir, you are one of those that will
not serve God, if the devil bid you. Because we
come to do you service and you think we are   110
ruffians, you'll have your daughter cover'd with a
Barbary horse; you'll have your nephews neigh to
you; you'll have coursers for cousins, and gennets
for germans.

   90 **snorting:** snoring.   106 **grange:** isolated farm.
   99 **distemp'ring:** intoxicating. 112 **nephews:** grandsons.
   100 [**bravery**] Q: swaggering. 113 **gennets:** Spanish horses.
   knavery F.   114 **germans:** relatives.
   101 **start:** startle.

BRABANTIO

    What profane wretch art thou?   115

IAGO

    I am one, sir, that comes to tell you your
    daughter and the Moor are [now] making the
    beast with two backs.

BRABANTIO

    Thou art a villain.

IAGO

                  You are—a senator.

BRABANTIO

    This thou shalt answer; I know thee, Roderigo.   120

RODERIGO

    Sir, I will answer anything. But, I beseech you,
    If 't be your pleasure and most wise consent,
    As partly I find it is, that your fair daughter,
    At this odd-even and dull watch o' th' night,
    Transported, with no worse nor better guard   125
    But with a knave of common hire, a gondolier,
    To the gross clasps of a lascivious Moor,—
    If this be known to you and your allowance,
    We then have done you bold and saucy wrongs;
    But if you know not this, my manners tell me   130
    We have your wrong rebuke. Do not believe
    That, from the sense of all civility,
    I thus would play and trifle with your reverence.
    Your daughter, if you have not given her leave,
    I say again, hath made a gross revolt,   135
    Tying her duty, beauty, wit, and fortunes
    In an extravagant and wheeling stranger
    Of here and everywhere. Straight satisfy yourself.
    If she be in her chamber or your house,
    Let loose on me the justice of the state   140
    For thus deluding you.

BRABANTIO

                Strike on the tinder, ho!
    Give me a taper! Call up all my people!
    This accident is not unlike my dream;
    Belief of it oppresses me already.
    Light, I say! light!

                                     [Exit [above].

IAGO

              Farewell; for I must leave you.   145
    It seems not meet, nor wholesome to my place,
    To be produc'd—as, if I stay, I shall—
    Against the Moor; for, I do know, the state,
    However this may gall him with some check,
    Cannot with safety cast him, for he's embark'd   150

117 **[now]** Q: Om. F.
124 **odd-even:** midnight; **dull:** dead.
128 **your allowance:** has your
approval.
132 **from:** contrary to.

137 **extravagant:** vagabond;
wheeling: roving.
149 **check:** rebuke.
150 **cast:** dismiss.

With such loud reason to the Cyprus wars,
Which even now [stand] in act, that, for their souls,
Another of his fathom they have none
To lead their business; in which regard,
Though I do hate him as I do hell-pains,   155
Yet, for necessity of present life,
I must show out a flag and sign of love,
Which is indeed but sign. That you shall surely find him,
Lead to the Sagittary the raised search;
And there will I be with him. So, farewell.   160
                  [Exit.
   Enter [below,] Brabantio in his night-gown, and Servants with torches.
BRABANTIO
 It is too true an evil; gone she is;
 And what's to come of my despised time
 Is nought but bitterness. Now, Roderigo,
 Where didst thou see her? O unhappy girl!
 With the Moor, say'st thou? Who would be a father!   165
 How didst thou know 'twas she? O, she deceives me
 Past thought! What said she to you? Get moe tapers;
 Raise all my kindred. Are they married, think you?
RODERIGO
 Truly, I think they are.
BRABANTIO
 O heaven! How got she out? O treason of the blood!   170
 Fathers, from hence trust not your daughters' minds
 By what you see them act. Is there not charms
 By which the property of youth and maidhood
 May be abus'd? Have you not read, Roderigo,
 Of some such thing?
RODERIGO
      Yes, sir, I have indeed.   175
BRABANTIO
 Call up my brother.—O, would you had had her!—
 Some one way, some another.—Do you know
 Where we may apprehend her and the Moor?
RODERIGO
 I think I can discover him, if you please
 To get good guard and go along with me.   180
BRABANTIO
 Pray you, lead on. At every house I'll call;
 I may command at most. Get weapons, ho!
 And raise some special officers of [night].
 On, good Roderigo; I'll deserve your pains.
                  [Exeunt.

152 [stand] (Pope): *stands* QF.
153 fathom: capacity.
159 Sagittary: an inn (with a Centaur on its sign). It has also been proposed that the word is a translation of *Frezzaria,* the Street of the Arrow-makers in Venice.

161 s.d. night-gown: dressing gown.
173 property: nature.
174 abus'd: deceived.
183 [night] Q: *might* F.
184 deserve: reward.

Scene II. [*Another street.*]
Enter Othello, Iago, and Attendants with torches.

IAGO

    Though in the trade of war I have slain men,
    Yet do I hold it very stuff o' th' conscience
    To do no contriv'd murder. I lack iniquity
    Sometimes to do me service. Nine or ten times
    I'd thought to have yerk'd him here under the ribs.   5

OTHELLO

    'Tis better as it is.

IAGO

                 Nay, but he prated,
    And spoke such scurvy and provoking terms
    Against your honour
    That, with the little godliness I have,
    I did full hard forbear him. But, I pray you, sir,   10
    Are you fast married? Be assur'd of this,
    That the magnifico is much belov'd,
    And hath in his effect a voice potential
    As double as the Duke's. He will divorce you,
    Or put upon you what restraint or grievance   15
    The law, with all his might to enforce it on,
    Will give him cable.

OTHELLO

                 Let him do his spite;
    My services which I have done the signiory
    Shall out-tongue his complaints. 'Tis yet to know,—
    Which, when I know that boasting is an honour,   20
    I shall promulgate—I fetch my life and being
    From men of royal siege, and my demerits
    May speak unbonneted to as proud a fortune
    As this that I have reach'd; for know, Iago,
    But that I love the gentle Desdemona,   25
    I would not my unhoused free condition
    Put into circumscription and confine
    For the sea's worth. But, look! what lights come yond?
    Enter Cassio, with lights, Officers, and torches.

IAGO

    Those are the raised father and his friends.
    You were best go in.

OTHELLO

                 Not I; I must be found.   30
    My parts, my title, and my perfect soul
    Shall manifest me rightly. Is it they?

IAGO

    By Janus, I think no.

OTHELLO

    The servants of the Duke, and my lieutenant.

---

ii.5 **yerk'd:** stabbed.
14 **double:** strong.
22 **siege:** rank; **demerits:** deserts.
23 **unbonneted:** without taking my
hat off, on equal terms.

26 **unhoused:** unconfined.
31 **perfect soul:** clear conscience.

The goodness of the night upon you, friends!   35
What is the news?
CASSIO
                    The Duke does greet you, general,
And he requires your haste-post-haste appearance,
Even on the instant.
OTHELLO
                    What is the matter, think you?
CASSIO
Something from Cyprus, as I may divine;
It is a business of some heat. The galleys   40
Have sent a dozen sequent messengers
This very night at one another's heels,
And many of the consuls, rais'd and met,
Are at the Duke's already. You have been hotly call'd for;
When, being not at your lodging to be found,   45
The Senate hath sent about three several quests
To search you out.
OTHELLO
                    'Tis well I am found by you.
I will but spend a word here in the house.
And go with you.   [*Exit.*
CASSIO
                    Ancient, what makes he here?
IAGO
Faith, he to-night hath boarded a land carack.   50
If it prove lawful prize, he's made for ever.
CASSIO
I do not understand.
IAGO
                    He's married.
CASSIO
                              To who?
            [*Re-enter Othello.*]
IAGO
Marry, to—Come, captain, will you go?
OTHELLO
                              Have with you.
CASSIO
Here comes another troop to seek for you.
            Enter Brabantio, Roderigo, and Officers with torches and weapons.
IAGO
It is Brabantio. General, be advis'd;   55
He comes to bad intent.
OTHELLO
                    Holla! stand there!
RODERIGO
Signior, it is the Moor.
BRABANTIO
                    Down with him, thief!
                              [*They draw on both sides.*]

40 **galleys:** i.e., officers of the   50 **carack:** large trading ship.
galleys.

IAGO

    You, Roderigo! come, sir, I am for you.

OTHELLO

    Keep up your bright swords, for the dew will rust them.
    Good signior, you shall more command with years   60
    Than with your weapons.

BRABANTIO

    O thou foul thief, where hast thou stow'd my daughter?
    Damn'd as thou art, thou hast enchanted her;
    For I'll refer me to all things of sense,
    If she in chains of magic were not bound,   65
    Whether a maid so tender, fair, and happy,
    So opposite to marriage that she shunn'd
    The wealthy curled darlings of our nation,
    Would ever have, t' incur a general mock,
    Run from her guardage to the sooty bosom   70
    Of such a thing as thou—to fear, not to delight.
    Judge me the world, if 'tis not gross in sense
    That thou hast practis'd on her with foul charms,
    Abus'd her delicate youth with drugs or minerals
    That weakens motion. I'll have 't disputed on;   75
    'Tis probable, and palpable to thinking.
    I therefore apprehend and do attach thee
    For an abuser of the world, a practiser
    Of arts inhibited and out of warrant.
    Lay hold upon him; if he do resist,   80
    Subdue him at his peril.

OTHELLO

                  Hold your hands,
    Both you of my inclining, and the rest.
    Were it my cue to fight, I should have known it
    Without a prompter. [Where] will you that I go
    To answer this your charge?

BRABANTIO

                To prison, till fit time   85
    Of law and course of direct session
    Call thee to answer.

OTHELLO

             What if [I] do obey?
    How may the Duke be therewith satisfi'd,
    Whose messengers are here about my side
    Upon some present business of the state   90
    To bring me to him?

OFFICER

             'Tis true, most worthy signior.
    The Duke 's in council; and your noble self,
    I am sure, is sent for.

---

72 **gross in sense:** perfectly clear.
75 **motion:** will power; **disputed on:** argued legally.
77 **attach:** arrest.
79 **inhibited:** prohibited; **out of warrant:** unjustifiable.

82 **inclining:** party.
84 [**Where**] Q: *Whether* F. *Whither* F$_2$.
86 **course . . . session:** due course of law.
87 [**I**] Q: Om. F.

BRABANTIO

                    How! the Duke in council!
In this time of the night! Bring him away;
Mine's not an idle cause. The Duke himself,   95
Or any of my brothers of the state,
Cannot but feel this wrong as 'twere their own;
For if such actions may have passage free,
Bond-slaves and pagans shall our statesmen be.   [*Exeunt.*

Scene III. [*A council-chamber.*]
The Duke and Senators set at a table, with lights; Officers attending.

DUKE

There is no composition in [these] news
That gives them credit.

FIRST SENATOR

                    Indeed, they are disproportion'd;
My letters say a hundred and seven galleys.

DUKE

And mine, a hundred forty.

SECOND SENATOR

                    And mine, two hundred!
But though they jump not on a just account,—   5
As in these cases, where the aim reports,
'Tis oft with difference—yet do they all confirm
A Turkish fleet, and bearing up to Cyprus.

DUKE

Nay, it is possible enough to judgement.
I do not so secure me in the error   10
But the main article I do approve
In fearful sense.

SAILOR (*Within.*)

                    What, ho! what, ho! what, ho!
          Enter a Sailor.

OFFICER

A messenger from the galleys.

DUKE

                              Now, what's the business?

SAILOR

The Turkish preparation makes for Rhodes;
So was I bid report here to the state   15
By Signior Angelo.

DUKE

How say you by this change?

FIRST SENATOR

                    This cannot be,
By no assay of reason; 'tis a pageant,
To keep us in false gaze. When we consider
Th' importancy of Cyprus to the Turk,   20

iii.1 **composition:** consistency;
[**these**] Q: *this* F.
5 **jump:** agree; **just:** exact.
6 **the . . . reports:** the reports are conjectural.

10 **so . . . error:** take such assurance from the disagreement.
11 **approve:** assent to.
18 **pageant:** pretence.

And let ourselves again but understand
That, as it more concerns the Turk than Rhodes,
So may he with more facile question bear it,
For that it stands not in such warlike brace,
But altogether lacks th' abilities 25
That Rhodes is dress'd in; if we make thought of this,
We must not think the Turk is so unskilful
To leave that latest which concerns him first,
Neglecting an attempt of ease and gain
To wake and wage a danger profitless. 30

DUKE
　　Nay, in all confidence, he's not for Rhodes.

OFFICER
　　Here is more news.
　　　　Enter a Messenger.

MESSENGER
　　The Ottomites, reverend and gracious,
　　Steering with due course towards the isle of Rhodes,
　　Have there injointed them with an after fleet. 35

FIRST SENATOR
　　Ay, so I thought. How many, as you guess?

MESSENGER
　　Of thirty sail; and now they do restem
　　Their backward course, bearing with frank appearance
　　Their purposes toward Cyprus. Signior Montano,
　　Your trusty and most valiant servitor, 40
　　With his free duty recommends you thus,
　　And prays you to believe him.

DUKE
　　'Tis certain, then, for Cyprus.
　　Marcus Luccicos, is not he in town?

FIRST SENATOR
　　He's now in Florence. 45

DUKE
　　Write from us to him; post-post-haste dispatch.

FIRST SENATOR
　　Here comes Brabantio and the valiant Moor.
　　　　Enter Brabantio, Othello, Cassio, Iago, Roderigo, and Officers.

DUKE
　　Valiant Othello, we must straight employ you
　　Against the general enemy Ottoman.
　　[*To Brabantio.*] I did not see you; welcome, gentle signior; 50
　　We lack'd your counsel and your help to-night.

BRABANTIO
　　So did I yours. Good your Grace, pardon me;
　　Neither my place nor aught I heard of business
　　Hath rais'd me from my bed, nor doth the general care
　　Take hold on me; for my particular grief 55
　　Is of so flood-gate and o'erbearing nature
　　That it engluts and swallows other sorrows
　　And it is still itself.

23 **with . . . it:** capture it more
easily.
24 **brace:** defense.

35 **after:** i.e., sent after.
55 **particular:** personal.

DUKE

                Why, what's the matter?

BRABANTIO

  My daughter! O, my daughter!

SENATOR

                      Dead?

BRABANTIO

                           Ay, to me;

  She is abus'd, stol'n from me, and corrupted   60

  By spells and medicines bought of mountebanks;

  For nature so prepost'rously to err,

  Being not deficient, blind, or lame of sense,

  Sans witchcraft could not.

DUKE

  Whoe'er he be that in this foul proceeding   65

  Hath thus beguil'd your daughter of herself

  And you of her, the bloody book of law

  You shall yourself read in the bitter letter

  After your own sense, yea, though our proper son

  Stood in your action.

BRABANTIO

                Humbly I thank your Grace.   70

  Here is the man,—this Moor, whom now, it seems,

  Your special mandate for the state affairs

  Hath hither brought.

ALL

              We are very sorry for 't.

DUKE [*To Othello.*]

  What, in your own part, can you say to this?

BRABANTIO

  Nothing, but this is so.   75

OTHELLO

  Most potent, grave, and reverend signiors,

  My very noble and approv'd good masters,

  That I have ta'en away this old man's daughter,

  It is most true; true, I have married her:

  The very head and front of my offending   80

  Hath this extent, no more. Rude am I in my speech,

  And little bless'd with the soft phrase of peace;

  For since these arms of mine had seven years' pith

  Till now, some nine moons wasted, they have us'd

  Their dearest action in the tented field,   85

  And little of this great world can I speak

  More than pertains to feats of broils and battle,

  And therefore little shall I grace my cause

  In speaking for myself. Yet, by your gracious patience,

  I will a round unvarnish'd tale deliver   90

  Of my whole course of love—what drugs, what charms,

  What conjuration, and what mighty magic,

  (For such proceeding I am charg'd withal,)

  I won his daughter.

BRABANTIO

             A maiden never bold;

90 **round:** plain.

Of spirit so still and quiet that her motion 95
Blush'd at herself; and she, in spite of nature,
Of years, of country, credit, everything,
To fall in love with what she fear'd to look on!
It is a judgement maim'd and most imperfect
That will confess perfection so could err 100
Against all rules of nature, and must be driven
To find out practices of cunning hell,
Why this should be. I therefore vouch again
That with some mixtures powerful o'er the blood,
Or with some dram conjur'd to this effect, 105
He wrought upon her.
[DUKE]
                To vouch this is no proof,
Without more wider and more overt test
Than these thin habits and poor likelihoods
Of modern seeming do prefer against him.
FIRST SENATOR
    But, Othello, speak. 110
Did you by indirect and forced courses
Subdue and poison this young maid's affections?
Or came it by request and such fair question
As soul to soul affordeth?
OTHELLO
                  I do beseech you,
Send for the lady to the Sagittary, 115
And let her speak of me before her father.
If you do find me foul in her report,
The trust, the office I do hold of you,
Not only take away, but let your sentence
Even fall upon my life.
DUKE
              Fetch Desdemona hither. 120

                       [*Exeunt two or three.*
OTHELLO
Ancient, conduct them; you best know the place.

                          [*Exit Iago.*]

And, till she come, as truly as to heaven
I do confess the vices of my blood,
So justly to your grave ears I'll present
How I did thrive in this fair lady's love, 125
And she in mine.
DUKE
    Say it, Othello.
OTHELLO
    Her father lov'd me; oft invited me;
Still question'd me the story of my life
From year to year, the battles, sieges, fortunes, 130
That I have pass'd.
I ran it through, even from my boyish days

---

95 **motion:** impulses.   108 **thin habits:** slight semblances.
106 [DUKE] Q: Om. F.   109 **modern:** ordinary, trivial.

To the very moment that he bade me tell it;
Wherein I spoke of most disastrous chances,
Of moving accidents by flood and field,   135
Of hair-breadth scapes i' th' imminent deadly breach,
Of being taken by the insolent foe
And sold to slavery, of my redemption thence
And portance in my travel's history;
Wherein of antres vast and deserts idle,   140
Rough quarries, rocks, [and] hills whose heads touch heaven,
It was my hint to speak,—such was my process,—
And of the Cannibals that each other eat,
The Anthropophagi, and men whose heads
[Do grow] beneath their shoulders. These to hear   145
Would Desdemona seriously incline;
But still the house-affairs would draw her thence,
Which ever as she could with haste dispatch,
She'd come again, and with a greedy ear
Devour up my discourse: which I observing,   150
Took once a pliant hour, and found good means
To draw from her a prayer of earnest heart
That I would all my pilgrimage dilate,
Whereof by parcels she had something heard,
But not [intentively]. I did consent,   155
And often did beguile her of her tears
When I did speak of some distressful stroke
That my youth suffer'd. My story being done,
She gave me for my pains a world of [sighs].
She swore, in faith, 'twas strange, 'twas passing strange,   160
'Twas pitiful, 'twas wondrous pitiful.
She wish'd she had not heard it; yet she wish'd
That Heaven had made her such a man. She thank'd me,
And bade me, if I had a friend that lov'd her,
I should but teach him how to tell my story,   165
And that would woo her. Upon this hint I spake:
She lov'd me for the dangers I had pass'd,
And I lov'd her that she did pity them.
This only is the witchcraft I have us'd.
Here comes the lady; let her witness it.   170
      Enter Desdemona, Iago, and Attendants.
DUKE
I think this tale would win my daughter too.
Good Brabantio,
Take up this mangled matter at the best;
Men do their broken weapons rather use
Than their bare hands.
BRABANTIO
                  I pray you, hear her speak.   175

139 **portance:** behavior.   151 **pliant:** convenient.
140 **antres:** caves; **idle:** barren.   155 [**intentively**] Q: attentively.
141 [**and**] Q: Om. F.   *instinctively* F.
142 **hint:** occasion.   159 [**sighs**] Q: *kisses* F.
145 [**Do grow**] Q: *Grew* F; **These** *Q²*:   166 **hint:** opportunity (not
These things F.   consciously given). Cf. l. 142.

If she confess that she was half the wooer,
Destruction on my head if my bad blame
Light on the man! Come hither, gentle mistress.
Do you perceive in all this noble company
Where most you owe obedience?

DESDEMONA

                    My noble father,   180
I do perceive here a divided duty.
To you I am bound for life and education;
My life and education both do learn me
How to respect you; you are the lord of duty;
I am hitherto your daughter. But here's my husband;   185
And so much duty as my mother show'd
To you, preferring you before her father,
So much I challenge that I may profess
Due to the Moor, my lord.

BRABANTIO

              God be with you! I have done.
Please it your Grace, on to the state-affairs.   190
I had rather to adopt a child than get it.
Come hither, Moor.
I here do give thee that with all my heart
Which, but thou hast already, with all my heart
I would keep from thee. For your sake, jewel,   195
I am glad at soul I have no other child;
For thy escape would teach me tyranny,
To hang clogs on them. I have done, my lord.

DUKE

Let me speak like yourself, and lay a sentence,
Which, as a grise or step, may help these lovers   200
[Into your favour].
When remedies are past, the griefs are ended
By seeing the worst, which late on hopes depended.
To mourn a mischief that is past and gone
Is the next way to draw new mischief on.   205
What cannot be preserv'd when fortune takes,
Patience her injury a mock'ry makes.
The robb'd that smiles steals something from the thief;
He robs himself that spends a bootless grief.

BRABANTIO

So let the Turk of Cyprus us beguile;   210
We lose it not, so long as we can smile.
He bears the sentence well that nothing bears
But the free comfort which from thence he hears,
But he bears both the sentence and the sorrow
That, to pay grief, must of poor patience borrow.   215
These sentences, to sugar or to gall
Being strong on both sides, are equivocal.
But words are words; I never yet did hear

---

199 **like yourself:** as you should.   216 **sentences:** maxims.
200 **grise:** degree.   217 **equivocal:** equal.
201 [**Into . . . favour**] Q: Om. F.

That the bruis'd heart was pierced through the ear.
I humbly beseech you, proceed to the affairs of state.   220
DUKE
The Turk with a most mighty preparation
makes for Cyprus. Othello, the fortitude of the
place is best known to you; and though we have
there a substitute of most allowed sufficiency, yet
opinion, a sovereign mistress of effects, throws a   225
more safer voice on you. You must therefore be
content to slubber the gloss of your new fortunes
with this more stubborn and boist'rous expedi-
tion.
OTHELLO
The tyrant custom, most grave senators,   230
Hath made the flinty and steel couch of war
My thrice-driven bed of down. I do agnize
A natural and prompt alacrity
I find in hardness, and do undertake
These present wars against the Ottomites.   235
Most humbly therefore bending to your state,
I crave fit disposition for my wife,
Due reference of place and exhibition,
With such accommodation and besort
As levels with her breeding.
DUKE
                              [If you please,   240
Be 't at her father's.]
BRABANTIO
                    I'll not have it so.
OTHELLO
     Nor I.
DESDEMONA
          Nor I; [I would not] there reside,
To put my father in impatient thoughts
By being in his eye. Most gracious Duke,
To my unfolding lend your prosperous ear;   245
And let me find a charter in your voice
T' assist my simpleness.
DUKE
What would you, Desdemona?
DESDEMONA
That I [did] love the Moor to live with him,
My downright violence and storm of fortunes   250
May trumpet to the world. My heart's subdu'd

---

222 **fortitude:** strength, fortification.
224 **allowed:** admitted.
225 **sovereign** Q: *more sovereign* F.
227 **slubber:** sully.
232 **thrice-driven:** thoroughly sifted;
agnize: acknowledge.
238 **reference:** assignment;
exhibition: provision.
239 **besort:** company.

240 **levels with:** befits.
240–241 [**If . . . father's.**] Q: *Why at her Fathers?* F.
242 [**I . . . not**] Q: *would I* F.
245 **prosperous:** propitious.
246 **charter:** privilege.
249 [**did**] Q: Om. F.
250 **My . . . fortunes:** my precipitate assault upon my fortunes.

Even to the very quality of my lord.
I saw Othello's visage in his mind,
And to his honours and his valiant parts
Did I my soul and fortunes consecrate.   255
So that, dear lords, if I were left behind,
A moth of peace, and he go to the war,
The rites for [which] I love him are bereft me,
And I a heavy interim shall support
By his dear absence. Let me go with him.   260

OTHELLO
 Let her have your voice.
Vouch with me, Heaven, I therefore beg it not
To please the palate of my appetite,
Nor to comply with heat, the young affects
In my defunct and proper satisfaction,   265
But to be free and bounteous to her mind;
And Heaven defend your good souls, that you think
I will your serious and great business scant
When she is with me. No, when light-wing'd toys
Of feather'd Cupid seel with wanton dullness   270
My speculative and offic'd instruments
That my disports corrupt and taint my business,
Let housewives make a skillet of my helm,
And all indign and base adversities
Make head against my estimation!   275

DUKE
 Be it as you shall privately determine,
Either for her stay or going. Th' affair cries haste,
And speed must answer it.

FIRST SENATOR
      You must away to-night.

DESDEMONA
 To-night, my lord?

DUKE
     This night.]

OTHELLO
      With all my heart.

DUKE
 At nine i' th' morning here we'll meet again.   280
Othello, leave some officer behind,
And he shall our commission bring to you,
And such things else of quality and respect
As doth import you.

OTHELLO
    So please your Grace, my ancient;
A man he is of honesty and trust.   285

---

258 [which] Q: *why* F.
265 **defunct** Q, F: The modern meaning is here excluded, and no convincing explanation has been found. [Some editors read "distinct."]
267 **defend:** forbid.
270 **seel:** blind (from falconry).

271 **My . . . instruments:** my faculties whose office is to perceive.
274 **indign:** unworthy.
275 **estimation:** reputation.
279 [DESDEMONA **To-night . . . night**] Q: Om. F.
284 **import:** concern.

To his conveyance I assign my wife,
With what else needful your good Grace shall think
To be sent after me.

DUKE

Let it be so.
Good-night to every one. [*To Brabantio*] And, noble signior,
If virtue no delighted beauty lack,   290
Your son-in-law is far more fair than black.

FIRST SENATOR

Adieu, brave Moor; use Desdemona well.

BRABANTIO

Look to her, Moor, if thou hast eyes to see;
She has deceiv'd her father, and may thee.

> [*Exeunt* [*Duke, Senators, Officers, etc.*].

OTHELLO

My life upon her faith! Honest Iago,   295
My Desdemona must I leave to thee.
I prithee, let thy wife attend on her;
And bring them after in the best advantage.
Come, Desdemona; I have but an hour
Of love, of worldly matters and direction,   300
To spend with thee. We must obey the time.

> [*Exeunt Othello and Desdemona.*

RODERIGO

Iago,—

IAGO

What say'st thou, noble heart?

RODERIGO

What will I do, think'st thou?

IAGO

Why, go to bed and sleep.   305

RODERIGO

I will incontinently drown myself.

IAGO

If thou dost, I shall never love thee after. Why,
thou silly gentleman!

RODERIGO

It is silliness to live when to live is torment;
and then have we a prescription to die when   310
Death is our physician.

IAGO

O villanous! I have look'd upon the world
for four times seven years; and since I could distinguish betwixt a benefit and an injury, I never
found man that knew how to love himself. Ere I   315
would say I would drown myself for the love of a
guinea-hen, I would change my humanity with a
baboon.

RODERIGO

What should I do? I confess it is my shame

---

290 **delighted:** delightful.   306 **incontinently:** straightway.
298 **advantage:** opportunity.

to be so fond, but it is not in my virtue to   320
amend it.

IAGO

Virtue! a fig! 'tis in ourselves that we are
thus or thus. Our bodies are our gardens, to the
which our wills are gardeners; so that if we will
plant nettles or sow lettuce, set hyssop and   325
weed up thyme, supply it with one gender of
herbs or distract it with many, either to have
it sterile with idleness or manured with industry,
why, the power and corrigible authority of this
lies in our wills. If the [balance] of our lives   330
had not one scale of reason to poise another
of sensuality, the blood and baseness of our
natures would conduct us to most preposterous
conclusions; but we have reason to cool our raging motions, our carnal stings, our unbitted   335
lusts, whereof I take this that you call love to
be a sect or scion.

RODERIGO

It cannot be.

IAGO

It is merely a lust of the blood and a permission of the will. Come, be a man! Drown thy-   340
self? drown cats and blind puppies! I have profess'd me thy friend, and I confess me knit to thy
deserving with cables of perdurable toughness; I
could never better stead thee than now. Put
money in thy purse; follow thou the wars; defeat   345
thy favour with an usurp'd beard. I say, put
money in thy purse. It cannot be long that Desdemona should continue her love to the Moor,—put
money in thy purse,—nor he his to her. It was a
violent commencement in her, and thou shalt   350
see an answerable sequestration. Put but money
in thy purse. These Moors are changeable in their
wills—fill thy purse with money;—the food that
to him now is as luscious as locusts, shall be to him
shortly as bitter as coloquintida. She must   355
change for youth; when she is sated with his body,
she will find the error of her choice; [she must have
change, she must:] therefore put money in thy
purse. If thou wilt needs damn thyself, do it a
more delicate way than drowning. Make all   360

---

325 **hyssop:** fragrant herb.
326 **gender:** kind.
329 **corrigible authority:** corrective
power.
330 [**balance**] Q: *braine* F.
335 **motions:** appetites.
337 **sect or scion:** cutting or
off-shoot.
343 **perdurable:** eternal.

345–346 **defeat thy favour:** disguise
thy face.
351 **sequestration:** separation.
354 **locusts:** the fruit of the carob
tree.
355 **coloquintida:** a bitter fruit.
357–358 [**she . . . she must:**] Q:
Om. F.

the money thou canst. If sanctimony and a frail
vow betwixt an erring barbarian and a super-subtle
Venetian be not too hard for my wits and all the
tribe of hell, thou shalt enjoy her; therefore make
money. A pox of drowning thyself! it is clean   365
out of the way. Seek thou rather to be hang'd in
compassing thy joy than to be drown'd and go
without her.

RODERIGO
    Wilt thou be fast to my hopes, if I depend
on the issue?   370

IAGO
    Thou art sure of me. Go, make money. I
had told thee often, and I re-tell thee again
and again, I hate the Moor. My cause is hearted;
thine hath no less reason. Let us be conjunctive
in our revenge against him. If thou canst   375
cuckold him, thou dost thyself a pleasure, me
a sport. There are many events in the womb
of time which will be delivered. Traverse! go,
provide thy money. We will have more of this
to-morrow. Adieu.   380

RODERIGO
    Where shall we meet i' th' morning?

IAGO
    At my lodging.

RODERIGO
    I'll be with thee betimes.

IAGO
    Go to; farewell. Do you hear, Roderigo?   385

[RODERIGO
    What say you?

IAGO
    No more of drowning, do you hear?

RODERIGO
    I am chang'd;] I'll sell all my land.

                                                          [Exit.

IAGO
    Thus do I ever make my fool my purse;
For I mine own gain'd knowledge should profane   390
If I would time expend with such a snipe
But for my sport and profit. I hate the Moor;
And it is thought abroad that 'twixt my sheets
He has done my office. I know not if 't be true;
But I, for mere suspicion in that kind,   395
Will do as if for surety. He holds me well;
The better shall my purpose work on him.
Cassio's a proper man: let me see now:

369–370 **depend . . . issue:** rely on
the outcome.
373 **hearted:** heart-felt.
374 **conjunctive:** united.
378 **Traverse:** forward.

386–388 [RODERIGO **What . . .
chang'd;]** Q: Om. F.
391 **snipe:** woodcock, a silly bird.
398 **proper:** handsome.

To get his place and to plume up my will
In double knavery—How, how?—Let's see:—   400
After some time, to abuse Othello's ear
That he is too familiar with his wife.
He hath a person and a smooth dispose
To be suspected, fram'd to make women false.
The Moor is of a free and open nature,   405
That thinks men honest that but seem to be so,
And will as tenderly be led by th' nose
As asses are.
I have't. It is engend'red. Hell and night
Must bring this monstrous birth to the world's light.   410

                                                        [*Exit.*

Act II

    Scene I. [*A sea-port in Cyprus. An open place near the quay.*]
    Enter Montano and two Gentlemen.

MONTANO
What from the cape can you discern at sea?
FIRST GENTLEMAN
Nothing at all; it is a high-wrought flood.
I cannot, 'twixt the heaven and the main,
Descry a sail.
MONTANO
Methinks the wind hath spoke aloud at land;   5
A fuller blast ne'er shook our battlements.
If it hath ruffian'd so upon the sea,
What ribs of oak, when mountains melt on them,
Can hold the mortise? What shall we hear of this?
SECOND GENTLEMAN
A segregation of the Turkish fleet.   10
For do but stand upon the foaming shore,
The chidden billow seems to pelt the clouds;
The wind-shak'd surge, with high and monstrous mane,
Seems to cast water on the burning Bear
And quench the guards of th' ever-fixed Pole.   15
I never did like molestation view
On the enchafed flood.
MONTANO
                    If that the Turkish fleet
Be not enshelter'd and embay'd, they are drown'd;
It is impossible to bear it out.
    Enter a third Gentleman.
THIRD GENTLEMAN
News, lads! our wars are done.   20
The desperate tempest hath so bang'd the Turks,

399–400 **plume . . . In:** brace
myself to.
403 **dispose:** disposition.
II. i. 9 **hold the mortise:** hold their
joints together.

10 **segregation:** dispersion.
15 **guards:** stars in the Little Bear in
line with the pole star.

That their designment halts. A noble ship of Venice
Hath seen a grievous wreck and sufferance
On most part of their fleet.
MONTANO
How! is this true?
THIRD GENTLEMAN
                  The ship is here put in.   25
A Veronese, Michael Cassio,
Lieutenant to the warlike Moor Othello,
Is come on shore; the Moor himself at sea,
And is in full commission here for Cyprus.
MONTANO
I am glad on't; 'tis a worthy governor.   30
THIRD GENTLEMAN
But this same Cassio, though he speak of comfort
Touching the Turkish loss, yet he looks sadly
And prays the Moor be safe, for they were parted
With foul and violent tempest.
MONTANO
                Pray heavens he be;
For I have serv'd him, and the man commands   35
Like a full soldier. Let's to the seaside, ho!
As well to see the vessel that's come in
As to throw out our eyes for brave Othello,
Even till we make the main and th' aerial blue
An indistinct regard.
THIRD GENTLEMAN
             Come, let's do so;   40
For every minute is expectancy
Of more arrivance.
    Enter Cassio.
CASSIO
Thanks, you the valiant of this warlike isle,
That so approve the Moor! O, let the heavens
Give him defence against the elements,   45
For I have lost him on a dangerous sea.
MONTANO
Is he well shipp'd?
CASSIO
His bark is stoutly timber'd, and his pilot
Of very expert and approv'd allowance;
Therefore my hopes, not surfeited to death,   50
Stand in bold cure.
                [*Within*, "A sail, a sail, a sail!"
    Enter a [*fourth Gentleman*].
CASSIO
What noise?

---

23 **sufferance:** disaster.
26 **A Veronese:** In I.i.20 Cassio is
called a Florentine.
49 **approv'd allowance:** tested
repute.

50–51 **my hopes . . . cure:** The
sense seems to be: "My hopes,
though far from being nourished to
excess, yet stand a good chance of
being fulfilled."

FOURTH GENTLEMAN

   The town is empty; on the brow o' th' sea
   Stand ranks of people, and they cry, "A sail!"

CASSIO

   My hopes do shape him for the governor.   55

                                    [*A shot.*

SECOND GENTLEMAN

   They do discharge their shot of courtesy.
   Our friends at least.

CASSIO

                  I pray you, sir, go forth,
   And give us truth who 'tis that is arriv'd.

SECOND GENTLEMAN

   I shall.

                                      [*Exit.*

MONTANO

   But, good Lieutenant, is your General wiv'd?   60

CASSIO

   Most fortunately. He hath achiev'd a maid
   That paragons description and wild fame;
   One that excels the quirks of blazoning pens,
   And in th' essential vesture of creation
   Does tire the [ingener].

       Re-enter second Gentleman.

               How now! who has put in?   65

SECOND GENTLEMAN

   'Tis one Iago, ancient to the general.

CASSIO

   He has had most favourable and happy speed.
   Tempests themselves, high seas, and howling winds,
   The gutter'd rocks and congregated sands,
   Traitors ensteep'd to enclog the guiltless keel,   70
   As having sense of beauty, do omit
   Their mortal natures, letting go safely by
   The divine Desdemona.

MONTANO

                  What is she?

CASSIO

   She that I spake of, our great captain's captain,
   Left in the conduct of the bold Iago,   75
   Whose footing here anticipates our thoughts
   A se'nnight's speed. Great Jove, Othello guard,
   And swell his sail with thine own powerful breath,
   That he may bless this bay with his tall ship,
   Make love's quick pants in Desdemona's arms,   80
   Give renew'd fire to our extincted spirits,
   [And bring all Cyprus comfort!]

62 **paragons:** excels.
63 **quirks:** flourishes; **blazoning:** praising.
64 **essential . . . creation:** i.e., just as she is, in her essential quality.
65 [**ingener**] (Steevens conj.): inventor (of praise). *Ingeniver* F. For

tire the [*ingener*] Q reads *beare an excellency.*
69 **gutter'd:** furrowed, jagged.
70 **ensteep'd:** submerged.
72 **mortal:** deadly.
82 [**And . . . comfort!**] Q: Om. F.

Enter Desdemona, Emilia, Iago, Roderigo [and Attendants].
                               O, behold,
The riches of the ship is come on shore!
You men of Cyprus, let her have your knees.
Hail to thee, lady! and the grace of heaven,   85
Before, behind thee, and on every hand,
Enwheel thee round!

DESDEMONA
                          I thank you, valiant Cassio.
What tidings can you tell [me] of my lord?

CASSIO
He is not yet arriv'd; nor know I aught
But that he's well and will be shortly here.   90

DESDEMONA
O, but I fear—How lost you company?

CASSIO
The great contention of sea and skies
Parted our fellowship.—But, hark! a sail.
                    [*Within,* "A sail, a sail!" [*Guns heard.*]

SECOND GENTLEMAN
They give [their] greeting to the citadel.   95
This likewise is a friend.

CASSIO
                          See for the news.
                                        [*Exit Gentleman.*]
Good ancient, you are welcome. [*To Emilia.*] Welcome, mistress.
Let it not gall your patience, good Iago,
That I extend my manners; 'tis my breeding
That gives me this bold show of courtesy.   100
                                        [*Kissing her.*]

IAGO
Sir, would she give you so much of her lips
As of her tongue she oft bestows on me,
You'd have enough.

DESDEMONA
                          Alas, she has no speech.

IAGO
In faith, too much;
I find it still, when I have [list] to sleep.   105
Marry, before your ladyship, I grant,
She puts her tongue a little in her heart,
And chides with thinking.

EMILIA
You have little cause to say so.

IAGO
Come on, come on; you are pictures out of door,   110
Bells in your parlours, wild-cats in your kitchens,

---

88 [**me**] Q: Om F.
95 [**their**] Q: *this* F.
105 [**list**] Q: inclination. *leave* F.
108 **with thinking:** i.e., without
words.

110–113 **Come . . . beds:** So Q.
Prose in F.
111 **Bells:** i.e., clanging tongues.

Saints in your injuries, devils being offended,
Players in your housewifery, and housewives in your beds.

DESDEMONA
O, fie upon thee, slanderer!

IAGO
Nay, it is true, or else I am a Turk.   115
You rise to play and go to bed to work.

EMILIA
You shall not write my praise.

IAGO
                                 No, let me not.

DESDEMONA
What wouldst thou write of me, if thou shouldst praise me?

IAGO
O gentle lady, do not put me to't;
For I am nothing if not critical.   120

DESDEMONA
Come on, assay.—There's one gone to the harbour?

IAGO
Ay, madam.

DESDEMONA
I am not merry; but I do beguile
The thing I am by seeming otherwise.—
Come, how wouldst thou praise me?   125

IAGO
I am about it; but indeed my invention
Comes from my pate as birdlime does from frieze;
It plucks out brains and all. But my Muse labours,
And thus she is deliver'd:
If she be fair and wise, fairness and wit,   130
The one 's for use, the other useth it.

DESDEMONA
Well prais'd! How if she be black and witty?

IAGO
If she be black, and thereto have a wit,
She'll find a white that shall her blackness fit.

DESDEMONA
Worse and worse.   135

EMILIA
How if fair and foolish?

IAGO
She never yet was foolish that was fair;
For even her folly help'd her to an heir.

DESDEMONA
These are old fond paradoxes to make fools
laugh i' th' alehouse. What miserable praise hast   140
thou for her that's foul and foolish?

112 **Saints . . . injuries:** i.e., you offend sanctimoniously.
113 **Players:** triflers; **housewives:** hussies.

126–129 **I am . . . deliver'd:** So Q. Prose in F.
132 **black:** brunette.
134 **white:** with a pun on *wight* (person).

IAGO

There's none so foul and foolish thereunto,
But does foul pranks which fair and wise ones do.

DESDEMONA

O heavy ignorance! thou praisest the worst
best. But what praise couldst thou bestow on a   145
deserving woman indeed, one that, in the authority
of her merit, did justly put on the vouch of very
malice itself?

IAGO

She that was ever fair and never proud,
Had tongue at will and yet was never loud,   150
Never lack'd gold and yet went never gay,
Fled from her wish and yet said, "Now I may;"
She that being ang'red, her revenge being nigh,
Bade her wrong stay and her displeasure fly;
She that in wisdom never was so frail   155
To change the cod's head for the salmon's tail;
She that could think and ne'er disclose her mind,
See suitors following and not look behind,
She was a wight, if ever such wights were,—

DESDEMONA

To do what?   160

IAGO

To suckle fools and chronicle small beer.

DESDEMONA

O most lame and impotent conclusion! Do not
learn of him, Emilia, though he be thy husband.
How say you, Cassio? Is he not a most profane
and liberal counsellor?   165

CASSIO

He speaks home, madam. You may relish him
more in the soldier than in the scholar.

IAGO [*Aside.*]

He takes her by the palm; ay, well said,
whisper. With as little a web as this will I
ensnare as great a fly as Cassio. Ay, smile upon   170
her, do; I will gyve thee in thine own courtship.
—You say true; 'tis so, indeed.—If such tricks as
these strip you out of your lieutenantry, it had been
better you had not kiss'd your three fingers so oft,
which now again you are most apt to play the sir   175
in. Very good; well kiss'd! an excellent curtsy! 'Tis
so, indeed. Yet again your fingers to your lips?
Would they were clyster-pipes for your sake!

147 **put . . . vouch:** compel the
testimony.
156 **To . . . tail:** to take the
worthless in exchange for the
worthy.
161 **chronicle small beer:** i.e., to
keep petty accounts.

165 **liberal:** free-spoken.
168 **well said:** well done.
171 **gyve:** fetter, entangle; **courtship:**
courtesy.
175 **sir:** gentleman.
178 **clyster-pipes:** syringes.

(*Trumpet within.*)—The Moor! I know his
  trumpet.   180

CASSIO
  'Tis truly so.

DESDEMONA
  Let's meet him and receive him.

CASSIO
  Lo, where he comes!
        Enter Othello and Attendants.

OTHELLO
  O my fair warrior!

DESDEMONA
               My dear Othello!

OTHELLO
  It gives me wonder great as my content   185
  To see you here before me. O my soul's joy!
  If after every tempest come such calms,
  May the winds blow till they have waken'd death!
  And let the labouring bark climb hills of seas
  Olympus-high, and duck again as low   190
  As hell's from heaven! If it were now to die,
  'Twere now to be most happy; for, I fear,
  My soul hath her content so absolute
  That not another comfort like to this
  Succeeds in unknown fate.

DESDEMONA
               The heavens forbid   195
  But that our loves and comforts should increase,
  Even as our days do grow!

OTHELLO
               Amen to that, sweet powers!
  I cannot speak enough of this content;
  It stops me here; it is too much of joy.
  And this, and this, the greatest discords be   200
                                   [*Kissing her.*
  That e'er our hearts shall make!

IAGO [*Aside.*]
  O, you are well tun'd now!
  But I'll set down the pegs that make this music,
  As honest as I am.

OTHELLO
             Come, let us to the castle.
  News, friends: our wars are done, the Turks are drown'd.
  How does my old acquaintance of this isle?   205
  Honey, you shall be well desir'd in Cyprus;
  I have found great love amongst them. O my sweet,
  I prattle out of fashion, and I dote
  In mine own comforts. I prithee, good Iago,
  Go to the bay and disembark my coffers.   210
  Bring thou the master to the citadel;
  He is a good one, and his worthiness

206 **desir'd:** beloved.   211 **master:** ship's master.

Does challenge much respect. Come, Desdemona,
Once more, well met at Cyprus.

[Exeunt Othello, Desdemona [and Attendants].

IAGO

Do thou meet me presently at the harbour.   215
—Come [hither]. If thou be'st valiant,—as, they
say, base men being in love have then a nobility in
their natures more than is native to them,—list me.
The lieutenant to-night watches on the court of
guard;—first, I must tell thee this: Desdemona is   220
directly in love with him.

RODERIGO

With him! why, 'tis not possible.

IAGO

Lay thy finger thus, and let thy soul be in-
structed. Mark me with what violence she first
lov'd the Moor, but for bragging and telling her   225
fantastical lies. To love him still for prating,—
let not thy discreet heart think it. Her eye must be
fed; and what delight shall she have to look on the
devil? When the blood is made dull with the act of
sport, there should be, [again] to inflame it and   230
to give satiety a fresh appetite, loveliness in favour,
sympathy in years, manners, and beauties; all
which the Moor is defective in. Now, for want of
these requir'd conveniences, her delicate tenderness
will find itself abus'd, begin to heave the gorge,   235
disrelish and abhor the Moor. Very nature will instruct her in it and compel her to some second
choice. Now, sir, this granted,—as it is a most
pregnant and unforc'd position—who stands so
eminent in the degree of this fortune as Cassio   240
does? a knave very voluble; no further conscionable than in putting on the mere form of civil and
humane seeming, for the better compassing of his
salt and most hidden loose affection? Why, none;
why, none; a slipper and subtle knave, a finder   245
of occasion, that has an eye can stamp and counterfeit advantages, though true advantage never present itself; a devilish knave. Besides, the knave is
handsome, young, and hath all those requisites   250
in him that folly and green minds look after; a
pestilent complete knave, and the woman hath
found him already.

RODERIGO

I cannot believe that in her; she's full of most
bless'd condition.   255

---

216 **[hither]** Q: *thither* F.   241 **conscionable:** conscientious.
230 **[again]** Q: *a game* F.   244 **salt:** lewd.
235 **heave the gorge:** be nauseated.   245 **slipper:** slippery.
239 **pregnant:** evident.   255 **condition:** character.

IAGO

Bless'd fig's-end! This wine she drinks is made
of grapes. If she had been bless'd, she would
never have lov'd the Moor. Bless'd pudding!
Didst thou not see her paddle with the palm
of his hand? Didst not mark that?   260

RODERIGO

Yes, that I did; but that was but courtesy.

IAGO

Lechery, by this hand; an index and obscure
prologue to the history of lust and foul
thoughts. They met so near with their lips
that their breaths embrac'd together. Villanous   265
thoughts, Roderigo! When these [mutualities]
so marshal the way, hard at hand comes the
master and main exercise, th' incorporate conclusion. Pish! But, sir, be you rul'd by me; I have
brought you from Venice. Watch you to-night; for   270
the command, I'll lay 't upon you. Cassio knows
you not. I'll not be far from you. Do you find
some occasion to anger Cassio, either by speaking
too loud, or tainting his discipline; or from what
other course you please, which the time shall more   275
favourably minister.

RODERIGO

Well?

IAGO

Sir, he's rash and very sudden in choler, and
haply may strike at you. Provoke him, that he
may; for even out of that will I cause these   280
of Cyprus to mutiny, whose qualification shall
come into no true taste again but by the dis-
planting of Cassio. So shall you have a shorter
journey to your desires by the means I shall
then have to prefer them; and the impedi-   285
ment most profitably removed, without the
which there were no expectation of our
prosperity.

RODERIGO

I will do this, if you can bring it to any
opportunity.   290

IAGO

I warrant thee. Meet me by and by at the
citadel; I must fetch his necessaries ashore. Farewell.

RODERIGO

Adieu.

[*Exit.*

IAGO

That Cassio loves her, I do well believe 't;   295

266 [**mutualities**] Q: exchanges.   281 **qualification:** appeasement.
mutabilities F.

That she loves him, 'tis apt and of great credit;
The Moor, howbeit that I endure him not,
Is of a constant, loving, noble nature,
And I dare think he'll prove to Desdemona
A most dear husband. Now, I do love her too; 300
Not out of absolute lust, though peradventure
I stand accountant for as great a sin,
But partly led to diet my revenge,
For that I do suspect the lusty Moor
Hath leap'd into my seat; the thought whereof 305
Doth, like a poisonous mineral, gnaw my inwards;
And nothing can or shall content my soul
Till I am even'd with him, wife for [wife];
Or failing so, yet that I put the Moor
At least into a jealousy so strong 310
That judgement cannot cure. Which thing to do,
If this poor trash of Venice, whom I [trash]
For his quick hunting, stand the putting on,
I'll have our Michael Cassio on the hip,
Abuse him to the Moor in the [rank] garb— 315
For I fear Cassio with my night-cap too—
Make the Moor thank me, love me, and reward me
For making him egregiously an ass
And practising upon his peace and quiet
Even to madness. 'Tis here, but yet confus'd; 320
Knavery's plain face is never seen till us'd.

[*Exit.*

Scene II. [*A street.*]
Enter Othello's Herald, with a proclamation [*People following*].
HERALD
It is Othello's pleasure, our noble and valiant
general, that, upon certain tidings now arriv'd
importing the mere perdition of the Turkish
fleet, every man put himself into triumph; some
to dance, some to make bonfires, each man to 5
what sport and revels his [addiction] leads him; for,
beside these beneficial news, it is the celebration of
his nuptial. So much was his pleasure should be
proclaimed. All offices are open, and there is full
liberty of feasting from this present hour of five 10
till the bell have told eleven. [Heaven] bless the isle
of Cyprus and our noble general Othello!

[*Exeunt.*

296 **apt:** natural; **of . . . credit:**
most credible.
308 [**wife**] Q: *wist* F.
312 **trash:** worthless fellow; [**trash**]
(Steevens): check. *trace* F. *crush* Q.
313 **putting on:** inciting.
315 [**rank**] Q: gross. *right* F; **garb:**
manner.

319 **practising upon:** plotting
against.
ii.3 **mere:** utter.
6 [**addiction**] Q$_2$: inclination. *addition*
F. *minde* Q.
9 **offices:** kitchens, etc.
11 [**Heaven**] Q: Om. F.

[*Scene III. A hall in the castle.*]
Enter Othello, Desdemona, Cassio, and Attendants.

OTHELLO

Good Michael, look you to the guard to-night.
Let's teach ourselves that honourable stop,
Not to outsport discretion.

CASSIO

Iago hath direction what to do;
But, notwithstanding, with my personal eye   5
Will I look to't.

OTHELLO

              Iago is most honest.
Michael, good-night; to-morrow with your earliest
Let me have speech with you. [*To Desdemona.*] Come, my dear love,
The purchase made, the fruits are to ensue;
That profit's yet to come 'tween me and you.   10
Good-night.

           [*Exeunt [Othello, Desdemona, and Attendants.*]]
Enter Iago.

CASSIO

Welcome, Iago; we must to the watch.

IAGO

Not this hour, Lieutenant; 'tis not yet ten o'
th' clock. Our general cast us thus early for the
love of his Desdemona; who let us not therefore   15
blame. He hath not yet made wanton the night
with her; and she is sport for Jove.

CASSIO

She's a most exquisite lady.

IAGO

And, I'll warrant her, full of game.

CASSIO

Indeed, she's a most fresh and delicate   20
creature.

IAGO

What an eye she has! Methinks it sounds
a parley to provocation.

CASSIO

An inviting eye; and yet methinks right
modest.   25

IAGO

And when she speaks, is it not an alarum to
love?

CASSIO

She is indeed perfection.

IAGO

Well, happiness to their sheets! Come,
lieutenant, I have a stoup of wine; and here   30
without are a brace of Cyprus gallants that
would fain have a measure to the health of
black Othello.

iii.14 **cast:** dismissed.

CASSIO

Not to-night, good Iago. I have very poor
and unhappy brains for drinking; I could well   35
wish courtesy would invent some other custom
of entertainment.

IAGO

O, they are our friends. But one cup; I'll
drink for you.

CASSIO

I have drunk but one cup to-night, and that   40
was craftily qualified too, and, behold, what
innovation it makes here. I am unfortunate in
the infirmity, and dare not task my weakness
with any more.

IAGO

What, man! 'tis a night of revels. The gallants   45
desire it.

CASSIO

Where are they?

IAGO

Here at the door; I pray you, call them in.

CASSIO

I'll do't; but it dislikes me.

[*Exit.*

IAGO

If I can fasten but one cup upon him,   50
With that which he hath drunk to-night already,
He'll be as full of quarrel and offence
As my young mistress' dog. Now, my sick fool Roderigo,
Whom love hath turn'd almost the wrong side out,
To Desdemona hath to-night carous'd   55
Potations pottle-deep; and he's to watch.
Three [lads] of Cyprus, noble swelling spirits
That hold their honours in a wary distance,
The very elements of this warlike isle,
Have I to-night fluster'd with flowing cups,   60
And they watch too. Now, 'mongst this flock of drunkards
Am I to put our Cassio in some action
That may offend the isle. But here they come.
      Re-enter Cassio; with him Montano and Gentlemen [Servants follow
      with wine].
If consequence do but approve my dream,
My boat sails freely, both with wind and stream.   65

CASSIO

'Fore [God], they have given me a rouse
already.

41 **craftily qualified:** slyly diluted.
49 **it dislikes me:** I don't want to.
56 **pottle-deep:** to the bottom of the
tankard.
57 [**lads**] Q: *else* F.

58 **hold . . . distance:** i.e., are quick
to quarrel.
59 **very elements:** true
representatives.
66 **rouse:** bumper.

MONTANO
    Good faith, a little one; not past a pint, as I
    am a soldier.
IAGO
    Some wine, ho!   70

[Sings.]

        "And let me the canakin clink, clink;
        And let me the canakin clink.
            A soldier's a man;
            O, man's life's but a span;
        Why, then, let a soldier drink."   75
    Some wine, boys!
CASSIO
    'Fore [God], an excellent song.
IAGO
    I learn'd it in England, where, indeed, they
    are most potent in potting; your Dane, your
    German, and your swag-belli'd Hollander—   80
    Drink, ho!—are nothing to your English.
CASSIO
    Is your Englishman so exquisite in his
    drinking?
IAGO
    Why, he drinks you, with facility, your Dane
    dead drunk; he sweats not to overthrow your   85
    Almain; he gives your Hollander a vomit ere
    the next pottle can be fill'd.
CASSIO
    To the health of our general!
MONTANO
    I am for it, Lieutenant; and I'll do you
    justice.   90
IAGO
    O sweet England!
    "King Stephen was and-a worthy peer,
        His breeches cost him but a crown;
    He held them sixpence all too dear,
        With that he call'd the tailor lown.   95

    "He was a wight of high renown,
        And thou art but of low degree.
    'Tis pride that pulls the country down;
        And take thy auld cloak about thee."
    Some wine, ho!   100
CASSIO
    Why, this is a more exquisite song than the
    other.
IAGO
    Will you hear 't again?
CASSIO
    No; for I hold him to be unworthy of his place

    86 **Almain:** German.   95 **lown:** fellow, rascal.

that does those things. Well, [God's] above all; 105
and there be souls must be saved, and there be
souls must not be saved.

IAGO

It's true, good Lieutenant.

CASSIO

For mine own part—no offence to the
general, nor any man of quality—I hope to be 110
saved.

IAGO

And so do I too, Lieutenant.

CASSIO

Ay, but, by your leave, not before me; the
lieutenant is to be saved before the ancient. Let's
have no more of this; let's to our affairs.— 115
[God] forgive us our sins!—Gentlemen, let's look to
our business. Do not think, gentlemen, I am drunk.
This is my ancient; this is my right hand, and this
is my left. I am not drunk now; I can stand well
enough, and I speak well enough. 120

GENTLEMEN

Excellent well.

CASSIO

Why, very well then; you must not think then
that I am drunk.

[*Exit.*

MONTANO

To the platform, masters; come, let's set the
watch. 125

IAGO

You see this fellow that is gone before:
He is a soldier fit to stand by Cæsar
And give direction; and do but see his vice.
'Tis to his virtue a just equinox,
The one as long as th' other; 'tis pity of him. 130
I fear the trust Othello puts him in,
On some odd time of his infirmity,
Will shake this island.

MONTANO

But is he often thus?

IAGO

'Tis evermore his prologue to his sleep.
He'll watch the horologe a double set 135
If drink rock not his cradle.

MONTANO

It were well
The general were put in mind of it.
Perhaps he sees it not; or his good nature
Prizes the virtue that appears in Cassio,
And looks not on his evils. Is not this true? 140

129 **equinox:** counterpart,
equivalent.

135 **horologe . . . set:** clock twice
around.

Enter Roderigo.

IAGO [*Aside to him*].
How now, Roderigo!
I pray you, after the lieutenant; go.

[*Exit Roderigo.*

MONTANO
And 'tis great pity that the noble Moor
Should hazard such a place as his own second
With one of an ingraft infirmity.   145
It were an honest action to say
So to the Moor.

IAGO
                    Not I, for this fair island.
I do love Cassio well; and would do much
To cure him of this evil.—But, hark! what noise?

[*Cry within:* "Help! help!"]

Re-enter Cassio, pursuing Roderigo.

CASSIO
'Zounds, you rogue! you rascal!

MONTANO
                              What's the matter, Lieutenant?   150

CASSIO
A knave teach me my duty!
I'll beat the knave into a twiggen bottle.

RODERIGO
Beat me!

CASSIO
          Dost thou prate, rogue?   ·   [*Striking Roderigo.*]

MONTANO
                              Nay, good Lieutenant;

[*Staying him.*]

I pray you, sir, hold your hand.

CASSIO
                         Let me go, sir,
Or I'll knock you o'er the mazzard.

MONTANO
                              Come, come, you're drunk.   155

CASSIO
Drunk!

[*They fight.*

IAGO [*Aside to Roderigo.*]
          Away, I say; go out, and cry a mutiny.

[*Exit Roderigo.*

Nay, good Lieutenant,—[God's will], gentlemen;—
Help, ho!—Lieutenant,—sir,—Montano,—[sir];—
Help, masters!—Here's a goodly watch indeed!

[*Bell rings.*

Who's that which rings the bell?—Diablo, ho!   160
The town will rise. Fie, fie, Lieutenant, [hold]!
You will be sham'd for ever.

152 **twiggen:** wicker-covered.   158 [**sir**] Q: Om. F.
155 **mazzard:** head.   161 [**hold**] Q: Om. F.
157 [**God's will**] Q: *Alas* F.

Re-enter Othello and Attendants.

OTHELLO

What is the matter here?

MONTANO

['Zounds], I bleed still; I am hurt to the death. He dies!

OTHELLO

Hold, for your lives!   165

IAGO

Hold, ho! Lieutenant,—sir,—Montano,—gentlemen,—
Have you forgot all [sense of place] and duty?
Hold! the general speaks to you; hold, for shame!

OTHELLO

Why, how now, ho! from whence ariseth this?
Are we turn'd Turks, and to ourselves do that   170
Which Heaven hath forbid the Ottomites?
For Christian shame, put by this barbarous brawl.
He that stirs next to carve for his own rage
Holds his soul light; he dies upon his motion.
Silence that dreadful bell; it frights the isle   175
From her propriety. What is the matter, masters?
Honest Iago, that looks dead with grieving,
Speak, who began this? On thy love, I charge thee.

IAGO

I do not know. Friends all but now, even now,
In quarter, and in terms like bride and groom   180
Devesting them for bed; and then, but now—
As if some planet had unwitted men—
Swords out, and tilting one at other's breast,
In opposition bloody. I cannot speak
Any beginning to this peevish odds;   185
And would in action glorious I had lost
Those legs that brought me to a part of it!

OTHELLO

How comes it, Michael, you are thus forgot?

CASSIO

I pray you, pardon me; I cannot speak.

OTHELLO

Worthy Montano, you were wont to be civil;   190
The gravity and stillness of your youth
The world hath noted, and your name is great
In mouths of wisest censure. What's the matter
That you unlace your reputation thus,
And spend your rich opinion for the name   195
Of a night-brawler? Give me answer to it.

MONTANO

Worthy Othello, I am hurt to danger.
Your officer, Iago, can inform you—
While I spare speech, which something now offends me—

167 [**sense of place**] (Hanmer): *place
of sense* QF.
173 **carve . . . rage:** act on his own
impulse.
180 **quarter:** peace.

185 **peevish odds:** stupid quarrel.
193 **censure:** judgment.
195 **opinion:** reputation.
199 **offends:** pains.

Of all that I do know; nor know I aught   200
By me that's said or done amiss this night,
Unless self-charity be sometimes a vice,
And to defend ourselves it be a sin
When violence assails us.

OTHELLO

                      Now, by heaven,
My blood begins my safer guides to rule;   205
And passion, having my best judgement collied,
Assays to lead the way. If I once stir
Or do but lift this arm, the best of you
Shall sink in my rebuke. Give me to know
How this foul rout began, who set it on;   210
And he that is approv'd in this offence,
Though he had twinn'd with me, both at a birth,
Shall lose me. What! in a town of war,
Yet wild, the people's hearts brimful of fear,
To manage private and domestic quarrel,   215
In night, and on the court and guard of safety!
'Tis monstrous. Iago, who began 't?

MONTANO

If partially affin'd, or leagu'd in office,
Thou dost deliver more or less than truth,
Thou art no soldier.

IAGO

                   Touch me not so near.   220
I had rather have this tongue cut from my mouth
Than it should do offence to Michael Cassio;
Yet, I persuade myself, to speak the truth
Shall nothing wrong him. [Thus] it is, General:
Montano and myself being in speech,   225
There comes a fellow crying out for help;
And Cassio following him with determin'd sword
To execute upon him. Sir, this gentleman
Steps in to Cassio and entreats his pause;
Myself the crying fellow did pursue,   230
Lest by his clamour—as it so fell out—
The town might fall in fright. He, swift of foot,
Outran my purpose; and I return'd the rather
For that I heard the clink and fall of swords,
And Cassio high in oath; which till to-night   235
I ne'er might say before. When I came back—
For this was brief—I found them close together,
At blow and thrust; even as again they were
When you yourself did part them.
More of this matter cannot I report.   240
But men are men; the best sometimes forget.
Though Cassio did some little wrong to him,
As men in rage strike those that wish them best,

---

206 **collied:** darkened.   218 **partially affin'd:** biased because
211 **approv'd:** found guilty.   of ties.
215 **manage:** carry on.   224 **[Thus]** Q: *This* F.

Yet surely Cassio, I believe, receiv'd
From him that fled some strange indignity   245
Which patience could not pass.

OTHELLO
                              I know, Iago,
Thy honesty and love doth mince this matter,
Making it light to Cassio. Cassio, I love thee;
But never more be officer of mine.
          Re-enter Desdemona, attended.
Look, if my gentle love be not rais'd up!   250
I'll make thee an example.

DESDEMONA
                         What's the matter, dear?

OTHELLO
All's well [now], sweeting; come away to bed.
Sir, for your hurts, myself will be your surgeon.—
Lead him off.
                    [To Montano, who is led off.]
Iago, look with care about the town,   255
And silence those whom this vile brawl distracted.
Come, Desdemona; 'tis the soldiers' life
To have their balmy slumbers wak'd with strife.
                    [Exeunt all but Iago and Cassio.

IAGO
What, are you hurt, Lieutenant?

CASSIO
Ay, past all surgery.   260

IAGO
Marry, God forbid!

CASSIO
Reputation, reputation, reputation! O,
I have lost my reputation! I have lost the im-
mortal part of myself, and what remains is bestial.
My reputation, Iago, my reputation!   265

IAGO
As I am an honest man, I thought you had
received some bodily wound; there is more sense
in that than in reputation. Reputation is an idle
and most false imposition; oft got without merit,
and lost without deserving. You have lost no   270
reputation at all, unless you repute yourself such a
loser. What, man! there are more ways to recover
the general again. You are but now cast in his
mood, a punishment more in policy than in malice;
even so as one would beat his offenceless dog to af-   275
fright an imperious lion. Sue to him again, and he's
yours.

CASSIO
I will rather sue to be despis'd than to deceive so good a commander with so slight, so

---

252 [**now**] Q: Om. F.   272 **recover:** regain favor with.
266 **thought** Q: *had thought* F.

drunken, and so indiscreet an officer. Drunk?   280
and speak parrot? and squabble? swagger? swear?
and discourse fustian with one's own shadow? O
thou invisible spirit of wine, if thou hast no name
to be known by, let us call thee devil!

IAGO

What was he that you follow'd with your   285
sword? What had he done to you?

CASSIO

I know not.

IAGO

Is't possible?

CASSIO

I remember a mass of things, but nothing
distinctly; a quarrel, but nothing wherefore. O   290
[God], that men should put an enemy in their
mouths to steal away their brains! That we should,
with joy, pleasance, revel, and applause, transform
ourselves into beasts!

IAGO

Why, but you are now well enough. How   295
came you thus recovered?

CASSIO

It hath pleas'd the devil drunkenness to give
place to the devil wrath. One unperfectness
shows me another, to make me frankly despise
myself.   300

IAGO

Come, you are too severe a moraler. As the
time, the place, and the condition of this country stands, I could heartily wish this had not
befallen; but since it is as it is, mend it for
your own good.   305

CASSIO

I will ask him for my place again; he shall
tell me I am a drunkard! Had I as many
mouths as Hydra, such an answer would stop
them all. To be now a sensible man, by and by
a fool, and presently a beast! O strange! Every   310
inordinate cup is unbless'd and the ingredient
is a devil.

IAGO

Come, come, good wine is a good familiar
creature, if it be well us'd; exclaim no more
against it. And, good Lieutenant, I think you   315
think I love you.

CASSIO

I have well approved it, sir. I drunk!

IAGO

You or any man living may be drunk at a
time, man. [I'll] tell you what you shall do. Our

281 **parrot:** nonsense.   319 [**I'll**] Q: *I* F.
282 **fustian:** nonsense.

general's wife is now the general;—I may say   320
so in this respect, for that he hath devoted and
given up himself to the contemplation, mark, and
[denotement] of her parts and graces;—confess
yourself freely to her; importune her help to put
you in your place again. She is of so free, so   325
kind, so apt, so blessed a disposition, she holds
it a vice in her goodness not to do more than she
is requested. This broken joint between you and
her husband entreat her to splinter; and, my fortunes against any lay worth naming, this crack of   330
your love shall grow stronger than it was before.

CASSIO
You advise me well.

IAGO
I protest, in the sincerity of love and honest
kindness.

CASSIO
I think it freely; and betimes in the morning   335
I will beseech the virtuous Desdemona to undertake for me. I am desperate of my fortunes if
they check me [here].

IAGO
You are in the right. Good-night, lieutenant;
I must to the watch.   340

CASSIO
Good-night, honest Iago.

                                            [*Exit.*

IAGO
And what's he then that says I play the villain?
When this advice is free I give and honest,
Probal to thinking and indeed the course
To win the Moor again? For 'tis most easy   345
Th' inclining Desdemona to subdue
In any honest suit; she's fram'd as fruitful
As the free elements. And then for her
To win the Moor, [were't] to renounce his baptism,
All seals and symbols of redeemed sin,   350
His soul is so enfetter'd to her love,
That she may make, unmake, do what she list,
Even as her appetite shall play the god
With his weak function. How am I then a villain
To counsel Cassio to this parallel course,   355
Directly to his good? Divinity of hell!
When devils will the blackest sins put on,
They do suggest at first with heavenly shows,
As I do now: for whiles this honest fool
Plies Desdemona to repair his fortune   360

323 [**denotement**] Q₂: *devotement* QF.   347 **fruitful:** generous.
329 **splinter:** bind with splints.   349 [**were't**] Q: *were* F.
330 **lay:** wager.   354 **function:** mental faculties.
338 [**here**] Q: Om. F.   357 **put on:** incite.
344 **Probal:** probable.

And she for him pleads strongly to the Moor,
I'll pour this pestilence into his ear,
That she repeals him for her body's lust;
And by how much she strives to do him good,
She shall undo her credit with the Moor. 365
So will I turn her virtue into pitch,
And out of her own goodness make the net
That shall enmesh them all.
      Re-enter Roderigo.
                        How now, Roderigo!

RODERIGO
I do follow here in the chase, not like a
hound that hunts, but one that fills up the cry. 370
My money is almost spent; I have been to-night
exceedingly well cudgell'd; and I think the issue
will be, I shall have so much experience for my
pains; and so, with no money at all and a little more
wit, return again to Venice. 375

IAGO
How poor are they that have not patience!
What wound did ever heal but by degrees?
Thou know'st we work by wit, and not by witchcraft;
And wit depends on dilatory time.
Does't not go well? Cassio hath beaten thee, 380
And thou, by that small hurt, hast cashier'd Cassio.
Though other things grow fair against the sun,
Yet fruits that blossom first will first be ripe.
Content thyself a while. In troth, 'tis morning;
Pleasure and action make the hours seem short. 385
Retire thee; go where thou art billeted.
Away, I say; thou shalt know more hereafter.
Nay, get thee gone. [*Exit Roderigo.*] Two things are to be done:
My wife must move for Cassio to her mistress;
I'll set her on; 390
Myself a while to draw the Moor apart,
And bring him jump when he may Cassio find
Soliciting his wife. Ay, that's the way;
Dull not device by coldness and delay.
                                        [*Exit.*

Act III

Scene I. [Cyprus before the castle.]
Enter Cassio, with Musicians.

CASSIO
Masters, play here; I will content your pains;
Something that's brief; and bid "Good morrow, general."
                                        [*They play.*

Enter Clown.

370 **cry:** pack.   III.i.1 **content:** requite.
392 **jump:** at the precise moment.

CLOWN
　Why, masters, have your instruments been
　in Naples, that they speak i' th' nose thus?
FIRST MUSICIAN
　How, sir, how?   5
CLOWN
　Are these, I pray you, wind-instruments?
FIRST MUSICIAN
　Ay, marry, are they, sir.
CLOWN
　O, thereby hangs a tail.
FIRST MUSICIAN
　Whereby hangs a tale, sir?
CLOWN
　Marry, sir, by many a wind-instrument that   10
　I know. But masters, here's money for you;
　and the General so likes your music, that he de-
　sires you, for love's sake, to make no more noise
　with it.
FIRST MUSICIAN
　Well, sir, we will not.   15
CLOWN
　If you have any music that may not be
　heard, to't again; but, as they say, to hear music
　the General does not greatly care.
FIRST MUSICIAN
　We have none such, sir.
CLOWN
　Then put up your pipes in your bag, for I'll   20
　away. Go, vanish into air, away!

　　　　　　　　　　　　　　　　　　[Exeunt Musicians.

CASSIO
　Dost thou hear mine honest friend?
CLOWN
　No, I hear not your honest friend; I hear
　you.
CASSIO
　Prithee, keep up thy quillets. There's a poor   25
　piece of gold for thee. If the gentlewoman
　that attends the [General's wife] be stirring,
　tell her there's one Cassio entreats her a little
　favour of speech. Wilt thou do this?
CLOWN
　She is stirring, sir. If she will stir hither, I   30
　shall seem to notify unto her.
CASSIO
　[Do, good my friend.]

　　　　　　　　　　　　　　　　　　　　[Exit Clown.

　　Enter Iago.
　　　　　　In happy time, Iago.

22 **hear** Q: *hear me* F.　　　　27 [**General's wife**] Q: *general* F.
25 **quillets:** quibbles.　　　　　32 [**Do . . . friend**] Q: Om. F.

IAGO

    You have not been a-bed, then?

CASSIO

    Why, no; the day had broke

    Before we parted. I have made bold, Iago,   35

    To send in to your wife. My suit to her

    Is that she will to virtuous Desdemona

    Procure me some access.

IAGO

                  I'll send her to you presently;

    And I'll devise a mean to draw the Moor

    Out of the way, that your converse and business   40

    May be more free.

CASSIO

    I humbly thank you for't. [*Exit Iago.*] I never knew

    A Florentine more kind and honest.

        Enter Emilia.

EMILIA

    Good morrow, good Lieutenant. I am sorry

    For your displeasure; but all will sure be well.   45

    The General and his wife are talking of it,

    And she speaks for you stoutly. The Moor replies

    That he you hurt is of great fame in Cyprus

    And great affinity, and that in wholesome wisdom

    He might not but refuse you; but he protests he loves you,   50

    And needs no other suitor but his likings

    [To take the safest occasion by the front]

    To bring you in again.

CASSIO

                  Yet, I beseech you,

    If you think fit, or that it may be done,

    Give me advantage of some brief discourse   55

    With Desdemon alone.

EMILIA

                Pray you, come in.

    I will bestow you where you shall have time

    To speak your bosom freely.

CASSIO

                I am much bound to you.

                              [*Exeunt.*

      Scene II. [A room in the castle.]

      Enter Othello, Iago, and Gentlemen.

OTHELLO

    These letters give, Iago, to the pilot;

    And by him do my duties to the Senate.

    That done, I will be walking on the works;

    Repair there to me.

IAGO

              Well, my good lord, I'll do't.

---

45 **displeasure:** disgrace.   52 [**To . . . front**] Q: Om. F; **front:**
49 **affinity:** connections.   forelock.
                            ii.3 **works:** fortifications.

OTHELLO
    This fortification, gentlemen, shall we see't?   5
GENTLEMEN
    We'll wait upon your lordship.

                           [Exeunt.

        Scene III. [The garden of the castle.]
        Enter Desdemona, Cassio, and Emilia.
DESDEMONA
    Be thou assur'd, good Cassio, I will do
    All my abilities in thy behalf.
EMILIA
    Good madam, do. I warrant it grieves my husband
    As if the cause were his.
DESDEMONA
    O, that's an honest fellow. Do not doubt, Cassio,   5
    But I will have my lord and you again
    As friendly as you were.
CASSIO
                  Bounteous madam,
    Whatever shall become of Michael Cassio,
    He's never anything but your true servant.
DESDEMONA
    I know 't; I thank you. You do love my lord;   10
    You have known him long; and be you well assur'd
    He shall in strangeness stand no farther off
    Than in a politic distance.
CASSIO
                  Ay, but, lady,
    That policy may either last so long,
    Or feed upon such nice and waterish diet,   15
    Or breed itself so out of circumstances,
    That, I being absent and my place supplied,
    My general will forget my love and service.
DESDEMONA
    Do not doubt that; before Emilia here
    I give thee warrant of thy place. Assure thee,   20
    If I do vow a friendship, I'll perform it
    To the last article. My lord shall never rest;
    I'll watch him tame, and talk him out of patience;
    His bed shall seem a school, his board a shrift;
    I'll intermingle everything he does   25
    With Cassio's suit. Therefore be merry, Cassio;
    For thy solicitor shall rather die
    Than give thy cause away.
        Enter Othello and Iago.
EMILIA
    Madam, here comes my lord.
CASSIO
    Madam, I'll take my leave.   30

      iii.12 **strangeness:** aloofness.   23 **watch him tame:** keep him awake
      19 **doubt:** fear.   till he gives in.
                                   24 **shrift:** confessional.

DESDEMONA
    Why, stay, and hear me speak.
CASSIO
    Madam, not now; I am very ill at ease,
    Unfit for mine own purposes.
DESDEMONA
    Well, do your discretion.

                                        [*Exit Cassio.*

IAGO
    Ha! I like not that.
OTHELLO
                            What dost thou say?   35
IAGO
    Nothing, my lord; or if—I know not what.
OTHELLO
    Was not that Cassio parted from my wife?
IAGO
    Cassio, my lord! No, sure, I cannot think it,
    That he would steal away so guilty-like,
    Seeing your coming.
OTHELLO
                        I do believe 'twas he.   40
DESDEMONA
    How now, my lord!
    I have been talking with a suitor here,
    A man that languishes in your displeasure.
OTHELLO
    Who is't you mean?
DESDEMONA
    Why, your lieutenant, Cassio. Good my lord,   45
    If I have any grace or power to move you,
    His present reconciliation take;
    For if he be not one that truly loves you,
    That errs in ignorance and not in cunning,
    I have no judgement in an honest face.   50
    I prithee, call him back.
OTHELLO
                            Went he hence now?
DESDEMONA
    Yes, faith; so humbled
    That he hath left part of his grief with me
    To suffer with him. Good love, call him back.
OTHELLO
    Not now, sweet Desdemon; some other time.   55
DESDEMONA
    But shall't be shortly?
OTHELLO
                        The sooner, sweet, for you.
DESDEMONA
    Shall't be to-night at supper?
OTHELLO
                        No, not to-night.

DESDEMONA
    To-morrow dinner, then?
OTHELLO
                                    I shall not dine at home;
    I meet the captains at the citadel.
DESDEMONA
    Why, then, to-morrow night; on Tuesday morn;   60
    On Tuesday noon, or night; on Wednesday morn.
    I prithee, name the time, but let it not
    Exceed three days. In faith, he's penitent;
    And yet his trespass, in our common reason—
    Save that, they say, the wars must make example   65
    Out of [their] best—is not almost a fault
    T' incur a private check. When shall he come?
    Tell me, Othello. I wonder in my soul
    What you would ask me that I should deny,
    Or stand so mamm'ring on. What! Michael Cassio,   70
    That came a-wooing with you, and so many a time,
    When I have spoke of you dispraisingly,
    Hath ta'en your part,—to have so much to do
    To bring him in! Trust me, I could do much,—
OTHELLO
    Prithee, no more; let him come when he will,   75
    I will deny thee nothing.
DESDEMONA
                                    Why, this is not a boon.
    'Tis as I should entreat you wear your gloves,
    Or feed on nourishing dishes, or keep you warm,
    Or sue to you to do a peculiar profit
    To your own person. Nay, when I have a suit   80
    Wherein I mean to touch your love indeed,
    It shall be full of poise and difficult weight
    And fearful to be granted.
OTHELLO
                                    I will deny thee nothing;
    Whereon, I do beseech thee, grant me this,
    To leave me but a little to myself.   85
DESDEMONA
    Shall I deny you? No. Farewell, my lord.
OTHELLO
    Farewell, my Desdemona; I'll come to thee straight.
DESDEMONA
    Emilia, come.—Be as your fancies teach you;
    Whate'er you be, I am obedient.
                                    [Exeunt Desdemona and Emilia.
OTHELLO
    Excellent wretch! Perdition catch my soul,   90
    But I do love thee! and when I love thee not,
    Chaos is come again.

66 [**their**] (Rowe): *her* QF; **not**   74 **bring . . . in:** i.e., into your
almost: hardly.   favor.
70 **mamm'ring:** hesitating.   82 **poise:** weight.

IAGO

    My noble lord,—

OTHELLO

                What dost thou say, Iago?

IAGO

    Did Michael Cassio, when [you] woo'd my lady,
    Know of your love?   95

OTHELLO

    He did, from first to last. Why dost thou ask?

IAGO

    But for a satisfaction of my thought;
    No further harm.

OTHELLO

                Why of thy thought, Iago?

IAGO

    I did not think he had been acquainted with her.

OTHELLO

    O, yes; and went between us very oft.   100

IAGO

    Indeed!

OTHELLO

    Indeed! ay, indeed. Discern'st thou aught in that?
    Is he not honest?

IAGO

              Honest, my lord?

OTHELLO

                            Honest! ay, honest.

IAGO

    My lord, for aught I know.

OTHELLO

    What dost thou think?

IAGO

            Think, my lord?

OTHELLO

                      Think, my lord!   105
    [By heaven, he echoes] me,
    As if there were some monster in [his] thought
    Too hideous to be shown.—Thou dost mean something.
    I heard thee say even now, thou lik'st not that,
    When Cassio left my wife. What didst not like?   110
    And when I told thee he was of my counsel
    [In] my whole course of wooing, thou criedst, "Indeed!"
    And didst contract and purse thy brow together,
    As if thou then hadst shut up in thy brain
    Some horrible conceit. If thou dost love me,   115
    Show me thy thought.

IAGO

    My lord, you know I love you.

---

    94 [you] Q: *he* F.   107 [his] Q: *thy* F.
    106 [By . . . echoes] Q: *Alas, thou*   112 [In] Q: *of* F.
    eccho'st F.

OTHELLO
                              I think thou dost;
And, for I know thou'rt full of love and honesty,
And weigh'st thy words before thou giv'st them breath,
Therefore these stops of thine fright me the more;   120
For such things in a false disloyal knave
Are tricks of custom; but in a man that's just
They're close dilations, working from the heart
That passion cannot rule.
IAGO
                              For Michael Cassio,
I dare be sworn I think that he is honest.   125
OTHELLO
I think so too.
IAGO
                    Men should be what they seem;
Or those that be not, would they might seem none!
OTHELLO
Certain, men should be what they seem.
IAGO
Why, then, I think Cassio's an honest man.
OTHELLO
Nay, yet there's more in this.   130
I prithee, speak to me as to thy thinkings,
As thou dost ruminate, and give thy worst of thoughts
The worst of words.
IAGO
                    Good my lord, pardon me.
Though I am bound to every act of duty,
I am not bound to that all slaves are free to.   135
Utter my thoughts? Why, say they are vile and false;
As where's that palace whereinto foul things
Sometimes intrude not? Who has that breast so pure
[But some] uncleanly apprehensions
Keep leets and law-days and in sessions sit   140
With meditations lawful?
OTHELLO
Thou dost conspire against thy friend, Iago,
If thou but think'st him wrong'd and mak'st his ear
A stranger to thy thoughts.
IAGO
                    I do beseech you—
Though I perchance am vicious in my guess,   145
As, I confess, it is my nature's plague
To spy into abuses, and [oft] my jealousy
Shapes faults that are not—that your wisdom yet,
From one that so imperfectly conceits,
Would take no notice, nor build yourself a trouble   150

123 **close dilations:** secret (i.e.,   140 **leets:** court-days.
unconscious) expressions.   147 **[oft]** Q: *of* F; **jealousy:**
139 **[But some]** Q: *Wherein* F.   suspicion.

Out of his scattering and unsure observance.
It were not for your quiet nor your good,
Nor for my manhood, honesty, and wisdom,
To let you know my thoughts.

OTHELLO

What dost thou mean?

IAGO

Good name in man and woman, dear my lord,   155
Is the immediate jewel of their souls.
Who steals my purse steals trash; 'tis something, nothing;
'Twas mine, 'tis his, and has been slave to thousands;
But he that filches from me my good name
Robs me of that which not enriches him,   160
And makes me poor indeed.

OTHELLO

[By heaven,] I'll know thy thoughts.

IAGO

You cannot, if my heart were in your hand;
Nor shall not, whilst 'tis in my custody.

OTHELLO

Ha!

IAGO

O, beware, my lord, of jealousy!   165
It is the green-ey'd monster which doth mock
The meat it feeds on. That cuckold lives in bliss
Who, certain of his fate, loves not his wronger;
But, O, what damned minutes tells he o'er
Who dotes, yet doubts, suspects, yet soundly loves!   170

OTHELLO

O misery!

IAGO

Poor and content is rich, and rich enough;
But riches fineless is as poor as winter
To him that ever fears he shall be poor.
Good heaven, the souls of all my tribe defend   175
From jealousy!

OTHELLO

Why, why is this?
Think'st thou I'd make a life of jealousy,
To follow still the changes of the moon
With fresh suspicions? No! to be once in doubt
Is [once] to be resolv'd. Exchange me for a goat   180
When I shall turn the business of my soul
To such exsufflicate and [blown] surmises,
Matching thy inference. 'Tis not to make me jealous
To say my wife is fair, feeds well, loves company,
Is free of speech, sings, plays, and dances [well];   185
Where virtue is, these are more virtuous.
Nor from mine own weak merits will I draw
The smallest fear or doubt of her revolt;

151 **scattering:** random.   182 **exsufflicate:** inflated; [**blown**]
173 **fineless:** unlimited.   Q: *blowed* F.
180 [**once**] Q: Om. F.   185 [**well**] Q: Om. F.

For she had eyes, and chose me. No, Iago;
I'll see before I doubt; when I doubt, prove;   190
And on the proof, there is no more but this,—
Away at once with love or jealousy!

IAGO
I am glad of this, for now I shall have reason
To show the love and duty that I bear you
With franker spirit; therefore, as I am bound,   195
Receive it from me. I speak not yet of proof.
Look to your wife; observe her well with Cassio;
Wear your eyes thus, not jealous nor secure.
I would not have your free and noble nature,
Out of self-bounty, be abus'd; look to't.   200
I know our country disposition well;
In Venice they do let Heaven see the pranks
They dare not show their husbands. Their best conscience
Is not to leave 't undone, but keep 't unknown.

OTHELLO
Dost thou say so?   205

IAGO
She did deceive her father, marrying you;
And when she seem'd to shake and fear your looks,
She lov'd them most.

OTHELLO
                    And so she did.

IAGO
                                        Why, go to then.
She that, so young, could give out such a seeming,
To seel her father's eyes up close as oak—   210
He thought 'twas witchcraft—but I am much to blame.
I humbly do beseech you of your pardon
For too much loving you.

OTHELLO
                            I am bound to thee for ever.

IAGO
I see this hath a little dash'd your spirits.

OTHELLO
Not a jot, not a jot.

IAGO
                    Trust me! I fear it has.   215
I hope you will consider what is spoke
Comes from [my] love. But I do see you're mov'd.
I am to pray you not to strain my speech
To grosser issues nor to larger reach
Than to suspicion.   220

OTHELLO
I will not.

IAGO
            Should you do so, my lord,
My speech should fall into such vile success

198 **secure:** careless.   217 [**my**] Q: *your* F.
200 **self-bounty:** inherent   222 **success:** consequence.
generosity.

Which my thoughts aim'd not at. Cassio's my worthy friend,—
My lord, I see you're mov'd.

OTHELLO

                              No, not much mov'd.
I do not think but Desdemona's honest.   225

IAGO

Long live she so! and long live you to think so!

OTHELLO

And yet, how nature erring from itself,—

IAGO

Ay, there's the point; as—to be bold with you—
Not to affect many proposed matches
Of her own clime, complexion, and degree,   230
Whereto we see in all things nature tends—
Foh! one may smell in such, a will most rank,
Foul disproportions, thoughts unnatural.
But pardon me; I do not in position
Distinctly speak of her; though I may fear   235
Her will, recoiling to her better judgement,
May fall to match you with her country forms,
And happily repent.

OTHELLO

                              Farewell, farewell!
If more thou dost perceive, let me know more;
Set on thy wife to observe. Leave me, Iago.   240

IAGO [Going.]

My lord, I take my leave.

OTHELLO

Why did I marry? This honest creature doubtless
Sees and knows more, much more, than he unfolds.

IAGO [Returning.]

My lord, I would I might entreat your honour
To scan this thing no farther; leave it to time.   245
Although 'tis fit that Cassio have his place,
For, sure, he fills it up with great ability,
Yet, if you please to [hold] him off a while,
You shall by that perceive him and his means.
Note if your lady strain his entertainment   250
With any strong or vehement importunity;
Much will be seen in that. In the mean time,
Let me be thought too busy in my fears—
As worthy cause I have to fear I am—
And hold her free, I do beseech your honour.   255

OTHELLO

Fear not my government.

IAGO

I once more take my leave.

                                                              [Exit.

225 **honest:** chaste.   250 **strain his entertainment:** press
232, 236 **will:** desire, appetite.   his reappointment.
232 **rank:** foul.   255 **free:** guiltless.
234 **position:** i.e., conviction.   256 **government:** management.
248 [**hold**] Q: Om. F.

OTHELLO
This fellow 's of exceeding honesty,
And knows all [qualities], with a learn'd spirit,
Of human dealings. If I do prove her haggard,   260
Though that her jesses were my dear heartstrings,
I'd whistle her off and let her down the wind
To prey at fortune. Haply, for I am black
And have not those soft parts of conversation
That chamberers have, or for I am declin'd   265
Into the vale of years,—yet that's not much—
She's gone. I am abus'd; and my relief
Must be to loathe her. O curse of marriage,
That we can call these delicate creatures ours,
And not their appetites! I had rather be a toad   270
And live upon the vapour of a dungeon
Than keep a corner in the thing I love
For others' uses. Yet, 'tis the plague [of] great ones;
Prerogativ'd are they less than the base.
'Tis destiny unshunnable, like death.   275
Even then this forked plague is fated to us
When we do quicken. Look where she comes,
        Re-enter Desdemona and Emilia.
If she be false, [O, then heaven mocks] itself!
I'll not believe 't.
DESDEMONA
                        How now, my dear Othello!
Your dinner, and the generous islanders   280
By you invited, do attend your presence.
OTHELLO
I am to blame.
DESDEMONA
                        Why do you speak so faintly?
Are you not well?
OTHELLO
I have a pain upon my forehead here.
DESDEMONA
Why, that's with watching; 'twill away again.   285
Let me but bind it hard, within this hour
It will be well.
OTHELLO
                        Your napkin is too little;
                [He puts the handkerchief from him; and it drops.]
Let it alone. Come, I'll go in with you.
DESDEMONA
I am very sorry that you are not well.
                                [Exeunt [Othello and Desdemona].

259 [**qualities**] Q: *quantities* F.
260 **haggard:** wild.
261 **jesses:** strings by which hawks were held.
264 **parts of conversation:** social graces.
265 **chamberers:** gallants.
273 [**of**] Q: *to* F.

276 **forked plague:** curse of cuckold's horns.
277 **quicken:** begin to live.
278 [**O . . . mocks**] Q: *Heaven mock'd* F.
280 **generous:** noble.
287 **napkin:** handkerchief.
288 **it:** i.e., his forehead.

EMILIA

    I am glad I have found this napkin;   290
    This was her first remembrance from the Moor.
    My wayward husband hath a hundred times
    Woo'd me to steal it; but she so loves the token,
    For he conjur'd her she should ever keep it,
    That she reserves it evermore about her   295
    To kiss and talk to. I'll have the work ta'en out
    And give 't Iago. What he will do with it
    Heaven knows, not I;
    I nothing but to please his fantasy.
        Re-enter Iago.

IAGO

    How now! what do you here alone?   300

EMILIA

    Do not you chide; I have a thing for you.

IAGO

    A thing for me? It is a common thing—

EMILIA

    Ha!

IAGO

    To have a foolish wife.

EMILIA

    O, is that all? What will you give me now   305
    For that same handkerchief?

IAGO

                       What handkerchief?

EMILIA

    What handkerchief!
    Why, that the Moor first gave to Desdemona;
    That which so often you did bid me steal.

IAGO

    Hast stol'n it from her?   310

EMILIA

    No, [faith;] she let it drop by negligence,
    And, to th' advantage, I, being here, took 't up.
    Look, here it is.

IAGO

              A good wench; give it me.

EMILIA

    What will you do with 't, that you have been so earnest
    To have me filch it?

IAGO [*Snatching it.*]

             Why, what is that to you?   315

EMILIA

    If it be not for some purpose of import,
    Give 't me again. Poor lady, she'll run mad
    When she shall lack it.

IAGO

    Be not acknown on't; I have use for it.
    Go, leave me.   320
                                    [*Exit Emilia.*

296 **work . . . out:** pattern copied.   312 **to th' advantage:** opportunely.
311 [**faith**] Q: *but* F.   319 **acknown:** aware.

I will in Cassio's lodging lose this napkin,
And let him find it. Trifles light as air
Are to the jealous confirmations strong
As proofs of holy writ; this may do something.
The Moor already changes with my poison.   325
Dangerous conceits are, in their natures poisons,
Which at the first are scarce found to distaste,
But with a little act upon the blood
Burn like the mines of sulphur. I did say so.
        Re-enter Othello.
Look, where he comes! Not poppy, nor mandragora,   330
Nor all the drowsy syrups of the world
Shall ever medicine thee to that sweet sleep
Which thou ow'dst yesterday.

OTHELLO
                    Ha! ha! false to me?

IAGO
Why, how now, General! no more of that.

OTHELLO
Avaunt! be gone! be gone! thou hast set me on the rack.   335
I swear 'tis better to be much abus'd
Than but to know 't a little.

IAGO
                    How now, my lord!

OTHELLO
What sense had I [of] her stol'n hours of lust?
I saw 't not, thought it not, it harm'd not me.
I slept the next night well, fed well, was free and merry; 340
I found not Cassio's kisses on her lips.
He that is robb'd, not wanting what is stolen,
Let him not know 't, and he's not robb'd at all.

IAGO
I am sorry to hear this.

OTHELLO
I had been happy, if the general camp,   345
Pioners and all, had tasted her sweet body,
So I had nothing known. O, now, for ever
Farewell the tranquil mind! farewell content!
Farewell the plumed troops and the big wars
That make ambition virtue! O, farewell!   350
Farewell the neighing steed and the shrill trump,
The spirit-stirring drum, th' ear-piercing fife,
The royal banner, and all quality,
Pride, pomp, and circumstance of glorious war!
And, O you mortal engines, whose rude throats   355
Th' immortal Jove's dread clamours counterfeit,
Farewell! Othello's occupation 's gone!

IAGO
Is 't possible, my lord?

---

328 **act:** action.
330 **mandragora:** a soporific.
333 **ow'dst:** hadst.

338 **[of]** Q: *in* F.
346 **Pioners:** the lowest rank of
soldiers.

OTHELLO
>   Villain, be sure thou prove my love a whore;
>   Be sure of it. Give me the ocular proof;   360
>   Or, by the worth of mine eternal soul,
>   Thou hadst been better have been born a dog
>   Than answer my wak'd wrath!

IAGO
>   Is 't come to this?

OTHELLO
>   Make me to see 't; or, at the least, so prove it
>   That the probation bear no hinge nor loop   365
>   To hang a doubt on; or woe upon thy life!

IAGO
>   My noble lord,—

OTHELLO
>   If thou dost slander her and torture me,
>   Never pray more; abandon all remorse;
>   On horror's head horrors accumulate;   370
>   Do deeds to make heaven weep, all earth amaz'd;
>   For nothing canst thou to damnation add
>   Greater than that.

IAGO
>   O grace! O Heaven forgive me!
>   Are you a man? Have you a soul or sense?
>   God buy you; take mine office. O wretched fool,   375
>   That lov'st to make thine honesty a vice!
>   O monstrous world! Take note, take note, O world,
>   To be direct and honest is not safe.
>   I thank you for this profit; and from hence
>   I'll love no friend, sith love breeds such offence.   380

OTHELLO
>   Nay, stay. Thou shouldst be honest.

IAGO
>   I should be wise, for honesty 's a fool
>   And loses that it works for.

OTHELLO
>   By the world,
>   I think my wife be honest and think she is not;
>   I think that thou art just and think thou art not.   385
>   I'll have some proof. [Her] name, that was as fresh
>   As Dian's visage, is now begrim'd and black
>   As mine own face. If there be cords, or knives,
>   Poison, or fire, or suffocating streams,
>   I'll not endure it. Would I were satisfied!   390

IAGO
>   I see, [sir], you are eaten up with passion;
>   I do repent me that I put it to you.
>   You would be satisfied?

OTHELLO
>   Would! nay, I will.

375 **buy:** be with.   391 **[sir]** Q: Om. F.
376 **lov'st** F: *livest* Q.   393 **nay** Q: *Nay, and* F.
386 **[Her]** Q: *My* F.

IAGO

And may; but, how? How satisfied, my lord?
Would you, the [supervisor], grossly gape on—   395
Behold her topp'd?

OTHELLO

Death and damnation! O!

IAGO

It were a tedious difficulty, I think,
To bring them to that prospect; [damn] them then,
If ever mortal eyes do see them bolster
More than their own! What then? How then?   400
What shall I say? Where's satisfaction?
It is impossible you should see this,
Were they as prime as goats, as hot as monkeys,
As salt as wolves in pride, and fools as gross
As ignorance made drunk. But yet, I say,   405
If imputation and strong circumstances
Which lead directly to the door of truth
Will give you satisfaction, you might have't.

OTHELLO

Give me a living reason she's disloyal.

IAGO

I do not like the office;   410
But, sith I am ent'red in this cause so far,
Prick'd to't by foolish honesty and love,
I will go on. I lay with Cassio lately;
And, being troubled with a raging tooth,
I could not sleep.   415
There are a kind of men so loose of soul,
That in their sleeps will mutter their affairs;
One of this kind is Cassio.
In sleep I heard him say, "Sweet Desdemona,
Let us be wary, let us hide our loves;"   420
And then, sir, would he gripe and wring my hand,
Cry, "O sweet creature!" then kiss me hard,
As if he pluck'd up kisses by the roots
That grew upon my lips; then lay his leg
Over my thigh, and sigh, and kiss; and then   425
Cry, "Cursed fate that gave thee to the Moor!"

OTHELLO

O monstrous! monstrous!

IAGO

Nay, this was but his dream.

OTHELLO

But this denoted a foregone conclusion.
'Tis a shrewd doubt, though it be but a dream.

IAGO

And this may help to thicken other proofs   430
That do demonstrate thinly.

395 [**supervisor**] Q: *supervision* F.
398 [**damn**] Q: Om. F.
399 **bolster**: lie on a bolster
(together).
403 **prime**: lecherous.

404 (**salt**: lecherous.); **pride**: heat.
428 **foregone conclusion**: earlier act.
429 **shrewd doubt**: strong reason for
suspicion.

OTHELLO

                        I'll tear her all to pieces.

IAGO

    Nay, [but] be wise; yet we see nothing done.
    She may be honest yet. Tell me but this,
    Have you not sometimes seen a handkerchief
    Spotted with strawberries in your wife's hand?   435

OTHELLO

    I gave her such a one; 'twas my first gift.

IAGO

    I know not that; but such a handkerchief—
    I am sure it was your wife's—did I to-day
    See Cassio wipe his beard with.

OTHELLO

                     If it be that,—

IAGO

    If it be that, or any [that] was hers,   440
    It speaks against her with the other proofs.

OTHELLO

    O, that the slave had forty thousand lives!
    One is too poor, too weak for my revenge.
    Now do I see 'tis true. Look here, Iago;
    All my fond love thus do I blow to heaven.   445
    'Tis gone.
    Arise, black vengeance, from the hollow hell!
    Yield up, O love, thy crown and hearted throne
    To tyrannous hate! Swell, bosom, with thy fraught,
    For 'tis of aspics' tongues!

IAGO

                     Yet be content.   450

OTHELLO

    O, blood, blood, blood!

IAGO

    Patience, I say; your mind [perhaps] may change.

OTHELLO

    Never, Iago. Like to the Pontic Sea,
    Whose icy current and compulsive course
    Ne'er [feels] retiring ebb, but keeps due on   455
    To the Propontic and the Hellespont,
    Even so my bloody thoughts, with violent pace,
    Shall ne'er look back, ne'er ebb to humble love,
    Till that a capable and wide revenge
    Swallow them up. Now, by yond marble heaven,   460
    In the due reverence of a sacred vow

                                          [Kneels.]

    I here engage my words.

IAGO

                  Do not rise yet.

432 [but] Q: *yet* F.   452 [perhaps] Q: Om. F.
440 [that] (Malone): *it* QF.   453 Pontic Sea: Black Sea.
449 fraught: burden.   455 [feels] Q_2. *keeps* F.
450 aspics': asps'.   459 capable: comprehensive.

Witness, you ever-burning lights above,
You elements that clip us round about,

                                     [Kneels.   465
Witness that here Iago doth give up
The execution of his wit, hands, heart,
To wrong'd Othello's service! Let him command,
And to obey shall be in me remorse,
What bloody business ever.

                                       [They rise.]

OTHELLO

                            I greet thy love,
Not with vain thanks, but with acceptance bounteous,   470
And will upon the instant put thee to't:
Within these three days let me hear thee say
That Cassio's not alive.

IAGO

My friend is dead; 'tis done at your request.
But let her live.

OTHELLO

Damn her, lewd minx! O, damn her! damn her!   475
Come, go with me apart; I will withdraw
To furnish me with some swift means of death
For the fair devil. Now art thou my lieutenant.

IAGO

I am your own for ever.

                                       [Exeunt.

        Scene IV.   [Before the castle.]
        Enter Desdemona, Emilia, and Clown.

DESDEMONA

Do you know, sirrah, where Lieutenant
Cassio lies?

CLOWN

I dare not say he lies anywhere.

DESDEMONA

Why, man?

CLOWN

He's a soldier, and for me to say a soldier   5
lies, 'tis stabbing.

DESDEMONA

Go to! Where lodges he?

CLOWN

To tell you where he lodges, is to tell you
where I lie.

DESDEMONA

Can anything be made of this?   10

CLOWN

I know not where he lodges, and for me to
devise a lodging and say he lies here or he lies
there, were to lie in mine own throat.

---

464 **clip:** embrace.   468 **remorse:** obligation.
466 **execution:** action.   iv.2 **lies:** lodges.

DESDEMONA

    Can you inquire him out, and be edified by
    report?   15

CLOWN

    I will catechize the world for him; that is,
    make questions, and by them answer.

DESDEMONA

    Seek him, bid him come hither. Tell him I
    have mov'd my lord on his behalf, and hope
    all will be well.   20

CLOWN

    To do this is within the compass of man's
    wit; and therefore I will attempt the doing it.

                                                       [Exit.

DESDEMONA

    Where should I lose the handkerchief, Emilia?

EMILIA

    I know not, madam.

DESDEMONA

    Believe me, I had rather have lost my purse   25
    Full of crusadoes; and, but my noble Moor
    Is true of mind and made of no such baseness
    As jealous creatures are, it were enough
    To put him to ill thinking.

EMILIA

                          Is he not jealous?

DESDEMONA

    Who, he? I think the sun where he was born   30
    Drew all such humours from him.

EMILIA

                          Look, where he comes.

    Enter Othello.

DESDEMONA

    I will not leave him now till Cassio
    Be call'd to him.—How is't with you, my lord?

OTHELLO

    Well, my good lady. [*Aside.*] O, hardness to dissemble!—
    How do you, Desdemona?

DESDEMONA

                      Well, my good lord.   35

OTHELLO

    Give me your hand. This hand is moist, my lady.

DESDEMONA

    It [yet] hath felt no age nor known no sorrow.

OTHELLO

    This argues fruitfulness and liberal heart;
    Hot, hot, and moist. This hand of yours requires
    A sequester from liberty, fasting and prayer,   40
    Much castigation, exercise devout;
    For here's a young and sweating devil here

---

26 **crusadoes:** Portuguese coins   37 [yet] Q: Om. F.
stamped with a cross.   40 **sequester:** separation.

That commonly rebels. 'Tis a good hand,
A frank one.

DESDEMONA
          You may, indeed, say so;
For 'twas that hand that gave away my heart.   45

OTHELLO
A liberal hand. The hearts of old gave hands;
But our new heraldry is hands, not hearts.

DESDEMONA
I cannot speak of this. Come now, your promise.

OTHELLO
What promise, chuck?

DESDEMONA
I have sent to bid Cassio come speak with you.   50

OTHELLO
I have salt and sorry rheum offends me;
Lend me thy handkerchief.

DESDEMONA
          Here, my lord.

OTHELLO
That which I gave you.

DESDEMONA
          I have it not about me.

OTHELLO
Not?

DESDEMONA
      No, indeed, my lord.

OTHELLO
That's a fault. That handkerchief   55
Did an Egyptian to my mother give;
She was a charmer, and could almost read
The thoughts of people. She told her, while she kept it
'Twould make her amiable and subdue my father
Entirely to her love, but if she lost it,   60
Or made a gift of it, my father's eye
Should hold her loathed and his spirits should hunt
After new fancies. She, dying, gave it me
And bid me, when my fate would have me wiv'd,
To give it her. I did so; and take heed on't;   65
Make it a darling like your precious eye.
To lose't or give't away were such perdition
As nothing else could match.

DESDEMONA
          Is't possible?

OTHELLO
'Tis true; there's magic in the web of it.
A sibyl, that had numb'red in the world   70
The sun to course two hundred compasses,
In her prophetic fury sew'd the work;

47 **our new heraldry:** Probably a
topical allusion.
51 **sorry:** distressing.

56 **Egyptian:** gypsy.
57 **charmer:** sorcerer.
59 **amiable:** lovable.

The worms were hallowed that did breed the silk;
And it was dy'd in mummy which the skilful
Conserv'd of maidens' hearts.

DESDEMONA
                              Indeed! is't true?   75

OTHELLO
Most veritable; therefore look to't well.

DESDEMONA
Then would to [God] that I had never seen 't!

OTHELLO
Ha! wherefore?

DESDEMONA
Why do you speak so startingly and rash?

OTHELLO
Is't lost? Is't gone? Speak, is't out o' th' way?   80

DESDEMONA
[Heaven] bless us!

OTHELLO
Say you?

DESDEMONA
It is not lost; but what an if it were?

OTHELLO
How?

DESDEMONA
I say, it is not lost.

OTHELLO
                              Fetch 't, let me see 't.   85

DESDEMONA
Why, so I can, [sir,] but I will not now.
This is a trick to put me from my suit.
Pray you, let Cassio be receiv'd again.

OTHELLO
Fetch me the handkerchief; my mind misgives.

DESDEMONA
Come, come;   90
You'll never meet a more sufficient man.

OTHELLO
The handkerchief!

[DESDEMONA
                              I pray, talk me of Cassio.

OTHELLO
The handkerchief!]

DESDEMONA
                              A man that all his time
Hath founded his good fortunes on your love,
Shar'd dangers with you,—   95

OTHELLO
The handkerchief!

74 **mummy:** embalming fluid.   92–93 [DESDEMONA I . . .
75 **Conserv'd:** prepared.   **handkerchief!**] Q: Om. F.
86 [**sir**] Q: Om. F.

DESDEMONA
    In sooth, you are to blame.
OTHELLO
    ['Zounds!]

                                                                [*Exit.*

EMILIA
    Is not this man jealous?
DESDEMONA
    I ne'er saw this before.   100
    Sure, there's some wonder in this handkerchief;
    I am most unhappy in the loss of it.
EMILIA
    'Tis not a year or two shows us a man.
    They are all but stomachs, and we all but food;
    They eat us hungerly, and when they are full   105
    They belch us.
        Enter Cassio and Iago.
                    Look you, Cassio and my husband!
IAGO
    There is no other way, 'tis she must do't;
    And, lo, the happiness! Go, and importune her.
DESDEMONA
    How now, good Cassio! What's the news with you?
CASSIO
    Madam, my former suit. I do beseech you   110
    That by your virtuous means I may again
    Exist, and be a member of his love
    Whom I with all the office of my heart
    Entirely honour. I would not be delay'd.
    If my offence be of such mortal kind   115
    That nor my service past, nor present sorrows,
    Nor purpos'd merit in futurity
    Can ransom me into his love again,
    But to know so must be my benefit;
    So shall I clothe me in a forc'd content,   120
    And shut myself up in some other course,
    To fortune's alms.
DESDEMONA
                    Alas, thrice-gentle Cassio!
    My advocation is not now in tune.
    My lord is not my lord; nor should I know him
    Were he in favour as in humour alter'd.   125
    So help me every spirit sanctified
    As I have spoken for you all my best
    And stood within the blank of his displeasure
    For my free speech! You must a while be patient.
    What I can do I will; and more I will   130
    Than for myself I dare. Let that suffice you.

98 ['Zounds!] Q: *Away* F.   125 favour: appearance.
108 happiness: luck.   128 blank: target; strictly, the white
111 virtuous: effective.   spot in the center.

IAGO

    Is my lord angry?

EMILIA

                  He went hence but now,
And certainly in strange unquietness.

IAGO

    Can he be angry? I have seen the cannon
When it hath blown his ranks into the air,   135
And, like the devil, from his very arm
Puff'd his own brother:—and is he angry?
Something of moment then. I will go meet him.
There's matter in't indeed, if he be angry.

                              [Exit Iago.

DESDEMONA

    I prithee, do so. Something, sure, of state,   140
Either from Venice, or some unhatch'd practice
Made demonstrable here in Cyprus to him,
Hath puddled his clear spirit; and in such cases
Men's natures wrangle with inferior things,
Though great ones are their object. 'Tis even so;   145
For let our finger ache, and it indues
Our other, healthful members even to a sense
Of pain. Nay, we must think men are not gods,
Nor of them look for such observancy
As fits the bridal. Beshrew me much, Emilia,   150
I was, unhandsome warrior as I am,
Arraigning his unkindness with my soul;
But now I find I had suborn'd the witness,
And he's indicted falsely.

EMILIA

    Pray Heaven it be state-matters, as you think,   155
And no conception nor no jealous toy
Concerning you.

DESDEMONA

    Alas the day! I never gave him cause.

EMILIA

    But jealous souls will not be answer'd so;
They are not ever jealous for the cause,   160
But jealous for they're jealous. It is a monster
Begot upon itself, born on itself.

DESDEMONA

    Heaven keep the monster from Othello's mind!

EMILIA

    Lady, amen.

DESDEMONA

    I will go seek him. Cassio, walk hereabout;   165
If I do find him fit, I'll move your suit
And seek to effect it to my uttermost.

CASSIO

    I humbly thank your ladyship.

                     [Exeunt [Desdemona and Emilia].

    141 **practice:** plot.

Enter Bianca.

BIANCA
    Save you, friend Cassio!
CASSIO
                    What make you from home?
    How is it with you, my most fair Bianca?   170
    Indeed, sweet love, I was coming to your house.
BIANCA
    And I was going to your lodging, Cassio.
    What, keep a week away? seven days and nights?
    Eightscore eight hours? and lovers' absent hours,
    More tedious than the dial eightscore times?   175
    O weary reck'ning!
CASSIO
                Pardon me, Bianca.
    I have this while with leaden thoughts been press'd;
    But I shall, in a more continuate time,
    Strike off this score of absence. Sweet Bianca,
                  [*Giving her Desdemona's handkerchief.*]
    Take me this work out.
BIANCA
                 O Cassio, whence came this?   180
    This is some token from a newer friend;
    To the felt absence now I feel a cause.
    Is't come to this? Well, well.
CASSIO
                Go to, woman!
    Throw your vile guesses in the devils' teeth,
    From whence you have them. You are jealous now   185
    That this is from some mistress, some remembrance.
    No, in good troth, Bianca.
BIANCA
             Why, whose is it?
CASSIO
    I know not, [sweet]; I found it in my chamber.
    I like the work well; ere it be demanded—
    As like enough it will—I'd have it copied.   190
    Take it, and do't; and leave me for this time.
BIANCA
    Leave you! Wherefore?
CASSIO
    I do attend here on the General;
    And think it no addition, nor my wish,
    To have him see me woman'd.
BIANCA
              Why, I pray you?   195
CASSIO
    Not that I love you not.
BIANCA
             But that you do not love me.

178 **continuate:** uninterrupted.   194 **addition:** credit.
188 [**sweet**] Q: *neither* F.

I pray you, bring me on the way a little,
And say if I shall see you soon at night.

CASSIO

'Tis but a little way that I can bring you,
For I attend here; but I'll see you soon.   200

BIANCA

'Tis very good; I must be circumstanc'd.

[*Exeunt.*

Act IV

Scene I. [Cyprus. Before the castle.]
Enter Othello and Iago.

IAGO

Will you think so?

OTHELLO

                Think so, Iago!

IAGO

                           What,
To kiss in private?

OTHELLO

                An unauthoriz'd kiss.

IAGO

Or to be naked with her friend in bed
An hour or more, not meaning any harm?

OTHELLO

Naked in bed, Iago, and not mean harm!   5
It is hypocrisy against the devil.
They that mean virtuously, and yet do so,
The devil their virtue tempts, and they tempt heaven.

IAGO

If they do nothing, 'tis a venial slip;
But if I give my wife a handkerchief,—   10

OTHELLO

What then?

IAGO

Why, then, 'tis hers, my lord; and, being hers,
She may, I think, bestow 't on any man.

OTHELLO

She is protectress of her honour too;
May she give that?   15

IAGO

Her honour is an essence that's not seen;
They have it very oft that have it not:
But, for the handkerchief,—

OTHELLO

By heaven, I would most gladly have forgot it.
Thou said'st—O, it comes o'er my memory,   20
As doth the raven o'er the infectious house,
Boding to all—he had my handkerchief.

201 **circumstanc'd:** reconciled.

IAGO

Ay, what of that?

OTHELLO

That's not so good now.

IAGO

What
If I had said I had seen him do you wrong?
Or heard him say,—as knaves be such abroad,   25
Who having, by their own importunate suit,
Or voluntary dotage of some mistress,
Convinced or suppli'd them, cannot choose
But they must blab—

OTHELLO

Hath he said anything?

IAGO

He hath, my lord; but be you well assur'd,   30
No more than he'll unswear.

OTHELLO

What hath he said?

IAGO

Why, that he did—I know not what he did.

OTHELLO

What? what?

IAGO

Lie—

OTHELLO

With her?

IAGO

With her, on her; what you will.

OTHELLO

Lie with her! lie on her! We say lie on her,   35
when they belie her. Lie with her! ['Zounds,]
that's fulsome!—Handkerchief—confessions—
handkerchief!—To confess, and be hang'd for his
labour;—first to be hang'd, and then to confess.—
I tremble at it. Nature would not invest herself
in such shadowing passion without some in-   40
struction. It is not words that shakes me thus.
Pish! Noses, ears, and lips.—Is't possible?—
Confess—handkerchief!—O devil!

[*Falls in a trance.*

IAGO

Work on,   45
My medicine, work! Thus credulous fools are caught;
And many worthy and chaste dames even thus,
All guiltless, meet reproach.—What, ho! my lord!
My lord, I say! Othello!
    Enter Cassio.

How now, Cassio!

IV.i.39–41 **invest . . . instruction:**
i.e., create such imaginings unless to
teach me.

CASSIO

    What's the matter? 50

IAGO

    My lord is fall'n into an epilepsy.
    This is his second fit; he had one yesterday.

CASSIO

    Rub him about the temples.

IAGO

                  [No, forbear;]
    The lethargy must have his quiet course;
    If not, he foams at mouth and by and by 55
    Breaks out to savage madness. Look, he stirs.
    Do you withdraw yourself a little while;
    He will recover straight. When he is gone,
    I would on great occasion speak with you.

                                              [*Exit Cassio.*

    How is it, General? Have you not hurt your head? 60

OTHELLO

    Dost thou mock me?

IAGO

                I mock you not, by heaven.
    Would you would bear your fortune like a man!

OTHELLO

    A horned man's a monster and a beast.

IAGO

    There's many a beast then in a populous city,
    And many a civil monster. 65

OTHELLO

    Did he confess it?

IAGO

             Good sir, be a man;
    Think every bearded fellow that's but yok'd
    May draw with you. There's millions now alive
    That nightly lie in those unproper beds
    Which they dare swear peculiar; your case is better. 70
    O, 'tis the spite of hell, the fiend's arch-mock,
    To lip a wanton in a secure couch,
    And to suppose her chaste! No, let me know;
    And knowing what I am, I know what she shall be.

OTHELLO

    O, thou art wise; 'tis certain.

IAGO

                Stand you a while apart; 75
    Confine yourself but in a patient list.
    Whilst you were here o'erwhelmed with your grief—
    A passion most [unsuiting] such a man—
    Cassio came hither. I shifted him away,

53 **[No, forbear;]** Q: Om. F.
55 **by and by:** straightway.
65 **civil:** civilized.
69 **unproper:** not exclusively their own.
70 **peculiar:** their own.

72 **secure:** supposed safe from others.
76 **a patient list:** the bounds of patience.
78 **[unsuiting]** Q: *resulting* F.

And laid good 'scuse upon your ecstasy;   80
Bade him anon return and here speak with me,
The which he promis'd. Do but encave yourself,
And mark the fleers, the gibes, and notable scorns
That dwell in every region of his face;
For I will make him tell the tale anew,   85
Where, how, how oft, how long ago, and when
He hath, and is again to cope your wife.
I say, but mark his gesture. Marry, patience;
Or I shall say you're all in all in spleen,
And nothing of a man.

OTHELLO
                              Dost thou hear, Iago?   90
I will be found most cunning in my patience;
But—dost thou hear?—most bloody.

IAGO
                              That's not amiss;
But yet keep time in all. Will you withdraw?

                                        [*Othello retires.*]

Now will I question Cassio of Bianca,
A housewife that by selling her desires   95
Buys herself bread and clothes. It is a creature
That dotes on Cassio, as 'tis the strumpet's plague
To beguile many and be beguil'd by one.
He, when he hears of her, cannot [refrain]
From the excess of laughter. Here he comes.   100
    Re-enter Cassio.
As he shall smile, Othello shall go mad;
And his unbookish jealousy must [conster]
Poor Cassio's smiles, gestures, and light behaviours
Quite in the wrong. How do you, Lieutenant?

CASSIO
The worser that you give me the addition   105
Whose want even kills me.

IAGO
Ply Desdemona well, and you are sure on't.
[*Speaking lower.*] Now, if this suit lay in Bianca's [power].
How quickly should you speed!

CASSIO
                              Alas, poor caitiff!

OTHELLO
Look how he laughs already!   110

IAGO
I never knew woman love man so.

CASSIO
Alas, poor rogue! I think, indeed, she loves
me.

OTHELLO
Now he denies it faintly, and laughs it out.

80 **ecstasy:** trance.
89 **spleen:** anger, passion.
99 [**refrain**] Q: *restraine* F.

102 [**conster**] Q: construe. *conserve* F.
108 [**power**] Q: *dowre* F.

IAGO

Do you hear, Cassio?   115

OTHELLO

Now he importunes him
To tell it o'er. Go to; well said, well said.

IAGO

She gives it out that you shall marry her.
Do you intend it?

CASSIO

Ha, ha, ha!   120

OTHELLO

Do ye triumph, Roman? Do you triumph?

CASSIO

I marry [her]!! What? a customer! Prithee,
bear some charity to my wit; do not think it
so unwholesome. Ha, ha, ha!   125

OTHELLO

So, so so, so; they laugh that win.

IAGO

Why, the cry goes that you [shall] marry her.

CASSIO

Prithee, say true.

IAGO

I am a very villain else.

OTHELLO

Have you scor'd me? Well.   130

CASSIO

This is the monkey's own giving out. She is
persuaded I will marry her, out of her own love
and flattery, not out of my promise.

OTHELLO

Iago [beckons] me; now he begins the
story.   135

CASSIO

She was here even now; she haunts me in
every place. I was the other day talking on the
sea-bank with certain Venetians; and thither
comes the bauble, and, falls me thus about
my neck—   140

OTHELLO

Crying, "O dear Cassio!" as it were; his
gesture imports it.

CASSIO

So hangs, and lolls, and weeps upon me;
so shakes and pulls me. Ha, ha, ha!

OTHELLO

Now he tells how she pluck'd him to my   145
chamber. Oh, I see that nose of yours, but not
that dog I shall throw it to.

---

122 [her] Q: Om. F; **customer:**   130 **scor'd:** branded.
harlot.   134 [**beckons**] Q: *becomes* F.
127 [**shall**] Q: Om. F.

CASSIO
  Well, I must leave her company.
IAGO
  Before me! look, where she comes.
      Enter Bianca.
CASSIO
  'Tis such another fitchew! Marry, a perfum'd   150
  one.—What do you mean by this haunting
  of me?
BIANCA
  Let the devil and his dam haunt you! What
  did you mean by that same handkerchief you
  gave me even now? I was a fine fool to take it.   155
  I must take out the work?—A likely piece of work,
  that you should find it in your chamber, and know
  not who left it there! This is some minx's token,
  and I must take out the work? There; give it
  your hobby-horse. Wheresoever you had it, I'll   160
  take out no work on't.
CASSIO
  How now, my sweet Bianca! how now!
  how now!
OTHELLO
  By heaven, that should be my handker-
  chief!   165
BIANCA
  If you'll come to supper to-night, you may;
  if you will not, come when you are next
  prepar'd for.
                                                              [*Exit.*
IAGO
  After her, after her.   170
CASSIO
  [Faith,] I must; she'll rail in the streets else.
IAGO
  Will you sup there?
CASSIO
  Yes, I intend so.
IAGO
  Well, I may chance to see you; for I would
  very fain speak with you.   175
CASSIO
  Prithee, come; will you?
IAGO
  Go to; say no more.
                                                        [*Exit Cassio.*
OTHELLO [*Advancing.*]
  How shall I murder him, Iago?
IAGO
  Did you perceive how he laugh'd at his   180
  vice?

      150 **fitchew:** polecat.

OTHELLO
O Iago!

IAGO
And did you see the handkerchief?

OTHELLO
Was that mine?

IAGO
Yours, by this hand. And to see how he   185
prizes the foolish woman your wife! She gave
it him, and he hath given it his whore.

OTHELLO
I would have him nine years a-killing. A
fine woman! a fair woman! a sweet woman!

IAGO
Nay, you must forget that.   190

OTHELLO
Ay, let her rot, and perish, and be damn'd
to-night; for she shall not live. No, my heart is
turn'd to stone; I strike it, and it hurts my hand.
O, the world hath not a sweeter creature! She
might lie by an emperor's side and command   195
him tasks.

IAGO
Nay, that's not your way.

OTHELLO
Hang her! I do but say what she is. So deli-
cate with her needle! an admirable musician!
O! she will sing the savageness out of a bear.   200
Of so high and plenteous wit and invention!

IAGO
She's the worse for all this.

OTHELLO
O, a thousand thousand times. And then,
of so gentle a condition!

IAGO
Ay, too gentle.   205

OTHELLO
Nay, that's certain. But yet the pity of it,
Iago! O Iago, the pity of it, Iago!

IAGO
If you are so fond over her iniquity, give
her patent to offend; for if it touch not you, it
comes near nobody.   210

OTHELLO
I will chop her into messes. Cuckold me!

IAGO
O, 'tis foul in her.

OTHELLO
With mine officer!

IAGO
That's fouler.   215

211 **messes:** portions of food.

OTHELLO
Get me some poison, Iago; this night. I'll
not expostulate with her, lest her body and
beauty unprovide my mind again. This
night, Iago.

IAGO
Do it not with poison; strangle her in her   220
bed, even the bed she hath contaminated.

OTHELLO
Good, good; the justice of it pleases; very
good.

IAGO
And for Cassio, let me be his undertaker.
You shall hear more by midnight.   225

                                          [A trumpet.

        Enter Lodovico, Desdemona, and Attendants.

OTHELLO
Excellent good. What trumpet is that same?

IAGO
I warrant, something from Venice. 'Tis
Lodovico, this, comes from the Duke. See,
your wife's with him.

LODOVICO
Save you, worthy General!

OTHELLO
                          With all my heart, sir.

LODOVICO
The Duke and Senators of Venice greet you.   230

                              [Gives him a letter.]

OTHELLO
I kiss the instrument of their pleasures.

                          [Opens the letter, and reads.]

DESDEMONA
And what's the news, good cousin Lodovico?

IAGO
I am very glad to see you, signior;
Welcome to Cyprus.

LODOVICO
I thank you. How does Lieutenant Cassio?   235

IAGO
Lives, sir.

DESDEMONA
Cousin, there's fall'n between him and my lord
An unkind breach; but you shall make all well.

OTHELLO
Are you sure of that?

DESDEMONA
My lord?

OTHELLO [Reads.]
"This fail you not to do, as you will."—   240

        224 undertaker: dispatcher.

LODOVICO
He did not call; he's busy in the paper.
Is there division 'twixt my lord and Cassio?
DESDEMONA
A most unhappy one. I would do much
T' atone them, for the love I bear to Cassio.
OTHELLO
Fire and brimstone!
DESDEMONA
                    My lord?
OTHELLO
                                    Are you wise?   245
DESDEMONA
What, is he angry?
LODOVICO
                            May be the letter mov'd him;
For, as I think, they do command him home,
Deputing Cassio in his government.
DESDEMONA
Trust me, I am glad on't.
OTHELLO
                                Indeed!
DESDEMONA
                                    My lord?
OTHELLO
I am glad to see you mad.
DESDEMONA
                            Why, sweet Othello,—   250
OTHELLO [Striking her.]
Devil!
DESDEMONA
I have not deserv'd this.
LODOVICO
My lord, this would not be believ'd in Venice
Though I should swear I saw 't. 'Tis very much.
Make her amends: she weeps.
OTHELLO
                                    O devil, devil!   255
If that the earth could teem with woman's tears,
Each drop she falls would prove a crocodile.
Out of my sight!
DESDEMONA
                    I will not stay to offend you.
                                    [Going.]
LODOVICO
Truly, [an] obedient lady:
I do beseech your lordship, call her back.   260
OTHELLO
Mistress!
DESDEMONA
        My lord?

244 **atone:** reconcile.   259 [**an**] Q: Om. F.
256 **teem:** breed.

OTHELLO
                    What would you with her, sir?
LODOVICO
    Who, I, my lord?
OTHELLO
    Ay; you did wish that I would make her turn.
    Sir, she can turn, and turn, and yet go on,
    And turn again; and she can weep, sir, weep;   265
    And she's obedient, as you say, obedient,
    Very obedient. Proceed you in your tears.
    Concerning this, sir,—O well-painted passion!—
    I am commanded home.—Get you away;
    I'll send for you anon.—Sir, I obey the mandate,   270
    And will return to Venice.—Hence, avaunt!—
                                            [Exit Desdemona.]
    Cassio shall have my place. And, sir, to-night
    I do entreat that we may sup together.
    You are welcome, sir, to Cyprus.—Goats and monkeys!
                                                        [Exit.
LODOVICO
    Is this the noble Moor whom our full Senate   275
    Call all in all sufficient? Is this the nature
    Whom passion could not shake? whose solid virtue
    The shot of accident nor dart of chance
    Could neither graze nor pierce?
IAGO
                            He is much chang'd.
LODOVICO
    Are his wits safe? Is he not light of brain?   280
IAGO
    He's that he is; I may not breathe my censure
    What he might be. If what he might he is not,
    I would to heaven he were!
LODOVICO
                        What, strike his wife!
IAGO
    Faith, that was not so well; yet would I knew
    That stroke would prove the worst!
LODOVICO
                                    Is it his use?   285
    Or did the letters work upon his blood
    And new-create [this] fault?
IAGO
                        Alas, alas!
    It is not honesty in me to speak
    What I have seen and known. You shall observe him,
    And his own courses will denote him so   290
    That I may save my speech. Do but go after,
    And mark how he continues.
LODOVICO
    I am sorry that I am deceiv'd in him.
                                                    [Exeunt.

        287 [this] Q: his F.

Scene II. [A room in the castle.]
Enter Othello and Emilia.

OTHELLO
You have seen nothing then?

EMILIA
Nor ever heard, nor ever did suspect.

OTHELLO
Yes, you have seen Cassio and she together.

EMILIA
But then I saw no harm, and then I heard
Each syllable that breath made up between them.   5

OTHELLO
What, did they never whisper?

EMILIA
                              Never, my lord.

OTHELLO
Nor send you out o' th' way?

EMILIA
Never.

OTHELLO
To fetch her fan, her gloves, her mask, nor nothing?

EMILIA
Never, my lord.   10

OTHELLO
That's strange.

EMILIA
I durst, my lord, to wager she is honest,
Lay down my soul at stake. If you think other,
Remove your thought; it doth abuse your bosom.
If any wretch have put this in your head,   15
Let Heaven requite it with the serpent's curse!
For, if she be not honest, chaste, and true,
There's no man happy; the purest of their wives
Is foul as slander.

OTHELLO
                    Bid her come hither; go.

                                            [*Exit Emilia.*

She says enough; yet she's a simple bawd   20
That cannot say as much. This is a subtle whore,
A closet lock and key of villanous secrets;
And yet she'll kneel and pray; I have seen her do't.
    Enter Desdemona with Emilia.

DESDEMONA
My lord, what is your will?

OTHELLO
                            Pray, chuck, come hither.

DESDEMONA
What is your pleasure?

OTHELLO
                       Let me see your eyes;   25
Look in my face.

ii. 24 **Pray** Q: *Pray you* F.

DESDEMONA
                    What horrible fancy's this?
OTHELLO [*To Emilia.*]
    Some of your function, mistress;
    Leave procreants alone and shut the door;
    Cough, or cry "hem," if anybody come.
    Your mystery, your mystery; nay, dispatch.   30
                                        [*Exit Emilia.*

DESDEMONA
    Upon my knee, what doth your speech import?
    I understand a fury in your words,
    [But not the words.]
OTHELLO
    Why, what art thou?
DESDEMONA
                    Your wife, my lord; your true
    And loyal wife.
OTHELLO
                    Come, swear it, damn thyself,   35
    Lest, being like one of heaven, the devils themselves
    Should fear to seize thee; therefore be double damn'd,
    Swear thou art honest.
DESDEMONA
                    Heaven doth truly know it.
OTHELLO
    Heaven truly knows that thou art false as hell.
DESDEMONA
    To whom, my lord? With whom? How am I false?   40
OTHELLO
    Ah, Desdemon! Away! away! away!
DESDEMONA
    Alas the heavy day! Why do you weep?
    Am I the motive of these tears, my lord?
    If haply you my father do suspect
    An instrument of this your calling back,   45
    Lay not your blame on me. If you have lost him,
    [Why,] I have lost him too.
OTHELLO
                    Had it pleas'd Heaven
    To try me with affliction; had they rain'd
    All kinds of sores and shames on my bare head,
    Steep'd me in poverty to the very lips,   50
    Given to captivity me and my utmost hopes,
    I should have found in some place of my soul
    A drop of patience; but, alas, to make me
    The fixed figure for the time of scorn
    To point his slow and moving finger at!   55
    Yet could I bear that too, well, very well;
    But there, where I have garner'd up my heart,

30 **mystery**: trade.   54 **time of scorn**: scorn of the age.
33 [**But . . . words.**] Q: Om. F.   55 **slow and moving**: slowly moving.
47 [**Why**] Q: Om. F.   Q reads *slow unmoving*.

Where either I must live or bear no life;
The fountain from the which my current runs
Or else dries up; to be discarded thence!   60
Or keep it as a cistern for foul toads
To knot and gender in! Turn thy complexion there,
Patience, thou young and rose-lipp'd cherubin,
[Ay, there] look grim as hell!

DESDEMONA
I hope my noble lord esteems me honest.   65

OTHELLO
O, ay; as summer flies are in the shambles,
That quicken even with blowing. O thou weed,
Who art so lovely fair and smell'st so sweet
That the sense aches at thee, would thou hadst ne'er been born!

DESDEMONA
Alas, what ignorant sin have I committed?   70

OTHELLO
Was this fair paper, this most goodly book,
Made to write "whore" upon? What committed!
Committed! O thou public commoner!
I should make very forges of my cheeks,
That would to cinders burn up modesty,   75
Did I but speak thy deeds. What committed!
Heaven stops the nose at it, and the moon winks;
The bawdy wind, that kisses all it meets,
Is hush'd within the hollow mine of earth
And will not hear it. What committed!   80
[Impudent strumpet!]

DESDEMONA
                          By heaven, you do me wrong.

OTHELLO
Are not you a strumpet?

DESDEMONA
                          No, as I am a Christian.
If to preserve this vessel for my lord
From any other foul unlawful touch
Be not to be a strumpet, I am none.   85

OTHELLO
What, not a whore?

DESDEMONA
                          No, as I shall be sav'd.

OTHELLO
Is't possible?

DESDEMONA
O, Heaven forgive us!

OTHELLO
                          I cry you mercy, then.

62 **Turn thy complexion:** change
thy color.
64 [**Ay, there**] (Theobald): *I here* Ff
Qq.
67 **quicken . . . blowing:** come to
life as soon as impregnated.

73 **commoner:** harlot.
77 **winks:** shuts her eyes.
81 [**Impudent strumpet!**] Q: Om. F.

I took you for that cunning whore of Venice
That married with Othello. [*Raising his voice.*]—You, mistress,   90
    Re-enter Emilia.
That have the office opposite to Saint Peter,
And keeps the gate of hell! You, you, ay, you!
We have done our course; there's money for your pains.
I pray you, turn the key and keep our counsel.

                                               [*Exit.*

EMILIA
Alas, what does this gentleman conceive?   95
How do you, madam? How do you, my good lady?
DESDEMONA
Faith, half asleep.
EMILIA
Good madam, what's the matter with my lord?
DESDEMONA
With who?
EMILIA
Why, with my lord, madam.   100
DESDEMONA
Who is thy lord?
EMILIA
                He that is yours, sweet lady.
DESDEMONA
I have none. Do not talk to me, Emilia;
I cannot weep, nor answers have I none
But what should go by water. Prithee, tonight
Lay on my bed my wedding sheets, remember;   105
And call thy husband hither.
EMILIA
                Here's a change indeed!
                                             [*Exit.*

DESDEMONA
'Tis meet I should be us'd so, very meet.
How have I been behav'd, that he might stick
The small'st opinion on my least misuse?
    Re-enter Emilia with Iago.
IAGO
What is your pleasure, madam? How is't with you?   110
DESDEMONA
I cannot tell. Those that do teach young babes
Do it with gentle means and easy tasks.
He might have chid me so; for, in good faith,
I am a child to chiding.
IAGO
                What's the matter, lady?
EMILIA
Alas, Iago, my lord hath so bewhor'd her,   115
Thrown such despite and heavy terms upon her,
That true hearts cannot bear it.

---

104 **go by water:** be rendered by tears.

109 **opinion:** censure; **misuse:** misconduct.

DESDEMONA
Am I that name, Iago?
IAGO
What name, fair lady?
DESDEMONA
Such as she said my lord did say I was.
EMILIA
He call'd her whore. A beggar in his drink   120
Could not have laid such terms upon his callet.
IAGO
Why did he so?
DESDEMONA
I do not know; I am sure I am none such.
IAGO
Do not weep, do not weep. Alas the day!
EMILIA
Hath she forsook so many noble matches,   125
Her father and her country and her friends,
To be call'd whore? Would it not make one weep?
DESDEMONA
It is my wretched fortune.
IAGO
Beshrew him for't!
How comes this trick upon him?
DESDEMONA
Nay, Heaven doth know.
EMILIA
I will be hang'd if some eternal villain,   130
Some busy and insinuating rogue,
Some cogging, cozening slave, to get some office,
Have not devis'd this slander. I'll be hang'd else.
IAGO
Fie, there is no such man; it is impossible.
DESDEMONA
If any such there be, Heaven pardon him!   135
EMILIA
A halter pardon him! and hell gnaw his bones!
Why should he call her whore? Who keeps her company?
What place? what time? what form? what likelihood?
The Moor's abus'd by some most villanous knave,
Some base notorious knave, some scurvy fellow.   140
O heavens, that such companions thou'dst unfold,
And put in every honest hand a whip
To lash the rascals naked through the world
Even from the east to th' west!
IAGO
Speak within door.
EMILIA
O, fie upon them! Some such squire he was   145

121 **callet:** whore.   141 **unfold:** expose.
132 **cogging:** lying; **cozening:**
cheating

That turn'd your wit the seamy side without,
And made you to suspect me with the Moor.

IAGO

You are a fool; go to.

DESDEMONA

                    Alas, Iago,
What shall I do to win my lord again?
Good friend, go to him; for, by this light of heaven,   150
I know not how I lost him. Here I kneel:
If e'er my will did trespass 'gainst his love,
Either in discourse of thought or actual deed,
Or that mine eyes, mine ears, or any sense
Delighted them [in] any other form;   155
Or that I do not yet, and ever did,
And ever will—though he do shake me off
To beggarly divorcement—love him dearly,
Comfort forswear me! Unkindness may do much;
And his unkindness may defeat my life,   160
But never taint my love. I cannot say "whore."
It does abhor me now I speak the word:
To do the act that might the addition earn
Not the world's mass of vanity could make me.

IAGO

I pray you, be content; 'tis but his humour.   165
The business of the state does him offence,
[And he does chide with you.]

DESDEMONA

If 'twere no other,—

IAGO

                    It is but so, I warrant.   [Trumpets within.]
Hark, how these instruments summon to supper!
The messengers of Venice stay the meat.   170
Go in, and weep not; all things shall be well.
                    [Exeunt Desdemona and Emilia.

    Enter Roderigo.
How now, Roderigo!

RODERIGO

I do not find that thou deal'st justly with
me.

IAGO

What in the contrary?   175

RODERIGO

Every day thou daff'st me with some device,
Iago; and rather, as it seems to me now, keep'st
from me all conveniency than suppliest me with
the least advantage of hope. I will indeed no
longer endure it, nor am I yet persuaded to   180
put up in peace what already I have foolishly
suff'red.

---

153 **discourse:** course.   167 [**And . . . you.**] Q: Om. F.
155 [**in**] Q₂: *or* F.   170 **stay the meat:** wait to dine.
160 **defeat:** destroy.   176 **daff'st me:** puttest me off.

IAGO

Will you hear me, Roderigo?

RODERIGO

I have heard too much, and your words and
performances are no kin together.   185

IAGO

You charge me most unjustly.

RODERIGO

With nought but truth. I have wasted myself
out of my means. The jewels you have had
from me to deliver Desdemona would half have
corrupted a votarist. You have told me she hath   190
receiv'd them and return'd me expectations and
comforts of sudden respect and acquaintance, but
I find none.

IAGO

Well; go to; very well.

RODERIGO

Very well! go to! I cannot go to, man; nor 'tis   195
not very well. Nay, I think it is scurvy, and
begin to find myself fopp'd in it.

IAGO

Very well.

RODERIGO

I tell you 'tis not very well. I will make myself known to Desdemona. If she will return   200
me my jewels, I will give over my suit and
repent my unlawful solicitation; if not, assure
yourself I will seek satisfaction of you.

IAGO

You have said now.

RODERIGO

Ay, and said nothing but what I protest   205
intendment of doing.

IAGO

Why, now I see there's mettle in thee, and
even from this instant do build on thee a better
opinion than ever before. Give me thy hand,
Roderigo. Thou hast taken against me a most   210
just exception; but yet, I protest, I have dealt
most directly in thy affair.

RODERIGO

It hath not appear'd.

IAGO

I grant indeed it hath not appear'd, and
your suspicion is not without wit and judgement.   215
But, Roderigo, if thou hast that in thee indeed,
which I have greater reason to believe now than
ever, I mean purpose, courage, and valour, this
night show it. If thou the next night following   220

190 **votarist:** nun.   197 **fopp'd:** duped.
192 **sudden respect:** speedy notice.

enjoy not Desdemona, take me from this world
with treachery and devise engines for my life.

RODERIGO
Well, what is it? Is it within reason and
compass?

IAGO
Sir, there is especial commission come from
Venice to depute Cassio in Othello's place.   225

RODERIGO
Is that true? Why, then Othello and Desdemona return again to Venice.

IAGO
O, no; he goes into Mauritania and taketh
away with him the fair Desdemona, unless his   230
abode be ling'red here by some accident; wherein
none can be so determinate as the removing of
Cassio.

RODERIGO
How do you mean, removing him?

IAGO
Why, by making him uncapable of Othello's   235
place; knocking out his brains.

RODERIGO
And that you would have me to do?

IAGO
Ay, if you dare do yourself a profit and a
right. He sups to-night with a harlotry, and
thither will I go to him; he knows not yet of his   240
honourable fortune. If you will watch his going
thence, which I will fashion to fall out between
twelve and one, you may take him at your pleasure.
I will be near to second your attempt, and he shall
fall between us. Come, stand not amaz'd at it,   245
but go along with me; I will show you such a neces-
sity in his death that you shall think yourself
bound to put it on him. It is now high supper-
time, and the night grows to waste. About it.   250

RODERIGO
I will hear further reason for this.

IAGO
And you shall be satisfi'd.

[Exeunt.

Scene III. [Another room in the castle.]
Enter Othello, Lodovico, Desdemona, Emilia, and Attendants.

LODOVICO
I do beseech you, sir, trouble yourself no further.

OTHELLO
O, pardon me, 'twill do me good to walk.

LODOVICO
Madam, good-night; I humbly thank your ladyship.

222 **engines:** plots.

DESDEMONA
Your honour is most welcome.
OTHELLO
                              Will you walk, sir?

O,—Desdemona,—   5
DESDEMONA
My lord?
OTHELLO
Get you to bed on th' instant; I will be return'd
forthwith. Dismiss your attendant there. Look 't
be done.
DESDEMONA
I will, my lord.   10
                    [Exeunt [Othello, Lodovico, and Attendants].
EMILIA
How goes it now? He looks gentler than he did.
DESDEMONA
He says he will return incontinent;
And hath commanded me to go to bed,
And bid me to dismiss you.
EMILIA
                              Dismiss me!

DESDEMONA
It was his bidding; therefore, good Emilia,   15
Give me my nightly wearing, and adieu.
We must not now displease him.
EMILIA
I would you had never seen him!
DESDEMONA
So would not I. My love doth so approve him,
That even his stubbornness, his checks, his frowns,—   20
Prithee, unpin me,—have grace and favour [in them].
EMILIA
I have laid those sheets you bade me on the bed.
DESDEMONA
All's one. Good [faith], how foolish are our minds!
If I do die before, prithee, shroud me
In one of these same sheets.
EMILIA
                              Come, come, you talk.   25

DESDEMONA
My mother had a maid call'd Barbary;
She was in love, and he she lov'd prov'd mad
And did forsake her. She had a song of "Willow";
An old thing 'twas, but it express'd her fortune,
And she died singing it. That song to-night   30
Will not go from my mind; I have much to do
But to go hang my head all at one side
And sing it like poor Barbary. Prithee, dispatch.

---

iii. 20 **stubbornness**: roughness.   23 [**faith**] Q: *Father* F.
21 [**in them**] Q: Om. F.

EMILIA
Shall I go fetch your night-gown?
DESDEMONA
                                    No, unpin me here.
This Lodovico is a proper man.   35
EMILIA
A very handsome man.
DESDEMONA
He speaks well.
EMILIA
I know a lady in Venice would have walk'd
barefoot to Palestine for a touch of his
nether lip.   40
DESDEMONA [*Singing.*]
        "The poor soul sat [sighing] by a sycamore tree,
            Sing all a green willow;
        Her hand on her bosom, her head on her knee,
            Sing willow, willow, willow.
        The fresh streams ran by her, and murmur'd her moans;   45
            Sing willow, willow, willow;
        Her salt tears fell from her, and soft'ned the stones;
            Sing willow, willow, willow;"
Lay by these;—
[*Singing.*] "Willow, willow;"—
Prithee, hie thee; he'll come anon;—   50
[*Singing.*]
        "Sing all a green willow must be my garland.
            Let nobody blame him, his scorn I approve,"—
Nay, that's not next.—Hark! who is't that knocks?
EMILIA
It's the wind.
DESDEMONA [*Singing.*]
        "I call'd my love false love; but what said he then?   55
            Sing willow, willow, willow.
        If I court moe women, you'll couch with moe men."—
So, get thee gone; good-night. Mine eyes do itch;
Doth that bode weeping?
EMILIA
                        'Tis neither here nor there.
DESDEMONA
I have heard it said so. O, these men, these men!   60
Dost thou in conscience think,—tell me, Emilia,—
That there be women do abuse their husbands
In such gross kind?
EMILIA
                    There be some such, no question.
DESDEMONA
Wouldst thou do such a deed for all the world?
EMILIA
Why, would not you?

41 [**sighing**] Q₂: *singing* F.

DESDEMONA

No, by this heavenly light!　　　　　65

EMILIA

Nor I neither by this heavenly light;
I might do't as well i' th' dark.

DESDEMONA

Wouldst thou do such a deed for all the world?

EMILIA

The world's a huge thing; it is a great price
For a small vice.

DESDEMONA

In troth, I think thou wouldst not.　　　70

EMILIA

In troth, I think I should; and undo't when I had
done. Marry, I would not do such a thing for a
joint-ring, nor for measures of lawn, nor for gowns,
petticoats, nor caps, nor any petty exhibition; but,
for all the whole world,—['ud's pity], who would　　75
not make her husband a cuckold to make him
a monarch? I should venture purgatory for't.

DESDEMONA

Beshrew me, if I would do such a wrong
For the whole world.

EMILIA

Why, the wrong is but a wrong i' th' world;　　　80
and having the world for your labour, 'tis a
wrong in your own world, and you might quickly
make it right.

DESDEMONA

I do not think there is any such woman.

EMILIA

Yes, a dozen; and as many to th' vantage　　　85
as would store the world they play'd for.
But I do think it is their husbands' faults
If wives do fall. Say that they slack their duties
And pour our treasures into foreign laps,
Or else break out in peevish jealousies,　　　90
Throwing restraint upon us; or say they strike us,
Or scant our former having in despite;
Why, we have galls, and though we have some grace,
Yet have we some revenge. Let husbands know
Their wives have sense like them; they see and smell　　95
And have their palates both for sweet and sour
As husbands have. What is it that they do
When they change us for others? Is it sport?
I think it is. And doth affection breed it?
I think it doth. Is't frailty that thus errs?　　　100
It is so too. And have not we affections,
Desires for sport, and frailty, as men have?

---

73 **joint-ring:** ring made in
separable halves.
74 **exhibition:** allowance.
75 **['ud's pity]** Q: God's pity. *Why* F.

85 **to th' vantage:** more, to boot.
90 **peevish:** silly.
92 **having:** allowance.
93 **galls:** spirits to resent injury.

Then let them use us well; else let them know,
The ills we do, their ills instruct us so.

DESDEMONA

Good-night, good-night. Heaven me such uses send,   105
Not to pick bad from bad, but by bad mend.

[*Exeunt.*

Act V

Scene I. [*Cyprus. A street.*]
Enter Iago and Roderigo.

IAGO

Here, stand behind this [bulk]; straight will he come.
Wear thy good rapier bare, and put it home.
Quick, quick; fear nothing; I'll be at thy elbow.
It makes us, or it mars us; think on that,
And fix most firm thy resolution.   5

RODERIGO

Be near at hand; I may miscarry in't.

IAGO

Here, at thy hand; be bold, and take thy stand.

[*Retires.*]

RODERIGO

I have no great devotion to the deed,
And yet he hath given me satisfying reasons.
'Tis but a man gone. Forth, my sword: he dies.   10

IAGO

I have rubb'd this young quat almost to the sense,
And he grows angry. Now, whether he kill Cassio,
Or Cassio him, or each do kill the other,
Every way makes my gain. Live Roderigo,
He calls me to a restitution large   15
Of gold jewels that I bobb'd from him
As gifts to Desdemona;
It must not be. If Cassio do remain,
He hath a daily beauty in his life
That makes me ugly; and, besides, the Moor   20
May unfold me to him; there stand I in much peril.
No, he must die. But so; I heard him coming.
Enter Cassio.

RODERIGO

I know his gait, 'tis he.—Villain, thou diest!

[*Makes a pass at Cassio.*]

CASSIO

That thrust had been mine enemy indeed,
But that my coat is better than thou know'st.   25
I will make proof of thine.

[*Draws, and wounds Roderigo.*]

V. I. 1 [**bulk**] Q: jutting part of a
building. *barke* F.
11 **quat:** pimple; **the sense:** the
quick.

16 **bobb'd:** cheated, swindled.
25 **coat:** i.e., of mail (worn under
outer clothing).

RODERIGO

O, I am slain.

[*Iago from behind wounds Cassio in the leg, and exit.*]

CASSIO

I am maim'd for ever. Help, ho! murder! murder!   [*Falls.*]
  Enter Othello.

OTHELLO

The voice of Cassio! Iago keeps his word.

RODERIGO

O, villain that I am!

OTHELLO

It is even so.

CASSIO

O, help, ho! light! a surgeon!   30

OTHELLO

'Tis he!—O brave Iago, honest and just,
That hast such noble sense of thy friend's wrong!
Thou teachest me. Minion, your dear lies dead,
And your unblest fate hies; strumpet, I come.
[Forth] of my heart those charms, thine eyes, are blotted;   35
Thy bed, lust-stain'd, shall with lust's blood be spotted.

[*Exit.*

  Enter Lodovico and Gratiano.

CASSIO

What, ho! no watch? no passage? Murder! murder!

GRATIANO

'Tis some mischance; the voice is very direful.

CASSIO

O, help!

LODOVICO

Hark!   40

RODERIGO

O wretched villain!

LODOVICO

Two or three groan. 'Tis heavy night,
These may be counterfeits; let's think 't unsafe
To come in to the cry without more help.

RODERIGO

Nobody come? Then shall I bleed to death.   45
  Re-enter Iago, with a light.

LODOVICO

Hark!

GRATIANO

Here's one comes in his shirt, with light and weapons.

IAGO

Who's there? Whose noise is this that cries on murder?

LODOVICO

We do not know.

IAGO

Do not you hear a cry?

33 **Minion:** hussy.   37 **passage:** passers-by.
35 **[Forth]** Q: *For* F.   42 **heavy:** dark.

CASSIO
Here, here! for Heaven's sake, help me!
IAGO
                                    What's the matter?   50
GRATIANO
This is Othello's ancient, as I take it.
LODOVICO
The same indeed; a very valiant fellow.
IAGO
What are you here that cry so grievously?
CASSIO
Iago? O, I am spoil'd, undone by villains!
Give me some help.   55
IAGO
O me, Lieutenant! what villains have done this?
CASSIO
I think that one of them is hereabout
And cannot make away.
IAGO
                    O treacherous villains!
What are you there?—Come in, and give some help.
                    [*To Lodovico and Gratiano.*]
RODERIGO
O, help me there!   60
CASSIO
That's one of them.
IAGO
                    O murd'rous slave! O villain!
                    [*Thrusts* [*Roderigo*] *in.*
RODERIGO
O damn'd Iago! O inhuman dog!
IAGO
Kill men i' th' dark!—Where be these bloody thieves?—
How silent is this town!—Ho! murder! murder!—
What may you be? Are you of good or evil?   65
LODOVICO
As you shall prove us, praise us.
IAGO
Signior Lodovico?
LODOVICO
He, sir.
IAGO
I cry you mercy. Here's Cassio hurt by villains.
GRATIANO
Cassio!   70
IAGO
How is't, brother!
CASSIO
My leg is cut in two.
IAGO
                    Marry, heaven forbid!
Light, gentlemen! I'll bind it with my shirt.
    Enter Bianca.

BIANCA
> What is the matter, ho? Who is't that cried?

IAGO
> Who is't that cried! 75

BIANCA
> O my dear Cassio! my sweet Cassio!
> O Cassio, Cassio, Cassio!

IAGO
> O notable strumpet! Cassio, may you suspect
> Who they should be that have thus mangled you?

CASSIO
> No. 80

GRATIANO
> I am sorry to find you thus; I have been to seek you.

IAGO
> Lend me a garter. So. O, for a chair,
> To bear him easily hence!

BIANCA
> Alas, he faints! O Cassio, Cassio, Cassio!

IAGO
> Gentlemen all, I do suspect this trash 85
> To be a party in this injury.
> Patience a while, good Cassio. Come, come;
> Lend me a light. Know we this face or no?
> Alas, my friend and my dear countryman
> Roderigo! No:—yes, sure:—yes, 'tis Roderigo. 90

GRATIANO
> What, of Venice?

IAGO
> Even he, sir; did you know him?

GRATIANO
>   Know him! ay.

IAGO
> Signior Gratiano? I cry your gentle pardon;
> These bloody accidents must excuse my manners
> That so neglected you.

GRATIANO
>   I am glad to see you. 95

IAGO
> How do you, Cassio? O, a chair, a chair!

GRATIANO
> Roderigo!

IAGO
> He, he, 'tis he. [*A chair brought in.*] O, that's well said; the chair.
> Some good man bear him carefully from hence;
> I'll fetch the General's surgeon. [*To Bianca.*] For you, mistress, 100
> Save you your labour. He that lies slain here, Cassio,
> Was my dear friend. What malice was between you?

CASSIO
> None in the world; nor do I know the man.

---

82 **chair:** sedan chair.

IAGO [*To Bianca.*]
What, look you pale? O, bear him out o' th' air.
                    [*Cassio and Roderigo are borne off.*]
Stay you, good gentlemen. Look you pale, mistress?   105
Do you perceive the gastness of her eye?
Nay, if you stare, we shall hear more anon.
Behold her well; I pray you, look upon her.
Do you see, gentlemen? Nay, guiltiness will speak,
Though tongues were out of use.   110
        Enter Emilia.
EMILIA
Alas, what's the matter? What's the matter, husband?
IAGO
Cassio hath here been set on in the dark
By Roderigo and fellows that are scap'd.
He's almost slain, and Roderigo quite dead.
EMILIA
Alas, good gentleman! alas, good Cassio!   115
IAGO
This is the fruits of whoring. Prithee, Emilia,
Go know of Cassio where he supp'd to-night.
[*To Bianca.*] What, do you shake at that?
BIANCA
He supp'd at my house; but I therefore shake not.
IAGO
O, did he so? I charge you, go with me.   120
EMILIA
Oh, fie upon thee, strumpet!
BIANCA
I am no strumpet, but of life as honest
As you that thus abuse me.
EMILIA
                As I? Fie upon thee!
IAGO
Kind gentlemen, let's go see poor Cassio dress'd.
Come, mistress, you must tell's another tale.   125
Emilia, run you to the citadel,
And tell my lord and lady what hath happ'd.
Will you go on afore? [*Aside.*] This is the night
That either makes me or fordoes me quite.
                                          [*Exeunt.*

        Scene II. [A bedchamber in the castle:] Desdemona in bed [asleep].
        Enter Othello with a light.
OTHELLO
It is the cause, it is the cause, my soul,—
Let me not name it to you, you chaste stars!—
It is the cause. Yet I'll not shed her blood,
Nor scar that whiter skin of hers than snow,
And smooth as monumental alabaster.   5

        106 **gastness:** ghastliness.   129 **fordoes:** destroys.

Yet she must die, else she'll betray more men.
Put out the light, and then put out the light.
If I quench thee, thou flaming minister,
I can again thy former light restore,
Should I repent me; but once put out thy light,   10
Thou cunning'st pattern of excelling nature,
I know not where is that Promethean heat
That can thy light relume. When I have pluck'd the rose
I cannot give it vital growth again,
It needs must wither. I'll smell [it] on the tree.   15

                                                              [*Kisses her.*

Oh, balmy breath, that dost almost persuade
Justice to break her sword! One more, one more.
Be thus when thou art dead, and I will kill thee
And love thee after. One more, and that's the last;
So sweet was ne'er so fatal. I must weep,   20
But they are cruel tears. This sorrow's heavenly;
It strikes where it doth love. She wakes.

DESDEMONA
Who's there? Othello?

OTHELLO
                          Ay, Desdemona.

DESDEMONA
Will you come to bed, my lord?

OTHELLO
Have you pray'd to-night, Desdemon?

DESDEMONA
                                      Ay, my lord.   25

OTHELLO
If you bethink yourself of any crime
Unreconcil'd as yet to Heaven and grace,
Solicit for it straight.

DESDEMONA
Alack, my lord, what may you mean by that?

OTHELLO
Well, do it, and be brief; I will walk by.   30
I would not kill thy unprepared spirit;
No; heavens forfend! I would not kill thy soul.

DESDEMONA
Talk you of killing?

OTHELLO
                    Ay, I do.

DESDEMONA
                         Then Heaven
Have mercy on me!

OTHELLO
                      Amen, with all my heart!

DESDEMONA
If you say [so], I hope you will not kill me.   35

ii. 12 **Promethean heat:** divine fire.   35 [so] Q: Om. F.
15 [it] Q: *thee* F.

OTHELLO

Hum!

DESDEMONA

And yet I fear you; for you're fatal then
When your eyes roll so. Why I should fear I know not,
Since guiltiness I know not; but yet I feel I fear.

OTHELLO

Think on thy sins.

DESDEMONA

                  They are loves I bear to you.   40

OTHELLO

Ay, and for that thou diest.

DESDEMONA

That death's unnatural that kills for loving.
Alas, why gnaw you so your nether lip?
Some bloody passion shakes your very frame.
These are portents; but yet I hope, I hope,   45
They do not point on me.

OTHELLO

                    Peace, and be still!

DESDEMONA

I will so. What's the matter?

OTHELLO

That handkerchief which I so lov'd and gave thee
Thou gav'st to Cassio.

DESDEMONA

               No, by my life and soul!
Send for the man, and ask him.

OTHELLO

                    Sweet soul, take heed,   50
Take heed of perjury; thou art on thy deathbed.

DESDEMONA

Ay, but not yet to die.

OTHELLO

                  [Yes], presently:
Therefore confess thee freely of thy sin;
For to deny each article with oath
Cannot remove nor choke the strong conception   55
That I do groan withal. Thou art to die.

DESDEMONA

O, Heaven, have mercy on me!

OTHELLO

                  I say, amen.

DESDEMONA

And have you mercy too! I never did
Offend you in my life; never lov'd Cassio
But with such general warranty of heaven   60
As I might love; I never gave him token.

OTHELLO

By heaven, I saw my handkerchief in 's hand.

52 [**Yes**] Q: Om. F.   55 **conception:** purpose.

O perjur'd woman! thou dost stone my heart,
And makes me call what I intend to do
A murder, which I thought a sacrifice.   65
I saw the handkerchief.

DESDEMONA
                              He found it then;
I never gave it him. Send for him hither;
Let him confess a truth.

OTHELLO
                              He hath confess'd.

DESDEMONA
What, my lord?

OTHELLO
That he hath us'd thee.

DESDEMONA
                              How? unlawfully?

OTHELLO
                                                            Ay.   70

DESDEMONA
He will not say so.

OTHELLO
                              No, his mouth is stopp'd;
Honest Iago hath ta'en order for't.

DESDEMONA
O! my fear interprets. What, is he dead?

OTHELLO
Had all his hairs been lives, my great revenge
Had stomach for them all.   75

DESDEMONA
Alas! he is betray'd and I undone.

OTHELLO
Out, strumpet! weep'st thou for him to my face?

DESDEMONA
O, banish me, my lord, but kill me not!

OTHELLO
Down, strumpet!

DESDEMONA
Kill me to-morrow; let me live to-night!   80

OTHELLO
Nay, if you strive,—

DESDEMONA
But half an hour!

OTHELLO
                              Being done, there is no pause.

DESDEMONA
But while I say one prayer!

OTHELLO
                              It is too late.

                                        [*He smothers her.*

EMILIA (*At the door.*)
My lord, my lord!
What, ho! my lord, my lord!

OTHELLO

What noise is this? Not dead? not yet quite dead?   85
I that am cruel am yet merciful;
I would not have thee linger in thy pain.
So, so.

EMILIA (*Within.*)

What, ho! my lord, my lord!

OTHELLO

Who's there?

EMILIA [*Within.*]

O, good my lord, I would speak a word with you!   90

OTHELLO

Yes:—'tis Emilia.—By and by.—She's dead.
'Tis like she comes to speak of Cassio's death.
The noise was high. Ha! no more moving?
Still as the grave. Shall she come in? Were't good?—
I think she stirs again:—no. What's best to do?   95
If she come in, she'll sure speak to my wife.
My wife! my wife! what wife? I have no wife.
O, insupportable! O heavy hour!
Methinks it should be now a huge eclipse
Of sun and moon, and that th' affrighted globe   100
Did yawn at alteration.

EMILIA [*Within.*]

I do beseech you
That I may speak with you, O, good my lord!

OTHELLO

I had forgot thee. O, come in, Emilia.
Soft; by and by.—Let me the curtains draw.—
Where art thou?

[*Unlocks the door.*]

Enter Emilia.

What's the matter with thee now?   105

EMILIA

O, my good lord, yonder's foul murders done!

OTHELLO

What, now?

EMILIA

But now, my lord.

OTHELLO

It is the very error of the moon;
She comes more nearer earth than she was wont,   110
And makes men mad.

EMILIA

Cassio, my lord, hath kill'd a young Venetian
Call'd Roderigo.

OTHELLO

Roderigo kill'd!
And Cassio kill'd!

EMILIA

No, Cassio is not kill'd.

109 **error:** aberration.

OTHELLO

    Not Cassio kill'd! Then murder's out of tune, 115
    And sweet revenge grows harsh.

DESDEMONA

    O, falsely, falsely murder'd!

EMILIA

                   O Lord, what cry is that?

OTHELLO

    That! what?

EMILIA

    Out, and alas! that was my lady's voice.
    Help! help, ho! help! O lady, speak again! 120
    Sweet Desdemona! O sweet mistress, speak!

DESDEMONA

    A guiltless death I die.

EMILIA

    O, who hath done this deed?

DESDEMONA

    Nobody; I myself. Farewell!
    Commend me to my kind lord. O, farewell! 125

                               [*Dies.*

OTHELLO

    Why, how should she be murd'red?

EMILIA

                 Alas, who knows?

OTHELLO

    You hear her say herself, it was not I.

EMILIA

    She said so; I must needs report the truth.

OTHELLO

    She's, like a liar, gone to burning hell.
    'Twas I that kill'd her.

EMILIA

             O, the more angel she, 130
    And you the blacker devil!

OTHELLO

    She turn'd to folly, and she was a whore.

EMILIA

    Thou dost belie her, and thou art a devil.

OTHELLO

    She was false as water.

EMILIA

             Thou art rash as fire to say
    That she was false: O, she was heavenly true! 135

OTHELLO

    Cassio did top her; ask thy husband else.
    O, I were damn'd beneath all depth in hell
    But that I did proceed upon just grounds
    To this extremity. Thy husband knew it all.

EMILIA

    My husband! 140

OTHELLO

    Thy husband.

EMILIA
That she was false to wedlock?
OTHELLO
Ay, with Cassio. Had she been true,
If Heaven would make me such another world
Of one entire and perfect chrysolite,   145
I'd not have sold her for it.
EMILIA
                          My husband!
OTHELLO
Ay, 'twas he that told me on her first.
An honest man he is, and hates the slime
That sticks on filthy deeds.
EMILIA
                          My husband!
OTHELLO
What needs this iterance, woman? I say thy husband.   150
EMILIA
O mistress, villainy hath made mocks with love!
My husband say [that] she was false!
OTHELLO
                                  He, woman;
I say thy husband; dost understand the word?
My friend, thy husband, honest, honest Iago.
EMILIA
If he say so, may his pernicious soul   155
Rot half a grain a day! He lies to the heart.
She was too fond of her most filthy bargain.
OTHELLO
Ha!
EMILIA
Do thy worst!
This deed of thine is no more worthy heaven   160
Than thou wast worthy her.
OTHELLO
                          Peace, you were best.
EMILIA
Thou hast not half that power to do me harm
As I have to be hurt. O gull! O dolt!
As ignorant as dirt! Thou hast done a deed—
I care not for thy sword; I'll make thee known   165
Though I lost twenty lives.—Help! help, ho! help!
The Moor hath kill'd my mistress! Murder! murder!
        Enter Montano, Gratiano, Iago, and others.
MONTANO
What is the matter? How now, general!
EMILIA
O, are you come, Iago? You have done well,
That men must lay their murders on your neck.   170
GRATIANO
What is the matter?

145 **chrysolite:** a precious stone.   152 [**that**] Q₂: Om. F.
150 **iterance:** repetition.

EMILIA

    Disprove this villain, if thou be'st a man.
    He says thou told'st him that his wife was false.
    I know thou didst not, thou'rt not such a villain.
    Speak, for my heart is full.   175

IAGO

    I told him what I thought, and told no more
    Than what he found himself was apt and true.

EMILIA

    But did you ever tell him she was false?

IAGO

    I did.

EMILIA

    You told a lie, an odious, damned lie;   180
    Upon my soul, a lie, a wicked lie.
    She false with Cassio!—did you say with Cassio?

IAGO

    With Cassio, mistress. Go to, charm your tongue.

EMILIA

    I will not charm my tongue; I am bound to speak.
    My mistress here lies murdered in her bed,—   185

ALL

    O heavens forfend!

EMILIA

    And your reports have set the murderer on.

OTHELLO

    Nay, stare not, masters; it is true, indeed.

GRATIANO

    'Tis a strange truth.

MONTANO

    O monstrous act!

EMILIA

                   Villany, villany, villany!   190
    I think upon't,—I think I smell 't,—O villany!
    I thought so then,—I'll kill myself for grief—
    O villany, villany!

IAGO

    What, are you mad? I charge you, get you home.

EMILIA

    Good gentlemen, let me have leave to speak;   195
    'Tis proper I obey him, but not now.
    Perchance, Iago, I will ne'er go home.

OTHELLO

    O! O! O!

                                    [*He falls on the bed.*

EMILIA

             Nay, lay thee down and roar;
    For thou hast kill'd the sweetest innocent
    That e'er did lift up eye.

OTHELLO [*Rising.*]

             O, she was foul!   200

192 **I . . . then:** See IV.ii.130–133.

I scarce did know you, uncle; there lies your niece,
Whose breath, indeed, these hands have newly stopp'd.
I know this act shows horrible and grim.

GRATIANO

Poor Desdemon! I am glad thy father's dead.   205
Thy match was mortal to him, and pure grief
Shore his old thread in twain. Did he live now,
This sight would make him do a desperate turn,
Yea, curse his better angel from his side,
And fall to reprobance.

OTHELLO

'Tis pitiful; but yet Iago knows   210
That she with Cassio hath the act of shame
A thousand times committed. Cassio confess'd it;
And she did gratify his amorous works
With that recognizance and pledge of love
Which I first gave her. I saw it in his hand;   215
It was a handkerchief, an antique token
My father gave my mother.

EMILIA

O [God]! O heavenly [God]!

IAGO

['Zounds,] hold your peace.

EMILIA

                'Twill out, 'twill out! I peace!
No, I will speak as liberal as the north.   220
Let Heaven and men and devils, let them all,
All, all, cry shame against me, yet I'll speak.

IAGO

Be wise, and get you home.

EMILIA

           I will not.

[Iago offers to stab Emilia.]

GRATIANO

                 Fie!
Your sword upon a woman?

EMILIA

O thou dull Moor! that handkerchief thou speak'st of   225
I found by fortune and did give my husband;
For often, with a solemn earnestness,
More than indeed belong'd to such a trifle,
He begg'd of me to steal 't.

IAGO

            Villanous whore!

EMILIA

She give it Cassio! No, alas! I found it,   230
And I did give't my husband.

IAGO

            Filth, thou liest!

---

209 **reprobance:** damnation.   219 ['**Zounds**] Q: *Come* F.
218 [**God**] . . . [**God**] Q: *Heaven*   220 **liberal:** freely.
. . . *Powers* F.

EMILIA
By heaven, I do not, I do not, gentlemen.
O murd'rous coxcomb! what should such a fool
Do with so good a wife?
OTHELLO
                    Are there no stones in heaven
But what serves for the thunder?—Precious villain!   235
                    [*He runs at Iago: Iago kills Emilia.*
GRATIANO
The woman falls; sure, he hath kill'd his wife.
EMILIA
Ay, ay! O, lay me by my mistress' side.
                                   [*Exit Iago.*
GRATIANO
He's gone, but his wife's kill'd.
MONTANO
'Tis a notorious villain. Take you this weapon
Which I have [here] recover'd from the Moor.   240
Come, guard the door without; let him not pass,
But kill him rather. I'll after that same villain,
For 'tis a damned slave.
                    [*Exeunt Montano and Gratiano.*
OTHELLO
                    I am not valiant neither,
But every puny whipster gets my sword.
But why should honour outlive honesty?   245
Let it go all.
EMILIA
              What did thy song bode, lady?
Hark, canst thou hear me? I will play the swan,
And die in music. [*Singing.*] "Willow, willow, willow!"—
Moor, she was chaste; she lov'd thee, cruel Moor:
So come my soul to bliss, as I speak true;   250
So speaking as I think, alas, I die.
                                   [*Dies.*
OTHELLO
I have another weapon in this chamber;
It was a sword of Spain, the ice-brook's temper,—
O, here it is. Uncle, I must come forth.
GRATIANO (*Within.*)
If thou attempt it, it will cost thee dear: 255
Thou hast no weapon, and perforce must suffer.
OTHELLO
Look in upon me then and speak with me,
Or, naked as I am, I will assault thee.
                    [*Re-enter Gratiano.*]
GRATIANO
What is the matter?
OTHELLO
              Behold, I have a weapon;
A better never did itself sustain   260

234 **stones:** bolts.
240 [**here**] Q: Om. F.
244 **whipster:** term of contempt.
253 **ice-brook's temper:** its steel tempered in icy water.
258 **naked:** unarmed.

Upon a soldier's thigh. I have seen the day
That, with this little arm and this good sword,
I have made my way through more impediments
Than twenty times your stop. But, O vain boast!
Who can control his fate? 'tis not so now. 265
Be not afraid though you do see me weapon'd;
Here is my journey's end, here is my butt
And very sea-mark of my utmost sail.
Do you go back dismay'd? 'Tis a lost fear;
Man but a rush against Othello's breast 270
And he retires. Where should Othello go?
Now, how dost thou look now? O ill-starr'd wench!
Pale as thy smock! when we shall meet at compt,
This look of thine will hurl my soul from heaven,
And fiends will snatch at it. Cold, cold, my girl! 275
Even like thy chastity. O cursed, cursed slave!
Whip me, ye devils,
From the possession of this heavenly sight!
Blow me about in winds! roast me in sulphur!
Wash me in steep-down gulfs of liquid fire! 280
O Desdemon! dead, Desdemon! dead!
Oh! Oh!

Enter Lodovico, Montano, Cassio carried in a chair, and Officers, with Iago [prisoner].

LODOVICO
Where is this rash and most unfortunate man?
OTHELLO
That's he that was Othello; here I am.
LODOVICO
Where is that viper? Bring the villain forth. 285
OTHELLO
I look down towards his feet; but that's a fable.
If that thou be'st a devil, I cannot kill thee.

[Wounds Iago.]

LODOVICO
Wrench his sword from him.
IAGO
                              I bleed, sir; but not kill'd.
OTHELLO
I am not sorry neither. I'd have thee live;
For, in my sense, 'tis happiness to die. 290
LODOVICO
O thou Othello, that [wast] once so good,
Fall'n in the practice of a cursed slave,
What shall be said to thee?
OTHELLO
                              Why, anything.
An honourable murderer, if you will;
For nought I did in hate, but all in honour. 295

264 **stop:** power to stop.
267 **butt:** goal.
273 **compt:** accounting, i.e.,
Judgment Day.

286 **I . . . feet:** i.e., to see if they
are cloven.
291 [**wast**]: *was* F. *wert* Q.
292 **practice:** plot.

LODOVICO
    This wretch hath part confess'd his villainy.
    Did you and he consent in Cassio's death?
OTHELLO
    Ay.
CASSIO
    Dear General, I never gave you cause.
OTHELLO
    I do believe it, and I ask your pardon.   300
    Will you, I pray, demand that demi-devil
    Why he hath thus ensnar'd my soul and body?
IAGO
    Demand me nothing; what you know, you know.
    From this time forth I never will speak word.
LODOVICO
    What, not to pray?
GRATIANO
                    Torments will ope your lips.   305
OTHELLO
    Well, thou dost best.
LODOVICO
    Sir, you shall understand what hath befall'n,
    Which, as I think, you know not. Here is a letter
    Found in the pocket of the slain Roderigo,
    And here another. The one of them imports   310
    The death of Cassio to be undertook
    By Roderigo.
OTHELLO
    O villain!
CASSIO
              Most heathenish and most gross!
LODOVICO
    Now here's another discontented paper,
    Found in his pocket too; and this, it seems,   315
    Roderigo meant t' have sent this damned villain;
    But that, belike, Iago in the interim
    Came in and satisfi'd him.
OTHELLO
                  O thou pernicious caitiff!—
    How came you, Cassio, by that handkerchief
    That was my wife's?
CASSIO
                I found it in my chamber,   320
    And he himself confess'd but even now
    That there he dropp'd it for a special purpose
    Which wrought to his desire.
OTHELLO
                O fool! fool! fool!
CASSIO
    There is besides in Roderigo's letter,
    How he upbraids Iago, that he made him   325

321 **but** Q: *it but* F.

Brave me upon the watch, whereon it came
That I was cast; and even but now he spake,
After long seeming dead, Iago hurt him,
Iago set him on.

LODOVICO
You must forsake this room and go with us.   330
Your power and your command is taken off,
And Cassio rules in Cyprus. For this slave,
If there be any cunning cruelty
That can torment him much and hold him long,
It shall be his. You shall close prisoner rest,   335
Till that the nature of your fault be known
To the Venetian state. Come, bring away.

OTHELLO
Soft you; a word or two before you go.
I have done the state some service, and they know 't.
Not more of that. I pray you, in your letters,   340
When you shall these unlucky deeds relate,
Speak of me as I am; nothing extenuate,
Nor set down aught in malice. Then must you speak
Of one that lov'd not wisely but too well;
Of one not easily jealous, but, being wrought,   345
Perplex'd in the extreme; of one whose hand,
Like the base [Indian], threw a pearl away
Richer than all his tribe; of one whose subdu'd eyes,
Albeit unused to the melting mood,
Drops tears as fast as the Arabian trees   350
Their medicinal gum. Set you down this;
And say besides, that in Aleppo once,
Where a malignant and a turban'd Turk
Beat a Venetian and traduc'd the state,
I took by th' throat the circumcised dog,   355
And smote him—thus.

                              [Stabs himself.

LODOVICO
O bloody period!

GRATIANO
              All that's spoke is marr'd.

OTHELLO
I kiss'd thee ere I kill'd thee: no way but this,
Killing myself, to die upon a kiss.

                    [Falls on the bed, and] dies.

CASSIO
This did I fear, but thought he had no weapon;   360
For he was great of heart.

LODOVICO [To Iago.]
              O Spartan dog,
More fell than anguish, hunger, or the sea!
Look on the tragic loading of this bed;

346 **Perplex'd:** distraught.   356 **period:** end.
347 [**Indian**] Q: *Iudean* F. The   361 **Spartan dog:** bloodhound.
allusion has not been identified.
[Some editors read *Judean.*]

This is thy work. The object poisons sight;
Let it be hid. Gratiano, keep the house, 365
And seize upon the fortunes of the Moor,
For they succeed on you. To you, Lord Governor,
Remains the censure of this hellish villain;
The time, the place, the torture. O, enforce it!
Myself will straight aboard; and to the state 370
This heavy act with heavy heart relate.

[*Exeunt.*

Action analysis and performance suggestions

Two scenes offer good opportunities to define and explore the actions and
the superobjective of *Othello:* Iago's second major evocation of Othello's
jealousy (act III, scene iii, from Emilia's exit to "I am your own for ever,"
lines 321–479) and Othello's confrontation with Desdemona over the lost
handkerchief (act III, scene iv, from Desdemona's "Where should I lose
the handkerchief, Emilia?" to Emilia's comments following Othello's exit,
lines 23–106). Before the first of these scenes, Iago has already bred a
monster in Othello's thought too hideous to be shown. Now he tries to
bring that monster jealousy forth, to arouse Othello to active revenge, to
entice the hidden doubts and fears from the recesses of Othello's soul, to
charm Othello into doing murder and mayhem. Othello is his willing accomplice after an initial attempt to assure himself that Iago tells the truth,
and his aim is to be satisfied that Desdemona and Cassio are guilty, not to
determine their guilt or innocence.

Act III, scene iii is the climax of *Othello.* We know this not just in
retrospect but at the time. The Othello who swears "Arise, black vengeance, from the hollow hell!" (III. iii 447) and kneels in satanic prayer
with Iago has already changed too much to reverse his course of action
before dire calamity befalls those with whom we sympathize—as it already
has befallen him psychologically. However, in great tragedy there is always
suspense and with suspense the hope that Othello will recover his senses or
that Iago's machinations will be exposed before chaotic destruction and
death have overtaken those we like. The first narrowing of this pitifully
bleak horizon takes place in Othello's interview with Desdemona over the
handkerchief.

DEFINING THE ACTIONS AND THE SUPEROBJECTIVE

Preceding Desdemona's opening lines to Emilia is a brief confrontation
with the witty, punning Clown we have seen once before. The exchange
resonates with the rest of the scene in the peculiarly comic way Shakespeare tended to use such moments of relief from tragic tension, for Desdemona's characteristically blunt and open approach to the subject of Cassio's whereabouts is answered with a double entendre that both reminds
us of Iago's earlier use of insinuation and presages Othello's use of double meaning later in this scene. These lines may be played in informal
performance. Desdemona's question to Emilia is an attempt to comfort
herself for the loss of the handkerchief rather than a strict interrogation.

366 **seize upon:** take legal possession of.   368 **censure:** sentencing.

More on her mind is her desire to make Othello comfortable (he had seemed ill and troubled in the previous scene) and to restore Cassio to his place, an action in part prompted by her belief that Cassio's firing is a cause rather than a symptom of Othello's present discomfort. Emilia answers Desdemona's question briefly—lying, of course—but then changes the subject. Emilia would not wish her mistress harm, but her more worldly, sophisticated, and sinful view of sexual love—*not* any great loyalty to her husband—makes her look on what Desdemona considers a great loss as a trifle. We may speculate on Emilia's motives further. Is she herself jealous of the beautiful, chaste Desdemona? Or is she merely trying to cover her transgressions? Why does she want to prove to Desdemona that all men are jealous? To see her mistress discomforted by love, as we know she has been (act IV, scene ii, lines 145–147)?

On his entrance, Othello tries to dissemble his jealousy, as he tells us in an aside (line 34). Iago has made him believe two things that will satisfy him as proofs of Desdemona's infidelity: that she has given the handkerchief to Cassio and that she will continue her suit to have Cassio restored to his office. One scene before Othello would have asked her directly if she gave the love token to Cassio; now he wants to trap her into a sinful confession, to uncover the evil disloyalty he thinks is in her soul. With his comments about the warmth and moistness of her hand—by Elizabethan physiology, qualities associated with lechery—he tries to draw her into a bawdy conversation. Desdemona does not understand and shifts instead to remind Othello of his promise to speak with Cassio about his position. Angered, Othello proceeds a bit more directly, first to ask for the handkerchief, then to impress on Desdemona its significance to him as a symbol of fidelity, although he still does not openly voice his suspicions. (Previously Othello had denied the use of witchcraft, but now that he believes Desdemona to be a "fair devil" and a "lewd minx," he summons its powers.) The intensity of his attack is designed to frighten Desdemona into a confession, perhaps to justify to himself his subsequent revenge if she refuses to admit its loss or shows confusion about it or lies. He catches on her "would to [God] that I had never seen 't" as a confession. Significantly, the innocent Desdemona is so moved by his attack that she lies, trying to calm Othello's wrath, then shifts to Cassio again to deflect his rage. Since it is her misfortune to be naïve and trusting, she can little know that this topic more than any other enrages him. Yet in her trifling efforts to dissemble the loss of the handkerchief and to calm him, here and elsewhere she returns to rub again and again precisely that open, dreadful sore in his soul from which flows his terrifying anger and jealousy. Even on her deathbed, she defends Cassio. The scene ends with Othello's exit, Desdemona's sorrowful wonder, and Emilia's attempt to emphasize the point she made earlier, that all men are jealous.

Desdemona's lie, Emilia's belief that all men are naturally jealous, and Othello's use of Iago's insinuating tools of interrogation (compare act III, scene iii, lines 90–277; act III, scene iii, lines 321–479; or Iago's manipulation of Cassio, Montano, and Othello in act II, scene iii) suggest an action for the scene as a whole and a tentative superobjective of the play: to uncover and bring forth the hidden evil in human souls. On a mundane social level, Emilia's desire to make her mistress accept her own more worldly view of sexual love is one illustration. Even Desdemona innocently and unknowingly participates in the superobjective when she continues to press Othello about Cassio, just as earlier her truthful, morally correct decision to give her obedience to Othello had brought out the worst in her father. However, the prime mover is Iago, whose action throughout the play is to incite riot and chaos by arousing the worst in people for his own purposes, and when Othello himself comes to adopt Iago's action, destruction is inevitable.

OVERCOMING OBSTACLES

Othello's immediate obstacle is Desdemona's true innocence, for he tries to uncover evil, not good. Damningly, he overcomes this obstacle and leads her to lie. His strange, insinuating behavior with its sexual grossness and his sudden, barely controlled anger represent obstacles to Desdemona almost as large as her growing guilt for losing the handkerchief. When Othello equates fidelity with the handkerchief, Desdemona cannot admit its loss. Almost innocently, as if to assert her chastity as a greater and more important truth than honesty about losing a trifle, she lies and tries to change the subject. Only perhaps in the case of Cordelia in *King Lear* did Shakespeare create a major virtuous character whose actions did not in some way morally contribute to an eventual unfortunate fate. Here Desdemona's lie in a foolish attempt to overcome the obstacles of her guilt for losing a handkerchief that Othello himself helped make disappear (see act III, scene iii, line 287) adds to the assurance of her destruction. What if she had admitted frankly that she did not know where it was or had asked Emilia in Othello's presence if she knew?

And why is Emilia silent on this occasion? Scholars and critics have argued that question for centuries. Shakespeare could easily have directed her off-stage during this interview so that she would not yet learn how important this handkerchief she has stolen is to Othello, but apparently he did not want to. Perhaps, then, her obstacle is her jealousy of Desdemona, the beautiful and innocent young wife of a great and successful warrior. Perhaps all that Emilia would wish to take from her mistress is the assurance of uncomplicated true love she herself lacks. Or perhaps Emilia merely wants to protect herself from exposure as a thief and to protect her husband. Her obstacle then is her own complicity in stealing the handkerchief, complicity she thinks can be exposed only at the cost of losing her own or her husband's position. Whether either of these motives influences Emilia, through her action she overcomes her obstacle and achieves her goal at a cost she will not realize until it is too late.

THE MAGIC IF AND THE GIVEN CIRCUMSTANCES

A great military leader is not necessarily a great lover, particularly when he is unfamiliar with the situation he faces. Located midway between the subtle civilization of Venice and the chaotic barbarism of Turkey (both conceptions are typically Elizabethan), Cyprus participates in the confusions of each society. Othello is quintessentially a warrior, not a courtier, but now there is no war. He tries to apply the lessons of military experience to a social and sexual situation using the simple dichotomous terms necessary for decisive action; his aggressiveness and political indirection—qualities that he capably displayed in his brilliant speech to the Venetian senate—replace the even-handed candor he showed in handling the Cyprian riot Iago provoked (see act II, scene iii). The circumstances in which Othello finds himself are inappropriate for such behavior; they call for calm, thoughtfulness, understanding, and candor—qualities that Desdemona would like to use as well. But all three participants in the scene view the circumstances through the impact of their own emotions. The resultant distortion leads to tragedy.

What IF you suspected you had caught your wife in marital infidelity and wanted to draw an admission from her that would utterly confirm your suspicions? What IF you had lost an important love token—say, your wedding ring—and your husband were acting strangely, questioning you about it, saying he would never love you again if you had lost it? What IF your newly married friend asserted that her husband could never be jealous, but you had stolen her lost wedding ring, given it to your own husband, and now wanted both to conceal your theft and to show her that, like your husband, all men are jealous? Such are the circumstances in which Othello, Desdemona, and Emilia find themselves.

CLASSROOM ADAPTATIONS TO ARRIVE AT STYLE

In both scenes suggested for informal performance, Othello's color should not pose a barrier in the absence of a Black student for the role. Actors of many races have performed the character with varying degrees of success. For the Elizabethan audience Othello's major racial characteristics were exoticism, warlike mien and courage, commanding presence, and naïveté about Western sexual customs. Clearly, several of the major characters in Shakespeare's play were racist in attributing to an individual characteristics unjustly assumed to be normative of a race as a whole. (Interestingly, Iago is the grossest offender here. See, for instance, his comments to Brabantio in act I, scene i, and act III, scene iii, lines 228–238.) But what Shakespeare gives us is an individual portrait of depth and understanding. Of more importance than Othello's color are the actions that can be attributed to his personality and the situation of stress in which he finds himself.

Costuming may be informal or as formal as swords, doublets, military insignia, and long dresses suggest. No special lighting is needed. Staging is best in three-quarter round, with the actors aware of and speaking to the audience in asides. No scenery but at least one property is essential: a handkerchief for Desdemona to offer Othello.

The most important quality of Shakespeare's theater remains his words. Before performance is attempted, students should try handling a speech or two while keeping in mind three key techniques: to think on rather than before the line, to modulate and build inflection and pitch, and to avoid naturalistic and line-end pauses. Consider Othello's speech about the handkerchief, in which his action is to scold and threaten Desdemona:

That's a fault. That handkerchief
Did an Egyptian to my mother give;
She was a charmer, and could almost read
The thoughts of people. She told her, while she kept it
'Twould make her amiable and subdue my father
Entirely to her love, but if she lost it,
Or made a gift of it, my father's eye
Should hold her loathed and his spirits should hunt
After new fancies. She, dying, gave it me
And bid me, when my fate would have me wiv'd,
To give it her. I did so; and take heed on't;
Make it a darling like your precious eye.

To lose't or give't away were such perdition
As nothing else could match.
    (III. iv. 55–68)

The curt and short "That's a fault" is followed by a full line completely
end-stopped. The effect is halting, as if he controls his rage with great effort; the "did"–indirect object–"give" grammatical inversion adds to the
sense of powerful subcurrents. The next sentence is similar in pattern and
about the same length. Still the pitch might be low, almost as if delivered
through clenched teeth. The next sentence, describing the charm the
gypsy attributed to the handkerchief, takes five full lines and six pauses,
building to the two phrases, "Or made a gift of it" and "Should hold her
loathèd." The strong position of "loathèd"—far more powerful than
"Should hate her"—suggests that the whole phrase should be spoken as
two spondees and an unaccentuated syllable (´´|´´|ˇ), and probably with
an increase in intensity and a lowering of pitch. The next sentence is just
two lines long but stopped fully six times, as if Othello leashes his anger
only with difficulty, and it reaches to the strongly spoken injunction "take
heed on't" with much power. Note the ambivalence so perfectly characteristic of the great tragic figure who will kill what he loves even while he
loves it. Desdemona's eye is precious to him as well as to her and although
he wants to scold and threaten her, he is unsure of himself. However, he
bitterly returns to his action in the next conditional with its reiteration of
"perdition" (which Othello had wished on himself to describe the depth of
his love) and the absolute "nothing else could match." The handkerchief
has grown to become fidelity itself, and Othello's fierce but controlled vir-
ulence frightens Desdemona more than did Brabantio's blustering, high-
pitched anger.

Jean Racine
Phaedra

PHAEDRA

     Each moment, terrified
by loose diseased emotions, now I cried
for death to save my glory and expel
my gloomy frenzy from this world, my hell.
    (I. iii. 317–320)

Thus Phaedra, her words rending the silken fabric of her deepest, reasoning being, concludes her confession of illicit love for her stepson Hippolytus. Her faithful nurse and confidant Oenone listens in horror: "What can you do, / but die? Your words have turned my blood to ice" (I. iii. 269–270). Earlier in the scene, before she has confessed her passion, Phaedra cries for her nurse to stop offering alternatives to death: "I've said too much. Oenone, let me die; / by dying I shall escape blasphemy" (I. iii. 228–229). What has Phaedra done to wish death so fervently?

    Nothing. Phaedra has not actually committed any deed; she has not acted on the passion she feels. In fact she has struggled time and again to suppress her adulterous desires. Her only morally culpable social act has been to counterfeit a hatred for "that hard-mouthed, proud / and pure Hippolytus" sufficient to stir some small dissension between her husband Theseus and her stepson. But for Phaedra, and indeed for most of the characters in Jean Racine's neoclassical tragedy (1677), to experience illicit emotion is to experience feelings of guilt with an intensity that is literally self-destructive. Over and over again in the first act of *Phaedra* we learn of and then see a woman who is wasting away from the morbid effects of passionate, never-to-be-fulfilled desires and consequent guilt. "Is your salvation from your terrified / conscience this passive, servile suicide?" (I. iii. 201–202) asks Oenone. Indeed, that is Phaedra's wish.

    A "terrified conscience" for a deed not committed surely is uncharacteristic of the mythical noble Grecian queen, wife of the great warrior Theseus, daughter of Cretan king Minos, but a terrified conscience does characterize the believing Christian who equates words, even feelings, with deeds. "Ye have heard that it was said by them of old time, Thou shalt not commit adultery," taught Jesus in his Sermon on the Mount. "But I say unto you, That whosoever looketh on a woman to lust after her hath committed adultery with her already in his heart" (Matt. 5:27–28). Phaedra has looked at Hippolytus with lust: "I have felt the heat / that drove my mother through the fields of Crete, / the bride of Minos, dying for the full / magnetic April thunders of the bull" (II. v. 707–710). The ugly, repellent image expresses the horror of losing control over one's emotions: Phaedra's mother, Pasiphaë, through no fault of her own but because of a quarrel her husband Minos had with the god

Poseidon, was made to fall in love with a bull; she conceived by the beast a monstrous child, the famous Minotaur whom Theseus slew. In Racine's version, Phaedra is not, like her mother, *fated* to feel an unnatural passion. She, not a god or goddess, controls her destiny. But Racine's Phaedra, by falling in love with Hippolytus, thinks she is losing control over her destiny, feels indeed that this loss of control is as monstrous as her mother's lust for a bull, and fears that her ancestry compels her toward this horrible, unnatural love. In giving her thoughts words, in voicing her deepest emotions, Phaedra is acting; she is losing control on a social level.

Despite the trappings of a mythological story—places, characters' names and backgrounds, even an off-stage death of supernatural origin—Jean Racine (1639–1699) has drawn characters who in all essential respects act and feel like seventeenth-century French aristocrats. Racine's Theseus thinks like a child of the Enlightenment, just as Shakespeare's Theseus in *A Midsummer-Night's Dream* rules with the even hand of a good Elizabethan liege lord. Both characters draw their names from the same mythological warrior and lover, but both reflect the cultural origins of their authors and the generic demands of the dramas in which they appear. By facing the horrible conflict between passions too strong to be controlled and a weakened reason, but valiantly trying to subdue those emotions, Phaedra acts out a particularly French neoclassical version of an archetypal human problem: Her illicit, unnamed love has driven her to the verge of madness.

Licit or illicit love as madness is, of course, an old metaphor. Shakespeare uses it (along with fairies) in *A Midsummer-Night's Dream*. Today we turn to Freud's divided portait of the human mind to explain how dark, hidden desires can inflame our being. But in Racine's time, a person's god-given ability to reason—what we would today recognize primarily as the conscious mind—completely defined existence. *"Cogito ergo sum,"* "I think, therefore I am," wrote the great French philosopher, René Descartes (1596–1650). Passion, which even thinking people naturally felt, was an animalistic attribute that could and should be controlled by reason for the good of humanity and for the good of the ordered society reasonably produced by civilized people.

Viewed in this cultural context, Phaedra's first crime is to express her passion to Oenone. The quality we most admire in Phaedra, her lasting moral nobility, is thus overcome by a temporary weakness, a weakness in her reason caused by a desire that again and again leads to tragic consequences. Oenone, lacking almost completely in moral scruple and acting vigorously only from her passionate devotion to Phaedra, leads her distraught mistress into further crimes. The crimes are Phaedra's, even though Oenone's actions help initiate them. Phaedra's "obscene confession" of her love to Hippolytus, the horrible temptation to dissemble to Theseus about the cause of her distraction, the final awful crime of omission when, enraged by jealousy at hearing that Hippolytus loves Aricia, she fails once again to confess the truth to Theseus: these are Phaedra's tragic acts. Because of them, Hippolytus lies on the sands, trampled to death by his own horses, the victim of the Phaedra who cried, "Have I lost my mind?" (IV. vi. 1302). Oenone has perished through her efforts to save her mistress at any cost. Theseus must live with the remorse of his blind and hasty judgment on his son. And Phaedra herself must die.

But the paradox of tragedy remains. The Phaedra who felt salvation lay in secrecy and repression obtains an enduring grace through confession and sacrificial death. As her "eyes at last give up their light, and see / the day they've soiled resume its purity" (V. vii. 1693–1694), one feels that Phaedra has come to terms with herself and has attained some measure of glory in death.

Everywhere in *Phaedra*, to countenance forbidden love is to invite madness, and reason is doomed. In part, *Phaedra* dramatizes what Francis Fergusson has called "the tragic life of the soul-as-rational" (*The Idea of a Theater*, p. 50), a disposition to believe that attempting to confront a person's passionate nature by asserting the power of reason to control errant emotion is inevitably doomed to pitiable and terrifying failure. The Jansenists, a Catholic sect of seventeenth-century France whose teachings were related to those of the protestant Calvinists, answered the tragic vision of the soul as reasoning with another ontology that denied the power of reason: A person has no free will but must depend solely on the grace of God for salvation and even then—since some are predestined for damnation no matter what their deeds on earth—has no assurance of salvation. Holy living, pure thoughts, and godly actions were some small evidence of a soul in the state of grace; impure emotions, harmful deeds, and evil thoughts suggested predestined damnation.

Jean Racine was raised in the teachings of Jansen, yet found in his own soul a different divine fire, the fire of artistic creation. In an era when drama was not officially tolerated (actors, for instance, could not receive Church burial, even though theirs was the most respected secular art), Racine chose the stage, an action that surely did not presage eternal salvation. Yet on earth, during his most brilliant and productive period (1667–1677), Racine surpassed even the great French tragic dramatist Pierre Corneille (1606–1684). Jean Baptiste Poquelin, the great comic playwright who called himself Molière (1622–1673), early championed his work. However, Racine triumphed without Molière's help, beginning with his first great characteristic work *Andromache* in 1667 and leaving the stage ten years and six tragedies later with *Phaedra* (although he produced two other minor Biblical dramas during his lifetime). He left the stage in part because he had been converted to his childhood Jansenism. *Phaedra* itself is obviously not about Racine's struggle between the Jansenism that denied efficacy of reason for salvation or governance of emotion and the secular doctrines that made reason supreme. Yet the struggle that led Racine to abjure the stage and spend the last twenty years of his life educating his children is clearly mirrored in the struggle between reason and passion in his tragedy.

Phaedra was produced in 1677 during an era of great intellectual activity. The Enlightenment in France believed it had created an ordered, reasonable society. At the head stood Louis XIV, the *Roi Soleil* ("Sun King") whose long life coincided with and greatly encouraged a remarkable period of cultural development. At the bottom, completely untouched by the great literature and art (unlike the Elizabethan common people who patronized Shakespeare) lay the serfs and peasants of France who a century later would usher in the modern era by staging the greatest revolution the world had ever seen. Louis XIV was the sun, the nobles and privileged few who surrounded him the planets; except as the dirt that made up the base substance of the satellites there was no room for the masses in the metaphor. For them order dictated a place far below, and in the controlled drama of the period, they were portrayed only in the comedies. To tragedy, the greatest achievement of the classical Greek and Roman world so admired by this despotic oligarchy, belonged characters as striking and famous as Louis himself—brilliant, carefully drawn aristocrats who, in art at least, spoke the compact, epigrammatic alexandrine couplets in which *Phaedra* was originally written. The best metaphor of artistic life is the order suggested by the existence of the French Academy, forty self-elected men who criticized art and articulated literary rules.

The purpose of using the rules by which, these men conceived, great literature had been written (and, with a failure of logic, by which great new literature could only be written) was to imitate great classical literature. But its most characteristic feature was its achievement of psychological realism. For drama, rules called *unities of time, place, and action* were devised (partly from a misreading of the greatest mimetic critic, Aristotle) to increase the *vraisemblance* and *le vrai* ("probability" and "truth") of the representation. The represented events of a play (according to the unity of time) should cover no more than a day; the represented scene (according to the unity of place) should be no larger than one city and ideally one location within that city; and all aspects of the events portrayed (according to the unity of action) must inextricably lead to a single denouement. Could an audience believe the action to be real if the scene shifted rapidly or characters aged before their eyes? Or, could an audience believe that a violent duel or ugly death was anything more than a stage event were it to take place on stage? *Decorum* (a concept championed by the Roman critic Horace) dictated that such events should take place offstage and be reported only; *verisimilitude* dictated that all events must be explicable, and Racine stepped very near the boundaries of the credible in *Phaedra* by attributing Hippolytus's death partly to the miraculous intervention of a pagan god.

The qualities that are most real in Racine's drama (and that of his contemporaries) are psychological and do not necessarily arise because the plays follow artificial rules like the unities, *liaison des scenes* (never leaving the stage empty during an act), or the exclusion of physical violence from the stage. Psychological realism is achieved because such neoclassical works dramatize with vigor and clarity the depths of human passion and the failure of human reason to control and order passions according to the best dictates of social duty.

Verisimilitude is not, of course, the same thing as the realism of television news reports, *cinéma verité,* or adult Westerns. The French *vraisemblance* might be better translated as *psychological* probability. Moreover, all art—even the naturalism of Chekhov or the realism of Shakespeare in some of the scenes from *A Midsummer-Night's Dream*—involves selection and hence cannot be completely "real." What is "real" is real according to the values of the viewer. That the aim of verisimilitude was a kind of realism seems strange since in so many ways the *vraisemblance* appears to work against what we would call realism today. However, in this ordered society and its ordered art, there were some unusual notions about what people would naturally say or do. Nobles were "naturally" refined, able to deal with subtle questions of reason and emotion; lower-class characters were "naturally" coarse, likely to think and feel grossly, suited for representation only in comedy—another Horatian dictum. Racine's age might not have fully approved contemporary American poet Robert Lowell's efforts to reveal the internal state of characters through the gross or bawdy language his free translation gives to Phaedra and others. Their objections would have been based on what they felt was true to human nature, and hence, on what was decorous in a tragedy.

Decorum, verisimilitude, and the other rules of neoclassical art sought to achieve not photographic realism of the particular but generalized psychological realism of what the age felt to be typical of human nature. To re-create the general conditions of a soul in torment, to paint the prominent and striking features, to neglect the odd or the unique, the eccentric or the untypical was to create lasting art. In the staging, too, generality of external trappings mattered more than minute realistic particularity. Tragic heroes, for instance, wore costumes that reflected broad outlines— Roman-style breastplates, fighting skirts, and short swords together with tall, obviously French headresses replete with plumes. The scene on which these heroes stood in their enclosed theaters was generalized and might be used for three or four different plays, the frontispiece, side wings, and backdrops fixed in place, depicting in a lush perspective style sometimes more than one location at once.

Perhaps the best clue to the essence of Racine's drama may be found in another facet of the physical conditions of staging. The theater itself was basically a rectangular hall measuring about one hundred by fifty feet. A forty-foot space at one end was reserved for acting and was enclosed by a proscenium or picture frame arch; the rest of the auditorium was ringed with boxes and galleries, with a central area called the *pit* providing more seats. The acting area was further limited to a space of about fifteen feet due to the custom of seating spectators on stage. Can duels and violent deaths be realistically represented in such a space? Will our concern be with the broad, sweeping gesture that brings audience and actor together with the gods or with the subtle argument, the curious and intense stroke of verbal expression, the nice distinction? *Phaedra* was shared with an audience but forced the members of that audience to look inward and measure their own knowledge of human nature against that portrayed by the skillful actors on-stage. In such close quarters thinking people discipline their responses; when discipline fails, chaos erupts. And in the events of *Phaedra,* that is what happened.

Phaedra

English version by Robert Lowell

for Miss Harriet Winslow

Acknowledgments: This translation was originally written for Mr. Eric Bent-ley. I was helped by innumerable suggestions made by friends and experts: Elizabeth Hardwick, Eric Bentley, Jacques Barzun, Stanley Kunitz, William Alfred, Adrienne Rich, Margaret Guiton, Mary Hivnor, and I. A. Rich-ards. R.L.

Characters
THESEUS, *son of Aegeus and King of Athens*
PHAEDRA, *wife of Theseus and daughter of Minos and Pasiphaë*
HIPPOLYTUS, *son of Theseus and Antiope, Queen of the Amazons*
ARICIA, *princess of the royal blood of Athens*
OENONE, *nurse of Phaedra*
THERAMENES, *tutor of Hippolytus*
ISMENE, *friend of Aricia*
PANOPE, *waiting-woman of Phaedra*
GUARDS

The scene is laid in Troezen, a city about forty miles from Athens, on the opposite side of the Gulf of Aegina.

Pronunciation:
Phaedra = Pheédra
Oenone = Eenónee
Ismene = Ismeénee
Pasiphaë = Pásiphá-ee
Aricia = Arisha
Theramenes = Therámeneés
Panope = Pánopée

Act I

Scene 1 Hippolytus, Theramenes
HIPPOLYTUS
No no, my friend, we're off! Six months have passed
since Father heard the ocean howl and cast
his galley on the Aegean's skull-white froth.
Listen! The blank sea calls us—off, off, off!
I'll follow Father to the fountainhead
and marsh of hell. We're off. Alive or dead,
I'll find him.
THERAMENES
                Where, my lord? I've sent a host
of veteran seamen up and down the coast;

each village, creek and cove from here to Crete
has been ransacked and questioned by my fleet;   10
my flagship skirted Hades' rapids, furled
sail there a day, and scoured the underworld.
Have you fresh news? New hopes? One even doubts
if noble Theseus wants his whereabouts
discovered. Does he need his helpers to share   15
the plunder of his latest love affair;
a shipload of spectators and his son
to watch him ruin his last Amazon—
some creature, taller than a man, whose tanned
and single bosom slithers from his hand,   20
when he leaps to crush her like a waterfall
of honeysuckle?

HIPPOLYTUS
                            You are cynical,
my friend. Your insinuations wrong a king,
sick as myself of his philandering.
His heart is Phaedra's and no rivals dare   25
to challenge Phaedra's sole possession there.
I sail to find my father. The command
of duty calls me from this stifling land.

THERAMENES
This stifling land? Is that how you deride
this gentle province where you used to ride   30
the bridle-paths, pursuing happiness?
You cured your orphaned childhood's loneliness
and found a peace here you preferred to all
the blaze of Athens' brawling protocol.
A rage for exploits blinds you. Your disease   35
is boredom.

HIPPOLYTUS
                        Friend, this kingdom lost its peace,
when Father left my mother, for defiled
bull-serviced Pasiphaë's child. The child
of homicidal Minos is our queen!

THERAMENES
Yes, Phaedra reigns and rules here. I have seen   40
you crouch before her outbursts like a cur.
When she first met you, she refused to stir
until your father drove you out of court.
The news is better now; our friends report
the queen is dying. Will you cross the seas,   45
desert your party and abandon Greece?
Why flee from Phaedra? Phaedra fears the night
less than she fears the day that strives to light
the universal ennui of her eyes—
this dying woman, who desires to die!   50

HIPPOLYTUS
No, I despise her Cretan vanity,
hysteria and idle cruelty.
I fear Aricia; she alone survives
the blood-feud that destroyed her brothers' lives.

THERAMENES

    Prince, Prince, forgive my laughter. Must you fly   55
beyond the limits of the world and die,
floating in flotsam, friendless, far from help,
and clubbed to death by Tartars in the kelp?
Why arm the shrinking violet with a knife?
Do you hate Aricia, and fear for your life,   60
Prince?

HIPPOLYTUS

        If I hated her, I'd trust myself
and stay.

THERAMENES

        Shall I explain you to yourself?
Prince, you have ceased to be that hard-mouthed, proud
and pure Hippolytus, who scorned the crowd
of common lovers once and rose above   65
your wayward father by despising love.
Now you justify your father, and you feel
love's poison running through you, now you kneel
and breathe the heavy incense, and a god
possesses you and revels in your blood!   70
Are you in love?

HIPPOLYTUS

        Theramenes, when I call
and cry for help, you push me to the wall.
Why do you plague me, and try to make me fear
the qualities you taught me to revere?
I sucked in prudence with my mother's milk.   75
Antiope, no harlot draped in silk,
first hardened me. I was my mother's son
and not my father's. When the Amazon,
my mother, was dethroned, my mind approved
her lessons more than ever. I still loved   80
her bristling chastity. Later, you told
stories about my father's deeds that made me hold
back judgment—how he stood for Hercules,
a second Hercules who cleared the Cretan seas
of pirates, throttled Scirron, Cercyon,   85
Procrustes, Sinnis, and the giant man
of Epidaurus writhing in his gore.
He pierced the maze and killed the Minotaur.
Other things turned my stomach: that long list
of women, all refusing to resist.   90
Helen, caught up with all her honeyed flesh
from Sparta; Periboea, young and fresh,
already tired of Salinis. A hundred more,
their names forgotten by my father—whore
and virgin, child and mother, all deceived,   95
if their protestations can be believed!
Ariadne declaiming to the rocks,
her sister, Phaedra, kidnapped. Phaedra locks
the gate at last! You know how often I
would weary, fall to nodding and deny   100

the possibility of hearing the whole
ignoble, dull, insipid boast unroll.
And now I too must fall. The gods have made me creep.
How can I be in love? I have no specious heap
of honors, friend. No mastered monsters drape   105
my shoulders—Theseus' excuse to rape
at will. Suppose I chose a woman. Why
choose an orphan? Aricia is eternally
cut off from marriage, lest she breed
successors to her fierce brothers, and seed   110
the land with treason. Father only grants
her life on one condition. This—he wants
no bridal torch to burn for her. Unwooed
and childless, she must answer for the blood
her brothers shed. How can I marry her,   115
gaily subvert our kingdom's character,
and sail on the high seas of love?

THERAMENES
                              You'll prove
nothing by reason, for you are in love.
Theseus' injustice to Aricia throws
her in the light; your eyes he wished to close   120
are open. She dazzles you. Her pitiful
seclusion makes her doubly terrible.
Does this innocent passion freeze your blood?
There's sweetness in it. Is your only good
the dismal famine of your chastity?   125
You shun your father's path? Where would you be,
Prince, if Antiope had never burned
chastely for Theseus? Love, my lord, has turned
the head of Hercules, and thousands—fired
the forge of Vulcan! All your uninspired, cold   130
moralizing is nothing, Prince. You have changed!
Now no one sees you riding, half-deranged
along the sand-bars, where you drove your horse
and foaming chariot with all your force,
tilting and staggering upright through the surf—   135
far from their usual course across the turf.
The woods are quiet. . . . How your eyes hang down!
You often murmur and forget to frown.
All's out, Prince. You're in love, you burn. Flames, flames,
Prince! A dissimulated sickness maims   140
the youthful quickness of your daring. Does
lovely Aricia haunt you?

HIPPOLYTUS
                        Friend, spare us.
I sail to find my father.

THERAMENES
                        Will you see
Phaedra before you go?

HIPPOLYTUS
                        I mean to be
here when she comes. Go, tell her. I will do   145

my duty. Wait, I see her nurse. What new
troubles torment her?

Scene 2 *Hippolytus, Theramenes, Oenone*

OENONE
      Who has griefs like mine,
my lord? I cannot help the queen in her decline.
Although I sit beside her day and night,
she shuts her eyes and withers in my sight.   150
An eternal tumult roisters through her head,
panics her sleep, and drags her from her bed.
Just now she fled me at the prime
of day to see the sun for the last time.
She's coming.

HIPPOLYTUS
     So! I'll steal away. My flight   155
removes a hateful object from her sight.

Scene 3 *Phaedra, Oenone*

PHAEDRA
Dearest, we'll go no further. I must rest.
I'll sit here. My emotions shake my breast,
the sunlight throws black bars across my eyes.
My knees give. If I fall, why should I rise,   160
Nurse?
   She sits down.

OENONE
   Heaven help us! Let me comfort you.

PHAEDRA
Tear off these gross, official rings, undo
these royal veils. They drag me to the ground.
Why have you frilled me, laced me, crowned me, and wound
my hair in turrets? All your skill torments   165
and chokes me. I am crushed by ornaments.
Everything hurts me, and drags me to my knees!

OENONE
Now this, now that, Madam. You never cease
commanding us, then cancelling your commands.
You feel your strength return, summon all hands   170
to dress you like a bride, then say you choke!
We open all the windows, fetch a cloak,
rush you outdoors. It's no use, you decide
that sunlight kills you, and only want to hide.

PHAEDRA
I feel the heaven's royal radiance cool   175
and fail, as if it feared my terrible
shame has destroyed its right to shine on men.
I'll never look upon the sun again.

OENONE
Renunciation on renunciation!
Now you slander the source of your creation.   180
Why do you run to death and tear your hair?

PHAEDRA
Oh God, take me to some sunless forest lair . . .
There hoof-beats raise a dust-cloud, and my eye
follows a horseman outlined on the sky!
OENONE
What's this, my lady?
PHAEDRA
                                    I have lost my mind.   185
Where am I? O forget my words! I find
I've lost the habit now of talking sense.
My face is red and guilty—evidence
of treason! I've betrayed my darkest fears,
Nurse, and my eyes, despite me, fill with tears.   190
OENONE
Lady, if you must weep, weep for your silence
that filled your days and mine with violence.
Ah deaf to argument and numb to care,
you have no mercy on us. Spare me, spare
yourself. Your blood is like polluted water,   195
fouling a mind desiring its own slaughter.
The sun has died and shadows filled the skies
thrice now, since you have closed your eyes;
the day has broken through the night's content
thrice now, since you have tasted nourishment.   200
Is your salvation from your terrified
conscience this passive, servile suicide?
Lady, your madness harms the gods who gave
you life, betrays your husband. Who will save
your children? Your downfall will orphan them,   205
deprive them of their kingdom, and condemn
their lives and future to the discipline
of one who abhors you and all your kin,
a tyrant suckled by an Amazon,
Hippolytus . . .
PHAEDRA
                Oh God!
OENONE
                            You still hate someone;   210
thank heaven for that, Madam!
PHAEDRA
                            You spoke his name!
OENONE
Hippolytus, Hippolytus! There's hope
in hatred, Lady. Give your anger rope.
I love your anger. If the winds of love
and fury stir you, you will live. Above   215
your children towers this foreigner, this child
of Scythian cannibals, now wild
to ruin the kingdom, master Greece, and choke
the children of the gods beneath his yoke.
Why dawdle? Why deliberate at length?   220
Oh, gather up your dissipated strength.

PHAEDRA
I've lived too long.
OENONE
Always, always agonized!
Is your conscience still stunned and paralyzed?
Do you think you have washed your hands in blood?
PHAEDRA
Thank God, my hands are clean still. Would to God   225
my heart were innocent!
OENONE
Your heart, your heart!
What have you done that tears your soul apart?
PHAEDRA
I've said too much. Oenone, let me die;
by dying I shall escape blasphemy.
ONEONE
Search for another hand to close your eyes.   230
Oh cruel Queen, I see that you despise
my sorrow and devotion. I'll die first,
and end the anguish of this service cursed
by your perversity. A thousand roads
always lie open to the killing gods.   235
I'll choose the nearest. Lady, tell me how
Oenone's love has failed you. Will you allow
your nurse to die, your nurse, who gave up all—
nation, parents, children, to serve in thrall.
I saved you from your mother, King Minos' wife!   240
Will your death pay me for giving up my life?
PHAEDRA
What I could tell you, I have told you. Nurse,
only my silence saves me from the curse
of heaven.
OENONE
How could you tell me anything
worse than watching you dying?
PHAEDRA
I would bring   245
my life and rank dishonor. What can I say
to save myself, or put off death a day?
OENONE
Ah Lady, I implore you by my tears,
and by your suffering body. Heaven hears,
and knows the truth already. Let me see.   250
PHAEDRA
Stand up.
OENONE
Your hesitation's killing me!
PHAEDRA
What can I tell you? How the gods reprove
me!
OENONE
Speak!

PHAEDRA

          Oh Venus, murdering Venus! love
gored Pasiphaë with the bull.

OENONE

                    Forget
your mother! When she died she paid her debt.   255

PHAEDRA

   Oh Ariadne, oh my Sister, lost
for love of Theseus on that rocky coast.

OENONE

   Lady, what nervous languor makes you rave
against your family; they are in the grave.

PHAEDRA

   Remorseless Aphrodite drives me. I,   260
my race's last and worst love-victim, die.

OENONE

   Are you in love?

PHAEDRA

              I am with love!

OENONE

                    Who
is he?

PHAEDRA

      I'll tell you. Nothing love can do
could equal . . . Nurse, I am in love. The shame
kills me. I love the. . . . Do not ask his name.   265

OENONE

   Who?

PHAEDRA

      Nurse, you know my old loathing for the son
of Theseus and the barbarous Amazon?

OENONE

   Hippolytus! My God, oh my God!

PHAEDRA

               You,
not I, have named him.

OENONE

          What can you do,
but die? Your words have turned my blood to ice.   270
Oh righteous heavens, must the blasphemies
of Pasiphaë fall upon her daughter?
Her Furies strike us down across the water.
Why did we come here?

PHAEDRA

   My evil comes from farther off. In May,   275
in brilliant Athens, on my marriage day,
I turned aside for shelter from the smile
of Theseus. Death was frowning in an aisle—
Hippolytus! I saw his face, turned white!
My lost and dazzled eyes saw only night,   280
capricious burnings flickered through my bleak
abandoned flesh. I could not breathe or speak.

I faced my flaming executioner,
Aphrodite, my mother's murderer!
I tried to calm her wrath by flowers and praise,   285
I built her a temple, fretted months and days
on decoration. I even hoped to find
symbols and stays for my distracted mind,
searching the guts of sacrificial steers.
Yet when my erring passions, mutineers   290
to virtue, offered incense at the shrine
of love, I failed to silence the malign
Goddess. Alas, my hungry open mouth,
thirsting with adoration, tasted drouth—
Venus resigned her altar to my new lord—   295
and even while I was praying, I adored
Hippolytus above the sacred flame,
now offered to his name I could not name.
I fled him, yet he stormed me in disguise,
and seemed to watch me with his father's eyes.   300
I even turned against myself, screwed up
my slack courage to fury, and would not stop
shrieking and raging, till half-dead with love
and the hatred of a stepmother, I drove
Hippolytus in exile from the rest   305
and strenuous wardship of his father's breast.
Then I could breathe, Oenone; he was gone;
my lazy, nerveless days meandered on
through dreams and daydreams, like a stately carriage
touring the level landscape of my marriage.   310
Yet nothing worked. My husband sent me here
to Troezen, far from Athens; once again the dear
face shattered me; I saw Hippolytus
each day, and felt my ancient, venomous
passion tear my body limb from limb;   315
naked, Venus was clawing down her victim.
What could I do? Each moment, terrified
by loose diseased emotions, now I cried
for death to save my glory and expel
my gloomy frenzy from this world, my hell.   320
And yet your tears and words bewildered me,
and so endangered my tranquillity,
at last I spoke. Nurse, I shall not repent,
if you will leave me the passive content
of dry silence and solitude.   325

Scene 4 Phaedra, Oenone, Panope

PANOPE
My heart breaks. Would to God, I could refuse
to tell your majesty my evil news.
The King is dead! Listen, the heavens ring
with shouts and lamentations for the King.

PHAEDRA
The King is dead? What's this?

PANOPE

                    In vain   330
you beg the gods to send him back again.
Hippolytus has heard the true report,
he is already heading for the port.

PHAEDRA

Oh God!

PANOPE

               They've heard in Athens. Everyone
is joining factions—some salute your son,   335
others are calling for Hippolytus;
they want him to reform and harden us—
even Aricia claims the loyalty
of a fanatical minority.
The Prince's captains have recalled their men.   340
His flag is up, and now he sails again
for Athens. Queen, if he appear there now,
he'll drag the people with him!

OENONE

                         Stop, allow
the Queen a little respite for her grief.
She hears you, and will act for our relief.   345

          Scene 5   Phaedra, Oenone

OENONE

I'd given up persuading you to live;
death was your refuge, only death could give
you peace and save your troubled glory. I
myself desired to follow you, and die.
But this catastrophe prescribes new laws: 350
the king is dead, and for the king who was,
fate offers you his kingdom. You have a son;
he should be king! If you abandon
him, he'll be a slave. The gods, his ancestors,
will curse and drive you on your fatal course.   355
Live! Who'll condemn you if you love and woo
the Prince? Your stepson is no kin to you,
now that your royal husband's death has cut
and freed you from the throttling marriage-knot.
Do not torment the Prince with persecution,   360
and give a leader to the revolution;
no, win his friendship, bind him to your side.
Give him this city and its countryside.
He will renounce the walls of Athens, piled
stone on stone by Minerva for your child.   365
Stand with Hippolytus, annihilate
Aricia's faction, and possess the state!

PHAEDRA

So be it! Your superior force has won.
I will live if compassion for my son,
devotion to the Prince, and love of power   370
can give me courage in this fearful hour.

Act II

Scene 1 Aricia, Ismene

ARICIA

What's this? The Prince has sent a messenger?
The Prince begs me to wait and meet him here?
The Prince begs! Goose, you've lost your feeble wits!

ISMENE

Lady, be calm. These are the benefits   375
of Theseus' death: first Prince Hippolytus
comes courting favors; soon the populous
cities of Greece will follow—they will eat
out of your hand, Princess, and kiss your feet.

ARICIA

This felon's hand, this slave's! My dear, your news   380
is only frivolous gossip, I refuse
to hope.

ISMENE

      Ah Princess, the just powers of hell
Have struck. Theseus has joined your brothers!

ARICIA

                      Tell
me how he died.

ISMENE

         Princess, fearful tales
are circulating. Sailors saw his sails,   385
his infamous black sails, spin round and round
in Charybdis' whirlpool; all hands were drowned.
Yet others say on better evidence
that Theseus and Pirithoüs passed the dense
darkness of hell to rape Persephone.   390
Pirithoüs was murdered by the hound;
Theseus, still living, was buried in the ground.

ARICIA

This is an old wives' tale. Only the dead
enter the underworld, and see the bed
of Queen Persephone. What brought him there?   395

ISMENE

Princess, the King is dead—dead! Everywhere
men know and mourn. Already our worshipping
townsmen acclaim Hippolytus for their king;
in her great palace, Phaedra, the self-styled
regent, rages and trembles for her child.   400

ARICIA

What makes you think the puritanical
son of Theseus is human? Will he recall
my sentence and relent?

ISMENE

            I know he will.

ARICIA

You know nothing about him. He would kill
a woman, rather than be kind to one.   405

That wolf-cub of a fighting Amazon
hates me above all women. He would walk
from here to hell, rather than hear me talk.

ISMENE

Do you know Hippolytus? Listen to me.
His famous, blasphemous frigidity,   410
what is it, when you've seen him close at hand?
I've watched him like a hawk, and seen him stand
shaking beside you—all his reputation
for hating womenkind bears no relation
to what I saw. He couldn't take his eyes   415
off you! His eyes speak what his tongue denies.

ARICIA

I can't believe you. Your story's absurd!
How greedily I listen to each word!
Ismene, you know me, you know how my heart
was reared on death and always set apart   420
from what it cherished—can this plaything of
the gods and furies feel the peace of love?
What sights I've seen, Ismene! "Heads will roll,"
my brothers told me, "we will rule." I, the sole
survivor of those fabulous kings, who tilled   425
the soil of Greece, have seen my brothers killed,
six brothers murdered! In a single hour,
the tyrant, Theseus, lopped them in their flower.
The monster spared my life, and yet decreed
the torments of this childless life I lead   430
in exile, where no Greek can look on me;
my forced, perpetual virginity
preserves his crown; no son shall bear my name
or blow my brothers' ashes into flame.
Ismene, you know how well his tyranny   435
favors my temperament and strengthens me
to guard the honor of my reputation;
his rigor fortified my inclination.
How could I test his son's civilities?
I'd never even seen him with my eyes!   440
I'd never seen him. I'd restrained my eye,
that giddy nerve, from dwelling thoughtlessly
upon his outward grace and beauty—on mere
embellishments of nature, a veneer
the Prince himself despises and ignores.   445
My heart loves nobler virtues, and adores
in him his father's hard intelligence.
He has his father's daring and a sense
of honor his father lacks. Let me confess,
I love him for his lofty haughtiness   450
never submitted to a woman's yoke.
How could Phaedra's splendid marriage provoke
my jealousy? Have I so little pride,
I'd snatch at a rake's heart, a heart denied
to none—all riddled, opened up to let   455

thousands pass in like water through a net?
To carry sorrows to a heart, alone
untouched by passion, inflexible as stone,
to fasten my dominion on a force
as nervous as a never-harnessed horse—   460
this stirs me, this enflames me. Devilish Zeus
is easier mastered than Hippolytus;
heaven's love-infatuated emperor
confers less glory on his conqueror!
Ismene, I'm afraid. Why should I boast?   465
His very virtues I admire the most
threaten to rise and throw me from the brink
of hope. What girlish folly made me think
Hippolytus could love Aricia?

ISMENE

                              Here
he is. He loves you, Princess. Have no fear.   470

     Scene 2 Aricia, Ismene, Hippolytus

HIPPOLYTUS

                                        Princess, before
I leave here, I must tell you what's in store
for you in Greece. Alas, my father's dead.
The fierce forebodings that disquieted
my peace are true. Death, only death, could hide   475
his valor from this world he pacified.
The homicidal Fates will not release
the comrade, friend and peer of Hercules.
Princess, I trust your hate will not resent
honors whose justice is self-evident.   480
A single hope alleviates my grief,
Princess, I hope to offer you relief.
I now revoke a law whose cruelty
has pained my conscience. Princess, you are free
to marry. Oh enjoy this province, whose   485
honest, unhesitating subjects choose
Hippolytus for king. Live free as air,
here, free as I am, much more free!

ARICIA

                              I dare
not hope. You are too gracious. Can you free
Aricia from your father's stern decree?   490

HIPPOLYTUS

Princess, the Athenian people, torn in two
between myself and Phaedra's son, want you.

ARICIA

Want me, my lord!

HIPPOLYTUS

                    I've no illusions. Lame
Athenian precedents condemn my claim,
because my mother was a foreigner.   495
But what is that? If my only rival were

my younger brother, his minority
would clear my legal disability.
However, a better claim than his or mine
now favors you, ennobled by the line   500
of great Erectheus. Your direct descent
sets you before my father; he was only lent
this kingdom by adoption. Once the common
Athenian, dazed by Theseus' superhuman
energies, had no longing to exhume   505
the rights that rushed your brothers to their doom.
Now Athens calls you home; the ancient feud
too long has stained the sacred olive wood;
blood festers in the furrows of our soil
to blight its fruits and scorch the farmer's toil.   510
This province suits me, let the vines of Crete
offer my brother a secure retreat.
The rest is yours. All Attica is yours;
I go to win you what your right assures.

ARICIA

Am I awake, my lord? Your sayings seem   515
like weird phantasmagoria in a dream.
How can your sparkling promises be true?
Some god, my lord, some god, has entered you!
How justly you are worshipped in this town;
oh how the truth surpasses your renown!   520
You wish to endow me with your heritage!
I only hoped you would not hate me. This rage
your father felt, how can you put it by
and treat me kindly?

HIPPOLYTUS

               Princess, is my eye
blind to beauty? Am I a bear, a bull, a boar,   525
some abortion fathered by the Minotaur?
Some one-eyed Cyclops, able to resist
Aricia's loveliness and still exist?
How can a man stand up against your grace?

ARICIA

My lord, my lord!

HIPPOLYTUS

              I cannot hide my face,   530
Princess! I'm driven. Why does my violence
so silence reason and intelligence?
Must I be still, and let my adoration
simmer away in silent resignation?
Princess, I've lost all power to restrain   535
myself. You see a madman, whose insane
pride hated love, and hoped to sit ashore,
watching the galleys founder in the war;
I was Diana's liegeman, dressed in steel.
I hoped to trample love beneath my heel—   540
alas, the flaming Venus burns me down,
I am the last dependent on her crown.

What left me charred and writhing in her clutch?
A single moment and a single touch.
Six months now, bounding like a wounded stag,   545
I've tried to shake this poisoned dart, and drag
myself to safety from your eyes that blind
when present, and when absent leave behind
volleys of burning arrows in my mind.
Ah Princess, shall I dive into the sea,   550
or steal the wings of Icarus to flee
love's Midas' touch that turns my world to gold?
Your image drives me stumbling through the cold,
floods my deserted forest caves with light,
darkens the day and dazzles through my night.   555
I'm grafted to your side by all I see;
all things unite us and imprison me.
I have no courage for the Spartan exercise
that trained my hand and steeled my energies.
Where are my horses? I forget their names.   560
My triumphs with my chariot at the games
no longer give me strength to mount a horse.
The ocean drives me shuddering from its shores.
Does such a savage conquest make you blush?
My boorish gestures, headlong cries that rush   565
at you like formless monsters from the sea?
Ah, Princess, hear me! Your serenity
must pardon the distortions of a weak
and new-born lover, forced by you to speak
love's foreign language, words that snarl and yelp . . .   570
I never could have spoken without your help.

    Scene 3 Aricia, Ismene, Hippolytus, Theramenes
THERAMENES
    I announce the Queen. She comes hurriedly,
    looking for you.
HIPPOLYTUS
            For me!
THERAMENES
                Don't ask me why;
    she insisted. I promised I'd prevail
    on you to speak with her before you sail.   575
HIPPOLYTUS
    What can she want to hear? What can I say?
ARICIA
    Wait for her, here! You cannot turn away.
    Forget her malice. Hating her will serve
    no purpose. Wait for her! Her tears deserve
    your pity.
HIPPOLYTUS
          You're going, Princess? And I must go   580
    to Athens, far from you. How shall I know
    if you accept my love?

ARICIA

My Lord, pursue
your gracious promise. Do what you must do,
make Athens tributary to my rule.
Nothing you offer is unacceptable,   585
yet this empire, so great, so glorious,
is the least precious of your gifts to us.

Scene 4 Hippolytus, Theramenes

HIPPOLYTUS

We're ready. Wait, the Queen's here. I need you.
You must interrupt this tedious interview.
Hurry down to the ship, then rush back, pale   590
and breathless. Say the wind's up and we must sail.

Scene 5 Hippolytus, Oenone, Phaedra

PHAEDRA *(To Oenone.)*

He's here! Why does he scowl and look
away from me? What shall I do? What shall I say?

OENONE

Speak for your son, he has no other patron.

PHAEDRA

Why are you so impatient to be gone   595
from us, my lord? Stay! we will weep together.
Pity my son; he too has lost his father.
My own death's near. Rebellion, sick with wrongs,
now like a sea-beast, lifts its slimey prongs,
its muck, its jelly. You alone now stand   600
to save the state. Who else can understand
a mother? I forget. You will not hear
me! An enemy deserves no pity. I fear
your anger. Must my son, your brother, Prince,
be punished for his cruel mother's sins?   605

HIPPOLYTUS

I've no such thoughts.

PHAEDRA

I persecuted you
blindly, and now you have good reason to
return my impudence. How could you find
the motivation of this heart and mind
that scourged and tortured you, till you began   610
to lose the calm composure of a man,
and dwindle to a harsh and sullen boy,
a thing of ice, unable to enjoy
the charms of any civilized resource
except the heavy friendship of your horse,   615
that whirled you far from women, court and throne,
to course the savage woods for wolves alone?
You have good reason, yet if pain's a measure,
no one has less deserved your stern displeasure.
My lord, no one has more deserved compassion.   620

HIPPOLYTUS
    Lady, I understand a mother's passion,
    a mother jealous for her children's rights.
    How can she spare a first wife's son? Long nights
    of plotting, devious days of quarrelling—
    a madhouse! What else can remarriage bring?   625
    Another would have shown equal hostility,
    pushed her advantage more outrageously.
PHAEDRA
    My lord, if you had known how far my love
    and yearning have exalted me above
    this usual weakness . . . Our afflicting kinship   630
    is ending . . .
HIPPOLYTUS
              Madam, the precious minutes slip
    by, I fatigue you. Fight against your fears.
    Perhaps Poseidon has listened to our tears,
    perhaps your husband's still alive. He hears
    us, he is surging home—only a short   635
    day's cruise conceals him, as he scuds for port.
PHAEDRA
    That's folly, my lord. Who has twice visited
    black Hades and the river of the dead
    and returned? No, the poisonous Acheron
    never lets go. Theseus drifts on and on,   640
    a gutted galley on that clotted waste—
    he woos, he wins Persephone, the chaste . . .
    What am I saying? Theseus is not dead.
    He lives in you. He speaks, he's taller by a head.
    I see him, touch him, and my heart—a reef . . .   645
    Ah Prince, I wander. Love betrays my grief . . .
HIPPOLYTUS
    No, no, my father lives. Lady, the blind
    furies release him; in your loyal mind,
    love's fullness holds him, and he cannot die.
PHAEDRA
    I hunger for Theseus. Always in my eye   650
    he wanders, not as he appeared in hell,
    lascivious eulogist of any belle
    he found there, from the lowest to the Queen;
    no, faithful, airy, just a little mean
    through virtue, charming all, yet young and new,   655
    as we would paint a god—as I now see you!
    Your valiant shyness would have graced his speech,
    he would have had your stature, eyes, and reach,
    Prince, when he flashed across our Cretan waters,
    the loved enslaver of King Minos' daughters.   660
    Where were you? How could he conscript the flower
    of Athens' youth against my father's power,
    and ignore you? You were too young, they say;
    you should have voyaged as a stowaway.
    No dawdling bypath would have saved our bull,   665

when your just vengeance thundered through its skull.
There, light of foot, and certain of your goal,
you would have struck my brother's monstrous soul,
and pierced our maze's slow meanders, led
by Ariadne and her subtle thread.   670
By Ariadne? Prince, *I* would have fought
for precedence; my every flaming thought,
love-quickened, would have shot you through the dark,
straight as an arrow to your quaking mark.
Could I have waited, panting, perishing,   675
entrusting your survival to a string,
like Ariadne, when she skulked behind,
there at the portal, to bemuse her mind
among the solemn cloisters of the porch?
No, Phaedra would have snatched your burning torch,   680
and lunged before you, reeling like a priest
of Dionysus to distract the beast.
I would have reached the final corridor
a lap before you, and killed the Minotaur!
Lost in the labyrinth, and at your side,   685
would it have mattered, if I lived or died?
HIPPOLYTUS
What are you saying, Madam? You forget
my father is your husband!
PHAEDRA
                                     I have let
you see my grief for Theseus! How could I
forget my honor and my majesty,   690
Prince?
HIPPOLYTUS
            Madam, forgive me! My foolish youth
conjectured hideous untruths from your truth.
I cannot face my insolence. Farewell . . .
PHAEDRA
You monster! You understood me too well!
Why do you hang there, speechless, petrified,   695
polite! My mind whirls. What have I to hide?
Phaedra in all her madness stands before you.
I love you! Fool, I love you, I adore you!
Do not imagine that my mind approved
my first defection, Prince, or that I loved   700
your youth light-heartedly, and fed my treason
with cowardly compliance, till I lost my reason.
I wished to hate you, but the gods corrupt
us; though I never suffered their abrupt
seductions, shattering advances, I   705
too bear their sensual lightnings in my thigh.
I too am dying. I have felt the heat
that drove my mother through the fields of Crete,
the bride of Minos, dying for the full
magnetic April thunders of the bull.   710
I struggled with my sickness, but I found

no grace or magic to preserve my sound
intelligence and honor from this lust,
plowing my body with its horny thrust.
At first I fled you, and when this fell short   715
of safety, Prince, I exiled you from court.
Alas, my violence to resist you made
my face inhuman, hateful. I was afraid
to kiss my husband lest I love his son.
I made you fear me (this was easily done);   720
you loathed me more, I ached for you no less.
Misfortune magnified your loveliness.
I grew so wrung and wasted, men mistook
me for the Sibyl. If you could bear to look
your eyes would tell you. Do you believe my passion   725
is voluntary? That my obscene confession
is some dark trick, some oily artifice?
I came to beg you not to sacrifice
my son, already uncertain of his life.
Ridiculous, mad embassy, for a wife   730
who loves her stepson! Prince, I only spoke
about myself! Avenge yourself, invoke
your father; a worse monster threatens you
than any Theseus ever fought and slew.
The wife of Theseus loves Hippolytus!   735
See, Prince! Look, this monster, ravenous
for her execution, will not flinch.
I want your sword's spasmodic final inch.

OENONE

Madam, put down this weapon. Your distress
attracts the people. Fly these witnesses.   740
Hurry! Stop kneeling! What a time to pray!

    Scene 6 Theramenes, Hippolytus

THERAMENES

Is this Phaedra, fleeing, or rather dragged away
sobbing? Where is your sword? Who tore
this empty scabbard from your belt?

HIPPOLYTUS

                      No more!

Oh let me get away! I face disaster.   745
Horrors unnerve me. Help! I cannot master
my terror. Phaedra . . . No, I won't expose
her. No! Something I do not dare disclose . . .

THERAMENES

Our ship is ready, but before you leave,
listen! Prince, what we never would believe   750
has happened: Athens has voted for your brother.
The citizens have made him king. His mother
is regent.

HIPPOLYTUS

       Phaedra is in power!

THERAMENES
>   An envoy sent from Athens came this hour
>   to place the scepter in her hands. Her son   755
>   is king.
HIPPOLYTUS
>   Almighty gods, you know this woman!
>   Is it her spotless virtue you reward?
THERAMENES
>   I've heard a rumor. Someone swam aboard
>   a ship off Epirus. He claims the King
>   is still alive. I've searched. I know the thing   760
>   is nonsense.
HIPPOLYTUS
>   Search! Nothing must be neglected.
>   If the king's dead, I'll rouse the disaffected
>   people, crown Aricia, and place our lands,
>   our people, and our lives in worthy hands.

Act III

Scene 1   Phaedra, Oenone

PHAEDRA
>   Why do my people rush to crown me queen?   765
>   Who can even want to see me? They have seen
>   my downfall. Will their praise deliver me?
>   Oh bury me at the bottom of the sea!
>   Nurse, I have said too much! Led on by you,
>   I've said what no one should have listened to.   770
>   *He* listened. How could he pretend my drift
>   was hidden? Something held him, and made him shift
>   his ground . . . He only wanted to depart
>   and hide, while I was pouring out my heart.
>   Oh how his blushing multiplied my shame!   775
>   Why did you hold me back? You are to blame,
>   Oenone. But for you, I would have killed
>   myself. Would he have stood there, iron-willed
>   and merciless, while I fell upon his sword?
>   He would have snatched it, touched me, and restored   780
>   my life! No, no!
OENONE
>   Control yourself! No peace
>   comes from surrendering to your disease,
>   Madam. Oh daughter of the kings of Crete,
>   why are you weeping and fawning at the feet
>   of this barbarian, less afraid of fate   785
>   than of a woman? You must rule the state.
PHAEDRA
>   Can I, who have no courage to restrain
>   the insurrection of my passions, reign?
>   Will the Athenians trust their sovereignty

to me? Love's despotism is crushing me,   790
I am ruined.

OENONE

        Fly!

PHAEDRA

          How can I leave him?

OENONE

Lady, you have already banished him;
can't you take flight?

PHAEDRA

              The time for flight has passed.
He knows me now. I rushed beyond the last
limits of modesty, when I confessed.   795
Hope was no longer blasting through my breast;
I was resigned to hopelessness and death,
and gasping out my last innocent breath,
Oenone, when you forced me back to life.
You thought I was no longer Theseus' wife,   800
and let me feel that I was free to love.

OENONE

I would have done anything to remove
your danger. Whether I'm guilty or innocent
is all the same to me. Your punishment
should fall on one who tried to kill you, not   805
on poor Oenone. Lady, you must plot
and sacrifice this monster, whose unjust
abhorrence left you dying in the dust.
Oh humble him, undo him, oh despise
him! Lady, you must see him with my eyes.   810

PHAEDRA

Oenone, he was nourished in the woods;
he is all shyness and ungracious moods
because the forests left him half-inhuman.
He's never heard love spoken by a woman!
We've gone too far. Oenone, we're unwise;   815
perhaps the young man's silence was surprise.

OENONE

His mother, the Amazon, was never moved
by men.

PHAEDRA

        The boy exists. She must have loved!

OENONE

He has a sullen hatred for our sex.

PHAEDRA

Oh, all the better; rivals will not vex   820
my chances. Your advice is out of season;
now you must serve my frenzy, not my reason!
You tell me love has never touched his heart;
we'll look, we'll find an undefended part.
He's turned his bronze prows seaward; look, the wind   825
already blows like a trumpeter behind
his bulging canvas! The Acropolis

of Athens and its empire shall be his!
Hurry, Oenone, hunt the young man down,
blind him with dazzling visions of the crown.   830
Go tell him I relinquish my command,
I only want the guidance of his hand.
Let him assume these powers that weary me;
he will instruct my son in sovereignty.
Perhaps he will adopt my son, and be   835
the son's and mother's one divinity!
Oenone, rush to him, use every means
to bend and win him; if he fears the Queen's
too proud, he'll listen to her slave. Plead, groan,
insist . . . say I am giving him my throne. . . .   840
No, say I'm dying!

       Scene 2 Phaedra

PHAEDRA

Implacable Aphrodite, now you see
the depths to which your tireless cruelty
has driven Phaedra—here is my bosom;
every thrust and arrow has struck home!   845
Oh Goddess, if you hunger for renown,
rise now, and shoot a worthier victim down!
Conquer the barbarous Hippolytus,
who mocks the graces and the power of Venus,
and gazes on your godhead with disgust.   850
Avenge me, Venus! See, my cause is just,
my cause is yours. Oh bend him to my will! . . .
You're back, Oenone? Does he hate me still?

       Scene 3 Phaedra, Oenone

OENONE

Your love is folly, dash it from your soul,
gather your scattered pride and self-control,   855
Madam! I've seen the royal ship arrive.
Theseus is back, Theseus is still alive!
Thousands of voices thunder from the docks.
People are waving flags and climbing rocks.
While I was looking for Hippolytus . . .   860

PHAEDRA

My husband's living! Must you trouble us
by talking? What am I living for?
He lives, Oenone, let me hear no more
about it.

OENONE

      Why?

PHAEDRA

          I told you, but my fears
were stilled, alas, and smothered by your tears.   865
Had I died this morning, I might have faced
the gods. I heeded you and die disgraced!

OENONE
      You are disgraced!
PHAEDRA
                                    Oh Gods of wrath,
      how far I've travelled on my dangerous path!
      I go to meet my husband; at his side   870
      will stand Hippolytus. How shall I hide
      my thick adulterous passion for this youth,
      who has rejected me, and knows the truth?
      Will the stern Prince stand smiling and approve
      the labored histrionics of my love   875
      for Theseus, see my lips, still languishing
      for his, betray his father and his King?
      Will he not draw his sword and strike me dead?
      Suppose he spares me? What if nothing's said?
      Am I a gorgon, or Circe, or the infidel   880
      Medea, stifled by the flames of hell,
      yet rising like Aphrodite from the sea,
      refreshed and radiant with indecency?
      Can I kiss Theseus with dissembled poise?
      I think each stone and pillar has a voice.   885
      The very dust rises to disabuse
      my husband—to defame me and accuse!
      Oenone, I want to die. Death will give
      me freedom; oh it's nothing not to live;
      death to the unhappy's no catastrophe!   890
      I fear the name that must live after me,
      and crush my son until the end of time.
      Is his inheritance his mother's crime?
      his right to curse me, when my pollution stains
      the blood of heaven bubbling in his veins?   895
      The day will come, alas, the day will come,
      when nothing will be left to save him from
      the voices of despair. If he should live
      he'll flee his subjects like a fugitive.
OENONE
      He has my pity. Who has ever built   900
      firmer foundations to expose her guilt?
      But why expose your son? Is your contribution
      for his defense to serve the prosecution?
      Suppose you kill yourself? The world will say
      you fled your outraged husband in dismay.   905
      Could there be stronger evidence and proof
      than Phaedra crushed beneath the horse's hoof
      of blasphemous self-destruction to convince
      the crowds who'll dance attendance on the Prince?
      The crowds will mob your children when they hear   910
      their defamation by a foreigner!
      Wouldn't you rather see earth bury us?
      Tell me, do you still love Hippolytus?
PHAEDRA
      I see him as a beast, who'd murder us.

OENONE

    Madam, let the positions be reversed!   915
    You fear the Prince; you must accuse him first.
    Who'll dare assert your story is untrue,
    if all the evidence shall speak for you:
    your present grief, your past despair of mind,
    the Prince's sword so luckily left behind?   920
    Do you think Theseus will oppose his son's
    second exile? He has consented once!

PHAEDRA

    How dare I take this murderous, plunging course?

OENONE

    I tremble, Lady, I too feel remorse.
    If death could rescue you from infamy,   925
    Madam, I too would follow you and die.
    Help me by being silent. I will speak
    in such a way the King will only seek
    a bloodless exile to assert his rights.
    A father is still a father when he smites.   930
    You shudder at this evil sacrifice,
    but nothing's evil or too high a price
    to save your menaced honor from defeat.
    Ah Minos, Minos, you defended Crete
    by killing young men! Help us! If the cost   935
    for saving Phaedra is a holocaust
    of virtue, Minos, you must sanctify
    our undertaking, or watch your daughter die.
    I see the King.

PHAEDRA

              I see Hippolytus.

Scene 4 Phaedra, Theseus, Hippolytus, Oenone, Theramenes

THESEUS

    Fate's heard me, Phaedra, and removed the bar   940
    that kept me from your arms.

PHAEDRA

              Theseus, stop where you are!
    Your raptures and endearments are profane.
    Your arm must never comfort me again.
    You have been wronged, the gods who spared your life
    have used your absence to disgrace your wife,   945
    unworthy now to please you or come near.
    My only refuge is to disappear.

Scene 5 Theseus, Hippolytus, Theramenes

THESEUS

    What a strange welcome! This bewilders me.
    My son, what's happened?

HIPPOLYTUS

             Phaedra holds the key.
    Ask Phaedra. If you love me, let me leave   950
    this kingdom. I'm determined to achieve

some action that will show my strength. I fear
Phaedra. I am afraid of living here.
THESEUS
My son, you want to leave me?
HIPPOLYTUS
I never sought
her grace or favor. Your decision brought   955
her here from Athens. Your desires prevailed
against my judgment, Father, when you sailed
leaving Phaedra and Aricia in my care.
I've done my duty, now I must prepare
for sterner actions, I must test my skill   960
on monsters far more dangerous to kill
than any wolf or eagle in this wood.
Release me, I too must prove my manhood!
Oh Father, you were hardly half my age,
when herds of giants writhed before your rage—   965
you were already famous as the scourge
of insolence. Our people saw you purge
the pirates from the shores of Greece and Thrace,
the harmless merchantman was free to race
the winds, and weary Hercules could pause   970
from slaughter, knowing you upheld his cause.
The world revered you. I am still unknown;
even my mother's deeds surpass my own.
Some tyrants have escaped you; let me meet
with them and throw their bodies at your feet.   975
I'll drag them from their wolf-holes; if I die,
my death will show I struggled worthily.
Oh, Father, raise me from oblivion;
my deeds shall tell the universe I am your son.
THESEUS
What do I see? Oh gods, what horror drives   980
my queen and children fleeing for their lives
before me? If so little warmth remains,
oh why did you release me from my chains?
Why am I hated, and so little loved?
I had a friend, just one. His folly moved   985
me till I aided his conspiracy
to ravish Queen Persephone.
The gods, tormented by our blasphemous
designs, befogged our minds and blinded us—
we invaded Epirus instead of hell.   990
There a diseased and subtle tyrant fell
upon us as we slept, and while I stood
by, helpless, monsters crazed for human blood
consumed Pirithoüs. I myself was chained
fast in a death-deep dungeon. I remained   995
six months there, then the gods had pity,
and put me in possession of the city.
I killed the tyrant; now his body feasts
the famished, pampered bellies of his beasts.

At last, I voyaged home, cast anchor, furled   1000
my sails. When I was rushing to my world—
what am I saying? When my heart and soul
were mine again, unable to control
themselves for longing—who receives me? All run
and shun me, as if I were a skeleton.   1005
Now I myself begin to feel the fear
I inspire. I wish I were a prisoner
again or dead. Speak! Phaedra says my home
was outraged. Who betrayed me? Someone come
and tell me. I have fought for Greece. Will Greece,   1010
sustained by Theseus, give my enemies
asylum in my household? Tell me why
I've no avenger? Is my son a spy?
You will not answer. I must know my fate.
Suspicion chokes me, while I hesitate   1015
and stand here pleading. Wait, let no one stir.
Phaedra shall tell me what has troubled her.

Scene 6 *Hippolytus, Theramenes*

HIPPOLYTUS

What now? His anger turns my blood to ice.
Will Phaedra, always uncertain, sacrifice
herself? What will she tell the King? How hot   1020
the air's becoming here! I feel the rot
of love seeping like poison through this house.
I feel the pollution. I cannot rouse
my former loyalties. When I try to gather
the necessary strength to face my father,   1025
my mind spins with some dark presentiment . . .
How can such terror touch the innocent?
I LOVE ARICIA! Father, I confess
my treason to you is my happiness!
I LOVE ARICIA! Will this bring you joy,   1030
our love you have no power to destroy?

Act IV

Scene 1 *Theseus, Oenone*

THESEUS

What's this, you tell me he dishonors me,
and has assaulted Phaedra's chastity?
Oh heavy fortune, I no longer know
who loves me, who I am, or where I go.   1035
Who has ever seen such disloyalty
after such love? Such sly audacity?
His youth made no impression on her soul,
so he fell back on force to reach his goal!
I recognize this perjured sword; I gave   1040
him this myself to teach him to be brave!
Oh Zeus, are blood-ties no impediment?

Even Phaedra to save him from punishment!
Why did her silence spare this parricide?

OENONE

She hoped to spare a trusting father's pride. 1045
She felt so sickened by your son's attempt,
his hot eyes leering at her with contempt,
she had no wish to live. She read out her will
to me, then lifted up her arm to kill
herself. I struck the sword out of her hand. 1050
Fainting, she babbled the secret she had planned
to bury with her in the grave. My ears
unwillingly interpreted her tears.

THESEUS

Oh traitor! I know why he seemed to blanch
and toss with terror like an aspen branch
when Phaedra saw him. Now I know why he stood 1055
back, then embraced me so coldly he froze my blood.
Was Athens the first stage for his obscene
attentions? Did he dare attack the Queen
before our marriage?

OENONE

                    Remember her disgust 1060
and hate then? She already feared his lust.

THESEUS

And when I sailed, this started up again?

OENONE

I've hidden nothing. Do you want your pain
redoubled? Phaedra calls me. Let me go,
and save her. I have told you what I know. 1065

Scene 2 Theseus, Hippolytus

THESEUS

My son returns! Oh God, reserved and cool,
dressed in a casual freedom that could fool
the sharpest. Is it right his brows should blaze
and dazzle me with virtue's sacred rays?
Are there not signs? Should not ADULTERER 1070
in looping scarlet script be branded there?

HIPPOLYTUS

What cares becloud your kingly countenance,
Father! What is this irritated glance?
Tell me! Are you afraid to trust your son?

THESEUS

How dare you stand here? May the great Zeus stone 1075
me, if I let my fondness and your birth
protect you! Is my strength which rid the earth
of brigands paralysed? Am I so sick
and senile, any coward with a stick
can strike me? Am I a schoolboy's target? Oh God, 1080
am I food for vultures? Some carrion you must prod
and poke to see if it's alive or dead?
Your hands are moist and itching for my bed,

Coward! Wasn't begetting you enough
dishonor to destroy me? Must I snuff   1085
your perjured life, my own son's life, and stain
a thousand glories? Let the gods restrain
my fury! Fly! live hated and alone—
there are places where my name may be unknown.
Go, find them, follow your disastrous star   1090
through filth; if I discover where you are,
I'll add another body to the hill
of vermin I've extinguished by my skill.
Fly from me, let the grieving storm-winds bear
your contagion from me. You corrupt the air.   1095
I call upon Poseidon. Help me, Lord
of Ocean, help your servant! Once my sword
heaped crucified assassins on your shore
and let them burn like beacons. God, you swore
my first request would be fulfilled. My first!   1100
I never made it. Even through the worst
torments of Epirus I held my peace;
no threat or torture brought me to my knees
beseeching favors; even then I knew
some greater project was reserved for you!   1105
Poseidon, now I kneel. Avenge me, dash
my incestuous son against your rocks, and wash
his dishonor from my household; wave on wave
of roaring nothingness shall be his grave.

HIPPOLYTUS
Phaedra accuses me of lawless love!   1110
Phaedra! My heart stops, I can hardly move
my lips and answer. I have no defense,
if you condemn me without evidence.

THESEUS
Oh coward, you were counting on the Queen
to hide your brutal insolence and screen   1115
your outrage with her weakness! You forgot
something. You dropped your sword and spoiled your plot.
You should have kept it. Surely you had time
to kill the only witness to your crime!

HIPPOLYTUS
Why do I stand this, and forbear to clear   1120
away these lies, and let the truth appear?
I could so easily. Where would you be,
if I spoke out? Respect my loyalty,
Father, respect your own intelligence.
Examine me. What am I? My defense   1125
is my whole life. When have I wavered, when
have I pursued the vices of young men?
Father, you have no scaffolding to rig
your charges on. Small crimes precede the big.
Phaedra accused me of attempting rape!   1130
Am I some Proteus, who can change his shape?
Nature despises such disparities.

Vice, like virtue, advances by degrees.
Bred by Antiope to manly arms,
I hate the fever of this lust that warms   1135
the loins and rots the spirit. I was taught
uprightness by Theramenes. I fought
with wolves, tamed horses, gave my soul to sport,
and shunned the joys of women and the court.
I dislike praise, but those who know me best   1140
grant me one virtue—it's that I detest
the very crimes of which I am accused.
How often you yourself have been amused
and puzzled by my love of purity,
pushed to the point of crudeness. By the sea   1145
and in the forests, I have filled my heart
with freedom, far from women.

THESEUS

                       When this part
was dropped, could only Phaedra violate
the cold abyss of your immaculate
reptilian soul? How could this funeral urn   1150
contain a heart, a living heart, or burn
for any woman but my wife?

HIPPOLYTUS

                  Ah no!
Father, I too have seen my passions blow
into a tempest. Why should I conceal
my true offense? I feel, Father, I feel   1155
what other young men feel. I love, I love
Aricia. Father, I love the sister of
your worst enemies. I worship her!
I only feel and breathe and live for her!

THESEUS

You love Aricia? God! No, this is meant   1160
to blind my eyes and throw me off the scent.

HIPPOLYTUS

Father, for six months I have done my worst
to kill this passion. You shall be the first
to know . . . You frown still. Nothing can remove
your dark obsession. Father, what will prove   1165
my innocence? I swear by earth and sky,
and nature's solemn, shining majesty. . . .

THESEUS

Oaths and religion are the common cant
of all betrayers. If you wish to taunt
me, find a better prop than blasphemy.   1170

HIPPOLYTUS

All's blasphemy to eyes that cannot see.
Could even Phaedra bear me such ill will?

THESEUS

Phaedra, Phaedra! Name her again, I'll kill
you! My hand's already on my sword.

HIPPOLYTUS

                                        Explain
   my terms of exile. What do you ordain?   1175
THESEUS
   Sail out across the ocean. Everywhere
   on earth and under heaven is too near.
HIPPOLYTUS
   Who'll take me in? Oh who will pity me,
   and give me bread, if you abandon me?
THESEUS
   You'll find fitting companions. Look for friends   1180
   who honor everything that most offends.
   Pimps and jackals who praise adultery
   and incest will protect your purity.
HIPPOLYTUS
   Adultery! Is it your privilege
   to fling this word in my teeth? I've reached the edge   1185
   of madness . . . No, I'll say no more. Compare
   my breeding with Phaedra's. Think and beware . . .
   She had a mother . . . No, I must not speak.
THESEUS
   You devil, you'll attack the queen still weak
   from your assault. How can you stand and face   1190
   your father? Must I drive you from this place
   with my own hand? Run off, or I will flog
   you with the flat of my sword like a dog!

       Scene 3 Theseus
THESEUS
   You go to your inevitable fate,
   Child—by the river immortals venerate.   1195
   Poseidon gave his word. You cannot fly;
   death and the gods march on invisibly.
   I loved you once; despite your perfidy,
   my bowels writhe inside me. Must you die?
   Yes; I am in too deep now to draw back.   1200
   What son has placed his father on such a rack?
   What father groans for such a monstrous birth?
   Oh gods, your thunder throws me to the earth.

       Scene 4 Theseus, Phaedra
PHAEDRA
   Theseus, I heard the deluge of your voice,
   and stand here trembling. If there's time for choice,   1205
   hold back your hand, still bloodless; spare your race!
   I supplicate you, here I kneel for grace.
   Oh, Theseus, Theseus, will you drench the earth
   with your own blood? His virtue, youth and birth
   cry out for him. Is he already slain   1210
   by you for me—spare me this incestuous pain!

THESEUS

    Phaedra, my son's blood has not touched my hand;
and yet I'll be avenged. On sea and land,
spirits, the swift of foot, shall track him down.
Poseidon owes me this. Why do you frown?   1215

PHAEDRA

    Poseidon owes you this? What have you done
in anger?

THESEUS

           What! You wish to help my son?
No, stir my anger, back me to the hilt,
call for blacker colors to paint his guilt.
Lash, strike and drive me on! You cannot guess   1220
the nerve and fury of his wickedness.
Phaedra, he slandered your sincerity,
he told me your accusation was a lie.
He swore he loved Aricia, he wants to wed
Aricia. . . .

PHAEDRA

         What, my lord?

THESEUS

                That's what he said.   1225
Of course, I scorn his shallow artifice.
Help me, Poseidon hear me, sacrifice
my son. I seek the altar. Come! Let us both
kneel down and beg the gods to keep their oath.

    Scene 5 Phaedra

PHAEDRA

    My husband's gone, still rumbling his own name   1230
and fame. He has no inkling of the flame
his words have started. If he hadn't spoken,
I might . . . I was on my feet, I'd broken
loose from Oenone, and had just begun
to say I know not what to save his son.   1235
Who knows how far I would have gone? Remorse,
longing and anguish shook me with such force,
I might have told the truth and suffered death,
before this revelation stopped my breath:
Hippolytus is not insensible,   1240
only insensible to me! His dull
heart chases shadows. He is glad to rest
upon Aricia's adolescent breast!
Oh thin abstraction! When I saw his firm
repugnance spurn my passion like a worm,   1245
I thought he had some magic to withstand
the lure of any woman in the land,
and now I see a schoolgirl leads the boy,
as simply as her puppy or a toy.
Was I about to perish for this sham,   1250
this panting hypocrite? Perhaps I am
the only woman that he could refuse!

Scene 6 Phaedra, Oenone

PHAEDRA

Oenone, dearest, have you heard the news?

OENONE

No, I know nothing, but I am afraid.
How can I follow you? You have betrayed   1255
your life and children. What have you revealed,
Madam?

PHAEDRA

        I have a rival in the field,
Oenone.

OENONE

      What?

PHAEDRA

          Oenone, he's in love—
this howling monster, able to disprove
my beauty, mock my passion, scorn each prayer,   1260
and face me like a tiger in its lair—
he's tamed, the beast is harnessed to a cart;
Aricia's found an entrance to his heart.

OENONE

Aricia?

PHAEDRA

      Nurse, my last calamity
has come. This is the bottom of the sea.   1265
All that preceded this had little force—
the flames of lust, the horrors of remorse,
the prim refusal by my grim young master,
were only feeble hints of this disaster.
They love each other! Passion blinded me.   1270
I let them blind me, let them meet and see
each other freely! Was such bounty wrong?
Oenone, you have known this all along,
you must have seen their meetings, watched them sneak
off to their forest, playing hide-and-seek!   1275
Alas, such rendezvous are no offence:
innocent nature smiles on innocence,
for them each natural impulse was allowed,
each day was summer and without a cloud.
Oenone, nature hated me. I fled   1280
its light, as if a price were on my head.
I shut my eyes and hungered for my end.
Death was the only God my vows could bend.
And even while my desolation served
me gall and tears, I knew I was observed;   1285
I never had security or leisure
for honest weeping, but must steal this pleasure.
Oh hideous pomp; a monarch only wears
the robes of majesty to hide her tears!

OENONE

How can their folly help them? They will never   1290
enjoy its fruit.

PHAEDRA

                      Ugh, they will love forever—
even while I am talking, they embrace,
they scorn me, they are laughing in my face!
In the teeth of exile, I hear them swear
they will be true forever, everywhere.   1295
Oenone, have pity on my jealous rage;
I'll kill this happiness that jeers at age.
I'll summon Theseus; hate shall answer hate!
I'll drive my husband to annihilate
Aricia—let no trivial punishment,   1300
her instant death, or bloodless banishment . . .
What am I saying? Have I lost my mind?
I am jealous, and call my husband! Bind
me, gag me; I am frothing with desire.
My husband is alive, and I'm on fire!   1305
For whom? Hippolytus. When I have said
his name, blood fills my eyes, my heart stops dead.
Imposture, incest, murder! I have passed
the limits of damnation; now at last,
my lover's lifeblood is my single food;   1310
nothing else cools my murderous thirst for blood.
Yet I live on. I live looked down upon
by my progenitor, the sacred sun,
by Zeus, by Europa, by the universe
of gods and stars, my ancestors. They curse   1315
their daughter. Let me die. In the great night
of Hades, I'll find shelter from their sight.
What am I saying? I've no place to turn:
Minos, my father, holds the judge's urn.
The gods have placed damnation in his hands,   1320
the shades in Hades follow his commands.
Will he not shake and curse his fatal star
that brings his daughter trembling to his bar?
His child by Pasiphaë forced to tell
a thousand sins unclassified in hell?   1325
Father, when you interpret what I speak,
I fear your fortitude will be too weak
to hold the urn. I see you fumbling for
new punishments for crimes unknown before.
You'll be your own child's executioner!   1330
You cannot kill me; look, my murderer
is Venus, who destroyed our family;
Father, she has already murdered me.
I killed myself—and what is worse I wasted
my life for pleasure I have never tasted.   1335
My love flees me still, and my last gasp,
is for the fleeting flesh I failed to clasp.

OENONE

Madam, Madam, cast off this groundless terror!
Is love now an unprecedented error?

You love! What then? You love! Accept your fate.   1340
You're not the first to sail into this strait.
Will chaos overturn the earth and Jove,
because a mortal woman is in love?
Such accidents are easy, all too common.
A woman must submit to being woman.   1345
You curse a failure in the source of things.
Venus has feasted on the hearts of kings;
even the gods, man's judges, feel desire,
Zeus learned to live with his adulterous fire.

PHAEDRA
Must I still listen, and drink your poisoned breath?   1350
My death redoubled on the edge of death—
I'd fled Hippolytus and I was free
till your entreaties stabbed and blinded me,
and dragged me howling to the pit of lust.
Oenone, I was learning to be just.   1355
You fed my malice. Attacking the young Prince
was not enough; you clothed him with my sins.
You wished to kill him; he is dying now,
because of you, and Theseus' brutal vow.
You watch my torture; I'm the last ungorged   1360
scrap rotting in this trap your plots have forged.
What binds you to me? Leave me, go, and die,
may your punishment be to terrify
all those who ruin princes by their lies,
hints, acquiescence, filth, and blasphemies—   1365
panders who grease the grooves of inclination,
and lure our willing bodies from salvation.
Go die, go frighten false flatterers, the worst
friends the gods can give to kings they've cursed!

OENONE (*Alone.*)
I have given all and left all for her service,   1370
almighty Gods! I have been paid my price!

Act V

Scene 1 Hippolytus, Aricia

ARICIA
Take a stand, speak the truth, if you respect
your father's glory and your life. Protect
yourself! I'm nothing to you. You consent
without a struggle to your banishment.   1375
If you are weary of Aricia, go;
at least do something to prevent the blow
that dooms your honor and existence—both
at a stroke! Your father must recall his oath;
there is time still, but if the truth's concealed,   1380
you offer your accuser a free field.
Speak to your father!

HIPPOLYTUS

                      I've already said
what's lawful. Shall I point to his soiled bed,
tell Athens how his marriage was foresworn,
make Theseus curse the day that he was born? 1385
My aching heart recoils. I only want
God and Aricia for my confidants.
See how I love you; love makes me confide
in you this horror I have tried to hide
from my own heart. My faith must not be broken; 1390
forget, if possible, what I have spoken.
Ah Princess, if even a whisper slips
past you, it will perjure your pure lips.
God's justice is committed to the cause
of those who love him, and uphold his laws; 1395
sooner or later, heaven itself will rise
in wrath and punish Phaedra's blasphemies.
I must not. If I rip away her mask,
I'll kill my father. Give me what I ask.
Do this! Then throw away your chains; it's right 1400
for you to follow me, and share my flight.
Fly from this prison; here the vices seethe
and simmer, virtue has no air to breathe.
In the confusion of my exile, none
will even notice that Aricia's gone. 1405
Banished and broken, Princess, I am still
a force in Greece. Your guards obey my will,
powerful intercessors wish us well:
our neighbors, Argos' citadel
is armed, and in Mycenae our allies 1410
will shelter us, if lying Phaedra tries
to harry us from our paternal throne,
and steal our sacred titles for her son.
The gods are ours, they urge us to attack.
Why do you tremble, falter and hold back? 1415
Your interests drive me to this sacrifice.
While I'm on fire, your blood has changed to ice.
Princess, is exile more than you can face?

ARICIA

    Exile with you, my lord? What sweeter place
is under heaven? Standing at your side, 1420
I'd let the universe and heaven slide.
You're my one love, my king, but can I hope
for peace and honor, Prince, if I elope
unmarried? This . . . I wasn't questioning
the decency of flying from the king. 1425
Is he my father? Only an abject
spirit honors tyrants with respect.
You say you love me. Prince, I am afraid.

HIPPOLYTUS

    Aricia, you shall never be betrayed;
accept me! Let our love be sanctified, 1430

then flee from your oppressor as my bride.
Bear witness, oh you gods, our love released
by danger, needs no temple or a priest.
It's faith, not ceremonial, that saves.
Here at the city gates, among these graves   1435
the resting places of my ancient line,
there stands a sacred temple and a shrine.
Here, where no mortal ever swore in vain,
here in these shadows, where eternal pain
is ready to engulf the perjurer;   1440
here heaven's scepter quivers to confer
its final sanction; here, my Love, we'll kneel,
and pray the gods to consecrate and seal
our love. Zeus, the father of the world will stand
here as your father and bestow your hand.   1445
Only the pure shall be our witnesses:
Hera, the guarantor of marriages,
Demeter and the virgin Artemis.

ARICIA

The King is coming. Fly. I'll stay and meet
his anger here and cover your retreat.   1450
Hurry. Be off, send me some friend to guide
my timid footsteps, husband, to your side.

        Scene 2 Theseus, Ismene, Aricia

THESEUS

Oh God, illuminate my troubled mind.
Show me the answer I have failed to find.

ARICIA

Go, Ismene, be ready to escape.   1455

        Scene 3 Theseus, Aricia

THESEUS

Princess, you are disturbed. You twist your cape
and blush. The Prince was talking to you. Why
is he running?

ARICIA

                We've said our last goodbye,
my lord.

THESEUS

          I see the beauty of your eyes
moves even my son, and you have gained a prize   1460
no woman hoped for.

ARICIA

                    He hasn't taken on
your hatred for me, though he is your son.

THESEUS

I follow. I can hear the oaths he swore.
He knelt, he wept. He has done this before
and worse. You are deceived.

ARICIA

                          Deceived, my lord?   1465

THESEUS
>Princess, are you so rich? Can you afford
>to hunger for this lover that my queen
>rejected? Your betrayer loves my wife.

ARICIA
>How can you bear to blacken his pure life?
>Is kingship only for the blind and strong, 1470
>unable to distinguish right from wrong?
>What insolent prerogative obscures
>a light that shines in every eye but yours?
>You have betrayed him to his enemies.
>What more, my lord? Repent your blasphemies. 1475
>Are you not fearful lest the gods so loathe
>and hate you they will gratify your oath?
>Fear God, my lord, fear God. How many times
>he grants men's wishes to expose their crimes.

THESEUS
>Love blinds you, Princess, and beclouds your reason. 1480
>Your outburst cannot cover up his treason.
>My trust's in witnesses that cannot lie.
>I have seen Phaedra's tears. She tried to die.

ARICIA
>Take care, your highness. When your killing hand
>drove all the thieves and reptiles from the land, 1485
>you missed one monster, one was left alive,
>one. . . . No, I must not name her, sire, or strive
>to save your helpless son; he wants to spare
>your reputation. Let me go. I dare
>not stay here. If I stayed I'd be too weak 1490
>to keep my promise. I'd be forced to speak.

Scene 4 Theseus

THESEUS
>What was she saying? I must try to reach
>the meaning of her interrupted speech.
>Is it a pitfall? A conspiracy?
>Are they plotting together to torture me? 1495
>Why did I let the rash, wild girl depart?
>What is this whisper crying in my heart?
>A secret pity fills my soul with pain.
>I must question Oenone once again.
>My guards, summon Oenone to the throne. 1500
>Quick, bring her. I must talk with her alone.

Scene 5 Theseus, Panope

PANOPE
>The Queen's deranged, your highness. Some accursed
>madness is driving her; some fury stalks
>behind her back, possesses her, and talks
>its evil through her, and blasphemes the world. 1505
>She cursed Oenone. Now Oenone's hurled

herself into the ocean, Sire, and drowned.
Why did she do it? No reason can be found.
THESEUS
        Oenone's drowned?
PANOPE
                            Her death has brought no peace.
The cries of Phaedra's troubled soul increase.   1510
Now driven by some sinister unrest,
she snatches up her children to her breast,
pets them and weeps, till something makes her scoff
at her affection, and she drives them off.
Her glance is drunken and irregular,   1515
she looks through us and wonders who we are;
thrice she has started letters to you, Sire,
thrice tossed the shredded fragments in the fire.
Oh call her to you. Help her!
THESEUS
        The nurse is drowned? Phaedra wishes to die?   1520
Oh gods! Summon my son. Let him defend
himself, tell him I'm ready to attend.
I want him!
        Exit Panope.
                    Neptune, hear me, spare my son!
My vengeance was too hastily begun.
Oh why was I so eager to believe   1525
Oenone's accusation? The gods deceive
the victims they are ready to destroy!

        Scene 6   Theseus, Theramenes
THESEUS
        Here is Theramenes. Where is my boy,
my first-born? He was yours to guard and keep.
Where is he? Answer me. What's this? You weep?   1530
THERAMENES
        Oh tardy, futile grief, his blood is shed.
My lord, your son, Hippolytus, is dead.
THESEUS
        Oh gods have mercy!
THERAMENES
                            I saw him die. The most
lovely and innocent of men is lost.
THESEUS
        He's dead? The gods have hurried him away   1535
and killed him? . . . just as I began to pray. . . .
What sudden thunderbolt has struck him down?
THERAMENES
        We'd started out, and hardly left the town.
He held the reins; a few feet to his rear,
a single, silent guard held up a spear.   1540
He followed the Mycenae highroad, deep
in thought, reins dangling, as if half asleep;

his famous horses, only he could hold,
trudged on with lowered heads, and sometimes rolled
their dull eyes slowly—they seemed to have caught   1545
their master's melancholy, and aped his thought.
Then all at once winds struck us like a fist,
we heard a sudden roaring through the mist;
from underground a voice in agony
answered the prolonged groaning of the sea.   1550
We shook, the horses' manes rose on their heads,
and now against a sky of blacks and reds,
we saw the flat waves hump into a mountain
of green-white water rising like a fountain,
as it reached land and crashed with a last roar   1555
to shatter like a galley on the shore.
Out of its fragments rose a monster, half
dragon, half bull; a mouth that seemed to laugh
drooled venom on its dirty yellow scales
and python belly, forking to three tails.   1560
The shore was shaken like a tuning fork,
ships bounced on the stung sea like bits of cork,
the earth moved, and the sun spun round and round,
a sulphur-colored venom swept the ground.
We fled; each felt his useless courage falter,   1565
and sought asylum at a nearby altar.
Only the Prince remained; he wheeled about,
and hurled a javelin through the monster's snout.
Each kept advancing. Flung from the Prince's arm,
dart after dart struck where the blood was warm.   1570
The monster in its death-throes felt defeat,
and bounded howling to the horses' feet.
There its stretched gullet and its armor broke,
and drenched the chariot with blood and smoke,
and then the horses, terror-struck, stampeded.   1575
Their master's whip and shouting went unheeded,
they dragged his breathless body to the spray.
Their red mouths bit the bloody surf, men say
Poseidon stood beside them, that the god
was stabbing at their bellies with a goad.   1580
Their terror drove them crashing on a cliff,
the chariot crashed in two, they ran as if
the Furies screamed and crackled in their manes,
their fallen hero tangled in the reins,
jounced on the rocks behind them. The sweet light   1585
of heaven never will expunge this sight:
the horses that Hippolytus had tamed,
now dragged him headlong, and their mad hooves maimed
his face past recognition. When he tried
to call them, calling only terrified;   1590
faster and ever faster moved their feet,
his body was a piece of bloody meat.
The cliffs and ocean trembled to our shout,
at last their panic failed, they turned about,

and stopped not far from where those hallowed graves,   1595
the Prince's fathers, overlook the waves.
I ran on breathless, guards were at my back,
my master's blood had left a generous track.
The stones were red, each thistle in the mud
was stuck with bits of hair and skin and blood.   1600
I came upon him, called; he stretched his right
hand to me, blinked his eyes, then closed them tight.
"I die," he whispered, "it's the gods' desire.
Friend, stand between Aricia and my sire—
some day enlightened, softened, disabused,   1605
he will lament his son, falsely accused;
then when at last he wishes to appease
my soul, he'll treat my lover well, release
and honor Arica. . . ." On this word, he died.
Only a broken body testified   1610
he'd lived and loved once. On the sand now lies
something his father will not recognize.
THESEUS
My son, my son! Alas, I stand alone.
Before the gods. I never can atone.
THERAMENES
Meanwhile Aricia, rushing down the path,   1615
approached us. She was fleeing from your wrath,
my lord, and wished to make Hippolytus
her husband in God's eyes. Then nearing us,
she saw the signs of struggle in the waste,
she saw (oh what a sight) her love defaced,   1620
her young love lying lifeless on the sand.
At first she hardly seemed to understand;
while staring at the body in the grass,
she kept on asking where her lover was.
At last the black and fearful truth broke through   1625
her desolation! She seemed to curse the blue
and murdering ocean, as she caught his head
up in her lap; then fainting lay half dead,
until Ismene somehow summoned back her breath,
restored the child to life—or rather death.   1630
I come, great King, to urge my final task,
your dying son's last outcry was to ask
mercy for poor Aricia, for his bride.
Now Phaedra comes. She killed him. She has lied.

Scene 7 Theseus, Phaedra, Panope, Theramenes, Guards
THESEUS
Ah Phaedra, you have won. He's dead. A man   1635
was killed. Were you watching? His horses ran
him down, and tore his body limb from limb.
Poseidon struck him, Theseus murdered him.
I served you! Tell me why Oenone died.
Was it to save you? Is her suicide   1640
a proof of your truth? No, since he's dead, I must

accept your evidence, just or unjust.
I must believe my faith has been abused;
you have accused him; he shall stand accused.
He's friendless, even in the world below.   1645
There the shades fear him! Am I forced to know
the truth? Truth cannot bring my son to life;
if fathers murder, shall I kill my wife
too? Leave me, Phaedra. Far from you, exiled
from Greece, I will lament my murdered child.   1650
I am a murdered gladiator, whirled
in black circles. I want to leave the world,
but my whole life rises to increase my guilt—
all those dazzled, dazzling eyes, my glory built
on killing killers. Less known, less magnified,   1655
I might escape, and find a place to hide.
Stand back, Poseidon. I know the gods are hard
to please. I pleased you. This is my reward:
I killed my son. I killed him! Only a god
spares enemies, and wants his servants' blood!   1660

PHAEDRA

No, Theseus, I must disobey your prayer.
Listen to me. I'm dying. I declare
Hippolytus was innocent.

THESEUS

Ah Phaedra, on your evidence, I sent
him to his death. Do you ask me to forgive   1665
my son's assassin? Can I let you live?

PHAEDRA

My time's too short, your highness. It was I,
who lusted for your son with my hot eye.
The flames of Aphrodite maddened me;
I loathed myself, and yearned outrageously   1670
like a starved wolf to fall upon the sheep.
I wished to hold him to me in my sleep
and dreamt I had him. Then Oenone's tears
troubled my mind; she played upon my fears,
until pleading forced me to declare   1675
I loved your son. He scorned me. In despair,
I plotted with my nurse, and our conspiracy
made you believe your son assaulted me.
Oenone's punished; fleeing from my wrath,
she drowned herself, and found a too easy path   1680
to death and hell. Perhaps you wonder why
I still survive her, and refuse to die?
Theseus, I stand before you to absolve
your noble son. Sire, only this resolve
upheld me, and made me throw down my knife.   1685
I've chosen a slower way to end my life—
Medea's poison; chills already dart
along my boiling veins and squeeze my heart.
A cold composure I have never known
gives me a moment's poise. I stand alone   1690

and seem to see my outraged husband fade
and waver into death's dissolving shade.
My eyes at last give up their light, and see
the day they've soiled resume its purity.

PANOPE

She's dead, my lord.

THESEUS

                      Would God, all memory   1695
of her and me had died with her! Now I
must live. This knowledge that has come too late
must give me strength and help me expiate
my sacrilegious vow. Let's go, I'll pay
my son the honors he has earned today.   1700
His father's tears shall mingle with his blood.
My love that did my son so little good
asks mercy from his spirit. I declare
Aricia is my daughter and my heir.

Action analysis and performance suggestions

Two portions of the play present significant challenges for informal
classroom performance: Phaedra's confession to Hippolytus of her incestuous love (act II, scene v) and Phaedra's failure to save Hippolytus by
confessing to Theseus (act IV, scenes iii–v). In the first scene, the fierce
struggle between reason and passion in both stepmother and stepson
finds expression in physical movement, in repulsion, in horrible revulsion
for passionate words that tear apart the social order on which all behavior
is dependent. Phaedra's "obscene confession" is to her mind, and to Hippolytus's, blatantly shocking; so horrid are her illicit passions to her that
her action in the scene may be to obtain the purity of death by using her
confession to force Hippolytus to kill her. Scenes iii, iv, and v in act IV
dramatize Phaedra's greatest temptation: Though she is doomed already,
though she has lost her dignity, she can still obtain purity through a confession to Theseus and thereby save Hippolytus from Theseus's wrath;
this is what she sets out to do.

DEFINING THE ACTIONS AND THE SUPEROBJECTIVE

The three contiguous scenes (act IV, scenes iii–v, lines 1194–1252) that
form a dramatic unit appropriate for informal performance open with
Theseus's soliloquy. He exults in the knowledge that Hippolytus is soon to
die, but he tries to justify to himself the horrible filicide that his vow to
Poseidon will cause. Phaedra enters, hoping first to prevent Theseus from
executing his revenge on Hippolytus because of her own, deeply ingrained sense of guilt. The battle between her reason (which would compel her to confess her illicit love for Hippolytus and her part in allowing
Oenone's accusation to stand) and her passions (which would compel her
to save Hippolytus in some fashion that would not expose her guilty love
and that would permit her to retain a sense of her femininity) seems on
the brink of being decided in favor of her reason. In her first speech, although she appeals to Theseus for grace, she moves toward confessing
her "incestuous pain." Theseus in his reply tries to vindicate his revenge,

first by denying responsibility, then by asserting the probability of vengeance by another. Here Phaedra reacts to new information: Theseus has called on Poseidon for revenge and this, Phaedra knows, means that Hippolytus's death is certain. The chance that she will prevent Theseus from executing his revenge without confessing her guilt is diminishing; her reply is a call for clarification: "What have you done in anger?" Theseus continues to attempt to justify his revenge on Hippolytus and to appeal to Phaedra for support, but again his appeal reveals new information to Phaedra. In his desire to expose Hippolytus as adulterous, incestuous, devious, dishonest, and unreasonable, a threat to the social fabric, Theseus tells of Hippolytus's confession of love for Aricia, a confession that if true is treasonous but one the father thinks is patently false. Phaedra's reaction to this new information is even more charged than before, yet she can only, hopelessly, ask for more information. (Her eagerness to have that clarification has halted Theseus's speech just as he exposed Hippolytus's confession.) Theseus interprets Phaedra's reaction as support, as justification for his behavior, and calls on her to approve the sacrifice. His action now is to exhort Phaedra to join him in prayer for revenge, but Phaedra cannot join him, and in soliloquy she tries to justify her criminal silence. Although she cannot yet admit it to herself, her failure to speak has doomed Hippolytus to death; she will have the blood of her lover that she calls for in the next scene. However, instead of coming to recognize her morally culpable crime of omission, she tries to hide behind her bruised femininity: "Was I about to perish for this sham, / this panting hypocrite? Perhaps I am / the only woman that he could refuse!" she concludes after attacking her husband ("rumbling his own name / and fame"), her nurse, her stepson, and her rival. As the scene comes to a close and before Phaedra can refocus her reasoning nature sufficiently to realize the destruction her passions have caused (as she partly will late in the following scene with Oenone), we see how both Theseus and Phaedra have vindicated their desires for revenge but have, ironically, denied themselves the chance to obtain the purity of grace and to retain their glory, the central action of the emotionally charged scene.

Indeed, the drive to obtain the purity of grace and to retain their glory articulates what may be the superobjective of the whole tragedy: Each character shares in the action and each dramatic element imitates it. For Oenone "glory" means only reputation; for Theseus "glory" may be too closely tied to sexual and physical exploits; but for Hippolytus and Phaedra "glory" is the glory of ordered, reasoned existence, upset now by their emotions and the events these emotions have caused. The suicides of Oenone and Phaedra and the vow of Theseus to name Aricia as ruler restores to them and to the society the purity of grace so long absent to these reasoning minds.

OVERCOMING OBSTACLES

The obstacles in these three contiguous scenes are all internal. That is, Theseus and Phaedra both must cope with their reason and passion; both feel they have justified their deeds or nondeeds to themselves by the end of the scenes; and both ironically have only immersed themselves further in the crimes of omission and commission that will bring about the terrifying ending. More specifically, Theseus's prime obstacle is his (justifiable) fear that his revenge is too severe, too unnatural—"my bowels writhe inside me" he admits to himself at the beginning of the scene. To overcome his fear he seeks Phaedra's approval (a secondary obstacle). By the end of the scene he has indeed justified his action to himself. Phaedra's obstacle is fear, too, in her case fear that her failure to vindicate Hippolytus of the charge of attempted rape will lead to Hippolytus's, Theseus's, and ultimately her own destruction through the loss of purity and glory. The news of Hippolytus's love for Aricia reactivates an old obstacle—passion, in this case jealousy—which Phaedra fails to recognize and which leads to her justification of her crime of silence.

THE MAGIC IF AND THE GIVEN CIRCUMSTANCES

It is hard, perhaps impossible, to imagine ourselves being involved in incest and filicide, far harder than imagining what it would be like to be blind or what it would be like to act before a group of fine ladies and gentlemen. But to understand the circumstances Theseus and Phaedra find themselves in, one must make an effort to articulate them. What IF you were sure your son was a rapist, indeed, that he had tried to rape your own wife, his stepmother? What IF you had a form of capital punishment, swift and sure, that would not require your actually acting? Remember, Theseus is a proud and overwhelmingly masculine man who has lived by his strength, cunning, and sexual attractiveness. He is a man of machismo, and his reaction to incest is based not just on abstract revulsion but on a hardly recognized sexual insecurity, which he never does discover for himself. For all the self-righteous horror in Theseus there is also a guilt, a fear that his passions have taken control of his reason, as indeed they have. Imagine this fear as the most important given circumstance.

A wider, even more intense range of emotions builds the magic IF for Phaedra. What IF you thought incestuous passion were a horrible crime? What IF you felt yourself guilty of such incestuous passion? IF you knew you had suppressed for years a longing most unfaithful to your husband? IF you now knew you had to confess that passion in order to save the object of that passion from exile and perhaps death? That your confession itself might cause your death and the death of the lover who had spurned you, hence gain you nothing but further damnation? Then, what IF you suddenly found out that your painful confession of love had been spurned apparently because you were not desirable? (Phaedra perhaps feels her seductive powers fading as she approaches middle age.) Here may lie a *reason* to justify a criminal act: the murder of your stepson.

CLASSROOM ADAPTATIONS TO ARRIVE AT STYLE

Style in *Phaedra* means introspection, artificiality, emphasis on the internal, a physically close but individualized relationship with the audience. The actor communicates not to the group response of an audience worshipping mystery together, but to the unconscious mind of each member of the audience. To translate these abstractions into the reality of informal classroom performance, costuming—suggestive rather than authentic, hints of military uniforms with swords, epaulets, long flowing gowns with low decolletage, but not Roman fighting dress or Greek-like togas—and three-quarter-round seating prove very helpful. At first these two aspects of style may seem to cancel each other since costuming is artificial and three-quarter-round seating productive of intimacy. But here the actors hold the key to style. They do not strive to make direct contact with the audience. There are no eye contacts, no melodramatic appeals. Instead, there is absolute concentration (with its consequent relaxation of self-identity) on the shifting, complex actions of the characters. Remember that Theseus is a middle-aged man of physical violence; keep in mind a Phaedra who doubts her sexual attractiveness and feels guilt for a deeply embedded failure to confess.

Here the verse provides a metaphoric clue. Normally artificial, highly epigrammatic, and especially concise, English heroic couplets (like the alexandrine, or iambic hexameter, couplets of Racine's original) seem particularly inappropriate to express the most intimate of human feelings. Shakespeare (and Grene in his translation of *Oedipus*) chose unrhymed iambic pentameter for the most intense scenes, but Robert Lowell's verse is wonderfully adapted to show the constant tension between reason and passion, control and disarray. Notice particularly how short sentences interrupt the normal patterns of balance and antithesis, how the lines are rarely end-stopped, how frequently dialogue divides but does not perfectly complete the dominant pattern. Like the conflicts inside Theseus and Phaedra, the verse reveals the chaos breaking upward through the patterned surfaces.

William Congreve
Love for Love

SCANDAL

> If indiscretion be a sign of love, you are the most a lover of anybody that
> I know: you fancy that parting with your estate will help you to your
> mistress.—In my mind he is a thoughtless adventurer,
>> Who hopes to purchase wealth by selling land,
>> Or win a mistress with a losing hand.
>
> (page 340)

ANGELICA

> Would anything but a madman complain of uncertainty? Uncertainty and
> expectation are the joys of life. Security is an insipid thing, and the over-
> taking and possessing of a wish, discovers the folly of the chase. Never let
> us know one another better: for the pleasure of a masquerade is done,
> when we come to show our faces; but I'll tell you two things before I
> leave you; I am not the fool you take me for; and you are mad, and don't
> know it.
>
> (pages 390–391)

Cynical, materialistic Scandal thinks Valentine is foolish; witty, beautiful,
and wealthy Angelica pretends to think he is mad; but Valentine's problem is simple: He is in love.

And yet, not so simple. He has led a libertine life, spending his time
and money in pursuits that have cost him more than one bastard child
and the total alienation of his crusty and embittered father. As the play
opens, a pack of lawyers and tradesmen crowd his doorway, clamoring for
their bills to be paid. What matter such worldly concerns? Now young
Valentine is in love, genuinely in love, and unable to convince the girl
that he desires honorable marriage not just for power, money, or position, but because he loves her. Perhaps, given his past follies, he deserves
to be scorned; his reputation for wit and profligacy give Angelica little
reason to trust him. What can Valentine do? He can but lay aside his last
possession—his wit—and wager love for love.

From her uncomfortable position as a wealthy heiress in a world of
fops and whores, Angelica has seen Valentine with a favorable but doubt-
ing eye. Unwilling to sacrifice her fortune to a man of intellectual or
physical show without substance or to give her person to one who would
not truly love her, she has not been the fool many have taken her for,
and contrary to the examples of her aunts Foresight and Frail, she has
not been content to build a life on loveless marriages, casual liaisons, and
fashionable intrigues. Like Valentine, Angelica is of her world but better
than it, and to make sure he is the man she hopes he is, she too has had
first to use her wit and then to wager love for love. In the end she gets
her wish, and we in the audience, with happiness for the lovers and

delighted satisfaction in the punishment of those who have stood in their way, applaud their successful match.

The courtship of Valentine and Angelica appears romantic, optimistic, even sentimental when viewed apart from its setting; it is simply the old boy-gets-girl story, ending happily as is the way of comedy. However, in the setting William Congreve has peopled with knaves and fools, it takes on added significance so that we cannot view Valentine and Angelica apart from the people who surround them. Standing in contrast to Angelica are Miss Prue, Mrs. Frail, and Mrs. Foresight. Prue is merely a child discovering her sexuality, and her drives are natural but not innocent, any more than the adulterous liaisons of her stepmother and aunt are innocent. Their goals—to grasp and hold power over men, to enjoy pleasure for its own sake regardless of the consequences as long as those consequences can be masked—are simply more sophisticated versions of Prue's, and the lessons of affectation and mendacity they teach her will not be in vain. In contrast to Valentine stand Scandal, Tattle, and Ben. Through his cynical wit and satiric disposition, Scandal comments sarcastically on all around him. We accept some of his judgments and applaud most of his actions, yet question why he spends the night with the faded Mrs. Foresight. Of Tattle's motives we have no such question. He is simply a foolish coxcomb whose feigned secrecy in his sexual affairs strikes us as ridiculous. When he becomes so self-deluded as to think he can direct his attentions toward Angelica, he earns our total scorn and fully deserves, we feel, the comic punishment of marriage to Mrs. Frail, a woman "whom we all know." Ben shares all the sexual appetites of his brother and father and is wholly natural in them. His pleasures, like the seas he sails, are elemental: drink, dance, and sex when available.

The six young people provide contrast to Valentine and Angelica, and so do the lawyers, nurses, servants, and tradesmen who surround them. Equally important are the two old men: Foresight, the superstitious and suggestible astrologer whose foolish vanity in his occult powers and lack of control over the women of his household so amuse us; and Sir Sampson—proud, arrogant, unnaturally lustful, egotistic, deluded, and a hearty warning of what (but for the grace of his wit and his true love for a worthy woman) Valentine might become. But who are they, then, these cynical libertines and imbecile cuckolds, these insatiable sexpots and calculating whores, these youthful fools and aged lunatics, these polished wits, awkward near wits, and naïve dolts? Clearly they are created characters acting according to motives devised to represent their personalities and actions comically conflicting in one particular situation. To ask if they are "real" or "artificial" is to miss the point. Of course they are artificial, just as any mimetic artistic creation is only an imitation, not a reality. But to ask if their activities, concerns, attitudes, and ideas were ever current or if their behavior is like that of a society that ever existed is useful. Clearly these are ladies and gentlemen of the English Restoration, just as Shakespeare's Theseus is an Elizabethan, and Racine's Phaedra is a troubled seventeenth-century French woman.

William Congreve (1670–1729) was the last of three great English comic playwrights of the Restoration who separately created eleven *comedies of wit,* dramas concerned with leisured, upper-class characters whose time seems filled with dressing and visiting, witty commentary on society, and endless sexual affairs. His two predecessors, Sir George Etherege (1635?–1691) and William Wycherley (1640–1716), wrote and produced most of their comedies in the late 1660s and early 1670s when King Charles II, the Merry Monarch, flaunted his mistresses, promoted members of the nobility on the basis of their wit, and generally led England through a period of reaction to the staid propriety of the Puritan Commonwealth period (1642–1660). Style—in dress, in conversation, in life, and in literature—was immensely important to Charles and his followers. Many a beautiful wig and vastly expensive suit of clothes covered a syphilis-ridden body, and many a brightly bawdy joke and quick devastating rejoinder graced councils on affairs of state or the bedchamber. Thomas Hobbes (1588–1679), their philosopher, had told them of humanity's natural base cravings, and they accepted his findings and concluded that a smoothly polished hedonism was the most reasonable course in a life whose meaning was obscure. For Hobbes and many of his readers, religion offered no consolation—particularly when in the name of religion England had groaned under the yoke of its premature experiment in republicanism. The supernatural was to be mistrusted; the here-and-now—facts demonstrable by observation and conclusions empirically arrived at—was for living and enjoying; egotism was as natural as the frank pursuit of sensual gratification; and rational pleasures ranked highest among all enjoyments because, according to Hobbes, although human beings are animals, they are animals who think; the individual who could not be entirely rational was not the most pitied, but the most ridiculed. Wit, satire, sarcasm, and irony—primarily verbal intellectual egotism—were the mode of the day.

One of the pleasures these rake-wit, cynical, libertine, rational hedonists most enjoyed was the drama. Closed during the Commonwealth period, public theaters reopened in 1660 with a novel feature: women actors. Candles burning on the slightly thrust proscenium stage illuminated the actors, the tongue-and-groove scenery (painted flats slid into place through grooves on the stage floor—the distant ancestors of the box set), and the five hundred or so auditors. Little physical distance separated spectator from performer. Indeed, many auditors sat on the stage itself, to be seen as much as to see, but artificial acting styles filled with set declamation provided aesthetic distance. The acting companies performed in repertory, offering older comedies and tragedies from the Elizabethan and Jacobean periods as well as newer comedies of wit and two peculiar British-grown phenomena: *heroic drama* replete with artificial rants, impossible conflicts of love and honor, and larger-than-life heroes; and *comedies of "humours,"* children of the great Jacobean playwright Ben Jonson, dramas whose satiric thrust was directed at absurd ruling passions such as lust, miserliness, or superstition. To the playhouse, then, went these cynical libertines to enjoy the sallies of wit and to see fools and knaves satirized and exposed.

However, society then as now was composed of more than cynical libertines, and the Restoration period in England created literature as diverse as *Paradise Lost* and Rochester's satiric poems, as *Pilgrim's Progress* and *The Country Wife.* As always the middle classes were rising, and with them a renewed respect for literature that was morally didactic. Puritans would not enter the playhouse, but solid and sober merchants—with their wives and daughters—increasingly would. They were neither sympathetic to nor fully capable of understanding the comedy of wit. Comic entertainment had to respond to an audience whose composition was changing. Playing side by side with the brilliant comedies of wit that we remember were many comedies we have forgotten. Vastly rotund Tom Shadwell (1642?–1692) supplied more than one amusing satiric piece, and his greater contemporary, the poet John Dryden (1631–1700), experimented with serious comedies that tried to integrate heroic plots with smutty stories of cuckoldry. By 1693, when twenty-three-year-old William Congreve produced his first play, *The Old Batchelor,* even these less witty comedies were no longer acceptable because a new influence was taking hold of English comedy. In 1696, just one year after *Love for Love* appeared as the premiere of a new acting company, a comedy called *Love's Last Shift* by a theatrically and sociologically canny actor named Colley Cibber was produced. Cibber combined his imitation of the superficial features of wit comedy—seductions, images of proper style contrasted with debased excessiveness in social behavior—and humours comedy with a relatively new feature: In a shower of tears from his heroine, he converted his rake-wit hero in the fifth act from a cynical libertine to a repentant husband. And so sentimental comedy, never entirely dead even in this period, was born anew. Audiences could enjoy both suggestiveness and sentimentality. Soon a Puritan divine named Jeremy Collier published a long tract called "A Short View of the Immorality and Profaneness of the English Stage," which called for an end to wit comedy if not drama itself. Congreve was among the contemporary authors Collier particularly attacked. After a pamphlet response, Congreve tried to answer both Cibber and Collier with one of the greatest comedies of manners ever written, *The Way of the World* (1700). But it was too late; unaccustomed to making sharp distinctions either between true and apparent morality or between true and false wit, Congreve's audience did not understand. They preferred the warmth of the unconvincing conversion, and increasingly they asked for and got exemplary comedy that portrayed old fathers, merchants, and even fops sympathetically—the very characters the earlier comedy of the Restoration had ridiculed. Somewhat embittered, Congreve retired from playwriting at the age of thirty. There would be sparkling witty comedies again on the English stage—George Farquhar's and, seventy years later, Oliver Goldsmith's and Richard Brinsley Sheridan's—but not until our century would wit so shape an effectively rendered dramatic action.

Indeed, wit is at the heart of *Love for Love.* Although they endlessly squabbled over the meaning of what was possibly the single most important aesthetic term of their time, Congreve and his contemporaries would generally have understood "wit" to consist of "judgment," human analytic capacity, and "fancy," human creative, imitative capacity, mixed together in one of three ways: as the product of general mental activity, properly balanced fancy and judgment; as the decorous expression of analytic judgment, the "natural thought naturally expressed," often in epigrammatic language; or as the carefully controlled fanciful perception of similarities between apparently dissimilar things. True wit in its social context might seem to be malicious satire, but it is always intellectually perceptive. False wit is uncreative, excessive or unbridled, personally malicious, or merely cheap like puns and quibbles. We may laugh to hear the purveyors of false wit, but we are laughing *at* them because they appear ridiculous, not because what they say reveals subtle implications we have missed. We laugh *with* the true wit, delighting in that certain intellectual excellence we hope we can share.

However difficult the wit of *Love for Love* or subtle the gradations of wit among the characters, the play finally reduces to another variation of the oldest plot of comedy: boy gets girl. Here the boy and girl are people of psychological substance far beyond that of Theseus and Hippolyta, Lysander and Hermia, or Demetrius and Helena. The social affectations that mask that substance, or that disguise the feelings beneath the reasoned artifice, barely cover the simple pleasures of the conclusion that Angelica articulates. Speaking for the last time in what may be a vain effort to maintain an independence that her coming marriage legally will deny, she analyzes the confusing events they have undergone this simply:

> The miracle to-day is, that we find
> A lover true: not that a woman's kind.

(page 405)

Love for Love

"*Nudus agris, nudus nummis paternis,*
. . .
Insanire parat certa ratione modoque."
Horat. lib. ii. Sat. 3.*

Dramatis personæ
SIR SAMPSON LEGEND, *father of Valentine and Ben*
VALENTINE, *fallen under his father's displeasure by his expensive way of living, in love with Angelica*
SCANDAL, *his friend, a free speaker*
TATTLE, *a half-witted beau, vain of his amours, yet valuing himself for secrecy*
BEN, *Sir Sampson's younger son, half home-bred, and half sea-bred, designed to marry Miss Prue*
FORESIGHT, *an illiterate old fellow, peevish and positive, superstitious, and pretending to understand astrology, palmistry, physiognomy, omens, dreams, &c., uncle to Angelica*
JEREMY, *servant to Valentine*
TRAPLAND, *a scrivener*
BUCKRAM, *a lawyer*
SNAP, *a bailiff*
ANGELICA, *niece to Foresight, of a considerable fortune in her own hands*
MRS. FORESIGHT, *second wife of Foresight*
MRS. FRAIL, *sister to Mrs. Foresight, a woman of the town*
MISS PRUE, *daughter of Foresight by a former wife, a silly awkward country girl*
NURSE *to Miss Prue*
JENNY, *maid to Angelica*
Stewards, Sailors, and Servants
    Scene: London

Act the first

Scene I. Valentine's lodgings.
Valentine discovered reading, Jeremy waiting: several books upon the table.
VALENTINE
  Jeremy!
JEREMY
  Sir?
VALENTINE
  Here, take away; I'll walk a turn, and digest what I have read.
JEREMY (*Aside.*)
  You'll grow devilish fat upon this paper diet.

                              [*Takes away the books.*

  * A madman, stripped of your paternal   should set about raving by right reason
  estate, stripped of your money, . . .   and rule.
  He will make no more of it, than if he

VALENTINE

And d'ye hear, you go to breakfast.—There's a page doubled down
in Epictetus that is a feast for an emperor.

JEREMY

Was Epictetus a real cook, or did he only write receipts?

VALENTINE

Read, read, sirrah! and refine your appetite; learn to live upon
instruction; feast your mind, and mortify your flesh; read, and
take your nourishment in at your eyes; shut up your mouth,
and chew the cud of understanding; so Epictetus advises.

JEREMY

O Lord! I have heard much of him, when I waited upon a gentleman at Cambridge. Pray what was that Epictetus?

VALENTINE

A very rich man—not worth a groat.

JEREMY

Humph, and so he has made a very fine feast where there is nothing
to be eaten?

VALENTINE

Yes.

JEREMY

Sir, you're a gentleman, and probably understand this fine feeding;
but if you please, I had rather be at board-wages. Does your Epictetus, or your Seneca here, or any of these poor rich rogues, teach you
how to pay your debts without money? Will they shut up the mouths
of your creditors? Will Plato be bail for you? or Diogenes, because
he understands confinement, and lived in a tub, go to prison for
you? 'Slife, sir, what do you mean? to mew yourself up here with three
or four musty books, in commendation of starving and poverty?

VALENTINE

Why, sirrah, I have no money, you know it; and therefore resolve to
rail at all that have; and in that I but follow the examples of the wisest and wittiest men in all ages; these poets and philosophers whom
you naturally hate, for just such another reason, because they
abound in sense, and you are a fool.

JEREMY

Ay, sir, I am a fool, I know it; and yet, Heaven help me, I'm
poor enough to be a wit;—but I was always a fool when I told
you what your expenses would bring you to; your coaches and
your liveries, your treats and your balls; your being in love with a lady
that did not care a farthing for you in your prosperity; and keeping
company with wits that cared for nothing but your prosperity, and
now, when you are poor, hate you as much as they do one another.

VALENTINE

Well, and now I am poor I have an opportunity to be revenged on
'em all; I'll pursue Angelica with more love than ever, and appear
more notoriously her admirer in this restraint, than when I openly
rivalled the rich fops that made court to her; so shall my poverty be
a mortification to her pride, and perhaps make her compassionate
the love, which principally reduced me to this lowness of fortune.
And for the wits, I'm sure I am in a condition to be even with them.

JEREMY

Nay, your position is pretty even with theirs, that's the truth on't.

VALENTINE

I'll take some of their trade out of their hands.

JEREMY

Now Heaven, of mercy, continue the tax upon paper! you don't mean to write?

VALENTINE

Yes, I do; I'll write a play.

JEREMY

Hem!—Sir, if you please to give me a small certificate of three lines;—only to certify those whom it may concern, that the bearer hereof, Jeremy Fetch by name, has for the space of seven years, truly and faithfully served Valentine Legend, Esq.; and that he is not now turned away for any misdemeanour, but does voluntarily dismiss his master from any future authority over him.

VALENTINE

No, sirrah, you shall live with me still.

JEREMY

Sir, it's impossible:—I may die with you, starve with you, or be damned with your works; but to live, even three days, the life of a play, I no more expect it, than to be canonised for a Muse after my decease.

VALENTINE

You are witty, you rogue! I shall want your help; I'll have you learn to make couplets, to tag the ends of acts; d'ye hear, get the maids to crambo in an evening, and learn the knack of rhyming: you may arrive at the height of a song sent by an unknown hand, or a choco-late-house lampoon.

JEREMY

But, sir, is this the way to recover your father's favour? why, Sir Sampson will be irreconcilable. If your younger brother should come from sea, he'd never look upon you again. You're undone, sir, you're ruined, you won't have a friend left in the world if you turn poet.—Ah, pox confound that Will's Coffee-house! [1] it has ruined more young men than the Royal Oak lottery;—nothing thrives that belongs to't. The man of the house would have been an alderman by this time with half the trade, if he had set up in the city. For my part, I never sit at the door that I don't get double the stomach that I do at a horse-race:—the air upon Banstead downs is nothing to it for a whetter. Yet I never see it, but the spirit of famine appears to me, sometimes like a decayed porter, worn out with pimping, and carrying billets-doux and songs; not like other porters for hire, but for the jest's sake:—now like a thin chairman, melted down to half his proportion with carrying a poet upon tick, to visit some great fortune, and his fare to be paid him, like the wages of sin, either at the day of marriage, or the day of death.

VALENTINE

Very well, sir; can you proceed?

JEREMY

Sometimes like a bilked bookseller, with a meagre terrified counte-nance, that looks as if he had written for himself, or were resolved

---

[1] Will's Coffee-house was situated at No. 1, Bow Street, at the corner of Russell Street, and was called after its proprietor William Urwin. It was fre-quented at this date by gamblers as well as wits.

to turn author, and bring the rest of his brethren into the same condition:—and lastly, in the form of a worn-out punk,[2] with verses in
her hand, which her vanity had preferred to settlements, without a
whole tatter to her tail, but as ragged as one of the Muses; or as if
she were carrying her linen to the papermill, to be converted into
folio books of warning to all young maids, not to prefer poetry to
good sense, or lying in the arms of a needy wit, before the embraces
of a wealthy fool.
    Enter Scandal.

SCANDAL
    What, Jeremy holding forth?

VALENTINE
    The rogue has (with all the wit he could muster up) been declaiming
    against wit.

SCANDAL
    Ay? why then I'm afraid Jeremy has wit: for wherever it is, it's
    always contriving its own ruin.

JEREMY
    Why, so I have been telling my master, sir; Mr. Scandal, for
    Heaven's sake, sir, try if you can dissuade him from turning poet.

SCANDAL
    Poet! he shall turn soldier first, and rather depend upon the outside
    of his head, than the lining. Why, what the devil! has not your pov-
    erty made you enemies enough? must you needs show your wit to
    get more?

JEREMY
    Ay, more indeed; for who cares for anybody that has more wit than
    himself?

SCANDAL
    Jeremy speaks like an oracle. Don't you see how worthless great
    men, and dull rich rogues, avoid a witty man of small fortune? Why,
    he looks like a writ of inquiry into their titles and estates; and seems
    commissioned by Heaven to seize the better half.

VALENTINE
    Therefore I would rail in my writings, and be revenged.

SCANDAL
    Rail? at whom? the whole world? Impotent and vain! who would die
    a martyr to sense in a country where the religion is folly? you may
    stand at bay for a while; but when the full cry is against you, you
    shan't have fair play for your life. If you can't be fairly run down by
    the hounds, you will be treacherously shot by the huntsmen. No,
    turn pimp, flatterer, quack, lawyer, parson, be chaplain to an atheist,
    or stallion to an old woman, anything but poet; a modern poet is
    worse, more servile, timorous and fawning, than any I have named:
    without you could retrieve the ancient honours of the name, recall
    the stage of Athens, and be allowed the force of open, honest satire.

VALENTINE
    You are as inveterate against our poets as if your character had been
    lately exposed upon the stage.—Nay, I am not violently bent upon
    the trade.—(*Knocking at the door.*) Jeremy, see who's there.—(*Exit
    Jeremy.*) But tell me what you would have me do? What does the
    world say of me, and my forced confinement?

_____
[2] Prostitute.

SCANDAL

The world behaves itself as it uses to do on such occasions; some pity you and condemn your father; others excuse him and blame you; only the ladies are merciful, and wish you well; since love and pleasurable expense have been your greatest faults.

Re-enter Jeremy.

VALENTINE

How now?

JEREMY

Nothing new, sir; I have despatched some half-a-dozen duns with as much dexterity as a hungry judge does causes at dinner time.

VALENTINE

What answer have you given 'em?

SCANDAL

Patience, I suppose? the old receipt.

JEREMY

No, faith, sir; I have put 'em off so long with patience and forbearance, and other fair words, that I was forced now to tell 'em in plain downright English—

VALENTINE

What?

JEREMY

That they should be paid.

VALENTINE

When?

JEREMY

To-morrow.

VALENTINE

And how the devil do you mean to keep your word?

JEREMY

Keep it! not at all; it has been so very much stretched that I reckon it will break of course by to-morrow, and nobody be surprised at the matter.—(*Knocking.*) Again!—Sir, if you don't like my negotiation, will you be pleased to answer these yourself?

VALENTINE

See who they are. [*Exit Jeremy.*

By this, Scandal, you may see what it is to be great; secretaries of state, presidents of the council, and generals of an army, lead just such a life as I do; have just such crowds of visitants in a morning, all soliciting of past promises; which are but a civiler sort of duns, that lay claim to voluntary debts.

SCANDAL

And you, like a true great man, having engaged their attendance, and promised more than ever you intend to perform, are more perplexed to find evasions than you would be to invent the honest means of keeping your word, and gratifying your creditors.

VALENTINE

Scandal, learn to spare your friends, and do not provoke your enemies: this liberty of your tongue will one day bring a confinement on your body, my friend.

Re-enter Jeremy.

JEREMY

O sir, there's Trapland the scrivener, with two suspicious fellows like lawful pads, that would knock a man down with pocket-tipstaves;—

and there's your father's steward, and the nurse with one of your children from Twitnam.

VALENTINE

Pox on her! could she find no other time to fling my sins in my face? Here, give her this (*Gives money.*), and bid her trouble me no more; —a thoughtless, two-handed whore! she knows my condition well enough, and might have overlaid the child a fortnight ago, if she had had any forecast in her.

SCANDAL

What, is it bouncing Margery with my godson?

JEREMY

Yes, sir.

SCANDAL

My blessing to the boy, with this token of my love. (*Gives money.*) And d'ye hear, bid Margery put more flocks in her bed, shift twice a-week, and not work so hard, that she may not smell so vigorously. I shall take the air shortly.

VALENTINE

Scandal, don't spoil my boy's milk.—(*To Jeremy.*) Bid Trapland come in. (*Exit Jeremy.*) If I can give that Cerberus a sop, I shall be at rest for one day.

    Re-enter Jeremy with Trapland.

VALENTINE

O Mr. Trapland, my old friend, welcome!—Jeremy, a chair quickly; a bottle of sack and a toast;—fly—a chair first.

TRAPLAND

A good morning to you, Mr. Valentine, and to you, Mr. Scandal.

SCANDAL

The morning's a very good morning, if you don't spoil it.

VALENTINE

Come sit you down, you know his way.

TRAPLAND (*Sits.*)

There is a debt, Mr. Valentine, of fifteen hundred pounds of pretty long standing—

VALENTINE

I cannot talk about business with a thirsty palate.—(*To Jeremy.*) Sirrah, the sack.

TRAPLAND

And I desire to know what course you have taken for the payment?

VALENTINE

Faith and troth, I am heartily glad to see you:—my service to you. (*Drinks.*) Fill, fill, to honest Mr. Trapland, fuller.

TRAPLAND

Hold, sweetheart;—this is not to our business. My service to you, Mr. Scandal. (*Drinks.*) I have forborne as long—

VALENTINE

T'other glass, and then we'll talk.—Fill, Jeremy.

TRAPLAND

No more, in truth.—I have forborne, I say—

VALENTINE (*To Jeremy.*)

Sirrah, fill when I bid you.—(*To Trapland.*) And how does your handsome daughter? Come, a good husband to her.   [*Drinks.*

TRAPLAND

Thank you.—I have been out of this money—

VALENTINE

Drink first.—Scandal, why do you not drink?

[They drink.

TRAPLAND

And in short, I can be put off no longer.

VALENTINE

I was much obliged to you for your supply: it did me signal service in my necessity. But you delight in doing good.—Scandal, drink to me my friend Trapland's health. An honester man lives not, nor one more ready to serve his friend in distress, though I say it to his face. Come, fill each man his glass.

SCANDAL

What, I know Trapland has been a whoremaster, and loves a wench still. You never knew a whoremaster that was not an honest fellow.

TRAPLAND

Fy, Mr. Scandal! you never knew—

SCANDAL

What, don't I know?—I know the buxum black widow in the Poultry—eight hundred pounds a-year, jointure, and twenty thousand pounds in money. Aha, old Trap!

VALENTINE

Say you so, i'faith? come, we'll remember the widow: I know whereabouts you are; come, to the widow—

TRAPLAND

No more, indeed.

VALENTINE

What, the widow's health.—(*To Jeremy.*) Give it him.—Off with it. (*They drink.*) A lovely girl, i'faith, black sparkling eyes, soft pouting ruby lips; better sealing there than a bond for a million, ha!

TRAPLAND

No, no, there's no such thing, we'd better mind our business;—you're a wag.

VALENTINE

No, faith, we'll mind the widow's business, fill again.—Pretty round heaving breasts, a Barbary shape, and a jut with her bum would stir an anchorite, and the prettiest foot! Oh, if a man could but fasten his eyes to her feet, as they steal in and out, and play at bo-peep under her petticoats! ah, Mr. Trapland?

TRAPLAND

Verily, give me a glass—you're a wag—and here's to the widow.

[Drinks.

SCANDAL (*Aside to Valentine.*)

He begins to chuckle; ply him close, or he'll relapse into a dun.

[Exit Jeremy.

Enter Snap.

SNAP

By your leave, gentlemen.—Mr. Trapland, if we must do our office, tell us: we have half-a-dozen gentlemen to arrest in Pall Mall and Covent Garden; and if we don't make haste, the chairmen will be abroad, and block up the chocolate-houses,[3] and then our labour's lost.

---

[3] The chief chocolate-houses were White's, St. James's Street; the Cocoa Tree, Pall Mall; and the Spread Eagle, Covent Garden.

TRAPLAND

Udso, that's true.—Mr. Valentine, I love mirth, but business must be done; are you ready to—

Re-enter Jeremy.

JEREMY

Sir, your father's steward says he comes to make proposals concerning your debts.

VALENTINE

Bid him come in.—Mr. Trapland, send away your officer; you shall have an answer presently.

TRAPLAND

Mr. Snap, stay within call.

[*Exit Snap.*

Enter Steward, who whispers to Valentine.

SCANDAL

Here's a dog now, a traitor in his wine; (*To Trapland.*)—sirrah, refund the sack.—Jeremy, fetch him some warm water, or I'll rip up his stomach, and go the shortest way to his conscience.

TRAPLAND

Mr. Scandal, you are uncivil; I did not value your sack; but you cannot expect it again, when I have drunk it.

SCANDAL

And how do you expect to have your money again, when a gentleman has spent it?

VALENTINE (*To Steward.*)

You need say no more, I understand the conditions, they are very hard, but my necessity is very pressing; I agree to 'em. Take Mr. Trapland with you, and let him draw the writing.—Mr. Trapland, you know this man, he shall satisfy you.

TRAPLAND

I am loth to be thus pressing, but my necessity—

VALENTINE

No apology, good Mr. Scrivener, you shall be paid.

TRAPLAND

I hope you forgive me, my business requires—

[*Exeunt Trapland, Steward, and Jeremy.*

Scene II. The same.
Valentine and Scandal seated.

SCANDAL

He begs pardon like a hangman at an execution.

VALENTINE

But I have got a reprieve.

SCANDAL

I am surprised; what, does your father relent?

VALENTINE

No; he has sent me the hardest conditions in the world. You have heard of a booby brother of mine that was sent to sea three years ago? this brother my father hears is landed; whereupon he very affectionately sends me word, if I will make a deed of conveyance of my right to his estate after his death to my younger brother, he will immediately furnish me with four thousand pounds to pay my debts, and make my fortune. This was once proposed before, and I refused it; but the present impatience of my creditors for their money, and my own impatience of confinement, and absence from Angelica, force me to consent.

SCANDAL

A very desperate demonstration of your love to Angelica; and I think she has never given you any assurance of hers.

VALENTINE

You know her temper; she never gave me any great reason either for hope or despair.

SCANDAL

Women of her airy temper, as they seldom think before they act, so they rarely give us any light to guess at what they mean; but you have little reason to believe that a woman of this age, who has had an indifference for you in your prosperity, will fall in love with your ill-fortune; besides, Angelica has a great fortune of her own; and great fortunes either expect another great fortune, or a fool.

Enter Jeremy.

JEREMY

More misfortunes, sir.

VALENTINE

What, another dun?

JEREMY

No, sir, but Mr. Tattle is come to wait upon you.

VALENTINE

Well, I can't help it;—you must bring him up; he knows I don't go abroad. *[Exit Jeremy.*

SCANDAL

Pox on him! I'll be gone.

VALENTINE

No, prithee stay: Tattle and you should never be asunder; you are light and shadow, and show one another: he is perfectly thy reverse both in humour and understanding; and, as you set up for defamation, he is a mender of reputations.

SCANDAL

A mender of reputations! ay, just as he is a keeper of secrets, another virtue that he sets up for in the same manner. For the rogue will speak aloud in the posture of a whisper; and deny a woman's name, while he gives you the marks of her person: he will forswear receiving a letter from her, and at the same time show you her hand in the superscription; and yet perhaps he has counterfeited the hand too, and sworn to a truth; but he hopes not to be believed; and refuses the reputation of a lady's favour, as a doctor says *No* to a bishopric, only that it may be granted him.—In short, he is a public professor of secrecy, and makes proclamation that he holds private intelligence.—He's here.

Enter Tattle.

TATTLE

Valentine, good morrow; Scandal, I am yours,—that is, when you speak well of me.

SCANDAL

That is, when I am yours; for while I am my own, or anybody's else, that will never happen.

TATTLE
How inhuman!

VALENTINE
Why, Tattle, you need not be much concerned at anything that he
says: for to converse with Scandal, is to play at Losing Loadum: you
must lose a good name to him, before you can win it for yourself.

TATTLE
But how barbarous that is, and how unfortunate for him, that the
world should think the better of any person for his calumniation!
—I thank heaven, it has always been a part of my character to handle
the reputation of others very tenderly indeed.

SCANDAL
Ay, such rotten reputations as you have to deal with, are to be
handled tenderly indeed.

TATTLE
Nay, but why rotten; why should you say rotten, when you know not
the persons of whom you speak? how cruel that is!

SCANDAL
Not know 'em? why, thou never hadst to do with anybody that did
not stink to all the town.

TATTLE
Ha! ha! ha! nay, now you make a jest of it indeed; for there is
nothing more known, than that nobody knows anything of that
nature of me.—As I hope to be saved, Valentine, I never exposed
a woman since I knew what woman was.

VALENTINE
And yet you have conversed with several.

TATTLE
To be free with you, I have;—I don't care if I own that;—nay more
(I'm going to say a bold word now), I never could meddle with a
woman that had to do with anybody else.

SCANDAL
How!

VALENTINE
Nay, faith, I'm apt to believe him.—Except her husband, Tattle.

TATTLE
Oh, that—

SCANDAL
What think you of that noble commoner Mrs. Drab?

TATTLE
Pooh, I know Madam Drab has made her brags in three or four
places, that I said this and that, and writ to her, and did I know not
what;—but upon my reputation she did me wrong.—Well, well, that
was malice:—but I know the bottom of it. She was bribed to that by
one we all know;—a man too—only to bring me into disgrace with a
certain woman of quality—

SCANDAL
Whom we all know.

TATTLE
No matter for that.—Yes, yes, everybody knows—no doubt on't,
everybody knows my secret.—But I soon satisfied the lady of my
innocence; for I told her—Madam, says I, there are some persons

who make it their business to tell stories, and say this and that of one and t'other, and everything in the world; and, say I, if your grace—

SCANDAL

Grace!

TATTLE

O Lord! what have I said? my unlucky tongue!

VALENTINE

Ha! ha! ha!

SCANDAL

Why, Tattle, thou hast more impudence than one can in reason expect: I shall have an esteem for thee. Well, and, ha! ha! ha! well, go on: and what did you say to her grace?

VALENTINE

I confess this is something extraordinary.

TATTLE

Not a word, as I hope to be saved; an arrant *lapsus linguæ*.—Come, let's talk of something else.

VALENTINE

Well, but how did you acquit yourself?

TATTLE

Pooh! pooh! nothing at all, I only rallied with you—a woman of ordinary rank was a little jealous of me, and I told her something or other, faith—I know not what.—Come, let's talk of something else.

[*Hums a song.*

SCANDAL

Hang him, let him alone, he has a mind we should inquire.

TATTLE

Valentine, I supped last night with your mistress, and her uncle old Foresight; I think your father lies at Foresight's.

VALENTINE

Yes.

TATTLE

Upon my soul, Angelica's a fine woman.—And so is Mrs. Foresight, and her sister Mrs. Frail.

SCANDAL

Yes, Mrs. Frail is a very fine woman; we all know her.

TATTLE

Oh, that is not fair!

SCANDAL

What?

TATTLE

To tell.

SCANDAL

To tell what? why, what do you know of Mrs. Frail?

TATTLE

Who, I? upon honour I don't know whether she be man or woman; but, by the smoothness of her chin, and roundness of her hips.

SCANDAL

No!

TATTLE

No.

SCANDAL

She says otherwise.

TATTLE

Impossible!

SCANDAL

Yes, faith. Ask Valentine else.

TATTLE

Why then, as I hope to be saved, I believe a woman only obliges a
man to secrecy, that she may have the pleasure of telling herself.

SCANDAL

No doubt on't. Well, but has she done you wrong, or no? you have
had her? ha?

TATTLE

Though I have more honour than to tell first, I have more manners
than to contradict what a lady has declared.

SCANDAL

Well, you own it?

TATTLE

I am strangely surprised!—Yes, yes, I can't deny't, if she taxes me
with it.

SCANDAL

She'll be here by-and-by, she sees Valentine every morning.

TATTLE

How?

VALENTINE

She does me the favour, I mean, of a visit sometimes. I did not think
she had granted more to anybody.

SCANDAL

Nor I, faith; but Tattle does not use to belie a lady; it is contrary to
his character.—How one may be deceived in a woman, Valentine!

TATTLE

Nay, what do you mean, gentlemen?

SCANDAL

I'm resolved I'll ask her.

TATTLE

O barbarous! why, did you not tell me—

SCANDAL

No, you told us.

TATTLE

And bid me ask Valentine?

VALENTINE

What did I say? I hope you won't bring me to confess an answer,
when you never asked me the question?

TATTLE

But, gentlemen, this is the most inhuman proceeding—

VALENTINE

Nay, if you have known Scandal thus long, and cannot avoid such a
palpable decoy as this was, the ladies have a fine time whose reputations are in your keeping.

Re-enter Jeremy.

JEREMY

Sir, Mrs. Frail has sent to know if you are stirring.

VALENTINE

Show her up when she comes.

[*Exit Jeremy.*

TATTLE

I'll be gone.

VALENTINE

You'll meet her.

TATTLE

Is there not a back way?

VALENTINE

If there were, you have more discretion than to give Scandal such an advantage; why, your running away will prove all that he can tell her.

TATTLE

Scandal, you will not be so ungenerous?—Oh, I shall lose my reputation of secrecy for ever!—I shall never be received but upon public days; and my visits will never be admitted beyond a drawing-room: I shall never see a bedchamber again, never be locked in a closet, nor run behind a screen, or under a table; never be distinguished among the waiting-women by the name of trusty Mr. Tattle more.—You will not be so cruel.

VALENTINE

Scandal, have pity on him; he'll yield to any conditions.

TATTLE

Any, any terms.

SCANDAL

Come, then, sacrifice half-a-dozen women of good reputation to me presently.—Come, where are you familiar?—and see that they are women of quality too, the first quality.

TATTLE

'Tis very hard.—Won't a baronet's lady pass?

SCANDAL

No, nothing under a right honourable.

TATTLE

O inhuman! you don't expect their names?

SCANDAL

No, their titles shall serve.

TATTLE

Alas! that's the same thing: pray spare me their titles; I'll describe their persons.

SCANDAL

Well, begin then: but take notice, if you are so ill a painter, that I cannot know the person by your picture of her, you must be condemned, like other bad painters, to write the name at the bottom.

TATTLE

Well, first then—

Enter Mrs. Frail.

O unfortunate! she's come already; will you have patience till another time;—I'll double the number.

SCANDAL

Well, on that condition.—Take heed you don't fail me.

MRS. FRAIL

I shall get a fine reputation by coming to see fellows in a morning.—Scandal, you devil, are you here too?—Oh, Mr. Tattle, everything is safe with you, we know.

SCANDAL
   Tattle!
TATTLE
   Mum.—O madam, you do me too much honour.
VALENTINE
   Well, lady galloper, how does Angelica?
MRS. FRAIL
   Angelica? manners!
VALENTINE
   What, will you allow an absent lover—
MRS. FRAIL
   No, I'll allow a lover present with his mistress to be particular;—but
   otherwise I think his passion ought to give place to his manners.
VALENTINE
   But what if he has more passion than manners?
MRS. FRAIL
   Then let him marry and reform.
VALENTINE
   Marriage indeed may qualify the fury of his passion, but it very
   rarely mends a man's manners.
MRS. FRAIL
   You are the most mistaken in the world; there is no creature
   perfectly civil but a husband. For in a little time he grows only rude
   to his wife, and that is the highest good breeding, for it begets his
   civility to other people.—Well, I'll tell you news; but I suppose you
   hear your brother Benjamin is landed. And my brother Foresight's
   daughter is come out of the country—I assure you there's a match
   talked of by the old people.—Well, if he be but as great a sea-beast
   as she is a land monster, we shall have a most amphibious breed.—
   The progeny will be all otters; he has been bred at sea, and she has
   never been out of the country.
VALENTINE
   Pox take 'em! their conjunction bodes me no good, I'm sure.
MRS. FRAIL
   Now you talk of conjunction, my brother Foresight has cast both
   their nativities, and prognosticates an admiral and an eminent justice
   of the peace to be the issue male of their two bodies.—'Tis the most
   superstitious old fool! he would have persuaded me, that this was an
   unlucky day, and would not let me come abroad; but I invented a
   dream, and sent him to Artemidorus for interpretation, and so stole
   out to see you. Well, and what will you give me now? come, I must
   have something.
VALENTINE
   Step into the next room—and I'll give you something.
SCANDAL
   Ay, we'll all give you something.
MRS. FRAIL
   Well, what will you all give me?
VALENTINE
   Mine's a secret.
MRS. FRAIL
   I thought you would give me something that would be a trouble to
   you to keep.

VALENTINE

And Scandal shall give you a good name.

MRS. FRAIL

That's more than he has for himself.—And what will you give me, Mr. Tattle?

TATTLE

I? my soul, madam.

MRS. FRAIL

Pooh, no, I thank you, I have enough to do to take care of my own. Well; but I'll come and see you one of these mornings: I hear you have a great many pictures.

TATTLE

I have a pretty good collection at your service, some originals.

SCANDAL

Hang him, he has nothing but the Seasons and the twelve Cæsars, paltry copies; and the Five Senses, as ill represented as they are in himself; and he himself is the only original you will see there.

MRS. FRAIL

Ay, but I hear he has a closet of beauties.

SCANDAL

Yes, all that have done him favours, if you will believe him.

MRS. FRAIL

Ay, let me see those, Mr. Tattle.

TATTLE

Oh, madam, those are sacred to love and contemplation. No man but the painter and myself was ever blest with the sight.

MRS. FRAIL

Well, but a woman—

TATTLE

Nor woman, 'till she consented to have her picture there too;—for then she's obliged to keep the secret.

SCANDAL

No, no; come to me if you'd see pictures.

MRS. FRAIL

You?

SCANDAL

Yes, faith, I can show you your own picture, and most of your acquaintance to the life, and as like as at Kneller's.

MRS. FRAIL

O lying creature!—Valentine, does not he lie?—I can't believe a word he says.

VALENTINE

No, indeed, he speaks truth now; for as Tattle has pictures of all that have granted him favours, he has the pictures of all that have refused him; if satires, descriptions, characters, and lampoons are pictures.

SCANDAL

Yes, mine are most in black and white;—and yet there are some set out in their true colours, both men and women. I can show you pride, folly, affectation, wantonness, inconstancy, covetousness, dissimulation, malice, and ignorance, all in one piece. Then I can show you lying, foppery, vanity, cowardice, bragging, lechery, impotence, and ugliness in another piece; and yet one of these is a celebrated beauty, and t'other a professed beau. I have paintings too, some pleasant enough.

MRS. FRAIL

Come, let's hear 'em.

SCANDAL

Why, I have a beau in a bagnio, cupping for a complexion, and sweating for a shape.

MRS. FRAIL

So.

SCANDAL

Then I have a lady burning brandy in a cellar with a hackney coachman.

MRS. FRAIL

O devil! Well, but that story is not true.

SCANDAL

I have some hieroglyphics too; I have a lawyer with a hundred hands, two heads, and but one face; a divine with two faces, and one head; and I have a soldier with his brains in his belly, and his heart where his head should be.

MRS. FRAIL

And no head?

SCANDAL

No head.

MRS. FRAIL

Pooh, this is all invention. Have you ne'er a poet?

SCANDAL

Yes, I have a poet weighing words, and selling praise for praise, and a critic picking his pocket. I have another large piece too, representing a school; where there are huge-proportioned critics, with long wigs, laced coats, Steenkirk cravats,[4] and terrible faces; with catcalls in their hands, and horn-books about their necks. I have many more of this kind, very well painted as you shall see.

MRS. FRAIL

Well, I'll come, if it be but to disprove you.

Re-enter Jeremy.

JEREMY

Sir, here's the steward again from your father.

VALENTINE

I'll come to him.—Will you give me leave? I'll wait on you again presently.

MRS. FRAIL

No, I'll be gone. Come, who squires me to the Exchange?[5] I must call my sister Foresight there.

SCANDAL

I will: I have a mind to your sister.

[4] The fashionable neckcloth of the day, so called from the battle of that name, which was fought August 3, 1692, when the English under William III were defeated. It was arranged with graceful carelessness, pretending to imitate the haste with which the French generals rushed into battle, they not having had time to tie their neckcloths.

[5] The Royal Exchange was at this time a favourite lounge; the galleries over its piazzas were filled with shops kept chiefly by women, not always of the most reputable character.

MRS. FRAIL
Civil!

TATTLE
I will, because I have a *tendre* for your ladyship.

MRS. FRAIL
That's somewhat the better reason, to my opinion.

SCANDAL
Well, if Tattle entertains you, I have the better opportunity to engage your sister.

VALENTINE
Tell Angelica, I am about making hard conditions to come abroad, and be at liberty to see her.

SCANDAL
I'll give an account of you and your proceedings. If indiscretion be a sign of love, you are the most a lover of anybody that I know: you fancy that parting with your estate will help you to your mistress.— In my mind he is a thoughtless adventurer,

> Who hopes to purchase wealth by selling land,
> Or win a mistress with a losing hand.

[*Exeunt.*

Act the second

Scene I. A room in Foresight's house.
Foresight and Servant.

FORESIGHT
Heyday! what are all the women of my family abroad? Is not my wife come home, nor my sister, nor my daughter?

SERVANT
No, sir.

FORESIGHT
Mercy on us, what can be the meaning of it? Sure the moon is in all her fortitudes. Is my niece Angelica at home?

SERVANT
Yes, sir.

FORESIGHT
I believe you lie, sir.

SERVANT
Sir?

FORESIGHT
I say you lie, sir. It is impossible that anything should be as I would have it; for I was born, sir, when the Crab was ascending, and all my affairs go backward.

SERVANT
I can't tell, indeed, sir.

FORESIGHT
No, I know you can't, sir; but I can tell, sir, and foretell, sir.
Enter Nurse.

FORESIGHT
Nurse, where's your young mistress?

NURSE
Wee'st heart, I know not, they're none of 'em come home yet. Poor

child! I warrant she's fond o' seeing the town;—marry, pray heaven,
they ha' given her any dinner.—Good lack-a-day, ha! ha! ha! Oh
strange! I'll vow and swear now,—ha! ha! ha! marry, and did you
ever see the like?

FORESIGHT

Why, how now, what's the matter?

NURSE

Pray Heaven send your worship good luck! marry and amen with all
my heart; for you have put on one stocking with the wrong side outward.

FORESIGHT

Ha, how? faith and troth I'm glad of it!—And so I have; that may be
good luck in troth, in troth it may, very good luck; nay, I have had
some omens: I got out of bed backwards too this morning, without
premeditation; pretty good that too; but then I stumbled coming
down stairs, and met a weasel; bad omens those: some bad, some
good, our lives are chequered: mirth and sorrow, want and plenty,
night and day, make up our time.—But in troth I am pleased at my
stocking; very well pleased at my stocking.—Oh, here's my niece!—
Sirrah, go tell Sir Sampson Legend I'll wait on him if he's at leisure;
'tis now three o'clock, a very good hour for business. Mercury gov-
erns this hour.

[*Exit Servant.*

Enter Angelica.

ANGELICA

Is it not a good hour for pleasure too, uncle? pray lend me your
coach, mine's out of order.

FORESIGHT

What, would you be gadding too? sure all females are mad to-day. It
is of evil portent, and bodes mischief to the master of a family.—I
remember an old prophecy written by Messahalah the Arabian, and
this translated by a reverend Buckinghamshire bard.

"When housewives all the house forsake,
  And leave goodman to brew and bake,
  Withouten guile then be it said,
  That house doth stond upon its head;
  And when the head is set in ground,
  Ne mar'l if it be fruitful found."

Fruitful, the head fruitful;—that bodes horns, the fruit of the head
is horns.—Dear niece, stay at home; for by the head of the house is
meant the husband; the prophecy needs no explanation.

ANGELICA

Well, but I can neither make you a cuckold, uncle, by going abroad;
nor secure you from being one, by staying at home.

FORESIGHT

Yes, yes; while there's one woman left, the prophecy is not in full
force.

ANGELICA

But my inclinations are in force; I have a mind to go abroad; and if
you won't lend me your coach, I'll take a hackney, or a chair, and
leave you to erect a scheme, and find who's in conjunction with your

wife. Why don't you keep her at home, if you're jealous of her when she's abroad? You know my aunt is a little retrograde (as you call it) in her nature. Uncle, I'm afraid you are not lord of the ascendant, ha! ha! ha!

FORESIGHT

Well, jill-flirt, you are very pert—and always ridiculing that celestial science.

ANGELICA

Nay, uncle, don't be angry;—if you are, I'll rip up all your false prophecies, ridiculous dreams, and idle divinations: I'll swear you are a nuisance to the neighbourhood.—What a bustle did you keep against the last invisible eclipse, laying in provision, as 'twere for a siege! What a world of fire and candle, matches and tinderboxes did you purchase! One would have thought we were ever after to live underground, or at least making a voyage to Greenland, to inhabit there all the dark season.

FORESIGHT

Why, you malapert slut!

ANGELICA

Will you lend me your coach, or I'll go on?—Nay, I'll declare how you prophesied popery was coming, only because the butler had mislaid some of the apostle spoons, and thought they were lost. Away went religion and spoonmeat together.—Indeed, uncle, I'll indict you for a wizard.

FORESIGHT

How, hussy! was there ever such a provoking minx!

NURSE

O merciful Father, how she talks!

ANGELICA

Yes, I can make oath of your unlawful midnight practices; you and the old nurse there—

NURSE

Marry, Heaven defend!—I at midnight practices!—O Lord, what's here to do!—I in unlawful doings with my master's worship!—Why, did you ever hear the like now?—Sir, did ever I do anything of your midnight concerns—but warm your bed, and tuck you up, and set the candle and your tobacco-box and your urinal by you, and now and then rub the soles of your feet?—O Lord, I?—

ANGELICA

Yes, I saw you together, through the keyhole of the closet, one night, like Saul and the witch of Endor, turning the sieve and shears, and pricking your thumbs to write poor innocent servants' names in blood, about a little nutmeg-grater, which she had forgot in the caudle-cup.—Nay, I know something worse, if I would speak of it.

FORESIGHT

I defy you, hussy! but I'll remember this, I'll be revenged on you, cockatrice; I'll hamper you.—You have your fortune in your own hands,—but I'll find a way to make your lover, your prodigal spendthrift gallant, Valentine, pay for all, I will.

ANGELICA

Will you? I care not but all shall out then.—Look to't, nurse; I can bring witness that you have a great unnatural teat under your left arm, and he another; and that you suckle a young devil in the shape of a tabbycat, by turns, I can.

NURSE

A teat! a teat! I an unnatural teat! O the false, slanderous thing; feel, feel here, if I have anything but like another Christian.

[Crying.

FORESIGHT

I will have patience, since it is the will of the stars I should be thus tormented.—This is the effect of the malicious conjunctions and op-positions in the third house of my nativity; there the curse of kindred was foretold.—But I will have my doors locked up—I'll punish you, not a man shall enter my house.

ANGELICA

Do, uncle, lock 'em up quickly before my aunt comes home;—you'll have a letter for alimony to-morrow morning,—but let me begone first, and then let no mankind come near the house, but converse with spirits and the celestial signs, the Bull, and the Ram, and the Goat. Bless me! there are a great many horned beasts among the Twelve Signs, uncle;—but cuckolds go to Heaven.

FORESIGHT

But there's but one virgin among the twelve signs, spitfire, but one virgin.

ANGELICA

Nor there had not been that one, if she had had to do with anything but astrologers, uncle. That makes my aunt go abroad.

FORESIGHT

How? how? is that the reason? Come, you know something: tell me and I'll forgive you; do, good niece.—Come, you shall have my coach and horses;—faith and troth you shall.—Does my wife com-plain? come, I know women tell one another.—She is young and sanguine, has a wanton hazel eye, and was born under Gemini, which may incline her to society; she has a mole upon her lip, with a moist palm, and an open liberality on the mount of Venus.

ANGELICA

Ha! ha! ha!

FORESIGHT

Do you laugh?—Well, gentlewoman, I'll—but come, be a good girl, don't perplex your poor uncle, tell me; won't you speak?—Odd, I'll—

Re-enter Servant.

SERVANT

Sir Sampson is coming down to wait upon you.

ANGELICA

Good b'w'ye, uncle.—Call me a chair.—(*Exit Servant.*) I'll find out my aunt, and tell her she must not come home.

[Exit.

FORESIGHT

I'm so perplexed and vexed, I am not fit to receive him; I shall scarce recover myself before the hour be past.—Go, nurse, tell Sir Sampson I'm ready to wait on him.

NURSE

Yes, sir.

[Exit.

FORESIGHT

Well—why, if I was born to be a cuckold there's no more to be said—he's here already.

Enter Sir Sampson with a paper.

SIR SAMPSON

Nor no more to be done, old boy; that's plain.—Here 'tis, I have it in my hand, old Ptolomee; I'll make the ungracious prodigal know who begat him; I will, old Nostrodamus. What, I warrant my son thought nothing belonged to a father but forgiveness and affection; no authority, no correction, no arbitrary power; nothing to be done, but for him to offend, and me to pardon. I warrant you, if he danced till doomsday, he thought I was to pay the piper. Well, but here it is under black and white, *signatum, sigillatum,* and *deliberatum;* that as soon as my son Benjamin is arrived, he is to make over to him his right of inheritance. Where's my daughter that is to be—ha! old Merlin! body o' me, I'm so glad I'm revenged on this undutiful rogue.

FORESIGHT

Odso, let me see; let me see the paper.—Ay, faith and troth, here 'tis, if it will but hold. I wish things were done, and the conveyance made. When was this signed, what hour? Odso, you should have consulted me for the time. Well, but we'll make haste.

SIR SAMPSON

Haste, ay, ay; haste enough, my son Ben will be in town to-night.—I have ordered my lawyer to draw up writings of settlement and jointure:—all shall be done tonight. No matter for the time: prithee, Brother Foresight, leave superstition. Pox o' th' time! there's no time but the time present, there's no more to be said of what's past, and all that is to come will happen. If the sun shine by day, and the stars by night, why, we shall know one another's faces without the help of a candle, and that's all the stars are good for.

FORESIGHT

How, how, Sir Sampson? that all? Give me leave to contradict you, and tell you, you are ignorant.

SIR SAMPSON

I tell you I am wise; and *sapiens dominabitur astris;* there's Latin for you to prove it, and an argument to confound your ephemeris. —Ignorant!—I tell you, I have travelled, old Fircu, and know the globe. I have seen the antipodes, where the sun rises at midnight, and sets at noonday.

FORESIGHT

But I tell you, I have travelled, and travelled in the celestial spheres, know the signs and the planets, and their houses. Can judge of motions direct and retrograde, of sextiles, quadrates, trines and oppositions, fiery trigons and aquatical trigons. Know whether life shall be long or short, happy or unhappy, whether diseases are curable or incurable. If journeys shall be prosperous, undertakings successful; or goods stolen recovered, I know—

SIR SAMPSON

I know the length of the Emperor of China's foot; have kissed the Great Mogul's slipper, and rid a hunting upon an elephant with the Cham of Tartary.—Body o' me, I have made a cuckold of a king, and the present majesty of Bantam is the issue of these loins.

FORESIGHT

I know when travellers lie or speak truth, when they don't know it themselves.

SIR SAMPSON

I have known an astrologer made a cuckold in the twinkling of a star; and seen a conjurer that could not keep the devil out of his wife's circle.

FORESIGHT (*Aside.*)

What, does he twit me with my wife too? I must be better informed of this.—(*Aloud.*) Do you mean my wife, Sir Sampson? Though you made a cuckold of the King of Bantam, yet by the body of the sun—

SIR SAMPSON

By the horns of the moon, you would say, brother Capricorn.

FORESIGHT

Capricorn in your teeth, thou modern Mandeville! Ferdinand Mendez Pinto was but a type of thee, thou liar of the first magnitude! Take back your paper of inheritance; send your son to sea again. I'll wed my daughter to an Egyptian mummy, ere she shall incorporate with a contemner of sciences, and a defamer of virtue.

SIR SAMPSON (*Aside.*)

Body o'me, I have gone too far;—I must not provoke honest Albumazar.[6]—(*Aloud.*) An Egyptian mummy is an illustrious creature, my trusty hieroglyphic; and may have significations of futurity about him; obsbud, I would my son were an Egyptian mummy for thy sake. What, thou art not angry for a jest, my good Haly?—I reverence the sun, moon, and stars with all my heart. What, I'll make thee a present of a mummy: now I think on't, body o'me, I have a shoulder of an Egyptian king, that I purloined from one of the pyramids, powdered with hieroglyphics; thou shalt have it brought home to thy house, and make an entertainment for all the philomaths, and students in physic and astrology, in and about London.

FORESIGHT

But what do you know of my wife, Sir Sampson?

SIR SAMPSON

Thy wife is a constellation of virtues; she's the moon, and thou art the man in the moon: nay, she is more illustrious than the moon; for she has her chastity without her inconstancy; 'sbud, I was but in jest.

Enter Jeremy.

How now, who sent for you? ha! what would you have?

[*Jeremy whispers to Sir Sampson.*

FORESIGHT

Nay, if you were but in jest—Who's that fellow? I don't like his physiognomy.

SIR SAMPSON (*To Jeremy.*)

My son, sir; what son, sir? my son Benjamin, hoh?

JEREMY

No, sir; Mr. Valentine, my master.—'Tis the first time he has been abroad since his confinement, and he comes to pay his duty to you.

SIR SAMPSON

Well, sir.

---

[6] A Persian astrologer who has given his name to a play.

Enter Valentine.

JEREMY

He is here, sir.

VALENTINE

Your blessing, sir.

SIR SAMPSON

You've had it already, sir. I think I sent it you to-day in a bill of four thousand pounds.—A great deal of money, Brother Foresight.

FORESIGHT

Ay, indeed, Sir Sampson, a great deal of money for a young man; I wonder what he can do with it.

SIR SAMPSON

Body o'me, so do I.—Hark ye, Valentine, if there be too much, refund the superfluity, dost hear, boy?

VALENTINE

Superfluity, sir! it will scarce pay my debts. I hope you will have more indulgence, than to oblige me to those hard conditions which my necessity signed to.

SIR SAMPSON

Sir, how, I beseech you, what were you pleased to intimate concerning indulgence?

VALENTINE

Why, sir, that you would not go to the extremity of the conditions, but release me at least from some part.

SIR SAMPSON

Oh, sir, I understand you—that's all, ha?

VALENTINE

Yes, sir, all that I presume to ask;—but what you, out of fatherly fondness, will be pleased to add shall be doubly welcome.

SIR SAMPSON

No doubt of it, sweet sir, but your filial piety and my fatherly fondness would fit like two tallies.—Here's a rogue, Brother Foresight, makes a bargain under hand and seal in the morning, and would be released from it in the afternoon; here's a rogue, dog, here's conscience and honesty; this is your wit now, this is the morality of your wits! You are a wit, and have been a beau, and may be a—why, sirrah, is it not here under hand and seal?—can you deny it?

VALENTINE

Sir, I don't deny it.

SIR SAMPSON

Sirrah, you'll be hanged; I shall live to see you go up Holborn Hill.[7]—Has he not a rogue's face?—Speak, brother, you understand physiognomy, a hanging look to me;—of all my boys the most unlike me; he has a damned Tyburn-face, without the benefit o' the clergy.

FORESIGHT

Hum—truly I don't care to discourage a young man. He has a violent death in his face; but I hope no danger of hanging.

VALENTINE

Sir, is this usage for your son?—for that old weather-headed fool, I know how to laugh at him; but you, sir—

---

[7] Meaning on the way to Tyburn.

SIR SAMPSON
You, sir; and you, sir;—why, who are you, sir?

VALENTINE
Your son, sir.

SIR SAMPSON
That's more than I know, sir, and I believe not.

VALENTINE
Faith, I hope not.

SIR SAMPSON
What, would you have your mother a whore!—Did you ever hear
the like! did you ever hear the like! Body o'me—

VALENTINE
I would have an excuse for your barbarity and unnatural usage.

SIR SAMPSON
Excuse! impudence! Why, sirrah, mayn't I do what I please? are not
you my slave? did not I beget you? and might not I have chosen
whether I would have begot you or no? 'Oons! who are you? whence
came you? what brought you into the world? how came you here,
sir? here, to stand here, upon those two legs, and look erect with
that audacious face, hah? Answer me that? Did you come a volun-
teer into the world? or did I, with the lawful authority of a parent,
press you to the service?

VALENTINE
I know no more why I came than you do why you called me. But
here I am, and if you don't mean to provide for me, I desire you
would leave me as you found me.

SIR SAMPSON
With all my heart: come, uncase, strip, and go naked out of the
world as you came into't.

VALENTINE
My clothes are soon put off;—but you must also divest me of reason,
thought, passions, inclinations, affections, appetites, senses, and the
huge train of attendants that you begot along with me.

SIR SAMPSON
Body o'me, what a many-headed monster have I propagated!

VALENTINE
I am of myself a plain, easy, simple creature, and to be kept at small
expense; but the retinue that you gave me are craving and invin-
cible; they are so many devils that you have raised, and will have employment.

SIR SAMPSON
'Oons, what had I to do to get children!—can't a private man be
born without all these followers?—Why, nothing under an emperor
should be born with appetites.—Why, at this rate, a fellow that has
but a groat in his pocket, may have a stomach capable of a ten-
shilling ordinary.

JEREMY
Nay, that's as clear as the sun; I'll make oath of it before any justice
in Middlesex.

SIR SAMPSON
Here's a cormorant too.—'S'heart, this fellow was not born with
you?—I did not beget him, did I?

JEREMY

By the provision that's made for me, you might have begot me too:—nay, and to tell your worship another truth, I believe you did, for I find I was born with those same whoreson appetites too that my master speaks of.

SIR SAMPSON

Why, look you there now—I'll maintain it, that by the rule of right reason, this fellow ought to have been born without a palate.— 'S'heart, what should he do with a distinguishing taste?—I warrant now he'd rather eat a pheasant than a piece of poor John: [8] and smell now—why, I warrant he can smell, and loves perfumes above a stink.—Why, there's it; and music—don't you love music, scoundrel?

JEREMY

Yes, I have a reasonable good ear, sir, as to jigs and country dances, and the like; I don't much matter your solos or sonatas; they give me the spleen.

SIR SAMPSON

The spleen, ha! ha! ha! a pox confound you!—solos or sonatas? 'Oons, whose son are you? how were you engendered, muckworm?

JEREMY

I am by my father the son of a chairman; my mother sold oysters in winter and cucumbers in summer; and I came up-stairs into the world; for I was born in a cellar.

FORESIGHT

By your looks, you should go up-stairs out of the world too, friend.

SIR SAMPSON

And if this rogue were anatomised now, and dissected, he has his vessels of digestion and concoction, and so forth, large enough for the inside of a cardinal, this son of a cucumber!—These things are unaccountable and unreasonable.—Body o'me, why was not I a bear? that my cubs might have lived upon sucking their paws. Nature has been provident only to bears and spiders; the one has its nutriment in his own hands, and t'other spins his habitation out of his own entrails.

VALENTINE

Fortune was provident enough to supply all the necessities of my nature, if I had my right of inheritance.

SIR SAMPSON

Again! 'Oons, han't you four thousand pounds—if I had it again, I would not give thee a groat.—What, wouldst thou have me turn pelican, and feed thee out of my own vitals?—'S'heart, live by your wits,—you were always fond of the wits:—now let's see if you have wit enough to keep yourself.—Your brother will be in town to-night or to-morrow morning, and then look you, perform covenants, and so your friend and servant.—Come, Brother Foresight.

[*Exeunt Sir Sampson and Foresight.*

JEREMY

I told you what your visit would come to.

VALENTINE

'Tis as much as I expected.—I did not come to see him: I came to Angelica; but since she was gone abroad it was easily turned another

[8] An inferior kind of dried hake.

way; and at least looked well on my side.—What's here? Mrs. Foresight and Mrs. Frail; they are earnest.—I'll avoid 'em.—Come this way, and go and inquire when Angelica will return.

[*Exeunt.*

Scene II. A room in Foresight's house.
Mrs. Foresight and Mrs. Frail

MRS. FRAIL

What have you to do to watch me! 'slife, I'll do what I please.

MRS. FORESIGHT

You will?

MRS. FRAIL

Yes, marry will I.—A great piece of business to go to Covent-Garden square in a hackney-coach, and take a turn with one's friend!

MRS. FORESIGHT

Nay, two or three turns, I'll take my oath.

MRS. FRAIL

Well, what if I took twenty?—I warrant if you had been there, it had been only innocent recreation.—Lord, where's the comfort of this life, if we can't have the happiness of conversing where we like?

MRS. FORESIGHT

But can't you converse at home?—I own it, I think there is no happiness like conversing with an agreeable man; I don't quarrel at that, nor I don't think but your conversation was very innocent; but the place is public, and to be seen with a man in a hackney-coach is scandalous: what if anybody else should have seen you alight, as I did?—How can anybody be happy, while they're in perpetual fear of being seen and censured?—Besides, it would not only reflect upon you, sister, but me.

MRS. FRAIL

Pooh, here's a clutter!—Why should it reflect upon you?—I don't doubt but you have thought yourself happy in a hackney-coach before now.—If I had gone to Knightsbridge, or to Chelsea, or to Spring Gardens, or Barn Elms, with a man alone—something might have been said.[9]

MRS. FORESIGHT

Why, was I ever in any of those places? what do you mean, sister?

MRS. FRAIL

Was I? what do you mean?

MRS. FORESIGHT

You have been at a worse place.

MRS. FRAIL

I at a worse place, and with a man!

MRS. FORESIGHT

I suppose you would not go alone to the World's-End.

[9] Spring Garden, a favourite haunt of pleasure between St. James's Park and Charing Cross, with butts and bowling-green. After the Restoration the entertainments were removed to the Spring Garden at Lambeth, subsequently called Vauxhall. Knightsbridge was then a retired and notorious district, where were two somewhat disreputable taverns, the Swan and the World's End, with gardens attached. Chelsea was also at that date a place of resort much patronised by cockneys; it was noted for its bun-house. Barn Elms had once a fashionable promenade, but at this time it was more famous for the duels that were fought there.

MRS. FRAIL
The world's-end! what, do you mean to banter me?

MRS. FORESIGHT
Poor innocent! you don't know that there's a place called the World's-End? I'll swear you can keep your countenance purely, you'd make an admirable player.

MRS. FRAIL
I'll swear you have a great deal of confidence, and in my mind too much for the stage.

MRS. FORESIGHT
Very well, that will appear who has most; you never were at the World's-End?

MRS. FRAIL
No.

MRS. FORESIGHT
You deny it positively to my face?

MRS. FRAIL
Your face! what's your face?

MRS. FORESIGHT
No matter for that, it's as good a face as yours.

MRS. FRAIL
Not by a dozen years' wearing.—But I do deny it positively to your face then.

MRS. FORESIGHT
I'll allow you now to find fault with my face;—for I'll swear your impudence has put me out of countenance:—but look you here now—where did you lose this gold bodkin?—O sister, sister!

MRS. FRAIL
My bodkin?

MRS. FORESIGHT
Nay, 'tis yours, look at it.

MRS. FRAIL
Well, if you go to that, where did you find this bodkin?—O sister, sister!—sister every way.

MRS. FORESIGHT (Aside.)
O devil on't, that I could not discover her without betraying myself!

MRS. FRAIL
I have heard gentlemen say, sister, that one should take great care, when one makes a thrust in fencing, not to lie open one's self.

MRS. FORESIGHT
It's very true, sister; well, since all's out, and as you say, since we are both wounded, let us do what is often done in duels, take care of one another, and grow better friends than before.

MRS. FRAIL
With all my heart: ours are but slight flesh wounds, and if we keep 'em from air, not at all dangerous: well, give me your hand in token of sisterly secrecy and affection.

MRS. FORESIGHT
Here 'tis with all my heart.

MRS. FRAIL
Well, as an earnest of friendship and confidence, I'll acquaint you with a design that I have. To tell truth, and speak openly one to an-

other, I'm afraid the world have observed us more than we have observed one another. You have a rich husband, and are provided for; I am at a loss, and have no great stock either of fortune or reputation; and therefore must look sharply about me. Sir Sampson has a son that is expected tonight; and by the account I have heard of his education, can be no conjuror; the estate you know is to be made over to him:—now if I could wheedle him, sister, ha? you understand me?

MRS. FORESIGHT

I do; and will help you to the utmost of my power.—And I can tell you one thing that falls out luckily enough; my awkward daughter-in-law, who you know is designed to be his wife, is grown fond of Mr. Tattle; now if we can improve that, and make her have an aversion for the booby, it may go a great way towards his liking you. Here they come together; and let us contrive some way or other to leave 'em together.

Enter Tattle and Miss Prue.

MISS PRUE

Mother, mother, mother, look you here!

MRS. FORESIGHT

Fy, fy, miss! how you bawl.—Besides, I have told you, you must not call me mother.

MISS PRUE

What must I call you then? are you not my father's wife?

MRS. FORESIGHT

Madam; you must say madam.—By my soul, I shall fancy myself old indeed, to have this great girl call me mother!—Well, but, miss, what are you so overjoyed at?

MISS PRUE

Look you here, madam, then, what Mr. Tattle has given me.—Look you here, cousin, here's a snuff-box; nay, there's snuff in't;—here, will you have any?—Oh good! how sweet it is.—Mr. Tattle is all over sweet, his peruke is sweet, and his gloves are sweet, and his handkerchief is sweet, pure sweet, sweeter than roses.—Smell him, mother, madam, I mean.—He gave me this ring for a kiss.

TATTLE

O fy, miss! you must not kiss and tell.

MISS PRUE

Yes; I may tell my mother.—And he says he'll give me something to make me smell so.—(*To Tattle.*) Oh pray lend me your handkerchief.—Smell, cousin; he says, he'll give me something that will make my smocks smell this way.—Is not it pure?—It's better than lavender, mun—I'm resolved I won't let nurse put any more lavender among my smocks—ha, cousin?

MRS. FRAIL

Fy, miss! amongst your linen, you must say;—you must never say smock.

MISS PRUE

Why, it is not bawdy, is it, cousin?

TATTLE

Oh, madam, you are too severe upon miss; you must not find fault with her pretty simplicity, it becomes her strangely.—Pretty miss, don't let 'em persuade you out of your innocency.

MRS. FORESIGHT
Oh, demn you, toad!—I wish you don't persuade her out of her innocency.

TATTLE
Who I, madam?—Oh Lord, how can your ladyship have such a thought—sure you don't know me?

MRS. FRAIL
Ah, devil! sly devil!—He's as close, sister, as a confessor.—He thinks we don't observe him.

MRS. FORESIGHT
A cunning cur! how soon he could find out a fresh harmless creature! and left us, sister, presently.

TATTLE
Upon reputation—

MRS. FORESIGHT
They're all so, sister, these men:—they love to have the spoiling of a young thing, they are as fond of it, as of being first in the fashion, or of seeing a new play the first day.—I warrant it would break Mr. Tattle's heart, to think that anybody else should be beforehand with him.

TATTLE
Oh Lord, I swear I would not for the world—

MRS. FRAIL
O hang you! who'll believe you?—You'd be hanged before you'd confess—we know you—she's very pretty!—Lord, what pure red and white!—she looks so wholesome;—ne'er stir, I don't know, but I fancy, if I were a man—

MISS PRUE
How you love to jeer one, cousin!

MRS. FORESIGHT
Hark ye, sister.—By my soul the girl is spoiled already—d'ye think she'll ever endure a great lubberly tarpaulin!—gad, I warrant you, she won't let him come near her, after Mr. Tattle.

MRS. FRAIL
O' my soul, I'm afraid not—eh!—filthy creature, that smells of all pitch and tar.—(*To Tattle.*) Devil take you, you confounded toad!—why did you see her before she was married?

MRS. FORESIGHT
Nay, why did we let him?—My husband will hang us;—he'll think we brought 'em acquainted.

MRS. FRAIL
Come, faith, let us begone.—If my brother Foresight should find us with them, he'd think so, sure enough.

MRS. FORESIGHT
So he would—but then leaving 'em together is as bad.—And he's such a sly devil, he'll never miss an opportunity.

MRS. FRAIL
I don't care; I won't be seen in't.

MRS. FORESIGHT
Well, if you should, Mr. Tattle, you'll have a world to answer for;—remember I wash my hands of it.—I'm thoroughly innocent.

[*Exeunt Mrs. Foresight and Mrs. Frail.*

MISS PRUE

What makes 'em go away, Mr. Tattle? what do they mean, do you know?

TATTLE

Yes, my dear,—I think I can guess;—but hang me if I know the reason of it.

MISS PRUE

Come, must not we go too?

TATTLE

No, no, they don't mean that.

MISS PRUE

No! what then? what shall you and I do together?

TATTLE

I must make love to you, pretty miss; will you let me make love to you?

MISS PRUE

Yes, if you please.

TATTLE (*Aside.*)

Frank, egad, at least. What a pox does Mrs. Foresight mean by this civility? Is it to make a fool of me? or does she leave us together out of good morality, and do as she would be done by?—Gad, I'll understand it so.

MISS PRUE

Well; and how will you make love to me? come, I long to have you begin. Must I make love too? you must tell me how.

TATTLE

You must let me speak, miss, you must not speak first; I must ask you questions, and you must answer.

MISS PRUE

What, is it like the catechism?—come then, ask me.

TATTLE

D'ye think you can love me?

MISS PRUE

Yes.

TATTLE

Pooh! pox! you must not say yes already; I shan't care a farthing for you then in a twinkling.

MISS PRUE

What must I say then?

TATTLE

Why, you must say no, or you believe not, or you can't tell.

MISS PRUE

Why, must I tell a lie then?

TATTLE

Yes, if you'd be well-bred;—all well-bred persons lie.—Besides, you are a woman, you must never speak what you think: your words must contradict your thoughts; but your actions may contradict your words. So, when I ask you, if you can love me, you must say no, but you must love me too. If I tell you you are handsome, you must deny it, and say I flatter you. But you must think yourself more charming than I speak you: and like me, for the beauty which I say you have, as much as if I had it myself. If I ask you to kiss me, you

must be angry, but you must not refuse me. If I ask you for more,
you must be more angry,—but more complying; and as soon as ever
I make you say you'll cry out, you must be sure to hold your
tongue.

MISS PRUE

O Lord, I swear this is pure!—I like it better than our old-fashioned
country way of speaking one's mind;—and must not you lie too?

TATTLE

Hum!—Yes; but you must believe I speak truth.

MISS PRUE

O Gemini! well, I always had a great mind to tell lies: but they
frighted me, and said it was a sin.

TATTLE

Well, my pretty creature; will you make me happy by giving me a
kiss?

MISS PRUE

No, indeed; I'm angry at you.

[*Runs and kisses him.*

TATTLE

Hold, hold, that's pretty well;—but you should not have given it me,
but have suffered me to have taken it.

MISS PRUE

Well, we'll do't again.

TATTLE

With all my heart.—Now then, my little angel!

[*Kisses her.*

MISS PRUE

Pish!

TATTLE

That's right—again, my charmer!

[*Kisses her again.*

MISS PRUE

O fy! nay, now I can't abide you.

TATTLE

Admirable! that was as well as if you had been born and bred in Covent Garden. And won't you show me, pretty miss, where your bedchamber is?

MISS PRUE

No, indeed, won't I; but I'll run there and hide myself from you behind the curtains.

TATTLE

I'll follow you.

MISS PRUE

Ah, but I'll hold the door with both hands, and be angry;—and you
shall push me down before you come in.

TATTLE

No, I'll come in first, and push you down afterwards.

MISS PRUE

Will you? then I'll be more angry, and more complying.

TATTLE

Then I'll make you cry out.

MISS PRUE

Oh, but you shan't; for I'll hold my tongue.

TATTLE

Oh, my dear apt scholar!

MISS PRUE

Well, now I'll run, and make more haste than you.

TATTLE

You shall not fly so fast as I'll pursue.

[*Exeunt.*

Act the third

Scene I. The gallery adjoining Prue's bedchamber.
Enter Nurse.

NURSE

Miss! miss! Miss Prue!—mercy on me, marry and amen!—Why, what's become of the child? why miss? Miss Foresight!—Sure, she has locked herself up in her chamber, and gone to sleep, or to prayers.—Miss! miss! I hear her;—come to your father, child; open the door—open the door, miss!—I hear you cry "Hush!"—O Lord who's there?—(*Peeps through the keyhole.*)—What's here to do?—O the father! a man with her!—Why, miss, I say! God's my life, here's fine doings towards!—O Lord, we're all undone!—O you young harlotry!—(*Knocks.*) Od's my life! won't you open the door?—I'll come in the back way.

[*Exit.*

Scene II. Prue's bedchamber.
Tattle and Miss Prue.

MISS PRUE

O Lord, she's coming!—and she'll tell my father; what shall I do now!

TATTLE

Pox take her!—if she had stayed two minutes longer, I should have wished for her coming.

MISS PRUE

Oh dear, what shall I say? tell me Mr. Tattle, tell me a lie.

TATTLE

There's no occasion for a lie; I could never tell a lie to no purpose;—but since we have done nothing, we must say nothing, I think. I hear her; I'll leave you together, and come off as you can.

[*Thrusts her back, and shuts the door.*

Scene III. A room in Foresight's house.
Tattle, Valentine, Scandal, and Angelica.

ANGELICA

You can't accuse me of inconstancy; I never told you that I loved you.

VALENTINE

But I can accuse you of uncertainty, for not telling me whether you did or not.

ANGELICA

You mistake indifference for uncertainty; I never had concern enough to ask myself the question.

SCANDAL
Nor good-nature enough to answer him that did ask you; I'll say that for you, madam.

ANGELICA
What, are you setting up for good-nature?

SCANDAL
Only for the affectation of it, as the women do for ill-nature.

ANGELICA
Persuade your friend that it is all affectation.

SCANDAL
I shall receive no benefit from the opinion; for I know no effectual difference between continued affectation and reality.

TATTLE (*Coming up.*)
Scandal, are you in private discourse? anything of secrecy?

[*Aside to Scandal.*

SCANDAL
Yes, but I dare trust you! we were talking of Angelica's love for Valentine; you won't speak of it?

TATTLE
No, no, not a syllable;—I know that's a secret, for it's whispered everywhere.

SCANDAL
Ha! ha! ha!

ANGELICA
What is, Mr. Tattle? I heard you say something was whispered everywhere.

SCANDAL
Your love of Valentine.

ANGELICA
How!

TATTLE
No, madam, his love for your ladyship.—Gad take me, I beg your pardon;—for I never heard a word of your ladyship's passion till this instant.

ANGELICA
My passion! and who told you of my passion, pray, sir?

SCANDAL (*Aside to Tattle.*)
Why, is the devil in you? did not I tell it you for a secret?

TATTLE (*Aside to Scandal.*)
Gad so, but I thought she might have been trusted with her own affairs.

SCANDAL
Is that your discretion? trust a woman with her self?

TATTLE
You say true, I beg your pardon;—I'll bring all off.—(*Aloud.*) It was impossible, madam, for me to imagine, that a person of your ladyship's wit and gallantry could have so long received the passionate addresses of the accomplished Valentine, and yet remain insensible; therefore you will pardon me, if, from a just weight of his merit, with your ladyship's good judgment, I formed the balance of a reciprocal affection.

VALENTINE

O the devil! what damned costive poet has given thee this lesson of fustian to get by rote?

ANGELICA

I dare swear you wrong him, it is his own; and Mr. Tattle only judges of the success of others from the effects of his own merit. For certainly Mr. Tattle was never denied anything in his life.

TATTLE

O Lord! yes, indeed, madam, several times.

ANGELICA

I swear I don't think 'tis possible.

TATTLE

Yes, I vow and swear I have: Lord, madam, I'm the most unfortunate man in the world, and the most cruelly used by the ladies.

ANGELICA

Nay, now you are ungrateful.

TATTLE

No, I hope not:—'tis as much ingratitude to own some favours as to conceal others.

VALENTINE

There, now it's out.

ANGELICA

I don't understand you now: I thought you had never asked anything but what a lady might modestly grant, and you confess.

SCANDAL

So, faith, your business is done here; now you may go brag somewhere else.

TATTLE

Brag! O heavens! why, did I name anybody?

ANGELICA

No, I suppose that is not in your power: but you would if you could, no doubt on't.

TATTLE

Not in my power, madam! what, does your ladyship mean that I have no woman's reputation in my power?

SCANDAL (*Aside to Tattle.*)

'Oons, why, you won't own it, will you?

TATTLE

Faith, madam, you're in the right: no more I have, as I hope to be saved; I never had it in my power to say anything to a lady's prejudice in my life. For, as I was telling you, madam, I have been the most unsuccessful creature living, in things of that nature; and never had the good fortune to be trusted once with a lady's secret, not once.

ANGELICA

No!

VALENTINE

Not once, I dare answer for him.

SCANDAL

And I'll answer for him; for I'm sure if he had, he would have told me.—I find, madam, you don't know Mr. Tattle.

TATTLE

No, indeed, madam, you don't know me at all, I find. For sure my intimate friends would have known—

ANGELICA

Then it seems you would have told, if you had been trusted.

TATTLE

O pox, Scandal! that was too far put.—Never have told particulars, madam. Perhaps I might have talked as of a third person, or have introduced an amour of my own, in conversation, by way of novel; but never have explained particulars.

ANGELICA

But whence comes the reputation of Mr. Tattle's secrecy, if he was never trusted?

SCANDAL

Why thence it arises: the thing is proverbially spoken; but may be applied to him.—As if we should say in general terms, "He only is secret who never was trusted"; a satirical proverb upon our sex.— There's another upon yours, as "She is chaste who was never asked the question." That's all.

VALENTINE

A couple of very civil proverbs truly: 'tis hard to tell whether the lady or Mr. Tattle be the more obliged to you. For you found her virtue upon the backwardness of the men, and his secrecy upon the mistrust of the women.

TATTLE

Gad, it's very true, madam, I think we are obliged to acquit ourselves; and for my part—but your ladyship is to speak first.

ANGELICA

Am I? well, I freely confess I have resisted a great deal of temptation.

TATTLE

And, egad, I have given some temptation that has not been resisted.

VALENTINE

Good!

ANGELICA

I cite Valentine here, to declare to the court how fruitless he has found his endeavours, and to confess all his solicitations and my denials.

VALENTINE

I am ready to plead not guilty for you, and guilty for myself.

SCANDAL

So, why this is fair, here's demonstration with a witness!

TATTLE

Well, my witnesses are not present. But I confess I have had favours from persons—but as the favours are numberless, so the persons are nameless.

SCANDAL

Pooh, this proves nothing.

TATTLE

No? I can show letters, lockets, pictures, and rings; and if there be occasion for witnesses, I can summon the maids at the chocolate-houses, all the porters at Pall-Mall and Covent-Garden, the door-keepers at the play-house, the drawers at Locket's, Pontac's, the

Rummer, Spring-Garden; [10] my own landlady, and valet-de-chambre; all who shall make oath, that I receive more letters than the Secretary's Office; and that I have more vizor-masks to inquire for me than ever went to see the Hermaphrodite, or the Naked Prince. And it is notorious, that in a country church, once, an inquiry being made who I was, it was answered, I was the famous Tattle, who had ruined so many women.

VALENTINE

It was there, I suppose, you got the nick-name of the Great Turk.

TATTLE

True, I was called Turk-Tattle all over the parish.—The next Sunday all the old women kept their daughters at home, and the parson had not half his congregation. He would have brought me into the spiritual court, but I was revenged upon him, for he had a handsome daughter, whom I initiated into the science. But I repented it afterwards, for it was talked of in town; and a lady of quality, that shall be nameless, in a raging fit of jealousy, came down in her coach and six horses, and exposed herself upon my account; gad, I was sorry for it with all my heart.—You know whom I mean—you know where we raffled—

SCANDAL

Mum, Tattle.

VALENTINE

'Sdeath, are not you ashamed?

ANGELICA

O barbarous! I never heard so insolent a piece of vanity.—Fy, Mr. Tattle!—I'll swear I could not have believed it.—Is this your secrecy?

TATTLE

Gad so, the heat of my story carried me beyond my discretion, as the heat of the lady's passion hurried her beyond her reputation.—But I hope you don't know whom I mean; for there were a great many ladies raffled.—Pox on't! now could I bite off my tongue.

SCANDAL

No, don't; for then you'll tell us no more.—Come, I'll recommend a song to you upon the hint of my two proverbs, and I see one in the next room that will sing it.

[*Exit.*

TATTLE

For Heaven's sake if you do guess, say nothing; gad, I'm very unfortunate.

Re-enter Scandal with one to sing.

SCANDAL

Pray sing the first song in the last new play.

SONG

A nymph and a swain to Apollo once prayed,
The swain had been jilted, the nymph been betrayed:

10 Noted taverns. Pontac's was a celebrated French eating-house in Abchurch Lane; Locket's a famous ordinary at Charing Cross, so called from Adam Locket the landlord; the Rummer Tavern was between Whitehall and Charing Cross. It was kept by Sam. Prior, the uncle of Matthew Prior the poet.

Their intent was to try if his oracle knew
E'er a nymph that was chaste, or a swain that was true.

Apollo was mute, and had like t'have been posed,
But sagely at length he this secret disclosed:
"He alone won't betray in whom none will confide:
And the nymph may be chaste that has never been tried."

[*Exit Singer.*

Enter Sir Sampson, Mrs. Frail, Miss Prue, and Servant

SIR SAMPSON
Is Ben come? odso, my son Ben come? odd I'm glad on't: where is
he? I long to see him.—Now, Mrs. Frail, you shall see my son Ben.—
Body o' me, he's the hopes of my family.—I han't seen him these
three years.—I warrant he's grown.—Call him in, bid him make
haste.—(*Exit Servant.*) I'm ready to cry for joy.

MRS. FRAIL
Now, Miss, you shall see your husband.

MISS PRUE (*Aside to Mrs. Frail.*)
Pish, he shall be none of my husband.

MRS. FRAIL (*Aside to Prue.*)
Hush: well he shan't, leave that to me.—I'll beckon Mr. Tattle to us.

ANGELICA
Won't you stay and see your brother?

VALENTINE
We are the twin-stars, and cannot shine in one sphere; when he rises
I must set.—Besides, if I should stay, I don't know but my father in
good-nature may press me to the immediate signing the deed of
conveyance of my estate; and I'll defer it as long as I can.—Well,
you'll come to a resolution?

ANGELICA
I can't. Resolution must come to me, or I shall never have one.

SCANDAL
Come, Valentine, I'll go with you; I've something in my head to
communicate to you.

[*Exeunt Valentine and Scandal.*

SIR SAMPSON
What, is my son Valentine gone? what, is he sneaked off, and would
not see his brother? There's an unnatural whelp! there's an ill-na-
tured dog!—What, were you here too, madam, and could not keep
him? could neither love, nor duty, nor natural affection, oblige him?
Odsbud, madam, have no more to say to him; he is not worth your
consideration. The rogue has not a drachm of generous love about
him: all interest, all interest; he's an undone scoundrel, and courts
your estate: body o' me, he does not care a doit for your person.

ANGELICA
I'm pretty even with him, Sir Sampson; for if ever I could have liked
anything in him, it should have been his estate, too: but since that's
gone, the bait's off, and the naked hook appears.

SIR SAMPSON
Odsbud, well spoken; and you are a wiser woman than I thought
you were; for most young women now-a-days are to be tempted with
a naked hook.

ANGELICA

If I marry, Sir Sampson, I'm for a good estate with any man, and for any man with a good estate: therefore if I were obliged to make a choice, I declare I'd rather have you than your son.

SIR SAMPSON

Faith and troth, you're a wise woman, and I'm glad to hear you say so; I was afraid you were in love with the reprobate; odd, I was sorry for you with all my heart: hang him, mongrel; cast him off; you shall see the rogue show himself, and make love to some desponding Cadua of four-score for sustenance. Odd, I love to see a young spendthrift forced to cling to an old woman for support, like ivy round a dead oak: faith I do; I love to see 'em hug and cotton together, like down upon a thistle.

Enter Ben and Servant.

BEN

Where's father?

SERVANT

There, sir, his back's toward you.

SIR SAMPSON

My son Ben! bless thee, my dear boy; body o' me, thou art heartily welcome.

BEN

Thank you, father, and I'm glad to see you.

SIR SAMPSON

Odsbud, and I am glad to see thee; kiss me, boy, kiss me again and again, dear Ben.

[*Kisses him.*

BEN

So, so, enough, father.—Mess,[11] I'd rather kiss these gentlewomen.

SIR SAMPSON

And so thou shalt.—Mrs. Angelica, my son Ben.

BEN

Forsooth, if you please.—(*Salutes her.*) Nay, mistress, I'm not for dropping anchor here; about ship i'faith.—(*Kisses Mrs. Frail.*) Nay, and you, too, my little cock-boat—so.

[*Kisses Miss Prue.*

TATTLE

Sir, you're welcome ashore.

BEN

Thank you, thank you, friend.

SIR SAMPSON

Thou hast been many a weary league, Ben, since I saw thee.

BEN

Ey, ey, been! been far enough, an that be all.—Well, father, and how do all at home? how does brother Dick, and brother Val?

SIR SAMPSON

Dick! body o' me, Dick has been dead these two years! I writ you word when you were at Leghorn.

BEN

Mess, that's true; marry, I had forgot. Dick's dead, as you say.—Well,

[11] A survival of the old oath, By the mass!

and how? I have many questions to ask you. Well, you ben't married again, father, be you?

SIR SAMPSON

No, I intend you shall marry, Ben; I would not marry for thy sake.

BEN

Nay, what does that signify?—An you marry again—why, then, I'll go to sea again, so there's one for t'other, an that be all.—Pray don't let me be your hindrance; e'en marry a' God's name, and the wind sit that way. As for my part, mayhap I have no mind to marry.

MRS. FRAIL

That would be a pity, such a handsome young gentleman.

BEN

Handsome! he! he! he! nay, forsooth, an you be for joking, I'll joke with you; for I love my jest, an the ship were sinking, as we say'n at sea. But I'll tell you why I don't much stand toward matrimony. I love to roam about from port to port, and from land to land: I could never abide to be port-bound, as we call it; now, a man that is married has, as it were, d'ye see, his feet in the bilboes, and mayhap mayn't get 'em out again when he would.

SIR SAMPSON

Ben's a wag.

BEN

A man that is married, d'ye see, is no more like another man than a galley-slave is like one of us free sailors; he is chained to an oar all his life; and mayhap forced to tug a leaky vessel into the bargain.

SIR SAMPSON

A very wag! Ben's a very wag! only a little rough, he wants a little polishing.

MRS. FRAIL

Not at all; I like his humour mightily, it's plain and honest; I should like such a humour in a husband extremely.

BEN

Say'n you so, forsooth? Marry, and I should like such a handsome gentlewoman for a bedfellow hugely; how say you, mistress, would you like going to sea? Mess, you're a tight vessel! and well rigged, an you were but as well manned.

MRS. FRAIL

I should not doubt that, if you were master of me.

BEN

But I'll tell you one thing, an you come to sea in a high wind, or that lady—you mayn't carry so much sail o' your head.—Top and top-gallant, by the mess.

MRS. FRAIL

No, why so?

BEN

Why, an you do, you may run the risk to be overset, and then you'll carry your keels above water, he! he! he!

ANGELICA

I swear, Mr. Benjamin is the veriest wag in nature; an absolute sea-wit.

SIR SAMPSON

Nay, Ben has parts, but as I told you before, they want a little polishing: you must not take anything ill, madam.

BEN

No, I hope the gentlewoman is not angry; I mean all in good part; for if I give a jest I'll take a jest: and so, forsooth, you may be as free with me.

ANGELICA

I thank you, sir, I am not at all offended.—But methinks, Sir Sampson, you should leave him alone with his mistress.—Mr. Tattle, we must not hinder lovers.

TATTLE (*Aside to Miss Prue.*)

Well, miss, I have your promise.

SIR SAMPSON

Body o' me, madam, you say true.—Look you, Ben, this is your mistress.—Come, miss, you must not be shamefaced; we'll leave you together.

MISS PRUE

I can't abide to be left alone, mayn't my cousin stay with me?

SIR SAMPSON

No, no.—Come, let's away.

BEN

Look you, father, mayhap the young woman mayn't take a liking to me.

SIR SAMPSON

I warrant thee, boy; come, come, we'll be gone; I'll venture that.

[*Exeunt Sir Sampson, Angelica, Tattle, and Mrs. Frail.*

BEN

Come, mistress, will you please to sit down? for an you stand astern a that'n, we shall never grapple together.—Come, I'll haul a chair; there, an you please to sit I'll sit by you.

MISS PRUE

You need not sit so near one; if you have anything to say I can hear you farther off, I an't deaf.

BEN

Why, that's true, as you say; nor I an't dumb; I can be heard as far as another;—I'll heave off to please you.—(*Sits farther off.*) An we were a league asunder, I'd undertake to hold discourse with you, an 'twere not a main high wind indeed, and full in my teeth. Look you, forsooth, I am, as it were, bound for the land of matrimony; 'tis a voyage, d'ye see, that was none of my seeking, I was commanded by father, and if you like of it mayhap I may steer into your harbour. How say you, mistress? The short of the thing is, that if you like me, and I like you, we may chance to swing in a hammock together.

MISS PRUE

I don't know what to say to you, nor I don't care to speak with you at all.

BEN

No? I'm sorry for that.—But pray, why are you so scornful?

MISS PRUE

As long as one must not speak one's mind, one had better not speak at all, I think, and truly I won't tell a lie for the matter.

BEN

Nay, you say true in that, 'tis but a folly to lie: for to speak one thing, and to think just the contrary way, is, as it were, to look one way and row another. Now, for my part, d'ye see, I'm for carrying things above board, I'm not for keeping anything under hatches,—so that if you ben't as willing as I, say so a' God's name, there's no harm done. Mayhap you may be shamefaced? some maidens, tho'f they love a man well enough, yet they don't care to tell'n so to's face: if that's the case, why silence gives consent.

MISS PRUE

But I'm sure it is not so, for I'll speak sooner than you should believe that; and I'll speak truth, though one should always tell a lie to a man; and I don't care, let my father do what he will; I'm too big to be whipped so I'll tell you plainly I don't like you, nor love you at all, nor never will, that's more: so, there's your answer for you; and don't trouble me no more, you ugly thing!

BEN

Look you, young woman, you may learn to give good words however. I spoke you fair, d'ye see, and civil.—As for your love or your liking, I don't value it of a rope's end;—and mayhap I like you as little as you do me.—What I said was in obedience to father; gad, I fear a whipping no more than you do. But I tell you one thing, if you should give such language at sea you'd have a cat o' ninetails laid across your shoulders. Flesh! who are you? You heard t'other handsome young woman speak civilly to me, of her own accord: whatever you think of yourself, gad, I don't think you are any more to compare to her than a can of small beer to a bowl of punch.

MISS PRUE

Well, and there's a handsome gentleman, and a fine gentleman, and a sweet gentleman, that was here, that loves me, and I love him; and if he sees you speak to me any more he'll thrash your jacket for you, he will, you great sea-calf!

BEN

What, do you mean that fair-weather spark that was here just now? will he thrash my jacket?—let'n—let'n. But an he comes near me, mayhap I may giv'n a salt eel for's supper, for all that. What does father mean to leave me alone as soon as I come home, with such a dirty dowdy? Sea-calf! I an't calf enough to lick your chalked face, you cheese-curd you!—Marry thee! 'oons, I'll marry a Lapland witch as soon, and live upon selling contrary winds and wrecked vessels.

MISS PRUE

I won't be called names, nor I won't be abused thus, so I won't.—If I were a man (*Cries.*), you durst not talk at this rate;—no, you durst not, you stinking tar-barrel!

Enter Mrs. Foresight and Mrs. Frail.

MRS. FORESIGHT (*Aside to Mrs. Frail.*)

They have quarrelled just as we could wish.

BEN

Tar-barrel? let your sweetheart there call me so if he'll take your part, your Tom Essence, and I'll say something to him; gad, I'll lace his musk doublet for him! I'll make him stink! he shall smell more like a weasel than a civet cat afore I ha' done with 'en.

MRS. FORESIGHT

Bless me, what's the matter, miss? What, does she cry?—Mr. Benjamin, what have you done to her?

BEN

Let her cry: the more she cries, the less she'll—she has been gathering foul weather in her mouth, and now it rains out at her eyes.

MRS. FORESIGHT
Come, miss, come along with me, and tell me, poor child.

MRS. FRAIL
Lord, what shall we do? there's my brother Foresight and Sir Sampson coming.—Sister, do you take miss down into the parlour, and I'll
carry Mr. Benjamin into my chamber, for they must not know that
they are fallen out.—Come, sir, will you venture yourself with me?
[*Looking kindly on him.*

BEN
Venture, mess, and that I will, though 'twere to sea in a storm.
[*Exeunt.*

Scene IV. The same.
Enter Sir Sampson and Foresight.

SIR SAMPSON
I left 'em together here; what, are they gone? Ben's a brisk boy; he
has got her into a corner; father's own son, faith, he'll touzle her,
and mouzle her; the rogue's sharp set, coming from sea; if he
should not stay for saying grace, old Foresight, but fall to without
the help of a parson, ha? Odd, if he should, I could not be angry
with him; 'twould be but like me, *a chip of the old block.* Ha! thou'rt
melancholic, old prognostication; as melancholic as if thou hadst spilt
the salt, or pared thy nails on a Sunday.—Come, cheer up, look
about thee: look up, old star-gazer.—(*Aside.*) Now is he poring upon
the ground for a crooked pin, or an old horse-nail, with the head
towards him.

FORESIGHT
Sir Sampson, we'll have the wedding to-morrow morning.

SIR SAMPSON
With all my heart.

FORESIGHT
At ten o'clock, punctually at ten.

SIR SAMPSON
To a minute, to a second; thou shalt set thy watch, and the bride-
groom shall observe its motions; they shall be married to a minute;
go to bed to a minute; and when the alarm strikes, they shall keep
time like the figures of St. Dunstan's clock, and *consummatum est* shall
ring all over the parish.
Enter Scandal.

SCANDAL
Sir Sampson, sad news!

FORESIGHT
Bless us!

SIR SAMPSON
Why, what's the matter?

SCANDAL
Can't you guess at what ought to afflict you and him, and all of us
more than anything else?

SIR SAMPSON
Body o' me, I don't know any universal grievance but a new tax, or
the loss of the Canary fleet. Unless popery should be landed in the
west, or the French fleet were at anchor at Blackwall.

SCANDAL
No! undoubtedly Mr. Foresight knew all this, and might have pre-
vented it.

FORESIGHT

'Tis no earthquake!

SCANDAL

No, not yet; nor whirlwind. But we don't know what it may come to.—But it has had a consequence already that touches us all.

SIR SAMPSON

Why, body o' me, out with't.

SCANDAL

Something has appeared to your son Valentine.—He's gone to bed upon't, and very ill.—He speaks little, yet says he has a world to say. Asks for his father and the wise Foresight; talks of Raymond Lully, and the ghost of Lilly. He has secrets to impart I suppose to you two. I can get nothing out of him but sighs. He desires he may see you in the morning, but would not be disturbed to-night, because he has some business to do in a dream.

SIR SAMPSON

Hoity, toity, what have I to do with his dreams or his divinations?— Body o' me, this is a trick to defer signing the conveyance. I warrant the devil will tell him in a dream, that he must not part with his estate; but I'll bring him a parson, to tell him that the devil's a liar; or, if that won't do, I'll bring a lawyer that shall outlie the devil. And so I'll try whether my blackguard or his shall get the better of the day.

[*Exit.*

SCANDAL

Alas, Mr. Foresight! I'm afraid all is not right.—You are a wise man, and a conscientious man; a searcher into obscurity and futurity; and if you commit an error, it is with a great deal of consideration and discretion and caution.

FORESIGHT

Ah, good Mr. Scandal—

SCANDAL

Nay, nay, 'tis manifest; I do not flatter you.—But Sir Sampson is hasty, very hasty; I'm afraid he is not scrupulous enough, Mr. Foresight.—He has been wicked, and Heaven grant he may mean well in his affair with you.—But my mind gives me, these things cannot be wholly insignificant. You are wise, and should not be over-reached, methinks you should not.

FORESIGHT

Alas, Mr. Scandal!—*Humanum est errare.*

SCANDAL

You say true, man will err; mere man will err—but you are something more.—There have been wise men; but they were such as you;—men who consulted the stars, and were observers of omens.— Solomon was wise, but how?—by his judgment in astrology:—so says Pineda in his third book and eighth chapter.

FORESIGHT

You are learned, Mr. Scandal!

SCANDAL

A trifler—but a lover of art.—And the wise men of the East owed their instruction to a star, which is rightly observed by Gregory the Great in favour of astrology! And Albertus Magnus makes it the most valuable science: because (says he) it teaches us to consider the causation of causes, in the causes of things.

FORESIGHT

I protest I honour you, Mr. Scandal:—I did not think you had been read in these matters.—Few young men are inclined—

SCANDAL

I thank my stars that have inclined me.—But I fear this marriage, and making over this estate, this transferring of a rightful inheritance, will bring judgments upon us. I prophesy it, and I would not have the fate of Cassandra, not to be believed. Valentine is disturbed, what can be the cause of that? and Sir Sampson is hurried on by an unusual violence.—I fear he does not act wholly from himself; methink he does not look as he used to do.

FORESIGHT

He was always of an impetuous nature.—But as to this marriage, I have consulted the stars, and all appearances are prosperous.

SCANDAL

Come, come, Mr. Foresight, let not the prospect of worldy lucre carry you beyond your judgment, nor against your conscience:—you are not satisfied that you act justly.

FORESIGHT

How?

SCANDAL

You are not satisfied, I say.—I am loath to discourage you—but it is palpable that you are not satisfied.

FORESIGHT

How does it appear, Mr. Scandal? I think I am very well satisfied.

SCANDAL

Either you suffer yourself to deceive yourself; or you do not know yourself.

FORESIGHT

Pray explain yourself.

SCANDAL

Do you sleep well o' nights?

FORESIGHT

Very well.

SCANDAL

Are you certain? you do not look so.

FORESIGHT

I am in health, I think.

SCANDAL

So was Valentine this morning; and looked just so.

FORESIGHT

How! am I altered any way? I don't perceive it.

SCANDAL

That may be, but your beard is longer than it was two hours ago.

FORESIGHT

Indeed! bless me!

Enter Mrs. Foresight.

MRS. FORESIGHT

Husband, will you go to bed? it's ten o'clock.—Mr. Scandal, your servant.

SCANDAL (*Aside.*)

Pox on her! she has interrupted my design:—but I must work her into the project.—(*Aloud.*) You keep early hours, madam.

MRS. FORESIGHT
Mr. Foresight is punctual, we sit up after him.

FORESIGHT
My dear, pray lend me your glass, your little looking-glass.

SCANDAL
Pray, lend it him, madam—I'll tell you the reason.—(*She gives him the glass: Scandal and she talk aside.*) My passion for you is grown so violent, that I am no longer master of myself.—I was interrupted in the morning, when you had charity enough to give me your attention, and I had hopes of finding another opportunity of explaining myself to you;—but was disappointed all this day; and the uneasiness that has attended me ever since, brings me now hither at this unseasonable hour.

MRS. FORESIGHT
Was there ever such impudence! to make love to me before my husband's face! I'll swear I'll tell him.

SCANDAL
Do; I'll die a martyr, rather than disclaim my passion. But come a little farther this way, and I'll tell you what project I had to get him out of the way, that I might have an opportunity of waiting upon you.

FORESIGHT (*Looking in the glass.*)
I do not see any revolution here;—methinks I look with a serene and benign aspect—pale, a little pale—but the roses of these cheeks have been gathered many years.—Ha! I do not like that sudden flushing;—gone already!—hem, hem, hem! faintish. My heart is pretty good; yet it beats; and my pulses, ha!—I have none—mercy on me!—hum—yes, here they are—gallop, gallop, gallop, gallop, gallop, gallop, hey! whither will they hurry me?—Now they're gone again—and now I'm faint again; and pale again, and, hem; and my, hem!—breath, hem!—grows short; hem! hem! he, he, hem!

SCANDAL (*Aside to Mrs. Foresight.*)
It takes; pursue it, in the name of love and pleasure!

MRS. FORESIGHT
How do you do, Mr. Foresight?

FORESIGHT
Hum, not so well as I thought I was. Lend me your hand.

SCANDAL
Look you there now—your lady says your sleep has been unquiet of late.

FORESIGHT
Very likely.

MRS. FORESIGHT
O mighty restless; but I was afraid to tell him so.—He has been subject to talking and starting.

SCANDAL
And did not use to be so?

MRS. FORESIGHT
Never, never, till within these three nights; I cannot say that he has once broken my rest since we have been married.

FORESIGHT
I will go to bed.

SCANDAL

Do so, Mr. Foresight, and say your prayers.—He looks better than he did.

MRS. FORESIGHT

Nurse, nurse!

[*Calls.*

FORESIGHT

Do you think so, Mr. Scandal?

SCANDAL

Yes, yes; I hope this will be gone by morning, taking it in time.

FORESIGHT

I hope so.

Enter Nurse

MRS. FORESIGHT

Nurse, your master is not well; put him to bed.

SCANDAL

I hope you will be able to see Valentine in the morning. You had best take a little diacodian and cowslip water, and lie upon your back, may be you may dream.

FORESIGHT

I thank you, Mr. Scandal, I will.—Nurse, let me have a watch-light, and lay *The Crumbs of Comfort* by me.

NURSE

Yes, sir.

FORESIGHT

And—hem, hem! I am very faint.

SCANDAL

No, no; you look much better.

FORESIGHT

Do I?—(*To Nurse.*) And, d'ye hear, bring me, let me see—within a quarter of twelve—hem—he, hem!—just upon the turning of the tide, bring me the urinal. And I hope neither the lord of my ascendant, nor the moon, will be combust; and then I may do well.

SCANDAL

I hope so. Leave that to me; I will erect a scheme; and I hope I shall find both Sol and Venus in the sixth house.

FORESIGHT

I thank you, Mr. Scandal; indeed that would be a great comfort to me. Hem, hem; good night.

[*Exit with Nurse.*

SCANDAL

Good night, good Mr. Foresight; and I hope Mars and Venus will be in conjunction, while your wife and I are together.

MRS. FORESIGHT

Well, and what use do you hope to make of this project? you don't think that you are ever like to succeed in your design upon me?

SCANDAL

Yes, faith, I do; I have a better opinion both of you and myself than to despair.

MRS. FORESIGHT

Did you ever hear such a toad? Hark ye, devil! do you think any woman honest?

SCANDAL

Yes, several very honest; they'll cheat a little at cards, sometimes; but that's nothing.

MRS. FORESIGHT

Pshaw! but virtuous, I mean.

SCANDAL

Yes, faith; I believe some women are virtuous too; but 'tis as I believe some men are valiant, through fear. For why should a man court danger, or a woman shun pleasure?

MRS. FORESIGHT

O monstrous! what are conscience and honour?

SCANDAL

Why, honour is a public enemy; and conscience a domestic thief; and he that would secure his pleasure, must pay a tribute to one, and go halves with t'other. As for honour, that you have secured; for you have purchased a perpetual opportunity for pleasure.

MRS. FORESIGHT

An opportunity for pleasure?

SCANDAL

Ay, your husband; a husband is an opportunity for pleasure; so you have taken care of honour, and 'tis the least I can do to take care of conscience.

MRS. FORESIGHT

And so you think we are free for one another.

SCANDAL

Yes, faith, I think so; I love to speak my mind.

MRS. FORESIGHT

Why, then I'll speak my mind. Now, as to this affair between you and me. Here you make love to me; why, I'll confess, it does not displease me. Your person is well enough, and your understanding is not amiss.

SCANDAL

I have no great opinion of myself; but I think I'm neither deformed nor a fool.

MRS. FORESIGHT

But you have a villainous character; you are a libertine in speech as well as practice.

SCANDAL

Come, I know what you would say; you think it more dangerous to be seen in conversation with me, than to allow some other men the last favour. You mistake; the liberty I take in talking is purely affected, for the service of your sex. He that first cries out, *Stop thief!* is often he that has stolen the treasure. I am a juggler, that act by confederacy; and, if you please, we'll put a trick upon the world.

MRS. FORESIGHT

Ay; but you are such a universal juggler, that I'm afraid you have a great many confederates.

SCANDAL

Faith, I'm sound.

MRS. FORESIGHT

O fy!—I'll swear you're impudent.

SCANDAL

I'll swear you're handsome.

MRS. FORESIGHT

Pish! you'd tell me so, though you did not think so.

SCANDAL

And you'd think so, though I should not tell you so. And now I think we know one another pretty well.

MRS. FORESIGHT

O Lord, who's here?

Enter Mrs. Frail and Ben

BEN

Mess, I love to speak my mind; father has nothing to do with me. Nay, I can't say that neither; he has something to do with me. But what does that signify? if so be, that I be'n't minded to be steered by him, 'tis as tho'f he should strive against wind and tide.

MRS. FRAIL

Ay, but my dear, we must keep it secret till the estate be settled; for you know marrying without an estate is like sailing in a ship without ballast.

BEN

He! he! he! why that's true; just so for all the world it is indeed, as like as two cable-ropes.

MRS. FRAIL

And though I have a good portion, you know one would not venture all in one bottom.

BEN

Why, that's true again; for mayhap one bottom may spring a leak. You have hit it indeed, mess, you've nicked the channel.

MRS. FRAIL

Well, but if you should forsake me after all, you'd break my heart.

BEN

Break your heart! I'd rather the Marygold should break her cable in a storm, as well as I love her. Flesh, you don't think I'm false-hearted like a landman! A sailor will be honest, tho'f mayhap he has never a penny of money in his pocket.—Mayhap I may not have so fair a face as a citizen or a courtier; but for all that, I've as good blood in my veins, and a heart as sound as a biscuit.

MRS. FRAIL

And will you love me always?

BEN

Nay, an I love once, I'll stick like pitch; I'll tell you that. Come, I'll sing you a song for a sailor.

MRS. FRAIL

Hold, there's my sister; I'll call her to hear it.

MRS. FORESIGHT

Well, I won't go to bed to my husband to-night; because I'll retire to my own chamber, and think of what you have said.

SCANDAL

Well; you'll give me leave to wait upon you to your chamber door, and leave you my last instructions?

MRS. FORESIGHT

Hold, here's my sister coming towards us.

MRS. FRAIL

If it won't interrupt you, I'll entertain you with a song.

BEN

> The song was made upon one of our ship's crew's wife; our boat-swain made the song; mayhap you may know her, sir. Before she was married, she was called buxom Joan of Deptford.

SCANDAL

> I have heard of her.
>
> *Ben sings.*

> A soldier and a sailor,
> A tinker and a tailor,
> Had once a doubtful strife, sir,
> To make a maid a wife, sir,
>   Whose name was buxom Joan.
> For now the time was ended,
> When she no more intended
> To lick her lips at men, sir,
> And gnaw the sheets in vain, sir,
>   And lie o' nights alone.

> The soldier swore like thunder,
> He loved her more than plunder;
> And showed her many a scar, sir,
> That he had brought from far, sir,
>   With fighting for her sake.
> The tailor thought to please her,
> With offering her his measure.
> The tinker too with mettle,
> Said he could mend her kettle
>   And stop up every leak.

> But while these three were prating,
> The sailor slily waiting,
> Thought if it came about, sir,
> That they should all fall out, sir,
>   He then might play his part.
> And just e'en as he meant, sir,
> To loggerheads they went, sir,
> And then he let fly at her
> A shot 'twixt wind and water,
>   That won this fair maid's heart.

> If some of our crew that came to see me are not gone, you shall see that we sailors can dance sometimes as well as other folks.—
> (*Whistles.*) I warrant that brings 'em, an they be within hearing.
>   *Enter Sailors.*
> Oh, here they be!—and fiddles along with 'em. Come, my lads, let's have a round, and I'll make one.

> [*They dance.*

BEN

> We're merry folks, we sailors, we han't much to care for. Thus we live at sea; eat biscuit, and drink flip; put on a clean shirt once a quarter—come home and lie with our landladies once a year, get rid of a little money; and then put off with the next fair wind. How d'ye like us?

MRS. FRAIL

O you are the happiest, merriest men alive!

MRS. FORESIGHT

We're beholden to Mr. Benjamin for this entertainment.—I believe it's late.

BEN

Why, forsooth, an you think so, you had best go to bed. For my part, I mean to toss a can, and remember my sweetheart, afore I turn in; mayhap I may dream of her.

MRS. FORESIGHT

Mr. Scandal, you had best go to bed and dream too.

SCANDAL

Why faith, I have a good lively imagination; and can dream as much to the purpose as another, if I set about it; but dreaming is the poor retreat of a lazy, hopeless, and imperfect lover; 'tis the last glimpse of love to worn-out sinners, and the faint dawning of a bliss to wishing girls and growing boys.

There's nought but willing, waking love that can
Make blest the ripened maid and finished man.

[*Exeunt.*

Act the fourth

Scene I. An ante-room at Valentine's lodgings.
Scandal and Jeremy.

SCANDAL

Well, is your master ready? does he look madly, and talk madly?

JEREMY

Yes, sir; you need make no great doubt of that; he that was so near turning poet yesterday morning, can't be much to seek in playing the madman to-day.

SCANDAL

Would he have Angelica acquainted with the reason of his design?

JEREMY

No, sir, not yet;—he has a mind to try, whether his playing the madman won't make her play the fool, and fall in love with him; or at least own that she has loved him all this while and concealed it.

SCANDAL

I saw her take coach just now with her maid; and think I heard her bid the coachman drive hither.

JEREMY

Like enough, sir, for I told her maid this morning my master was run stark mad only for love of her mistress. I hear a coach stop; if it should be she, sir, I believe he would not see her, till he hears how she takes it.

SCANDAL

Well, I'll try her:—'tis she, here she comes.

Enter Angelica and Jenny.

ANGELICA

Mr. Scandal, I suppose you don't think it a novelty to see a woman visit a man at his own lodgings in a morning?

SCANDAL

Not upon a kind occasion, madam. But when a lady comes tyrannically to insult a ruined lover, and make manifest the cruel triumphs of her beauty, the barbarity of it something surprises me.

ANGELICA

I don't like raillery from a serious face.—Pray tell me what is the matter?

JEREMY

No strange matter, madam; my master's mad, that's all: I suppose your ladyship has thought him so a great while.

ANGELICA

How d'ye mean, mad?

JEREMY

Why, faith, madam, he's mad for want of his wits, just as he was poor for want of money; his head is e'en as light as his pockets; and anybody that has a mind to a bad bargain, can't do better than to beg him for his estate.

ANGELICA

If you speak truth, your endeavouring at wit is very unseasonable.

SCANDAL (*Aside.*)

She's concerned, and loves him.

ANGELICA

Mr. Scandal, you cannot think me guilty of so much inhumanity, as not to be concerned for a man I must own myself obliged to; pray tell me the truth.

SCANDAL

Faith, madam, I wish telling a lie would mend the matter. But this is no new effect of an unsuccessful passion.

ANGELICA (*Aside.*)

I know not what to think.—Yet I should be vexed to have a trick put upon me.—(*Aloud.*) May I not see him?

SCANDAL

I'm afraid the physician is not willing you should see him yet.— Jeremy, go in and inquire.

[Exit Jeremy.

ANGELICA (*Aside.*)

Ha! I saw him wink and smile—I fancy 'tis a trick—I'll try.—(*Aloud.*) I would disguise to all the world a failing which I must own to you.—I fear my happiness depends upon the recovery of Valentine. Therefore I conjure you, as you are his friend, and as you have compassion upon one fearful of affliction, to tell me what I am to hope for.—I cannot speak—but you may tell me, for you know what I would ask.

SCANDAL (*Aside.*)

So, this is pretty plain.—(*Aloud.*) Be not too much concerned, madam, I hope his condition is not desperate: an acknowledgment of love from you, perhaps, may work a cure; as the fear of your aversion occasioned his distemper.

ANGELICA (*Aside.*)

Say you so? nay, then I'm convinced; and if I don't play trick for trick, may I never taste the pleasure of revenge!—(*Aloud.*) Acknowledgment of love! I find you have mistaken my compassion, and think me guilty of a weakness I'm a stranger to. But I have too much sincerity to deceive you, and too much charity to suffer him to be deluded with vain hopes. Good-nature and humanity oblige me to be concerned for him; but to love is neither in my power nor inclination; and if he can't be cured without I suck the poison from his wounds, I'm afraid he won't recover his senses till I lose mine.

SCANDAL (*Aside.*)

Hey, brave woman, i'faith!—(*Aloud.*) Won't you see him then, if he desire it?

ANGELICA

What signify a madman's desires? besides, 'twould make me uneasy. If I don't see him, perhaps my concern for him may lessen. If I forget him, 'tis no more than he has done by himself; and now the surprise is over, methinks I am not half so sorry as I was.

SCANDAL

So, faith, good nature works apace; you were confessing just now an obligation to his love.

ANGELICA

But I have considered that passions are unreasonable and involuntary; if he loves, he can't help it; and if I don't love, I can't help it; no more than he can help his being a man, or I my being a woman; or no more than I can help my want of inclination to stay longer here.—Come, Jenny.

[*Exeunt Angelica and Jenny.*

SCANDAL

Humph!—An admirable composition, faith, this same womankind!
Re-enter Jeremy.

JEREMY

What, is she gone, sir?

SCANDAL

Gone? why she was never here; nor anywhere else; nor I don't know her if I see her; nor you neither.

JEREMY

Good lack! what's the matter now? are any more of us to be mad? Why, sir, my master longs to see her; and is almost mad in good earnest with the joyful news of her being here.

SCANDAL

We are all under a mistake. Ask no questions, for I can't resolve you; but I'll inform your master. In the mean time, if our project succeed no better with his father than it does with his mistress, he may descend from his exaltation of madness into the road of common sense, and be content only to be made a fool with other reasonable people.—I hear Sir Sampson. You know your cue; I'll to your master.

[*Exit.*

Enter Sir Sampson and Buckram

SIR SAMPSON

D'ye see, Mr. Buckram, here's the paper signed with his own hand.

BUCKRAM

Good, sir. And the conveyance is ready drawn in this box, if he be ready to sign and seal.

SIR SAMPSON

Ready, body o' me, he must be ready! his sham-sickness shan't excuse him.—O, here's his scoundrel.—Sirrah, where's your master?

JEREMY

> Ah, sir, he's quite gone.

SIR SAMPSON

> Gone! what, he is not dead?

JEREMY

> No, sir, not dead.

SIR SAMPSON

> What, is he gone out of town? run away, ha! he has tricked me? speak, varlet.

JEREMY

> No, no, sir, he's safe enough, sir, an he were but as sound, poor gentleman. He is, indeed, here, sir, and not here, sir.

SIR SAMPSON

> Heyday, rascal, do you banter me? sirrah, d'ye banter me?—Speak, sirrah, where is he? for I will find him.

JEREMY

> Would you could, sir! for he has lost himself. Indeed, sir, I have almost broke my heart about him—I can't refrain tears when I think of him, sir: I'm as melancholy for him as a passing-bell, sir; or a horse in a pound.

SIR SAMPSON

> A pox confound your similitudes, sir!—Speak to be understood, and tell me in plain terms what the matter is with him, or I'll crack your fool's skull.

JEREMY

> Ah, you've hit it, sir! that's the matter with him, sir; his skull's cracked, poor gentleman! he's stark mad, sir.

SIR SAMPSON

> Mad!

BUCKRAM

> What, is he *non compos?*

JEREMY

> Quite *non compos,* sir.

BUCKRAM

> Why, then all's obliterated, Sir Sampson; if he be *non compos mentis,* his act and deed will be of no effect, it is not good in law.

SIR SAMPSON

> 'Oons, I won't believe it! let me see him, sir.—Mad! I'll make him find his senses.

JEREMY

> Mr. Scandal is with him, sir; I'll knock at the door.

> [*Goes to the Scene, which opens.*

> *Scene II. Another room at Valentine's lodgings.*
> *Sir Sampson, Valentine, Scandal, Jeremy, and Buckram. Valentine*
> *upon a couch, disorderly dressed.*

SIR SAMPSON

> How now! what's here to do?

VALENTINE (*Starting.*)

> Ha! who's that?

SCANDAL

> For Heaven's sake softly, sir, and gently! don't provoke him.

VALENTINE

Answer me, who is that, and that?

SIR SAMPSON

Gadsobs, does he not know me? Is he mischievous? I'll speak
gently.—Val, Val, dost thou not know me, boy? not know thy own
father, Val? I am thy own father, and this is honest Brief Buckram
the lawyer.

VALENTINE

It may be so—I did not know you—the world is full.—There are
people that we do know and people that we do not know; and yet
the sun shines upon all alike.—There are fathers that have many
children; and there are children that have many fathers.—'Tis
strange! but I am Truth, and come to give the world the lie.

SIR SAMPSON

Body o' me, I know not what to say to him!

VALENTINE

Why does that lawyer wear black?—does he carry his conscience
withoutside?—Lawyer, what art thou? dost thou know me?

BUCKRAM

O Lord! what must I say?—Yes, sir.

VALENTINE

Thou liest, for I am Truth. 'Tis hard I cannot get a livelihood
amongst you. I have been sworn out of Westminster-Hall the first
day of every term—let me see—no matter how long—but I'll tell you
one thing; it's a question that would puzzle an arithmetician, if you
should ask him, whether the Bible saves more souls in Westminster-
Abbey or damns more in Westminster-Hall; for my part, I am
Truth, and can't tell; I have very few acquaintance.

SIR SAMPSON

Body o' me, he talks sensibly in his madness! has he no intervals?

JEREMY

Very short, sir.

BUCKRAM

Sir, I can do you no service while he's in this condition; here's your
paper, sir—he may do me a mischief if I stay—the conveyance is
ready, sir, if he recover his senses.   [Exit Buckram.

SIR SAMPSON

Hold, hold, hold, don't you go yet.

SCANDAL

You'd better let him go, sir; and send for him if there be occasion;
for I fancy his presence provokes him more.

VALENTINE

Is the lawyer gone? 'tis well; then we may drink about without going
together by the ears—heigh-ho! What o'clock is't?—My father here!
your blessing, sir.

SIR SAMPSON

He recovers.—Bless thee, Val,—how dost thou do, boy?

VALENTINE

Thank you, sir, pretty well—I have been a little out of order—won't
you please to sit, sir?

SIR SAMPSON

Ay, boy.—Come, thou shalt sit down by me.

VALENTINE

Sir, 'tis my duty to wait.

SIR SAMPSON

No, no, come, come, sit thee down, honest Val; how dost thou do?
let me feel thy pulse.—Oh, pretty well now, Val; body o' me, I was
sorry to see thee indisposed! but I'm glad thou art better, honest
Val.

VALENTINE

I thank you, sir.

SCANDAL (*Aside.*)

Miracle! the monster grows loving.

SIR SAMPSON

Let me feel thy hand again, Val; it does not shake—I believe thou
canst write, Val; ha, boy, thou canst write thy name, Val?—Jeremy,
step and overtake Mr. Buckram, bid him make haste back with the
conveyance! quick! quick!

[*Whispers to Jeremy, who goes out.*

SCANDAL (*Aside.*)

That ever I should suspect such a heathen of any remorse!

SIR SAMPSON

Dost thou know this paper, Val? I know thou'rt honest, and wilt perform articles.

Shows him the paper, but holds it out of his reach.

VALENTINE

Pray, let me see it, sir. You hold it so far off, that I can't tell whether
I know it or no.

SIR SAMPSON

See it, boy? ay, ay, why thou dost see it—'tis thy own hand, Vally.
Why, let me see, I can read it as plain as can be; look you here—
(*Reads.*) "The conditions of this obligation"—look you, as plain as can
be, so it begins—and then at the bottom—"As witness my hand, Valentine Legend," in great letters; why, 'tis as plain as the nose in one's
face; what, are my eyes better than thine? I believe I can read it farther off yet—let me see.

[*Stretches out his arm as far as he can.*

VALENTINE

Will you please to let me hold it, sir?

SIR SAMPSON

Let thee hold it, sayest thou?—ay, with all my heart.—What matter is
it who holds it? what need anybody hold it?—i'll put it in my pocket,
Val, and then nobody need hold it.—(*Puts the paper in his pocket.*)
There, Val, it's safe enough, boy—but thou shalt have it as soon as
thou hast set thy hand to another paper, little Val.

Re-enter Jeremy and Buckram.

VALENTINE

What, is my bad genius here again! Oh, no, it is the lawyer with his
itching palm; and he's come to be scratched—my nails are not long
enough—let me have a pair of red-hot tongs, quickly! quickly! and
you shall see me act St. Dunstan, and lead the devil by the nose.

BUCKRAM

O Lord, let me be gone! I'll not venture myself with a madman.

[*Exit.*

VALENTINE

Ha! ha! ha! you need not run so fast, honesty will not overtake you.—Ha! ha! ha! the rogue found me out to be *in formâ pauperis* presently.

SIR SAMPSON

Oons! what a vexation is here! I know not to do or say, or which way to go.

VALENTINE

Who's that, that's out of his way! I am Truth, and can set him right.—Hark ye, friend, the straight road is the worst way you can go:—He that follows his nose always, will very often be led into a stink.—*Probatum est.*—But what are you for, religion or politics? There's a couple of topics for you, no more like one another than oil and vinegar; and yet those two beaten together by a state-cook, make sauce for the whole nation.

SIR SAMPSON

What the devil had I to do, ever to beget sons? why did I ever marry?

VALENTINE

Because thou wert a monster, old boy; the two greatest monsters in the world are a man and a woman: what's thy opinion?

SIR SAMPSON

Why, my opinion is that those two monsters joined together, make a yet greater, that's a man and his wife.

VALENTINE

Aha, old truepenny! sayest thou so? thou hast nicked it.—But, it's wonderful strange, Jeremy.

JEREMY

What is, sir?

VALENTINE

That grey hairs should cover a green head, and I make a fool of my father.—What's here! *Erra Pater,* or a bearded Sibyl? If Prophecy comes, Truth must give place.

[*Exeunt.*

Scene III. An ante-room at Valentine's lodgings.
Enter Sir Sampson, Scandal, Foresight, Mrs. Foresight, and Mrs.
Frail.

FORESIGHT

What says he? what, did he prophesy?—Ha, Sir Sampson, bless us! how are we?

SIR SAMPSON

Are we! a pox o' your prognostication—why, we are fools as we used to be.—Oons, that you could not foresee that the moon would predominate, and my son be mad!—Where's your oppositions, your trines, and your quadrates?—What did your Cardan and your Ptolemy tell you? your Messahalah and your Longomontanus, your harmony of chiromancy with astrology? Ah! pox on't, that I that know the world, and men and manners, that don't believe a syllable in the sky and stars, and suns, and almanacs, and trash, should be directed by a dreamer, an omen-hunter, and defer business in expectation of a lucky hour! when, body o' me, there never was a lucky hour after the first opportunity.

[*Exit Sir Sampson.*

FORESIGHT

Ah, Sir Sampson, Heaven help your head! This is none of your lucky hour! *Nemo omnibus horis sapit.* What, is he gone, and in contempt of science? Ill stars and unconvertible ignorance attend him!

SCANDAL

You must excuse his passion, Mr. Foresight, for he has been heartily vexed.—His son is *non compos mentis,* and thereby incapable of making any conveyance in law; so that all his measures are disappointed.

FORESIGHT

Ha! say you so?

MRS. FRAIL (*Aside to Mrs. Foresight.*)

What, has my sea-lover lost his anchor of hope then?

MRS. FORESIGHT

Oh, sister, what will you do with him?

MRS. FRAIL

Do with him! send him to sea again in the next foul weather.—He's used to an inconstant element, and won't be surprised to see the tide turned.

FORESIGHT

Wherein was I mistaken, not to foresee this?

[*Considers.*

SCANDAL (*Aside to Mrs. Foresight.*)

Madam, you and I can tell him something else that he did not foresee, and more particularly relating to his own fortune.

MRS. FORESIGHT (*Aside to Scandal.*)

What do you mean? I don't understand you.

SCANDAL

Hush, softly—the pleasures of last night, my dear! too considerable to be forgot so soon.

MRS. FORESIGHT

Last night! and what would your impudence infer from last night! last night was like the night before, I think.

SCANDAL

'Sdeath, do you make no difference between me and your husband?

MRS. FORESIGHT

Not much;—he's superstitious, and you are mad, in my opinion.

SCANDAL

You make me mad.—You are not serious;—pray, recollect yourself.

MRS. FORESIGHT

O yes, now I remember, you were very impertinent and impudent,—and would have come to bed to me.

SCANDAL

And did not?

MRS. FORESIGHT

Did not! with what face can you ask the question?

SCANDAL (*Aside.*)

This I have heard of before, but never believed. I have been told she had that admirable quality of forgetting to a man's face in the morning that she had lain with him all night, and denying that she

had done favours with more impudence than she could grant 'em.—
Madam, I'm your humble servant, and honour you.—(*Aloud.*) You
look pretty well, Mr. Foresight.—How did you rest last night?

FORESIGHT

Truly, Mr. Scandal, I was so taken up with broken dreams and distracted visions, that I remember little.

SCANDAL

'Twas a very forgetting night.—But would you not talk with Valentine, perhaps you may understand him? I'm apt to believe there is
something mysterious in his discourses, and sometimes rather think
him inspired than mad.

FORESIGHT

You speak with singular good judgment, Mr. Scandal, truly.—I am
inclining to your Turkish opinion in this matter, and do reverence a
man whom the vulgar think mad. Let us go to him.

[*Exeunt Foresight and Scandal.*

MRS. FRAIL

Sister, do you stay with them; I'll find out my lover, and give him his
discharge, and come to you.—O' my conscience here he comes.

[*Exit Mrs. Foresight.*

Enter Ben.

BEN

All mad, I think.—Flesh, I believe all the calentures of the sea are
come ashore, for my part!

MRS. FRAIL

Mr. Benjamin in choler!

BEN

No, I'm pleased well enough now I have found you.—Mess, I have
had such a hurricane upon your account yonder!

MRS. FRAIL

My account! pray what's the matter?

BEN

Why, father came and found me squabbling with yon chitty-faced
thing as he would have me marry,—so he asked what was the matter.—He asked in a surly sort of a way.—It seems brother Val is
gone mad, and so that put'n into a passion: but what did I know
that, what's that to me?—So he asked in a surly sort of manner,—
and gad I answered 'en as surlily; what tho'f he be my father? I an't
bound prentice to 'en:—so faith I told'n in plain terms, if I were
minded to marry I'd marry to please myself, not him: and for the
young woman that he provided for me, I thought it more fitting for
her to learn her sampler and make dirt-pies, than to look after a
husband; for my part I was none of her man.—I had another
voyage to make, let him take it as he will.

MRS. FRAIL

So then, you intend to go to sea again?

BEN

Nay, nay, my mind run upon you,—but I would not tell him so
much.—So he said he'd make my heart ache; and if so be that he
could get a woman to his mind, he'd marry himself. Gad, says I, an
you play the fool and marry at these years, there's more danger of
your head's aching than my heart.—He was woundy angry when I

gav'n that wipe.—He hadn't a word to say, and so I left'n and the green girl together; mayhap the bee may bite, and he'll marry her himself; with all my heart.

MRS. FRAIL

And were you this undutiful and graceless wretch to your father?

BEN

Then why was he graceless first?—If I am undutiful and graceless, why did he beget me so? I did not get myself.

MRS. FRAIL

O impiety! how have I been mistaken! what an inhuman merciless creature have I set my heart upon! O, I am happy to have discovered the shelves and quicksands that lurk beneath that faithless smiling face!

BEN

Hey toss? what's the matter now? why, you ben't angry, be you?

MRS. FRAIL

O see me no more! for thou wert born amongst rocks, suckled by whales, cradled in a tempest, and whistled to by winds; and thou art come forth with fins and scales, and three rows of teeth, a most outrageous fish of prey.

BEN

O Lord, O Lord, she's mad! poor young woman; love has turned her senses, her brain is quite overset! Well-a-day, how shall I do to set her to rights?

MRS. FRAIL

No, no, I am not mad, monster, I am wise enough to find you out. Hadst thou the impudence to aspire at being a husband with that stubborn and disobedient temper?—You that know not how to submit to a father, presume to have a sufficient stock of duty to undergo a wife? I should have been finely fobbed indeed, very finely fobbed.

BEN

Hark ye, forsooth; if so be that you are in your right senses, d'ye see; for aught as I perceive I'm like to be finely fobbed,—if I have got anger here upon your account, and you are tacked about already.—What d'ye mean, after all your fair speeches and stroking my cheeks, and kissing, and hugging, what, would you sheer off so? would you, and leave me aground?

MRS. FRAIL

No, I'll leave you adrift, and go which way you will.

BEN

What, are you false-hearted, then?

MRS. FRAIL

Only the wind's changed.

BEN

More shame for you:—the wind's changed! It's an ill wind blows nobody good,—mayhap I have a good riddance on you, if these be your tricks. What did you mean all this while, to make a fool of me?

MRS. FRAIL

Any fool but a husband.

BEN

Husband! gad, I would not be your husband, if you would have me, now I know your mind, tho'f you had your weight in gold and jewels, and tho'f I loved you never so well.

MRS. FRAIL

Why, canst thou love, porpoise?

BEN

No matter what I can do; don't call names,—I don't love you so well as to bear that, whatever I did. I'm glad you showed yourself, mistress.—Let them marry you, as don't know you:—gad, I know you too well, by sad experience: I believe he that marries you will go to sea in a hen-pecked frigate—I believe that, young woman—and mayhap may come to an anchor at Cuckold's-point; so there's a dash for you, take it as you will, mayhap you may holla after me when I won't come to.

[*Exit.*

MRS. FRAIL

Ha! ha! ha! no doubt on't;—
        (*Sings.*) My true love is gone to sea—
        Re-enter Mrs. Foresight.
O sister, had you come a minute sooner, you would have seen the resolution of a lover.—Honest Tar and I are parted,—and with the same indifference that we met.—O' my life I am half vexed at the insensibility of a brute that I despised.

MRS. FORESIGHT

What, then, he bore it most heroically?

MRS. FRAIL

Most tyrannically,—for you see he has got the start of me; and I the poor forsaken maid am left complaining on the shore. But I'll tell you a hint that he has given me; Sir Sampson is enraged, and talks desperately of committing matrimony himself;—if he has a mind to throw himself away, he can't do it more effectually than upon me, if we could bring it about.

MRS. FORESIGHT

Oh, hang him, old fox! he's too cunning; besides he hates both you and me. But I have a project in my head for you, and I have gone a good way towards it. I have almost made a bargain with Jeremy, Valentine's man, to sell his master to us.

MRS. FRAIL

Sell him! how?

MRS. FORESIGHT

Valentine raves upon Angelica, and took me for her, and Jeremy says will take anybody for her that he imposes on him. Now I have promised him mountains, if in one of his mad fits he will bring you to him in her stead, and get you married together, and put to bed together; and after consummation, girl, there's no revoking. And if he should recover his senses, he'll be glad at least to make you a good settlement.—Here they come: stand aside a little, and tell me how you like the design.
        Enter Valentine, Scandal, Foresight, and Jeremy.

SCANDAL (*To Jeremy.*)

And have you given your master a hint of their plot upon him?

JEREMY

Yes, sir; he says he'll favour it, and mistake her for Angelica.

SCANDAL

It may make us sport.

FORESIGHT

Mercy on us!

VALENTINE

Hush!—interrupt me not: I'll whisper prediction to thee, and thou
shalt prophesy. I am Truth, and can teach thy tongue a new trick:—
I have told thee what's past—now I'll tell what's to come. Dost thou
know what will happen to-morrow?—answer me not—for I will tell
thee. To-morrow, knaves will thrive through craft, and fools through
fortune, and honesty will go as it did, frost-nipped in a summer suit.
Ask me questions concerning to-morrow.

SCANDAL

Ask him, Mr. Foresight.

FORESIGHT

Pray, what will be done at court?

VALENTINE

Scandal will tell you:—I am Truth, I never come there.

FORESIGHT

In the city?

VALENTINE

Oh, prayers will be said in empty churches, at the usual hours. Yet
you will see such zealous faces behind the counters, as if religion
were to be sold in every shop. Oh, things will go methodically, in the
city; the clocks will strike twelve at noon, and the horned herd buzz
in the Exchange at two. Husbands and wives will drive distinct
trades, and care and pleasure separately occupy the family. Coffee-
houses will be full of smoke and stratagem. And the cropt prentice,
that sweeps his master's shop in the morning, may, ten to one, dirty
his sheets before night. But there are two things that you will see very
strange; which are wanton wives with their legs at liberty, and tame
cuckolds with chains about their necks.—But hold, I must examine
you before I go further; you look suspiciously. Are you a husband?

FORESIGHT

I am married.

VALENTINE

Poor creature! is your wife of Covent-garden parish?

FORESIGHT

No; St. Martin's-in-the-fields.

VALENTINE

Alas, poor man! his eyes are sunk, and his hands shrivelled; his legs
dwindled, and his back bowed; pray, pray, for a metamorphosis.
Change thy shape, and shake off age; get thee Medea's kettle, and
be boiled anew; come forth with labouring callous hands, a chine of
steel, and Atlas shoulders. Let Taliacotius trim the calves of twenty
chairmen, and make thee pedestals to stand erect upon, and look
matrimony in the face. Ha! ha! ha! that a man should have a stomach to a wedding supper, when the pigeons ought rather to be laid
to his feet, ha! ha! ha!

FORESIGHT

His frenzy is very high now, Mr. Scandal.

SCANDAL

I believe it is a spring-tide.

FORESIGHT

Very likely, truly; you understand these matters;—Mr. Scandal, I shall be very glad to confer with you about these things which he has uttered—his sayings are very mysterious and hieroglyphical.

VALENTINE

Oh, why would Angelica be absent from my eyes so long?

JEREMY

She's here, sir.

MRS. FORESIGHT

Now, sister.

MRS. FRAIL

O Lord, what must I say?

SCANDAL

Humour him, madam, by all means.

VALENTINE

Where is she? oh, I see her;—she comes like riches, health, and liberty at once, to a despairing, starving, and abandoned wretch. Oh welcome, welcome.

MRS. FRAIL

How d'ye, sir? can I serve you?

VALENTINE

Hark ye—I have a secret to tell you—Endymion and the moon shall meet us upon Mount Latmos, and we'll be married in the dead of night—but say not a word. Hymen shall put his torch into a dark lantern, that it may be secret; and Juno shall give her peacock poppy-water, that he may fold his ogling tail, and Argus's hundred eyes be shut, ha! Nobody shall know but Jeremy.

MRS. FRAIL

No, no, we'll keep it secret, it shall be done presently.

VALENTINE

The sooner the better.—Jeremy, come hither—closer—that none may overhear us—Jeremy, I can tell you news; Angelica is turned nun, and I am turning friar, and yet we'll marry one another in spite of the pope. Get me a cowl and beads, that I may play my part; for she'll meet me two hours hence in black and white, and a long veil to cover the project, and we won't see one another's faces, till we have done something to be ashamed of, and then we'll blush once for all.

Enter Tattle and Angelica.

JEREMY

I'll take care, and—

VALENTINE

Whisper.

ANGELICA

Nay, Mr. Tattle, if you make love to me, you spoil my design, for I intend to make you my confidant.

TATTLE

But, madam, to throw away your person, such a person, and such a fortune, on a madman?

ANGELICA

I never loved him till he was mad; but don't tell anybody so.

SCANDAL (*Aside.*)

How's this! Tattle making love to Angelica?

TATTLE

Tell, madam! alas, you don't know me—I have much ado to tell your ladyship how long I have been in love with you; but encouraged by the impossibility of Valentine's making any more addresses to you, I have ventured to declare the very inmost passion of my heart. Oh, madam, look upon us both; there you see the ruins of a poor decayed creature,—here a complete and lively figure, with youth and health, and all his five senses in perfection, madam; and to all this, the most passionate lover—

ANGELICA

O fy, for shame! hold your tongue; a passionate lover and five senses in perfection! when you are as mad as Valentine, I'll believe you love me, and the maddest shall take me.

VALENTINE

It is enough.—Ha, who's here?

MRS. FRAIL (*Aside to Jeremy.*)

O Lord, her coming will spoil all!

JEREMY (*Aside to Mrs. Frail.*)

No, no, madam, he won't know her; if he should, I can persuade him.

VALENTINE

Scandal, who are these? foreigners? If they are, I'll tell you what I think.—(*Whispers.*) Get away all the company but Angelica, that I may discover my design to her.

SCANDAL (*Whispers.*)

I will: I have discovered something of Tattle that is of a piece with Mrs. Frail. He courts Angelica; if we could contrive to couple 'em together; hark ye.

MRS. FORESIGHT

He won't know you, cousin, he knows nobody.

FORESIGHT

But he knows more than anybody. Oh, niece, he knows things past and to come, and all the profound secrets of time.

TATTLE

Look you, Mr. Foresight, it is not my way to make many words of matters, so I shan't say much; but, in short, d'ye see, I will hold you a hundred pounds now, that I know more secrets than he.

FORESIGHT

How! I cannot read that knowledge in your face, Mr. Tattle. Pray, what do you know?

TATTLE

Why, d'ye think I'll tell you, sir? Read it in my face! no, sir, 'tis written in my heart; and safer there, sir, than letters writ in juice of lemon; for no fire can fetch it out. I am no blab, sir.

VALENTINE (*Aside to Scandal.*)

Acquaint Jeremy with it, he may easily bring it about.—(*Aloud.*) They are welcome, and I'll tell 'em so myself. What, do you look strange upon me? then I must be plain.—(*Coming up to them.*) I am Truth, and hate an old acquaintance with a new face.

[*Scandal goes aside with Jeremy.*

TATTLE

Do you know me, Valentine?

VALENTINE

You, who are you? no, I hope not.

TATTLE

I am Jack Tattle, your friend.

VALENTINE

My friend? what to do? I am no married man, and thou canst not lie with my wife; I am very poor, and thou canst not borrow money of me; then what employment have I for a friend?

TATTLE

Ha! a good open speaker, and not to be trusted with a secret.

ANGELICA

Do you know me, Valentine?

VALENTINE

Oh, very well.

ANGELICA

Who am I?

VALENTINE

You're a woman,—one to whom Heaven gave beauty, when it grafted roses on a briar. You are the reflection of Heaven in a pond, and he that leaps at you is sunk. You are all white, a sheet of lovely, spotless paper, when you first are born; but you are to be scrawled and blotted by every goose's quill. I know you; for I loved a woman, and loved her so long, that I found out a strange thing; I found out what a woman was good for.

TATTLE

Ay, prithee, what's that?

VALENTINE

Why, to keep a secret.

TATTLE

O Lord!

VALENTINE

O, exceeding good to keep a secret: for though she should tell, yet she is not to be believed.

TATTLE

Ha! good again, faith.

VALENTINE

I would have music.—Sing me the song that I like.

SONG

I tell thee, Charmion, could I time retrieve,
And could again begin to love and live,
To you I should my earliest offering give;

I know, my eyes would lead my heart to you,
And I should all my vows and oaths renew;
But, to be plain, I never would be true.

For by our weak and weary truth I find,
Love hates to centre in a point assigned;
But runs with joy the circle of the mind:

Then never let us chain what should be free,
But for relief of either sex agree:
Since women love to change, and so do we.

VALENTINE
No more, for I am melancholy.

[*Walks musing.*

JEREMY (*Aside to Scandal.*)
I'll do't, sir.

SCANDAL
Mr. Foresight, we had best leave him. He may grow outrageous, and do mischief.

FORESIGHT
I will be directed by you.

JEREMY (*Aside to Mrs. Frail*)
You'll meet, madam? I'll take care everything shall be ready.

MRS. FRAIL
Thou shalt do what thou wilt; in short, I will deny thee nothing.

TATTLE (*To Angelica.*)
Madam, shall I wait upon you?

ANGELICA
No, I'll stay with him; Mr. Scandal will protect me.—Aunt, Mr. Tattle desires you would give him leave to wait on you.

TATTLE (*Aside.*)
Pox on't! there's no coming off, now she has said that.—(*Aloud.*)
Madam, will you do me the honour?

MRS. FORESIGHT
Mr. Tattle might have used less ceremony.

[*Exeunt Foresight, Mrs. Frail, Mrs. Foresight, and Tattle.*

SCANDAL
Jeremy, follow Tattle.

[*Exit Jeremy.*

ANGELICA
Mr. Scandal, I only stay till my maid comes, and because I had a mind to be rid of Mr. Tattle.

SCANDAL
Madam, I am very glad that I overheard a better reason, which you gave to Mr. Tattle; for his impertinence forced you to acknowledge a kindness for Valentine which you denied to all his sufferings and my solicitations. So I'll leave him to make use of the discovery, and your ladyship to the free confession of your inclinations.

ANGELICA
Oh Heavens! you won't leave me alone with a madman?

SCANDAL
No, madam, I only leave a madman to his remedy.

[*Exit Scandal.*

VALENTINE
Madam, you need not be very much afraid, for I fancy I begin to come to myself.

ANGELICA (*Aside.*)
> Ay, but if I don't fit you, I'll be hanged.

VALENTINE
> You see what disguises love makes us put on: gods have been in counterfeited shapes for the same reason; and the divine part of me, my mind, has worn this mask of madness, and this motley livery, only as the slave of love, and menial creature of your beauty.

ANGELICA
> Mercy on me, how he talks! poor Valentine!

VALENTINE
> Nay, faith, now let us understand one another, hypocrisy apart.— The comedy draws toward an end, and let us think of leaving acting, and be ourselves; and since you have loved me, you must own, I have at length deserved you should confess it.

ANGELICA (*Sighs.*)
> I would I had loved you!—for Heaven knows I pity you; and could I have foreseen the bad effects, I would have striven; but that's too late.

> > [*Sighs.*

VALENTINE
> What bad effects?—what's too late? My seeming madness has deceived my father, and procured me time to think of means to reconcile me to him, and preserve the right of my inheritance to his estate; which otherwise by articles I must this morning have resigned: and this I had informed you of to-day, but you were gone, before I knew you had been here.

ANGELICA
> How! I thought your love of me had caused this transport in your soul; which it seems you only counterfeited, for mercenary ends and sordid interest!

VALENTINE
> Nay, now you do me wrong; for if any interest was considered it was yours; since I thought I wanted more than love to make me worthy of you.

ANGELICA
> Then you thought me mercenary.—But how am I deluded by this interval of sense, to reason with a madman!

VALENTINE
> Oh, 'tis barbarous to misunderstand me longer.
> > *Enter Jeremy.*

ANGELICA
> Oh, here's a reasonable creature—sure he will not have the impudence to persevere.—Come, Jeremy, acknowledge your trick, and confess your master's madness counterfeit.

JEREMY
> Counterfeit, madam! I'll maintain him to be as absolutely and substantially mad as any freeholder in Bethlehem; nay, he's as mad as any projector, fanatic, chemist, lover, or poet in Europe.

VALENTINE
> Sirrah, you lie! I am not mad.

ANGELICA
> Ha! ha! ha! you see he denies it.

JEREMY

O Lord, madam, did you ever know any madman mad enough to own it?

VALENTINE

Sot, can't you comprehend?

ANGELICA

Why, he talked very sensible just now.

JEREMY

Yes, madam, he has intervals; but you see he begins to look wild again now.

VALENTINE

Why, you thick-skulled rascal, I tell you the farce is done, and I will be mad no longer.

[Beats him.

ANGELICA

Ha! ha! ha! is he mad or no, Jeremy?

JEREMY

Partly I think—for he does not know his own mind two hours.—I'm sure I left him just now in the humour to be mad; and I think I have not found him very quiet at this present!—(Knocking at the door.) Who's there?

VALENTINE

Go see, you sot.—(Exit Jeremy.) I'm very glad that I can move your mirth, though not your compassion.

ANGELICA

I did not think you had apprehension enough to be exceptious: but madmen show themselves most, by overpretending to a sound understanding; as drunken men do by over-acting sobriety. I was half-inclining to believe you, till I accidentally touched upon your tender part; but now you have restored me to my former opinion and compassion.

Re-enter Jeremy.

JEREMY

Sir, your father has sent to know if you are any better yet.—Will you please to be mad, sir, or how?

VALENTINE

Stupidity! you know the penalty of all I'm worth must pay for the confession of my senses; I'm mad, and will be mad to everybody but this lady.

JEREMY

So,—just the very backside of truth.—But lying is a figure in speech, that interlards the greatest part of my conversation.—Madam, your ladyship's woman.

[Exit.

Enter Jenny.

ANGELICA

Well, have you been there?—Come hither.

JENNY (Aside to Angelica.)

Yes, madam, Sir Sampson will wait upon you presently.

VALENTINE

You are not leaving me in this uncertainty?

ANGELICA

Would anything but a madman complain of uncertainty? Uncertainty and expectation are the joys of life. Security is an insipid thing, and the overtaking and possessing of a wish, discovers the folly of the chase. Never let us know one another better: for the pleasure of a masquerade is done, when we come to show our faces; but I'll tell you two things before I leave you; I am not the fool you take me for; and you are mad, and don't know it.

[*Exeunt Angelica and Jenny.*

VALENTINE

From a riddle you can expect nothing but a riddle. There's my instruction, and the moral of my lesson.

Re-enter Jeremy.

JEREMY

What, is the lady gone again, sir? I hope you understood one another before she went?

VALENTINE

Understood! she is harder to be understood than a piece of Egyptian antiquity, or an Irish manuscript; you may pore till you spoil your eyes, and not improve your knowledge.

JEREMY

I have heard 'em say, sir, they read hard Hebrew books backwards; may be you begin to read at the wrong end.

VALENTINE

They say so of a witch's prayer: and dreams and Dutch almanacs are to be understood by contraries. But there's regularity and method in that; she is a medal without a reverse or inscription, for indifference has both sides alike. Yet while she does not seem to hate me, I will pursue her, and know her if it be possible, in spite of the opinion of my satirical friend, Scandal, who says,

> That women are like tricks by sleight of hand,
> Which, to admire, we should not understand.

[*Exeunt.*

Act the fifth

Scene I. A room in Foresight's house.
Enter Angelica and Jenny.

ANGELICA

Where is Sir Sampson? did you not tell me he would be here before me?

JENNY

He's at the great glass in the dining-room, madam, setting his cravat and wig.

ANGELICA

How! I'm glad on't.—If he has a mind I should like him, it's a sign he likes me; and that's more than half my design.

JENNY

I hear him, madam.

ANGELICA

Leave me; and d'ye hear, if Valentine should come or send, I am not to be spoken with.

[*Exit Jenny.*

Enter Sir Sampson.

SIR SAMPSON

I have not been honoured with the commands of a fair lady, a great while:—odd, madam, you have revived me!—not since I was five-and-thirty.

ANGELICA

Why, you have no great reason to complain, Sir Sampson, that is not long ago.

SIR SAMPSON

Zooks, but it is, madam, a very great while to a man that admires a fine woman as much as I do.

ANGELICA

You're an absolute courtier, Sir Sampson.

SIR SAMPSON

Not at all, madam; odsbud you wrong me; I am not so old neither to be a bare courtier, only a man of words: odd, I have warm blood about me yet, and can serve a lady any way.—Come, come, let me tell you, you women think a man old too soon, faith and troth, you do!—Come, don't despise fifty: odd, fifty, in a hale constitution, is no such contemptible age.

ANGELICA

Fifty a contemptible age! not at all, a very fashionable age, I think.—I assure you, I know very considerable beaux that set a good face upon fifty:—fifty! I have seen fifty in a side-box, by candle-light, out-blossom five-and-twenty.

SIR SAMPSON

Outsides, outsides; a pize take 'em, mere outsides! hang your side-box beaux! no, I'm none of those, none of your forced trees, that pretend to blossom in the fall, and bud when they should bring forth fruit; I am of a long-lived race, and inherit vigour: none of my ancestors married till fifty; yet they begot sons and daughters till fourscore; I am of your patriarchs, I, a branch of one of your antediluvian families, fellows that the flood could not wash away. Well, madam, what are your commands? has any young rogue affronted you, and shall I cut his throat? or—

ANGELICA

No, Sir Sampson, I have no quarrel upon my hands—I have more occasion for your conduct than your courage at this time. To tell you the truth, I'm weary of living single, and want a husband.

SIR SAMPSON

Odsbud, and 'tis pity you should!—(*Aside.*) Odd, would she would like me, then I should hamper my young rogues: odd, would she would; faith and troth she's devilish handsome!—(*Aloud.*) Madam, you deserve a good husband, and 'twere pity you should be thrown away upon any of these young idle rogues about the town. Odd, there's ne'er a young fellow worth hanging!—that is a very young fellow.—Pize on 'em! they never think beforehand of anything;—and if they commit matrimony, 'tis as they commit murder; out of a frolic, and are ready to hang themselves, or to be hanged by the law, the next morning:—odso, have a care, madam.

ANGELICA

Therefore I ask your advice, Sir Sampson: I have fortune enough to make any man easy that I can like; if there were such a thing as a young agreeable man with a reasonable stock of good-nature and sense.—For I would neither have an absolute wit nor a fool.

SIR SAMPSON

Odd, you are hard to please, madam; to find a young fellow that is neither a wit in his own eye, nor a fool in the eye of the world, is a very hard task. But, faith and troth, you speak very discreetly; for I hate both a wit and a fool.

ANGELICA

She that marries a fool, Sir Sampson, forfeits the reputation of her honesty or understanding: and she that marries a very witty man is a slave to the severity and insolent conduct of her husband. I should like a man of wit for a lover, because I would have such a one in my power; but I would no more be his wife than his enemy. For his malice is not a more terrible consequence of his aversion than his jealousy is of his love.

SIR SAMPSON

None of old Foresight's Sibyls ever uttered such a truth. Odsbud, you have won my heart! I hate a wit; I had a son that was spoiled among 'em; a good hopeful lad, till he learned to be a wit—and might have risen in the state.—But a pox on't! his wit run him out of his money, and now his poverty has run him out of his wits.

ANGELICA

Sir Sampson, as your friend, I must tell you, you are very much abused in that matter: he's no more mad than you are.

SIR SAMPSON

How, madam! would I could prove it!

ANGELICA

I can tell you how that may be done.—But it is a thing that would make me appear to be too much concerned in your affairs.

SIR SAMPSON (*Aside.*)

Odsbud, I believe she likes me! (*Aloud.*) Ah, madam, all my affairs are scarce worthy to be laid at your feet; and I wish, madam, they were in a better posture, that I might make a more becoming offer to a lady of your incomparable beauty and merit.—If I had Peru in one hand, and Mexico in t'other, and the eastern empire under my feet, it would make me only a more glorious victim to be offered at the shrine of your beauty.

ANGELICA

Bless me, Sir Sampson, what's the matter?

SIR SAMPSON

Odd, madam, I love you!—and if you would take my advice in a husband—

ANGELICA

Hold, hold, Sir Sampson. I asked your advice for a husband, and you are giving me your consent.—I was indeed thinking to propose something like it in jest, to satisfy you about Valentine: for if a match were seemingly carried on between you and me, it would oblige him to throw off his disguise of madness, in apprehension of losing me: for you know he has long pretended a passion for me.

SIR SAMPSON

Gadzooks, a most ingenious contrivance!—if we were to go through with it. But why must the match only be seemingly carried on?— Odd, let it be a real contract.

ANGELICA

O fy, Sir Sampson! what would the world say?

SIR SAMPSON

Say! they would say you were a wise woman and I a happy man. Odd, madam, I'll love you as long as I live, and leave you a good jointure when I die.

ANGELICA

Ay; but that is not in your power, Sir Sampson; for when Valentine confesses himself in his senses, he must make over his inheritance to his younger brother.

SIR SAMPSON

Odd, you're cunning, a wary baggage! faith and troth, I like you the better.—But, I warrant you, I have a proviso in the obligation in favour of myself.—Body o' me, I have a trick to turn the settlement upon issue male of our two bodies begotten. Odsbud, let us find children, and I'll find an estate.

ANGELICA

Will you? well do you find the estate, and leave the other to me.

SIR SAMPSON

O rogue! but I'll trust you. And will you consent! is it a match then?

ANGELICA

Let me consult my lawyer concerning this obligation; and if I find what you propose practicable, I'll give you my answer.

SIR SAMPSON

With all my heart: come in with me, and I'll lend you the bond.— You shall consult your lawyer, and I'll consult a parson. Odzooks I'm a young man: odzooks, I'm a young man, and I'll make it appear. Odd, you're devilish handsome: faith and troth, you're very handsome; and I'm very young, and very lusty. Odsbud, hussy, you know how to choose, and so do I;—odd, I think we are very well met. Give me your hand, odd, let me kiss it; 'tis as warm and as soft—as what?—Odd, as t'other hand; give me t'other hand, and I'll mumble 'em and kiss 'em till they melt in my mouth.

ANGELICA

Hold, Sir Sampson: you're profuse of your vigour before your time: you'll spend your estate before you come to it.

SIR SAMPSON

No, no, only give you a rent-roll of my possessions,—ha! baggage!—I warrant you for little Sampson: odd, Sampson's a very good name for an able fellow: your Sampsons were strong dogs from the beginning.

ANGELICA

Have a care, and don't overact your part. If you remember, Sampson, the strongest of the name, pulled on old house over his head at last.

SIR SAMPSON

Say you so, hussy? Come, let's go then; odd, I long to be pulling too, come away.—Odso, here's somebody coming. [*Exeunt.*

Scene II. The same.
Enter Tattle and Jeremy.

TATTLE

Is not that she, gone out just now?

JEREMY

Ay, sir, she's just going to the place of appointment. Ah, sir, if you are not very faithful and close in this business, you'll certainly be the death of a person that has a most extraordinary passion for your honour's service.

TATTLE

Ay, who's that?

JEREMY

Even my unworthy self, sir. Sir, I have had an appetite to be fed with your commands a great while; and now, sir, my former master having much troubled the fountain of his understanding, it is a very plausible occasion for me to quench my thirst at the spring of your bounty. I thought I could not recommend myself better to you, sir, than by the delivery of a great beauty and fortune into your arms, whom I have heard you sigh for.

TATTLE

I'll make thy fortune; say no more. Thou art a pretty fellow, and canst carry a message to a lady, in a pretty soft kind of phrase, and with a good persuading accent.

JEREMY

Sir, I have the seeds of rhetoric and oratory in my head; I have been at Cambridge.

TATTLE

Ay! 'tis well enough for a servant to be bred at a university: but the education is a little too pedantic for a gentleman. I hope you are secret in your nature, private, close, ha?

JEREMY

O sir, for that, sir, 'tis my chief talent: I'm as secret as the head of Nilus.

TATTLE

Ay! who is he, though? a privy counsellor?

JEREMY (Aside.)

O ignorance!—(Aloud.) A cunning Egyptian, sir, that with his arms would overrun the country. yet nobody could ever find out his head-quarters.

TATTLE

Close dog! a good whoremaster, I warrant him. The time draws nigh, Jeremy. Angelica will be veiled like a nun; and I must be hooded like a friar; ha, Jeremy?

JEREMY

Ay, sir, hooded like a hawk, to seize at first sight upon the quarry. It is the whim of my master's madness to be so dressed; and she is so in love with him, she'll comply with anything to please him. Poor lady, I'm sure she'll have reason to pray for me, when she finds what a happy exchange she has made, between a madman and so accomplished a gentleman.

TATTLE

Ay, faith, so she will, Jeremy; you're a good friend to her, poor creature. I swear I do it hardly so much in consideration of myself as compassion to her.

JEREMY

'Tis an act of charity, sir, to save a fine woman with thirty thousand pounds, from throwing herself away.

TATTLE

So 'tis, faith. I might have saved several others in my time; but egad, I could never find in my heart to marry anybody before.

JEREMY

Well, sir, I'll go and tell her my master is coming; and meet you in half a quarter of an hour, with your disguise, at your own lodgings. You must talk a little madly, she won't distinguish the tone of your voice.

TATTLE

No, no, let me alone for a counterfeit; I'll be ready for you.

[*Exit Jeremy.*

Enter Miss Prue.

MISS PRUE

O Mr. Tattle, are you here! I'm glad I have found you; I have been looking up and down for you like anything, 'till I am as tired as anything in the world.

TATTLE (*Aside.*)

O pox, how shall I get rid of this foolish girl!

MISS PRUE

O I have pure news, I can tell you, pure news. I must not marry the seaman now—my father says so. Why won't you be my husband? you say you love me, and you won't be my husband. And I know you may be my husband now if you please.

TATTLE

O fy, miss! who told you so, child?

MISS PRUE

Why, my father. I told him that you loved me.

TATTLE

O fy, miss! why did you do so? and who told you so, child?

MISS PRUE

Who! why you did; did not you?

TATTLE

O pox! that was yesterday, miss, that was a great while ago, child. I have been asleep since; slept a whole night, and did not so much as dream of the matter.

MISS PRUE

Pshaw! O but I dreamt that it was so though.

TATTLE

Ay, but your father will tell you that dreams come by contraries, child. O fy! what, we must not love one another now—pshaw, that would be a foolish thing indeed! Fy! fy! you're a woman now, and must think of a new man every morning, and forget him every night.—No, no, to marry is to be a child again, and play with the same rattle always; O fy! marrying is a paw thing.

MISS PRUE

Well, but don't you love me as well as you did last night then?

TATTLE

No, no, child, you would not have me.

MISS PRUE

No! yes, but I would though.

TATTLE

Pshaw! but I tell you, you would not—You forget you're a woman, and don't know your own mind.

MISS PRUE

But here's my father, and he knows my mind.

Enter Foresight.

FORESIGHT

O, Mr. Tattle, your servant, you are a close man; but methinks your love to my daughter was a secret I might have been trusted with; or had you a mind to try if I could discover it by my art? Hum, ha! I think there is something in your physiognomy that has a resemblance of her; and the girl is like me.

TATTLE

And so you would infer, that you and I are alike?—(*Aside.*) What does the old prig mean? I'll banter him, and laugh at him, and leave him.—(*Aloud.*) I fancy you have a wrong notion of faces.

FORESIGHT

How? what? a wrong notion! how so?

TATTLE

In the way of art: I have some taking features, not obvious to vulgar eyes; that are indications of a sudden turn of good fortune in the lottery of wives; and promise a great beauty and a great fortune reserved alone for me, by a private intrigue of destiny, kept secret from the piercing eye of perspicuity; from all astrologers and the stars themselves.

FORESIGHT

How? I will make it appear that what you say is impossible.

TATTLE

Sir, I beg your pardon, I'm in haste—

FORESIGHT

For what?

TATTLE

To be married, sir, married.

FORESIGHT

Ay, but pray take me along with you,[12] sir—

TATTLE

No, sir: 'tis to be done privately. I never make confidants.

FORESIGHT

Well, but my consent, I mean.—You won't marry my daughter without my consent.

TATTLE

Who, I, sir? I'm an absolute stranger to you and your daughter, sir.

FORESIGHT

Heyday! what time of the moon is this?

TATTLE

Very true, sir, and desire to continue so. I have no more love for your daughter than I have likeness of you; and I have a secret in my heart, which you would be glad to know, and shan't know; and yet you shall know it too, and be sorry for it afterwards. I'd have you to know, sir, that I am as knowing as the stars, and as secret as the night. And I'm going to be married just now, yet did not know of it half an hour ago; and the lady stays for me, and does not know of it yet. There's a mystery for you!—I know you love to untie difficulties

12 i.e., Let me understand you.

—or if you can't solve this, stay here a quarter of an hour, and I'll come and explain it to you.

[*Exit.*

MISS PRUE

O father, why will you let him go? won't you make him to be my husband?

FORESIGHT

Mercy on us! what do these lunacies portend?—Alas! he's mad, child, stark wild.

MISS PRUE

What, and must not I have e'er a husband then? What, must I go to bed to nurse again, and be a child as long as she's an old woman? Indeed but I won't; for now my mind is set upon a man, I will have a man some way or other. Oh! methinks I'm sick when I think of a man; and if I can't have one I would go to sleep all my life: for when I'm awake it makes me wish and long, and I don't know for what:—and I'd rather be always asleep, than sick with thinking.

FORESIGHT

O fearful! I think the girl's influenced too.—Hussy, you shall have a rod.

MISS PRUE

A fiddle of a rod! I'll have a husband: and if you won't get me one I'll get one for myself. I'll marry our Robin the butler; he says he loves me, and he's a handsome man, and shall be my husband: I warrant he'll be my husband, and thank me too, for he told me so.

Enter Scandal, Mrs. Foresight, and Nurse.

FORESIGHT

Did he so? I'll dispatch him for it presently; rogue!—Oh, nurse, come hither.

NURSE

What is your worship's pleasure?

FORESIGHT

Here take your young mistress, and lock her up presently, till farther orders from me.—Not a word, hussy. Do what I bid you; no reply; away! And bid Robin make ready to give an account of his plate and linen, d'ye hear: begone when I bid you.

MRS. FORESIGHT

What is the matter, husband?

FORESIGHT

'Tis not convenient to tell you now.—Mr. Scandal, heaven keep us all in our senses!—I fear there is a contagious frenzy abroad. How does Valentine?

SCANDAL

Oh, I hope he will do well again:—I have a message from him to your niece Angelica.

FORESIGHT

I think she has not returned since she went abroad with Sir Sampson.—Nurse, why are you not gone?

[*Exeunt Nurse and Miss Prue.*

Enter Ben.

MRS. FORESIGHT

Here's Mr. Benjamin; he can tell us if his father be come home.

BEN

Who, father? ay, he's come home with a vengeance.

MRS. FORESIGHT

Why, what's the matter?

BEN

Matter! why, he's mad.

FORESIGHT

Mercy on us! I was afraid of this.

BEN

And there's the handsome young woman, she, as they say, brother Val went mad for, she's mad too, I think.

FORESIGHT

O my poor niece, my poor niece, is she gone too? Well, I shall run mad next.

MRS. FORESIGHT

Well, but how mad? how d'ye mean?

BEN

Nay, I'll give you leave to guess:—I'll undertake to make a voyage to Antegoa—no, hold, I mayn't say so neither—but I'll sail as far as Leghorn, and back again, before you shall guess at the matter, and do nothing else; mess, you may take in all the points of the compass and not hit right.

MRS. FORESIGHT

Your experiment will take up a little too much time.

BEN

Why then I'll tell you: there's a new wedding upon the stocks, and they two are a-going to be married to-night.

SCANDAL

Who?

BEN

My father, and—the young woman. I can't hit of her name.

SCANDAL

Angelica?

BEN

Ay, the same.

MRS. FORESIGHT

Sir Sampson and Angelica: impossible!

BEN

That may be—but I'm sure it is as I tell you.

SCANDAL

'Sdeath, it's a jest! I can't believe it.

BEN

Look you, friend, it's nothing to me whether you believe it or no. What I say is true, d'ye see; they are married, or just going to be married, I know not which.

FORESIGHT

Well, but they are not mad, that is not lunatic?

BEN

I don't know what you may call madness; but she's mad for a husband, and he's horn mad, I think, or they'd ne'er make a match together.—Here they come.

Enter Sir Sampson, Angelica, and Buckram.

SIR SAMPSON

Where is this old soothsayer? this uncle of mine elect?—Aha! old
Foresight, Uncle Foresight, wish me joy, Uncle Foresight, double joy,
both as uncle and astrologer; here's a conjunction that was not foretold in all your Ephemeris. The brightest star in the blue fir-
mament—*is shot from above in a jelly of love,* and so forth; and I'm
lord of the ascendant. Odd, you're an old fellow, Foresight, uncle I
mean; a very old fellow, Uncle Foresight; and yet you shall live to
dance at my wedding, faith and troth you shall. Odd, we'll have the
music of the spheres for thee, old Lilly, that we will, and thou shalt
lead up a dance *in via lactea!*

FORESIGHT

I'm thunderstruck!—You are not married to my niece?

SIR SAMPSON

Not absolutely married, uncle; but very near it, within a kiss of the
matter, as you see.

[*Kisses Angelica.*

ANGELICA

'Tis very true, indeed, uncle; I hope you'll be my father, and give
me.

SIR SAMPSON

That he shall, or I'll burn his globes. Body o' me, he shall be thy father, I'll make him thy father, and thou shalt make me a father, and
I'll make thee a mother, and we'll beget sons and daughters enough
to put the weekly bills out of countenance.

SCANDAL

Death and hell! where's Valentine?

[*Exit.*

MRS. FORESIGHT

This is so surprising—

SIR SAMPSON

How! what does my aunt say? Surprising, aunt! not at all, for a
young couple to make a match in winter: not at all.—It's a plot to
undermine cold weather, and destroy that usurper of a bed called a
warming-pan.

MRS. FORESIGHT

I'm glad to hear you have so much fire in you, Sir Sampson.

BEN

Mess, I fear his fire's little better than tinder; mayhap it will only
serve to light up a match for somebody else. The young woman's a
handsome young woman, I can't deny it; but, father, if I might be
your pilot in this case, you should not marry her. It's just the same
thing, as if so be you should sail so far as the Straits without provision.

SIR SAMPSON

Who gave you authority to speak, sirrah? To your element, fish! be
mute, fish, and to sea! rule your helm, sirrah, don't direct me.

BEN

Well, well, take you care of your own helm, or you mayn't keep your
new vessel steady.

SIR SAMPSON

Why, you impudent tarpaulin! sirrah, do you bring your forecastle
jests upon your father? but I shall be even with you, I won't give you

a groat.—Mr. Buckram, is the conveyance so worded that nothing can possibly descend to this scoundrel? I would not so much as have him the prospect of an estate; though there were no way to come to it but by the north-east passage.

BUCKRAM

Sir, it is drawn according to your directions, there is not the least cranny of the law unstopped.

BEN

Lawyer, I believe there's many a cranny and leak unstopped in your conscience.—If so be that one had a pump to your bosom, I believe we should discover a foul hold. They say a witch will sail in a sieve,—but I believe the devil would not venture aboard o' your conscience. And that's for you.

SIR SAMPSON

Hold your tongue, sirrah!—How now? who's here?
Enter Tattle and Mrs. Frail.

MRS. FRAIL

O sister, the most unlucky accident!

MRS. FORESIGHT

What's the matter?

TATTLE

Oh, the two most unfortunate poor creatures in the world we are!

FORESIGHT

Bless us! how so?

MRS. FRAIL

Ah, Mr. Tattle and I, poor Mr. Tattle and I are—I can't speak it out.

TATTLE

Nor I—but poor Mrs. Frail and I are—

MRS. FRAIL

Married.

MRS. FORESIGHT

Married! How?

TATTLE

Suddenly—before we knew where we were—that villain Jeremy, by the help of disguises, tricked us into one another.

FORESIGHT

Why, you told me just now, you went hence in haste to be married.

ANGELICA

But I believe Mr. Tattle meant the favour to me: I thank him.

TATTLE

I did, as I hope to be saved, madam; my intentions were good.—But this is the most cruel thing, to marry one does not know how, nor why, nor wherefore.—The devil take me if ever I was so much concerned at anything in my life!

ANGELICA

'Tis very unhappy, if you don't care for one another.

TATTLE

The least in the world;—that is, for my part; I speak for myself. Gad, I never had the least thought of serious kindness:—I never liked anybody less in my life. Poor woman! gad, I'm sorry for her, too; for I have no reason to hate her neither; but I believe I shall lead her a damned sort of life.

MRS. FORESIGHT (*Aside to Mrs. Frail.*)

Hε's better than no husband at all—though he's a coxcomb.

MRS. FRAIL (*Aside to Mrs. Foresight.*)

Ay, ay, it's well it's no worse.—(*Aloud.*) Nay, for my part I always despised Mr. Tattle of all things; nothing but his being my husband could have made me like him less.

TATTLE

Look you there, I thought as much!—Pox on't, I wish we could keep it secret! why, I don't believe any of this company would speak of it.

MRS. FRAIL

But, my dear, that's impossible; the parson and that rogue Jeremy will publish it.

TATTLE

Ay, my dear, so they will, as you say.

ANGELICA

O you'll agree very well in a little time; custom will make it easy to you.

TATTLE

Easy! pox on't! I don't believe I shall sleep to-night.

SIR SAMPSON

Sleep, quotha! no; why you would not sleep o' your wedding night! I'm an older fellow than you, and don't mean to sleep.

BEN

Why, there's another match now, as tho'f a couple of privateers were looking for a prize, and should fall foul of one another. I'm sorry for the young man with all my heart. Look you, friend, if I may advise you, when she's going, for that you must expect, I have experience of her, when she's going, let her go. For no matrimony is tough enough to hold her, and if she can't drag her anchor along with her, she'll break her cable, I can tell you that.—Who's here? the madman?

Enter Valentine, Scandal, and Jeremy.

VALENTINE

No; here's the fool; and, if occasion be, I'll give it under my hand.

SIR SAMPSON

How now!

VALENTINE

Sir, I'm come to acknowledge my errors, and ask your pardon.

SIR SAMPSON

What, have you found your senses at last then? in good time, sir.

VALENTINE

You were abused, sir, I never was distracted.

FORESIGHT

How, not mad! Mr. Scandal?

SCANDAL

No, really, sir; I'm his witness, it was all counterfeit.

VALENTINE

I thought I had reasons.—But it was a poor contrivance; the effect has shown it such.

SIR SAMPSON

Contrivance! what, to cheat me? to cheat your father? sirrah, could you hope to prosper?

VALENTINE

Indeed, I thought, sir, when the father endeavoured to undo the son, it was a reasonable return of nature.

SIR SAMPSON

Very good, sir!—Mr. Buckram, are you ready?—(*To Valentine.*) Come, sir, will you sign and seal?

VALENTINE

If you please, sir; but first I would ask this lady one question.

SIR SAMPSON

Sir, you must ask me leave first.—That lady! no, sir; you shall ask that lady no questions, till you have asked her blessing, sir; that lady is to be my wife.

VALENTINE

I have heard as much, sir; but I would have it from her own mouth.

SIR SAMPSON

That's as much as to say, I lie, sir, and you don't believe what I say.

VALENTINE

Pardon me, sir. But I reflect that I very lately counterfeited madness; I don't know but the frolic may go round.

SIR SAMPSON

Come, chuck, satisfy him, answer him.—Come, come, Mr. Buckram, the pen and ink.

BUCKRAM

Here it is, sir, with the deed; all is ready.

[Valentine goes to Angelica.

ANGELICA

'Tis true, you have a great while pretended love to me; nay, what if you were sincere; still you must pardon me, if I think my own inclinations have a better right to dispose of my person, than yours.

SIR SAMPSON

Are you answered now, sir?

VALENTINE

Yes, sir.

SIR SAMPSON

Where's your plot, sir; and your contrivance now, sir? Will you sign, sir? come, will you sign and seal?

VALENTINE

With all my heart, sir.

SCANDAL

'Sdeath, you are not mad indeed, to ruin yourself?

VALENTINE

I have been disappointed of my only hope; and he that loses hope may part with anything. I never valued fortune, but as it was subservient to my pleasure; and my only pleasure was to please this lady; I have made many vain attempts, and find at last that nothing but my ruin can effect it; which, for that reason I will sign to.—Give me the paper.

ANGELICA (*Aside.*)

Generous Valentine!

BUCKRAM

Here is the deed, sir.

VALENTINE

But where is the bond, by which I am obliged to sign this?

BUCKRAM
> Sir Sampson, you have it.

ANGELICA
> No, I have it; and I'll use it, as I would everything that is an enemy to Valentine.

> [*Tears the paper.*

SIR SAMPSON
> How now!

VALENTINE
> Ha!

ANGELICA (*To Valentine.*)
> Had I the world to give you, it could not make me worthy of so generous and faithful a passion; here's my hand, my heart was always yours, and struggled very hard to make this utmost trial of your virtue.

VALENTINE
> Between pleasure and amazement, I am lost.—But on my knees I take the blessing.

SIR SAMPSON
> Oons, what is the meaning of this?

BEN
> Mess, here's the wind changed again! Father, you and I may make a voyage together now.

ANGELICA
> Well, Sir Sampson, since I have played you a trick, I'll advise you how you may avoid such another. Learn to be a good father, or you'll never get a second wife. I always loved your son, and hated your unforgiving nature. I was resolved to try him to the utmost; I have tried you too, and know you both. You have not more faults than he has virtues; and 'tis hardly more pleasure to me, that I can make him and myself happy, than that I can punish you.

VALENTINE
> If my happiness could receive addition, this kind surprise would make it double.

SIR SAMPSON
> Oons, you're a crocodile!

FORESIGHT
> Really, Sir Sampson, this a sudden eclipse.

SIR SAMPSON
> You're an illiterate old fool, and I'm another!

> [*Exit.*

TATTLE
> If the gentleman is in disorder for want of a wife, I can spare him mine.—(*To Jeremy.*) Oh, are you there, sir? I'm indebted to you for my happiness.

JEREMY
> Sir, I ask you ten thousand pardons; 'twas an arrant mistake.—You see, sir, my master was never mad, or anything like it:—then how could it be otherwise?

VALENTINE
> Tattle, I thank you, you would have interposed between me and Heaven; but Providence laid purgatory in your way:—you have but justice.

SCANDAL

I hear the fiddles that Sir Sampson provided for his own wedding; methinks 'tis pity they should not be employed when the match is so much mended.—Valentine, though it be morning, we may have a dance.

VALENTINE

Anything, my friend, everything that looks like joy and transport.

SCANDAL

Call 'em, Jeremy.

[*Exit Jeremy.*

ANGELICA

I have done dissembling now, Valentine; and if that coldness which I have always worn before you, should turn to an extreme fondness, you must not suspect it.

VALENTINE

I'll prevent that suspicion:—for I intend to dote to that immoderate degree, that your fondness shall never distinguish itself enough to be taken notice of. If ever you seem to love too much, it must be only when I can't love enough.

ANGELICA

Have a care of promises; you know you are apt to run more in debt than you are able to pay.

VALENTINE

Therefore I yield my body as your prisoner, and make your best on't.

Re-enter Jeremy.

JEREMY

The music stays for you.

[*A dance.*

SCANDAL

Well, madam, you have done exemplary justice, in punishing an in-human father, and rewarding a faithful lover: but there is a third good work, which I, in particular, must thank you for; I was an in-fidel to your sex, and you have converted me.—For now I am convinced that all women are not like Fortune, blind in bestowing favours, either on those who do not merit, or who do not want 'em.

ANGELICA

'Tis an unreasonable accusation, that you lay upon our sex: you tax us with injustice, only to cover your own want of merit. You would all have the reward of love; but few have the constancy to stay till it becomes your due. Men are generally hypocrites and infidels, they pretend to worship, but have neither zeal nor faith: how few, like Valentine, would persevere even to martyrdom, and sacrifice their interest to their constancy! In admiring me you misplace the novelty:—

The miracle to-day is, that we find
A lover true: not that a woman's kind.

[*Exeunt omnes*

Action analysis and performance suggestions

Two scenes that demonstrate effectively the interrelationship of wit and action in *Love for Love* occur near the middle of the play. In both, as throughout the rest of the comedy, Angelica stands in control, mistress of the situation not by virtue of her beauty and wealth but by virtue of her quick-witted intelligence, the only true resource an otherwise powerless woman has in this society of men. Neither scene depends on the idiosyncrasies of the characters for its comic effect (as do the rehearsal scenes of *A Midsummer-Night's Dream* or the scenes involving Ben, Prue, Foresight, and Sir Sampson here) as much as on the witty conflict of characters with differing actions. The latter of the two scenes in the play—the portion of act IV, scene iii (pages 388–391) in which Angelica interviews Valentine (from the exit of Foresight, Mrs. Frail, Mrs. Foresight, and Tattle to the end of the act)—shows the various ways three characters try to hide their real emotions beneath a mask of wit.

Angelica masks her feelings with incredulity as Valentine, caught in his act of insanity, attempts to convince her of his affection. Ironically and comically, when the truth of his madness comes into question, Jeremy tries to convince Angelica that Valentine is mad—exactly what his master now wants him to deny. Angelica gets her revenge on Valentine for trying to trick an admission of love from her, and the comic conflict ends with her neat, epigrammatic, ambiguous exit lines (quoted as the epigraph to the introduction).

The first of the two scenes, act III, scene iii, to Scandal's exit (pages 355–359), which will be examined here at length, brings together Angelica, Valentine, Scandal, and Tattle and shows how deeply the comedy depends on witty dialogue.

DEFINING THE ACTIONS AND THE SUPEROBJECTIVE

As the scene opens, Valentine wishes to tax Angelica for her refusal to admit she loves him in order to encourage her to commit herself; on their entrance, he is pursuing her into the stage area. Angelica, always trying to assure herself that Valentine's love is not merely a desire for power masked by wit, hopes at first to avoid talk of love. Scandal, as Valentine's ally, tries to join Valentine in taxing Angelica. While Valentine continues pressing Angelica (in dumb show), we see a brief tête-à-tête between Tattle (who wants to join in the gossip) and Scandal. Scandal sees his chance to use Tattle to tax Angelica and cleverly maneuvers the fool into the conversation, and Tattle wants to show himself a lover, wit, and man of confidence. This action provides Angelica with an opportunity to expose the sterility of wit without love, a way to test Valentine's fine language by exposing the emptiness of Tattle's rhetoric, and by implication, the emptiness of Valentine's protestations. Although their conversation in the scene deals with the minute particulars of Tattle's sordid little affairs, its real subject is constancy in love. In one sense, nothing happens in the encounter. We already know that Tattle is incapable of keeping the secrets of his encounters, however capable he thinks he is in initiating them. We are well aware of Valentine's love for Angelica, and equally aware that she is not sure of his true affection. We have seen already how capable Scandal's satiric tongue is: His ability to turn the jest on another (as he does with Angelica when she challenges him to prove to Valentine that her behavior is merely the affectation of ill-nature) makes Tattle's foolishness more than clear. The central action of the whole scene, however, is one that ironically Scandal supports, Valentine unconsciously demonstrates, and Angelica plans—to expose the sterility of wit without love—and it is accomplished in large part by exposing not Valentine but Tattle. The reason for Angelica's demur to Valentine's repeated protestations lies in a question she does not articulate but which she surely asks herself: Is Valentine merely a Tattle in disguise, incapable of real love? She doubts because like all the play's characters she masks emotion with wit and participates in the superobjective of the comedy—to use wit to win the games of love and to teach Valentine to wager love for love.

OVERCOMING OBSTACLES

Since the actors seek to unmask another individual, the obstacles in the scene are largely internal. For example, one may consider Angelica's obstacle as her perception, or lack of perception, of Valentine's character: Does he love her? More specifically, she feels the need to expose his soul, so she is intent on the reactions of one for whom a little playlet of Tattle's stupidity is being staged. Valentine considers Angelica's character as his obstacle. Unsure of her love, and perhaps even at this point of slightly mixed motives himself (how much does his need for monetary security enter into his love of the wealthy Angelica?), he must strive to trick her by using his wit. To articulate the obstacles in a slightly different fashion, Angelica's wit is Valentine's superficial obstacle, Valentine's wit is Angelica's. Is the wit of the other a mask or a reality? For Scandal, the major obstacle is Angelica's wit as well, for he wants to help Valentine's cause, although we cannot be sure if Scandal understands love. For Tattle the obstacle is an internal one, which he never understands: his stupidity, foppishness, and desire to appear witty, clever, and experienced. He is not playing the game with a full deck of cards. He *thinks*, of course, that his obstacle is the neutral opinion of Angelica and of Scandal (who is twitting him).

THE MAGIC IF AND THE GIVEN CIRCUMSTANCES

What IF you were a member of a leisured society that frowned but slightly on male sexual freedoms, had no regular occupations beyond parties and visiting, and valued most highly matters of physical and intellectual appearance—fashion and wit? What IF you had led a highly libertine life, the first and foremost in intelligence, wit, fashion, and debauchery, but now had fallen in love with a beautiful, chaste, witty, and wealthy woman to whom you had no way to prove your love and sincere renunciation of your past, and who also had reason to suspect your motives because you were now poverty stricken?

What IF your best friend were in that situation?

What IF you were heiress to a large fortune and besieged with offers of marriage from men whose truthfulness you doubted? What IF you loved one of them—the best and the brightest, but a man of dubious morality who also needed money? What IF, too, divorce were impossible and a miserable existence similar to Mrs. Foresight's or Mrs. Frail's the probable outcome of most marriages in your society?

What IF, finally, you thought yourself to be an equal to all in this society, but perhaps felt in your heart that you were not paid the attention you deserved?

These are the general magic IFs of Valentine, Angelica, Scandal, and

Tattle throughout most of *Love for Love*. We should remember that this scene is Valentine's first interview with Angelica since he learned of his father's intent to disinherit him. Hence his anxiety to assure himself of her love and to tax her for not admitting she loves him must be mixed with his realization of a coming poverty from which there is no recourse.

CLASSROOM ADAPTATIONS TO ARRIVE AT STYLE

"I know no effectual difference between continued affectation and reality" (page 356), says Scandal. In adapting this scene for informal classroom representation, attention to the appearances as well as the realities of the characters provides clues to effective performances. Costuming in Congreve's time was not only lavish but also an indication of both social status and social expertise. An informal classroom adaptation might emphasize the artificial appearances of these characters with suggestive modern equivalents of fancy dress. Valentine and Scandal surely should wear suits or sportcoats. Tattle—the fop of the comedy—certainly should wear a suit, even a laced cuff, carry a long walking stick, snuff box, and handkerchief. Angelica should wear a long gown with wide skirts and perhaps a significant decolletage; she should also be tightly corseted and might do well to carry a fan. (If the student-actress portraying Angelica has long hair, it should be rolled up; both actors and actresses of this period wore wigs, and a woman who appeared with her hair hanging down was thought to have just appeared from her bed or to be insane.) The properties (and these costumes surely are props to social behavior) become valuable tools for punctuating the actions of the characters. Angelica may dismiss Valentine's protestations of love with a rapid folding of her fan, she may hide an imagined blush behind her open fan when Tattle impugns a lady's virtue, she may indeed rap Scandal's knuckles in vexation when he retorts with a witty remark. Tattle's cane might provide good striking evidence of his pride in bringing the virtue of a whole town of women into question; his snuff box might be a small depository of silent sneezing answers when he lacks a reply.

Seating for informal performance could be three-quarter round, though a quasi proscenium arrangement is just as effective. None of the actors is aware of the audience. It is important to remember the extent to which this scene, like much of the whole play, involves game playing, serious game playing with high stakes albeit, but game playing at love nonetheless. Valentine wants to chase Angelica on his own terms; Angelica wants the rules changed; Scandal plays by the rules for the sake of his friend; Tattle, although he doesn't know it, understands neither the rules of the game his brighter compeers play nor the real substance of the rules his society has made to hide the realities. Appearance, as Scandal says, may become reality if continued too long, and the affectations of these characters make their delightful course through the oldest comic story of all time—boy gets girl—dangerous and ludicrous, serious and harmless.

Henrik Ibsen
The Wild Duck

GREGERS

>Look, Father. The gentlemen are playing blind man's buff with Mrs.
>Soerby. Good night, and good-bye.
>
>>(page 429)

So observes Gregers Werle, as he melodramatically exits from a party
given in honor of his return home by his elderly father. What Gregers
thinks he has discovered in conversation with his childhood friend, Hjalmar Ekdal, whom he has insisted on having at the party, and then in conversation with his father, is an attempt on old Werle's part to use him
for the sake of appearances, just as he has used the Ekdal family for his
own purposes. Old Werle wants to marry his housekeeper, Mrs. Soerby,
and it would look very well to have the son hastening home "on the wings
of filial piety to attend his aging father's wedding feast," Gregers remarks
bitterly. He insists that they were never a family and that Werle's only desire is to put to rest talk of his previous wife's sufferings. He also accuses
his father of impure motives in helping the Ekdals. Perhaps old Ekdal was
not the only one guilty in the business scandal that sent him to jail but left
his partner, old Werle, free. More certainly Werle has contrived to marry
Hjalmar Ekdal to Gina Hansen, the housekeeper in the Werle home with
whom the old man has had an affair. Whether or not Hedvig, the child
Gina bore, is Werle's or Hjalmar's remains as ambiguous as Werle's guilt
in the business scandal, but Gregers, convinced that his father's motives
are evil, sets out to save Hjalmar and his family from the tissue of lies in
which he thinks they live.

The structure of *The Wild Duck* is not unlike that of *Oedipus the King*.
As in the Greek play, revelations of the past are used to bring the present
to its moment of crisis. Also like the earlier play, many of the ironies of
the action revolve around images of vision and blindness, lightness and
darkness, and ways of seeing. Indeed, the game of blind man's buff played
by Mrs. Soerby and the hangers-on who enjoy old Werle's hospitality becomes a significant poetic image for the entire drama. But here the high
tragic search of Oedipus for his city and himself has become a game of
hide-and-seek played out in the narrow, middle-class landscape of the
modern parlor. Unwilling to recognize his own father as the old man
passes through a scene of gaiety on his way out with some copy work,
Hjalmar is hardly of the heroic stature to recognize the truth about himself or the human condition. And Gregers, who storms from his father's
presence with his new mission at the outset of the play, remains blind at
the end to the harm he has caused. Gregers and Hjalmar become the
somewhat ridiculous antiheroes of modern drama and the child Hedvig
becomes the victim of their melodramatic actions.

409

As the acknowledged father of modern drama, Henrik Ibsen (1828–1906) was concerned throughout his writing career with the struggle of the individual for self-realization in a middle-class society. While his plays may roughly be classified as romantic (1850–1873), realistic (1877–1890), and symbolistic (1890–1899), he was always concerned with the tensions of a human being as a member of society and he remained, even in his prose plays, a poet of the inherent contradictions of modern social life.

Ibsen's early plays, mostly written in poetry when he was stage manager and playwright for the Norwegian theaters in Bergen (1851–1857) and Christiana (1857–1862), dwelled on Norwegian history, legend, fairy tales, and sagas and expressed something of the emerging sense of nationalism that his native Norway was experiencing. The most famous of these, *Peer Gynt* (1867), deals with a romantic quest but has a modern skeptical tone. Following the troll maxim, "to thyself be enough," Peer comes to find no self at the center of the peeled onion that becomes his image, and the romantic "round about" path must give way to the narrow path that is "straight ahead."

However, Ibsen's major influence on modern drama stems from his middle or realistic period, from such plays as *A Doll's House* (1879), *Ghosts* (1881), *An Enemy of the People* (1882), *The Wild Duck* (1884), and *Hedda Gabler* (1890). Here the playwright moved away from the romantic epic to focus on society and domestic life. Although he still employed many of the techniques of the contemporary popular French playwright, Eugene Scribe, whose well-made plays employed exciting plot devices, character types, poetic justice, and happy endings, he turned from verse to prose and from the two-dimensional illusionistic staging inherited from the eighteenth century to a box set with an imaginary fourth wall. His aim in using prose was to create the illusion of reality. Human beings should no longer use the language of the gods and the viewer should be led to believe that the events of the drama really happened. The box setting, with its three continuous walls and a ceiling, its practical doors and windows, and its real rather than painted furniture and properties, was employed to augment this illusion of reality. Gas and then electric lighting, with their greater potential for control than oil lamps, allowed Ibsen to use lighting both realistically and symbolically (witness the explicit stage directions about lighting at the beginning of each act of *The Wild Duck*).

Spectacle, then, which Aristotle considered the least important of the elements that imitate an action, takes on special importance in Ibsen's method of imitation. The romantics had broken ground for the realists not only in subject matter with their interest in the rights of the individual but also in scene design with their interest in authentic detail and mood. That Ibsen's settings were no longer mere background but a living environment where the characters interacted is partly a reflection of late nineteenth-century thinking in which people were considered to be largely a product of their heredity and environment.

And so the audience, now largely middle-class, came to a theater where the gulf between the actor and themselves was complete. The actors retired behind the proscenium, which became a frame they pierced with neither soliloquy nor aside. The auditorium was darkened and the lights were on the picture of reality before the audience, helping to give it shadow, depth, and dimension.

Still, Ibsen's drama proved to be far from a drama of photographic illusion. Although his later plays, such as *The Master Builder* (1892) or *When We Dead Awaken* (1899), are considered to be more symbolic and mysterious than his earlier dramas, Ibsen's artistic vision had never aimed at a mere copying of the surface reality of life and he employed symbolism throughout his works. *The Wild Duck* (1884), which straddles his more realist and symbolist periods, illustrates very well the nature of Ibsen's realism.

The setting of Hjalmar Ekdal's photographic studio with its attic loft housing old Christmas trees, rabbits, pigeons, and a wounded wild duck gives ample room for Ibsen to develop both the daily life of the Ekdal family and their inner lives as well. The wild duck belongs to Hedvig, but she lends it to her grandfather, who relives his old hunting days before the scandal hunting rabbits in the confines of the duck's loft. She also lends it to her father who uses it to escape from the photographic retouching work, which he feels is beneath his talents. For Hedvig, the girl whose daily life consists of loving submission to her father's childish egotism, the wild duck becomes an embodiment of romance, reminiscent of the sea depths from which it had been retrieved in its wounded state.

Ibsen uses the image of photography itself to suggest much of the sham superficiality and false illusion in which the Ekdals live. From the time Hjalmar touches up the story of his evening out at the Werle's to the later self-pitying image he presents when he comes home to collect his things, we come to see him as one who touches up life's pictures to suit himself. Such touching up would be merely comic, and often is so in the play, if it were not for the tragic consequences to Hedvig when Hjalmar refuses to look at the child after he rejects her. Gregers' picture of reality is equally blurred since his "claim of the ideal" is as full of false illusions as the life he would save Hjalmar from.

At a time when industry and science were making rapid and revolutionary advances, it is a tribute to Ibsen as a dramatic poet that he turned his eye with new candor on the reality of everyday existence but made no claim either to achieving total objectivity or finding solutions to problems. Ibsen did not, as some critics have claimed, either attempt to solve the problems of life or present a thesis on those problems. Gregers is satirized for just such an attempt. Ibsen saw himself as less a social philosopher than a poet and freely acknowledged his spiritual involvement with his material. The inscription he wrote in one of his books best defines that involvement:

Living is a war with the trolls
    In the depths of the mind and heart;
Writing means summoning oneself
    To court and playing the judge's part.

The Wild Duck

Translated by Michael Meyer

Characters

HAAKON WERLE, *a wholesale merchant*
GREGERS WERLE, *his son*
OLD EKDAL
HJALMAR EKDAL, *his son, a photographer*
GINA EKDAL, *Hjalmar's wife*
HEDVIG, *their daughter, aged 14*
MRS. SOERBY, *housekeeper to Haakon Werle*
RELLING, *a doctor*
MOLVIK, *sometime student of theology*
GRAABERG, *a clerk*
PETTERSEN, *servant to Haakon Werle*
JENSEN, *a hired waiter*
A PALE, FLABBY GENTLEMAN
A BALDING GENTLEMAN
A SHORT-SIGHTED GENTLEMAN
SIX OTHER GENTLEMEN, *dinner guests of Haakon Werle*
SEVERAL HIRED WAITERS

> *The first act takes place in Haakon Werle's house, the remaining acts in Hjalmar Ekdal's studio.*

Act one

> *The home of Haakon Werle, a wholesale merchant. A study, expensively and comfortably furnished; bookcases, upholstered furniture. A desk, with papers and ledgers on it, stands in the middle of the room. Lighted lamps with green shades throw a soft light. In the rear wall folding doors stand open; the curtains across the entrance are drawn aside, and within can be seen a large and elegant room, brilliantly lit by lamps and candelabra. Downstage right in the study a small concealed door leads to the offices. Downstage left, a fireplace with coals glowing in it. Upstage of this a double door leads to the dining room. Werle's servant, Pettersen, in livery, and a hired waiter, Jensen, in black, are arranging the study. In the larger room two or three other hired waiters are moving around putting things in order and lighting more lamps. From the dining room can be heard the buzz of conversation and laughter. Someone taps a knife against a glass; silence; a toast is proposed; cries of "Bravo!"; then the buzz of conversation begins again.*

PETTERSEN (*Lights a lamp on the mantelpiece above the fireplace, and puts a shade over it.*)

You hear that, Jensen? Now the old man's at it, proposing a toast to Mrs. Soerby.

JENSEN (*Moves a chair forward.*)

Is it true what they say, that there's something between them?

PETTERSEN

I wouldn't know.

JENSEN

> They say he's been a regular old billy goat in his time.

PETTERSEN

> Could be.

JENSEN

> Did you say he's giving this party for his son?

PETTERSEN

> Yes. He came home yesterday.

JENSEN

> I never knew old Werle had a son.

PETTERSEN

> Oh yes, he's got a son. The boy spends all his time up at the sawmill, though, out at Hoydal. He's never set foot in town all the years I've worked in this house.

A HIRED WAITER (*In the doorway to the large room.*)

> Pettersen, there's an old fellow here who wants to—

PETTERSEN (*Beneath his breath.*)

> What the devil—oh, not now!
>
>> *Old Ekdal enters from the large room, right. He is wearing a thread-bare coat with a high collar, and woollen gloves, and carries a stick and a fur hat in his hand and a brown paper parcel under his arm. He has a dirty, reddish-brown wig and small grey moustaches. Goes towards him.*
>
> Oh, Jesus! What do *you* want here?

EKDAL (*In the doorway.*)

> Got to get into the office, Pettersen. It's very important.

PETTERSEN

> The office has been shut for an hour—

EKDAL

> They told me that downstairs, my boy. But Graaberg's still in there. Be a good lad, Pettersen, and let me nip in this way.
>
>> *Points at the concealed door.*
>
> I've been this way before.

PETTERSEN

> Oh, all right.
>
>> *Opens the door.*
>
> But make sure you leave by the proper way. We've got company.

EKDAL

> Yes, I know that—hm! Thanks, Pettersen, my boy. You're a good pal.
>
>> *Mutters quietly.*
>
> Damn fool!
>
>> *Goes into the office. Pettersen shuts the door after him.*

JENSEN

> Does he work in the office, too?

PETTERSEN

> No, he just takes stuff home to copy, when they've more than they can manage. Mind you, he's been quite a gentleman in his time, has old Ekdal.

JENSEN

> Yes, he looked as if he might have been around a bit.

PETTERSEN

> Oh, yes. He was a lieutenant.

JENSEN
> What—him a lieutenant?

PETTERSEN
> That's right. But then he went into timber or something of that sort. They say he did the dirty on old Werle once. The two of them used to work together at Hoydal. Oh, I know old Ekdal well. We often have a nip and a bottle of beer together down at Madame Eriksen's.

JENSEN
> But he can't have much to spend, surely?

PETTERSEN
> I'm the one who does the spending. The way I look at it is, it's only right to lend a helping hand to gentry who've come down in the world.

JENSEN
> What, did he go bankrupt?

PETTERSEN
> Worse. He went to prison.

JENSEN
> Went to prison!

PETTERSEN
> Ssh, they're getting up now.
> *The doors to the dining room are thrown open from inside by waiters. Mrs. Soerby comes out, engaged in conversation by two gentlemen. A few moments later, the rest of the company follow, Haakon Werle among them. Last come Hjalmar Ekdal and Gregers Werle.*

MRS. SOERBY (*As she goes through.*)
> Pettersen, have the coffee served in the music room.

PETTERSEN
> Very good, Mrs. Soerby.
> *She and the two gentlemen go into the large room and out towards the right. Pettersen and Jensen follow them.*

A PALE, FLABBY GENTLEMAN (*To one with little hair.*)
> Whew—that dinner! Pretty exhausting work, eh?

BALDING GENTLEMAN
> Ah, it's remarkable what one can get through in three hours, when one puts one's mind to it.

FLABBY GENTLEMAN
> Yes, but afterwards, my dear sir! Afterwards!

A THIRD GENTLEMAN
> I hear the—er—mocha and maraschino are to be served in the music room.

FLABBY GENTLEMAN
> Capital! Then perhaps Mrs. Soerby will play something for us.

BALDING GENTLEMAN (*Sotto voce.*)
> Let's hope it isn't a marching song!

FLABBY GENTLEMAN
> No fear of that. Berta won't give her old friends the shoulder.
> *They laugh and pass into the large room.*

WERLE (*Quietly, unhappily.*)
> I don't think anyone noticed, Gregers.

GREGERS (*Looks at him.*)
> What?

WERLE

Didn't you notice, either?

GREGERS

Notice what?

WERLE

We were thirteen at table.

GREGERS

Thirteen? Oh, really?

WERLE (*Glances at Hjalmar Ekdal.*)

We're usually twelve.

To the others.

Gentlemen—please!

He and the rest, except for Hjalmar and Gregers, go out upstage right.

HJALMAR (*Who has overheard their conversation.*)

You shouldn't have invited me, Gregers.

GREGERS

What! But this dinner is said to be in my honour. So why shouldn't I invite my one and only friend?

HJALMAR

I don't think your father approves. I mean, I never get invited to this house.

GREGERS

No, so I've heard. But I had to see you and speak with you; I'm not staying very long, you know. Yes, we've lost touch with each other since we were at school, Hjalmar. We haven't seen each other for— why, it must be sixteen or seventeen years.

HJALMAR

Is it as long as that?

GREGERS

I'm afraid so. Well, how is everything with you? You look well. You've filled out a bit; you're quite stout now.

HJALMAR

Oh—I wouldn't say stout. I dare say I'm a bit broader across the shoulders than I used to be. After all, I'm a man now.

GREGERS

Oh, yes. You're as handsome as ever.

HJALMAR (*Sadly.*)

But within, Gregers! There has been a change there. You must know how disastrously my world has crashed about me—and my family—since we last met.

GREGERS (*More quietly.*)

How is your father now?

HJALMAR

My dear friend, let us not talk about it. My poor unfortunate father lives with me, of course. He has no one else in the world to lean on. But all this is so distressing for me to talk about. Tell me now, how have things been for you up at the sawmill?

GREGERS

Oh, I've been wonderfully lonely. I've had plenty of time to brood over things. Come, let's make ourselves comfortable.

He sits in an armchair by the fire and motions Hjalmar into another beside him.

HJALMAR (*Softly.*)

Thank you all the same, Gregers. I'm grateful to you for inviting me to your father's house. I know now that you no longer have anything against me.

GREGERS (*Amazed.*)

What makes you think I have anything against you?

HJALMAR

You did at first.

GREGERS

At first?

HJALMAR

After the great disaster. Oh, it was only natural that you should. It was only by a hairsbreadth that your father himself escaped being dragged into all this—this dreadful business.

GREGERS

And I should hold that against you? Who gave you this idea?

HJALMAR

I know—I know you did, Gregers. Your father himself told me so.

GREGERS

Father! I see. Hm. Was that why you never wrote me a line?

HJALMAR

Yes.

GREGERS

Not even when you went and became a photographer?

HJALMAR

Your father said there would be no purpose in my writing to you about anything whatever.

GREGERS (*Thoughtfully.*)

No, no; perhaps he was right. But, tell me, Hjalmar—are you quite satisfied the way things are now?

HJALMAR (*With a little sigh.*)

Oh yes, indeed I am. I can't complain. At first, you know, I found it a little strange. It was such a different way of life from what I'd been used to. But everything had changed. The great disaster that ruined my father—the disgrace and the shame, Gregers—

GREGERS (*Upset.*)

Yes, yes, of course, yes.

HJALMAR

Naturally, I had to give up any idea of continuing with my studies. We hadn't a shilling to spare—quite the reverse in fact. Debts. Mostly to your father, I believe—

GREGERS

Hm—

HJALMAR

Well, so I thought it'd be best, you see, to make a clean break. Cut myself off from everything that had to do with my old way of life. In fact, it was your father who advised me to do it—and as he was being so very helpful to me—

GREGERS

Father?

HJALMAR

Yes, surely you must know? How else could I have found the money to learn photography and equip a studio and set myself up? That costs a lot of money, you know.

GREGERS

And Father paid for all this?

HJALMAR

Yes, my dear fellow, didn't you know? I understood him to say he'd written to you.

GREGERS

He never said he was behind it. He must have forgotten. We never write to each other except on business. So it was Father—

HJALMAR

Why, yes. He's never wanted people to know about it; but it was he. And of course it was he who made it possible for me to get married. But—perhaps you don't know that either?

GREGERS

I had no idea.

> *Shakes him by the arm.*

But, my dear Hjalmar, I can't tell you how happy I feel—and guilty. Perhaps I've been unjust to Father after all—in some respects. This proves that he has a heart, you see. A kind of conscience—

HJALMAR

Conscience?

GREGERS

Yes, or whatever you like to call it. No, I can't tell you how happy I am to hear this about Father. Well, and you're married, Hjalmar! That's more than I shall ever dare to do. Well, I trust you've found happiness in marriage.

HJALMAR

Oh, indeed I have. She's as capable and good a wife as any man could wish for. And she's not by any means uncultured.

GREGERS (*A little surprised.*)

I'm sure she isn't.

HJALMAR

Yes. Life is a great teacher. Being with me every day—and we have a couple of very gifted friends who visit us daily. I can assure you, you wouldn't recognise Gina.

GREGERS

Gina?

HJALMAR

Yes, my dear fellow, don't you remember? Her name's Gina.

GREGERS

Whose name is Gina? I have no idea what you're—

HJALMAR

But don't you remember? She used to work here once.

GREGERS (*Looks at him.*)

You mean Gina Hansen?

HJALMAR

Of course I mean Gina Hansen.

GREGERS

Who kept house for us when my mother was ill? The year before she died?

HJALMAR

Yes, that's right. But, my dear fellow, I'm absolutely certain your father wrote and told you I'd got married.

GREGERS (*Has got up.*)

Yes, he told me that. But what he didn't tell me was that—

Begins to pace up and down.

Ah, but wait a minute. Perhaps he did after all, now I think about it. But Father always writes such brief letters.

Half sits on the arm of his chair.

Look, tell me now, Hjalmar—this is very funny—how did you come to meet Gina—I mean, your wife?

HJALMAR

Oh, it was quite straightforward. As you know, Gina didn't stay long with your father—everything was so upside down at that time—your mother's illness—it was all too much for Gina, so she gave notice and left. It was the year before your mother died. Or was it the same year?

GREGERS

The same year. And I was up at the sawmill. But then what happened?

HJALMAR

Yes, well, then Gina went home to live with her mother, a Mrs. Hansen, a very excellent hard-working woman who ran a little café. Well, she had a room to let; a very nice, comfortable room.

GREGERS

And you were lucky enough to find out about it?

HJALMAR

Yes—in fact, it was your father who suggested it. And it was there, you see, that I really got to know Gina.

GREGERS

And the engagement followed?

HJALMAR

Yes. Well, you know how quickly young people become fond of each other—hm—

GREGERS (*Gets up and walks up and down for a little.*)

Tell me—when you were engaged—was that when Father got you to—I mean, was that when you began to take up photography?

HJALMAR

Yes, that's right. I was very keen to get married as soon as possible. And your father and I both came to the conclusion that photography would be the most convenient profession for me to take up. And Gina thought so too. Oh, and there was another thing. By a lucky chance, Gina had learned how to retouch photographs.

GREGERS

What a fortunate coincidence.

HJALMAR (*Pleased, gets up.*)

Yes, wasn't it? Amazingly lucky, don't you think?

GREGERS

I certainly do. Father seems almost to have been a kind of fairy godfather to you.

HJALMAR (*Emotionally.*)

He did not forget his old friend's son in his time of need. He's got a heart, you see, Gregers.

MRS. SOERBY (*Enters with Haakon Werle on her arm.*)
>Not another word, now, Mr. Werle. You mustn't walk around any longer in there with all those bright lights. It's not good for you.

WERLE (*Lets go of her arm and passes his hand over his eyes.*)
>Yes, I think you may be right.
>>*Pettersen and Jensen enter with trays.*

MRS. SOERBY (*To the guests in the other room.*)
>Gentlemen, please! If anyone wants a glass of punch, he must come in here.

FLABBY GENTLEMAN (*Comes over to Mrs. Soerby.*)
>Dammit, madame, is it true that you have deprived us of our sacred privilege, the cigar?

MRS. SOERBY
>Yes. This is Mr. Werle's sanctum, sir, and here there is no smoking.

BALDING GENTLEMAN
>When did you introduce this austere edict, Mrs. Soerby?

MRS. SOERBY
>After our last dinner, sir; when certain persons permitted themselves to overstep the mark.

BALDING GENTLEMAN
>And it is not permitted to overstep the mark a little, Madame Berta? Not even an inch or two?

MRS. SOERBY
>No. Not in any direction, my dear Chamberlain.
>>*Most of the guests have come into the study. The servants hand round glasses of punch.*

WERLE (*To Hjalmar, who is standing apart, by a table.*)
>What's that you're looking at, Ekdal?

HJALMAR
>It's only an album, sir.

BALDING GENTLEMAN (*Who is wandering around.*)
>Ah, photographs! Yes, that's rather down your street, isn't it?

FLABBY GENTLEMAN (*In an armchair.*)
>Haven't you brought any of your own with you?

HJALMAR
>No, I haven't.

FLABBY GENTLEMAN
>You should have. It's so good for the digestion to sit and look at pictures.

BALDING GENTLEMAN
>Adds to the fun. We've each got to contribute our mite, haven't we?

A SHORT-SIGHTED GENTLEMAN
>All contributions will be gratefully received.

MRS. SOERBY
>I think the gentlemen mean that if one is invited out one should work for one's dinner, Mr. Ekdal.

FLABBY GENTLEMAN
>Where the table is so exquisite, that duty becomes a pleasure.

BALDING GENTLEMAN
>Yes, by God! Particularly when it's a question of fighting for survival—

MRS. SOERBY
>*Touché!*

They continue amid joking and laughter.

GREGERS (*Quietly.*)

You must join in, Hjalmar.

HJALMAR (*Twists uncomfortably.*)

What should I talk about?

FLABBY GENTLEMAN

Wouldn't you agree, Mr. Werle, that Tokay may be regarded as a comparatively safe drink for the stomach?

WERLE (*By the fireplace.*)

I'd guarantee the Tokay you drank tonight, anyway. It's an exceptional year, quite exceptional. But of course you would have noticed that.

FLABBY GENTLEMAN

Yes, it had a remarkably *soigné* bouquet.

HJALMAR (*Uncertainly.*)

Is there some difference between the various years?

FLABBY GENTLEMAN (*Laughs.*)

I say, that's good!

WERLE (*Smiles.*)

It's a waste to offer you good wine.

BALDING GENTLEMAN

Tokay's like photography, Mr. Ekdal. It needs sunshine. Isn't that right?

HJALMAR

Oh yes, light is important, of course.

MRS. SOERBY

But that's like you, gentlemen. You're drawn towards the sun, too.

BALDING GENTLEMAN

For shame! That's not worthy of you.

SHORT-SIGHTED GENTLEMAN

Mrs. Soerby is displaying her wit.

FLABBY GENTLEMAN

At our expense.

>   *Threateningly.*

Oh, madame, madame!

MRS. SOERBY

But it's perfectly true. Vintages do differ greatly. The oldest are the best.

SHORT-SIGHTED GENTLEMAN

Do you count me among the old ones?

MRS. SOERBY

By no means.

BALDING GENTLEMAN

Indeed? And what about me, dear Mrs. Soerby?

FLABBY GENTLEMAN

Yes, and me. What vintage are we?

MRS. SOERBY

A sweet vintage, gentlemen!

>   *She sips a glass of punch. The gentlemen laugh and flirt with her.*

WERLE

Mrs. Soerby always finds a way out—when she wants to. Fill your glasses, gentlemen! Pettersen, look after them. Gregers, let us take a glass together.

Gregers does not move.

Won't you join us, Ekdal? I didn't get a chance to drink with you at dinner.

Graaberg, the bookkeeper, looks in through the concealed door.

GRAABERG (*To Haakon Werle.*)

Excuse me, sir, but I can't get out.

WERLE

What, have you got locked in again?

GRAABERG

Yes. Flakstad's gone off with the keys.

WERLE

Well, you'd better come through here, then.

GRAABERG

But there's someone else—

WERLE

Well, let him come, too. Don't be frightened.

Graaberg and old Ekdal come out of the office.
Involuntarily.

Oh, God!

The laughter and chatter of the guests dies away. Hjalmar shrinks at the sight of his father, puts down his glass and turns away towards the fireplace.

EKDAL (*Does not look up, but makes little bows to either side as he walks, mumbling.*)

Beg pardon. Come the wrong way. Door locked. Beg pardon.

He and Graaberg go out upstage right.

WERLE (*Between his teeth.*)

Damn that Graaberg!

GREGERS (*Stares open-mouthed at Hjalmar.*)

Surely that wasn't—?

FLABBY GENTLEMAN

What's all this? Who was that?

GREGERS

Oh, no one. Just the bookkeeper and someone else.

SHORT-SIGHTED GENTLEMAN (*To Hjalmar.*)

Did you know that man?

HJALMAR

I don't know—I didn't notice—

FLABBY GENTLEMAN (*Gets up.*)

What the devil's going on?

He goes over to some of the others, who are talking quietly amongst themselves.

MRS. SOERBY (*Whispers to Pettersen.*)

Take something out to him. Something really nice.

PETTERSEN (*Nods.*)

Very good, ma'am.

Goes out.

GREGERS (*Quietly, emotionally, to Hjalmar.*)

Then it *was* he!

HJALMAR

Yes.

GREGERS

And you stood here and denied him!

HJALMAR (*Whispers violently.*)

    What could I do?

GREGERS

    You denied your own father?

HJALMAR (*In pain.*)

    Oh—if you were in my place, you'd—

        The talk among the guests, which has been carried on in a low tone,
        now switches over to a forced loudness.

BALDING GENTLEMAN (*Goes amiably over to Hjalmar and Gregers.*)

    Hullo, reviving old college memories, what? Don't you smoke, Mr.
Ekdal? Want a light? Oh, I'd forgotten—we mustn't—

HJALMAR

    Thank you, I won't.

FLABBY GENTLEMAN

    Haven't you some nice little poem you could recite to us, Mr. Ekdal?
You used to recite so beautifully.

HJALMAR

    I'm afraid I can't remember one.

FLABBY GENTLEMAN

    Pity. What else can we find to amuse ourselves with, Balle?

        The two gentlemen walk into the next room.

HJALMAR (*Unhappily.*)

    Gregers, I want to go. You know, when a man has been as buffeted
and tossed by the winds of Fate as I have— Say good-bye to your father for me.

GREGERS

    I will. Are you going straight home?

HJALMAR

    Yes.

GREGERS

    In that case I may drop in on you later.

HJALMAR

    No, don't do that. You mustn't come to my home. It's a miserable
place, Gregers; especially after a brilliant gathering like this. We can
always meet somewhere in town.

MRS. SOERBY (*Has come over to them, and says quietly.*)

    Are you leaving, Ekdal?

HJALMAR

    Yes.

MRS. SOERBY

    Give my regards to Gina.

HJALMAR

    Thank you.

MRS. SOERBY

    Tell her I'm coming out to see her one of these days.

HJALMAR

    I will. Thank you.

        To Gregers.

    Stay here. I don't want anyone to see me go.

        Saunters into the other room and out to the right.

MRS. SOERBY (*To Pettersen, who has returned.*)

    Well, did you give the old man something?

PETTERSEN
Yes, I put a bottle of brandy into his pocket.

MRS. SOERBY
Oh, you might have found him something nicer than that.

PETTERSEN
Why no, Mrs. Soerby. Brandy's what he likes best.

FLABBY GENTLEMAN (*In the doorway, with a sheet of music in his hand.*)
Shall we play a duet together, Mrs. Soerby?

MRS. SOERBY
Yes, with pleasure.

GUESTS
Bravo, bravo!
> *She and all the guests go out to the right. Gregers remains standing by the fireplace. Haakon Werle starts looking for something on his desk, and seems to wish that Gregers would go. Seeing that Gregers does not move, he goes towards the door.*

GREGERS
Father, would you mind waiting a moment?

WERLE (*Stops.*)
What is it?

GREGERS
I've got to speak with you.

WERLE
Can't it wait till we're alone together?

GREGERS
No, it can't. We may never be alone together.

WERLE (*Comes closer.*)
What does that mean?
> *During the following scene, piano music can be heard distantly from the music room.*

GREGERS
How has that family been allowed to sink into this pitiable condition?

WERLE
You mean the Ekdals, I presume?

GREGERS
Yes, I mean the Ekdals. Lieutenant Ekdal and you used to be such close friends.

WERLE
Unfortunately, yes. Too close. All these years I've had to pay for it. It's him I have to thank for the stain I have suffered on my name and reputation.

GREGERS (*Quietly.*)
Was he really the only one who was guilty?

WERLE
Who else?

GREGERS
You and he bought those forests together.

WERLE
But it was Ekdal who drew up that misleading map. It was he who had all that timber felled illegally on government property. He was in charge of everything up there. I was absolutely in the dark as to what Lieutenant Ekdal was doing.

GREGERS

Lieutenant Ekdal seems to have been pretty much in the dark himself.

WERLE

Quite possibly. But the fact remains that he was found guilty and I was acquitted.

GREGERS

Oh yes, I know nothing was proved against you.

WERLE

An acquittal means not guilty. Why do you rake up these old troubles, which turned me grey before my time? Is that what you've been brooding about all these years up there? I can assure you, Gregers, in this town the whole business has been forgotten long ago, as far as my reputation is concerned.

GREGERS

But what about those wretched Ekdals?

WERLE

What would you have had me do for them? When Ekdal was released he was a broken man, past help. There are some people in this world who sink to the bottom the moment they get a couple of pellets in their body, and never rise to the surface again. Upon my honour, Gregers, I did everything I could short of exposing myself to gossip and suspicion—

GREGERS

Suspicion? Oh, I see.

WERLE

I've arranged for Ekdal to do copying for the office, and I pay him a great deal more than the work's worth—

GREGERS (*Without looking at him.*)

I don't doubt it.

WERLE

You laugh? You don't think it's true? Oh, you won't find anything about it in the books. I don't keep account of that kind of payment.

GREGERS (*Smiles coldly.*)

No, there are certain payments of which it's best to keep no account.

WERLE

What do you mean by that?

GREGERS (*Screwing up his courage.*)

Have you any account of what it cost you to have Hjalmar Ekdal taught photography?

WERLE

Why should I have any account of that?

GREGERS

I know now that it was you who paid for it. And I also know that it was you who so generously enabled him to set himself up.

WERLE

And still you say I've done nothing for the Ekdals? I can assure you, that family's cost me a pretty penny.

GREGERS

Have you accounted any of those pennies in your books?

WERLE

Why do you ask that?

GREGERS

Oh, I have my reasons. Tell me—when you began to take such a warm interest in your old friend's son—wasn't that just about the time he was about to get married?

WERLE

Yes, how the devil—how do you expect me to remember after all these years—?

GREGERS

You wrote me a letter at the time—a business letter, of course—and in a postscript you said—quite briefly—that Hjalmar Ekdal had married a Miss Hansen.

WERLE

Yes, so he did. That was her name.

GREGERS

But what you didn't say was that this Miss Hansen was Gina Hansen—our former maid.

WERLE (*Laughs scornfully, but with an effort.*)

No. It didn't occur to me that you were particularly interested in our former maid.

GREGERS

I wasn't. But—

Lowers his voice.

—there was someone else in this house who was interested in her.

WERLE

What do you mean?

Angrily.

You're not referring to me?

GREGERS (*Quietly but firmly.*)

Yes, I am referring to you.

WERLE

You dare to—you have the impertinence—! That ungrateful—that photographer—how dare he make such insinuations!

GREGERS

Hjalmar has never said a word about this. I don't think he suspects anything.

WERLE

Where do you get it from, then? Who has said such a thing to you?

GREGERS

My unhappy mother told me. The last time I saw her.

WERLE

Your mother! I might have known it. She and you always clung together. She turned you against me from the first.

GREGERS

No. It was all the suffering and humiliation she had to endure before she finally succumbed and came to such a pitiful end.

WERLE

Oh, she didn't have to suffer. Not more than most people, anyway. But one can't do anything with people who are oversensitive and romantic. I've learned that much. And you nurse these suspicions and go around rooting up all kinds of old rumors and slanders about your own father! At your age, Gregers, it's time you found something more useful to do.

GREGERS
Yes, it's about time.

WERLE
It might enable you to be a little more at peace with yourself than you seem to be now. What good can it do for you to stay up at the sawmill, year after year, drudging away like a common clerk and refusing to accept a penny more than the standard wage? It's absolutely idiotic.

GREGERS
I wish I was sure of that.

WERLE
I understand how you feel. You want to be independent, you don't want to be in my debt. But now there is an opportunity for you to become independent, and be your own master in everything.

GREGERS
Oh? How?

WERLE
When I wrote and told you it was necessary for you to travel here at once—hm—

GREGERS
Yes, what do you want me for? I've been waiting all day to find out.

WERLE
I want to suggest that you become a partner in the firm.

GREGERS
I? Your partner?

WERLE
Yes. It wouldn't mean we'd have to be together all the time. You could take over the business here, and I'd move up to the mill.

GREGERS
You?

WERLE
Yes. You see, I'm not able to work as hard as I used to. I've got to take care of my eyes, Gregers. They've begun to grow a little weak.

GREGERS
They always were.

WERLE
Not like now. Besides—circumstances might make it desirable for me to live up there. For a while, anyway.

GREGERS
I hadn't imagined anything like this.

WERLE
Listen, Gregers. I know there are so many things that stand between us. But we're father and son. It seems to me we must be able to come to an understanding.

GREGERS
You mean, we must appear to come to an understanding?

WERLE
Well, that is something. Think it over, Gregers. Don't you think it might be possible? Well?

GREGERS (*Looks at him coldly.*)
What's behind all this?

WERLE
How do you mean?

GREGERS
You want to use me, don't you?

WERLE
In a relationship as close as ours, one can always be useful to the other.

GREGERS
That's what they say.

WERLE
I should like to have you living at home with me for a while. I'm a lonely man, Gregers. I've always felt lonely, all my life, but especially now that I'm growing old. I need to have someone near me—

GREGERS
You've got Mrs. Soerby.

WERLE
Yes, I have her. And she's become—well, almost indispensable to me. She's witty and good-humoured; she brightens the house for me. I need that—badly.

GREGERS
Well, then you have things the way you want them.

WERLE
Yes, but I'm afraid it can't continue like this. A woman in her situation may easily find herself compromised in the eyes of the world. Yes; and I dare say it's not very good for a man's reputation, either.

GREGERS
Oh, when a man gives dinners like this, he needn't worry about what people think.

WERLE
Yes, but what about her, Gregers? I'm afraid she won't want to put up with this for much longer. And even if she did—even if, for my sake, she were to set herself above the gossip and the slander—Don't you think then, Gregers—you with your stern sense of right and wrong—that—?

GREGERS (*Interrupts.*)
Answer me one thing. Are you thinking of marrying her?

WERLE
Suppose I were? Would you be so insuperably opposed to that?

GREGERS
Not in the least.

WERLE
I didn't know if perhaps—out of respect to your late mother's memory—

GREGERS
I'm not a romantic.

WERLE
Well, whatever you are, you've taken a great weight from my mind. I'm delighted that I may count on your agreement to the action I propose to take.

GREGERS (*Looks at him.*)
Now I see what you want to use me for.

WERLE
Use you? What kind of talk is that?

GREGERS
Oh, let's not be squeamish. Not when we're alone together.

> *Gives a short laugh.*

I see. So that's why, at all costs, I had to come along and show myself here. So as to have a nice family reunion in Mrs. Soerby's honour. Father and son—*tableau!* That's something new, isn't it?

WERLE

How dare you take that tone?

GREGERS

When has there been any family life here? Not for as long as I can remember. But now of course there's got to be a little. It'll look splendid if people can say that the son of the family has flown home on the wings of filial piety to attend his ageing father's wedding feast. What'll become then of all those dreadful rumours about the wrongs his poor dead mother had to put up with? They will vanish. Her son will dissipate them into thin air.

WERLE

Gregers—I believe there's no one in the world you hate as much as you do me.

GREGERS (*Quietly.*)

I've seen you at close quarters.

WERLE

You have seen me with your mother's eyes.

> *Lowers his voice a little.*

But you should remember that her vision was sometimes a little—blurred.

GREGERS (*Trembling.*)

I know what you're trying to say. But who was to blame for that? You were! You and all those—! And the last of them you palmed off on to Hjalmar Ekdal, when you no longer—oh!

WERLE (*Shrugs his shoulders.*)

Word for word as though I were listening to your mother.

GREGERS (*Not heeding him.*)

And there he sits, childlike and trusting, caught in this web of deceit—sharing his roof with a woman like that, never suspecting that what he calls his home is built upon a lie!

> *Comes a step closer.*

When I look back on your career, I see a battlefield strewn with shattered lives.

WERLE

It seems the gulf between us is too wide.

GREGERS (*Bows coldly.*)

I agree. Therefore I take my hat and go.

WERLE

Go? Leave the house?

GREGERS

Yes. Because now at last I see my vocation.

WERLE

And what is that vocation?

GREGERS

You'd only laugh if I told you.

WERLE

A lonely man does not laugh easily, Gregers.

GREGERS (*Points upstage.*)

Look, Father. The gentlemen are playing blind man's buff with Mrs. Soerby. Good night, and good-bye.

He goes out upstage right. Sounds of laughter and merriment are heard from the guests, as they come into sight in the other room.

WERLE (*Mutters scornfully after Gregers.*)

Hm! Poor wretch! And he says he's not a romantic!

Act two

Hjalmar Ekdal's studio. It is quite a large room, and is evidently an attic. To the right is a sloping ceiling containing large panes of glass, which are half covered by a blue curtain. In the corner upstage right is the front door. Downstage of this is a door to the living room. In the left-hand wall are two more doors, with an iron stove between them. In the rear wall are broad double sliding doors. The studio is humbly but comfortably furnished. Between the doors on the right, a little away from the wall, stands a sofa, with a table and some chairs. On the table is a lighted lamp, with a shade. In the corner by the stove is an old armchair. Here and there, various pieces of photographic apparatus are set up. Against the rear wall, to the left of the sliding doors, is a book-case, containing some books, boxes, bottles containing chemicals, various tools, instruments and other objects. Photographs and small articles such as brushes, sheets of paper and so forth, lie on the table. Gina Ekdal is seated on a chair at the table, sewing. Hedvig is seated on the sofa with her hands shading her eyes and her thumbs in her ears, reading a book.

GINA (*Glances at her a couple of times, as though with secret anxiety.*)

Hedvig!

Hedvig does not hear. Gina repeats more loudly.

Hedvig!

HEDVIG (*Drops her hands and looks up.*)

Yes, Mother?

GINA

Hedvig darling, don't read any more.

HEDVIG

Oh, but Mother, can't I go on a little longer? Just a little?

GINA

No, no; put the book away. Your father doesn't like it. He never reads in the evenings.

HEDVIG (*Closes the book.*)

No, Father doesn't bother much about reading, does he?

GINA (*Puts down her sewing and picks up a pencil and a small notebook from the table.*)

Can you remember how much we paid for that butter?

HEDVIG

One crown sixty-five öre.

GINA

That's right.

Makes a note of it.

It's shocking how much butter gets eaten in this house. Then there was the sausages, and the cheese—let me see—
> *Writes.*

And the ham—hm—
> *Adds it up.*

Mm, that makes nearly—

HEDVIG

Don't forget the beer.

GINA

Oh yes, of course.
> *Writes.*

It mounts up. But we've got to have it.

HEDVIG

But you and I didn't have to have a proper meal this evening, as Father was out.

GINA

Yes; that helped. Oh, and I got eight and a half crowns for those photographs.

HEDVIG

I say! As much as that?

GINA

Exactly eight and a half crowns.
> *Silence. Gina takes up her sewing again. Hedvig picks up a pencil and paper and starts to draw, her left hand shading her eyes.*

HEDVIG

Isn't it lovely to think of Father being invited by Mr. Werle to that big dinner?

GINA

He wasn't invited by Mr. Werle. It was his son who sent the invitation.
> *Short pause.*

You know we've nothing to do with Mr. Werle.

HEDVIG

I'm so looking forward to Father coming home. He promised he'd ask Mrs. Soerby for something nice to bring me.

GINA

Yes, there's never any shortage of nice things in that house.

HEDVIG (*Still drawing.*)

I think I'm beginning to get a bit hungry.
> *Old Ekdal, his package of papers under his arm and another parcel in his coat pocket, comes in through the front door.*

GINA

Hullo, Grandfather, you're very late tonight.

EKDAL

They'd shut the office. Graaberg kept me waiting. I had to go through the—hm.

HEDVIG

Did they give you anything new to copy, Grandfather?

EKDAL

All this. Look!

GINA

Well, that's good.

HEDVIG

And you've another parcel in your pocket.

EKDAL

Have I? Oh, nonsense—that's nothing.

Puts down his stick in a corner.

This'll keep me busy for a long time, this will, Gina.

Slides one of the doors in the rear wall a little to one side.

Ssh!

Looks inside for a moment, then closes the door again carefully.

He, he! They're all asleep. And she's lied down in her basket. He, he!

HEDVIG

Are you sure she won't be cold in that basket, Grandfather?

EKDAL

What an idea! Cold? With all that straw?

Goes towards the door upstage left.

Are there any matches?

GINA

They're on the chest-of-drawers.

Ekdal goes into his room.

HEDVIG

Isn't it splendid Grandfather getting all that stuff to copy again, after so long?

GINA

Yes, poor old Father. It'll mean a bit of pocket money for him.

HEDVIG

And he won't be able to spend all morning down at that horrid Mrs. Eriksen's restaurant, will he?

GINA

Yes, there's that too.

Short silence.

HEDVIG

Do you think they're still stitting at table?

GINA

God knows. It wouldn't surprise me.

HEDVIG

Think of all that lovely food Father's getting to eat! I'm sure he'll be in a good humour when he comes back. Don't you think, Mother?

GINA

Oh, yes. But if only we were able to tell him we'd managed to let that room.

HEDVIG

But we don't have to worry about *that* tonight.

GINA

It wouldn't do any harm. It's no use to us standing empty.

HEDVIG

No, I mean we don't have to worry about it because Father'll be jolly anyway. It'll be better if we can save the news about the room for another time.

GINA (*Glances across at her.*)

Does it make you happy to have good news to tell Father when he comes home in the evening?

HEDVIG

Yes, it makes things more cheerful here.

GINA

Yes, there's something in that.

Old Ekdal comes in again and goes towards the door downstage left. Half turns in her chair.

Do you want something out of the kitchen, Grandfather?

EKDAL

Er—yes, yes. Don't get up.

Goes out.

GINA

He's not messing about with the fire, is he?

Waits a moment.

Hedvig, go and see what he's up to.

Ekdal returns with a little jug of steaming water.

HEDVIG

Are you getting some hot water, Grandfather?

EKDAL

Yes, I am. Need it for something. Got some writing to do; and the ink's like porridge—hm!

GINA

But, Grandfather, you should eat your supper first. I've put it in there for you.

EKDAL

Can't be bothered with supper, Gina. I'm busy, I tell you. I don't want anyone to disturb me. Not anyone—hm!

He goes into his room. Gina and Hedvig look at each other.

GINA (*Quietly.*)

Where do you think he's got the money from?

HEDVIG

From Graaberg, I suppose.

GINA

No, he can't have. Graaberg always sends the money to me.

HEDVIG

He must have got a bottle on tick somewhere, then.

GINA

Poor Grandfather! No one'll give him anything on credit.

Hjalmar Ekdal, wearing an overcoat and a grey felt hat, enters right. Gina drops her sewing and gets up.

Why, Hjalmar, are you here already?

HEDVIG (*Simultaneously, jumping to her feet.*)

Oh Father, fancy your coming back so soon!

HJALMAR (*Takes off his hat.*)

Yes, well, most of them had begun to leave.

HEDVIG

As early as this?

HJALMAR

Yes. It was a dinner party, you know.

Begins to take off his overcoat.

GINA

Let me help you.

HEDVIG

Me too.

They take off his coat. Gina hangs it up on the rear wall.

Were there many people there, Father?

HJALMAR

Oh no, not many. We were, oh, twelve or fourteen at table.

GINA

And you talked to them all?

HJALMAR

Oh yes, a little. But Gregers monopolised me most of the time.

GINA

Is he still as ugly as ever?

HJALMAR

Well, he's not very much to look at. Hasn't the old man come home?

HEDVIG

Yes, Grandfather's in his room, writing.

HJALMAR

Did he say anything?

GINA

No, what should he say?

HJALMAR

Didn't he mention anything about—? I thought I heard someone say he'd been up to see Graaberg. I'll go in and have a word with him.

GINA

No, no—don't.

HJALMAR

Why not? Did he say he didn't want to see me?

GINA

I don't think he wants to see anyone this evening.

Hedvig makes signs to Hjalmar, Gina does not notice.

He's been out and fetched some hot water.

HJALMAR

Oh. He's—?

GINA

Yes.

HJALMAR

Dear God! Poor old Father! Bless his white hairs! Let him have his little pleasure.

Old Ekdal, wearing a dressing gown and smoking a pipe, enters from his room.

EKDAL

So you're home? I thought I heard your voice.

HJALMAR

Yes, I've just got back.

EKDAL

You didn't see me, did you?

HJALMAR

No. But they said you'd been through, and so I thought I'd follow you.

EKDAL

Hm. Decent of you, Hjalmar. Who were all those people?

HJALMAR

Oh, all sorts. There was Mr. Flor—the Chamberlain—and Mr. Balle—he's one, too—and so's Mr. Kaspersen—and Mr.—what's his name, I don't remember what they were all called—

EKDAL (*Nods.*)
> You hear that, Gina? People from the palace—and Hjalmar!

GINA
> Yes, they're very grand up there nowadays.

HEDVIG
> Did the Chamberlains sing, Father? Or recite anything?

HJALMAR
> No, they just chattered. They tried to get me to recite something. But I said: "No."

EKDAL
> You said "No," did you?

GINA
> Oh, you might have obliged them.

HJALMAR
> No. One can't go round pandering to everyone.
>> *Begins to walk up and down the room.*
>
> I won't, anyway.

EKDAL
> No, no. You won't get round Hjalmar as easily as that.

HJALMAR
> I don't see why *I* should have to provide the entertainment on the few occasions when I go out to enjoy myself. Let the others do some work for a change. Those fellows go from one dinner table to the next stuffing themselves every night. Let them work for their food and drink.

GINA
> You didn't say all this?

HJALMAR (*Hums to himself.*)
> I gave them a piece of my mind.

EKDAL
> You said this to their faces?

HJALMAR
> Could be.
>> *Nonchalantly.*
>
> Afterwards we had a little altercation about Tokay.

EKDAL
> Tokay, did you say? That's a fine wine.

HJALMAR (*Stops walking.*)
> It *can* be a fine wine. But, let me tell you, all vintages are not equally fine. It depends on how much sunshine the grapes have had.

GINA
> Oh, Hjalmar! You know about everything!

EKDAL
> And they tried to argue about that?

HJALMAR
> They tried. But they soon learned that it's the same as with Chamberlains. All vintages are not equally fine.

GINA
> The things you think of!

EKDAL (*Chuckles.*)
> He, he! And they had to put that in their pipe and smoke it?

HJALMAR
> Yes. It was said straight to their faces.

EKDAL

You hear that, Gina? He said it straight to the Chamberlains' faces.

GINA

Just fancy! Straight to their faces!

HJALMAR

Yes, but I don't want it talked about. One doesn't repeat such things. It was all very friendly, of course. They're decent, friendly people. Why should I hurt them?

EKDAL

But straight to their faces!

HEDVIG (*Trying to please him.*)

What fun it is to see you in tails! You look splendid in tails, Father!

HJALMAR

Yes, I do, don't I? And it fits me perfectly; almost as though it had been made for me. Just a little tight under the arms, perhaps. Give me a hand, Hedvig.

Takes them off.

I think I'll put my jacket on. Where's my jacket, Gina?

GINA

Here it is.

Brings the jacket and helps him on with it.

HJALMAR

That's better! Don't forget to let Molvik have the tails back tomorrow morning.

GINA (*Puts them away.*)

I'll see he gets them.

HJALMAR (*Stretches.*)

Ah, now I feel more at home. Loose-fitting clothes suit my figure better. Don't you think, Hedvig?

HEDVIG

Yes, Father.

HJALMAR

When I loosen my tie so that the ends flow like this—Look! What do you think of that?

HEDVIG

Oh yes, that looks very good with your moustache and those big curls of yours.

HJALMAR

I wouldn't call them curls. Waves.

HEDVIG

Yes, they're such big curls.

HJALMAR

They are waves.

HEDVIG (*After a moment, tugs his jacket.*)

Father!

HJALMAR

Well, what is it?

HEDVIG

Oh, you know quite well what it is.

HJALMAR

No, I don't. Really.

HEDVIG (*Laughs and whimpers.*)

Oh yes, you do, Father. You mustn't tease me!

HJALMAR

But what *is* it?

HEDVIG

Oh, stop it! Give it to me, Father! You know! All those nice things you promised me!

HJALMAR

Oh, dear! Fancy my forgetting that!

HEDVIG

Oh, no, you're only teasing, Father! Oh, it's beastly of you! Where have you hidden it?

HJALMAR

No, honestly, I forgot. But wait a moment! I've something else for you, Hedvig.
Goes over to the tails and searches in the pockets.

HEDVIG (*Jumps and claps her hands.*)

Oh, Mother, Mother!

GINA

There, you see. Just be patient, and—

HJALMAR (*Holds out a card.*)

Look, here it is.

HEDVIG

That? That's only a piece of paper.

HJALMAR

It's the menu, Hedvig. The whole menu. Look here. It says *Déjeuner.* That means menu.

HEDVIG

Is that all?

HJALMAR

Well, I forgot the other things. But believe me, Hedvig, they're not much fun really, all those sickly sweet things. Sit over there at the table and read this menu, and then I'll describe to you how each dish tasted. Here you are, now, Hedvig.

HEDVIG (*Swallows her tears.*)

Thank you.
She sits down but does not read. Gina makes a sign to her. Hjalmar notices.

HJALMAR (*Starts walking up and down.*)

Really, it's incredible the things a breadwinner's expected to remember. If one forgets the slightest little thing, there are sour faces all round one. Well, one gets used to it.
Stops by the stove, where old Ekdal is sitting.
Have you looked in there this evening, Father?

EKDAL

Yes, of course I have. She's gone into the basket.

HJALMAR

Gone into the basket, has she? She's beginning to get used to it, then.

EKDAL

What did I tell you? Well, now, you see, there are one or two little—

HJALMAR

Little improvements, yes.

EKDAL

We've got to have them, Hjalmar.

HJALMAR

Yes. Let's have a word about those improvements, Father. Come along, let's sit on the sofa.

EKDAL

Yes, let's. Er—I think I'll fill my pipe first. Oh, I'd better clean it, too. Hm.

Goes into his room.

GINA (*Smiles at Hjalmar.*)

Clean his pipe!

HJALMAR

Oh, Gina, let him. Poor, shipwrecked old man! Yes, those improvements—I'd better get them done tomorrow.

GINA

But you won't have time tomorrow, Hjalmar.

HEDVIG (*Interrupts.*)

Oh, yes, he will, Mother!

GINA

Don't forget those prints have to be retouched. They've sent for them so many times.

HJALMAR

Oh, are you on about those prints again? They'll be ready. Have there been any new orders at all?

GINA

No, I'm afraid not. I've nothing tomorrow but those two portraits I told you about.

HJALMAR

Is that all? Well, if one doesn't put one's mind to it—

GINA

But what can I do? I advertise as much as I can—

HJALMAR

Advertise, advertise! You see what good that does. I don't suppose anyone's come to look at the room either?

GINA

No, not yet.

HJALMAR

I might have known it. If one doesn't bother to keep one's eyes and ears open— One must try to make an effort, Gina.

HEDVIG (*Goes towards him.*)

Can I bring your flute, Father?

HJALMAR

No. No flute. *I* don't need the pleasures of this world.

Starts walking again.

Yes, I'm going to work tomorrow. Don't you worry about that. I'll work as long as there's strength in these arms—

GINA

But my dear Hjalmar, I didn't mean it like that.

HEDVIG

Father, would you like a bottle of beer?

HJALMAR

Certainly not. I want nothing of anyone.

Stops.

Beer? Did you say beer?

HEDVIG (*Alive.*)

Yes, Father, Lovely, cool beer.

HJALMAR

Well—if you want to, bring in a bottle.

GINA

Yes, do. That's a nice idea.

Hedvig runs towards the kitchen door.

HJALMAR (*By the stove, stops her, looks at her, takes her head in his hands and presses her to him.*)

Hedvig! Hedvig!

HEDVIG (*Happy, crying.*)

Oh, dear, kind, Father!

HJALMAR

No, don't call me that. I have been eating at the rich man's table. Gorging my belly at the groaning board. And yet I could—

GINA (*Sitting at the table.*)

Oh, nonsense, nonsense, Hjalmar.

HJALMAR

It's true. But you mustn't judge me too harshly. You know I love you both. In spite of everything—

HEDVIG (*Throws her arms round him.*)

And we love you very, very much, Father.

HJALMAR

And if I should, once in a while, be unreasonable—dear God!— remember that I am a man besieged by a host of sorrows. Oh, well.

Dries her eyes.

This is not the moment for beer. Give me my flute.

Hedvig runs to the bookcase and fetches it.

Thank you. Ah, this is better. With my flute in my hand, and you two by my side—ah!

Hedvig sits at the table by Gina. Hjalmar walks up and down, then begins to play a Bohemian folk dance, with spirit, in a slow and mournful tempo, and sensitively. Stops playing, stretches out his left hand to Gina and says emotionally.

Life may be poor and humble under our roof. But it is home. And I tell you, Gina—it is good to be here.

He begins to play again.

After a few moments, there is a knock on the front door.

GINA (*Gets up.*)

Hush, Hjalmar. I think there's someone at the door.

HJALMAR (*Puts the flute away in the bookcase.*)

Oh, here we go again.

GREGERS (*Outside on the landing.*)

Excuse me, but—

GINA (*Starts back slightly.*)

Oh!

GREGERS

Doesn't Mr. Ekdal live here? The photographer.

GINA

Yes, he does.

HJALMAR (*Goes over to the door.*)

Gregers! Are you here? Well, you'd better come in.

GREGERS (*Enters.*)
> But I told you I'd visit you.

HJALMAR
> But—tonight? Have you left the party?

GREGERS
> Yes. I have left the party. And my home, too. Good evening, Mrs. Ekdal. I don't suppose you recognise me?

GINA
> Why, yes, Mr. Gregers. I recognise you.

GREGERS
> Yes. I'm like my mother. And I've no doubt you remember her.

HJALMAR
> Did you say you had left your father's house?

GREGERS
> Yes. I've moved to a hotel.

HJALMAR
> Oh, I see. Well, since you've come, take off your coat and sit down.

GREGERS
> Thank you.
>> *He takes off his coat. He has changed into a simple grey suit of a pro-vincial cut.*

HJALMAR
> Here, on the sofa. Make yourself comfortable.
>> *Gregers sits on the sofa, Hjalmar on a chair by the table.*

GREGERS (*Looks around.*)
> So this is it, Hjalmar. This is where you live.

HJALMAR
> This room is my studio, as you see.

GINA
> We usually sit here, because there's more space.

HJALMAR
> We had a nicer place before, but this apartment has one great advantage. The bedrooms—

GINA
> And we've a spare room on the other side of the passage that we can let.

GREGERS (*To Hjalmar.*)
> Oh, I see. You take lodgers as well?

HJALMAR
> No, not yet. It takes time, you know. One's got to keep one's eyes and ears open.
>> *To Hedvig.*
> Let's have that beer now.
>> *Hedvig nods and goes out into the kitchen.*

GREGERS
> So that's your daughter?

HJALMAR
> Yes, that is Hedvig.

GREGERS
> Your only child?

HJALMAR
> Yes, she is the only one. Our greatest joy.

Drops his voice.
And also our greatest sorrow, Gregers.

GREGERS
What do you mean?

HJALMAR
There is a grave risk that she may lose her eyesight.

GREGERS
Go blind?

HJALMAR
Yes. As yet there are only the first symptoms, and she may be all right for some while. But the doctor has warned us. It will happen in the end.

GREGERS
What a terrible tragedy. What's the cause?

HJALMAR (*Sighs.*)
It's probably hereditary.

GREGERS (*Starts.*)
Hereditary?

GINA
Hjalmar's mother had weak eyes, too.

HJALMAR
So my father says. Of course, I can't remember.

GREGERS
Poor child. And how does she take it?

HJALMAR
Oh, you don't imagine we have the heart to tell her? She suspects nothing. Carefree and gay, singing like a little bird, she will fly into the night.
Overcome.
Oh, it will be the death of me, Gregers.
Hedvig brings a tray with beer and glasses, and sets it on the table.
Hjalmar strokes her head.
Thank you, Hedvig.
She puts her arm round his neck and whispers in his ear.
No, no sandwiches now.
Glances at Gregers.
Unless you'd like some, Gregers?

GREGERS
No, no, thank you.

HJALMAR (*Still melancholy.*)
Well, you might bring a few in, anyway. A crust will be enough for me. Put plenty of butter on it, mind.
Hedvig nods happily and goes back into the kitchen.

GREGERS (*Follows her with his eyes.*)
She looks quite strong and healthy, apart from that, I think.

GINA
Yes, there's nothing else the matter with her, thank God.

GREGERS
She's going to look very like you, Mrs. Ekdal. How old would she be now?

GINA
Almost exactly fourteen. It's her birthday the day after tomorrow.

GREGERS
Quite big for her age.

GINA

Yes, she's certainly shot up this last year.

GREGERS

Seeing these young people grow up makes one realise how old one's getting oneself. How long have you two been married now?

GINA

We've been married—er—yes, nearly fifteen years.

GREGERS

Good Lord, is it as long as that?

GINA (*Suddenly alert; looks at him.*)

Yes, that's right.

HJALMAR

It certainly is. Fifteen years, all but a few months.

Changes his tone.

They must have seemed long to you, those years up at the mill, Gregers.

GREGERS

They seemed long at the time. Looking back on them, I hardly know where they went.

Old Ekdal enters from his room, without his pipe but wearing his old army helmet. He walks a little unsteadily.

EKDAL

Well, Hjalmar, now we can sit down and talk about that—er—. What was it we were going to talk about?

HJALMAR (*Goes over to him.*)

Father, we have a guest. Gregers Werle. I don't know if you remember him.

EKDAL (*Looks at Gregers, who has got up.*)

Werle? The son? What does he want with me?

HJALMAR

Nothing. He's come to see me.

EKDAL

Oh. Nothing's wrong, then?

HJALMAR

No, of course not. Nothing at all.

EKDAL (*Waves an arm.*)

Mind you, I'm not afraid. It's just that—

GREGERS (*Goes over to him.*)

I only wanted to bring you a greeting from your old hunting grounds, Lieutenant Ekdal.

EKDAL

Hunting grounds?

GREGERS

Yes—up around Hoydal.

EKDAL

Oh, up there. Yes, I used to know that part well, in the old days.

GREGERS

You were a famous hunter then.

EKDAL

Oh, well. Maybe I was. I won't deny it. You're looking at my uniform. I don't ask anyone's permission to wear it in here. As long as I don't go out into the street in it—

Hedvig brings a plate of sandwiches and puts it on the table.

HJALMAR

    Sit down now, Father, and have a glass of beer. Gregers, please.

       Ekdal mumbles to himself and stumbles over to the sofa. Gregers sits in the chair nearest to him, Hjalmar on the other side of Gregers. Gina sits a little away from the table, sewing. Hedvig stands beside her father.

GREGERS

    Do you remember, Lieutenant Ekdal, how Hjalmar and I used to come up and visit you during the summer, and at Christmas?

EKDAL

    Did you? No, no, no, I don't remember it. But though I say it myself, I was a first-rate shot. I've killed bears too, you know. Nine of them.

GREGERS (*Looks at him sympathetically.*)

    And now your hunting days are over?

EKDAL

    Oh, I wouldn't say that, my boy. Do a bit of hunting now and again. Not quite the way I used to. You see, the forest—the forest, you see, the forest—

       Drinks.

    How does the forest look up there now? Still good, eh?

GREGERS

    Not as good as in your day. It's been thinned out a lot.

EKDAL

    Thinned out? Chopped down?

       More quietly, as though in fear.

    That's dangerous. Bad things'll come of that. The forest'll have its revenge.

HJALMAR (*Fills his glass.*)

    Have a little more, Father.

GREGERS

    How can a man like you, a man who loves the open air as you do, bear to live in the middle of a stuffy town, boxed between four walls?

EKDAL (*Gives a short laugh and glances at Hjalmar.*)

    Oh, it's not too bad here. Not bad at all.

GREGERS

    But what about the cool, sweeping breezes, the free life in the forest, and up on the wide, open spaces among animals and birds? These things which had become part of you?

EKDAL (*Smiles.*)

    Hjalmar, shall we show it to him?

HJALMAR (*Quickly, a little embarrassed.*)

    Oh, no, Father, no. Not tonight.

GREGERS

    What does he want to show me?

HJALMAR

    It's only something that—. You can see it another time.

GREGERS (*Continues speaking to Ekdal.*)

    What I was going to suggest, Lieutenant Edkal, was that you should come with me back to the mill. I shall be returning there soon. I'm sure we could find you some copying to do up there, too. And there's nothing here to keep you cheerful and interested.

EKDAL (*Stares at him, amazed.*)

Nothing here—?

GREGERS

Of course you have Hjalmar; but then he has his own family. And a man like you, who has always been drawn to a life that is wild and free—

EKDAL (*Strikes the table.*)

Hjalmar, he *shall* see it!

HJALMAR

But, Father, what's the point of showing it to him now? It's dark.

EKDAL

Nonsense, there's the moonlight.

> *Gets up.*

He shall see it, I tell you. Let me come through. Come and help me, Hjalmar.

HEDVIG

Oh, yes, do, Father!

HJALMAR (*Gets up.*)

Oh, very well.

GREGERS (*To Gina.*)

What are they talking about?

GINA

Oh, don't take any notice. It's nothing very much.

> *Ekdal and Hjalmar go to the rear wall, and each of them pushes back one of the sliding doors. Hedvig helps the old man. Gregers remains standing by the sofa. Gina continues calmly with her sewing. Through the open doors can be seen a long and irregularly shaped loft, full of dark nooks and crannies, with a couple of brick chimney-pipes coming through the floor. Through small skylights bright moonlight shines on to various parts of the loft, while the rest lies in shadow.*

EKDAL (*To Gregers.*)

You can come right in, if you like.

GREGERS (*Goes over to them.*)

What is it, exactly?

EKDAL

Have a look. Hm.

HJALMAR (*Somewhat embarrassed.*)

This belongs to my father, you understand.

GREGERS (*In the doorway, peers into the loft.*)

Why, you keep chickens, Lieutenant Ekdal.

EKDAL

I should think we do keep chickens! They've gone to roost now. But you should just see them by daylight!

HEDVIG

And then there's the—!

EKDAL

Ssh! Don't say anything yet.

GREGERS

And you've pigeons, too, I see.

EKDAL

Why, yes! Of course we've pigeons. They've got their roosting-boxes up there under the roof. Pigeons like to nest high, you know.

HJALMAR

They're not all ordinary pigeons.

EKDAL

Ordinary! No, I should say not! We've tumblers. And a pair of
pouters, too. But come over here! Do you see that hutch over there
against the wall?

GREGERS

Yes. What do you use that for?

EKDAL

The rabbits go there at night.

GREGERS

Oh, you have rabbits, too?

EKDAL

You're damn right we've got rabbits. You hear that, Hjalmar? He
asks if we've got rabbits! Hm! But now I'll show you! This is really
something. Move over, Hedvig. Stand here. That's right. Now look
down there. Can you see a basket with straw in it?

GREGERS

Yes. And there's a bird lying in the straw.

EKDAL

Hm! A bird!

GREGERS

Isn't it a duck?

EKDAL (*Hurt.*)

Of course it's a duck.

HJALMAR

Ah, but what *kind* of a duck?

HEDVIG

It's not just an ordinary duck—

EKDAL

Ssh!

GREGERS

It's not one of those Muscovy ducks, is it?

EKDAL

No, Mr. Werle, it's not a Muscovy duck. It's a wild duck.

GREGERS

Oh, is it really? A wild duck?

EKDAL

Yes, that's what it is. That "bird," as you called it—that's a wild duck,
that is. That's our wild duck, my boy.

HEDVIG

My wild duck. I own it.

GREGERS

But can it live up here in this loft? Is it happy here?

EKDAL

Well, naturally she has a trough of water to splash about in.

HJALMAR

Fresh water every other day.

GINA (*Turns towards Hjalmar.*)

Hjalmar dear, it's getting icy cold up here.

EKDAL

Mm. Well, let's shut up, then. It's best not to disturb them when
they're sleeping, anyway. Give me a hand, Hedvig.

Hjalmar and Hedvig slide the doors together.

Some other time you must have a proper look at her.

Sits in the armchair by the stove.

Ah, they're strange creatures, you know, these wild ducks.

GREGERS

But how did you manage to catch it, Lieutenant Ekdal?

EKDAL

I didn't catch it. There's a certain gentleman in this town whom we have to thank for that.

GREGERS (*Starts slightly.*)

You don't mean my father, surely?

EKDAL

Indeed I do. Your father. Hm.

HJALMAR

How odd that you should guess that, Gregers.

GREGERS

You told me earlier that you were indebted to my father for so many things, so I thought perhaps—

GINA

Oh, we didn't get it from Mr. Werle himself—

EKDAL

All the same, it's Haakon Werle we have to thank for her, Gina.

To Gregers.

He was out in his boat, you see, and he shot her. But his eyesight isn't very good. Hm. So he only winged her.

GREGERS

Oh, I see. She got a couple of pellets in her.

HJALMAR

Yes, two or three.

HEDVIG

She got them under her wing, so that she couldn't fly.

GREGERS

Oh, and so she dived to the bottom, I suppose?

EKDAL (*Sleepily, in a thick voice.*)

Of course. Wild ducks always do that. Dive down to the bottom, as deep as they can go, and hold on with their beaks to the seaweed or whatever they can find down there. And they never come up again.

GREGERS

But your wild duck did come up again, Lieutenant Ekdal.

EKDAL

He had such a damned clever dog, your father. And that dog—he dived down after the duck, and brought her to the surface.

GREGERS (*Turns to Hjalmar.*)

And then you took her in here?

HJALMAR

Not at once. To begin with, they took her home to your father's house. But she didn't seem to thrive there. So Pettersen was told to wring her neck.

EKDAL (*Half asleep.*)

Hm. Yes. Pettersen. Damn fool—

HJALMAR (*Speaks more softly.*)

That was how we got her, you see. Father knows Pettersen, and when he heard all this about the wild duck he got him to give it to us.

GREGERS

And now she's thriving in your loft.

HJALMAR

Yes, she's doing extraordinarily well. She's got fat. Well, she's been in there so long now that she's forgotten what it's like to live the life she was born for; that's the whole trick.

GREGERS

Yes, you're right there, Hjalmar. Just make sure she never gets a glimpse of the sky or the sea. But I mustn't stay longer. I think your father's fallen asleep.

HJALMAR

Oh, never mind about that.

GREGERS

By the bye, you said you had a room to let.

HJALMAR

Yes, why? Do you know anyone who—?

GREGERS

Could I have it?

HJALMAR

You?

GINA

No, but Mr. Werle, it isn't—

GREGERS

Can I have that room? I'd like to move in right away. Tomorrow morning.

HJALMAR

Why, yes, with the greatest pleasure—

GINA

Oh, no, Mr. Werle, it's not at all the kind of room for you.

HJALMAR

Why, Gina, how can you say that?

GINA

Well, it's dark and poky.

GREGERS

That won't bother me, Mrs. Ekdal.

HJALMAR

Personally I think it's quite a nice room. Not too badly furnished, either.

GINA

Don't forget those two who live down below.

GREGERS

Who are they?

GINA

Oh, one of them used to be a tutor—

HJALMAR

A Mr. Molvik.

GINA

And the other's a doctor called Relling.

GREGERS

Relling? I know him slightly. He had a practice up at Hoydal once.

GINA

They're a real couple of good-for-nothings. They often go out on
the spree and come home very late at night, and aren't always—

GREGERS

One soon gets accustomed to that sort of thing. I hope I shall manage to acclimatise myself like the wild duck.

GINA

Well, I think you ought to sleep on it first, all the same.

GREGERS

You evidently don't want to have me living here, Mrs. Edkal.

GINA

For heaven's sake! How can you think that?

HJALMAR

You're really behaving very strangely, Gina.

> *To Gregers.*

But tell me, are you thinking of staying in town for a while?

GREGERS (*Puts on his overcoat.*)

Yes, now I'm staying.

HJALMAR

But not at home with your father? What do you intend to do?

GREGERS

Ah, if only I knew that, Hjalmar, it wouldn't be so bad. But when
one has the misfortune to be called Gregers—with Werle on top of
it—Hjalmar, have you ever heard anything so awful?

HJALMAR

Oh, I don't think it's awful at all.

GREGERS

Oh, nonsense. Ugh! I'd want to spit on anyone who had a name like
that.

HJALMAR (*Laughs.*)

If you weren't Gregers Werle, what would you like to be?

GREGERS

If I could choose, I think most of all I'd like to be a clever dog.

GINA

A dog?

HEDVIG (*Involuntarily.*)

Oh, no!

GREGERS

Oh, yes. A tremendously clever dog. The sort that dives down after
wild ducks when they have plunged to the bottom and gripped
themselves fast in the seaweed and the mud.

HJALMAR

Honestly, Gregers, I don't understand a word of all this.

GREGERS

Oh, well, it doesn't mean much really. I'll move in tomorrow morning, then.

> *To Gina.*

I shan't cause you any trouble. I do everything for myself.

> *To Hjalmar.*

We'll talk about everything else tomorrow. Good night, Mrs. Ekdal.

> *Nods to Hedvig.*

Good night.

GINA

Good night, Mr. Werle.

HEDVIG

Good night.

HJALMAR (*Who has lit a candle.*)

Wait a moment. I'll have to light you down. It's very dark on the stairs.

> *Gregers and Hjalmar go out through the front door.*

GINA (*Thoughtfully, her sewing in her lap.*)

Wasn't that a funny thing, saying he'd like to be a dog?

HEDVIG

You know, Mother—I think when he said that he meant something else.

GINA

What could he mean?

HEDVIG

I don't know. But I felt as though he meant something different from what he was saying all the time.

GINA

You think so? Yes, it certainly was strange.

HJALMAR (*Comes back.*)

The light was still on.

> *Snuffs the candle and puts it down.*

Ah, now I can get a little food inside me at last.

> *Begins eating the sandwiches.*

Well, there you are, Gina. If one only keeps one's eyes and ears open—

GINA

How do you mean?

HJALMAR

Well, it's jolly lucky we've managed to let that room at last, isn't it? And, what's more, to a man like Gregers. A dear old friend.

GINA

Well, I don't know what to say about it.

HEDVIG

Oh, Mother! You'll see—it'll be such fun!

HJALMAR

You're very awkward. You were aching to let the room, and now we've done it you're not happy.

GINA

Oh, yes I am, Hjalmar. I only wish it had been to someone else. But what do you suppose the old man will say?

HJALMAR

Old Werle? It's none of his business.

GINA

Can't you see? They must have quarrelled again if his son's walked out of the house. You know how things are between those two.

HJALMAR

That may well be, but—

GINA

Now perhaps Mr. Werle'll think you're behind it all.

HJALMAR

All right, let him think so, if he wants to! Old Werle's done a great deal for me, I admit it. But that doesn't make me his vassal for life.

GINA

But, dear Hjalmar, he might take it out on Grandfather. Maybe now he'll lose the little bit of money he gets through Graaberg.

HJALMAR

Good riddance—I've half a mind to say. Don't you think it's a little humiliating for a man like me to see his grey old father treated like a leper? But I've a feeling the time is getting ripe.
  Takes another sandwich.
As sure as I have a mission in life, it shall be fulfilled.

HEDVIG

Oh, Father, yes! It must, it must!

GINA

Ssh! For heaven's sake, don't wake him.

HJALMAR (*More quietly.*)

It shall be accomplished. The day will come, I tell you—and that's why it's good we've let that room—it makes me more independent.
  Over by the armchair, emotionally.
My poor old father! Bless his white hairs! Put your trust in your son. He has broad shoulders—well, strong shoulders, anyway. One fine day you will wake up—
  To Gina.
Don't you believe it?

GINA (*Gets up.*)

Of course I believe it. But let's get him to bed first.

HJALMAR

Yes, let's.
  They take hold of the old man gently.

Act three

> *Hjalmar Ekdal's studio. It is morning. The daylight is shining in through the large window in the sloping ceiling, from which the curtain is drawn back. Hjalmar is seated at the table re-touching a photograph. Several others lie in front of him. After a few moments, Gina enters through the front door wearing a hat and coat. She has a lidded basket on her arm.*

HJALMAR

Back already, Gina?

GINA

Yes, I've no time to waste.
  Puts the basket down on a chair and takes off her coat.

HJALMAR

Did you look in on Gregers?

GINA

I'll say I did. Lovely it looks. He's made it really nice and cosy for himself right from the start.

HJALMAR

Oh, how?

GINA

Manage for himself, he said he would. So he starts lighting the stove.
Well, he shoved that damper in so far the whole room got full of
smoke. Ugh! It stank like a—

HJALMAR

Oh dear, oh dear!

GINA

That's not all. Then he wants to put out the fire, so he throws all his
washing water into the stove. That floor's swimming like a pigsty.

HJALMAR

Oh, I'm sorry about that.

GINA

I've got the caretaker's wife to clean up after him, the pig. But that
room won't be fit to live in till this afternoon.

HJALMAR

What's he doing with himself meanwhile?

GINA

He said he'd go out for a bit.

HJALMAR

I went in there too for a moment. After you'd gone.

GINA

So I gathered. I hear you've invited him for lunch.

HJALMAR

Just a little snack, I thought. After all, it's his first day here—we can't
very well not. You've got something, I suppose?

GINA

I'll have to find something, won't I?

HJALMAR

Don't skimp it too much. Relling and Molvik may be looking in, too,
I think. I ran into Relling on the stairs just now, you see, so I
couldn't very well—

GINA

Oh, we're having those two as well, are we?

HJALMAR

Good God, a couple more or less, what difference does that make?

EKDAL (*Opens his door and looks out.*)

I say, Hjalmar—

Notices Gina.

Oh.

GINA

Do you want something, Grandfather?

EKDAL

Oh, no. It doesn't matter. Hm!

Goes inside again.

GINA (*Picks up the basket.*)

Watch him. See he doesn't go out.

HJALMAR

All right, all right. I say, Gina, a little of that herring salad of yours
mightn't be a bad idea. I think Relling and Molvik were out on the
tiles again last night.

GINA

Well, as long as they don't come too soon—

HJALMAR

Of course, of course. You take your time.

GINA

Yes, well; and you can get a little work done in the meantime.

HJALMAR

I *am* working! I'm working as hard as I can!

GINA

I only meant, then you'll have it out of the way.

She goes out with her basket to the kitchen. Hjalmar sits working at the photograph with a brush, slowly and listlessly.

EKDAL (*Pokes his head in, looks around the room and says in a whisper.*)

Are you working?

HJALMAR

Yes, can't you see I'm struggling away at these pictures?

EKDAL

Oh. Well, never mind. If you're working so hard, I—hm.

Goes out again. His door remains open.

HJALMAR (*Continues silently for a few moments, then puts down his brush and goes across to the door.*)

Are *you* working, Father?

EKDAL (*Grumblingly, from the other room.*)

If you're working, I'm working, too. Hm!

HJALMAR

Yes, yes, of course.

Goes back to his work.

EKDAL (*After a moment, reappears in the doorway.*)

You know—I'm not working as hard as all that, Hjalmar.

HJALMAR

I thought you were writing.

EKDAL

Damn it, that Graaberg can wait a day or two. It's not a matter of life and death, is it?

HJALMAR

No. Anyway, you're not a slave, are you?

EKDAL

And then there's that thing in there—

HJALMAR

I was just thinking of that. Did you want to go in? Shall I open the door for you?

EKDAL

That's not a bad idea.

HJALMAR (*Gets up.*)

Then we'd have it out of the way.

EKDAL

That's what I was thinking. We've got to have it ready by tomorrow morning. It is tomorrow, isn't it? Eh?

HJALMAR

Yes, of course it's tomorrow.

Hjalmar and Ekdal each slide back one of the doors. Within, the morning sun is shining in through the skylights. Some pigeons are flying back and forth, while others perch, cooing, on the rafters. Now and then the hens cackle further back in the loft.

Well now. Get on with it, Father.

EKDAL (*Goes inside.*)
>Aren't you going to help?

HJALMAR
>You know, I think I—
>>*Sees Gina in the kitchen doorway.*
>Me? No, I've no time. I've got to work. Oh—my contraption—
>>*He pulls a cord. A curtain falls in the attic; the lower section of this consists of a strip of old sailcloth, the upper of a piece of fishing net, stretched taut. The floor of the attic is thus no longer visible.*
>>*Goes over to the table.*
>Good. Now perhaps I can be allowed to work in peace for a few minutes.

GINA
>Is he messing around in there again?

HJALMAR
>Would you rather he sneaked off down to Madame Eriksen's?
>>*Sits.*
>Did you want something? You were saying—

GINA
>I only wanted to ask whether you think it'd be all right if we eat in here.

HJALMAR
>Yes, we haven't any early sittings today, have we?

GINA
>Only those two young lovers who want to be taken together.

HJALMAR
>Why the devil can't they be taken together some other day?

GINA
>It's all right, dear. I've fixed for them to come after lunch, when you'll be having your nap.

HJALMAR
>Oh, good. Very well, then, let's eat in here.

GINA
>All right. But there's no hurry about laying the table just yet. You can go on using it for a bit longer.

HJALMAR
>Surely you can see I'm working as hard as I can!

GINA
>I only meant, then you'll be free later.
>>*She goes back into the kitchen. Short pause.*

EKDAL (*Peers through the net in the loft.*)
>Hjalmar!

HJALMAR
>What is it?

EKDAL
>Afraid we'll have to move that water trough after all.

HJALMAR
>That's what I've said all along.

EKDAL
>Hm—hm—hm.
>>*Goes away from the door again.*
>>*Hjalmar works for a few moments, then glances towards the attic and half rises. Hedvig comes in from the kitchen.*

HJALMAR (*Sits quickly down.*)
> What do you want?

HEDVIG
> I only wanted to be with you, Father.

HJALMAR (*After a moment.*)
> What are you nosing around for? Have you been told to keep an eye
> on me?

HEDVIG
> No, of course not.

HJALMAR
> What's your mother up to now?

HEDVIG
> Oh, she's in the middle of the herring salad.
>> *Goes over to the table.*
> Isn't there some little thing I could help you with, Father?

HJALMAR
> Oh, no. I'd better cope with it alone. While I still can. All will be
> well, Hedvig. As long as your father's strength holds out—

HEDVIG
> Oh, no, Father, you mustn't say such dreadful things.
>> *She wanders around for a little, then stops by the open doorway and
>> looks into the loft.*

HJALMAR
> What's he up to, Hedvig?

HEDVIG
> I think he's making a new path up to the water trough.

HJALMAR
> He'll never manage that by himself! And I'm forced to sit here—

HEDVIG (*Comes over to him.*)
> Let me take the brush, Father. I know how to do it.

HJALMAR
> Oh, no, you'll only ruin your eyes.

HEDVIG
> Nonsense. Come on, give me the brush.

HJALMAR (*Gets up.*)
> Yes, well it won't take more than a minute or two.

HEDVIG
> Oh, what does it matter?
>> *Takes the brush.*
> There, now.
>> *Sits.*
> Here's one I can start on.

HJALMAR
> But listen—if you ruin your eyes, I won't take the responsibility. On
> your own head be it. You hear?

HEDVIG (*Busy on the photograph.*)
> Yes, yes, I know.

HJALMAR
> You're a clever girl, Hedvig. It'll only take a couple of minutes—
>> *He squeezes into the loft past the edge of the curtain. Hedvig sits work-
>> ing. Hjalmar and Ekdal can be heard arguing in the loft.
>> Hjalmar comes back through the curtain.*

Hedvig, get me those pliers from that shelf. And the chisel.

> *Turns round towards the loft.*

Now you'll see, Father. Just let me show you.

> *Hedvig gets the tools from the bookcase and hands them to him.*

Ah, thanks. Good thing I came, Hedvig.

> *He goes away from the doorway. They can be heard working and chatting inside. Hedvig stands watching them. After a moment, there is a knock on the front door. She does not hear it.*

GREGERS (*Enters bareheaded and without an overcoat. He pauses in the doorway.*)
Hm—

HEDVIG (*Turns and goes towards him.*)
Good morning. Please come in.

GREGERS

Thank you.

> *Looks towards the attic.*

Have you got workmen in the house?

HEDVIG

No, that's only Father and Grandfather. I'll tell them you're here.

GREGERS

No, no, don't do that. I'd rather wait.

> *Sits on the sofa.*

HEDVIG

It's so untidy in here.

> *Begins to clear away the photographs.*

GREGERS

Oh, never mind that. Are those photographs that have to be—er—finished off?

HEDVIG

Yes, just a few I'm helping Father with.

GREGERS

Please don't let me disturb you.

HEDVIG

All right.

> *Arranges the things again and sits down to work. Gregers watches her in silence.*

GREGERS

Did the wild duck sleep well last night?

HEDVIG

Yes, thank you, I think so.

GREGERS (*Turns towards the loft.*)
It looks quite different in there by daylight.

HEDVIG

Oh, yes. It varies a lot. In the morning it looks quite different from what it does in the afternoon. And when it's raining it looks different from when it's fine.

GREGERS

You've noticed that, have you?

HEDVIG

Yes, you can't help seeing it.

GREGERS

Do you like being in there with the wild duck, too?

HEDVIG
Yes, when I'm able to—
GREGERS
But you haven't so much spare time, I dare say. You go to school, of course?
HEDVIG
No, not any longer. Father's afraid I shall ruin my eyes.
GREGERS
Oh. So he reads with you himself?
HEDVIG
Father's promised to read with me, but he hasn't found time for it yet.
GREGERS
But isn't there someone else who could help you a little?
HEDVIG
Yes, there's Mr. Molvik—he's a student who lives downstairs—but he isn't always—er—altogether quite—
GREGERS
Does he drink?
HEDVIG
I think he does.
GREGERS
Oh. Then you've time for all sorts of things. In there, it's like a different world, I suppose?
HEDVIG
Quite, quite different. And there are so many strange things in there.
GREGERS
Oh?
HEDVIG
Yes. There are big cupboards with books in them. And a lot of the books have got pictures.
GREGERS
Ah.
HEDVIG
And there's an old bureau with drawers and bits that slide out, and a big clock with figures that are meant to pop out. But the clock doesn't work any more.
GREGERS
So time has stopped in there with the wild duck.
HEDVIG
Yes. And there are old paintboxes and things like that. And all the books.
GREGERS
And you read books, I suppose?
HEDVIG
Oh yes, when I can get the chance. But most of them are in English, and I can't understand that. But I look at the pictures. There's a great big book called *Harrison's History of London*–I should think it must be a hundred years old—and that's got heaps and heaps of pictures in it. On the front there's a picture of death with an hourglass, and a girl. That's horrid, I think. But then there are lots of other

pictures of churches and castles and streets and great ships sailing on the sea.

GREGERS

But tell me, where have all these wonderful things come from?

HEDVIG

Oh, there was an old sea captain who used to live here once, and he brought them home. They called him The Flying Dutchman. It's funny, because he wasn't a Dutchman.

GREGERS

Wasn't he?

HEDVIG

No. But in the end he got lost at sea and left all these things behind.

GREGERS

Tell me—as you sit in there and look at the pictures, don't you feel you want to get out and see the world as it really is?

HEDVIG

Oh, no! I want to stay at home always, and help Father and Mother.

GREGERS

Help them retouch photographs?

HEDVIG

No, not only that. Most of all I'd like to learn to engrave pictures like the ones in the English books.

GREGERS

Hm. What does your father say to that?

HEDVIG

I don't think Father likes the idea. He's so strange about anything like that. Imagine, he talks about my learning how to plait straw and make baskets! I don't think there can be any future in that.

GREGERS

No, neither do I.

HEDVIG

But Father's right when he says that if I'd learned basket-making I could have made the new basket for the wild duck.

GREGERS

Yes, so you could. It was your job really, wasn't it?

HEDVIG

Yes, because it's my wild duck.

GREGERS

Of course it is.

HEDVIG

Oh, yes. I own it. But Father and Grandfather are allowed to borrow it whenever they want.

GREGERS

Oh, and what do they do with it?

HEDVIG

Oh, they look after it and build things for it, and that kind of thing.

GREGERS

I should think so. The wild duck's the most important thing in there, isn't it?

HEDVIG

Oh, yes. She's a real wild bird, you see. That's why I feel so sorry for her. She's got no one to care for, poor thing.

GREGERS

No family like the rabbits.

HEDVIG

No. The hens have got friends they used to be chicks with; but she's been separated from all her family. And there's so much that's strange about the wild duck. No one knows her. And no one knows where she came from.

GREGERS

And she's been down to the bottom of the deep blue sea.

HEDVIG (*Glances quickly at him and represses a smile.*)

Why do you say "the deep blue sea"?

GREGERS

What should I have said?

HEDVIG

You could have said the "sea bed," or just the "bottom of the sea."

GREGERS

Oh, why can't I say "the deep blue sea"?

HEDVIG

Yes, but it always sounds so odd to me when other people talk about "the deep blue sea."

GREGERS

Why? Tell me.

HEDVIG

No, I won't. It's silly.

GREGERS

Not at all. Tell me now, why did you smile?

HEDVIG

It's because if I suddenly—without thinking—remember what's in there, I always think of it all as being "the deep blue sea." But that's just silly.

GREGERS

No, you mustn't say that.

HEDVIG

Well, it's only a loft.

GREGERS (*Looks hard at her.*)

Are you so sure?

HEDVIG (*Astonished.*)

That it's only a loft?

GREGERS

Yes. You are quite certain about that?

> *Hedvig stares silently at him, open-mouthed. Gina comes from the kitchen with cutlery and tablecloth.*
> *Gregers gets up.*

I'm afraid I've come too early.

GINA

Oh, you've got to sit somewhere. Anyway, I'll be ready in a minute. Clear the table, Hedvig.

> *Hedvig clears the table. She and Gina lay the cloth, etc., during the following scene. Gregers sits in an armchair and turns the pages of an album.*

GREGERS

I hear you know how to retouch photographs, Mrs. Ekdal.

GINA (*Gives him a quick glance.*)
> Why—yes, I know how.

GREGERS
> That was a lucky chance, wasn't it?

GINA
> Why lucky?

GREGERS
> Since Hjalmar was to become a photographer, I mean.

HEDVIG
> Mother can take photographs, too.

GINA
> Oh, yes, I've had to teach myself that.

GREGERS
> Then it's really you who run the business?

GINA
> Yes, when Hjalmar hasn't time himself, I—

GREGERS
> His old father takes up a lot of his time, I dare say.

GINA
> Yes. And anyway it's no real job for a man like Hjalmar to have to take the portraits of just anyone.

GREGERS
> I quite agree. But after all, he has chosen this profession—

GINA
> Hjalmar isn't just an ordinary photographer, you know, Mr. Werle.

GREGERS
> I'm sure he isn't. But—
> > *A shot is fired inside the loft.*
> > *Gregers jumps up.*
> What's that?

GINA
> Ugh, they're shooting again.

GREGERS
> Do they shoot too?

HEDVIG
> They go hunting.

GREGERS
> What!
> > *By the door of the loft.*
> Are you hunting, Hjalmar?

HJALMAR (*From beyond the curtain.*)
> Are you here? Oh, I didn't know. I was so busy with—
> > *To Hedvig.*
> Why didn't you tell us?
> > *Comes into the studio.*

GREGERS
> Do you go shooting in the loft?

HJALMAR (*Shows him a double-barrelled pistol.*)
> Oh, only with this.

GINA
> You and Grandfather'll do yourselves an injury one of these fine days with that popgun.

HJALMAR (*Irritated.*)

This is a pistol, as I think I've told you before.

GINA

I don't see that that improves matters.

GREGERS

So you've turned hunter, too, Hjalmar?

HJALMAR

Oh, I just go out after rabbits now and then. Mostly for the old man's sake, you know.

GINA

Men are funny creatures. Always got to have something to diverge themselves with.

HJALMAR (*Bad-temperedly.*)

Quite so. As Gina says, we've always got to have something to divert ourselves with.

GINA

Isn't that what I said?

HJALMAR

Hm. Well—.

To Gregers.

Yes, you see, as luck would have it the loft's placed in such a way that no one can hear us when we shoot.

Puts down the pistol on the top shelf of the bookcase.

Don't touch that pistol, Hedvig. One of the barrels is loaded. Now don't forget.

GREGERS (*Peers in through the net.*)

You've a shotgun too, I see.

HJALMAR

That's Father's old gun. It's no use any longer, something's gone wrong with the lock. But it's quite fun to have it around. We can take it to pieces now and then and clean it and grease it and put it together again. Of course it's mostly Father who fiddles around like that.

HEDVIG (*To Gregers.*)

Now you can see the wild duck properly.

GREGERS

Yes, I was just looking at her. She droops a little on one wing, doesn't she?

HJALMAR

No wonder. That's where she was shot.

GREGERS

And she trails one foot a little. Am I right?

HJALMAR

Perhaps just a little.

HEDVIG

Yes, that's where the dog bit her.

HJALMAR

But otherwise there's nothing wrong with her. It's really marvellous when you think she's had a charge of shot in her and has been between the teeth of a dog—

GREGERS (*Glances at Hedvig.*)

And has been on the bottom of the deep blue sea for so long.

HEDVIG (*Smiles.*)
>Yes.

GINA (*Laying the table.*)
>Oh, that blessed wild duck. You make too much of a song and dance about her.

HJALMAR
>Hm. Are you nearly ready with that?

GINA
>Yes, I shan't be a minute. Hedvig, come and give me a hand.
>>*Gina and Hedvig go out into the kitchen.*

HJALMAR (*In a low voice.*)
>I think you'd better not stand there watching Father. He doesn't like it.
>>*Gregers comes away from the loft door.*
>I'd better close up before the others arrive.
>>*Claps his hands to frighten the birds.*
>Shoo, shoo! Get away with you!
>>*Pulls up the curtain and closes the doors as he speaks.*
>I invented these gadgets myself. It's really rather fun to have something like this to fiddle with, and fix when it goes wrong. We've got to have it, because Gina doesn't like rabbits and hens in here.

GREGERS
>No, no. It's your wife who runs the studio, I suppose?

HJALMAR
>I generally leave the details of the business to her. Then I can lock myself away in the parlour and think about more important things.

GREGERS
>What kind of things, Hjalmar?

HJALMAR
>I wonder you haven't asked me that before. But perhaps you haven't heard about my invention?

GREGERS
>Your invention? No.

HJALMAR
>Really? Haven't you? Oh no, I suppose being cut off up there in those forests—

GREGERS
>So you've invented something?

HJALMAR
>It's not quite finished yet. But I'm working on it. As you can imagine, when I decided to give up my life to the service of photography it wasn't because I wanted to take portraits of the *bourgeoisie*.

GREGERS
>No, that's what your wife said just now.

HJALMAR
>I made a vow that if I was going to dedicate my powers to this craft, I would exalt it to the level of both an art and a science. And so I decided to make this astonishing invention.

GREGERS
>But what *is* this invention? What's the idea behind it?

HJALMAR
>Oh, my dear fellow, you mustn't ask me about details yet. It takes

time, you know. And you mustn't think it's vanity that's inspiring me to do this. It isn't for myself that I'm doing it. Oh, no. I have a mission in life that I can never forget.

GREGERS

What kind of mission?

HJALMAR

Have you forgotten that old man with the silver hair?

GREGERS

Your poor father. Yes, but there isn't very much you can do for him, is there?

HJALMAR

I can rekindle his self-respect by restoring to the name of Ekdal the honour and dignity which it once had.

GREGERS

And that's your mission?

HJALMAR

I want to save that shipwrecked soul, yes. Right from the moment the storm broke over him, he was a wreck. And during those terrible investigations he was no longer himself. That pistol over there, Gregers—the one we use for shooting rabbits—has played its part in the tragedy of the House of Ekdal.

GREGERS

Really? That pistol?

HJALMAR

When sentence had been pronounced and he was about to be taken to prison—he had the pistol in his hand—

GREGERS

You mean—?

HJALMAR

Yes. But he didn't dare. He was a coward. His spirit had been broken. Can you understand it? He, a soldier, who had killed nine bears, and was descended from two lieutenant colonels—one after the other, of course— Can you understand it, Gregers?

GREGERS

Yes, I understand it very well.

HJALMAR

I can't. But that wasn't the last time that pistol played a part in the history of our family. When he was in his grey garb, under lock and key—oh, it was a terrible time for me, believe me. I kept the blinds drawn over both my windows. When I peeped out I saw that the sun still shone. I couldn't understand it. I saw people in the street, laughing and chatting, about trivial things. I couldn't understand it. I thought the whole world ought to stand still, as though in eclipse.

GREGERS

That is how I felt when my mother died.

HJALMAR

At such a moment, Hjalmar Ekdal held the pistol pointed at his own breast.

GREGERS

You mean you, too, thought of—?

HJALMAR

Yes.

GREGERS

But you didn't fire?

HJALMAR

No. At the critical moment, I triumphed over myself. I decided to remain alive. But I can tell you, Gregers, it takes courage under such circumstances to choose life.

GREGERS

Yes, well—that depends on how one—

HJALMAR

Believe me, Gregers, I am right. Anyway, it was better so. Now I shall make my invention; and then, Dr. Relling agrees with me, Father may be allowed to wear his uniform again. I shall demand it as my sole reward.

GREGERS

So it's the uniform he—?

HJALMAR

Yes, that's what he longs for most. You can't imagine how my heart bleeds for him. Every time we have any little family celebration—for example, Gina's and my wedding anniversary, or whatever it may be—the old man appears as the lieutenant he used to be in happier days. But if there's a knock on the door he scampers back to his room as fast as his old legs will carry him, because he daren't show himself to strangers. Oh, it's heart-rending for a son to have to witness such things, Gregers.

GREGERS

How soon do you expect this invention to be ready?

HJALMAR

Good heavens, you can't expect me to work to a schedule. An invention is something that even the inventor himself isn't completely master of. It depends largely on intuition—on inspiration—and it's almost impossible to predict when that's going to come.

GREGERS

But you're making progress?

HJALMAR

Of course I am. I think about it every day. It's always with me. Every afternoon, after I've eaten, I shut myself up in the parlour where I can meditate in peace. But I mustn't be rushed. That won't help at all. Relling says so too.

GREGERS

And you don't think that all that business in the loft distracts you too much, and dissipates your energies?

HJALMAR

No, no, no—quite the contrary. I can't spend all my time brooding over the same exhausting problem. I must have some distraction while I wait for the inspiration to come. Inspiration, you see, comes when it comes.

GREGERS

My dear Hjalmar, I really believe there is something of the wild duck in you.

HJALMAR

The wild duck? How do you mean?

GREGERS

You've plunged to the bottom and are holding on to the seaweed.

HJALMAR
Are you referring to that stroke of fate which crippled Father—and me as well?

GREGERS
Not that so much. I wouldn't say you've been crippled. You've wandered into a poisonous swamp, Hjalmar. You've got a creeping disease in your body, and you've sunk to the bottom to die in the dark.

HJALMAR
Me? Die in the dark? Now really, Gregers, you must stop that talk.

GREGERS
Don't worry. I shall get you up again. I've found a mission in life, too, you see. I found it yesterday.

HJALMAR
I dare say, but please leave me out of it. I can assure you that—apart from a certain melancholy, which is easily explained—I'm as contented with life as anyone could wish to be.

GREGERS
That's another effect of the poison.

HJALMAR
Oh, my dear Gregers, do stop talking about diseases and poisons. I'm not used to this kind of conversation. In my house we don't talk about disagreeable matters.

GREGERS
No, I can well believe that.

HJALMAR
Yes—it's not good for me, you see. And you won't find any poisonous fumes here, as you insinuate. In the poor photographer's home the roof is low, I know that well. And the circumstances are narrow. But I am an inventor, Gregers—the breadwinner for my family—and that lifts me above the poverty of my surroundings. Ah, lunch!

Gina and Hedvig bring in bottles of beer, a decanter of aquavit, glasses, etc. . . . At the same time Relling and Molvik enter from the passage. Neither has a hat or overcoat. Molvik is dressed in black.

GINA *(Putting the things on the table.)*
Trust those two to come on time!

RELLING
Molvik thought he could smell herring salad, so there was no holding him. Good morning again, Ekdal.

HJALMAR
Gregers, may I present Mr. Molvik? Dr.—but of course you know Relling.

GREGERS
Yes, we have met.

RELLING
Oh, it's Mr. Werle Junior. Yes, we two have clashed before, up at Hoydal. You moved in here?

GREGERS
I moved in this morning.

RELLING
Molvik and I live underneath, so you haven't far to go for a doctor or a priest, if you should ever need either of them.

GREGERS

Thank you, I well may. Yesterday we were thirteen at table.

HJALMAR

Oh, don't start that awful business again.

RELLING

Take it easy, Edkal. You were one of the twelve.

HJALMAR

I hope so, for my family's sake. But now let's sit down, and eat and drink and be merry.

GREGERS

Oughtn't we to wait for your father?

HJALMAR

No, he wants his taken in to him later. Come along now, everybody!

The men sit down at the table, and start eating and drinking. Gina and Hedvig come and go, waiting on them.

RELLING

Molvik was as tight as a drum again last night, Mrs. Ekdal.

GINA

Oh? Last night again?

RELLING

Didn't you hear him when I brought him home?

GINA

No, I can't say I did.

RELLING

That's as well. Molvik was *awful* last night.

GINA

Is this true, Molvik?

MOLVIK

Let us draw a veil over the events of last night. It was not a manifestation of my better self.

RELLING (*To Gregers.*)

It comes on him like an inspiration. And then I have to go out and paint the town with him. Molvik's daemonic, you see.

GREGERS

Daemonic?

RELLING

Yes, daemonic.

GREGERS

Hm.

RELLING

And people who are born daemonic can't keep a straight course through life. They have to go off the rails now and then. Well, so you're still sticking it out at that ugly black mill, are you?

GREGERS

I have stuck it out until now.

RELLING

And did you manage to enforce that claim you went round pestering everyone with?

GREGERS

Claim?

Understands him.

I see.

HJALMAR

Have you been acting as a debt collector, Gregers?

GREGERS

Oh, nonsense.

RELLING

Oh yes, he has. He went round all the workmen's cottages, shoving something in their faces which he called the "claim of the ideal."

GREGERS

I was young then.

RELLING

You're right there. You were very young. And as for that claim of the ideal—you never got anyone to honour it before I left.

GREGERS

Nor since, either.

RELLING

Then I hope you've grown wise enough to reduce your demands a little.

GREGERS

Not when I stand face to face with a man.

HJALMAR

Well, that sounds reasonable enough. A little butter, Gina.

RELLING

And a slice of pork for Molvik.

MOLVIK

Oh no, not pork!
There is a knock on the door of the loft.

HJALMAR

Open the door, Hedvig. Father wants to come out.
Hedvig goes across and opens the door a little. Old Ekdal comes out with a fresh rabbit skin. She closes the door behind him.

EKDAL

Morning, gentlemen. Good hunting today. I've shot a big one.

HJALMAR

Why did you have to skin it before I came?

EKDAL

Salted it, too. It's good, tender meat, rabbit meat. Sweet, too. Tastes like sugar. Enjoy your dinner, gentlemen!
Goes into his room.

MOLVIK (*Gets up.*)

Excuse me—I can't—I must—quickly—

RELLING

Drink some soda water, man!

MOLVIK (*Hurries out.*)

Ah—ah!
Goes out through the front door.

RELLING (*To Hjalmar.*)

Let's drink to the old huntsman.

HJALMAR (*Clinks glasses with him.*)

A great sportsman at the end of the road.

RELLING

His hair tempered with grey—
Drinks.
By the way, tell me, is his hair grey or white?

HJALMAR

Oh—somewhere between the two. Actually, he hasn't very many hairs left on his head.

RELLING

Well, one can get through the world with a wig, as one can with a mask. You're a lucky man, Ekdal. A beautiful mission to fight for—

HJALMAR

And I do fight for it, believe me.

RELLING

And a clever wife, jogging quietly in and out in her felt slippers, rocking her hips and making everything nice and comfortable for you.

HJALMAR

Yes, Gina.

Nods to her.

You are a good companion to have on life's journey.

GINA

Oh, get along with you!

RELLING

And then you have your little Hedvig.

HJALMAR (*Moved.*)

My child, yes. Above all, my child. Hedvig, come to me.

Strokes her hair.

What day is it tomorrow, Hedvig?

HEDVIG (*Shakes him.*)

Oh no, Father, you mustn't tell them!

HJALMAR

It wounds me like a knife through the heart when I think how poor it must be. Just a little party in the attic—

HEDVIG

But Father, that's just what's so wonderful!

RELLING

And just you wait till your father's ready with his great invention, Hedvig.

HJALMAR

Yes, then you'll see! Hedvig, I have resolved to secure your future. You shall never want. I shall make it a condition that you get—er—something or other. That shall be the poor inventor's sole reward.

HEDVIG (*Whispers, her arm round his neck.*)

Oh, dear, kind Father!

RELLING (*To Gregers.*)

Well, don't you find it pleasant for a change to sit down to a good meal surrounded by a happy family?

HJALMAR

Yes, I think I appreciate these hours at the table more than anything.

GREGERS

Personally I don't like poisonous fumes.

RELLING

Poisonous fumes!

HJALMAR

Oh, for heaven's sake, don't start that again.

GINA

By God, you'll find no fumes in here, Mr. Werle. I give the whole place a good airing every day.

GREGERS (*Leaving the table.*)

You can't drive out the stench I mean by opening the windows.

HJALMAR

Stench!

GINA

How do you like that, Hjalmar!

RELLING

I beg your pardon—you couldn't possibly have brought the stench in yourself from those pits up there?

GREGERS

Yes, it's like you to call what I bring with me a stench.

RELLING (*Goes over to him.*)

Listen, Mr. Werle Junior. I've a strong suspicion you're still carrying that "claim of the ideal" unabridged in your back pocket.

GREGERS

I carry it in my heart.

RELLING

Well, wherever you have the bloody thing I'm damned if I'll let you blackmail anyone with it as long as I'm in this house.

GREGERS

And if I choose to ignore your warning?

RELLING

Then you'll go headfirst down those stairs. Now you know.

HJALMAR (*Gets up.*)

But—but, Relling—

GREGERS

All right, throw me out.

GINA (*Goes between them.*)

Relling, you can't do that. But I must say, Mr. Werle, after the mess you made with your stove you're in no position to come and complain to me about fumes.

There is a knock on the front door.

HEDVIG

Mother, someone's knocking.

HJALMAR

Oh, now that's going to start.

GINA

Let me take care of it.

Goes over, opens the door and steps back in surprise.

Oh! Oh, no!

Haakon Werle, in a fur-lined coat with a fur collar, takes a step into the room.

WERLE

I beg your pardon, but I believe my son is living in this house.

GINA (*Swallows.*)

Yes.

HJALMAR (*Goes towards him.*)

Wouldn't you do us the honour, sir, to—?

WERLE

Thank you, I only want to speak to my son.

GREGERS
Well? I'm here. What is it?
WERLE
I want to speak to you in your room.
GREGERS
Oh? In my room?
Moves towards the door.
GINA
No, for heaven's sake, that's in no state—
WERLE
Out in the passage, then. I want to speak with you alone.
HJALMAR
You can do that here, sir. Relling, come into the parlour.
Hjalmar and Relling go out to the right. Gina takes Hedvig into the kitchen.
GREGERS (*After a short pause.*)
Well. Now we're alone.
WERLE
You let drop a few remarks last night about— And since you've now come to lodge with the Ekdals I can only assume that you intend some action directed against me.
GREGERS
I intend to open the eyes of Hjalmar Ekdal. He must see his situation as it really is. That is all.
WERLE
And that is the mission in life you spoke of yesterday?
GREGERS
Yes. It's the only one you have left me.
WERLE
So it's I who have soured your mind, Gregers?
GREGERS
You have soured my whole life. Oh, I'm not just thinking of what happened to my mother. But it's you I have to thank for the fact that I'm continually haunted by a guilty conscience.
WERLE
Oh, so it's your conscience that's queasy, is it?
GREGERS
I ought to have stood up to you when those traps were laid for Lieutenant Ekdal. I ought to have warned him. I knew in my mind what was going on.
WERLE
Then you ought to have spoken out.
GREGERS
I was frightened. I was a coward. I was so miserably afraid of you then. And long afterwards.
WERLE
You seem to have got over that very well now.
GREGERS
Yes, thank God, I have. The crimes that have been committed against old Ekdal, by me and by—others—can never be undone. But at least I can free Hjalmar from the conspiracy of silence and deceit which is killing him here.

WERLE

And you think that'd be doing him a service?

GREGERS

I have no doubt of it.

WERLE

You think this photographer is the kind of man who would thank you for such a proof of friendship?

GREGERS

Yes. He is that kind of man.

WERLE

Well. We shall see.

GREGERS

And besides—if I am to go on living, I must try to find some cure for my sick conscience.

WERLE

Your conscience has been sickly ever since you were a child. There's no cure for it. That's an heirloom from your mother, Gregers. The only thing she left you.

GREGERS (*With a scornful smile.*)

Haven't you got over your disappointment yet? You miscalculated badly, didn't you, when you thought you'd get rich through her.

WERLE

Don't try to distract me with irrelevancies. Are you still resolved to carry out your intention of guiding Ekdal on to what you suppose to be the right path?

GREGERS

Yes. I am resolved.

WERLE

In that case I might have saved myself the trouble of climbing the stairs. I don't suppose it's any use now asking if you'll come back home?

GREGERS

No.

WERLE

And you won't enter the firm either, I suppose?

GREGERS

No.

WERLE

Very good. But since I am intending to enter into a new marriage, I will arrange for the estate to be divided between us.

GREGERS (*Quickly.*)

No, I don't want that.

WERLE

You don't want it?

GREGERS

No. My conscience won't allow me.

WERLE (*After a moment.*)

Are you going back to the mill?

GREGERS

No. I have left your service.

WERLE

But what will you do?

GREGERS
    I shall simply fulfil my mission. That is all.

WERLE
    But afterwards? How will you live?

GREGERS
    I have saved a little out of my salary.

WERLE
    Yes, but how long will that last?

GREGERS
    I think it will see me through.

WERLE
    What does that mean?

GREGERS
    I think you've asked me enough questions.

WERLE
    Good-bye, then, Gregers.

GREGERS
    Good-bye.
        Haakon Werle goes out.

HJALMAR (*Looks in.*)
    Has he gone?

GREGERS
    Yes.
        *Hjalmar and Relling come in. Gina and Hedvig enter from the
        kitchen.*

RELLING
    Well, that's the end of our lunch.

GREGERS
    Get your coat, Hjalmar. You and I must take a long walk together.

HJALMAR
    Yes, let's. What did your father want? Was it anything to do with
    me?

GREGERS
    Come along. We must have a little talk. I'll go and fetch my coat.
        Goes out through the front door.

GINA
    I don't like you going out with him, Hjalmar.

RELLING
    She's right. Stay here with us.

HJALMAR (*Takes his hat and overcoat.*)
    What! When an old schoolfellow feels the need to pour out his heart
    to me—?

RELLING
    But, for Christ's sake—don't you see the fellow's mad, twisted, out of
    his mind?

GINA
    There you are! Well, what do you expect? His mother had weird fits
    like that too, sometimes.

HJALMAR
    All the more need for someone to keep a friendly eye on him, then.
        To Gina.
    Make sure dinner's ready in good time. Good-bye for now.
        Goes out through the front door.

RELLING

What a pity that fellow didn't fall into one of his own mines and drop right down to Hell!

GINA

Mercy on us! Why do you say that?

RELLING (*Mutters.*)

Oh, I have my reasons.

GINA

Do you think young Mr. Werle's really mad?

RELLING

No, worse luck. He's no madder than most people. He's sick all right, though.

GINA

What do you think's wrong with him?

RELLING

I'll tell you, Mrs. Ekdal. He's suffering from a surfeit of self-right-eousness.

GINA

Surfeit of self-righteousness?

HEDVIG

Is that a disease?

RELLING

Yes. It's a national disease. But it only very seldom becomes acute.
Nods to Gina.
Thanks for the lunch.
Goes out through the front door.

GINA (*Walks round uneasily.*)

Ugh! That Gregers Werle. He always was a queer fish.

HEDVIG (*Stands by the table and looks searchingly at her.*)

I think this is all very strange.

Act four

> *Hjalmar Ekdal's studio. A photograph has just been taken; a camera with a cloth over it, a stand, two or three chairs, a folding table, etc., stand round the room. Afternoon light; the sun is just going down; a little later it begins to grow dark. Gina is standing in the open doorway with a small box and a wet glass plate in her hand, talking to someone outside.*

GINA

Yes, definitely. When I make a promise I always keep it. I'll have the first dozen ready by Monday. Good-bye, good-bye.
> *The other person goes downstairs. Gina closes the door, puts the glass plate in the box and places the latter in the covered camera.*

HEDVIG (*Comes in from the kitchen.*)

Have they gone?

GINA (*Tidying up.*)

Yes, thank God, I got rid of them at last.

HEDVIG

Why do you suppose Father hasn't come home yet?

GINA

Are you sure he's not down with Relling?

HEDVIG

No, he's not there. I've just run down the back stairs to ask.

GINA

And his dinner's getting cold too, I suppose?

HEDVIG

It's funny—Father's always on time for dinner.

GINA

Oh, he'll be here soon. You'll see.

HEDVIG

I wish he'd come. Everything seems so strange suddenly.

GINA (*Cries out.*)

Here he is!

Hjalmar Ekdal comes in through the front door.

HEDVIG (*Runs towards him.*)

Oh, Father! Oh, we've waited and waited for you!

GINA (*Gives him a glance.*)

You've been a long time, Hjalmar.

HJALMAR (*Without looking at her.*)

Yes, I have rather, haven't I?

He takes off his overcoat. Gina and Hedvig try to help him, but he gestures them away.

GINA

Have you eaten with Werle?

HJALMAR (*Hangs up his coat.*)

No.

GINA (*Goes towards the kitchen door.*)

I'll bring in your food, then.

HJALMAR

No, never mind the food. I don't want any.

HEDVIG (*Goes closer.*)

Aren't you well, Father?

HJALMAR

Well? Oh yes, tolerably. We had rather a tiring walk, Gregers and I.

GINA

You shouldn't do that, Hjalmar. You're not used to it.

HJALMAR

But there are a lot of things in life a man's got to get used to.

Wanders round a little.

Anyone been here while I was out?

GINA

Only those two sweethearts.

HJALMAR

No new orders?

GINA

No, not today.

HEDVIG

There'll be some tomorrow, Father. You'll see.

HJALMAR

Let's hope so. Because tomorrow I intend to start working in real earnest.

HEDVIG

Tomorrow? But don't you remember what day it is tomorrow?

HJALMAR

Ah, that's true. Well, the day after tomorrow, then. From now on I'm going to do everything myself. I'm going to manage the whole business on my own.

GINA

But why should you do that, Hjalmar? It'll only make you miserable. No, I'll take care of the photography, and you can go on puzzling with your invention.

HEDVIG

And think of the wild duck, Father. And all the hens and rabbits, and—

HJALMAR

Don't talk to me about all that nonsense. From now on I shall never set foot in that loft again.

HEDVIG

But Father, you promised tomorrow we'd have a party—

HJALMAR

Hm, that's true. Well, from the day after tomorrow, then. I'd like to wring the neck of that damned wild duck.

HEDVIG (*Screams.*)

The wild duck!

GINA

I never heard such nonsense!

HEDVIG (*Shaking him.*)

But Father! It's my wild duck!

HJALMAR

That's why I won't do it. I haven't the heart to—I haven't the heart—because of you, Hedvig. But I know in my heart that I ought to do it. I ought not to allow any creature to live under my roof which has been in *his* hands.

GINA

For heaven's sake! Just because Grandfather got it from that wretched Pettersen—

HJALMAR (*Wandering around.*)

There are certain demands—demands a man makes of himself—how shall I put it?—a striving for perfection—one might say the demands of an ideal—which a man may not ignore without danger to his soul.

HEDVIG (*Goes after him.*)

But Father, the wild duck! The poor wild duck!

HJALMAR (*Stops.*)

I've told you I shall spare it. For your sake. I shall not touch a hair of its—well, as I told you, I shall spare it. I have more important tasks than that to get down to. But you'd better go and take your walk now, Hedvig. It's getting dark—the light won't hurt your eyes now.

HEDVIG

No, I won't bother to go out today.

HJALMAR

Yes, you must. You screw up your eyes so; all these fumes in here are bad for you. The air under this roof is unclean.

HEDVIG

All right, all right. I'll run down the back stairs and go for a little walk. My coat and hat? Oh, they're in my room. Father, you won't hurt the wild duck while I'm out?

HJALMAR

Not a feather of its head shall be touched.

> *Presses her to him.*

You and I, Hedvig—we two—! Well, run along.

> *Hedvig nods to her parents and goes out through the kitchen.*
> *Hjalmar walks around without looking up.*

Gina.

GINA

Yes?

HJALMAR

From tomorrow—or let's say the day after tomorrow—I'd like to keep the household accounts myself.

GINA

You want to look after the household accounts too now?

HJALMAR

Yes. I want to find out where the money comes from.

GINA

Well, heaven knows that won't take you long.

HJALMAR

One would imagine it would. You seem to make it go a remarkably long way.

> *Stops and looks at her.*

How do you do it?

GINA

It's because Hedvig and I need so little.

HJALMAR

Is it true that Father gets paid very generously for the copying he does for Mr. Werle?

GINA

I don't know if it's so very generous. But then I don't know what that kind of work is worth.

HJALMAR

Well, roughly how much does he get? Come on, tell me!

GINA

It varies. On an average about what it costs us to keep him, and a bit of pocket money over.

HJALMAR

What it costs us to keep him! And you never told me!

GINA

How could I? You were so happy because you thought he got everything from you.

HJALMAR

And all the time he gets it from Mr. Werle!

GINA

Oh, there's more where that comes from.

HJALMAR

I suppose we'd better light that lamp.

GINA (*Lights it.*)

Of course, we don't know if it's the old man himself. It might easily be Graaberg—

HJALMAR

Why drag in Graaberg?

GINA

No, I don't know. I just thought—

HJALMAR

Hm!

GINA

I didn't get this work for Grandfather. It was Berta—when she came to live there.

HJALMAR

Your voice has gone funny.

GINA (*Puts the shade on the lamp.*)

My voice?

HJALMAR

And your hands are trembling. Do you deny it?

GINA (*Firmly.*)

Don't beat about the bush, Hjalmar. What's he been telling you about me?

HJALMAR

Is it true—can it be true—that there was a kind of relationship between you and Mr. Werle when you were in his service?

GINA

No, it's not true. Not at that time. Oh, he was after me, all right. And Mrs. Werle thought there was something doing; she created a great hullaballoo, and pulled my hair, she did, so I gave my notice and went.

HJALMAR

But it happened afterwards!

GINA

Yes, well I went home. And Mother—she wasn't such a simple soul as you thought, Hjalmar. She kept talking to me about one thing and another. Well, the old man was a widower by then, you see—

HJALMAR

Go on!

GINA

Well, I suppose you'd better know. He wouldn't give in till he'd had his way.

HJALMAR

And this is the mother of my child! How could you keep such a thing from me?

GINA

Yes, it was very wrong. I ought to have told you about it long ago.

HJALMAR

You ought to have told me at once. Then I'd have known what kind of woman you were.

GINA

If I had, would you have married me?

HJALMAR

What do you think?

GINA

Yes, well, that's why I didn't dare to say anything to you at the time. You know how fond I'd grown of you. How could I throw away my whole life?

HJALMAR (*Walking about.*)

And this is the mother of my Hedvig! And to know that everything I see around me—

Kicks a chair.

—my entire home—I owe to a predecessor in your favours! Oh, that seductive old Werle!

GINA

Do you regret the fifteen years we have lived together?

HJALMAR (*Stops in front of her.*)

Have you not every day, every moment, regretted the web of concealment and deceit that you've spun around me like a spider? Answer me that! Do you mean to tell me that all this time you haven't been living in anguish and remorse?

GINA

Oh, my dear Hjalmar, I've had enough to think about trying to run the house without—

HJALMAR

Then you never probe your past with a questioning eye?

GINA

You know, I'd almost forgotten the whole dirty business.

HJALMAR

Oh, this soulless, unfeeling complacency! It always fills me with moral indignation. And what is more, you don't even regret it!

GINA

Yes, but tell me, Hjalmar. What would have become of you if you hadn't had a wife like me?

HJALMAR

Like you?

GINA

Yes; I've always been a little more down-to-earth and practical than you. Well, it's natural, I suppose, I'm just that much older.

HJALMAR

What would have become of me!

GINA

Yes. You'd gone a bit off the rails when you met me. You surely won't deny that.

HJALMAR

You call that going off the rails? Oh, you don't understand what it's like when a man is full of sorrow and despair. Particularly a man of my fiery temperament.

GINA

No, no. Perhaps I don't. Anyway, I'm not complaining; you became such a good man once you'd got a house and home of your own. And now it was getting to be so homely and nice here; and Hedvig and I were just thinking we might be able to spend a little on food and clothes.

HJALMAR

Yes, in this swamp of deceit.

GINA

Oh, why did that repulsive little man have to come to our house?

HJALMAR

I too used to think this was a good home. It was a delusion. Where shall I now find the strength I need to transfer my invention into terms of reality? Perhaps it will die with me. And it will be your past, Gina, which will have killed it.

GINA (*On the verge of tears.*)

No, you mustn't say things like that, Hjalmar. All our married life I've never thought of anyone but you.

HJALMAR

I ask you—what will become of the breadwinner's dream now? As I lay in there on the sofa brooding over the invention I had a feeling that it would devour my energies to the last drop. I sensed that the day on which I held the patent in my hands—that day would spell my release. And it was my dream that you should live on as the late inventor's prosperous widow.

GINA (*Drying her tears.*)

Now you mustn't talk like that, Hjalmar. May the good Lord never let me live to see myself a widow.

HJALMAR

Oh, what does it matter? It's all finished now. Everything!

Gregers Werle cautiously opens the front door and looks in.

GREGERS

May one come in?

HJALMAR

Yes, come in.

GREGERS (*Comes forward with a radiant, gratified expression and holds out his hands to them.*)

Well, my dear friends!

Looks from one to the other and whispers to Hjalmar.

Hasn't it happened yet?

HJALMAR

Oh, it has happened.

GREGERS

It has!

HJALMAR

I have just lived through the bitterest moment of my life.

GREGERS

But also, surely, the most sublime.

HJALMAR

Well, we've put that behind us. For the time being, anyway.

GINA

May God forgive you, Mr. Werle.

GREGERS (*Greatly amazed.*)

But what I don't see is—

HJALMAR

What don't you see?

GREGERS

From such a crisis there must spring a mutual understanding on which a whole new life can be founded—a partnership built on truth, without concealment.

HJALMAR

Yes, I know, Gregers. I know.

GREGERS

I felt so sure, that when I walked through that door you would be standing there transfigured, and that my eyes would be dazzled by the light. And instead I see nothing but this dull heaviness and misery—

GINA

Oh, I see.

Takes the shade off the lamp.

GREGERS

You don't want to understand me, Mrs. Ekdal. Ah, well. I suppose you need a bit more time. But you, Hjalmar, you? Surely you must have gained a higher understanding now that the crisis is over?

HJALMAR

Yes, of course I have. That is—in a kind of way.

GREGERS

For there is nothing in the world that can compare with the joy of forgiving someone who has sinned, and raising her to one's heart in love.

HJALMAR

Do you think that a man can so easily digest the bitter draught that I have just drained?

GREGERS

Not an ordinary man, perhaps. But a man like you—

HJALMAR

Oh yes, I know, I know. But you mustn't rush me, Gregers. It takes time, you see.

GREGERS

There's a lot of the wild duck in you, Hjalmar.

Relling has entered through the front door.

RELLING

So the wild duck's in the air again?

HJALMAR

Yes. Mr. Werle's winged victim.

RELLING

Mr. Werle? Are you talking about him?

HJALMAR

About him and—the rest of us.

RELLING (*Aside, to Gregers.*)

You bloody fool, why don't you go to Hell?

HJALMAR

What did you say?

RELLING

I was expressing my heartfelt desire to see this quack doctor back where he belongs. If he stays here he's quite capable of messing up both your lives.

GREGERS

You needn't fear for these two, Dr. Relling. I shan't speak about Hjalmar. We both know him. But in her too, deep in her heart, there is something of honesty and truthfulness.

GINA (*Near to tears.*)

Then you ought to have let me stay as I was.

RELLING

Would it be impertinent to ask exactly what it is you're trying to do in this house?

GREGERS
I want to lay the foundations of a true marriage.

RELLING
Then you don't think their marriage is good enough as it stands?

GREGERS
It's probably as good a marriage as most others, I'm afraid. But it is not yet a true marriage.

HJALMAR
You've never had much faith in ideals, Dr. Relling.

RELLING
Rubbish, my boy! May I ask, Mr. Werle—how many true marriages have you seen in your life? Just roughly.

GREGERS
I hardly think I've seen a single one.

RELLING
Neither have I.

GREGERS
But I've seen so many, many marriages of the opposite kind. And I've had the opportunity to study one at sufficiently close quarters to realise how it can demoralise two human beings.

HJALMAR
The whole moral foundation of a man's life can crumble under his feet. That's the terrible thing.

RELLING
Yes, well, I've never been what you'd call married, so I wouldn't presume to judge. But I do know this, that children are as much a part of any marriage as their parents. So you leave that child alone.

HJALMAR
Ah! Hedvig! My poor Hedvig!

RELLING
Yes, I'll thank you to keep Hedvig out of this. You two are adults; muck about with your own lives if you enjoy it. But I'm warning you, be gentle with Hedvig, or you may do her irreparable harm.

HJALMAR
Harm?

RELLING
Yes, or she may come to do herself harm—and perhaps others too.

GINA
What would you know about that, Relling?

HJALMAR
There isn't any immediate danger to her eyes, is there?

RELLING
This has nothing to do with her eyes. Hedvig's at a difficult age just now. She's capable of getting up to anything.

GINA
Yes, that's true—I've noticed it already. She's started fooling around with the kitchen stove. She calls it playing with fire. I'm often afraid she'll burn down the house.

RELLING
There you are. You see. I thought as much.

GREGERS (*To Relling.*)
But how would you explain that kind of behaviour?

RELLING (*Quietly.*)
> My boy. Her voice is breaking.

HJALMAR
> As long as the child has me— As long as my head is above the ground—
> *There is a knock on the door.*

GINA
> Quiet, Hjalmar. There's someone on the landing.
> *Calls.*
> Come in.
> *Mrs. Soerby enters, in an overcoat.*

MRS. SOERBY
> Good evening.

GINA (*Goes to greet her.*)
> Berta, is it you?

MRS. SOERBY
> Yes, it's me. But perhaps I've come at an inconvenient moment?

HJALMAR
> Of course not. Any messenger from that house is always—

MRS. SOERBY (*To Gina.*)
> To be honest, I hoped I might find you alone at this hour of the evening, so I looked in to have a chat and to say good-bye.

GINA
> Oh? Are you going away?

MRS. SOERBY
> Yes. Tomorrow morning. Up to Hoydal. Mr. Werle left this afternoon.
> *Casually, to Gregers.*
> He asked to be remembered to you.

GINA
> Well, fancy that!

HJALMAR
> So Mr. Werle has gone away. And you're going after him?

MRS. SOERBY
> Yes. What have you got to say about that, Ekdal?

HJALMAR
> I say: take care!

GREGERS
> I'd better explain. My father is marrying Mrs. Soerby.

HJALMAR
> Going to *marry* her?

GINA
> Berta! So it's happened at last!

RELLING (*With a slight tremor in his voice.*)
> This isn't true, surely?

MRS. SOERBY
> Yes, dear Relling, it's perfectly true.

RELLING
> You want to get married again?

MRS. SOERBY
> Yes, I've decided I do. Mr. Werle has obtained a special licence, and we're going to get married quite quietly up at Hoydal.

GREGERS

Well, in that case nothing remains but to wish you happiness, as a dutiful stepson.

MRS. SOERBY

Thank you; if you really mean it. I certainly hope it will bring happiness to Mr. Werle and to me.

RELLING

Oh, I'm sure it will. Mr. Werle never gets drunk—as far as I know—and I don't think he's in the habit of beating up his wives, as the late lamented horse-doctor used to.

MRS. SOERBY

Oh, let Soerby rest in peace. He had his good points.

RELLING

But Mr. Werle, we gather, has better ones.

MRS. SOERBY

At least he hasn't wasted all that was best in him. Men who do that must accept the consequences.

RELLING

I'm going out with Molvik tonight.

MRS. SOERBY

Don't do that, Relling. Please, for my sake.

RELLING

What else do you suggest?

To Hjalmar.

Care to join us?

GINA

No, thank you. Hjalmar doesn't go on that kind of spree.

HJALMAR (*Aside, irritated.*)

Oh, be quiet.

RELLING

Good-bye, Mrs.—Werle.

Goes out through front door.

GREGERS (*To Mrs. Soerby.*)

It seems that you and Dr. Relling know each other pretty well.

MRS. SOERBY

Yes, we've known each other for many years. At one time it even seemed as though our friendship might lead to something more permanent.

GREGERS

Lucky for you it didn't.

MRS. SOERBY

I know. But I've always been wary of acting on impulse. A woman can't just throw herself away, can she?

GREGERS

Aren't you afraid I might tell my father about this old friendship?

MRS. SOERBY

You don't imagine I haven't told him myself?

GREGERS

Oh?

MRS. SOERBY

Anything anyone could truthfully say about me I have already told him. It was the first thing I did when I gathered his intentions.

GREGERS

In that case you've been uncommonly frank.

MRS. SOERBY

I've always been frank. It's by far the best policy for a woman.

HJALMAR

What do you say to that, Gina?

GINA

Oh, we women are so different. We can't all be like Berta.

MRS. SOERBY

Well, Gina, I really believe I did the only sensible thing. Mr. Werle hasn't hidden anything from me, either. And perhaps that's what binds us so closely. Now he can talk to me as freely as a child. He's never been able to do that with anyone before. Fancy a strong and vigorous man like him having to spend all his youth and the best years of his life listening to sermons—very often occasioned by quite imaginary offences, from what I've heard.

GINA

Yes, that's true enough.

GREGERS

If you ladies are going to discuss that subject, I had better go.

MRS. SOERBY

Don't bother. I've had my say. I haven't lied to him or kept anything from him. I dare say you think I've done very well for myself. Well, perhaps I have. But I don't think I'm taking more than I shall be able to give him. I shall never fail him. I shall serve him and look after him better than anyone, now that he's growing helpless.

HJALMAR

He? Growing helpless?

GREGERS (To Mrs. Soerby.)

Look, I'd rather we didn't discuss that.

MRS. SOERBY

It's no use trying to hide it any longer, though I know he wants to. He's going blind.

HJALMAR (Starts.)

Going blind? That's strange. Is he going blind, too?

GINA

It happens to lots of people.

MRS. SOERBY

It's not hard to imagine what that must mean to a man like him. Well, I shall try to make my eyes serve for the two of us as best I can. But I mustn't stay any longer, I've so much to do just now. Oh, what I wanted to tell you, Ekdal, was that if there's anything Mr. Werle can ever do for you, just go and speak to Graaberg.

GREGERS

I hardly think Hjalmar Ekdal will want to accept that offer.

MRS. SOERBY

Oh? I haven't noticed in the past that he—

GINA

Yes, Berta. Hjalmar doesn't need to take anything from Mr. Werle any longer.

HJALMAR (Slowly and emphatically.)

Will you present my compliments to your future husband and tell him that I intend at the earliest opportunity to visit Mr. Graaberg—

GREGERS
Hjalmar!
HJALMAR
I repeat, to visit Mr. Graaberg and demand from him an account of the sum I owe his employer. I shall repay this debt of honour—
    Laughs.
—debt of honour! But enough of that. I shall repay it to the last penny, with five per cent interest.
GINA
But my dear Hjalmar, we haven't the money to do that.
HJALMAR
Will you please tell your fiancé that I am working indefatigably at my invention. Will you tell him that my spirit is sustained throughout this exhausting struggle by the desire to be rid of the embarrassing burden of this debt. That is why I have become an inventor. The entire profits shall be used to free me from the money of which your prospective husband has seen fit to disgorge himself.
MRS. SOERBY
What's been going on in this house?
HJALMAR
Never mind.
MRS. SOERBY
Well, good-bye. There was something else I wanted to talk to you about, Gina; but it'll have to wait till another time. Good-bye.
    Hjalmar and Gregers bow silently. Gina accompanies Mrs. Soerby to the door.
HJALMAR
Not beyond the threshold, Gina.
    Mrs. Soerby goes. Gina closes the door behind her.
There, Gregers. Thank God I've managed to get that debt off my conscience.
GREGERS
Well, you will soon, anyway.
HJALMAR
I think I can claim I behaved correctly.
GREGERS
You behaved exactly as I always knew you would.
HJALMAR
A time comes when a man can no longer ignore the command of his ideals. As the family breadwinner I am continually tormented by this command. I tell you, Gregers, it isn't easy for a man of small means to repay an old debt on which, as one might say, there has settled the dust of oblivion. But there's no other way. I must do what is right.
GREGERS (*Puts his hand on Hjalmar's shoulders.*)
My dear Hjalmar. Aren't you glad I came?
HJALMAR
Yes.
GREGERS
Aren't you glad to see yourself as you really are?
HJALMAR (*A little impatiently.*)
Of course I'm glad. But there's one thing which troubles my sense of

justice. Well, but I don't know whether I should speak so bluntly about your father.

GREGERS

Say what you like. I don't mind.

HJALMAR

Well, then—it offends me to think that it is he, and not I, who is going to make a true marriage.

GREGERS

What are you saying!

HJALMAR

But it's true. Your father and Mrs. Soerby are entering upon a marriage founded on absolute trust, with complete frankness on both sides. They are keeping nothing from each other. They have confessed their sins, if I may so put it, and have forgiven each other.

GREGERS

Well, what of it?

HJALMAR

But that's the whole point. You just said yourself that it's only by overcoming all that that you can found a true marriage.

GREGERS

But that's quite different, Hjalmar. You surely don't compare yourself or her with these two—? Well, you know what I mean.

HJALMAR

I can't get away from the fact that there's something here which wounds and offends my sense of justice. Well, it looks as though there's no just power ruling this world.

GINA

Oh, Hjalmar, really! You mustn't speak like that!

GREGERS

Hm—let's not get on to that subject!

HJALMAR

But on the other hand I seem to see the finger of fate at work restoring the balance. He is going blind.

GINA

Oh, we don't know for sure about that.

HJALMAR

Can we doubt it? At least, we ought not to; for there lie justice and retribution. He has blinded a loyal and trusting friend—

GREGERS

I'm afraid he has blinded many.

HJALMAR

And now comes the inexorable, the unfathomable, and demands his own eyes.

GINA

Oh, how can you say such a horrible thing? You make me feel quite frightened.

HJALMAR

It is useful to face up to the darker aspects of existence now and then.

Hedvig, in her hat and coat, enters happy and breathless through the front door.

GINA

Are you back already?

HEDVIG
Yes, I didn't want to walk any more. And a good thing too, for I met someone coming out of the front door.
HJALMAR
That Mrs. Soerby, I suppose.
HEDVIG
Yes.
HJALMAR (*Walking up and down.*)
I hope you have seen her for the last time.
> *Silence. Hedvig looks timidly from one to the other as though to find out what is the matter.*
HEDVIG (*Goes nearer him; wooingly.*)
Father.
HJALMAR
Well, what is it, Hedvig?
HEDVIG
Mrs. Soerby brought something for me.
HJALMAR (*Stops.*)
For you?
HEDVIG
Yes. Something for tomorrow.
GINA
Berta always brings something for your birthday.
HJALMAR
What is it?
HEDVIG
No, you mustn't know yet. Mother's going to bring it to me in bed tomorrow morning.
HJALMAR
Oh, this conspiracy to keep me out of everything!
HEDVIG (*Quickly.*)
No, of course you can see it. It's a big letter.
> *Takes the letter from her coat pocket.*
HJALMAR
A letter too?
HEDVIG
Only a letter. The present'll come later, I suppose. But fancy—a letter! I've never had a letter before. And there's "Miss" written on the outside!
> *Reads.*
"Miss Hedvig Ekdal." That's me!
HJALMAR
Let me see that letter.
HEDVIG (*Holds it out to him.*)
Here—look!
HJALMAR
This is Mr. Werle's writing.
GINA
Are you sure, Hjalmar?
HJALMAR
Look for yourself.
GINA
How should I know?

HJALMAR
>Hedvig, may I open this letter and read it?

HEDVIG
>Yes, certainly, if you want to.

GINA
>No, Hjalmar, not tonight. It's for tomorrow.

HEDVIG (*Quietly.*)
>Oh, do let him read it, please! It's sure to be something nice, and then Father'll be happy, and it'll be nice here again.

HJALMAR
>I may open it, then?

HEDVIG
>Yes, do, Father. It'll be fun to know what's in it.

HJALMAR
>Right.
>>*Opens the letter, takes out a sheet of paper, reads it and looks bewildered.*
>What on earth—?

GINA
>What does it say?

HEDVIG
>Oh yes, Father! Do tell us!

HJALMAR
>Be quiet!
>>*Reads it through again. Then, pale but controlled, he says.*
>It's a deed of gift, Hedvig.

HEDVIG
>I say! What do I get?

HJALMAR
>See for yourself.
>>*Hedvig goes over to the lamp and reads the letter under it.*
>>*Hjalmar softly, clenching his fists.*
>The eyes! The eyes! And this letter!

HEDVIG (*Looks up from her reading.*)
>But I think Grandfather ought to have it.

HJALMAR (*Takes the letter from her.*)
>Gina, can you make any sense of this?

GINA
>You know I don't understand anything. Tell me what it's about.

HJALMAR
>Mr. Werle writes to Hedvig that her old grandfather need no longer trouble to copy letters but that he can henceforth draw from the office the sum of one hundred crowns per month—

GINA
>Really?

HEDVIG
>A hundred crowns, Mother! That's what it says!

GINA
>Well, that'll be nice for Grandfather.

HJALMAR
>One hundred crowns, for as long as he needs it. That means, of course, for as long as he lives.

GINA

Well, at least he's provided for then, poor old man.

HJALMAR

But there's something else. You didn't read this part, Hedvig. Afterwards, this money is to be paid to you.

HEDVIG

To me? All of it?

HJALMAR

"You are assured of this sum for the rest of your life," he writes. Did you hear that, Gina?

GINA

Yes, I heard.

HEDVIG

Imagine all the money I'm going to have!
     Shakes him.
Oh, Father, Father, aren't you happy—?

HJALMAR (*Avoids her.*)

Happy!
     Walks about.
Oh, what vistas, what perspectives begin to unroll before my eyes! It's Hedvig! She's the one he remembers so generously!

GINA

Yes—well, it's Hedvig's birthday.

HEDVIG

But you shall have it all, Father! I want to give all the money to you and Mother!

HJALMAR

Yes, to Mother! There we have it!

GREGERS

Hjalmar, this is a trap which has been laid for you.

HJALMAR

You think this is another trap?

GREGERS

When he was here this morning, he said to me: "Hjalmar Ekdal is not the man you think he is."

HJALMAR

Not the man—!

GREGERS

"You'll see," he said.

HJALMAR

Meaning that I would let myself be fobbed off with money!

HEDVIG

Mother, what are they talking about?

GINA

Go in there and take your coat off.
     Hedvig goes out through the kitchen door, almost in tears.

GREGERS

Well, Hjalmar, now we shall see which of us is right. He or I.

HJALMAR (*Slowly tears the letter in two and puts the pieces on the table.*)

There is my reply.

GREGERS

I knew it would be.

HJALMAR (*Goes over to Gina who is standing by the stove and says in a low voice.*)
And now let's have the truth. If it was all over between you and him when you—began to grow fond of me, as you put it—why did he make it possible for us to get married?

GINA
I suppose he thought he could have a key.

HJALMAR
Was that all? Wasn't he afraid of a certain possibility?

GINA
I don't know what you mean.

HJALMAR
I want to know if—your child has the right to live beneath my roof.

GINA (*Draws herself up; her eyes flash.*)
You ask me that?

HJALMAR
Answer me! Is Hedvig mine or—? Well?

GINA (*Looks at him in cold defiance.*)
I don't know.

HJALMAR (*Trembles slightly.*)
You don't know!

GINA
How could I? You know yourself what I'm like.

HJALMAR (*Quietly, turning away from her.*)
Then I have no further business in this house.

GREGERS
Consider, Hjalmar!

HJALMAR (*Puts on his overcoat.*)
There's nothing for a man like me to consider.

GREGERS
You're wrong. There's a great deal to consider. You three must stay together if you are to win the forgiveness that comes with self-sacrifice.

HJALMAR
I don't want to win it! Never, never! My hat!
    Takes his hat.
My home has crashed in ruins about me!
    Bursts into tears.
Gregers, I have no child!

HEDVIG (*Who has opened the kitchen door.*)
What are you saying!
    Runs over to him.
Daddy, daddy!

GINA
There, you see!

HJALMAR
Don't come near me, Hedvig! Go—go far away! I can't bear to look at you! Ah—those eyes! Good-bye!
    Goes towards the door.

HEDVIG (*Clings tightly to him and screams.*)
No! No! Don't leave me!

GINA (*Cries.*)
Look at the child, Hjalmar! Look at the child!

HJALMAR

> I won't! I can't! I must get away! Away from all this!
>> *Tears himself free from Hedvig and goes out through the front door.*

HEDVIG (*With despair in her eyes.*)

> He's leaving us, Mother! He's leaving us! He'll never come back again!

GINA

> Don't cry, Hedvig. Daddy will come back.

HEDVIG (*Throws herself sobbing on the sofa.*)

> No, no. He'll never come back to us again.

GREGERS

> Will you believe that I meant it all for your good, Mrs. Ekdal?

GINA

> Yes, I believe it. But God forgive you.

HEDVIG (*Lying on the sofa.*)

> Oh, I shall die, I shall die! What have I done to him? Mother, you must make him come back home!

GINA

> Yes, yes, yes, all right. Calm yourself, and I'll go out and look for him.
>> *Puts on her overcoat.*
>
> Perhaps he's just gone down to Relling. But you mustn't lie there and cry. Promise me?

HEDVIG (*Sobbing convulsively.*)

> Yes, I'll stop. When Father comes back.

GREGERS (*To Gina, as she is about to go.*)

> Wouldn't it be better to let him fight his bitter battle to the end?

GINA

> Oh, that'll have to wait. Now we must think of the child.
>> *Goes out through the front door.*

HEDVIG (*Sits up and dries her tears.*)

> I want to know what all this means. Why won't Father look at me any more?

GREGERS

> You mustn't ask that till you're grown up.

HEDVIG (*Catches her breath.*)

> But I can't go on being unhappy like this all the time till I'm grown up. I know what it is. I'm not really Daddy's child.

GREGERS (*Uneasily.*)

> How on earth could that be?

HEDVIG

> Mummy might have found me. And perhaps Father's got to know about it. I've read of things like that.

GREGERS

> Well, but even if it were true—

HEDVIG

> Yes, I think he should love me just the same. Or even more. After all, we got the wild duck sent to us as a present, but I love it very much.

GREGERS (*Changing the conversation.*)

> Yes, that's true. Let's talk for a moment about the wild duck, Hedvig.

HEDVIG

> The poor wild duck. He can't bear to look at her any longer, either.
> Do you know, he wants to wring her neck!

GREGERS

> Oh, I'm sure he won't do that.

HEDVIG

> No, but he said it. And I think it was such a horrid thing for Father
> to say. I say a prayer for the wild duck every evening. I pray that
> she may be delivered from death and from all evil.

GREGERS (*Looks at her.*)

> Do you always say your prayers at night?

HEDVIG

> Oh, yes.

GREGERS

> Who taught you to do that?

HEDVIG

> I taught myself. Once when Father was very ill, and had leeches on
> his neck. He said death was staring him in the face.

GREGERS

> Yes?

HEDVIG

> So I said a prayer for him after I'd gone to bed. And since then I've
> kept it up.

GREGERS

> And now you pray for the wild duck, too?

HEDVIG

> I thought I'd better include her, because she was so ill when she first
> came to us.

GREGERS

> Do you say your prayers in the morning, too?

HEDVIG

> Oh, no. Of course not.

GREGERS

> Well, why not in the morning?

HEDVIG

> In the morning it's light, and then there's nothing to be afraid of
> any more.

GREGERS

> And your father wanted to wring the neck of the wild duck, which
> you love so much?

HEDVIG

> No, he said he ought to, but he'd spare her for my sake. That was
> kind of him, wasn't it?

GREGERS (*A little closer.*)

> Yes, but what if you now gave up the wild duck for his sake?

HEDVIG (*Rises.*)

> The wild duck?

GREGERS

> Yes. Suppose you sacrificed for him the most precious of your pos-
> sessions—the thing you love most dearly?

HEDVIG

> Do you think that would help?

GREGERS
> Try it, Hedvig.

HEDVIG (*Quietly, her eyes aglow.*)
> Yes, I will try it.

GREGERS
> Do you think you have the strength to do it?

HEDVIG
> I'll ask Grandfather to shoot the wild duck for me.

GREGERS
> Yes, do that. But not a word to your mother about this!

HEDVIG
> Why not?

GREGERS
> She doesn't understand us.

HEDVIG
> The wild duck! I'll do it tomorrow morning.
> *Gina comes in through the front door.*
> *Hedvig goes to meet her.*
> Did you find him, Mother?

GINA
> No. But I heard he'd called in to see Relling and they'd gone off together.

GREGERS
> Are you sure?

GINA
> Yes, the caretaker told me. Molvik went with them too, she said.

GREGERS
> Now, when he needs to wrestle with his soul alone!

GINA (*Takes off her coat.*)
> Well, men are difficult creatures. God knows where Relling's dragged him off to. I ran over to Mrs. Eriksen's, but they weren't there.

HEDVIG (*Trying not to cry.*)
> Oh, suppose he never comes back!

GREGERS
> He'll come back. I shall tell him the news tomorrow, and then you'll see how quickly he will come. Don't worry, Hedvig. You can sleep in peace. Good night.
> *Goes out through the front door.*

HEDVIG (*Throws her arms, sobbing, round Gina's neck.*)
> Mummy, mummy!

GINA (*Pats her on the back and sighs.*)
> Oh, yes, Relling was right. This is what happens when people go round preaching about the commands of the ideal.

Act five

Hjalmar Ekdal's studio. A cold, grey morning light. Wet snow lies on the large panes of glass in the roof. Gina, wearing an apron, enters from the kitchen with a brush and duster and goes towards the parlour door. At the same moment, Hedvig runs in from the passage.

GINA (*Stops.*)

> Well?

HEDVIG

> Yes, Mother, I think he's down with Relling—

GINA

> There you are!

HEDVIG

> The caretaker said Relling had two people with him when he came back last night.

GINA

> I thought as much.

HEDVIG

> But that's no good, if he won't come up and see us.

GINA

> You leave it to me. I'll go down and have a word with him.
>
> *Old Ekdal, in a dressing gown and slippers and with a lighted pipe, appears in the doorway of his room.*

EKDAL

> Hjalmar, I! Isn't Hjalmar at home?

GINA

> No, he seems to have gone out.

EKDAL

> What, already? And in this blizzard? Oh, well. Let him. I can go for a walk by myself.
>
> *He pushes aside the door of the loft. Hedvig helps him. He goes in, and she closes the door behind him.*

HEDVIG (*Softly.*)

> Poor Grandfather! What will he say when he hears Father's leaving us?

GINA

> Don't be silly, Grandfather mustn't be told about that. Thank God he wasn't here yesterday when all the hullaballoo was going on.

HEDVIG

> Yes, but—
>
> *Gregers enters through the front door.*

GREGERS

> Well? Have you found where he is?

GINA

> They say he's downstairs with Relling.

GREGERS

> With Relling! Has he really been out with those people?

GINA

> So it seems.

GREGERS

> But he needed so much to be alone, and to collect his thoughts—

GINA

> Yes, you may well say that.
>
> *Relling enters from the passage.*

HEDVIG (*Goes towards him.*)

> Is Father with you?

GINA (*Simultaneously.*)

> Is he there?

RELLING
> He certainly is.

HEDVIG
> And you didn't tell us!

RELLING
> Yes, I'm a beast. But I had to put the other beast to bed first—I refer of course to our daemonic friend—and then I fell asleep—

GINA
> What has Hjalmar got to say today?

RELLING
> Nothing.

HEDVIG
> Doesn't he say anything?

RELLING
> Not a damn thing.

GREGERS
> No, no. I can understand that so well.

GINA
> But what's he doing, then?

RELLING
> He's on the sofa, snoring.

GINA
> Is he? Yes, Hjalmar's a terrible snorer.

HEDVIG
> You mean he's asleep?

RELLING
> It certainly sounds like it.

GREGERS
> It's quite understandable. After the spiritual conflict that's been rending him—

GINA
> And he's not used to wandering around outside at night.

HEDVIG
> Perhaps it's a good thing he's getting some sleep, Mother.

GINA
> Yes, I was just thinking that. We'd better not wake him up too soon. Thanks, Relling. I must just clean the place up a bit, and then I'll— Come and give me a hand, Hedvig.
> *Gina and Hedvig go into the parlour.*

GREGERS (*Turns to Relling.*)
> Can you explain this spiritual turmoil in Hjalmar Ekdal?

RELLING
> Can't say I've ever noticed any spiritual turmoil in him.

GREGERS
> What! At such a crisis, when his whole life has been given a new moral foundation—! How do you suppose a man of Hjalmar's personality—?

RELLING
> Personality—*him?* If he ever had any tendency to the kind of abnormalities you call personality, they were nipped out of him, root and branch, before his voice broke. You take my word for it.

GREGERS

That's surprising, considering the love and care with which he was brought up.

RELLING

By those two twisted, hysterical maiden aunts, you mean?

GREGERS

At least they were idealists—but I suppose you'll laugh at me again for saying that.

RELLING

No, I'm not in the mood for that. I know all about it. I've had to endure vomits of rhetoric about his "two spiritual mothers." But I don't think he's got much to be grateful to them for. Hjalmar's tragedy is that all his life he's been regarded by everyone around him as a genius—

GREGERS

Well, isn't he? Deep down inside?

RELLING

I've never noticed any evidence of it. Oh, his father thought so, but—well, *he's* been a bloody fool all his life.

GREGERS

No, he has kept the innocence of a child all his life. That's something you can't understand.

RELLING

All right, have it your way. But when dear little Hjalmar somehow got to university, he was at once hailed as the great white hope there too. Well, he was handsome of course—that helps—you know, peaches and cream, the shopgirl's dream—and with his romantic temperament and throbbing voice and talent for declaiming other people's poetry and ideas—

GREGERS (*Indignantly.*)

Are you talking about Hjalmar Ekdal?

RELLING

Yes. With your permission, that's what this idol you grovel to really looks like when you take him apart.

GREGERS

Well, I don't think I'm completely blind.

RELLING

You're not far off. You're a sick man too, you know.

GREGERS

Yes, you're right there.

RELLING

Oh, yes. Yours is a complicated case. To begin with, you've this tiresome rash of righteousness; and what's worse, you live in a perpetual delirium of hero-worship. You've always got to have something outside yourself that you can idolise.

GREGERS

That's true. I have to seek it outside myself.

RELLING

It's pathetic the way you make a fool of yourself over these supermen you imagine you see all around you. This is just another of those workmen's cottages where you started hawking your ideals. We're all insolvent here.

GREGERS

    If that's your opinion of Hjalmar Ekdal, how can you spend so much time with him?

RELLING

    I'm meant to be a doctor of sorts, God forgive me. I've got to do something for these wretched cripples I share a roof with.

GREGERS

    I see. So Hjalmar Ekdal is sick too?

RELLING

    Well, who isn't?

GREGERS

    And what medicine are you giving him?

RELLING

    My usual one. I feed the life-lie in him.

GREGERS

    Life-*lie,* did you say?

RELLING

    Yes, that's right. The universal stimulant.

GREGERS

    And what is the life-lie with which Hjalmar Ekdal is infected, if I may ask?

RELLING

    You may not. I don't betray professional secrets to quacks. I wouldn't put it past you to make an even worse mess of him. But my remedy's infallible. I've used it on Molvik for years. I've made him daemonic. That's the serum I've injected into his skull.

GREGERS

    Isn't he daemonic, then?

RELLING

    What the hell does it mean, daemonic? It's just a bit of claptrap I thought up to keep him alive. If I hadn't done it the poor swine would have succumbed to self-contempt and despair years ago. And what about the old lieutenant? Well, he found the cure himself.

GREGERS

    Lieutenant Ekdal? How do you mean?

RELLING

    What about that? The great bear hunter going into that musty old loft to chase rabbits? There isn't a happier sportsman in the world than that old man when they let him potter around in there among all that junk. Those four or five withered Christmas trees smell the same to him as the great forests of Hoydal; the chickens are the wild game in the pine tops; and the rabbits that flop across the floor are bears to challenge the strength and skill of the mighty hunter.

GREGERS

    Poor Lieutenant Ekdal! Yes, he's had to abandon his youthful ideals.

RELLING

    While I remember it, Mr. Werle Junior, forget that foreign word "ideals." Why not use that good old Norwegian word: "lies"?

GREGERS

    Do you suggest the two are related?

RELLING

    About as closely as typhus and putrid fever.

GREGERS

Dr. Relling, I will not give up until I have rescued Hjalmar Ekdal from your clutches.

RELLING

So much the worse for him. Deprive the average human being of his life-lie, and you rob him of his happiness.

To Hedvig, as she enters from the parlour.

Well, little wild-duck-mother, I'm off downstairs to see if your father's still pondering his great invention on my sofa.

Goes out through front door.

GREGERS (*Goes closer to Hedvig.*)

I can see it, Hedvig. You haven't done it.

HEDVIG

What? Oh, that thing about the wild duck. No.

GREGERS

Your strength of purpose failed you when the moment for action came, I suppose.

HEDVIG

No, it wasn't that. It was just that when I woke this morning and remembered what we'd been talking about, I thought it all seemed so strange.

GREGERS

Strange?

HEDVIG

I don't know. Yesterday evening, when you first mentioned it, I thought there was something so beautiful in the idea; but when I'd slept on it and thought about it again, it didn't seem so good.

GREGERS

Oh, no. Of course you can't have grown up in this house without some rot setting in.

HEDVIG

I don't care about that. If only Father would come back, I'd—

GREGERS

Oh, if only your eyes could be opened to what really matters in life! If only you had the courage to make your sacrifice truly and joyfully, you'd see—he'd come back to you! But I still believe in you, Hedvig. I believe in you.

He goes out through the front door.

Hedvig walks around for a little; then she is about to go into the kitchen when there is a knock on the door of the loft. Hedvig goes over and opens it slightly. Old Ekdal comes out. She closes the door again.

EKDAL

Hm! It's not much fun having to take my exercise alone.

HEDVIG

Didn't you feel like hunting today, Grandfather?

EKDAL

It's bad weather for hunting today. Dark. You can hardly see your hand in front of your face.

HEDVIG

Don't you ever feel you'd like to shoot something else besides rabbits?

EKDAL

What's wrong with rabbits? Aren't they good enough?

HEDVIG
   Yes, but what about—well, the wild duck?
EKDAL (*Laughs.*)
   Oh, so you're afraid I'll shoot your wild duck, are you? Don't you
   worry, my child. I'd never do that.
HEDVIG
   No, of course, you couldn't. I've heard it's very difficult to shoot wild
   ducks.
EKDAL
   Couldn't? What do you mean? Of course I could.
HEDVIG
   How would you go about it, Grandfather? I don't mean with my
   wild duck, but with other ones?
EKDAL
   I'd shoot them under the breast, Hedvig. That's the safest place.
   And you've got to shoot against the feathers, mind, not with them.
HEDVIG
   Do they die then, Grandfather?
EKDAL
   You bet they die, if you shoot them properly. Well, I must go in
   and—hm—clean myself up. You understand—hm?
      *He goes into his room. Hedvig waits a few moments, glances towards
      the door of the parlour, goes over to the bookcase, reaches up on tiptoe,
      takes down the double-barrelled pistol from the shelf and looks at it.
      Gina enters from the parlour with her duster and brush. Hedvig
      quickly puts down the pistol, unnoticed.*
GINA
   Don't stand there messing about with your father's things, Hedvig.
HEDVIG (*Leaves the bookcase.*)
   I only wanted to tidy up a little.
GINA
   Go into the kitchen and see if the coffee's still hot. I'll take the tray
   when I go down.
      *Hedvig goes out. Gina begins to sweep and clean the studio. After a
      few moments, the front door is cautiously opened and Hjalmar looks in.
      He is wearing his overcoat but is hatless and unwashed. His hair is
      tousled and his eyes are dull and tired.
      Stands with the brush in her hand and looks at him.*
   Oh. Hullo, Hjalmar. You've come.
HJALMAR (*Walks in and answers in a flat voice.*)
   I've come—but only to go at once.
GINA
   Yes, yes, of course. But, my goodness, look at you!
HJALMAR
   At me?
GINA
   And your nice winter coat! Well, that's done for.
HEDVIG (*In the kitchen doorway.*)
   Mother, hadn't I better—?
      Sees Hjalmar, gives a cry of joy and runs towards him.
   Oh, Father, Father!
HJALMAR (*Turns away with a gesture of rejection.*)
   Get away, get away, get away!

To Gina.

Get her away from me!

GINA (*Softly.*)

Go into the parlour, Hedvig.

Hedvig goes silently out.

HJALMAR (*Feverishly pulls out the drawer of the table.*)

I must take my books with me. Where are my books?

GINA

What books?

HJALMAR

My scientific books, of course. The technical magazines I need for my invention.

GINA (*Looks in the bookcase.*)

Are these the ones, without any covers?

HJALMAR

Of course they are.

GINA (*Puts a heap of magazines on the table.*)

Shall I get Hedvig to cut the pages for you?

HJALMAR

I don't want them cut.

Short silence.

GINA

So you're really leaving us, Hjalmar?

HJALMAR (*Rummaging among the books.*)

Have I any choice?

GINA

No, no.

HJALMAR (*Vehemently.*)

I can't go on being pierced to the heart every hour of every day!

GINA

May God forgive you for thinking so vilely of me!

HJALMAR

Give me proof—!

GINA

I think you're the one who needs to do the proving.

HJALMAR

With your past! There are certain things a man has a right to demand—one might be tempted to call them demands of the ideal—

GINA

What about Grandfather? What's going to become of him, poor old man?

HJALMAR

I know my duty. That helpless old man leaves with me. I shall go into town and make arrangements. Hm—

Unwillingly.

Has anyone seen my hat on the stairs?

GINA

No. Have you lost your hat?

HJALMAR

I had it on when I came back last night. Naturally. There can be no doubt about that. But I haven't been able to find it today.

GINA
>For mercy's sake, where on earth did you get to with those two scal-
>lywags?

HJALMAR
>Don't bother me with trivialities. Do you suppose I'm in a mood to
>recall details?

GINA
>Well, I only hope you haven't caught cold, Hjalmar.
>>*Goes out into the kitchen.*

HJALMAR (*Mutters to himself, half audibly and furiously as he empties the
>>drawer beneath the table.*)
>You're a scoundrel, Relling! A cad, that's what you are! Oh, you vile
>seducer! I wish I could hire someone to stick a knife in your back!
>>*He puts some old letters on one side, finds the letter he tore up yester-
>>day, picks it up and looks at the pieces, then puts it quickly down again
>>as Gina returns.*

GINA (*Puts a tray with coffee, etc., on the table.*)
>I've brought you a cup of something warm, in case you feel inclined.
>And some bread and butter and a bit of cold fish.

HJALMAR (*Glances at the tray.*)
>Cold fish? Under this roof? Never! I've had no solid food for nearly
>twenty-four hours, but no matter. My notes! The first chapter of my
>memoirs! Where's my diary? Where are all my important papers?
>>*Opens the parlour door, but shrinks back.*
>There she is again!

GINA
>But for heaven's sake, the child's got to be somewhere.

HJALMAR
>Come out.
>>*He moves aside to make way for her. Hedvig enters, frightened.*
>>*With his hand on the door handle, Hjalmar says to Gina:*
>During my last minutes in what *was* my home, I wish to be spared
>the presence of outsiders.
>>*Goes out into the parlour.*

HEDVIG (*Runs to her mother and asks softly, trembling.*)
>Does he mean me?

GINA
>Stay in the kitchen, Hedvig. No, you'd better go to your room.
>>*To Hjalmar, as she goes in to him.*
>Stop rummaging in those drawers. I know where everything is.

HEDVIG (*Stands motionless for a moment, anguished and bewildered, biting her
>>lips to keep back her tears. Then she clenches her fists convulsively and
>>says quietly.*)
>The wild duck!
>>*She steals over and takes the pistol from the shelf, opens the loft door a
>>few inches, creeps in and pulls it shut behind her. In the parlour off-
>>stage, Hjalmar and Gina begin to argue.*

HJALMAR (*Comes out with some notebooks and old loose papers, which he puts
>>down on the table.*)
>Oh, that old bag's no use. There are hundreds of things I've got to
>lug away.

GINA (*Comes after him with the bag.*)
>   Well, just take a shirt and a pair of pants with you. You can come back for the rest later.

HJALMAR
>   Phew! It's so exhausting, all this packing!
>   *Tears off his overcoat and throws it on the sofa.*

GINA
>   And now your coffee's getting cold, too.

HJALMAR
>   Hm.
>   *Automatically takes a mouthful; then another.*

GINA (*Dusting the backs of the chairs.*)
>   The big difficulty'll be to find another big loft like this for the rabbits.

HJALMAR
>   What! Do you expect me to drag all those rabbits along too?

GINA
>   Well, you know Grandfather can't live without his rabbits.

HJALMAR
>   Well, he'll have to learn. I'm giving up more important things than rabbits.

GINA (*Dusting the bookshelves.*)
>   Shall I pack the flute?

HJALMAR
>   No. No flute for me. Give me the pistol, though.

GINA
>   Are you going to take the pistol?

HJALMAR
>   Yes. My loaded pistol.

GINA (*Looks for it.*)
>   It's gone. He must have taken it with him.

HJALMAR
>   Is he in the loft?

GINA
>   Yes, of course he's in the loft.

HJALMAR
>   Hm. The lonely old man!
>   *Takes a piece of bread and butter, eats it and empties his cup.*

GINA
>   If only we hadn't let that room, you could have moved in there.

HJALMAR
>   What! Live under the same roof as—? Never! Never!

GINA
>   Couldn't you manage in the parlour for a day or two? You'd be alone there.

HJALMAR
>   Within these walls? Never!

GINA
>   Well, how about downstairs with Relling and Molvik?

HJALMAR
>   Don't mention their names to me! The mere thought of them makes me lose my appetite. No, I must go out into the wind and snow,

wandering from door to door seeking shelter for myself and my old
father.

GINA

But you've no hat, Hjalmar. You've lost your hat.

HJALMAR

Scum! Vice-ridden scum, that's what they are! We must find a hat.

Takes another piece of bread and butter.

Something must be done. I don't intend to die of exposure.

GINA

What are you looking for?

HJALMAR

Butter.

GINA

Coming up right away.

Goes out into the kitchen.

HJALMAR (*Shouts after her.*)

Oh, it doesn't matter. I can eat dry bread.

GINA (*Comes back with a butter-dish.*)

Here, this is meant to be fresh.

*She pours him another cup of coffee. He sits on the sofa, spreads more
butter on his bread, and eats and drinks for a few moments in silence.*

HJALMAR

Would I really not be bothered by anyone if I stayed a couple of
days in that room? Anyone at all?

GINA

No, of course not. Why don't you?

HJALMAR

I can't see any hope of getting all Father's things moved out all at
once.

GINA

And don't forget you've got to break the news to him about your not
wanting to live with us any longer.

HJALMAR (*Pushes away his coffee cup.*)

Yes, there's that too. I've got to dig up all those complications again.
I must think things over. I must give myself breathing-space. I can't
cope with so many different burdens in one day.

GINA

No, of course not. Especially with the weather what it is.

HJALMAR (*Touches Werle's letter*).

I see that letter's still lying around.

GINA

Yes, I haven't touched it.

HJALMAR

Of course, it's nothing to do with me—

GINA

Well, I certainly don't want to make anything out of it.

HJALMAR

Still, there's no point in letting it get lost. In the confusion of my
moving, it might easily—

GINA

I'll see it doesn't.

HJALMAR

Of course, this deed of gift really belongs to Father. It's up to him to decide whether it's to be used or not.

GINA (*Sighs.*)

Yes, poor old Father!

HJALMAR

Perhaps for safety's sake—where can I find some glue?

GINA (*Goes over to the bookcase.*)

The pot's here.

HJALMAR

And a brush.

GINA

The brush is here, too.

Brings them to him.

HJALMAR (*Takes a pair of scissors.*)

Just a strip of paper along the back—

Cuts and glues.

Far be it from me to deprive other people of what belongs to them. Least of all a destitute old man. Or—any other person. There, now! Let that stand for a few minutes. And when it's dry, take it away. I never want to see the thing again. Never!

Gregers Werle enters from the passage.

GREGERS (*A little surprised.*)

Oh! Are you here, Hjalmar?

HJALMAR (*Gets up quickly.*)

I was overcome by fatigue.

GREGERS

I see you've had breakfast, however.

HJALMAR

The body makes its demands too, you know.

GREGERS

Well, what have you decided?

HJALMAR

For a man like me, there is no choice. I'm just getting my most important belongings together. But that takes time, you know.

GINA (*A little impatiently.*)

Well, shall I make the room ready or shall I pack your bag?

HJALMAR (*Gives an annoyed glance at Gregers.*)

Pack. *And* make it ready.

GINA (*Takes the bag.*)

Well, well. I'll put in a shirt and p— and the other thing.

Goes into the parlour and closes the door behind her.

GREGERS (*After a short silence.*)

I'd never envisaged it ending like this. Must you really leave your home?

HJALMAR (*Wanders around restlessly.*)

Well, what do you want me to do? I wasn't cut out to suffer, Gregers. I must have peace and calm and comfort around me.

GREGERS

Well, why not? Try! It seems to me that now you have firm ground to build on. Start afresh! And remember, you have your invention to live for too.

HJALMAR

Oh, don't talk about the invention. That may be further off than you think.

GREGERS

Oh?

HJALMAR

Well, dammit, what *is* there for me to invent? Other people have invented almost everything already. It's becoming more and more difficult every day—

GREGERS

But you've put so much work into it.

HJALMAR

It was that drunkard Relling who started me off on it.

GREGERS

Relling?

HJALMAR

Yes. It was he who first made me conscious that I had the talent to make some invention that would revolutionise photography.

GREGERS

I see. So it was Relling.

HJALMAR

Oh, it's made me so happy thinking about it! Not so much for the sake of the invention itself, but because Hedvig believed in it— believed in it as passionately and trustingly as only a child can believe in a thing. What I mean to say is—I was fool enough to delude myself into thinking she believed in it.

GREGERS

Do you seriously believe that Hedvig hasn't been sincere?

HJALMAR

I can believe anything now. Hedvig's the one who stands in my way. Her shadow is going to shut the sunlight out of my life.

GREGERS

Hedvig? Are you talking about Hedvig?

HJALMAR

I loved that child beyond words. I felt so incredibly happy every time I came back to this humble home and she ran to greet me with those sweet eyes peering at me. Oh, what a credulous fool I was! I loved her so, I loved her so. And I dreamed, I deluded myself into believing that she loved me too.

GREGERS

You call that a delusion?

HJALMAR

How can I know? I can't get anything out of Gina—and anyway, she's so totally insensitive to the idealistic aspect of all these complicated— But to you, Gregers, I feel impelled to open my heart. There's this dreadful doubt in my mind that perhaps Hedvig has never really and truly loved me.

GREGERS

Perhaps you may be given proof that she does.

Listens.

What was that? I think I can hear the wild duck crying.

HJALMAR

Yes, that's her quacking. Father's there in the loft.

GREGERS

Is he?

His eyes shine with joy.

I tell you, you may perhaps be given proof that your poor, mis-judged Hedvig does love you.

HJALMAR

Oh, what proof can she give me? I couldn't believe anything from those lips.

GREGERS

Hedvig is incapable of deceit.

HJALMAR

Oh, Gregers, that's just what I can't be sure of. Who knows what Gina and that Mrs. Soerby may not have said when they were gossiping up here? And that child keeps her ears open. That deed of gift may not have come as such a surprise to her as she made out. I thought I noticed something odd in her manner.

GREGERS

What on earth has come over you?

HJALMAR

I've had my eyes opened. Just you wait—you'll see. That deed of gift is only the beginning. Mrs. Soerby's always had a soft spot for Hedvig, and now she's in a position to do anything she likes for the child. They can take her from me any moment they want.

GREGERS

Hedvig will never leave you.

HJALMAR

I wouldn't be too sure of that. If they stand there beckoning to her with their hands full of—and I, who loved her so much, so much! I couldn't imagine any greater happiness than to take her gently by the hand and lead her as a man leads a child who is afraid of the dark through a large, empty room. I can see it now so clearly—the poor photographer in his attic has never really meant very much to her. She was just cunning enough to keep on good terms with him until the time was ripe.

GREGERS

Oh, Hjalmar, you don't believe that.

HJALMAR

The tragedy is that I don't know what to believe—and that I never will know. Oh, you're too much of an idealist, my dear Gregers. If they came to her with their hands full of gold and cried to the child: "Leave him! We can offer you life!"—

GREGERS (*Swiftly.*)

Yes? What do you think she would reply?

HJALMAR

If I were to ask her: "Hedvig, will you sacrifice your life for me?"—

He laughs scornfully.

Oh, yes! You'd hear what answer she'd give me!

A pistol shot is heard from the loft.

GREGERS (*Cries joyfully.*)

Hjalmar!

HJALMAR (*Enviously.*)

Oh, now he's started hunting.

GINA (*Enters, worried.*)

    Oh, Hjalmar, Grandfather's banging away in there on his own.

HJALMAR

    I'll go and have a look.

GREGERS (*Alive, excited.*)

    Wait! Do you know what that was?

HJALMAR

    Of course I do.

GREGERS

    No, you don't. But I know. It was the proof you wanted.

HJALMAR

    What proof?

GREGERS

    A child's sacrifice. She has got your father to shoot the wild duck.

HJALMAR

    Shoot the wild duck?

GINA

    What an idea!

HJALMAR

    But why?

GREGERS

    She wanted to sacrifice for you the most precious of her possessions, because she thought that then you would have to love her again.

HJALMAR (*Gently, emotionally.*)

    Oh, child, child!

GINA

    The things she gets up to!

GREGERS

    She only wanted you to love her again, Hjalmar. She couldn't live without it.

GINA (*Almost in tears.*)

    There, Hjalmar, you see.

HJALMAR

    Where is she, Gina?

GINA (*Sniffs.*)

    Sitting outside in the kitchen, I suppose, poor child.

HJALMAR (*Walks across and flings open the kitchen door.*)

    Hedvig, come here. Come and talk to me.

        Looks round.

    No, she isn't here.

GINA

    She must be in her room, then.

HJALMAR (*Outside.*)

    No, she isn't there, either.

        Comes back.

    She must have gone out.

GINA

    Well, you didn't want to have her in the house.

HJALMAR

    Oh, I wish she'd come home again soon, so that I can tell her! Now everything will be all right, Gregers. Now I think we can start life afresh.

GREGERS (*Quietly.*)

I knew it. Through the child will come resurrection.

> *Old Ekdal appears in the doorway of his room. He is in full uniform, and is busy buckling on his sword.*

HJALMAR (*Amazed.*)

Father! Have you been in there?

GINA

Have you been shooting in your room?

EKDAL (*Indignantly, comes closer.*)

So you go hunting alone now, do you, Hjalmar?

HJALMAR (*Confused.*)

Then it wasn't you who fired that shot in the loft?

EKDAL

Wasn't me? Hm!

GREGERS (*Cries to Hjalmar.*)

Hjalmar! She has shot the wild duck herself!

HJALMAR

What's going on round here?

> *Runs over to the door of the loft, pulls it open, looks in and cries.*

Hedvig!

GINA (*Runs over to the door.*)

Oh, God! What is it?

HJALMAR (*Goes inside.*)

She's lying on the floor.

GREGERS

Lying on the floor? Hedvig?

> *Joins Hjalmar inside.*

GINA (*Simultaneously.*)

Hedvig!

> *Goes into the loft.*

Oh, no, no, no!

EKDAL (*Laughs.*)

Now she's started hunting too!

> *Hjalmar, Gina and Gregers drag Hedvig into the studio. Her right hand is hanging down with the pistol tightly clasped between her fingers.*

HJALMAR (*Distraught.*)

The pistol's gone off! She's shot herself! Call for help! Help!

GINA (*Runs out into the passage and calls down.*)

Relling! Relling! Dr. Relling! Come upstairs! As quick as you can!

> *Hjalmar and Gregers lay Hedvig on the sofa.*

EKDAL (*Quietly.*)

The forest has taken its revenge.

HJALMAR (*On his knees beside her.*)

She's coming round now! She'll be all right!

GINA (*Comes back.*)

Where's the wound? I can't see anything—

> *Relling hurries in. Molvik follows, with no waistcoat or tie, and with his coat hanging open.*

RELLING

What's happened?

GINA

They say Hedvig's shot herself.

HJALMAR
Come here and help us.

RELLING
Shot herself!
Pushes the table aside and begins to examine her.

HJALMAR (*Lying on the floor, gazes up at him in anguish.*)
It can't be dangerous? Can it, Relling? She's hardly bleeding at all. It can't be dangerous, can it?

RELLING
How did it happen?

HJALMAR
Oh, how do I know?

GINA
She was going to shoot the wild duck.

RELLING
The wild duck?

HJALMAR
The pistol must have gone off.

RELLING
Hm. I see.

EKDAL
The forest has taken its revenge. But I'm not afraid of it.
Goes into the loft and closes the door behind him.

HJALMAR
Well, Relling, why don't you say something?

RELLING
The bullet has entered her breast.

HJALMAR
But she'll be all right?

RELLING
Surely you can see that Hedvig is dead.

GINA (*Bursts into tears.*)
Oh, my child, my child!

GREGERS (*Hoarsely.*)
The deep blue sea—!

HJALMAR (*Jumps up.*)
Yes, yes, she must live! Oh, God bless you, Relling, only for a moment! Only long enough for me to tell her how much I loved her—always—always!

RELLING
The bullet entered her heart. Internal haemorrhage. She died instantaneously.

HJALMAR
And I drove her from me like an animal! And she crept into the loft in terror, and died there—because she loved me!
Sobs.
I can never atone for this—never tell her—!
Clasps his hands and cried upwards.
Oh—You up there—if You exist! Why have You done this to me?

GINA
Hush, hush, don't carry on like that. We had no right to keep her—I suppose—

MOLVIK

    The child is not dead, but sleepeth.

RELLING

    Rubbish!

HJALMAR (*Becomes calm, goes across to the sofa and looks down at Hedvig, with folded hands.*)

    How stiff and still she lies!

RELLING (*Tries to free the pistol from her fingers.*)

    She's holding on to it so tightly. So tightly.

GINA

    No, no, Relling, don't break her fingers. Let the pistol stay there.

HJALMAR

    Let her keep it.

GINA

    Yes, let her. But the child mustn't lie here like a show. We'll take her into her own room. Help me, Hjalmar.

    Hjalmar and Gina pick Hedvig up.

HJALMAR (*As they carry her out.*)

    Oh, Gina, Gina! How shall we live after this?

GINA

    We must help each other. Now she belongs to both of us, you know.

MOLVIK (*Stretches out his arms and mumbles.*)

    Praised be the Lord! To dust thou shalt return! To dust thou shalt return!

RELLING (*Whispers.*)

    Shut up, man. You're drunk.

    Hjalmar and Gina carry the body out through the kitchen door. Relling shuts it behind them. Molvik slinks out into the passage. Relling goes over to Gregers and says:

    No one's ever going to make me believe that this was an accident.

GREGERS (*Who has stood overcome by horror, shaking convulsively.*)

    No one will ever know how this dreadful thing happened.

RELLING

    The powder had burned her dress. She must have pressed the pistol against her breast before she fired.

GREGERS

    Hedvig has not died in vain. Did you see how grief set free all that is most noble in him?

RELLING

    Most men are noble when they stand by a death-bed. But how long do you think this nobility will last?

GREGERS

    For as long as he lives. And it will grow, and grow.

RELLING

    In nine months, little Hedvig will be nothing more to him than a theme for a recitation.

GREGERS

    You dare to say that about Hjalmar Ekdal!

RELLING

    Let's talk about it again when the first grasses have withered on her grave. Then you'll hear him gulping about "the child untimely ripped from her father's bosom." You'll see him stewing in emotion and self-admiration and self-pity. Just you wait.

GREGERS
> If you are right and I am wrong, life is not worth living.

RELLING
> Oh, life would be all right if we didn't have to put up with these damned creditors who keep pestering us with the demands of their ideals.

GREGERS (*Stares ahead of him.*)
> In that case, I am glad that my destiny is what it is.

RELLING
> And what, if I may ask, is your destiny?

GREGERS (*As he goes toward the door.*)
> To be the thirteenth at table.
>> *Relling laughs and spits.*

Action analysis and performance suggestions

The following scenes are particularly recommended for informal classroom performance: act III, the scene between Hjalmar and Hedvig and Gregers and Hedvig, pages 453–457, and the final scene of the play, beginning on page 497.

If *The Wild Duck* were merely a problem-solving play with a thesis, then one would probably read it as a criticism of Gregers' "claim of the ideal." Dr. Relling, with his belief in the need for living with life lies, would be the hero for Ibsen. But the drama, as already noted, is more than one of ideas. It is also more than one of character or language. After working on the play for two years, Ibsen wrote in a letter that he would now proceed to the further individualizing of the characters and dialogue. His concern in *The Wild Duck,* despite the choice of prose, was a poet's concern for the imitation of an action; language, thought, and character were elements that imitated it. To understand the play, then, one must seek to identify its specific actions and its central action or superobjective.

DEFINING THE ACTIONS AND THE SUPEROBJECTIVE

One may best define *The Wild Duck*'s action by reference to the duck itself. Gregers identifies himself with the dog who retrieves wounded wild ducks from the poisonous marshes to which they cling in the depths of the sea. In Gregers' eyes Hjalmar is like that duck and he wants to save him and restore him to his whole and noble state. But the wild duck becomes a symbol with various meanings for the different characters and a complex of meanings for the reader or audience. To some extent everybody wants to save the wild duck, but each character perceives the duck in a different way. Close analysis of individual scenes for performance should give important clues to the resulting richness of this central action.

Much is revealed about the relationship between father and daughter in their seemingly simple interchange on pages 453–454. Hjalmar has little appetite for the retouching work and would rather join his father in making improvements in the wild duck's loft. About to escape, he pauses at Hedvig's entrance and is afraid she is snooping, although she says that she merely wants to be with him. Hjalmar responds to her offers of help with a typically melodramatic martyr's refusal: "Oh, no. I'd better cope with it alone. While I still can. All will be well, Hedvig. As long as your father's strength holds out. . . ." He is well aware that such work is bad for

Hedvig's failing eyes, but he cannot resist his desire and tries here to claim her sympathy, to use her to do his work so that he can escape. Hjalmar's efforts to save or to care for the wild duck are revealed as essentially egotistic. He is willing to use his daughter in order to pursue his own comfortable escape.

It is imperative that the actor not play the action to use Hedvig. Hjalmar is unaware of his baser motives. He is more fool than villain, and he continually fools himself. What the actor must play is to claim Hedvig's sympathy and help in order to escape and to help his father with the wild duck.

To some degree the little interchange between father and daughter reveals Hjalmar's larger action in the entire play. His unconscious use of others and his demands for their sympathy to build himself up and make himself comfortable are evident in his false and self-serving rendition to Gina and Hedvig of his dinner at the Werle's. He forgets to bring Hedvig something to eat as he had promised and offers her a menu instead. His demands for food, butter in particular, mean that Gina and Hedvig must go without. The invention he claims he is about to make is a ruse for getting out of work and building himself up, one of Dr. Relling's necessary "life lies." At the end, Dr. Relling predicts that Hjalmar will use the girl's death to wallow "in emotion and self-admiration and self-pity," a prediction that seems entirely plausible in view of his previous actions.

Hedvig's action in much of the play, as in this interchange, is to please her father. But Gregers' subsequent questioning about her life and the wild duck bring out some of her deeper aspirations. Hedvig too is drawn to the wild duck, who has "no one to care for her, poor thing" and whose origins are unknown. Hedvig assures Gregers that she has no wish to travel but only wants to stay home to help her parents. Her deeper wish, however, is to spend time with the duck and all its romantic surroundings, which to her represent the mysterious depths of the sea. Time has ceased to exist in the attic where a clock has stopped, so the reality she aspires to is primordial and mythically ideal. Yet death threatens in the picture in an old history book of "death with an hourglass, and a girl." Hedvig finds the picture horrible but her own prefigured doom is offset by romantic pictures of churches, castles, ships, and the sea.

When Hedvig confesses to Gregers that she would like "to engrave pictures like the ones in the English books," she reveals her creative spirit and her aspiration to a vision beyond the daily one reflected in the photographer's studio. Her action in the scene is partly to make Gregers understand her dream world and her aspirations, but she is astonished when he takes her dream world seriously and asks her if she is sure "that it's only a loft?" Hedvig has partly tried to mask her dreams and she is astonished when she is unmasked.

Gregers questions Hedvig closely and sympathetically about the attic and its contents. On one level he tries to probe the situation for information that will help him on his mission to save Hjalmar. Yet he does reveal some sensitive understanding of a young girl's dreams. Gregers is not unlike the wild duck since he feels himself to be sick or wounded, without family and alone. His ostensible action in the play is to save Hjalmar but his deeper and confessed objective is to save himself. "And besides, if I am to go on living," he explains to old Werle, "I must try to find some cure for my sick conscience."

Gregers' action in the scene is to capture Hedvig's imagination, to win her over, to use her for his own ends. He is able to do so partly because he too identifies with the wounded bird she loves. If the actor playing Gregers is aware of this identification, he will be less tempted to play the cold villain Gregers seems to become. Like Hjalmar, Gregers fools himself and must always act from the highest conscious motives: to save Hjalmar whom he identifies with the wild duck.

OVERCOMING OBSTACLES

In this particular scene, Hjalmar, Gregers, and Hedvig all focus on the wild duck. Underneath the specific actions lies the deeper objective of each of the characters: to save the wild duck with which each one identifies. The obstacle that prevents Hjalmar from continually using Hedvig and anybody else he can to make his life in captivity comfortable is an occasional insight about his selfishness tinged with a sense of guilt. Hjalmar knows it is not good for Hedvig to use her eyes in close work. Hence his insistence that she is responsible if she ruins her eyes by helping him is a coverup for his own guilt, which is based on real love and concern for Hedvig. In a sense, the obstacle to Hjalmar's total action of escape is his better nature and truer vision.

While occasional insight is Hjalmar's obstacle, blindness is the major obstacle to Gregers. Since he cannot see that Hjalmar is not languishing in the poisonous marshes, but is happy in captivity, all his efforts to save him misfire. Old Werle suggests that Gregers' unhealthy attachment to the memory of a sick mother will be fatal to him. The source of Gregers' blindness may then be an oedipal struggle on the son's part to vindicate the memory of a sick mother and undermine the purposes of his father. Such hidden motives would be an obstacle to the conscious one that the actor must play.

Hedvig's obstacle is her incipient blindness and innocence—also a kind of blindness. She aspires to be an engraver, which is beyond physical possibility, and she aspires to please a father who is unworthy of her adoration. The imagery and the designated lighting help focus on this major obstacle in the lives of the characters: their inability to see. Note the shaded lamp at the opening of act I, the growing darkness in act IV, and the "cold, grey morning light" of act V.

THE MAGIC IF AND THE GIVEN CIRCUMSTANCES

Illusion—the life lie that Dr. Relling prescribes—is what keeps the world of *The Wild Duck* alive. Gregers' illusion is that he is a savior and that Hjalmar is eager and able to be saved. Hjalmar's illusion is that he will save his family through a great invention. Hedvig's illusion is that her father is worthy of her adoration. Old Ekdal imagines himself a great hunter in the make-believe wilds of the attic. Old Werle, Mrs. Soerby, Gina, and Dr. Relling are more honest in their appraisals of reality, but Dr. Relling must drink to bear it all, and Gina must constantly bend to survive and save the family which lives on illusions. What IF you suffered from one of the illusions described? What IF you suffered from the lack of them?

The other major given circumstance involves the captivity of the wild duck. Like the wild duck, all the characters are trapped in one way or another. The Ekdals are a family retrieved by old Werle but dependent on his generosity for survival. Wounded like the wild duck and living in captivity, most of them hang on to illusions in order to survive with dignity.

What IF you were very proud but were being kept in hopeless captivity? What illusions might you cling to in such a situation?

CLASSROOM ADAPTATIONS TO ARRIVE AT STYLE

There should be as much separation as possible between actors and audience. The actors should pretend that there is a fourth wall between them and the audience. Hence their concentration should be entirely within the area designated as the stage so as to produce an illusion of reality.

To enhance that illusion of reality, classroom lights should be turned off and Ibsen's instructions for lighting should be improvised (note that "daylight is shining in through the large window in the sloping ceiling, from which the curtain is drawn back"). Furniture and properties should be employed, for example, Hjalmar's table, retouching materials, and portraits lying on the table. The sloping roof and doors to other rooms and to the wild duck's area could be drawn on the blackboard, but it should be noted that they would be working doors in a full production. If comfortable furniture is too difficult to obtain, classroom chairs could be covered with soft materials to give some effect of the warm and comfortable room. Costumes can be late nineteenth-century or contemporary, with Gregers in a suit, Hjalmar in a smock or working clothes, and Hedvig in a skirt and blouse or jumper. Hjalmar and Hedvig should use the properties on the table and relate to elements of the setting as environment rather than background.

Movement and gesture should be simple, natural, and close to everyday conversational tones and movement in order to aid the illusion that the audience is eavesdropping on a scene from life. Since the actors still must be heard and seen, a student-director should help them with projection and arrange the movement so that focus is on the right action at the right moment.

The actors must be aware of the fine line between the comic and the tragic that Ibsen maintains in *The Wild Duck*. Ibsen did not believe Hjalmar should be acted with any trace of parody or affectation; he should be unaware of his sentimentality and attractive in his melancholy. The comic, then, should not be played but will emerge through the exaggerations of Hjalmar's speech, exaggerations of which he is unaware.

Anton Chekhov
The Cherry Orchard

LYUBOFF ANDREEVNA (MADAME RANEVSKAYA)
> I love this house, I can't imagine my life without the cherry orchard and
> if it is very necessary to sell it, then sell me along with the orchard— . . .
>   (page 547)

Madame Ranevskaya appeals in vain to the student Trofimoff to understand her love for the cherry orchard, which is being sold at auction to
pay her debts. Just as the duck in Ibsen's *The Wild Duck* becomes the focus
of the action, so the cherry orchard becomes the action's focus in the last
play of the Russian playwright Anton Chekhov. Also as in *The Wild Duck*,
the symbolic significance of the central image shifts with the interests and
motivations of the various characters. However, in *The Cherry Orchard*, one
realizes that the fate of the orchard involves not only the personal fates of
the characters and the fate of social classes but also the fate of Russia itself or even, on one level, the fate of the modern world.

Chekhov himself lived through the social changes he depicted
(1860–1904). His father had been a serf and then an unsuccessful shop-
keeper, and Chekhov wrote humorous pieces both as the chief support of
his family and as a means to see himself through medical school. Although he received his medical degree, he turned to writing short stories
and then dramatic literature. He became successful as a playwright when
his last plays were produced by the Moscow Art Theater under the direction of Constantin Stanislavski. Chekhov married one of its leading actresses, Olga Knipper, a few short years before his death from tubercu-
losis at the age of forty-four.

No critics dispute Chekhov's ability to depict the prerevolutionary
Russia of the last decades of the nineteenth century. In his four major
plays, *The Seagull* (1896), *Uncle Vanya* (1899), *The Three Sisters* (1901), and
The Cherry Orchard (1904), Chekhov captures particularly well the apathy,
monotony, and frustration of the landowning class. *The Cherry Orchard*'s
social spectrum includes not only Madame Ranevskaya and her brother
Gayeff as landed gentry but also Lopahin, a successful merchant who
buys the very orchard and estate his father served on as a serf, and Trofimoff, the former tutor of Madame Ranevskaya's drowned son, who as a
perennial student and revolutionary idealist contrasts with Lopahin, the
conservative materialist. The tensions of social change are depicted as well
in the ancient and faithful servant Fiers, who regards the emancipation of
the serfs as a disaster, and in the brash young valet Yasha, who wishes
only to return to the more exciting life in Paris. At stake is the cherry orchard, which is associated with a past, a present, and a future: an affluent, leisured, cultured life remembered as an ideal by Madame Ranevskaya and her brother; an unproductive present in which even the recipe

for drying the cherries has been lost; and a transformed future in which Lopahin will cut down the trees to build summer cottages and Trofimoff will continue to work and dream of transforming all of Russia into an orchard.

While the critics agree that Chekhov masterfully catches both the social types of his time and, more important, the social change from an agrarian, feudal age to a more commercial and industrial one, they do not agree on Chekhov's attitude toward that change. Postrevolutionary Russian critics have tended to regard him as negative toward the landed gentry—even to the point of mocking them out of existence. Others have found his plays to be full of a great nostalgia for what had passed, a view that would put Chekhov's sympathies mainly with Madame Ranevskaya and her brother.

However, just as Ibsen tended not to take sides, so Chekhov adopts a largely objective point of view. The child of a scientific age and a doctor, Chekhov hoped to attain that truth he saw as fiction's aim by being scientifically objective but without becoming indifferent or inhumane. His ability to see his creations with both a skeptical and a humane eye is well illustrated in his attitude toward Lopahin, whom he makes a somewhat comic and ridiculous figure with flailing arms but defends as "a very decent person in every sense" who should "behave with perfect decorum, like an educated man, with no petty ways or tricks of any sort . . ." (*Letters of Anton Chekhov to His Family and Friends*, pp. 407–408).

Chekhov had not entirely given up melodramatic endings of acts or plays in his earlier dramatic efforts, though he did relegate what he complained of as the inevitable pistol shots and marriages to off-stage. But while Ibsen maintained and reworked the well-made play for his own realistic purposes, Chekhov's tendency was more and more to capture the flow of life, the latent drama in its day-to-day trivialities and rhythms. Like Ibsen, whom he did not particularly admire, he was most interested in the inner life of his characters, and by the time he wrote *The Cherry Orchard* there were neither gun shots nor marriages at the end. "A play," he said, "should be written in which people arrive, go away, have dinner, talk about the weather, and play cards. Life must be exactly the way it is, and people as they are—not on stilts. . . . Let everything on the stage be just as complicated, and at the same time just as simple as it is in life" (cited by Elisaveta Fen in her edition, *The Seagull and Other Plays*, p. 20). While Ibsen had tried to capture life as it is lived in its moments of crisis, Chekhov revolutionized playwriting even more by what appeared to some as plotless plays or "slices of life."

Actually Chekhov's plays are very carefully and subtly plotted, as can be seen in *The Cherry Orchard* where Madame Ranevskaya comes home in order to save the orchard and departs when attempts to save it fail. Emphasis, however, despite the crisis of the sale and the passing of a way of life that the sale suggests, remains on the reactions of the various characters to that change rather than on reasoned efforts to save it or on the events themselves. We are less interested in Lopahin's victorious purchase of the estate and orchard than in his very mixed feelings about his victory.

Chekhov had decided to give up writing for the theater with the failure of *The Seagull* in 1896, which was badly misunderstood and poorly performed by the Alexandrinsky Theater. Two years later it was produced by the Moscow Art Theater with success. The event was of extreme significance both for Chekhov, who wrote three more major plays to be produced by that theater under the direction of Stanislavski, and for the Moscow Art Theater itself, which found its particular style through its continuing association with the playwright. Vladimir Nemirovich-Danchenko and Stanislavski had been working together, partly under the influence of the famous Meiningen Company, to create an ensemble that could act in a natural and lifelike manner in scenic background of total realism and historical accuracy. What they found in Chekhov, who shared their desire to leave theatrical artifice and affectation behind and who admired the unity of production that they emphasized, was a poet of mood and psychology, and they learned to use their naturalistic techniques of acting and production to communicate the poetic moods and music of his plays.

The production style, then, for *The Cherry Orchard* was naturalistic. Its three settings were placed on a revolving stage, and its atmosphere was enhanced with the modulations made possible by electric lighting. The audiences in Stanislavski's theater were expected to be on time and to give the plays their silent attention. Despite the Moscow Art Theater's immediate success with *The Seagull,* it usually took a second season to educate the audience to the nuances of plays so devoid of exterior action and so dependent on a musical counterpoint of language to build their action, their moods, and their meaning.

The theatrical marriage of the Moscow Art Theater and Chekhov was not without dissension, and Chekhov's preference for understatement in all aspects of production caused him some aggravation with Stanislavski's sometimes overzealous attempts at authenticity. When actors started killing mosquitoes in the second act of *The Cherry Orchard,* Chekhov said that in his next play "somebody will say, what a marvelous site, there are no mosquitoes" (Marc Slonim, *Russian Theater: From the Empire to the Soviets,* p. 126). Chekhov also deplored Stanislavski's insistence that his play, conceived as a comedy and in places "almost a farce," was tragic, as well as Stanislavski's drawing out of the brief final act into a length that distorted the playwright's intent. Stanislavski is not the only interpreter of *The Cherry Orchard* who failed to grasp its comic aspects. The problem was that like Ibsen in *The Wild Duck,* Chekhov was creating a drama that was neither tragic nor comic, but both. Many playwrights in the past have combined tragic and comic elements in their dramas, Shakespeare included, but Chekhov's comic perspective on what could so easily have been a tragic interpretation of social change is peculiarly modern. As with Ibsen, there are no more heroes—only victims, well-meaning but weak characters who are incapable of taking life tragically. In their situation Chekhov clearly sees the pathos as well as the irony of life.

Chekhov was concerned with the limitations of an artist who has no particular religious or social beliefs, but his particular achievement as an artist may ironically be attributed to what he considered a disadvantage. Going far beyond a photographic reproduction of life, Chekhov has not only charted the losses of individuals and the changing state of Russia in his play; he has also projected the rather helpless state of the modern world in which people unwittingly contribute so much to the fatalities that tend to overwhelm them.

A note on Russian names

Russian names cause confusion to many until their logic is understood. A Russian name is composed of a given or Christian first name, a patronymic second name, and a last name:

LYU-boff an-dray-YEV-na rahn-nyev-SKY-ya

Lyuboff, daughter of Andre, wife of Ranevsky

Patronymic and last names are given in either a masculine or feminine gender:

Lyuboff Andreevna *but* Leonid Andreevich (an-DRAY-yeh-vitch)

Close friends and family members address one another by diminutive forms of first names:

Lyuba

Petya

Strangers or acquaintances call one another by first and patronymic names or by the last name preceded by a title:

Lyuboff Andreevna *or* Madame Ranevskaya

Often names are accented on the penultimate syllable.

LEY-o-nid an-DRAY-yeh-vitch GAH-yeff

YER-mo-lay a-ylex-YEH-vitch lo-PAH-een

BORE-is bore-EES-oh-vitch SEM-yoh-noff PISH-chick

Shar-LAH-tah ee-vah-NOV-na

SEM-yon pahn-teh-LYEE-vitch eh-peh-HO-doff

The Cherry Orchard

Translated by Stark Young

Characters
RANEVSKAYA, LYUBOFF ANDREEVNA, *a landowner*
ANYA, *her daughter, seventeen years old*
VARYA, *her adopted daughter, twenty-four years old*
GAYEFF, LEONID ANDREEVICH, *brother of Ranevskaya*
LOPAHIN, YERMOLAY ALEXEEVICH, *a merchant*
TROFIMOFF, PYOTR SERGEEVICH, *a student*
SEMYONOFF-PISHTCHIK, BORIS BORISOVICH, *a landowner*
CHARLOTTA IVANOVNA, *a governess*
EPIHODOFF, SEMYON PANTELEEVICH, *a clerk*
DUNYASHA, *a maid*
FIERS, *a valet, an old man of eighty-seven*
YASHA, *a young valet*
A PASSERBY *or* STRANGER
THE STATIONMASTER
A POST-OFFICE CLERK
Visitors, Servants
   The action takes place on the estate of L. A. Ranevskaya.

Act one

A room that is still called the nursery. One of the doors leads into Anya's room. Dawn, the sun will soon be rising. It is May, the cherry trees are in blossom but in the orchard it is cold, with a morning frost. The windows in the room are closed. Enter Dunyasha with a candle and Lopahin with a book in his hand.

LOPAHIN
The train got in, thank God! What time is it?

DUNYASHA
It's nearly two. (*Blows out his candle.*) It's already daylight.

LOPAHIN
But how late was the train? Two hours at least. (*Yawning and stretching.*) I'm a fine one, I am, look what a fool thing I did! I drove here on purpose just to meet them at the station, and then all of a sudden I'd overslept myself! Fell asleep in my chair. How provoking!—You could have waked me up.

DUNYASHA
I thought you had gone. (*Listening.*) Listen, I think they are coming now.

LOPAHIN (*Listening.*)
No—No, there's the luggage and one thing and another. (*A pause.*) Lyuboff Andreevna has been living abroad five years. I don't know what she is like now—She is a good woman. An easy-going, simple woman. I remember when I was a boy about fifteen, my father, who

is at rest—in those days he ran a shop here in the village—hit me in the face with his fist, my nose was bleeding—We'd come to the yard together for something or other, and he was a little drunk. Lyuboff Andreevna, I can see her now, still so young, so slim, led me to the washbasin here in this very room, in the nursery. "Don't cry," she says, "little peasant, it will be well in time for your wedding"—(*A pause.*) Yes, little peasant—My father was a peasant truly, and here I am in a white waistcoat and yellow shoes. Like a pig rooting in a pastry shop—I've got this rich, lots of money, but if you really stop and think of it, I'm just a peasant—(*Turning the pages of a book.*) Here I was reading a book and didn't get a thing out of it. Reading and went to sleep. (*A pause.*)

DUNYASHA

And all night long the dogs were not asleep, they know their masters are coming.

LOPAHIN

What is it, Dunyasha, you're so—

DUNYASHA

My hands are shaking. I'm going to faint.

LOPAHIN

You're just so delicate, Dunyasha. And all dressed up like a lady, and your hair all done up! Mustn't do that. Must know your place.
> *Enter Epihodoff, with a bouquet: he wears a jacket and highly polished boots with a loud squeak. As he enters he drops the bouquet.*

EPIHODOFF (*Picking up the bouquet.*)

Look, the gardener sent these, he says to put them in the dining room.
> *Giving the bouquet to Dunyasha.*

LOPAHIN

And bring me some kvass.

DUNYASHA

Yes, sir. (*Goes out.*)

EPIHODOFF

There is a morning frost now, three degrees of frost (*Sighing.*) and the cherries all in bloom. I cannot approve of our climate—I cannot. Our climate can never quite rise to the occasion. Listen, Yermolay Alexeevich, allow me to subtend, I bought myself, day before yesterday, some boots and they, I venture to assure you, squeak so that it is impossible. What could I grease them with?

LOPAHIN

Go on. You annoy me.

EPIHODOFF

Every day some misfortune happens to me. But I don't complain, I am used to it and I even smile.
> *Dunyasha enters, serves Lopahin the kvass.*

I'm going. (*Stumbling over a chair and upsetting it.*) There. (*As if triumphant.*) There, you see, pardon the expression, a circumstance like that, among others—It is simply quite remarkable. (*Goes out.*)

DUNYASHA

And I must tell you, Yermolay Alexeevich, that Epihodoff has proposed to me.

LOPAHIN

Ah!

DUNYASHA

I don't know really what to—He is a quiet man but sometimes when he starts talking, you can't understand a thing he means. It's all very nice, and full of feeling, but just doesn't make any sense. I sort of like him. He loves me madly. He's a man that's unfortunate, every day there's something or other. They tease him around here, call him twenty-two misfortunes—

LOPAHIN (Cocking his ear.)

Listen, I think they are coming—

DUNYASHA

They are coming! But what's the matter with me—I'm cold all over.

LOPAHIN

They're really coming. Let's go meet them. Will she recognize me? It's five years we haven't seen each other.

DUNYASHA (Excitedly.)

I'm going to faint this very minute. Ah, I'm going to faint!

> *Two carriages can be heard driving up to the house. Lopahin and Dunyasha hurry out. The stage is empty. In the adjoining rooms a noise begins. Fiers hurries across the stage, leaning on a stick; he has been to meet Lyuboff Andreevna, and wears an old-fashioned livery and a high hat; he mutters something to himself, but you cannot understand a word of it. The noise offstage gets louder and louder. A voice: "Look! Let's go through here—" Lyuboff Andreevna, Anya and Charlotta Ivan-ovna, with a little dog on a chain, all of them dressed for traveling, Varya, in a coat and kerchief, Gayeff, Semyonoff-Pishtchik, Lopahin, Dunyasha, with a bundle and an umbrella, servants with pieces of luggage—all pass through the room.*

ANYA

Let's go through here. Mama, do you remember what room this is?

LYUBOFF ANDREEVNA (Happily, through her tears.)

The nursery!

VARYA

How cold it is, my hands are stiff. (To Lyuboff Andreevna.) Your rooms, the white one and the violet, are just the same as ever, Mama.

LYUBOFF ANDREEVNA

The nursery, my dear beautiful room—I slept here when I was little— (Crying.) And now I am like a child— (Kisses her brother and Varya, then her brother again.) And Varya is just the same as ever, looks like a nun. And I knew Dunyasha— (Kisses Dunyasha.)

GAYEFF

The train was two hours late. How's that? How's that for good management?

CHARLOTTA (To Pishtchik.)

My dog he eats nuts too.

PISHTCHIK (Astonished.)

Think of that!

> *Everybody goes out except Anya and Dunyasha.*

DUNYASHA

We waited so long— (Taking off Anya's coat and hat.)

ANYA

I didn't sleep all four nights on the way. And now I feel so chilly.

DUNYASHA

It was Lent when you left, there was some snow then, there was frost, and now? My darling (*Laughing and kissing her.*), I waited so long for you, my joy, my life—I'm telling you now, I can't keep from it another minute.

ANYA (*Wearily.*)

There we go again—

DUNYASHA

The clerk Epihodoff proposed to me after Holy Week.

ANYA

You're always talking about the same thing— (*Arranging her hair.*) I've lost all my hairpins— (*She is tired to the point of staggering.*)

DUNYASHA

I just don't know what to think. He loves me, loves me so!

ANYA (*Looks in through her door, tenderly.*)

My room, my windows, it's just as if I had never been away. I'm home! Tomorrow morning I'll get up, I'll run into the orchard— Oh, if I only could go to sleep! I haven't slept all the way, I was tormented by anxiety.

DUNYASHA

Day before yesterday, Pyotr Sergeevich arrived.

ANYA (*Joyfully.*)

Petya!

DUNYASHA

He's asleep in the bathhouse, he lives there. I am afraid, he says, of being in the way. (*Taking her watch from her pocket and looking at it.*) Somebody ought to wake him up. It's only that Varvara Mikhailovna told us not to. Don't you wake him up, she said.

Enter Varya with a bunch of keys at her belt.

VARYA

Dunyasha, coffee, quick—Mama is asking for coffee.

DUNYASHA

This minute. (*Goes out.*)

VARYA

Well, thank goodness, you've come back. You are home again. (*Caressingly.*) My darling is back! My precious is back!

ANYA

I've had such a time.

VARYA

I can imagine!

ANYA

I left during Holy Week, it was cold then. Charlotta talked all the way and did her tricks. Why did you fasten Charlotta on to me—?

VARYA

But you couldn't have traveled alone, darling; not at seventeen!

ANYA

We arrived in Paris, it was cold there and snowing. I speak terrible French. Mama lived on the fifth floor; I went to see her; there were some French people in her room, ladies, an old priest with his prayer book, and the place was full of tobacco smoke—very dreary. Suddenly I began to feel sorry for Mama, so sorry, I drew her to me, held her close and couldn't let her go. Then Mama kept hugging me, crying—yes—

VARYA (*Tearfully.*)

Don't—oh, don't—

ANYA

Her villa near Mentone she had already sold, she had nothing left, nothing. And I didn't have a kopeck left. It was all we could do to get here. And Mama doesn't understand! We sit down to dinner at a station and she orders, insists on the most expensive things and gives the waiters rouble tips. Charlotta does the same. Yasha too demands his share; it's simply dreadful. Mama has her butler, Yasha, we've brought him here—

VARYA

I saw the wretch.

ANYA

Well, how are things? Has the interest on the mortgage been paid?

VARYA

How could we?

ANYA

Oh, my God, my God—!

VARYA

In August the estate is to be sold—

ANYA

My God—!

LOPAHIN (*Looking in through the door and mooing like a cow.*)

Moo-o-o— (*Goes away.*)

VARYA (*Tearfully.*)

I'd land him one like that— (*Shaking her fist.*)

ANYA (*Embracing Varya gently.*)

Varya, has he proposed? (*Varya shakes her head.*) But he loves you— Why don't you have it out with him, what are you waiting for?

VARYA

I don't think anything will come of it for us. He is very busy, he hasn't any time for me—And doesn't notice me. God knows, it's painful for me to see him—Everybody talks about our marriage, everybody congratulates us, and the truth is, there's nothing to it—it's all like a dream— (*In a different tone.*) You have a brooch looks like a bee.

ANYA (*Sadly.*)

Mama bought it. (*Going toward her room, speaking gaily, like a child.*) And in Paris I went up in a balloon!

VARYA

My darling is back! My precious is back! (*Dunyasha has returned with the coffee pot and is making coffee. Varya is standing by the door.*) Darling, I'm busy all day long with the house and I go around thinking things. If only you could be married to a rich man, I'd be more at peace too, I would go all by myself to a hermitage—then to Kiev—to Moscow, and I'd keep going like that from one holy place to another—I would go on and on. Heavenly!

ANYA

The birds are singing in the orchard. What time is it now?

VARYA

It must be after two. It's time you were asleep, darling. (*Going into Anya's room.*) Heavenly!

Yasha enters with a lap robe and a traveling bag.

YASHA (*Crossing the stage airily.*)

> May I go through here?

DUNYASHA

> We'd hardly recognize you, Yasha; you've changed so abroad!

YASHA

> Hm— And who are you?

DUNYASHA

> When you left here, I was like that— (*Her hand so high from the floor.*)
> I'm Dunyasha, Fyodor Kozoyedoff's daughter. You don't remember!

YASHA

> Hm— You little peach!
>> *Looking around before he embraces her; she shrieks and drops a saucer;*
>> *Yasha hurries out.*

VARYA (*At the door, in a vexed tone.*)

> And what's going on here?

DUNYASHA (*Tearfully.*)

> I broke a saucer—

VARYA

> That's good luck.

ANYA (*Emerging from her room.*)

> We ought to tell Mama beforehand: Petya is here—

VARYA

> I told them not to wake him up.

ANYA (*Pensively.*)

> Six years ago our father died, a month later our brother Grisha was
> drowned in the river, such a pretty little boy, just seven. Mama
> couldn't bear it, she went away, went away without ever looking
> back— (*Shuddering.*) How I understand her, if she only knew I did.
> (*A pause.*) And Petya Trofimoff was Grisha's tutor, he might re-
> mind—
> *Enter Fiers; he is in a jacket and white waistcoat. Goes to the coffee*
> *urn, busy with it.*

FIERS

> The mistress will have her breakfast here— (*Putting on white gloves.*)
> Is the coffee ready? (*To Dunyasha, sternly.*) You! What about the
> cream?

DUNYASHA

> Oh, my God— (*Hurrying out.*)

FIERS (*Busy at the coffee urn.*)

> Oh, you good-for-nothing—! (*Muttering to himself.*) Come back from
> Paris—And the master used to go to Paris by coach— (*Laughing.*)

VARYA

> Fiers, what are you—?

FIERS

> At your service. (*Joyfully.*) My mistress is back! It's what I've been
> waiting for! Now I'm ready to die— (*Crying for joy.*)
> *Lyuboff Andreevna, Gayeff and Semyonoff-Pishtchik enter; Semyonoff-*
> *Pishtchik is in a podyovka of fine cloth and sharovary. Gayeff enters;*
> *he makes gestures with his hands and body as if he were playing*
> *billiards.*

LYUBOFF ANDREEVNA

> How is it? Let me remember—Yellow into the corner! Duplicate in
> the middle!

GAYEFF

I cut into the corner. Sister, you and I slept here in this very room once, and now I am fifty-one years old, strange as that may seem—

LOPAHIN

Yes, time passes.

GAYEFF

What?

LOPAHIN

Time, I say, passes.

GAYEFF

And it smells like patchouli here.

ANYA

I'm going to bed. Good night, Mama. (*Kissing her mother.*)

LYUBOFF ANDREEVNA

My sweet little child. (*Kissing her hands.*) You're glad you are home? I still can't get myself together.

ANYA

Good-by, Uncle.

GAYEFF (*Kissing her face and hands.*)

God be with you. How like your mother you are! (*To his sister.*) Lyuba, at her age you were exactly like her.

  Anya shakes hands with Lopahin and Pishtchik, goes out and closes the door behind her.

LYUBOFF ANDREEVNA

She's very tired.

PISHTCHIK

It is a long trip, I imagine.

VARYA (*To Lopahin and Pishtchik.*)

Well, then, sirs? It's going on three o'clock, time for gentlemen to be going.

LYUBOFF ANDREEVNA (*Laughing.*)

The same old Varya. (*Drawing her to her and kissing her.*) There, I'll drink my coffee, then we'll all go. (*Fiers puts a small cushion under her feet.*) Thank you, my dear. I am used to coffee. Drink it day and night. Thank you, my dear old soul.

  Kissing Fiers.

VARYA

I'll go see if all the things have come. (*Goes out.*)

LYUBOFF ANDREEVNA

Is it really me sitting here? (*Laughing.*) I'd like to jump around and wave my arms. (*Covering her face with her hands.*) But I may be dreaming! God knows I love my country, love it deeply, I couldn't look out of the car window, I just kept crying. (*Tearfully.*) However, I must drink my coffee. Thank you, Fiers, thank you, my dear old friend. I'm so glad you're still alive.

FIERS

Day before yesterday.

GAYEFF

He doesn't hear well.

LOPAHIN

And I must leave right now. It's nearly five o'clock in the morning, for Harkoff. What a nuisance! I wanted to look at you—talk— You are as beautiful as ever.

PISHTCHIK (*Breathing heavily.*)

Even more beautiful— In your Paris clothes— It's a feast for the eyes—

LOPAHIN

Your brother, Leonid Andreevich here, says I'm a boor, a peasant money grubber, but that's all the same to me, absolutely. Let him say it. All I wish is you'd trust me as you used to, and your wonderful, touching eyes would look at me as they did. Merciful God! My father was a serf; belonged to your grandfather and your father; but you, your own self, you did so much for me once that I've forgotten all that and love you like my own kin—more than my kin.

LYUBOFF ANDREEVNA

I can't sit still—I can't. (*Jumping up and walking about in great excitement.*) I'll never live through this happiness— Laugh at me, I'm silly—My own little bookcase—! (*Kissing the bookcase.*) My little table!

GAYEFF

And in your absence the nurse here died.

LYUBOFF ANDREEVNA (*Sitting down and drinking coffee.*)

Yes, may she rest in Heaven! They wrote me.

GAYEFF

And Anastasy died. Cross-eyed Petrushka left me and lives in town now at the police officer's. (*Taking out of his pocket a box of hard candy and sucking a piece.*)

PISHTCHIK

My daughter, Dashenka—sends you her greetings—

LOPAHIN

I want to tell you something very pleasant, cheerful. (*Glancing at his watch.*) I'm going right away. There's no time for talking. Well, I'll make it two or three words. As you know, your cherry orchard is to be sold for your debts; the auction is set for August 22nd, but don't you worry, my dear, you just sleep in peace, there's a way out of it. Here's my plan. Please listen to me. Your estate is only thirteen miles from town. They've run the railroad by it. Now if the cherry orchard and the land along the river were cut up into building lots and leased for summer cottages, you'd have at the very lowest twenty-five thousand roubles per year income.

GAYEFF

Excuse me, what rot!

LYUBOFF ANDREEVNA

I don't quite understand you, Yermolay Alexeevich.

LOPAHIN

At the very least you will get from the summer residents twenty-five roubles per year for a two-and-a-half acre lot and if you post a notice right off, I'll bet you anything that by autumn you won't have a single patch of land free, everything will be taken. In a word, my congratulations, you are saved. The location is wonderful, the river's so deep. Except, of course, it all needs to be tidied up, cleared— For instance, let's say, tear all the old buildings down and this house, which is no good any more, and cut down the old cherry orchard—

LYUBOFF ANDREEVNA

Cut down? My dear, forgive me, you don't understand at all. If there's one thing in the whole province that's interesting—not to say remarkable—it's our cherry orchard.

LOPAHIN

The only remarkable thing about this cherry orchard is that it's very big. There's a crop of cherries once every two years and even that's hard to get rid of. Nobody buys them.

GAYEFF

This orchard is even mentioned in the encyclopedia.

LOPAHIN (*Glancing at his watch.*)

If we don't cook up something and don't get somewhere, the cherry orchard and the entire estate will be sold at auction on the twenty-second of August. Do get it settled then! I swear there is no other way out. Not a one!

FIERS

There was a time, forty-fifty years ago when the cherries were dried, soaked, pickled, cooked into jam and it used to be—

GAYEFF

Keep quiet, Fiers.

FIERS

And it used to be that the dried cherries were shipped by the wagon-load to Moscow and to Kharkov. And the money there was! And the dried cherries were soft then, juicy, sweet, fragrant— They had a way of treating them then—

LYUBOFF ANDREEVNA

And where is that way now?

FIERS

They have forgotten it. Nobody remembers it.

PISHTCHIK (*To Lyuboff Andreevna.*)

What's happening in Paris? How is everything? Did you eat frogs?

LYUBOFF ANDREEVNA

I ate crocodiles.

PISHTCHIK

Think of it—!

LOPAHIN

Up to now in the country there have been only the gentry and the peasants, but now in summer the villa people too are coming in. All the towns, even the least big ones, are surrounded with cottages. In about twenty years very likely the summer resident will multiply enormously. He merely drinks tea on the porch now, but it might well happen that on this two-and-a-half acre lot of his, he'll go in for farming, and then your cherry orchard would be happy, rich, splendid—

GAYEFF (*Getting hot.*)

What rot!

Enter Varya and Yasha.

VARYA

Here, Mama. Two telegrams for you. (*Choosing a key and opening the old bookcase noisily.*) Here they are.

LYUBOFF ANDREEVNA

From Paris. (*Tearing up the telegrams without reading them.*) Paris, that's all over—

GAYEFF

Do you know how old this bookcase is, Lyuba? A week ago I pulled out the bottom drawer and looked, and there the figures were burned on it. The bookcase was made exactly a hundred years ago.

How's that? Eh? You might celebrate its jubilee. It's an inanimate object, but all the same, be that as it may, it's a bookcase.

PISHTCHIK (*In astonishment.*)

A hundred years—! Think of it—!

GAYEFF

Yes—quite something— (*Shaking the bookcase.*) Dear, honored bookcase! I salute your existence, which for more than a hundred years has been directed toward the clear ideals of goodness and justice; your silent appeal to fruitful endeavor has not flagged in all the course of a hundred years, sustaining (*Tearfully.*) through the generations of our family, our courage and our faith in a better future and nurturing in us ideals of goodness and of a social consciousness.

A pause.

LOPAHIN

Yes.

LYUBOFF ANDREEVNA

You're the same as ever, Lenya.

GAYEFF (*Slightly embarrassed.*)

Carom to the right into the corner pocket. I cut into the side pocket!

LOPAHIN (*Glancing at his watch.*)

Well, it's time for me to go.

YASHA (*Handing medicine to Lyuboff Andreevna*)

Perhaps you'll take the pills now—

PISHTCHIK

You should never take medicaments, dear madam— They do neither harm nor good— Hand them here, dearest lady. (*He takes the pillbox, shakes the pills out into his palm, blows on them, puts them in his mouth and washes them down with kvass.*) There! Now!

LYUBOFF ANDREEVNA (*Startled.*)

Why, you've lost your mind!

PISHTCHIK

I took all the pills.

LOPAHIN

Such a glutton!

Everyone laughs.

FIERS

The gentleman stayed with us during Holy Week, he ate half a bucket of pickles— (*Muttering.*)

LYUBOFF ANDREEVNA

What is he muttering about?

VARYA

He's been muttering like that for three years. We're used to it.

YASHA

In his dotage.

Charlotta Ivanovna in a white dress—she is very thin, her corset laced very tight—with a lorgnette at her belt, crosses the stage.

LOPAHIN

Excuse me, Charlotta Ivanovna, I haven't had a chance yet to welcome you. (*Trying to kiss her hand.*)

CHARLOTTA (*Drawing her hand away.*)

If I let you kiss my hand, 'twould be my elbow next, then my shoulder—

LOPAHIN

No luck for me today. (*Everyone laughs.*) Charlotta Ivanovna, show us a trick!

CHARLOTTA

No. I want to go to bed. (*Exit.*)

LOPAHIN

In three weeks we shall see each other. (*Kissing Lyuboff Andreevna's hand.*) Till then, good-by. It's time. (*To Gayeff.*) See you soon. (*Kissing Pishtchik.*) See you soon. (*Shaking Varya's hand, then Fiers' and Yasha's.*) I don't feel like going. (*To Lyuboff Andreevna.*) If you think it over and make up your mind about the summer cottages, let me know and I'll arrange a loan of something like fifty thousand roubles. Think it over seriously.

VARYA (*Angrily.*)

Do go on, anyhow, will you!

LOPAHIN

I'm going, I'm going— (*Exit.*)

GAYEFF

Boor. However, pardon—Varya is going to marry him, it's Varya's little fiancé.

VARYA

Don't talk too much, Uncle.

LYUBOFF ANDREEVNA

Well, Varya, I should be very glad. He's a good man.

PISHTCHIK

A man, one must say truthfully—A most worthy—And my Dashenka—says also that—she says all sorts of things— (*Snoring but immediately waking up.*) Nevertheless, dearest lady, oblige me—With a loan of two hundred and forty roubles— Tomorrow the interest on my mortgage has got to be paid—

VARYA (*Startled.*)

There's not any money, none at all.

LYUBOFF ANDREEVNA

Really, I haven't got anything.

PISHTCHIK

I'll find it, somehow. (*Laughing.*) I never give up hope. There, I think to myself, all is lost, I am ruined and lo and behold—a railroad is put through my land and—they paid me. And then, just watch, something else will turn up—if not today, then tomorrow—Dashenka will win two hundred thousand— She has a ticket.

LYUBOFF ANDREEVNA

We've finished the coffee, now we can go to bed.

FIERS (*Brushing Gayeff's clothes, reprovingly.*)

You put on the wrong trousers again. What am I going to do with you!

VARYA (*Softly.*)

Anya is asleep. (*Opening the window softly.*) Already the sun's rising—it's not cold. Look, Mama! What beautiful trees! My Lord, what air! The starlings are singing!

GAYEFF (*Opening another window.*)

The orchard is all white. You haven't forgotten, Lyuba? That long lane there runs straight—as a strap stretched out. It glistens on moonlight nights. Do you remember? You haven't forgotten it?

LYUBOFF ANDREEVNA (*Looking out of the window on to the orchard.*)

Oh, my childhood, my innocence! I slept in this nursery and looked out on the orchard from here, every morning happiness awoke with me, it was just as it is now, then, nothing has changed. (*Laughing with joy.*) All, all white! Oh, my orchard! After a dark, rainy autumn and cold winter, you are young again and full of happiness. The heavenly angels have not deserted you— If I only could lift the weight from my breast, from my shoulders, if I could only forget my past!

GAYEFF

Yes, and the orchard will be sold for debt, strange as that may seem.

LYUBOFF ANDREEVNA

Look, our dear mother is walking through the orchard—In a white dress! (*Laughing happily.*) It's she.

GAYEFF

Where?

VARYA

God be with you, Mama!

LYUBOFF ANDREEVNA

There's not anybody, it only seemed so. To the right, as you turn to the summerhouse, a little white tree is leaning there, looks like a woman—

Enter Trofimoff, in a student's uniform, well worn, and glasses.

What a wonderful orchard! The white masses of blossoms, the sky all blue.

TROFIMOFF

Lyuboff Andreevna! (*She looks around at him.*) I will just greet you and go immediately. (*Kissing her hand warmly.*) I was told to wait until morning, but I hadn't the patience—

Lyuboff Andreevna looks at him puzzled.

VARYA (*Tearfully.*)

This is Petya Trofimoff—

TROFIMOFF

Petya Trofimoff, the former tutor of your Grisha— Have I really changed so?

Lyuboff Andreevna embraces him; and crying quietly.

GAYEFF (*Embarrassed.*)

There, there, Lyuba.

VARYA (*Crying.*)

I told you, Petya, to wait till tomorrow.

LYUBOFF ANDREEVNA

My Grisha—My boy—Grisha—Son—

VARYA

What can we do, Mama? It's God's will.

TROFIMOFF (*In a low voice tearfully.*)

There, there—

LYUBOFF ANDREEVNA (*Weeping softly.*)

My boy was lost, drowned— Why? Why, my friend? (*More quietly.*) Anya is asleep there, and I am talking so loud—Making so much noise— But why, Petya? Why have you lost your looks? Why do you look so much older?

TROFIMOFF

A peasant woman on the train called me a mangy-looking gentleman.

LYUBOFF ANDREEVNA

You were a mere boy then, a charming young student, and now your hair's not very thick any more and you wear glasses. Are you really a student still? (*Going to the door.*)

TROFIMOFF

Very likely I'll be a perennial student.

LYUBOFF ANDREEVNA (*Kissing her brother, then Varya.*)

Well, go to bed— You've grown older too, Leonid.

PISHTCHIK (*Following her.*)

So that's it, we are going to bed now. Oh, my gout! I'm staying here— I'd like, Lyuboff Andreevna, my soul, tomorrow morning— Two hundred and forty roubles—

GAYEFF

He's still at it.

PISHTCHIK

Two hundred and forty roubles— To pay interest on the mortgage.

LYUBOFF ANDREEVNA

I haven't any money, my dove.

PISHTCHIK

I'll pay it back, my dear— It's a trifling sum—

LYUBOFF ANDREEVNA

Oh, very well, Leonid will give—You give it to him, Leonid.

GAYEFF

Oh, certainly, I'll give it to him. Hold out your pockets.

LYUBOFF ANDREEVNA

What can we do, give it, he needs it— He'll pay it back.

> *Lyuboff Andreevna, Trofimoff, Pishtchik and Fiers go out. Gayeff, Varya and Yasha remain.*

GAYEFF

My sister hasn't yet lost her habit of throwing money away. (*To Yasha.*) Get away, my good fellow, you smell like hens.

YASHA (*With a grin.*)

And you are just the same as you used to be, Leonid Andreevich.

GAYEFF

What? (*To Varya.*) What did he say?

VARYA (*To Yasha.*)

Your mother has come from the village, she's been sitting in the servants' hall ever since yesterday, she wants to see you—

YASHA

The devil take her'

VARYA

Ach, shameless creature!

YASHA

A lot I need her! She might have come tomorrow.

> *Goes out.*

VARYA

Mama is just the same as she was, she hasn't changed at all. If she could, she'd give away everything she has.

GAYEFF

Yes— If many remedies are prescribed for an illness, you may know the illness is incurable. I keep thinking, I wrack my brains, I have many remedies, a great many, and that means, really, I haven't any at all. It would be fine to inherit a fortune from somebody, it would

be fine to marry off our Anya to a very rich man, it would be fine to
go to Yaroslavl and try our luck with our old aunt, the Countess.
Auntie is very, very rich.

VARYA (*Crying.*)

If God would only help us!

GAYEFF

Don't bawl! Auntie is very rich but she doesn't like us. To begin
with, Sister married a lawyer, not a nobleman— (*Anya appears at the
door.*) Married not a nobleman and behaved herself, you could say,
not very virtuously. She is good, kind, nice, I love her very much,
but no matter how much you allow for the extenuating circumstances, you must admit she's a depraved woman. You feel it in her
slightest movement.

VARYA (*Whispering.*)

Anya is standing in the door there.

GAYEFF

What? (*A pause.*) It's amazing, something got in my right eye. I am
beginning to see poorly. And on Thursday, when I was in the District Court—

Anya enters.

VARYA

But why aren't you asleep, Anya?

ANYA

I don't feel like sleeping. I can't.

GAYEFF

My little girl— (*Kissing Anya's face and hands.*) My child— (*Tearfully.*)
You are not my niece, you are my angel, you are everything to me.
Believe me, believe—

ANYA

I believe you, Uncle. Everybody loves you, respects you— But dear
Uncle, you must keep quiet, just keep quiet— What were you saying,
just now, about my mother, about your own sister? What did you say
that for?

GAYEFF

Yes, yes— (*Putting her hand up over his face.*) Really, it's terrible! My
God! Oh, God, save me! And today I made a speech to the
bookcase— So silly! And it was only when I finished it that I could
see it was silly.

VARYA

It's true, Uncle, you ought to keep quiet. Just keep quiet. That's all.

ANYA

If you kept quiet, you'd have more peace.

GAYEFF

I'll keep quiet. (*Kissing Anya's and Varya's hands.*) I'll keep quiet. Only
this, it's about business. On Thursday I was in the District Court;
well, a few of us gathered around and a conversation began about
this and that, about lots of things; apparently it will be possible to arrange a loan on a promissory note to pay the bank the interest due.

VARYA

If the Lord would only help us!

GAYEFF

Tuesday I shall go and talk it over again. (*To Varya.*) Don't bawl! (*To
Anya.*) Your mother will talk to Lopahin; of course, he won't refuse

her . . . And as soon as you rest up, you will go to Yaroslavl to your great-aunt, the Countess. There, that's how we will move from three directions, and the business is in the bag. We'll pay the interest. I am convinced of that— (*Putting a hard candy in his mouth.*) On my honor I'll swear, by anything you like, that the estate shall not be sold! (*Excitedly.*) By my happiness, I swear! Here's my hand, call me a worthless, dishonorable man, if I allow it to come up for auction! With all my soul I swear it!

ANYA (*A quieter mood returns to her; she is happy.*)

How good you are, Uncle, how clever! (*Embracing her uncle.*) I feel easy now! I feel easy! I'm happy!

    Fiers enters.

FIERS (*Reproachfully.*)

Leonid Andreevich, have you no fear of God! When are you going to bed?

GAYEFF

Right away, right away. You may go, Fiers. For this once I'll undress myself. Well, children, beddy bye— More details tomorrow, and now, go to bed. (*Kissing Anya and Varya.*) I am a man of the eighties— It is a period that's not admired, but I can say, nevertheless, that I've suffered no little for my convictions in the course of my life. It is not for nothing that the peasant loves me. One must know the peasant! One must know from what—

ANYA

Again, Uncle!

VARYA

You, Uncle dear, keep quiet.

FIERS (*Angrily.*)

Leonid Andreevich!

GAYEFF

I'm coming, I'm coming— Go to bed. A double bank into the side pocket! A clean shot—

    Goes out, Fiers hobbling after him.

ANYA

I feel easy now. I don't feel like going to Yaroslavl; I don't like Great-aunt, but still I feel easy. Thanks to Uncle. (*Sits down.*)

VARYA

I must get to sleep. I'm going. And there was unpleasantness here during your absence. In the old servants' quarters, as you know, live only the old servants: Yephemushka, Polya, Yevstignay, well, and Karp. They began to let every sort of creature spend the night with them—I didn't say anything. But then I hear they've spread the rumor that I'd given orders to feed them nothing but beans. Out of stinginess, you see— And all that from Yevstignay— Very well, I think to myself. If that's the way it is, I think to myself, then you just wait. I call in Yevstignay— (*Yawning.*) He comes— How is it, I say, that you, Yevstignay— You're such a fool— (*Glancing at Anya.*) Anitchka!—(*A pause.*) Asleep! (*Takes Anya by her arm.*) Let's go to bed— Come on!— (*Leading her.*) My little darling fell asleep! Come on—

    They go. Far away beyond the orchard a shepherd is playing on a pipe.
    Trofimoff walks across the stage and, seeing Varya and Anya, stops.

Shh— She is asleep—asleep— Let's go, dear.

ANYA (*Softly, half dreaming.*)

I'm so tired— All the bells!—Uncle—dear— And Mama and Uncle—
Varya.

VARYA

Come on, my dear, come on.
They go into Anya's room.

TROFIMOFF (*Tenderly.*)

My little sun! My spring!

Act two

*A field. An old chapel, long abandoned, with crooked walls, near it a
well, big stones that apparently were once tombstones, and an old
bench. A road to the estate of Gayeff can be seen. On one side poplars
rise, casting their shadows, the cherry orchard begins there. In the distance a row of telegraph poles; and far, far away, faintly traced on the
horizon, is a large town, visible only in the clearest weather. The sun
will soon be down. Charlotta, Yasha and Dunyasha are sitting on the
bench; Epihodoff is standing near and playing the guitar; everyone
sits lost in thought. Charlotta wears an old peak cap* (fourrage); *she
has taken a rifle from off her shoulders and is adjusting the buckle on
the strap.*

CHARLOTTA (*Pensively.*)

I have no proper passport, I don't know how old I am—it always
seems to me I'm very young. When I was a little girl, my father and
mother traveled from fair to fair and gave performances, very good
ones. And I did *salto mortale* and different tricks. And when Papa
and Mama died, a German lady took me to live with her and began
teaching me. Good. I grew up. And became a governess. But where
I came from and who I am I don't know— Who my parents were,
perhaps they weren't even married—I don't know. (*Taking a cucumber out of her pocket and beginning to eat it.*) I don't know a thing. (*A
pause.*) I'd like so much to talk but there's not anybody. I haven't
anybody.

EPIHODOFF (*Playing the guitar and singing.*)

"What care I for the noisy world, what care I for friends and foes."—
How pleasant it is to play the mandolin!

DUNYASHA

That's a guitar, not a mandolin. (*Looking into a little mirror and powdering her face.*)

EPIHODOFF

For a madman who is in love this is a mandolin— (*Singing.*) "If only
my heart were warm with the fire of requited love."
Yasha sings with him.

CHARLOTTA

How dreadfully these people sing— Phooey! Like jackals.

DUNYASHA (*To Yasha.*)

All the same what happiness to have been abroad.

YASHA

Yes, of course. I cannot disagree with you.
Yawning and then lighting a cigar.

EPIHODOFF

That's easily understood. Abroad everything long since attained its complete development.

YASHA

That's obvious.

EPIHODOFF

I am a cultured man. I read all kinds of remarkable books, but the trouble is I cannot discover my own inclinations, whether to live or to shoot myself, but nevertheless, I always carry a revolver on me. Here it is—(*Showing a revolver.*)

CHARLOTTA

That's done. Now I am going. (*Slinging the rifle over her shoulder.*) You are a very clever man, Epihodoff, and a very terrible one; the women must love you madly. Brrrr-r-r-r! (*Going.*) These clever people are all so silly, I haven't anybody to talk with. I'm always alone, alone, I have nobody and— Who I am, why I am, is unknown— (*Goes out without hurrying.*)

EPIHODOFF

Strictly speaking, not touching on other subjects, I must state about myself, in passing, that fate treats me mercilessly, as a storm does a small ship. If, let us suppose, I am mistaken, then why, to mention one instance, do I wake up this morning, look and there on my chest is a spider of terrific size— There, like that. (*Showing the size with both hands.*) And also I take some kvass to drink and in it I find something in the highest degree indecent, such as a cockroach. (*A pause.*) Have you read Buckle? (*A pause.*) I desire to trouble you, Avdotya Feodorovna, with a couple of words.

DUNYASHA

Speak.

EPIHODOFF

I have a desire to speak with you alone—

    Sighing.

DUNYASHA (*Embarrassed.*)

Very well— But bring me my cape first—by the cupboard— It's rather damp here—

EPIHODOFF

Very well— I'll fetch it— Now I know what I should do with my revolver— (*Takes the guitar and goes out playing.*)

YASHA

Twenty-two misfortunes! Between us he's a stupid man, it must be said. (*Yawning.*)

DUNYASHA

God forbid he should shoot himself. (*A pause.*) I've grown so uneasy, I'm always fretting. I was only a girl when I was taken into the master's house, and now I've lost the habit of simple living—and here are my hands white, white as a lady's. I've become so delicate, fragile, ladylike, afraid of everything—Frightfully so. And, Yasha, if you deceive me, I don't know what will happen to my nerves.

YASHA (*Kissing her.*)

You little cucumber! Of course every girl must behave properly. What I dislike above everything is for a girl to conduct herself badly.

DUNYASHA

I have come to love you passionately, you are educated, you can discuss anything. (*A pause.*)

YASHA (*Yawning.*)

Yes, sir—To my mind it is like this: If a girl loves someone, it means she is immoral. (*A pause.*) It is pleasant to smoke a cigar in the clear air—(*Listening.*) They are coming here— It is the ladies and gentlemen—

Dunyasha impulsively embraces him.

YASHA

Go to the house, as though you had been to bathe in the river, go by this path, otherwise, they might meet you and suspect me of making a rendezvous with you. That I cannot tolerate.

DUNYASHA (*With a little cough.*)

Your cigar has given me the headache. (*Goes out.*)

Yasha remains, sitting near the chapel. Lyuboff Andreevna, Gayeff and Lopahin enter.

LOPAHIN

We must decide definitely, time doesn't wait. Why, the matter's quite simple. Are you willing to lease your land for summer cottages or are you not? Answer in one word, yes or no? Just one word!

LYUBOFF ANDREEVNA

Who is it smokes those disgusting cigars out here—? (*Sitting down.*)

GAYEFF

The railroad running so near is a great convenience. (*Sitting down.*) We made a trip to town and lunched there— Yellow in the side pocket! Perhaps I should go in the house first and play one game—

LYUBOFF ANDREEVNA

You'll have time.

LOPAHIN

Just one word! (*Imploringly.*) Do give me your answer!

GAYEFF (*Yawning.*)

What?

LYUBOFF ANDREEVNA (*Looking in her purse.*)

Yesterday there was lots of money in it. Today there's very little. My poor Varya! For the sake of economy she feeds everybody milk soup, and in the kitchen the old people get nothing but beans, and here I spend money—senselessly— (*Dropping her purse and scattering gold coins.*) There they go scattering! (*She is vexed.*)

YASHA

Allow me, I'll pick them up in a second. (*Picking up the coins.*)

LYUBOFF ANDREEVNA

If you will, Yasha. And why did I go in town for lunch—? Your restaurant with its music is trashy, the tablecloths smell of soap— Why drink so much, Lyonya? Why eat so much? Why talk so much? Today in the restaurant you were talking a lot again, and all of it beside the point. About the seventies, about the decadents. And to whom? Talking to waiters about the decadents!

LOPAHIN

Yes.

GAYEFF (*Waving his hand.*)

I am incorrigible, that's evident— (*To Yasha irritably.*) What is it?—You are forever swirling around in front of us.

YASHA (*Laughing.*)

I cannot hear your voice without laughing.

GAYEFF (*To his sister.*)

Either I or he—

LYUBOFF ANDREEVNA

Go away, Yasha. Go on—

YASHA (*Giving Lyuboff Andreevna her purse.*)

I am going right away. (*Barely suppressing his laughter.*) This minute. (*Goes out.*)

LOPAHIN

The rich Deriganoff intends to buy your estate. They say he is coming personally to the auction.

LYUBOFF ANDREEVNA

And where did you hear that?

LOPAHIN

In town they are saying it.

GAYEFF

Our Yaroslavl aunt promised to send us something, but when and how much she will send, nobody knows—

LOPAHIN

How much will she send? A hundred thousand? Two hundred?

LYUBOFF ANDREEVNA

Well—maybe ten, fifteen thousand—we'd be thankful for that.

LOPAHIN

Excuse me, but such light-minded people as you are, such odd, unbusinesslike people, I never saw. You are told in plain Russian that your estate is being sold up and you just don't seem to take it in.

LYUBOFF ANDREEVNA

But what are we to do? Tell us what?

LOPAHIN

I tell you every day. Every day I tell you the same thing. Both the cherry orchard and the land have got to be leased for summer cottages, it has to be done right now, quick— The auction is right under your noses. Do understand! Once you finally decide that there are to be summer cottages, you will get all the money you want, and then you'll be saved.

LYUBOFF ANDREEVNA

Summer cottages and summer residents—it is so trivial, excuse me.

GAYEFF

I absolutely agree with you.

LOPAHIN

I'll either burst out crying, or scream, or faint. I can't bear it! You are torturing me! (*To Gayeff.*) You're a perfect old woman!

GAYEFF

What?

LOPAHIN

A perfect old woman! (*About to go.*)

LYUBOFF ANDREEVNA (*Alarmed.*)

No, don't go, stay, my lamb, I beg you. Perhaps we will think of something!

LOPAHIN

What is there to think about?

LYUBOFF ANDREEVNA

Don't go, I beg you. With you here it is more cheerful anyhow— (*A pause.*) I keep waiting for something, as if the house were about to tumble down on our heads.

GAYEFF (*Deep in thought.*)

Double into the corner pocket— Bank into the wide pocket—

LYUBOFF ANDREEVNA

We have sinned so much—

LOPAHIN

What sins have you—?

GAYEFF (*Puts a hard candy into his mouth.*)

They say I've eaten my fortune up in hard candies— (*Laughing.*)

LYUBOFF ANDREEVNA

Oh, my sins—I've always thrown money around like mad, recklessly, and I married a man who accumulated nothing but debts. My husband died from champagne—he drank fearfully—and to my misfortune I fell in love with another man. I lived with him, and just at that time—it was my first punishment—a blow over the head: right here in the river my boy was drowned and I went abroad—went away for good, never to return, never to see this river again—I shut my eyes, ran away, beside myself, and he after me—mercilessly, brutally. I bought a villa near Mentone, because he fell ill there, and for three years I knew no rest day or night, the sick man exhausted me, my soul dried up. And last year when the villa was sold for debts, I went to Paris and there he robbed me of everything, threw me over, took up with another woman; I tried to poison myself—so stupid, so shameful— And suddenly I was seized with longing for Russia, for my own country, for my little girl— (*Wiping away her tears.*) Lord, Lord, have mercy, forgive me my sins! Don't punish me any more! (*Getting a telegram out of her pocket.*) I got this today from Paris, he asks forgiveness, begs me to return— (*Tears up the telegram.*) That sounds like music somewhere.

Listening.

GAYEFF

It is our famous Jewish orchestra. You remember, four violins, a flute and double bass.

LYUBOFF ANDREEVNA

Does it still exist? We ought to get hold of it sometime and give a party.

LOPAHIN (*Listening.*)

Can't hear it— (*Singing softly.*) "And for money the Germans will frenchify a Russian." (*Laughing.*) What a play I saw yesterday at the theatre, very funny!

LYUBOFF ANDREEVNA

And most likely there was nothing funny about it. You shouldn't look at plays, but look oftener at yourselves. How gray all your lives are, what a lot of idle things you say!

LOPAHIN

That's true. It must be said frankly this life of ours is idiotic— (*A pause.*) My father was a peasant, an idiot, he understood nothing, he taught me nothing, he just beat me in his drunken fits and always with a stick. At bottom I am just as big a dolt and idiot as he was. I wasn't taught anything, my handwriting is vile, I write like a pig—I am ashamed for people to see it.

LYUBOFF ANDREEVNA

You ought to get married, my friend.

LOPAHIN

Yes—That's true.

LYUBOFF ANDREEVNA

To our Varya, perhaps. She is a good girl.

LOPAHIN

Yes.

LYUBOFF ANDREEVNA

She comes from simple people, and she works all day long, but the main thing is she loves you. And you, too, have liked her a long time.

LOPAHIN

Why not? I am not against it— She's a good girl. (*A pause.*)

GAYEFF

They are offering me a position in a bank. Six thousand a year— Have you heard that?

LYUBOFF ANDREEVNA

Not you! You stay where you are—

Fiers enters, bringing an overcoat.

FIERS (*To Gayeff.*)

Pray, Sir, put this on, it's damp.

GAYEFF (*Putting on the overcoat.*)

You're a pest, old man.

FIERS

That's all right— This morning you went off without letting me know. (*Looking him over.*)

LYUBOFF ANDREEVNA

How old you've grown, Fiers!

FIERS

At your service.

LOPAHIN

She says you've grown very old!

FIERS

I've lived a long time. They were planning to marry me off before your papa was born. (*Laughing.*) And at the time the serfs were freed I was already the head footman. I didn't want to be freed then, I stayed with the masters—(*A pause.*) And I remember, everybody was happy, but what they were happy about they didn't know themselves.

LOPAHIN

In the old days it was fine. At least they flogged.

FIERS (*Not hearing.*)

But, of course. The peasants stuck to the masters, the masters stuck to the peasants, and now everything is all smashed up, you can't tell about anything.

GAYEFF

Keep still, Fiers. Tomorrow I must go to town. They have promised to introduce me to a certain general who might make us a loan.

LOPAHIN
Nothing will come of it. And you can rest assured you won't pay the interest.

LYUBOFF ANDREEVNA
He's just raving on. There aren't any such generals.
Trofimoff, Anya and Varya enter.

GAYEFF
Here they come.

ANYA
There is Mama sitting there.

LYUBOFF ANDREEVNA (*Tenderly.*)
Come, come—My darlings—(*Embracing Anya and Varya.*) If you only knew how I love you both! Come sit by me—there—like that.
Everybody sits down.

LOPAHIN
Our perennial student is always strolling with the young ladies.

TROFIMOFF
It's none of your business.

LOPAHIN
He will soon be fifty and he's still a student.

TROFIMOFF
Stop your stupid jokes.

LOPAHIN
But why are you so peevish, you queer duck?

TROFIMOFF
Don't you pester me.

LOPAHIN (*Laughing.*)
Permit me to ask you, what do you make of me?

TROFIMOFF
Yermolay Alexeevich, I make this of you: you are a rich man, you'll soon be a millionaire. Just as it is in the metabolism of nature, a wild beast is needed to eat up everything that comes his way; so you, too, are needed.
Everyone laughs.

VARYA
Petya, you'd better tell us about the planets.

LYUBOFF ANDREEVNA
No, let's go on with yesterday's conversation.

TROFIMOFF
What was it about?

GAYEFF
About the proud man.

TROFIMOFF
We talked a long time yesterday, but didn't get anywhere. In a proud man, in your sense of the word, there is something mystical. Maybe you are right, from your standpoint, but if we are to discuss it in simple terms, without whimsy, then what pride can there be, is there any sense in it, if man physiologically is poorly constructed, if in the great majority he is crude, unintelligent, profoundly miserable. One must stop admiring oneself. One must only work.

GAYEFF
All the same, you will die.

TROFIMOFF

Who knows? And what does it mean—you will die? Man may have a hundred senses, and when he dies only the five that are known to us may perish, and the remaining ninety-five go on living.

LYUBOFF ANDREEVNA

How clever you are, Petya!

LOPAHIN (*Ironically.*)

Terribly!

TROFIMOFF

Humanity goes forward, perfecting its powers. Everything that's unattainable now will some day become familiar, understandable; it is only that one must work and must help with all one's might those who seek the truth. With us in Russia so far only a very few work. The great majority of the intelligentsia that I know are looking for nothing, doing nothing, and as yet have no capacity for work. They call themselves intelligentsia, are free and easy with the servants, treat the peasants like animals, educate themselves poorly, read nothing seriously, do absolutely nothing; about science they just talk and about art they understand very little. Every one of them is serious, all have stern faces; they all talk of nothing but important things, philosophize, and all the time everybody can see that the workmen eat abominably, sleep without any pillows, thirty or forty to a room, and everywhere there are bedbugs, stench, dampness, moral uncleanness— And apparently with us, all the fine talk is only to divert the attention of ourselves and of others. Show me where we have the day nurseries they are always talking so much about, where are the reading rooms? They only write of these in novels, for the truth is there are not any at all. There is only filth, vulgarity, orientalism— I am afraid of very serious faces and dislike them. I'm afraid of serious conversations. Rather than that let's just keep still.

LOPAHIN

You know I get up before five o'clock in the morning and work from morning till night. Well, I always have money, my own and other people's, on hand, and I see what the people around me are. One has only to start doing something to find out how few honest and decent people there are. At times when I can't go to sleep, I think: Lord, thou gavest us immense forests, unbounded fields and the widest horizons, and living in the midst of them we should indeed be giants—

LYUBOFF ANDREEVNA

You feel the need for giants— They are good only in fairy tales, anywhere else they only frighten us.

> *At the back of the stage Epihodoff passes by, playing the guitar.*
>
> (*Lyuboff Andreevna, lost in thought, says:*)

Epihodoff is coming—

ANYA (*Lost in thought.*)

Epihodoff is coming.

GAYEFF

The sun has set, ladies and gentlemen.

TROFIMOFF

Yes.

GAYEFF (*Not loud and as if he were declaiming.*)

Oh, Nature, wonderful, you gleam with eternal radiance, beautiful and indifferent, you, whom we call Mother, combine in yourself both life and death, you give life and you take it away.

VARYA (*Beseechingly.*)

Uncle!

ANYA

Uncle, you're doing it again!

TROFIMOFF

You'd better bank the yellow into the side pocket.

GAYEFF

I'll be quiet, quiet.

> *All sit absorbed in their thoughts. There is only the silence. Fiers is heard muttering to himself softly. Suddenly a distant sound is heard, as if from the sky, like the sound of a snapped string, dying away, mournful.*

LYUBOFF ANDREEVNA

What's that?

LOPAHIN

I don't know. Somewhere far off in a mine shaft a bucket fell. But somewhere very far off.

GAYEFF

And it may be some bird—like a heron.

TROFIMOFF

Or an owl—

LYUBOFF ANDREEVNA (*Shivering.*)

It's unpleasant, somehow. (*A pause.*)

FIERS

Before the disaster it was like that. The owl hooted and the samovar hummed without stopping, both.

GAYEFF

Before what disaster?

FIERS

Before the emancipation.

> *A pause.*

LYUBOFF ANDREEVNA

You know, my friends, let's go. Twilight is falling. (*To Anya.*) You have tears in your eyes— What is it, my dear little girl? (*Embracing her.*)

ANYA

It's just that, Mama. It's nothing.

TROFIMOFF

Somebody is coming.

> *A Stranger appears in a shabby white cap, and an overcoat; he is a little drunk.*

THE STRANGER

Allow me to ask you, can I go straight through here to the station?

GAYEFF

You can. Go by that road.

THE STRANGER

I am heartily grateful to you. (*Coughing.*) The weather is splendid— (*Declaiming.*) Brother of mine, suffering brother— Go out to the Volga, whose moans— (*To Varya.*) Mademoiselle, grant a hungry Russian man some thirty kopecks—

Varya is frightened and gives a shriek.

LOPAHIN (*Angrily.*)

There's a limit to everything.

LYUBOFF ANDREEVNA (*Flustered.*)

Take this— Here's this for you— (*Searching in her purse.*) No silver— It's all the same, here's a gold piece for you—

THE STRANGER

I am heartily grateful to you. (*Goes out. Laughter.*)

VARYA (*Frightened.*)

I'm going—I'm going— Oh, Mama, you poor little Mama! There's nothing in the house for people to eat, and you gave him a gold piece.

LYUBOFF ANDREEVNA

What is to be done with me, so silly? I shall give you all I have in the house. Yermolay Alexeevich, you will lend me some this once more!—

LOPAHIN

Agreed.

LYUBOFF ANDREEVNA

Let's go, ladies and gentlemen, it's time. And here, Varya, we have definitely made a match for you, I congratulate you.

VARYA (*Through her tears.*)

Mama, that's not something to joke about.

LOPAHIN

Achmelia, get thee to a nunnery.

GAYEFF

And my hands are trembling; it is a long time since I have played billiards.

LOPAHIN

Achmelia, Oh nymph, in thine orisons be all my sins remember'd—

LYUBOFF ANDREEVNA

Let's go, my dear friends, it will soon be suppertime.

VARYA

He frightened me. My heart is thumping so!

LOPAHIN

I remind you, ladies and gentleman: August 22nd the cherry or- chard will be auctioned off. Think about that!—Think!—

All go out except Trofimoff and Anya.

ANYA (*Laughing.*)

My thanks to the stranger, he frightened Varya, now we are alone.

TROFIMOFF

Varya is afraid we might begin to love each other and all day long she won't leave us to ourselves. With her narrow mind she cannot understand that we are above love. To sidestep the petty and illu- sory, which prevent our being free and happy, that is the aim and meaning of our life. Forward! We march on irresistibly toward the bright star that burns there in the distance. Forward! Do not fall be- hind, friends!

ANYA (*Extending her arms upward.*)

How well you talk! (*A pause.*) It's wonderful here today!

TROFIMOFF

Yes, the weather is marvelous.

ANYA

What have you done to me, Petya, why don't I love the cherry orchard any longer the way I used to? I loved it so tenderly, it seemed to me there was not a better place on earth than our orchard.

TROFIMOFF

All Russia is our orchard. The earth is immense and beautiful, and on it are many wonderful places. (*A pause.*) Just think, Anya: your grandfather, great-grandfather and all your ancestors were slave owners, in possession of living souls, and can you doubt that from every cherry in the orchard, from every leaf, from every trunk, human beings are looking at you, can it be that you don't hear their voices? To possess living souls, well, that depraved all of you who lived before and who are living now, so that your mother and you, and your uncle no longer notice that you live by debt, at somebody else's expense, at the expense of those very people whom you wouldn't let past your front door— We are at least two hundred years behind the times, we have as yet absolutely nothing, we have no definite attitude toward the past, we only philosophize, complain of our sadness or drink vodka. Why, it is quite clear that to begin to live in the present we must first atone for our past, must be done with it; and we can atone for it only through suffering, only through uncommon, incessant labor. Understand that, Anya.

ANYA

The house we live in ceased to be ours long ago, and I'll go away, I give you my word.

TROFIMOFF

If you have the household keys, throw them in the well and go away. Be free as the wind.

ANYA (*Transported.*)

How well you said that!

TROFIMOFF

Believe me, Anya, believe me! I am not thirty yet, I am young, I am still a student, but I have already borne so much! Every winter I am hungry, sick, anxious, poor as a beggar, and—where has destiny not chased me, where haven't I been! And yet, my soul has always, every minute, day and night, been full of inexplicable premonitions. I have a premonition of happiness, Anya, I see it already—

ANYA (*Pensively.*)

The moon is rising.

Epihodoff is heard playing on the guitar, always the same sad song. The moon rises. Somewhere near the poplars Varya is looking for Anya and calling: "Anya! Where are you?"

TROFIMOFF

Yes, the moon is rising. (*A pause.*) Here is happiness, here it comes, comes always nearer and nearer, I hear its footsteps now. And if we shall not see it, shall not come to know it, what does that matter? Others will see it!

VARYA (*Off.*)

Anya! Where are you?

TROFIMOFF

Again, that Varya! (*Angrily.*) It's scandalous!

ANYA
Well, let's go to the river. It's lovely there.
TROFIMOFF
Let's go. (*They go out.*)
VARYA (*Off.*)
Anya! Anya!

Act three

The drawing room, separated by an arch from the ballroom. A chandelier is lighted. A Jewish orchestra is playing—the same that was mentioned in Act Two. Evening. In the ballroom they are dancing grand rond. The voice of Semyonoff-Pishtchik: "Promenade à une paire!" They enter the drawing room; in the first couple are Pishtchik and Charlotta Ivanovna; in the second, Trofimoff and Lyuboff Andreevna; in the third, Anya with the Post-Office Clerk; in the fourth, Varya with the Stationmaster, et cetera—Varya is crying softly and wipes away her tears while she is dancing. Dunyasha is in the last couple through the drawing room, Pishtchik shouts: "Grand rond, balancez!" and "Les Cavaliers à genoux et remerciez vos dames!" Fiers in a frock coat goes by with seltzer water on a tray. Pishtchik and Trofimoff come into the drawing room.

PISHTCHIK
I am full-blooded, I have had two strokes already, and dancing is hard for me, but as they say, if you are in a pack of dogs, you may bark and bark, but you must still wag your tail. At that, I have the health of a horse. My dear father—he was a great joker—may he dwell in Heaven—used to talk as if our ancient line, the Semyonoff-Pishtchiks, were descended from the very horse that Caligula made a Senator—(*Sitting down.*) But here's my trouble: I haven't any money. A hungry dog believes in nothing but meat—(*Snoring but waking at once.*) And the same way with me—I can't talk about anything but money.
TROFIMOFF
Well, to tell you the truth, there is something of a horse about your figure.
PISHTCHIK
Well—a horse is a fine animal— You can sell a horse—
The sound of playing billiards comes from the next room. Varya appears under the arch to the ballroom.
TROFIMOFF (*Teasing.*)
Madam Lopahin! Madam Lopahin!
VARYA (*Angrily.*)
A mangy-looking gentleman!
TROFIMOFF
Yes, I am a mangy-looking gentleman, and proud of it!
VARYA (*In bitter thought.*)
Here we have gone and hired musicians and what are we going to pay them with?
Goes out.

TROFIMOFF (*To Pishtchik.*)

If the energy you have wasted in the course of your life trying to find money to pay the interest had gone into something else, you could very likely have turned the world upside down before you were done with it.

PISHTCHIK

Nietzsche—the philosopher—the greatest—the most celebrated—a man of tremendous mind—says in his works that one may make counterfeit money.

TROFIMOFF

And have you read Nietzsche?

PISHTCHIK

Well—Dashenka told me. And I'm in such a state now that I could make counterfeit money myself— Day after tomorrow three hundred and ten roubles must be paid—one hundred and thirty I've on hand— (*Feeling in his pockets, alarmed.*) The money is gone! I have lost the money! (*Tearfully.*) Where is the money? (*Joyfully.*) Here it is, inside the lining— I was in quite a sweat—

Lyuboff Andreevna and Charlotta Ivanovna come in.

LYUBOFF ANDREEVNA (*Humming lazginka, a Georgian dance.*)

Why does Leonid take so long? What's he doing in town? (*To Dunyasha.*) Dunyasha, offer the musicians some tea—

TROFIMOFF

In all probability the auction did not take place.

LYUBOFF ANDREEVNA

And the musicians came at an unfortunate moment and we planned the ball at an unfortunate moment— Well, it doesn't matter. (*Sitting down and singing softly.*)

CHARLOTTA (*Gives Pishtchik a deck of cards.*)

Here is a deck of cards for you, think of some one card.

PISHTCHIK

I have thought of one.

CHARLOTTA

Now, shuffle the deck. Very good. Hand it here; oh, my dear Monsieur Pishtchik. *Eins, zwei, drei!* Now look for it, it's in your coat pocket—

PISHTCHIK (*Getting a card out of his coat pocket.*)

The eight of spades, that's absolutely right! (*Amazed.*) Fancy that!

CHARLOTTA (*Holding a deck of cards in her palm; to Trofimoff.*)

Tell me quick now, which card is on top?

TROFIMOFF

What is it? Well—the Queen of Spades.

CHARLOTTA

Right! (*To Pishtchik.*) Well? Which card's on top?

PISHTCHIK

The Ace of Hearts.

CHARLOTTA

Right! (*Strikes the deck against her palm; the deck of cards disappears.*) And what beautiful weather we are having today!

A mysterious feminine voice answers her, as if from under the floor: "Oh, yes. The weather is splendid, madame." "You are so nice, you're my ideal—" The voice: "Madame, you too please me greatly."

THE STATIONMASTER (*Applauding.*)

Madam Ventriloquist, bravo!

PISHTCHIK (*Amazed.*)

Fancy that! Most charming Charlotta Ivanovna—I am simply in love with you.

CHARLOTTA

In love? (*Shrugging her shoulders.*) Is it possible that you can love? *Guter Mensch aber schlechter Musikant.*

TROFIMOFF (*Slapping Pishtchik on the shoulder.*)

You horse, you—

CHARLOTTA

I beg your attention, one more trick. (*Taking a lap robe from the chair.*) Here is a very fine lap robe—I want to sell it— (*Shaking it out.*) Wouldn't somebody like to buy it?

PISHTCHIK (*Amazed.*)

Fancy that!

CHARLOTTA

Eins, zwei, drei!

> She quickly raises the lowered robe, behind it stands Anya, who curtseys, runs to her mother, embraces her and runs back into the ballroom amid the general delight.

LYUBOFF ANDREEVNA (*Applauding.*)

Bravo, bravo—!

CHARLOTTA

Now again! *Eins, zwei, drei!*

> Lifting the robe: behind it stands Varya, she bows.

PISHTCHIK (*Amazed.*)

Fancy that!

CHARLOTTA

That's all.

> Throwing the robe at Pishtchik, curtseying and running into the ballroom.

PISHTCHIK (*Hurrying after her.*)

You little rascal—What a girl! What a girl! (*Goes out.*)

LYUBOFF ANDREEVNA

And Leonid is not here yet. What he's doing in town so long, I don't understand! Everything is finished there, either the estate is sold by now, or the auction didn't take place. Why keep it from us so long?

VARYA (*Trying to comfort her.*)

Uncle has bought it, I am sure of that.

TROFIMOFF (*Mockingly.*)

Yes.

VARYA

Great-aunt sent him power of attorney to buy it in her name and transfer the debt. She did this for Anya. And I feel certain, God willing, that Uncle will buy it.

LYUBOFF ANDREEVNA

Our Yaroslavl great-aunt has sent fifteen thousand to buy the estate in her name— She doesn't trust us, but that wouldn't be enough to pay the interest even— (*Covering her face with her hands.*) Today my fate will be decided, my fate—

TROFIMOFF (*Teasing Varya.*)

Madam Lopahin!

VARYA (*Angrily.*)

Perennial student! You have already been expelled from the University twice.

LYUBOFF ANDREEVNA

But why are you angry, Varya? He teases you about Lopahin, what of it? Marry Lopahin if you want to, he is a good man, interesting. If you don't want to, don't marry him; darling, nobody is making you do it.

VARYA

I look at this matter seriously, Mama, one must speak straight out. He's a good man, I like him.

LYUBOFF ANDREEVNA

Then marry him. What there is to wait for I don't understand!

VARYA

But I can't propose to him myself, Mama. It's two years now; everyone has been talking to me about him, everyone talks, and he either remains silent or jokes. I understand. He's getting rich, he's busy with his own affairs, and has no time for me. If there were money, ever so little, even a hundred roubles, I would drop everything, and go far away. I'd go to a nunnery.

TROFIMOFF

How saintly!

VARYA (*To Trofimoff.*)

A student should be intelligent! (*In a low voice, tearfully.*) How homely you have grown, Petya, how old you've got. (*To Lyuboff Andreevna, no longer crying.*) It is just that I can't live without working, Mama. I must be doing something every minute.

Yasha enters.

YASHA (*Barely restraining his laughter.*)

Epihodoff has broken a billiard cue!— (*Goes out.*)

VARYA

But why is Epihodoff here? Who allowed him to play billiards? I don't understand these people— (*Goes out.*)

LYUBOFF ANDREEVNA

Don't tease her, Petya; you can see she has troubles enough without that.

TROFIMOFF

She is just too zealous. Sticking her nose into things that are none of her business. All summer she gave us no peace, neither me nor Anya; she was afraid a romance would spring up between us. What business is that of hers? And besides I haven't shown any signs of it. I am so remote from triviality. We are above love!

LYUBOFF ANDREEVNA

Well, then, I must be beneath love. (*Very anxiously.*) Why isn't Leonid here? Just to tell us whether the estate is sold or not? Calamity seems to me so incredible that I don't know what to think, I'm lost—I could scream this minute—I could do something insane. Save me, Petya. Say something, do say. . . .

TROFIMOFF

Whether the estate is sold today or is not sold—is it not the same? There is no turning back, the path is all grown over. Calm yourself, my dear, all that was over long ago. One mustn't deceive oneself, one must for once at least in one's life look truth straight in the eye.

LYUBOFF ANDREEVNA

What truth? You see where the truth is and where the untruth is, but as for me, it's as if I had lost my sight, I see nothing. You boldly decide all important questions, but tell me, my dear boy, isn't that because you are young and haven't had time yet to suffer through any one of your problems? You look boldly ahead, and isn't that because you don't see and don't expect anything terrible, since life is still hidden from your young eyes? You are braver, more honest, more profound than we are, but stop and think, be magnanimous, have a little mercy on me, just a little. Why, I was born here. My father and mother lived here and my grandfather. I love this house, I can't imagine my life without the cherry orchard and if it is very necessary to sell it, then sell me along with the orchard— (*Embracing Trofimoff and kissing him on the forehead.*) Why, my son was drowned here—(*Crying.*) Have mercy on me, good, kind man.

TROFIMOFF

You know I sympathize with you from the bottom of my heart.

LYUBOFF ANDREEVNA

But that should be said differently, differently—(*Taking out her handkerchief; a telegram falls on the floor.*) My heart is heavy today, you can't imagine how heavy. It is too noisy for me here, my soul trembles at every sound, I tremble all over and yet I can't go off to myself, when I am alone the silence frightens me. Don't blame me, Petya—I love you as one of my own. I should gladly have given you Anya's hand, I assure you, only, my dear, you must study and finish your course. You do nothing. Fate simply flings you about from place to place, and that's so strange— Isn't that so? Yes? And you must do something about your beard, to make it grow somehow— (*Laughing.*) You look funny!

TROFIMOFF (*Picking up the telegram.*)

I do not desire to be beautiful.

LYUBOFF ANDREEVNA

This telegram is from Paris. I get one every day. Yesterday and today too. That wild man has fallen ill again, something is wrong again with him— He asks forgiveness, begs me to come, and really I ought to make a trip to Paris and stay awhile near him. Your face looks stern, Petya, but what is there to do, my dear, what am I to do, he is ill, he is alone, unhappy and who will look after him there, who will keep him from doing the wrong thing, who will give him his medicine on time? And what is there to hide or keep still about? I love him, that's plain. I love him, love him— It's a stone about my neck, I'm sinking to the bottom with it, but I love that stone and live without it I cannot. (*Pressing Trofimoff's hand.*) Don't think harshly of me, Petya, don't say anything to me, don't—

TROFIMOFF (*Tearfully.*)

Forgive my frankness, for God's sake! Why, he picked your bones.

LYUBOFF ANDREEVNA

No, no, no, you must not talk like that. (*Stopping her ears.*)

TROFIMOFF

But he is a scoundrel, only you, you are the only one that doesn't know it. He is a petty scoundrel, a nonentity—

LYUBOFF ANDREEVNA (*Angry but controlling herself.*)

You are twenty-six years old or twenty-seven, but you are still a schoolboy in the second grade!

TROFIMOFF

Very well!

LYUBOFF ANDREEVNA

You should be a man—at your age you should understand people who love. And you yourself should love someone—you should fall in love! (*Angrily.*) Yes, yes! And there is no purity in you; you are simply smug, a ridiculous crank, a freak—

TROFIMOFF (*Horrified.*)

What is she saying!

LYUBOFF ANDREEVNA

"I am above love!" You are not above love, Petya, you are, as our Fiers would say, just a good-for-nothing. Imagine, at your age, not having a mistress—!

TROFIMOFF (*Horrified.*)

This is terrible! What is she saying! (*Goes quickly into the ballroom, clutching his head.*) This is horrible—I can't bear it, I am going—(*Goes out but immediately returns.*) All is over between us. (*Goes out into the hall.*)

LYUBOFF ANDREEVNA (*Shouting after him.*)

Petya, wait! You funny creature, I was joking! Petya!

In the hall you hear someone running up the stairs and suddenly falling back down with a crash. You hear Anya and Varya scream but immediately you hear laughter.

What's that?

Anya runs in.

ANYA (*Laughing.*)

Petya fell down the stairs! (*Runs out.*)

LYUBOFF ANDREEVNA

What a funny boy that Petya is—!

The Stationmaster stops in the center of the ballroom and begins to recite "The Sinner" by A. Tolstoi. They listen to him but he has recited only a few lines when the strains of a waltz are heard from the hall and the recitation is broken off. They all dance. Trofimoff, Anya, Varya and Lyuboff Andreevna come in from the hall.

But, Petya—but, dear soul—I beg your forgiveness— Let's go dance.

She dances with Trofimoff. Anya and Varya dance. Fiers enters, leaving his stick by the side door. Yasha also comes into the drawing room and watches the dancers.

YASHA

What is it, Grandpa?

FIERS

I don't feel very well. In the old days there were generals, barons, admirals dancing at our parties, and now we send for the post-office clerk and the stationmaster, and even they are none too anxious to come. Somehow I've grown feeble. The old master, the grandfather, treated everybody with sealing-wax for all sicknesses. I take sealing-wax every day, have done so for twenty-odd years or more; it may be due to that that I'm alive.

YASHA
> You are tiresome, Grandpa. (*Yawning.*) Why don't you go off and die?

FIERS
> Aw, you—good-for-nothing!— (*Muttering.*)
>> *Trofimoff and Lyuboff Andreevna dance in the ballroom and then in the drawing room.*

LYUBOFF ANDREEVNA
> *Merci.* I'll sit down awhile— (*Sitting down.*) I'm tired.
>> *Anya enters.*

ANYA (*Agitated.*)
> And just now in the kitchen some man was saying that the cherry orchard had been sold today.

LYUBOFF ANDREEVNA
> Sold to whom?

ANYA
> He didn't say who to. He's gone.
>> *Dancing with Trofimoff, they pass into the ballroom.*

YASHA
> It was some old man babbling there. A stranger.

FIERS
> And Leonid Andreevich is still not here, he has not arrived. The overcoat he has on is light, mid-season—let's hope he won't catch cold. Ach, these young things!

LYUBOFF ANDREEVNA
> I shall die this minute. Go, Yasha, find out who it was sold to.

YASHA
> But he's been gone a long time, the old fellow.
>> *Laughing.*

LYUBOFF ANDREEVNA (*With some annoyance.*)
> Well, what are you laughing at? What are you so amused at?

YASHA
> Epihodoff is just too funny. An empty-headed man. Twenty-two misfortunes!

LYUBOFF ANDREEVNA
> Fiers, if the estate is sold, where will you go?

FIERS
> Wherever you say, there I'll go.

LYUBOFF ANDREEVNA
> Why do you look like that? Aren't you well? You know you ought to go to bed—

FIERS
> Yes—(*With a sneer.*) I go to bed and without me who's going to serve, who'll take care of things? I'm the only one in the whole house.

YASHA (*To Lyuboff Andreevna.*)
> Lyuboff Andreevna, let me ask a favor of you, do be so kind! If you ever go back to Paris, take me with you, please do! It's impossible for me to stay here. (*Looking around him, and speaking in a low voice.*) Why talk about it? You can see for yourself it's an uncivilized country, an immoral people and not only that, there's the boredom of it. The food they give us in that kitchen is abominable and there's that Fiers,

too, walking about and muttering all kinds of words that are out of place. Take me with you, be so kind!

Pishtchik enters.

PISHTCHIK

Allow me to ask you—for a little waltz, most beautiful lady— (*Lyuboff Andreevna goes with him.*) Charming lady, I must borrow a hundred and eighty roubles from you—will borrow— (*Dancing.*) a hundred and eighty roubles— (*They pass into the ballroom.*)

YASHA (*Singing low.*)

"Wilt thou know the unrest in my soul!"

In the ballroom a figure in a gray top hat and checked trousers waves both hands and jumps about; there are shouts of "Bravo, Charlotta Ivanovna!"

DUNYASHA (*Stopping to powder her face.*)

The young lady orders me to dance—there are a lot of gentlemen and very few ladies—but dancing makes my head swim and my heart thump. Fiers Nikolaevich, the post-office clerk said something to me just now that took my breath away.

The music plays more softly.

FIERS

What did he say to you?

DUNYASHA

You are like a flower, he says.

YASHA (*Yawning.*)

What ignorance—! (*Goes out.*)

DUNYASHA

Like a flower—I am such a sensitive girl, I love tender words awfully.

FIERS

You'll be getting your head turned.

Epihodoff enters.

EPIHODOFF

Avdotya Feodorovna, you don't want to see me— It's as if I were some sort of insect. (*Sighing.*) Ach, life!

DUNYASHA

What do you want?

EPIHODOFF

Undoubtedly you may be right. (*Sighing.*) But of course, if one considers it from a given point of view, then you, I will allow myself so to express it, forgive my frankness, absolutely led me into a state of mind. I know my fate, every day some misfortune happens to me, but I have long since become accustomed to that, and so I look on my misfortunes with a smile. You gave me your word and, although I—

DUNYASHA

I beg you, we'll talk later on, but leave me now in peace. I'm in a dream now. (*Playing with her fan.*)

EPIHODOFF

I have a something wrong happens every day—I will allow myself so to express it—I just smile, I even laugh.

Varya enters from the ballroom.

VARYA

You are not gone yet, Semyon? What a really disrespectful man you are! (*To Dunyasha.*) Get out of here, Dunyasha. (*To Epihodoff.*) You either play billiards and break a cue or you walk about the drawing room like a guest.

EPIHODOFF

Allow me to tell you, you cannot make any demands on me.

VARYA

I'm not making any demands on you, I'm talking to you. All you know is to walk from place to place but not do any work. We keep a clerk, but what for, nobody knows.

EPIHODOFF (*Offended.*)

Whether I work, whether I walk, whether I eat, or whether I play billiards are matters to be discussed only by people of understanding and my seniors.

VARYA

You dare to say that to me! (*Flying into a temper.*) You dare? So I don't understand anything? Get out of here! This minute!

EPIHODOFF (*Alarmed.*)

I beg you to express yourself in a delicate manner.

VARYA (*Beside herself.*)

This very minute, get out of here! Get out! (*He goes to the door; she follows him.*) Twenty-two misfortunes! Don't you dare breathe in here! Don't let me set eyes on you!

> *Epihodoff has gone out, but his voice comes from outside the door: "I shall complain about you."*

Ah, you are coming back? (*Grabbing the stick that Fiers put by the door.*) Come on, come—come on, I'll show you— Ah, you are coming? You are coming? Take that then—!

> *She swings the stick, at the very moment when Lopahin is coming in.*

LOPAHIN

Most humbly, I thank you.

VARYA (*Angrily and ironically.*)

I beg your pardon!

LOPAHIN

It's nothing at all. I humbly thank you for the pleasant treat.

VARYA

It isn't worth your thanks. (*Moving away, then looking back and asking gently.*) I haven't hurt you?

LOPAHIN

No, it's nothing. There's a great bump coming though.

> *Voices in the ballroom: "Lopahin has come back." "Yermolay Alexeevich!"*
> *Pishtchik enters.*

PISHTCHIK

See what we see, hear what we hear—! (*He and Lopahin kiss one another.*) You smell slightly of cognac, my dear, my good old chap. And we are amusing ourselves here too.

> *Lyuboff Andreevna enters.*

LYUBOFF ANDREEVNA

Is that you, Yermolay Alexeevich? Why were you so long? Where is Leonid?

LOPAHIN

Leonid Andreevich got back when I did, he's coming.

LYUBOFF ANDREEVNA (*Agitated.*)

Well, what? Was there an auction? Do speak!

LOPAHIN (*Embarrassed, afraid of showing the joy he feels.*)

The auction was over by four o'clock— We were late for the train, had to wait till half-past nine. (*Sighing heavily.*) Ugh, my head's swimming a bit!

> *Gayeff enters; with his right hand he carries his purchases, with his left he wipes away his tears.*

LYUBOFF ANDREEVNA

Lyona, what? Lyona, eh? (*Impatiently, with tears in her eyes.*) Quick, for God's sake—

GAYEFF (*Not answering her, merely waving his hand; to Fiers, crying.*)

Here, take it— There are anchovies, some Kertch herrings— I haven't eaten anything all day—What I have suffered!

> *The door into the billiard room is open; you hear the balls clicking and Yasha's voice: "Seven and eighteen!" Gayeff's expression changes, he is no longer crying.*

I'm terribly tired. You help me change, Fiers.

> *Goes to his room through the ballroom, Fiers behind him.*

PISHTCHIK

What happened at the auction? Go on, tell us!

LYUBOFF ANDREEVNA

Is the cherry orchard sold?

LOPAHIN

It's sold.

LYUBOFF ANDREEVNA

Who bought it?

LOPAHIN

I bought it.

> *A pause. Lyuboff Andreevna is overcome. She would have fallen had she not been standing near the chair and table. Varya takes the keys from her belt, throws them on the floor in the middle of the drawing room and goes out.*

I bought it. Kindly wait a moment, ladies and gentlemen, everything is muddled up in my head, I can't speak—(*Laughing.*) We arrived at the auction, Deriganoff was already there. Leonid Andreevich had only fifteen thousand and Deriganoff right off bids thirty over and above indebtedness. I see how things are, I match him with forty thousand. He forty-five. I fifty-five. That is to say he raises it by fives, I by tens.—So it ended. Over and above the indebtedness, I bid up to ninety thousand, it was knocked down to me. The cherry orchard is mine now. Mine! (*Guffawing.*) My God, Lord, the cherry orchard is mine! Tell me I'm drunk, out of my head, that I'm imagining all this— (*Stamps his feet.*) Don't laugh at me! If only my father and grandfather could rise from their graves and see this whole business, see how their Yermolay, beaten, half-illiterate Yermolay, who used to run around barefoot in winter, how that very Yermolay has bought an estate that nothing in the world can beat. I bought the estate where grandfather and father were slaves, where you wouldn't even let me in the kitchen. I am asleep, it's only some dream of mine, it only seems so to me— That's nothing but the fruit of your imagination, covered with the darkness of the unknown— (*Picking up the keys, with a gentle smile.*) She threw down the keys, wants to show she is not mistress any more— (*Jingling the keys.*) Well, it's all the same. (*The orchestra is heard tuning up.*) Hey, musicians, play, I want to hear you! Come on, everybody, and see how Yermolay Lopahin will swing the ax in the cherry orchard, how the trees will fall to the ground! We are going to build villas and our grandsons and great-grandsons will see a new life here— Music, play! (*The music is playing. Lyuboff Andreevna has sunk into a chair, crying bitterly. Lopahin, reproachfully.*) Why, then, didn't you listen to me? My poor dear, it can't be undone now. (*With tears.*) Oh, if this could all be over soon, if somehow our awkward, unhappy life would be changed!

PISHTCHIK (*Taking him by the arm, in a low voice.*)

She is crying. Come on in the ballroom, let her be by herself— Come on— (*Taking him by the arm and leading him into the ballroom.*)

LOPAHIN

What's the matter? Music, there, play up! (*Sarcastically.*) Everything is to be as I want it! Here comes the new squire, the owner of the cherry orchard. (*Quite accidentally, he bumps into the little table, and very nearly upsets the candelabra.*) I can pay for everything!

> *Goes out with Pishtchik. There is nobody left either in the ballroom or the drawing room but Lyuboff Andreevna, who sits all huddled up and crying bitterly. The music plays softly. Anya and Trofimoff enter hurriedly. Anya comes up to her mother and kneels in front of her. Trofimoff remains at the ballroom door.*

ANYA

Mama—! Mama, you are crying? My dear, kind, good Mama, my beautiful, I love you—I bless you. The cherry orchard is sold, it's not ours any more, that's true, true; but don't cry, Mama, you've your life still left you, you've your good, pure heart ahead of you— Come with me, come on, darling, away from here, come on— We will plant a new orchard, finer than this one, you'll see it, you'll understand; and joy, quiet, deep joy will sink into your heart, like the sun at evening, and you'll smile, Mama! Come, darling, come on!

Act four

> *The same setting as in Act One. There are neither curtains on the windows nor are there any pictures on the walls. Only a little furniture remains piled up in one corner as if for sale. A sense of emptiness is felt. Near the outer door, at the rear of the stage, is a pile of suitcases, traveling bags, and so on. The door on the left is open, and through it Varya's and Anya's voices are heard. Lopahin is standing waiting. Yasha is holding a tray with glasses of champagne. In the hall Epihodoff is tying up a box, offstage at the rear there is a hum. It is the peasants who have come to say good-by. Gayeff's voice: "Thanks, brothers, thank you."*

YASHA

The simple folk have come to say good-by. I am of the opinion, Yermolay Alexeevich, that the people are kind enough but don't understand anything.

The hum subsides. Lyuboff Andreevna enters through the hall with Gayeff; she is not crying, but is pale, her face quivers, she is not able to speak.

GAYEFF

You gave them your purse, Lyuba. Mustn't do that! Mustn't do that!

LYUBOFF ANDREEVNA

I couldn't help it! I couldn't help it!

Both go out.

LOPAHIN (*Calling through the door after them.*)

Please, I humbly beg you! A little glass at parting. I didn't think to bring some from town, and at the station I found just one bottle. Please! (*A pause.*) Well, then, ladies and gentlemen! You don't want it? (*Moving away from the door.*) If I'd known that, I wouldn't have bought it. Well, then I won't drink any either. (*Yasha carefully sets the tray down on a chair.*) At least, you have some, Yasha.

YASHA

To those who are departing! Pleasant days to those who stay behind! (*Drinking.*) This champagne is not the real stuff, I can assure you.

LOPAHIN

Eight roubles a bottle. (*A pause.*) It's devilish cold in here.

YASHA

They didn't heat up today, we are leaving anyway. (*Laughing.*)

LOPAHIN

What are you laughing about?

YASHA

For joy.

LOPAHIN

Outside it's October, but it's sunny and still, like summer. Good for building. (*Looking at his watch, then through the door.*) Ladies and gentlemen, bear in mind we have forty-six minutes in all till train time! Which means you have to go to the station in twenty minutes. Hurry up a little.

TROFIMOFF (*In an overcoat, entering from outside.*)

Seems to me it is time to go. The carriages are ready. The devil knows where my rubbers are. They've disappeared. (*In the door.*) Anya, my rubbers are not here! I can't find them.

LOPAHIN

And I have to go to Harkoff. I'm going on the same train with you. I'm going to live in Harkoff all winter. I've been dilly-dallying along with you, I'm tired of doing nothing. I can't be without work, look, I don't know what to do with my hands here, see, they are dangling somehow, as if they didn't belong to me.

TROFIMOFF

We are leaving right away, and you'll set about your useful labors again.

LOPAHIN

Here, drink a glass.

TROFIMOFF

I shan't.

LOPAHIN

It's to Moscow now?

TROFIMOFF

Yes. I'll see them off to town, and tomorrow to Moscow.

LOPAHIN

Yes— Maybe the professors are not giving their lectures. I imagine they are waiting till you arrive.

TROFIMOFF

That's none of your business.

LOPAHIN

How many years is it you've been studying at the University?

TROFIMOFF

Think of something newer. This is old and flat. (*Looking for his rubbers.*) You know, perhaps, we shall not see each other again; therefore, permit me to give you one piece of advice at parting! Don't wave your arms! Cure yourself of that habit—of arm waving. And also of building summer cottages, figuring that the summer residents will in time become individual landowners; figuring like that is arm waving too— Just the same, however, I like you. You have delicate soft fingers like an artist, you have a delicate soft heart—

LOPAHIN (*Embracing him.*)

Good-by, my dear boy. Thanks for everything. If you need it, take some money from me for the trip.

TROFIMOFF

Why should I? There's no need for it.

LOPAHIN

But you haven't any!

TROFIMOFF

I have. Thank you. I got some for a translation. Here it is in my pocket. (*Anxiously.*) But my rubbers are gone.

VARYA (*From another room.*)

Take your nasty things! (*Throws a pair of rubbers on to the stage.*)

TROFIMOFF

But what are you angry about, Varya? Hm— Why, these are not my rubbers.

LOPAHIN

In the spring I planted twenty-seven hundred acres of poppies and now I've made forty thousand clear. And when my poppies were in bloom, what a picture it was! So look, as I say, I've made forty thousand, which means I'm offering you a loan because I can afford to. Why turn up your nose? I'm a peasant—I speak straight out.

TROFIMOFF

Your father was a peasant, mine—an apothecary—and from that absolutely nothing follows. (*Lopahin takes out his wallet.*) Leave it alone, leave it alone—If you gave me two hundred thousand even, I wouldn't take it. I am a free man. And everything that you all value so highly and dearly, both rich man and beggars, has not the slightest power over me, it's like a mere feather floating in the air. I can get along without you, I can pass you by, I am strong and proud. Humanity is moving toward the loftiest truth, toward the loftiest happiness that is possible on earth and I am in the front ranks.

LOPAHIN

Will you get there?

TROFIMOFF

I'll get there. (*A pause.*) I'll get there, or I'll show the others the way to get there.

In the distance is heard the sound of an ax on a tree.

LOPAHIN

Well, good-by, my dear boy. It's time to go. We turn up our noses at one another, but life keeps on passing. When I work a long time without stopping, my thoughts are clearer, and it seems as if I, too, know what I exist for, and, brother, how many people are there in Russia who exist, nobody knows for what! Well, all the same, it's not that that keeps things circulating. Leonid Andreevich, they say, has accepted a position—he'll be in a bank, six thousand a year—the only thing is he won't stay there, he's very lazy—

ANYA (*In the doorway.*)

Mama begs of you until she's gone, not to cut down the orchard.

TROFIMOFF

Honestly, haven't you enough tact to—
    Goes out through the hall.

LOPAHIN

Right away, right away— What people, really!
    Goes out after him.

ANYA

Has Fiers been sent to the hospital?

YASHA

I told them to this morning. They must have sent him.

ANYA (*To Epihodoff, who is passing through the room.*)

Semyon Panteleevich, please inquire whether or not they have taken Fiers to the hospital.

YASHA (*Huffily.*)

This morning, I told Igor. Why ask ten times over!

EPIHODOFF

The venerable Fiers, according to my conclusive opinion, is not worth mending, he ought to join his forefathers. And I can only envy him. (*Putting a suitcase on a hatbox and crushing it.*) Well, there you are, of course. I knew it. (*Goes out.*)

YASHA (*Mockingly.*)

Twenty-two misfortunes—

VARYA (*On the other side of the door.*)

Have they taken Fiers to the hospital?

ANYA

They have.

VARYA

Then why didn't they take the letter to the doctor?

ANYA

We must send it on after them— (*Goes out.*)

VARYA (*From the next room.*)

Where is Yasha? Tell him his mother has come, she wants to say good-by to him.

YASHA (*Waving his hand.*)

They merely try my patience.
    Dunyasha has been busying herself with the luggage; now when Yasha is left alone, she goes up to him.

DUNYASHA

If you'd only look at me once, Yasha. You are going away—leaving me— (*Crying and throwing herself on his neck.*)

YASHA

Why are you crying? (*Drinking champagne.*) In six days I'll be in Paris again. Tomorrow we will board the express train and dash off out of sight; somehow, I can't believe it. *Vive la France!* It doesn't suit me here—I can't live here—Can't help that. I've seen enough ignorance —enough for me. (*Drinking champagne.*) Why do you cry? Behave yourself properly, then you won't be crying.

DUNYASHA (*Powdering her face, looking into a small mirror.*)

Send me a letter from Paris. I loved you, Yasha, you know, loved you so! I am a tender creature, Yasha!

YASHA

They are coming here. (*Bustling about near the suitcases, humming low.*)

Lyuboff Andreevna, Gayeff, Anya and Charlotta Ivanovna enter.

GAYEFF

We should be going. There is very little time left. (*Looking at Yasha.*) Who is it smells like herring!

LYUBOFF ANDREEVNA

In about ten minutes let's be in the carriage— (*Glancing around the room.*) Good-by, dear house, old Grandfather. Winter will pass, spring will be here, but you won't be here any longer, they'll tear you down. How much these walls have seen! (*Kissing her daughter warmly.*) My treasure, you are beaming, your eyes are dancing like two diamonds. Are you happy? Very?

ANYA

Very! It's the beginning of a new life, Mama!

GAYEFF (*Gaily.*)

Yes, indeed, everything is fine now. Before the sale of the cherry orchard, we all were troubled, distressed, and then when the question was settled definitely, irrevocably, we all calmed down and were even cheerful— I'm a bank official. I am a financier now— Yellow ball into the side pocket, anyway, Lyuba, you look better, no doubt about that.

LYUBOFF ANDREEVNA

Yes. My nerves are better, that's true. (*They hand her her hat and coat.*) I sleep well. Carry out my things, Yasha. It's time. (*To Anya.*) My little girl, we shall see each other again soon— I am going to Paris, I shall live there on the money your Yaroslavl great-aunt sent for the purchase of the estate—long live Great-aunt! But that money won't last long.

ANYA

Mama, you'll come back soon, soon— Isn't that so? I'll prepare myself, pass the examination at high school, and then I'll work, I will help you. We'll read all sorts of books together. Mama, isn't that so? (*Kissing her mother's hands.*) We'll read in the autumn evenings, read lots of books, and a new, wonderful world will open up before us— (*Daydreaming.*) Mama, do come—

LYUBOFF ANDREEVNA

I'll come, my precious. (*Embracing her daughter.*)

Lopahin enters with Charlotta who is softly humming a song.

GAYEFF

Lucky Charlotta: she's singing!

CHARLOTTA (*Taking a bundle that looks like a baby wrapped up.*)

My baby, bye, bye— (*A baby's cry is heard: Ooah, ooah—!*) Hush, my darling, my dear little boy. (*Ooah, ooah—!*) I am so sorry for you!

(*Throwing the bundle back.*) Will you please find me a position? I cannot go on like this.

LOPAHIN

We will find something, Charlotta Ivanovna, don't worry.

GAYEFF

Everybody is dropping us, Varya is going away.—All of a sudden we are not needed.

CHARLOTTA

I have no place in town to live. I must go away. (*Humming.*) It's all the same—

> Pishtchik enters.

LOPAHIN

The freak of nature—!

PISTCHIK (*Out of breath.*)

Ugh, let me catch my breath—I'm exhaused— My honored friends— Give me some water—

GAYEFF

After money, I suppose? This humble servant will flee from sin!

> *Goes out.*

PISHTCHIK

It's a long time since I was here— Most beautiful lady— (*To Lopahin.*) You here—? Glad to see you—a man of the greatest intellect— Here— Take it— (*Giving Lopahin some money.*) Four hundred roubles— That leaves eight hundred and forty I still owe you—

LOPAHIN (*With astonishment, shrugging his shoulders.*)

I must be dreaming. But where did you get it?

PISHTCHIK

Wait—I'm hot— Most extraordinary event. Some Englishmen came and found on my land some kind of white clay— (*To Lyuboff Andreevna.*) And four hundred for you—Beautiful lady—Wonderful lady— (*Handing over the money.*) The rest later. (*Taking a drink of water.*) Just now a young man was saying on the train that some great philosopher recommends jumping off roofs—"Jump!" he says, and "therein lies the whole problem." (*With astonishment.*) You don't say! Water!

LOPAHIN

And what Englishmen were they?

PISHTCHIK

I leased them the parcel of land with the clay for twenty-four years— And now, excuse me, I haven't time—I must run along—I'm going to Znoykoff's—To Kardamonoff's— I owe everybody— (*Drinking.*) I wish you well—I'll drop in on Thursday—

LYUBOFF ANDREEVNA

We are moving to town right away, and tomorrow I'm going abroad—

PISHTCHIK

What? (*Alarmed.*) Why to town? That's why I see furniture— Suitcases— Well, no matter—(*Tearfully.*) No matter— Men of the greatest minds—those Englishmen— No matter— Good luck! God will help you— No matter— Everything in this world comes to an end— (*Kissing Lyuboff Andreevna's hand.*) And should the report reach you that my end has come, think of that well-known horse and say: "There was once on earth a so and so— Semyonoff Pishtchik— The kingdom of Heaven be his." Most remarkable weather—yes— (*Going out greatly disconcerted, but immediately returning and speaking from the door.*) Dashenka sends her greetings!

> *Goes out.*

LYUBOFF ANDREEVNA

And now we can go. I am leaving with two worries. First, that Fiers is sick. (*Glancing at her watch.*) We still have five minutes—

ANYA

Mama, Fiers has already been sent to the hospital. Yasha sent him off this morning.

LYUBOFF ANDREEVNA

My second worry—is Varya. She is used to getting up early and working, and now without any work she is like a fish out of water. She has grown thin, pale and cries all the time, poor thing— (*A pause.*) You know this, Yermolay Alexeevich: I dreamed— of marrying her to you. And there was every sign of your getting married.

> *Whispering to Anya, who beckons to Charlotta; both go out.*

She loves you, you are fond of her, and I don't know, don't know why it is you seem to avoid each other—I don't understand it!

LOPAHIN

I don't understand it either, I must confess. It's all strange somehow— If there's still time, I am ready right now even— Let's finish it up—and *basta,* but without you I feel I won't propose.

LYUBOFF ANDREEVNA

But that's excellent. Surely it takes only a minute. I'll call her at once.

LOPAHIN

And to fit the occasion there's the champagne. (*Looking at the glasses.*) Empty, somebody has already drunk them. (*Yasha coughs.*) That's what's called lapping it up—

LYUBOFF ANDREEVNA (*Vivaciously.*)

Splendid! We'll go out— Yasha, *allez!* I'll call her— (*Through the door.*) Varya, drop everything and come here. Come on!

> *Goes out with Yasha.*

LOPAHIN (*Looking at his watch.*)

Yes—

> *A pause. Behind the door you hear smothered laughter, whispering, finally Varya enters.*

VARYA (*Looking at the luggage a long time.*)

That's strange, I just can't find it—

LOPAHIN

What are you looking for?

VARYA

I packed it myself and don't remember where.

> *A pause.*

LOPAHIN

Where do you expect to go now, Varvara Mikhailovna?

VARYA

I? To Regulin's. I agreed to go there to look after the house— As a sort of housekeeper.

LOPAHIN

That's in Yashnevo? It's nigh on to seventy miles. (*A pause.*) And here ends life in this house—

VARYA (*Examining the luggage.*)

But where is it? Either I put it in the trunk, perhaps— Yes, life in this house is ended—it won't be any more—

LOPAHIN

And I am going to Harkoff now— By the next train. I've a lot to do. And I am leaving Epihodoff—on the ground here—I've hired him.

VARYA

Well!

LOPAHIN

Last year at this time it had already been snowing, if you remember, and now it's quiet, it's sunny. It's only that it's cold, about three degrees of frost.

VARYA

I haven't noticed. (*A pause.*) And besides our thermometer is broken— (*A pause. A voice from the yard through the door: "Yermolay Alexeevich—"*)

LOPAHIN (*As if he had been expecting this call for a long time.*)

This minute! (*Goes out quickly.*)

    Varya, sitting on the floor, putting her head on a bundle of clothes, sobs quietly. The door opens, Lyuboff Andreevna enters cautiously.

VARYA (*She is not crying any longer, and has wiped her eyes.*)

Yes, it's time, Mama. I can get to Regulin's today, if we are just not too late for the train— (*Through the door.*) Anya, put your things on!

    Anya, then Gayeff and Charlotta Ivanovna enter. Gayeff has on a warm overcoat, with a hood. The servants gather, also the drivers. Epihodoff busies himself with the luggage.

Now we can be on our way.

ANYA (*Joyfully.*)

On our way!

GAYEFF

My friends, my dear, kind friends! Leaving this house forever, can I remain silent, can I restrain myself from expressing, as we say, farewell, those feelings that fill now my whole being—

ANYA (*Beseechingly.*)

Uncle!

VARYA

Dear Uncle, don't!

GAYEFF (*Dejectedly.*)

Bank the yellow into the side pocket— I am silent—

    Trofimoff and then Lopahin enter.

TROFIMOFF

Well, ladies and gentlemen, it's time to go!

LOPAHIN

Epihodoff, my coat!

LYUBOFF ANDREEVNA

I'll sit here just a minute more. It's as if I had never seen before what the walls in this house are like, what kind of ceilings, and now I look at them greedily, with such tender love—

GAYEFF

I remember when I was six years old, on Trinity Day, I sat in this window and watched my father going to Church—

LYUBOFF ANDREEVNA

Are all the things taken out?

LOPAHIN

Everything, I think. (*Putting on his overcoat. To Epihodoff.*) Epihodoff, you see that everything is in order.

EPIHODOFF (*Talking in a hoarse voice.*)

Don't worry, Yermolay Alexeevich!

LOPAHIN

Why is your voice like that?

EPIHODOFF

Just drank some water, swallowed something.

YASHA (*With contempt.*)

The ignorance—

LYUBOFF ANDREEVNA

We are going and there won't be a soul left here—

LOPAHIN

Till spring.

VARYA (*She pulls an umbrella out from a bundle, it looks as if she were going to hit someone; Lopahin pretends to be frightened.*)

What do you, what do you— I never thought of it.

TROFIMOFF

Ladies and gentlemen, let's get in the carriages— It's time! The train is coming any minute.

VARYA

Petya, here they are, your rubbers, by the suitcase. (*Tearfully.*) And how dirty yours are, how old—!

TROFIMOFF (*Putting on the rubbers.*)

Let's go, ladies and gentlemen!

GAYEFF (*Greatly embarrassed, afraid he will cry.*)

The train— The station— Cross into the side, combination off the white into the corner—

LYUBOFF ANDREEVNA

Let's go!

LOPAHIN

Everybody here? Nobody there? (*Locking the side door on the left.*) Things are stored here, it must be locked up, let's go!

ANYA

Good-by, house! Good-by, the old life!

TROFIMOFF

Long live the new life!

> Goes out with Anya. Varya casts a glance around the room and, without hurrying, goes out. Yasha and Charlotta, with her dog, go out.

LOPAHIN

And so, till spring. Out, ladies and gentlemen— Till we meet. (*Goes out.*)

> Lyuboff Andreevna and Gayeff are left alone. As if they had been waiting for this, they throw themselves on one another's necks sobbing, but smothering their sobs as if afraid of being heard.

GAYEFF (*In despair.*)

Oh, Sister, Sister—

LYUBOFF ANDREEVNA

Oh, my dear, my lovely, beautiful orchard! My life, my youth, my happiness, good-by!

ANYA (*Anya's voice, gaily, appealingly.*)

Mama—!

TROFIMOFF (*Trofimoff's voice, gaily, excitedly.*)

Aaooch!

LYUBOFF ANDREEVNA

For the last time, just to look at the walls, at the window— My dear mother used to love to walk around in this room—

GAYEFF

Oh, Sister, Sister—!

ANYA (*Anya's voice.*)

Mama—!

TROFIMOFF (*Trofimoff's voice.*)

Aaooch—!

LYUBOFF ANDREEVNA

We are coming! (*They go out.*)

> *The stage is empty. You hear the keys locking all the doors, then the carriages drive off. It grows quiet. In the silence you hear the dull thud of an ax on a tree, a lonely, mournful sound. Footsteps are heard. From the door on the right Fiers appears. He is dressed as usual, in a jacket and a white waistcoat, slippers on his feet. He is sick.*

FIERS (*Going to the door and trying the knob.*)

Locked. They've gone. (*Sitting down on the sofa.*) They forgot about me— No matter— I'll sit here awhile— And Leonid Andreevich, for sure, didn't put on his fur coat, he went off with his topcoat— (*Sighing anxiously.*) And I didn't see to it— The young saplings! (*He mutters something that cannot be understood.*) Life has gone by, as if I hadn't lived at all— (*Lying down.*) I'll lie down awhile— You haven't got any strength, nothing is left, nothing— Ach, you—good-for-nothing— (*He lies still.*)

> *There is a far-off sound as if out of the sky, the sound of a snapped string, dying away, sad. A stillness falls, and there is only the thud of an ax on a tree, far away in the orchard.*
> *Curtain*

Action analysis and performance suggestions

The following scenes are particularly recommended for informal classroom performance: Madame Ranevskaya's interchange with Trofimoff in act III, pages 546–548, and the opening of act II to the entry of Fiers, pages 532–537).

If Stanislavski missed some of the comic irony in *The Cherry Orchard*, his basic approach to Chekhov was what made and what still makes the dramas work on stage. If one plays the despair, boredom, or anguish that the characters so frequently complain of in a Chekhov play, then the result will not only be a bored audience but also a misinterpretation of the characters and of the play's action. Stanislavski saw that despite the inertia of the characters in the face of disaster, they are filled with longings, desires, and a thirst for life that is revealed in both their introspective philosophic ramblings and in their concern with the trivia of their existence, be it lunch or the weather. In *My Life in Art*, Stanislavski recalls the discovery he made about Chekhov's plays when he was struggling with *The Three Sisters:* "The men of Chekhov do not bathe, as we did at that time, in their own sorrow. Just the opposite; they, like Chekhov himself, seek life, joy, laughter, courage. The men and women of Chekhov want to live and not to die. They are active and surge to overcome the hard and unbearable impasses into which life has plunged them" (pp. 373–374).

DEFINING THE ACTIONS AND THE SUPEROBJECTIVE

Just as the duck had different meanings for the different characters who tried to save it in Ibsen's play, so the cherry orchard has different meanings for the characters who try to control its fate in Chekhov's play. For Madame Ranevskaya and her brother, the orchard represents the past, their childhood, and the values of a leisured and cultured class. Their efforts to save it are seen from the start by others as hopeless since the way of life it represents is clearly past. Lopahin wants to cut down the orchard's trees and transform it into a profitable real estate venture. One might be tempted to say that Trofimoff would have no interest in controlling the orchard's fate if he were not so drawn to its occupants, to Anya in particular, whom he wishes to convert from her attachment to the orchard to an attachment to Russia itself as a potential garden. Like Lopahin, but in a different vein, he too hopes to see the life of the old orchard transformed, but Trofimoff wants the transformation to be one that benefits all of Russia and the texture of its life.

In the exchange between Madame Ranevskaya and Trofimoff in act III, an exchange that is part of the broader scene in which the news of the sale is dreaded and received, the aspirations of the two characters come into conflict. At first Madame Ranevskaya wants to cling to Trofimoff like a drowning woman. She senses that the estate has been sold and begs Trofimoff to help her: "Calamity seems to me so incredible that I don't know what to think, I'm lost—I could scream this minute—I could do something insane. Save me, Petya. Say something, do say. . . ." The plea is especially moving in that Trofimoff was the tutor of her drowned son, a drowning she feels was retribution for her sinful life, especially a love affair. Yet when her plea for help from Trofimoff evokes a lesson on truth from him, she attacks him in order to defend herself and her way of life. Though drawn to Madame Ranevskaya's daughter Anya, Trofimoff insists that he and Anya "are above love," but Madame Ranevskaya, who is drawn back to her worthless lover in Paris, replies, "Well, then, I must be beneath love." She knows she will return to her lover and that he will not save her either: "I love him, love him—It's a stone about my neck, I'm sinking to the bottom with it, but I love that stone and live without it I cannot." What she wants in the scene is to make Trofimoff understand her need. "Don't think harshly of me Petya, don't say anything to me, don't—."

Although deeply moved, Trofimoff can neither understand nor accept Madame Ranevskaya's point of view or actions. Perhaps if he had believed more in her way of life in Russia, he could have given her the strength to resist her lover and suffer the loss of the orchard with tragic dignity and strength. But he does not understand. He sees what Madame Ranevskaya senses, that the changes implied in the sale of the orchard have already begun and cannot be stopped. "Whether the estate is sold today or is not sold—is it not the same?" he asks her. "There is no turning back, the path is all grown over. Calm yourself, my dear, all that was over long ago. One mustn't deceive oneself, one must for once at least in one's life look truth straight in the eye." Trofimoff recognizes Madame Ranevskaya's plea for help and understanding, but his action is to help her face the truth rather than offer sympathy and understanding. As a student, a revolutionary, and a man of ideas, he offers his ideas, and his action is to convince her of the truth as he sees it. Not only is the sale of the orchard of no consequence, but Madame Ranevskaya's lover is "a scoundrel." "TROFIMOFF *(Tearfully.)* Forgive my frankness, for God's sake! Why, he picked your bones." The stage direction, "tearfully," shows how important it is to Trofimoff to make Madame Ranevskaya understand his point of view.

Madame Ranevskaya challenges Trofimoff's truth even as Dr. Relling challenges Gregers' truth in *The Wild Duck:* "What truth? You see where the truth is and where the untruth is, but as for me, it's as if I had lost my sight, I see nothing." She accuses him of the mercilessness of youth, of knowing the answers because he has not suffered. She further seeks to undermine his truth with her suggestion that he is a failure. "You do nothing. Fate simply flings you about from place to place, and that's so strange—Isn't that so?" She attacks his physical appearance and finally, in order to defend her weakness in love, attacks what she considers his weakness: " 'I am above love!' " she taunts him. "You are not above love, Petya, you are as our Fiers would say, just a good-for-nothing. Imagine at your age, not having a mistress—!"

High tragedy? Hardly. Trofimoff exits in anguish, returns to inform Madame Ranevskaya that all is over between them, proceeds to fall down the stairs, and is back dancing with the apologetic lady almost immediately. Although they have pitted their ways of life against each other, on some level they both understand and forgive each other the distance between them.

OVERCOMING OBSTACLES

Madame Ranevskaya's obstacles in the scene are interior (her sense of guilt) and exterior (Trofimoff's smug youth). As someone who expended her energies and love first on a drunken husband and then on an unscrupulous lover, she feels that her son's death and the loss of the orchard itself are judgments on her. This may account for her attack on Trofimoff, who refuses the kind of sympathy she craves. Since her main objective in the scene and perhaps in the play is to find the means for survival, her defense of herself is at the expense of one whose youth makes him incapable of understanding. Her love of and even her respect for Trofimoff is another obstacle. She cannot dismiss him without pain when she knows her own weaknesses and has much feeling for him as well.

Trofimoff, who begins by trying to calm Madame Ranevskaya and ends in such emotional upheaval that he falls down a flight of stairs, also finds his feelings an obstacle to his ideas. He has come back to the estate in order to see this woman whom he loves (his berating of her lover may even contain seeds of jealousy) and has possibly fallen in love with her daughter, despite his attempts to be "above love." Since he really has accomplished little as a revolutionary student, he is vulnerable on all counts and he collapses when the woman he would guide attacks him.

THE MAGIC IF AND THE GIVEN CIRCUMSTANCES

Madame Ranevskaya completely identifies herself with the orchard; hence her feeling of intolerable loss. But one cannot act the feeling of loss. What IF the most precious thing you owned were being sold or taken from you, something you associate with the most pleasant memories of your childhood? What IF you turned for help and understanding to someone who does not understand the beauty and the importance of the possession? The circumstances are such that the loss of the object means an uncertain future and a total change in circumstances. The image of drowning is helpful since Madame Ranevskaya feels as if the sale of the estate presents a life-and-death situation.

What IF on the other hand you felt sorry for a woman who was on dry land but thought she was drowning? Wouldn't you point out to her that she is on dry land? What IF you saw only hope where others saw despair but cared very much for the misguided ones and hoped to open their eyes? But what IF you yourself suffered from some of youth's blindness and lack of self-knowledge? What IF in the process of pointing out to Madame Ranevskaya that she is not drowning but on dry land, you, Trofimoff, quite literally have the rug pulled out from under you and find yourself at sea? The result should be the tragicomic effect that this crucial scene depends on.

CLASSROOM ADAPTATIONS TO ARRIVE AT STYLE

As in *The Wild Duck,* a clear separation between acting area and audience should be made. Classroom lights should be off, windows should be covered, and, if possible, special lights should be focused on the acting area. The actors should imagine a fourth wall and focus entirely on one another and the setting.

The setting should be as precisely detailed as possible. Since it is a drawing room with much activity coming from an adjoining ballroom, screens could be used to suggest the opening to the other room. In the original settings for *The Cherry Orchard,* an effort was made to obtain even more realism than in earlier Ibsen productions by creating rooms that were not simply boxes but which had walls set at angles. The screens might be effectively used in the classroom to suggest both the division between the two rooms and an interesting shape for the drawing room.

The Jewish orchestra is supposedly playing in the ballroom and it is important to have some music, laughter, and movement coming from that area. Madame Ranevskaya's anxiety and sense of loss may be heightened if the false mood of celebration she has surrounded herself with is highlighted. Chekhov's style often derives from just such a juxtaposition of inner and outer moods.

Chekhov had complained of the excess of naturalistic detail in Stanislavski's production. The key, then, in selecting furniture and properties is necessity and simplicity. Classroom chairs may be covered with elegant cloth and pillows if period furniture is not available. The actors should move naturally: Madame Ranevskaya expressing her emotions physically, caressing, scolding, and so on, and Trofimoff appearing more reticent and uncomfortable. Madame Ranevskaya should wear a long dress and Trofimoff, who really should have a beard, might wear a shirt, pants, and vest, unless the performers want to update the scene and dress in contemporary clothing.

In order to arrive at the proper production style, very careful attention should be given to the interplay of the speeches, their rhythms, and the levels they suggest. The stage directions show Madame Ranevskaya going from tears to laughter to anger but the hysterical effect that is suggested may be achieved if the actor plays each action, noting that first Madame Ranevskaya begs Trofimoff to speak and later begs him not to do so. Trofimoff also has a wide range as he moves from a position of

calm teacher to one of hysterical, berated child, but as with Madame Ranevskaya all the necessary steps are indicated.

In the less confrontational second act, careful attention must be
given to the pauses as well as to the sounds, such as the breaking string
that is heard both in this act and at the play's end. Despite the contempla-
tive philosophizing of the second act, much is suggested beneath the
speeches, and the pauses are part of the rhythm that exposes this subtex-
tual material. In Shakespeare's plays the rhythms lead to the meanings,
which are mostly contained in the line itself. However, Chekhov's characters, despite their introspective speeches, often reveal themselves between
and beneath the lines, in pauses or in the way they speak about the
weather. Capturing the rhythms and their suggested undercurrents thus
becomes an important clue to Chekhov's style.

The comic dimension of the third act scene will emerge if the actors
playing Madame Ranevskaya and Trofimoff never forget that the two
characters are not enemies but friends. Their interchange dramatizes differences of age and youth as well as different points of view on social
change. They are like mother and son and their feelings for each other
are stronger than their quarrel.

Another source of the tragicomic effect of the play lies in the tendency of Chekhov's characters not to take one another entirely seriously.
They do not bring forth the laughter that the posing, self-dramatizing
Hjalmar Ekdal or the neurotic and pompous Gregers Werle evoke in *The
Wild Duck*. Instead we share the characters' amusement at one another, at
the bumbling Epihodoff and his exaggeration of his misfortunes, or at the
distraught Trofimoff falling down a flight of stairs. Despite their extreme
stands, the characters themselves have a certain self-awareness and balance that also undermine a completely tragic tone. Epihodoff may fling
himself off in act I, indicating he will shoot himself, but the humor of the
role lies not only in the fact that the *audience* knows Epihodoff will never
shoot himself—*he* knows it himself. Madame Ranevskaya bemoans the loss
of self, which the loss of the orchard implies, but she knows she will go on
and return to her lover. And Trofimoff may tell Madame Ranevskaya
that all is over between them after their heated interchange, but his fall
down the stairs chastens him and he is back dancing with her in no time
at all.

Tennessee Williams
The Glass Menagerie

JIM

Being different is nothing to be ashamed of. Because other people aren't such wonderful people. They're a hundred times one thousand. You're one times one!

(page 624)

The Glass Menagerie takes its name from Laura Wingfield's collection of small glass animals. Laura is painfully shy, physically and socially crippled, and terrified of a world that sees her differences as peculiarities. She has sought relief from these disabilities in the comforting tones of her old Victrola and the undemanding reflectiveness of her glass collection. Twice this glass menagerie takes on obvious allegorical significance. Enraged by their mother's nagging, Laura's brother Tom throws down his coat and it strikes the display case where the delicate animals are housed, eliciting a scream from Laura. Later in the play, Jim O'Connor, the gentleman caller, leads Laura in a clumsy waltz that ends when they accidentally break the horn off the glass unicorn, rendering it, and Laura briefly, less unique and less different. In each case, the injury to the glass collection stands as a correlative for the emotional injury to Laura.

Laura is different, but so is her brother Tom. Bored by a repetitive job in a shoe warehouse and oppressed by the responsibility of supporting his sister and mother, Tom seeks solace and adventure in movies and liquor. These sensual stimulants also compensate for his frustrated literary aspirations. While we do not see the fruition of his aspirations, we do see their effects; Tom's bitterest quarrel with his mother comes over her interruption of his creative activity, and his dismissal from the warehouse is sparked by his writing poems on shoebox lids. Like Laura's, Tom's differences make continued existence in a neatly if unimaginatively ordered society difficult.

Amanda Wingfield fails to understand fully the differences in either of her children. Moreover, emotionally she cannot afford to countenance the sort of difference that upsets family solidarity, for that solidarity is her only hope in a world that has been undeniably cruel to her. Lurking behind Amanda's failure to understand her children is a "fifth character" in the play, the absent father, "a telephone man who fell in love with long distance" and deserted his wife and children. Amanda's aspirations for material comfort—aspirations unrealistically stimulated by a Southern-belle milieu—have been smashed. Now all she can hope for is survival. Still Amanda is optimistic that some change can be achieved through the channels of change she knows best: business acuity and success, and marital security. When Amanda wishes for "success and happiness for my precious children," her sincerity is undoubted, but the means she uses to measure "success and happiness" are all wrong for her particular children—they will not be successful or happy following the streams of business or marriage. As a result, given our point of view, Amanda appears alternately as a shrewish harpy or a pathetic relic of lost Southern gentility. Both pictures must be balanced with the final stage direction, *"she has dignity and tragic beauty."* Amanda's characterization lacks the force of Phaedra's, but she shares with Madame Ranevskaya a dignity larger than one-sided comic simplicity can encompass.

For some viewers of *The Glass Menagerie* the play appears to be a "portrait of the artist as a young man," not just a portrait of family conflict. Tennessee Williams, born Thomas Lanier Williams in 1911, lived in St. Louis in the 1930s with a Southern-bred mother, sister, and brother in a lower-middle-class family whose father was absent in spirit if not in body. Like his Tom, Williams worked as a shoeclerk for $65 a month, and like Tom he wrote poetry (as well as drama and short fiction). The choice of Tom as narrator to provide a frame for the story of Laura, the conscious use of poetic and dramatic devices to break the theatrical illusion of reality, even the ambiguity of a conclusion that neither condemns Laura and Amanda to eat the crust of humility forever nor relieves the uncertainty of their situation—these all suggest an artist's explanation of his emotional coming of age. Indeed, many of the apparent difficulties of the dramatic presentation (for instance, how could Tom in a "memory play" remember conversations at which he was not present?) may be explained by making the representation of Tom's artistic maturation and escape from a stifling family situation the primary focus of the play, and relegating the representation of Laura to a secondary, supporting role.

In fact, the autobiographical details matter relatively little. Williams subtly modifies them as do many creative artists who shape and turn their own experience into literary visions far removed from the social or psychological realities of their own lives. Williams never deserted his family or joined the merchant marine; their financial circumstances were strained but did not approach the penury of the Wingfields; and his mother and sister bear little resemblance to Amanda and Laura. However, the subordination of event to characterization is typical of autobiographical impulse and of much modern literary art; here as elsewhere it makes interpretation difficult. In production, *The Glass Menagerie* may be dominated by any one of the three major characters with rich if contradictory results. Ideally a balance should be maintained among the three.

Perhaps this ambiguity can be explained by Williams's preoccupation with the problems inherent in each character, for the character types are favorites of his and appear in significantly different but still recognizable shapes in many of his plays. Although he had previously written stories, movie scripts, and prize-winning plays, *The Glass Menagerie* (1945) was Williams's first major success. Since then he has produced better than one play every two years and has become one of America's foremost living playwrights. The great critical and financial successes have been *A Streetcar Named Desire* (1947), *Cat on a Hot Tin Roof* (1955), and *The Night of the Iguana* (1961). In each play there are characters (like Tom) whose artistic impulses conflict with social norms, and characters (like Laura) who are physically or emotionally crippled. In all but one play, the moribund state of old Southern gentility is mirrored in the events or in a character (as it is in Amanda).

But character depiction in Williams's work in general and in *The Glass Menagerie* in particular leads not so much to the extraordinary depth of individualized psychological probing we associate with Shakespeare or Racine but rather to a richer understanding of character in a social situation. Amanda's monologues, for instance, reveal her history twenty-five years earlier. Yet instead of getting a great sense of an individualized Amanda who married the smiling doughboy, we gain a much better understanding of a society in which the "pretty traps" caught soon-to-be rich bankers and planters. Tom's monologues—especially his last—reveal more generalized emotions typical of a time and place (America just before World War II) and less particularized emotions that pinpoint and individualize his guilt. "For now the world is lit by lightning" beautifully and metaphorically evokes young America experiencing the mixed emotions generated by a war that dragged the country out of a depression and gave it adventure to compensate for capitalistic drudgery. However, we are less sure how to interpret Tom's injunction, "Blow out your candles, Laura," in relation to the earlier metaphor. Does he have to exorcise his sister's spirit because the world has changed? We do, of course, know all the characters of *The Glass Menagerie* far more fully than we know, say, Mak, Tattle, old Ekdal, or Charlotta Ivanovna, but we know them less fully than we do Oedipus, Bottom, Hippolytus, Gregers Werle, or Gayeff.

The emphasis on character in a social situation as opposed to character in individualized depth arises in part from Williams's use of literary and theatrical devices. "I have a poet's weakness for symbols," says Tom in his role of narrator, speaking very much for the author. The glass menagerie, the unicorn, the fire escape, the candles, the smiling picture of the absent father are joined with a wide range of realistic and nonrealistic dramatic techniques. Lighting, music, costuming, the very use of a narrator have the effect of heightening the unreality of the situation, of heightening the emblematic rather than particularized nature of the characters.

The use of such devices makes calling *The Glass Menagerie* either realistic, naturalistic, or expressionistic only partly true. Like many modern *postrealistic* dramas, the play mixes techniques originally associated with one or another of the different dramatic stylistic movements. At one time there is a fourth wall behind which we glimpse the characters acting out their conflict of insecurity in what appears to be an Ibsen-like realism; in another instance, Tom steps out and beyond, breaking the fourth-wall convention, to explain, to interpret, or to flash us forward or backward in his story. Such techniques have been called *expressionistic;* that is, they portray an individual's subjective account of his subjective experience, a mode that was pioneered by German dramatists in the 1910s. Breaking from realism, Williams returns to Shakespeare's device of the soliloquy, but he also extends Chekhov's naturalism and reveals through his emphasis on conflict and interaction the illusions that forge Amanda's, Laura's, and Tom's understanding of what is real in their lives. The carefully controlled poetry of the dialogue is one such technique designed to heighten psychological realism without sinking the characters into a morass of environment-bound particularity. Yet paradoxically the poetry does not always lead to an increased understanding of the characters as individuals but rather to an enlarged, symbolic view of the characters and events.

The Glass Menagerie

Production notes

Being a "memory play," *The Glass Menagerie* can be presented with unusual freedom of convention. Because of its considerably delicate or tenuous material, atmospheric touches and subtleties of direction play a particularly important part. Expressionism and all other unconventional techniques in drama have only one valid aim, and that is a closer approach to truth. When a play employs unconventional techniques, it is not, or certainly shouldn't be, trying to escape its responsibility of dealing with reality, or interpreting experience, but is actually or should be attempting to find a closer approach, a more penetrating and vivid expression of things as they are. The straight realistic play with its genuine Frigidaire and authentic ice-cubes, its characters who speak exactly as its audience speaks, corresponds to the academic landscape and has the same virtue of a photographic likeness. Everyone should know nowadays the unimportance of the photographic in art: that truth, life, or reality is an organic thing which the poetic imagination can represent or suggest, in essence, only through transformation, through changing into other forms than those which were merely present in appearance.

These remarks are not meant as a preface only to this particular play. They have to do with a conception of a new, plastic theatre which must take the place of the exhausted theatre of realistic conventions if the theatre is to resume vitality as a part of our culture.

THE SCREEN DEVICE

There is only one important difference between the original and the acting version of the play and that is the omission in the latter of the device that I tentatively included in my original script. This device was the use of a screen on which were projected magic-lantern slides bearing images or titles. I do not regret the omission of this device from the original Broadway production. The extraordinary power of Miss Taylor's performance [1] made it suitable to have the utmost simplicity in the physical production. But I think it may be interesting to some readers to see how this device was conceived. So I am putting it into the published manuscript.[2] These images and legends, projected from behind, were cast on a section of wall between the front-room and dining-room areas, which should be indistinguishable from the rest when not in use.

The purpose of this will probably be apparent. It is to give accent to certain values in each scene. Each scene contains a particular point (or several) which is structurally the most important. In an episodic play, such as this, the basic structure or narrative line may be obscured from the audience; the effect may seem fragmentary rather than architectural. This may not be the fault of the play so much as a lack of attention in the audience. The legend or image upon the screen will strengthen the effect of

---

[1] Laurette Taylor, "Amanda" of the Broadway version. EDS.
[2] These legends are not included in the acting version of the play, which is the version used in this book. EDS.

what is merely allusion in the writing and allow the primary point to be made more simply and lightly than if the entire responsibility were on the spoken lines. Aside from this structural value, I think the screen will have a definite emotional appeal, less definable but just as important. An imaginative producer or director may invent many other uses for this device than those indicated in the present script. In fact the possibilities of the device seem much larger to me than the instance of this play can possibly utilize.

THE MUSIC

Another extra-literary accent in this play is provided by the use of music. A single recurring tune, "The Glass Menagerie," is used to give emotional emphasis to suitable passages. This tune is like circus music, not when you are on the grounds or in the immediate vicinity of the parade, but when you are at some distance and very likely thinking of something else. It seems under those circumstances to continue almost interminably and it weaves in and out of your preoccupied consciousness; then it is the lightest, most delicate music in the world and perhaps the saddest. It expresses the surface vivacity of life with the underlying strain of immutable and inexpressible sorrow. When you look at a piece of delicately spun glass you think of two things: how beautiful it is and how easily it can be broken. Both of those ideas should be woven into the recurring tune, which dips in and out of the play as if it were carried on a wind that changes. It serves as a thread of connection and allusion between the narrator with his separate point in time and space and the subject of his story. Between each episode it returns as reference to the emotion, nostalgia, which is the first condition of the play. It is primarily Laura's music and therefore comes out most clearly when the play focuses upon her and the lovely fragility of glass which is her image.

THE LIGHTING

The lighting in the play is not realistic. In keeping with the atmosphere of memory, the stage is dim. Shafts of light are focused on selected areas or actors, sometimes in contradistinction to what is the apparent center. For instance, in the quarrel scene between Tom and Amanda, in which Laura has no active part, the clearest pool of light is on her figure. This is also true of the supper scene, when her silent figure on the sofa should remain the visual center. The light upon Laura should be distinct from the others, having a peculiar pristine clarity such as light used in early religious portraits of female saints or madonnas. A certain correspondence to light in religious paintings, such as El Greco's, where the figures are radiant in atmosphere that is relatively dusky, could be effectively used throughout the play. (It will also permit a more effective use of the screen.) A free, imaginative use of light can be of enormous value in giving a mobile, plastic quality to plays of a more or less static nature.

Tennessee Williams

Characters
THE MOTHER
HER SON
HER DAUGHTER
THE GENTLEMAN CALLER
  Scene: An alley in St. Louis.
  Act I: Preparation for a Gentleman Caller.
  Act II: The Gentleman Calls.
  Time: Now and the Past.

Act I

Scene 1
The Wingfield apartment is in the rear of the building, one of those vast hive-like conglomerations of cellular living-units that flower as warty growths in over-crowded urban centers of lower middle-class population and are symptomatic of the impulse of this largest and fundamentally enslaved section of American society to avoid fluidity and differentiation and to exist and function as one interfused mass of automatism. The apartment faces an alley and is entered by a fire-escape, a structure whose name is a touch of accidental poetic truth, for all of these huge buildings are always burning with the slow and implacable fires of human desperation. The fire-escape is included in the set—that is, the landing of it and steps descending from it. (Note that the stage L. *alley may be entirely omitted, since it is never used except for Tom's first entrance, which can take place stage* R.) *The scene is memory and is therefore nonrealistic. Memory takes a lot of poetic license. It omits some details, others are exaggerated, according to the emotional value of the articles it touches, for memory is seated predominantly in the heart. The interior is therefore rather dim and poetic. (Cue #1. As soon as the house lights dim, dance-hall music heard on-stage* R. *Old popular music of, say,* 1915–1920 *period. This continues until Tom is at fire-escape landing, having lighted cigarette, and begins speaking.)*

At rise: At the rise of the house curtain, the audience is faced with the dark, grim rear wall of the Wingfield tenement. (The stage set proper is screened out by a gauze curtain, which suggests the front part, outside, of the building.) This building, which runs parallel to the foot-lights, is flanked on both sides by dark, narrow alleys which run into murky canyons of tangled clotheslines, garbage cans and the sinister lattice-work of neighboring fire-escapes. (The alleys are actually in darkness, and the objects just mentioned are not visible.) It is up and down these side alleys that exterior entrances and exits are made, during the play. At the end of Tom's opening commentary, the dark tenement wall slowly reveals (by means of a transparency) the interior of the ground floor Wingfield apartment. (Gauze curtain, which suggests front part of building, rises on the interior set.) Downstage is the living room, which also serves as a sleeping room for Laura, the day-bed unfolding to make her bed. Just above this is a small stool or table on which is a telephone. Up-stage, C., *and divided by a wide arch or second proscenium with transparent faded portieres (or second curtain, "second curtain" is actually the inner gauze curtain between the living-room and the dining-room, which is upstage of it), is the dining-room. In an old-fashioned what-not in the living-room are seen scores of transparent glass animals. A blown-up photograph of the father hangs on the wall of the living-room, facing the audience, to the* L. *of the archway. It is the face of a very handsome young man in a doughboy's First World War cap. He is gallantly smiling, ineluctably smiling, as if to say, "I will be smiling forever." (Note that all that is essential in connection with dance-hall is that the window be shown lighting lower part of alley. It is not necessary to show any considerable part of dance-hall.) The audience hears and sees the opening scene in the dining-room through both the transparent fourth wall (this is the gauze curtain which suggests outside of building) of the building and the transparent gauze portieres of the dining-room arch. It is during this revealing scene that the fourth wall slowly ascends, out of sight. This transparent exterior wall is not brought down again until the very end of the play, during Tom's final speech. The narrator is an undisguised convention of the play. He takes whatever license with dramatic convention as is convenient to his purposes.*

Tom enters dressed as a merchant sailor from alley, stage L. *(i.e., stage* R. *if* L. *alley is omitted), and strolls across the front of the stage to the fire-escape. There he stops and lights a cigarette. He addresses the audience.*

TOM

I have tricks in my pocket—I have things up my sleeve—but I am the opposite of the stage magician. He gives you illusion that has the appearance of truth. I give you truth in the pleasant disguise of illusion. I take you back to an alley in St. Louis. The time that quaint period when the huge middle class of America was matriculating from a school for the blind. Their eyes had failed them, or they had failed their eyes, and so they were having their fingers pressed forcibly down on the fiery Braille alphabet of a dissolving economy.—In Spain there was revolution.—Here there was only shouting and confusion and labor disturbances, sometimes violent, in otherwise peaceful cities such as Cleveland—Chicago—Detroit. . . . That is the social background of this play. . . . The play is memory. (*Music cue #2.*) Being a memory play, it is dimly lighted, it is sentimental, it is not realistic.—In memory everything seems to happen to music.—That explains the fiddle in the wings. I am the narrator of the play, and also a character in it. The other characters in the play are my mother, Amanda, my sister, Laura, and a gentleman caller who appears in the final scenes. He is the most realistic character in the play, being an emissary from a world that we were somehow set apart from.—But having a poet's weakness for symbols, I am using this character as a symbol—as the long-delayed but always expected something that we live for.—There is a fifth character who doesn't appear other than in a photograph hanging on the wall. When you see the picture of this grinning gentleman, please remember this is our father who left us a long time ago. He was a telephone man who fell in love with long distance—so he gave up his job with the telephone company and skipped the light fantastic out of town. . . .

The last we heard of him was a picture postcard from the Pacific coast of Mexico, containing a message of two words—"Hello—Good-bye!" and no address.

> *Lights up in dining-room. Tom exits* R. *He goes off downstage, takes off his sailor overcoat and skull-fitting knitted cap and remains off-stage by dining-room* R. *door for his entrance cue. Amanda's voice becomes audible through the portieres—i.e., gauze curtains separating dining-room from living-room. Amanda and Laura are seated at a drop-leaf table. Amanda is sitting in* C. *chair and Laura in* L. *chair. Eating is indicated by gestures without food or utensils. Amanda faces the audience. The interior of the dining-room has lit up softly and through the scrim—gauze curtains—we see Amanda and Laura seated at the table in the upstage area.*

AMANDA

You know, Laura, I had the funniest experience in church last Sunday. The church was crowded except for one pew way down front and in that was just one little woman. I smiled very sweetly at her and said, "Excuse me, would you mind if I shared this pew?" "I certainly would," she said, "this space is rented." Do you know that is the first time that I ever knew that the Lord rented space. (*Dining-room gauze curtains open automatically.*) These Northern Episcopalians! I can understand the Southern Episcopalians, but these Northern ones, no. (*Tom enters dining-room* R., *slips over to table and sits in chair* R.) Honey, don't push your food with your fingers. If you have to push your food with something, the thing to use is a crust of bread. You must chew your food. Animals have secretions in their stomachs which enable them to digest their food without mastication, but human beings must chew their food before they swallow it down, and chew, chew. Oh, eat leisurely. Eat leisurely. A well-cooked meal has many delicate flavors that have to be held in the mouth for appreciation, not just gulped down. Oh, chew, chew—chew!

> *At this point the scrim curtain—if the director decides to use it—the one suggesting exterior wall, rises here and does not come down again until just before the end of the play.*

Don't you want to give your salivary glands a chance to function?

TOM

Mother, I haven't enjoyed one bite of my dinner because of your constant directions on how to eat it. It's you that makes me hurry through my meals with your hawk-like attention to every bite I take. It's disgusting—all this discussion of animals' secretion—salivary glands—mastication! (*Comes down to arm-chair in living room* R., *lights cigarette.*)

AMANDA

Temperament like a Metropolitan star! You're not excused from this table.

TOM

I'm getting a cigarette.

AMANDA

You smoke too much.

LAURA (*Rising.*)

Mother, I'll bring in the coffee.

AMANDA
No, no, no, no. You sit down. I'm going to be the colored boy today and you're going to be the lady.

LAURA
I'm already up.

AMANDA
Resume your seat. Resume your seat. You keep yourself fresh and pretty for the gentlemen callers.
Laura sits.

LAURA
I'm not expecting any gentlemen callers.

AMANDA (*Who has been gathering dishes from table and loading them on tray.*)
Well, the nice thing about them is they come when they're least expected. Why, I remember one Sunday afternoon in Blue Mountain when your mother was a girl . . . (*Goes out for coffee,* U.R.)

TOM
I know what's coming now!
Laura rises.

LAURA
Yes. But let her tell it. (*Crosses to* L. *of day-bed, sits.*)

TOM
Again?

LAURA
She loves to tell it.

AMANDA (*Entering from* R. *in dining-room and coming down into living-room with tray and coffee.*)
I remember one Sunday afternoon in Blue Mountain when your mother was a girl she received—seventeen—gentlemen callers!
Amanda crosses to Tom at armchair R., *gives him coffee, and crosses* C. *Laura comes to her, takes cup, resumes her place on* L. *of day-bed. Amanda puts tray on small table* R. *of day-bed, sits* R. *on day-bed. Inner curtain closes, light dims out.*
Why, sometimes there weren't chairs enough to accommodate them all and we had to send the colored boy over to the parish house to fetch the folding chairs.

TOM
How did you entertain all those gentlemen callers? (*Tom finally sits in armchair* R.)

AMANDA
I happened to understand the art of conversation!

TOM
I bet you could talk!

AMANDA
Well, I could. All the girls in my day could, I tell you.

TOM
Yes?

AMANDA
They knew how to entertain their gentlemen callers. It wasn't enough for a girl to be possessed of a pretty face and a graceful figure—although I wasn't slighted in either respect. She also needed to have a nimble wit and a tongue to meet all occasions.

TOM
What did you talk about?

AMANDA
Why, we'd talk about things of importance going on in the world!
Never anything common or coarse or vulgar. My callers were gen-
tlemen—all! Some of the most prominent men on the Mississippi
Delta—planters and sons of planters! There was young Champ
Laughlin. (*Music cue #3.*) He later became Vice-President of the
Delta Planters' Bank. And Hadley Stevenson; he was drowned in
Moon Lake.—My goodness, he certainly left his widow well provided
for—a hundred and fifty thousand dollars in government bonds.
And the Cutrere Brothers—Wesley and Bates. Bates was one of my
own bright particular beaus! But he got in a quarrel with that wild
Wainwright boy and they shot it out on the floor of Moon Lake Ca-
sino. Bates was shot through the stomach. He died in the ambulance
on his way to Memphis. He certainly left his widow well provided
for, too—eight or ten thousand acres, no less. He never loved that
woman; she just caught him on the rebound. My picture was found
on him the night he died. Oh and that boy, that boy that every girl
in the Delta was setting her cap for! That beautiful (*Music fades out.*)
brilliant young Fitzhugh boy from Greene County!

TOM
What did he leave his widow?

AMANDA
He never married! What's the matter with you—you talk as though
all my old admirers had turned up their toes to the daisies!

TOM
Isn't this the first you've mentioned that still survives?

AMANDA
He made an awful lot of money. He went North to Wall Street and
made a fortune. He had the Midas touch—everything that boy
touched just turned to gold! (*Gets up.*) And I could have been Mrs. J.
Duncan Fitzhugh—mind you! (*Crosses L.C.*) But—what did I do?—I
just went out of my way and picked your father! (*Looks at picture on
L. wall. Goes to small table R. of day-bed for tray.*)

LAURA (*Rises from day-bed.*)
Mother, let me clear the table.

AMANDA (*Crossing L. for Laura's cup, then crossing R. for Tom's.*)
No, dear, you go in front and study your typewriter chart. Or practice your shorthand a little. Stay fresh and pretty! It's almost time
for our gentlemen callers to start arriving. How many do you suppose we're going to entertain this afternoon?
> Tom opens curtains between dining-room and living-room for her.
> These close behind her, and she exits into kitchen R. Tom stands U.C. in
> living-room.

LAURA (*To Amanda, off-stage.*)
I don't believe we're going to receive any, Mother.

AMANDA (*Off-stage.*)
Not any? Not one? Why, you must be joking! Not one gentleman
caller? What's the matter? Has there been a flood or a tornado?

LAURA (*Crossing to typing table.*)
It isn't a flood. It's not a tornado, Mother. I'm just not popular like

you were in Blue Mountain. Mother's afraid that I'm going to be an old maid. (*Music cue #4.*)

> *Lights dim out. Tom exits* U.C. *in blackout. Laura crosses to menagerie* R.

Act I

Scene 2
Scene is the same. Lights dim up on living-room.
Laura discovered by menagerie, polishing glass. Crosses to phonograph, plays record. She times this business so as to put needle on record as music cue #4 ends. Enter Amanda down alley R. *Rattles key in lock. Laura crosses guiltily to typewriter and types. (Small typewriter table with typewriter on it is still on stage in living-room* L.) *Amanda comes into room* R. *closing door. Crosses to armchair, putting hat, purse and gloves on it. Something has happened to Amanda. It is written in her face: a look that is grim and hopeless and a little absurd. She has on one of those cheap or imitation velvety-looking cloth coats with imitation fur collar. Her hat is five or six years old, one of those dreadful cloche hats that were worn in the late twenties and she is clasping an enormous black patent-leather pocketbook with nickel clasps and initials. This is her full-dress outfit, the one she usually wears to the D.A.R. She purses her lips, opens her eyes very wide, rolls them upward and shakes her head. Seeing her mother's expression, Laura touches her lips with a nervous gesture.*

LAURA
Hello, Mother, I was just . . .

AMANDA
I know. You were just practicing your typing, I suppose.
> *Behind chair* R.

LAURA
Yes.

AMANDA
Deception, deception, deception!

LAURA (*Shakily.*)
How was the D.A.R. meeting, Mother?

AMANDA (*Crosses to Laura.*)
D.A.R. meeting!

LAURA
Didn't you go to the D.A.R. meeting, Mother?

AMANDA (*Faintly, almost inaudibly.*)
No, I didn't go to any D.A.R. meeting. (*Then more forcibly.*) I didn't have the strength—I didn't have the courage. I just wanted to find a hole in the ground and crawl in it and stay there the rest of my entire life. (*Tears type charts, throws them on floor.*)

LAURA (*Faintly.*)
Why did you do that, Mother?

AMANDA (*Sits on* R. *end of day-bed.*)
Why? Why? How old are you, Laura?

LAURA
Mother, you know my age.

AMANDA

I was under the impression that you were an adult, but evidently I was very much mistaken. (*She stares at Laura.*)

LAURA

Please don't stare at me, Mother!

Amanda closes her eyes and lowers her head. Pause.

AMANDA

What are we going to do? What is going to become of us? What is the future?

Pause.

LAURA

Has something happened, Mother? Mother, has something happened?

AMANDA

I'll be all right in a minute. I'm just bewildered—by life . . .

LAURA

Mother, I wish that you would tell me what's happened!

AMANDA

I went to the D.A.R. this afternoon, as you know; I was to be inducted as an officer. I stopped off at Rubicam's Business College to tell them about your cold and to ask how you were progressing down there.

LAURA

Oh . . .

AMANDA

Yes, oh—oh—oh. I went straight to your typing instructor and introduced myself as your mother. She didn't even know who you were. Wingfield, she said? We don't have any such scholar enrolled in this school. I assured her she did. I said my daughter Laura's been coming to classes since early January. "Well, I don't know," she said, "unless you mean that terribly shy little girl who dropped out of school after a few days' attendance?" No, I said, I don't mean that one. I mean my daughter, Laura, who's been coming here every single day for the past six weeks! "Excuse me," she said. And she took down the attendance book and there was your name, unmistakable, printed, and all the dates you'd been absent. I still told her she was wrong. I still said, "No, there must have been some mistake! There must have been some mix-up in the records!" "No," she said, "I remember her perfectly now. She was so shy and her hands trembled so that her fingers couldn't touch the right keys! When we gave a speed-test—she just broke down completely—was sick at the stomach and had to be carried to the washroom! After that she never came back. We telephoned the house every single day and never got any answer." (*Rises from day-bed, crosses* R.C.) That was while I was working all day long down at that department store, I suppose, demonstrating those —— (*With hands indicates brassiere.*) Oh! I felt so weak I couldn't stand up! (*Sits in armchair.*) I had to sit down while they got me a glass of water! (*Laura crosses up to phonograph.*) Fifty dollars' tuition. I don't care about the money so much, but all my hopes for any kind of future for you—gone up the spout, just gone up the spout like that. (*Laura winds phonograph up.*) Oh, don't *do* that, Laura!—Don't play that victrola!

LAURA

Oh! (*Stops phonograph, crosses to typing table, sits.*)

AMANDA

What have you been doing every day when you've gone out of the house pretending that you were going to business college?

LAURA

I've just been going out walking.

AMANDA

That's not true!

LAURA

Yes, it is, Mother, I just went walking.

AMANDA

Walking? Walking? In winter? Deliberately courting pneumonia in that light coat? Where did you walk to, Laura?

LAURA

All sorts of places—mostly in the park.

AMANDA

Even after you'd started catching that cold?

LAURA

It was the lesser of two evils, Mother. I couldn't go back. I threw up on the floor!

AMANDA

From half-past seven till after five every day you mean to tell me you walked around in the park, because you wanted to make me think that you were still going to Rubicam's Business College?

LAURA

Oh, Mother, it wasn't as bad as it sounds. I went inside places to get warmed up.

AMANDA

Inside where?

LAURA

I went in the art museum and the bird-houses at the Zoo. I visited the penguins every day! Sometimes I did without lunch and went to the movies. Lately I've been spending most of my afternoons in the Jewel-box, that big glass house where they raise the tropical flowers.

AMANDA

You did all that to deceive me, just for deception! Why? Why? Why? Why?

LAURA

Mother, when you're disappointed, you get that awful suffering look on your face, like the picture of Jesus' mother in the Museum!

    Rises.

AMANDA

Hush!

LAURA (*Crosses* R. *to menagerie.*)

I couldn't face it. I couldn't.

    Music cue #5.

AMANDA (*Rising from day-bed.*)

So what are we going to do now, honey, the rest of our lives? Just sit down in this house and watch the parades go by? Amuse ourselves with the glass menagerie? Eternally play those worn-out records your father left us as a painful reminder of him? (*Slams phonograph lid.*)

We can't have a business career. (*End music cue #5.*) No, we can't do that—that just gives us indigestion. (*Around* R. *day-bed.*) What is there left for us now but dependency all our lives? I tell you, Laura, I know so well what happens to unmarried women who aren't prepared to occupy a position in life. (*Crosses* L., *sits on day-bed.*) I've seen such pitiful cases in the South—barely tolerated spinsters living on some brother's wife or a sister's husband—tucked away in some mouse-trap of a room—encouraged by one in-law to go on and visit the next in-law—little bird-like women—without any nest—eating the crust of humility all their lives! Is that the future that we've mapped out for ourselves? I swear I don't see any other alternative. And I don't think that's a very pleasant alternative. Of course—some girls *do* marry. My goodness, Laura, haven't you ever liked some boy?

LAURA

Yes, Mother, I liked one once.

AMANDA

You did?

LAURA

I came across his picture a while ago.

AMANDA

He gave you his picture, too? (*Rises from day-bed, crosses to chair* R.)

LAURA

No, it's in the year-book.

AMANDA (*Sits in armchair.*)

Oh—a high-school boy.

LAURA

Yes. His name was Jim. (*Kneeling on floor, gets year-book from under menagerie.*) Here he is in "The Pirates of Penzance."

AMANDA (*Absently.*)

The what?

LAURA

The operetta the senior class put on. He had a wonderful voice. We sat across the aisle from each other Mondays, Wednesdays and Fridays in the auditorium. Here he is with a silver cup for debating! See his grin?

AMANDA

So he had a grin, too! (*Looks at picture of father on wall behind phonograph. Hands year-book back.*)

LAURA

He used to call me—Blue Roses.

AMANDA

Blue Roses? What did he call you a silly name like that for?

LAURA (*Still kneeling.*)

When I had that attack of pleurosis—he asked me what was the matter when I came back. I said pleurosis—he thought that I said "Blue Roses." So that's what he always called me after that. Whenever he saw me, he'd holler, "Hello, Blue Roses!" I didn't care for the girl that he went out with. Emily Meisenbach. Oh, Emily was the best-dressed girl at Soldan. But she never struck me as being sincere. . . . I read in a newspaper once that they were engaged. (*Puts year-book back on a shelf of glass menagerie.*) That's a long time ago—they're probably married by now.

AMANDA

That's all right, honey, that's all right. It doesn't matter. Little girls who aren't cut out for business careers sometimes end up married to very nice young men. And I'm just going to see that you do that, too!

LAURA

But, Mother——

AMANDA

What is it now?

LAURA

I'm—crippled!

AMANDA

Don't say that word! (*Rises, crosses to* c. *Turns to Laura.*) How many times have I told you never to say that word! You're not crippled, you've just got a slight defect. (*Laura rises.*) If you lived in the days when I was a girl and they had long graceful skirts sweeping the ground, it might have been considered an asset. When you've got a slight disadvantage like that, you've just got to cultivate something else to take its place. You have to cultivate charm—or vivacity—or *charm!* (*Spotlight on photograph. Then dim out.*) That's the only thing your father had plenty of—charm!

> *Amanda sits on day-bed. Laura crosses to armchair and sits. Music cue #6. Blackout.*

Act I

> *Scene 3*
> *Scene: The same. Lights up again but only on* R. *alley and fire-escape landing, rest of the stage dark. (Typewriter table and typewriter have been taken off-stage.) Enter Tom, again wearing merchant sailor over-coat and knitted cap, in alley* R. *As music cue #6 ends, Tom begins to speak.*

TOM (*Leans against grill of fire-escape, smoking.*)

After the fiasco at Rubicam's Business College, the idea of getting a gentleman caller for my sister Laura began to play a more and more important part in my mother's calculations. It became an obsession. Like some archetype of the universal unconscious, the image of the gentleman caller haunted our small apartment. An evening at home rarely passed without some allusion to this image, this spectre, this hope. . . . And even when he wasn't mentioned, his presence hung in my mother's preoccupied look and in my sister's frightened, apologetic manner. It hung like a sentence passed upon the Wingfields! But my mother was a woman of action as well as words. (*Music cue #7.*) She began to take logical steps in the planned direction. Late that winter and in the early spring—realizing that extra money would be needed to properly feather the nest and plume the bird— she began a vigorous campaign on the telephone, roping in subscribers to one of those magazines for matrons called "The Homemaker's Companion," the type of journal that features the serialized sublimations of ladies of letters who think in terms of delicate cup-like breasts, slim, tapering waists, rich creamy thighs, eyes like wood-smoke in autumn, fingers that soothe and caress like soft, soft strains of music. Bodies as powerful as Etruscan sculpture.

He exits down R. into wings. Light in alley R. is blacked out, and a head-spot falls on Amanda, at phone in living-room. Music cue #7 ends as Tom stops speaking.

AMANDA

Ida Scott?

During this speech Tom enters dining room U.R. unseen by audience, not wearing overcoat or hat. There is an unlighted reading lamp on table. Sits C. of dining-room table with writing materials.

This is Amanda Wingfield. We missed you at the D.A.R. last Monday. Oh, first I want to know how's your sinus condition? You're just a Christian martyr. That's what you are. You're just a Christian martyr. Well, I was just going through my little red book, and I saw that your subscription to the "Companion" is about to expire just when that wonderful new serial by Bessie Mae Harper is starting. It's the first thing she's written since "Honeymoon for Three." Now, that was unusual, wasn't it? Why, Ida, this one is even lovelier. It's all about the horsey set on Long Island and a debutante is thrown from her horse while taking him over the jumps at the—regatta. Her spine—her spine is injured. That's what the horse did—he stepped on her. Now, there is only one surgeon in the entire world that can keep her from being completely paralyzed, and that's the man she's engaged to be married to and he's tall and he's blond and he's handsome. That's unusual, too, huh? Oh, he's not perfect. Of course he has a weakness. He has the most terrible weakness in the entire world. He just drinks too much. What? Oh, no, Honey, don't let them burn. You go take a look in the oven and I'll hold on . . . Why, that woman! Do you know what she did? She hung up on me.

Dining-room and living-room lights dim in. Reading lamp lights up at same time.

LAURA

Oh, Mother, Mother, Tom's trying to write. *(Rises from armchair where she was left at curtain of previous scene, goes to curtain between dining-room and living-room, which is already open.)*

AMANDA

Oh! So he is. So he is. *(Crosses from phone, goes to dining-room and up to Tom.)*

TOM *(At table.)*

Now what are you up to?

AMANDA

I'm trying to save your eyesight. *(Business with lamp.)* You've only got one pair of eyes and you've got to take care of them. Oh, I know that Milton was blind, but that's not what made him a genius.

TOM

Mother, will you please go away and let me finish my writing?

AMANDA *(Squares his shoulders.)*

Why can't you sit up straight? So your shoulders don't stick through like sparrows' wings?

TOM

Mother, please go busy yourself with something else. I'm trying to write.

AMANDA (*Business with Tom.*)

Now, I've seen a medical chart, and I know what that position does to your internal organs. You sit up and I'll show you. Your stomach presses against your lungs, and your lungs press against your heart, and that poor little heart gets discouraged because it hasn't got any room left to go on beating for you.

TOM

What in hell . . . !

Inner curtains between living-room and dining-room close. Lights dim down in dining-room. Laura crosses, stands C. *of curtains in living-room listening to following scene between Tom and Amanda.*

AMANDA

Don't you talk to me like that——

TOM

—am I supposed to do?

AMANDA

What's the matter with you? Have you gone out of your senses?

TOM

Yes, I have. You've driven me out of them.

AMANDA

What is the matter with you lately, you big—big—idiot?

TOM

Look, Mother—I haven't got a thing, not a single thing left in this house that I can call my own.

AMANDA

Lower your voice!

TOM

Yesterday you confiscated my books! You had the nerve to ——

AMANDA

I did. I took that horrible novel back to the library—that awful book by that insane Mr. Lawrence. I cannot control the output of a diseased mind or people who cater to them, but I won't allow such filth in my house. No, no, no, no, no!

TOM

House, house! Who pays the rent on the house, who makes a slave of himself to ——!

AMANDA

Don't you dare talk to me like that!

Laura crosses D.L. *to back of armchair.*

TOM

No, *I* mustn't say anything! *I've* just got to keep quiet and let you do all the talking.

AMANDA

Let me tell you something!

TOM

I don't want to hear any more.

AMANDA

You will hear more ——

Laura crosses to phonograph.

TOM (*Crossing through curtains between dining-room and living-room. Goes up stage of door* R. *where, in a dark spot, there is supposedly a closet.*)

Well, I'm not going to listen. I'm going out. (*Gets out coat.*)

AMANDA (*Coming through curtains into living-room, stands* C.)

You are going to listen to me, Tom Wingfield. I'm tired of your impudence.—And another thing—I'm right at the end of my patience!

TOM (*Putting overcoat on back of armchair and crossing back to Amanda.*)

What do you think I'm at the end of, Mother? Aren't I supposed to have any patience to reach the end of? I know, I know. It seems unimportant to you, what I'm *doing*—what I'm trying to do—having a difference between them! You don't think that.

AMANDA

I think you're doing things that you're ashamed of, and that's why you act like this. (*Tom crosses to day-bed and sits.*) I don't believe that you go every night to the movies. Nobody goes to the movies night after night. Nobody in their right minds goes to the movies as often as you pretend to. People don't go to the movies at nearly midnight and movies don't let out at two A.M. Come in stumblng, muttering to yourself like a maniac. You get three hours' sleep and then go to work. Oh, I can picture the way you're doing down there. Moping, doping, because you're in no condition.

TOM

That's true—that's very, very true. I'm in no condition!

AMANDA

How dare you jeopardize your job? Jeopardize our security? How do you think we'd manage ——? (*Sits armchair* R.)

TOM

Look, Mother, do you think I'm *crazy* about the *ware-house?* You think I'm in love with the Continental Shoemakers? You think I want to spend fifty-five years of my life down there in that—*celotex interior!* with *fluorescent tubes?!* Honest to God, I'd rather somebody picked up a crow-bar and battered out my brains—than go back mornings! But I *go!* Sure, every time you come in yelling that bloody *Rise and Shine!* Rise and shine!! I think how lucky dead people are! But I get up. (*Rises from day-bed.*) I *go!* For sixty-five dollars a month I give up all that I dream of doing and being *ever!* And you say that is all I think of. Oh, God! Why, Mother, if self is all I ever thought of, Mother, *I'd* be where *he* is—GONE! (*Crosses to get overcoat on back of armchair.*) As far as the system of transportation reaches! (*Amanda rises, crosses to him and grabs his arm.*) Please don't grab at me, Mother!

AMANDA (*Following him.*)

I'm not grabbing at you. I want to know where you're going now.

TOM (*Taking overcoat and starts crossing to door* R.)

I'm going to the movies!

AMANDA (*Crosses* C.)

I don't believe that lie!

TOM (*Crosses back to Amanda.*)

No? Well, you're right. For once in your life you're right. I'm not going to the movies! I'm going to opium dens! Yes, Mother, opium dens, dens of vice and criminals' hang-outs, Mother. I've joined the Hogan gang. I'm a hired assassin, I carry a tommy-gun in a violin case! I run a string of cathouses in the valley! They call me Killer, Killer Wingfield, I'm really leading a double life. By day I'm a simple, honest ware-house worker, but at night I'm a dynamic czar of the underworld. Why, I go to gambling casinos and spin away a fortune on the roulette table! I wear a patch over one eye and a false moustache, sometimes I wear green whiskers. On those occasions they call me—El Diablo! Oh, I could tell you things to make you sleepless! My enemies plan to dynamite this place some night! Some night they're going to blow us all sky-high. And will I be glad! Will I be happy! And so will you be. You'll go up—up—over Blue Mountain on a broomstick! With seventeen gentlemen callers. You ugly babbling old witch!

> *He goes through a series of violent, clumsy movements, seizing his overcoat, lunging to* R. *door, pulling it fiercely open. The women watch him, aghast. His arm catches in the sleeve of the coat as he struggles to pull it on. For a moment he is pinioned by the bulky garment. With an outraged groan he tears the coat off again, splitting the shoulder of it, and hurls it across the room. It strikes against the shelf of Laura's glass collection, there is a tinkle of shattering glass. Laura cries out as if wounded.*

LAURA

My glass!—menagerie . . .

> *She covers her face and turns away. Music cue #8 through to end of scene.*

AMANDA (*In an awful voice.*)

I'll never speak to you again as long as you live unless you apologize to me!

> *Amanda exits through living-room curtains. Tom is left with Laura. He stares at her stupidly for a moment. Then he crosses to shelf holding glass menagerie. Drops awkwardly on his knees to collect fallen glass, glancing at Laura as if he would speak, but couldn't. Blackout. Tom, Amanda and Laura exit in blackout.*

Act I

> Scene 4
> *The interior is dark. Faint light in alley* R. *A deep-voiced bell in a church is tolling the hour of five as the scene commences.*
> *Tom appears at the top of* R. *alley. After each solemn boom of the bell in the tower he shakes a little toy noise-maker or rattle as if to express the tiny spasm of man in contrast to the sustained power and dignity of the Almighty. This and the unsteadiness of his advance make it evident that he has been drinking. As he climbs the few steps to the fire-escape landing light steals up inside. Laura appears in night-dress, entering living-room from* L. *door of dining-room, observing Tom's empty bed (day-bed) in the living-room. Tom fishes in his pockets for door-key, removing a motley assortment of articles in the search, including a perfect shower of movie-ticket stubs and an empty bottle. At last he finds the key, but just as he is about to insert it, it slips from his fingers. He strikes a match and crouches below the door.*

TOM (*Bitterly.*)

One crack—and it falls through!

> *Laura opens door* R.

LAURA

Tom! Tom, what are you doing?

TOM

Looking for a door-key.

LAURA
> Where have you been all this time?

TOM
> I have been to the movies.

LAURA
> All this time at the movies?

TOM
> There was a very long program. There was a Garbo picture and a Mickey Mouse and a travelogue and a newsreel and a preview of coming attractions. And there was an organ solo and a collection for the milk-fund—simultaneously—which ended up in a terrible fight between a fat lady and an usher!

LAURA (*Innocently.*)
> Did you have to stay through everything?

TOM
> Of course! And, oh, I forgot! There was a big stage show! The headliner on this stage show was Malvolio the Magician. He performed wonderful tricks, many of them, such as pouring water back and forth between pitchers. First it turned to wine and then it turned to beer and then it turned to whiskey. I know it was whiskey it finally turned into because he needed somebody to come up out of the audience to help him, and I came up—both shows! It was Kentucky Straight Bourbon. A very generous fellow, he gave souvenirs. (*He pulls from his back pocket a shimmering rainbow-colored scarf.*) He gave me this. This is his magic scarf. You can have it, Laura. You wave it over a canary cage and you get a bowl of gold-fish. You wave it over the gold-fish bowl and they fly away canaries. . . . But the wonderfullest trick of all was the coffin trick. We nailed him into a coffin and he got out of the coffin without removing one nail. (*They enter.*) There is a trick that would come in handy for me—get me out of this 2 by 4 situation! (*Flops onto day-bed and starts removing shoes.*)

LAURA
> Tom—shhh!

TOM
> What're you shushing me for?

LAURA
> You'll wake up Mother.

TOM
> Goody goody! Pay'er back for all those "Rise an' Shines." (*Lies down groaning.*) You know it don't take much intelligence to get yourself into a nailed-up coffin, Laura. But who in hell ever got himself out of one without removing one nail?
> > *As if in answer, the father's grinning photograph lights up. Laura exits up* L. *Lights fade except for blue glow in dining-room. Pause after lights fade, then clock chimes six times. This is followed by the alarm clock. Dim in fore-stage.*

Act I

Scene 5
Scene is the same. Immediately following. The church-bell is heard striking six. At the sixth stroke the alarm-clock goes off in Amanda's

> room off R. of dining-room and after a few moments we hear her calling,
> "Rise and shine! Rise and shine! Laura, go tell your brother to rise and
> shine!"

TOM (*Sitting up slowly in day-bed.*)

I'll rise—but I won't shine.

> *The light increases.*

AMANDA (*Offstage.*)

Laura, tell your brother his coffee is ready.

> *Laura, fully dressed, a cape over her shoulders, slips into living-room.*
> *Tom is still in bed, covered with blanket, having taken off only shoes*
> *and coat.*

LAURA

Tom!—It's nearly seven. Don't make Mother nervous. (*He stares at
her stupidly. Beseechingly.*) Tom, speak to Mother this morning. Make
up with her, apologize, speak to her!

TOM (*Putting on shoes.*)

She won't to me. It's her that started not speaking.

LAURA

If you just say you're sorry she'll start speaking.

TOM

Her not speaking—is that such a tragedy?

LAURA

Please—please!

AMANDA (*Calling offstage R. from kitchen.*)

Laura, are you going to do what I asked you to do, or do I have to
get dressed and go out myself?

LAURA

Going, going—soon as I get on my coat! (*She rises and crosses to door
R.*) Butter and what else? (*To Amanda.*)

AMANDA (*Offstage.*)

Just butter. Tell them to charge it.

LAURA

Mother, they make such faces when I do that.

AMANDA (*Offstage.*)

Sticks and stones can break our bones, but the expression on Mr.
Garfinkel's face won't harm us! Tell your brother his coffee is getting cold.

LAURA (*At door R.*)

Do what I asked you, will you, will you, Tom?

> *He looks sullenly away.*

AMANDA

Laura, go now or just don't go at all!

LAURA (*Rushing out R.*)

Going—going!

> *A second later she cries out. Falls on fire-escape landing. Tom springs*
> *up and crosses to door R. Amanda rushes anxiously in from dining-*
> *room, puts dishes on dining-room table. Tom opens door R.*

TOM

Laura?

LAURA

I'm all right. I slipped, but I'm all right. (*Goes up R. alley, out of sight.*)

AMANDA (*On fire-escape.*)

I tell you if anybody falls down and breaks a leg on those fire-escape steps, the landlord ought to be sued for every cent he —— (*Sees Tom.*) Who are you?

>*Leaves fire-escape landing, crosses to dining-room and returns with bowls, coffee cup, cream, etc. Puts them on small table* R. *of day-bed, crosses to armchair, sits. Counts 3. Music cue #9. As Tom reenters* R., *listlessly for his coffee, she turns her back to him, as she sits in armchair. The light on her face with its aged but childish features is cruelly sharp, satirical as a Daumier print. Tom glances sheepishly but sullenly at her averted figure and sits on day-bed next to the food. The coffee is scalding hot, he sips it and gasps and spits it back in the cup. At his gasp, Amanda catches her breath and half turns. Then catches herself and turns away. Tom blows on his coffee, glancing sidewise at his mother. She clears her throat. Tom clears his. He starts to rise. Sinks back down again, scratches his head, clears his throat again. Amanda coughs. Tom raises his cup in both hands to blow on it, his eyes staring over the rim of it at his mother for several moments. Then he slowly sets the cup down and awkwardly and hesitantly rises from day-bed.*

TOM (*Hoarsely.*)

I'm sorry, Mother. I'm sorry for all those things I said. I didn't mean it. I apologize.

AMANDA (*Sobbingly.*)

My devotion has made me a witch and so I make myself hateful to my children!

TOM

No, you don't.

AMANDA

I worry so much, I don't sleep, it makes me nervous!

TOM (*Gently.*)

I understand that.

AMANDA

You know I've had to put up a solitary battle all these years. But you're my right hand bower! Now don't fail me. Don't fall down.

TOM (*Gently.*)

I try, Mother.

AMANDA (*With great enthusiasm.*)

That's all right! You just keep on trying and you're bound to succeed. Why, you're—you're just full of natural endowments! Both my children are—they're very precious children and I've got an awful lot to be thankful for; you just must promise me one thing.

>*Music cue #9 stops.*

TOM

What is it, Mother?

AMANDA

Promise me you're never going to become a drunkard!

TOM

I promise, Mother. I won't ever become a drunkard, Mother.

AMANDA

That's what frightened me so, that you'd be drinking! Eat a bowl of Purina.

TOM

Just coffee, Mother.

AMANDA

Shredded Wheat Biscuit?

TOM
No, no, Mother, just coffee.

AMANDA
You can't put in a day's work on an empty stomach. You've got ten minutes—don't gulp! Drinking too-hot liquids makes cancer of the stomach. . . . Put cream in.

TOM
No, thank you.

AMANDA
To cool it.

TOM
No! No, thank you, I want it black.

AMANDA
I know, but it's not good for you. We have to do all that we can to build ourselves up. In these trying times we live in, all that we have to cling to is—each other. . . . That's why it's so important to —— Tom, I—I sent out your sister so I could discuss something with you. If you hadn't spoken I would have spoken to you. (*Sits down.*)

TOM (*Gently.*)
What is it, Mother, that you want to discuss?

AMANDA
Laura!
> *Tom puts his cup down slowly. Music cue #10.*

TOM
—Oh.—Laura . . .

AMANDA (*Touching his sleeve.*)
You know how Laura is. So quiet but—still water runs deep! She notices things and I think she—broods about them. (*Tom looks up.*) A few days ago I came in and she was crying.

TOM
What about?

AMANDA
You.

TOM
Me?

AMANDA
She has an idea that you're not happy here.
> *Music cue #10 stops.*

TOM
What gave her that idea?

AMANDA
What gives her any idea? However, you do act strangely. (*Tom slaps cup down on small table.*) I—I'm not criticizing, understand that! I know your ambitions do not lie in the warehouse, that like everybody in the whole wide world—you've had to—make sacrifices, but— Tom—Tom—life's not easy, it calls for—Spartan endurance! There's so many things in my heart that I cannot describe to you! I've never told you but I—loved your father . . .

TOM (*Gently.*)
I know that, Mother.

AMANDA
And you—when I see you taking after his ways! Staying out late —and—well, you had been drinking the night you were in that

—terrifying condition! Laura says that you hate the apartment and that you go out nights to get away from it! Is that true, Tom?

TOM

No. You say there's so much in your heart that you can't describe to me. That's true of me, too. There's so much in my heart that I can't describe to you! So let's respect each other's ——

AMANDA

But, why—why, Tom—are you always so restless? Where do you go to, nights?

TOM

I—go to the movies.

AMANDA

Why do you go to the movies so much, Tom?

TOM

I go to the movies because—I like adventure. Adventure is something I don't have much of at work, so I go to the movies.

AMANDA

But, Tom, you go to the movies entirely too much!

TOM

I like a lot of adventure.

> *Amanda looks baffled, then hurt. As the familiar inquisition resumes he becomes hard and impatient again. Amanda slips back into her querulous attitude toward him.*

AMANDA

Most young men find adventure in their careers.

TOM

Then most young men are not employed in a warehouse.

AMANDA

The world is full of young men employed in warehouses and offices and factories.

TOM

Do all of them find adventure in their careers?

AMANDA

They do or they do without it! Not everybody has a craze for adventure.

TOM

Man is by instinct a lover, a hunter, a fighter, and none of those instincts are given much play at the warehouse!

AMANDA

Man is by instinct! Don't quote instinct to me! Instinct is something that people have got away from! It belongs to animals! Christian adults don't want it!

TOM

What do Christian adults want, then, Mother?

AMANDA

Superior things! Things of the mind and the spirit! Only animals have to satisfy instincts! Surely your aims are somewhat higher than theirs! Than monkeys—pigs ——

TOM

I reckon they're not.

AMANDA

You're joking. However, that isn't what I wanted to discuss.

TOM (*Rising.*)

I haven't much time.

AMANDA (*Pushing his shoulders.*)
> Sit down.

TOM
> You want me to punch in red at the warehouse, Mother?

AMANDA
> You have five minutes. I want to talk about Laura.

TOM
> All right! What about Laura?

AMANDA
> We have to be making some plans and provisions for her. She's older than you, two years, and nothing has happened. She just drifts along doing nothing. It frightens me terribly how she just drifts along.

TOM
> I guess she's the type that people call home girls.

AMANDA
> There's no such type, and if there is, it's a pity! That is unless the home is hers, with a husband!

TOM
> What?

AMANDA (*Crossing* D. R. *to armchair.*)
> Oh, I can see the handwriting on the wall as plain as I see the nose in front of my face! It's terrifying! More and more you remind me of your father! He was out all (*Sits in armchair.*) hours without explanation!—Then left! Good-bye! And me with the bag to hold. I saw that letter you got from the Merchant Marine. I know what you're dreaming of. I'm not standing here blindfolded. Very well, then. Then do it! But not till there's somebody to take your place.

TOM
> What do you mean?

AMANDA
> I mean that as soon as Laura has got somebody to take care of her, married, a home of her own, independent—why, then you'll be free to go wherever you please, (*Rises, crosses to Tom.*) on land, on sea, whichever way the wind blows you! But until that time you've got to look out for your sister. (*Crosses* R. *behind armchair.*) I don't say me because I'm old and don't matter! I say for your sister because she's young and dependent. I put her in business college—a dismal failure! Frightened her so it made her sick at the stomach. I took her over to the Young People's League at the church. Another fiasco. She spoke to nobody, nobody spoke to her. (*Sits in armchair.*) Now all she does is fool with those pieces of glass and play those worn-out records. What kind of a life is that for a girl to lead?

TOM
> What can I do about it?

AMANDA
> Overcome selfishness! Self, self, self is all that you ever think of! (*Tom springs up and crosses* R. *to get his coat and put it on. It is ugly and bulky. He pulls on a cap with earmuffs.*) Where is your muffler? Put your wool muffler on! (*He snatches it angrily from the hook and tosses it around his neck and pulls both ends tight.*) Tom! I haven't said what I had in mind to ask you.

TOM
> I'm too late to ——

AMANDA (*Catching his arm—very importunately. Then shyly.*)
Down at the warehouse, aren't there some—nice young men?

TOM
No!

AMANDA
There must be—some . . .

TOM
Mother —— (*Gesture.*)

AMANDA
Find out one that's clean-living—doesn't drink and—ask him out for sister!

TOM
What?

AMANDA
For sister! To meet! Get acquainted!

TOM (*Stamping to door* R.)
Oh, my go-osh!

AMANDA
Will you? (*He opens door. Imploringly.*) Will you? (*He starts out.*) Will you? Will you, dear?

> Tom exits up alley R. Amanda is on fire-escape landing.

TOM (*Calling back.*)
Yes!

AMANDA (*Re-entering* R. *and crossing to phone. Music cue* #11.)
Ella Cartwright? Ella, this is Amanda Wingfield. First, first, how's that kidney trouble? Oh, it has? It has come back? Well, you're just a Christian martyr, you're just a Christian martyr. I was noticing in my little red book that your subscription to the "Companion" has run out just when that wonderful new serial by Bessie Mae Harper was starting. It's all about the horsey set on Long Island. Oh, you have? You have read it? Well, how do you think it turns out? Oh, no. Bessie Mae Harper never lets you down. Oh, of course, we have to have complications. You have to have complications—oh, you can't have a story without them—but Bessie Mae Harper always leaves you with such an uplift —— What's the matter, Ella? You sound so mad. Oh, because it's seven o'clock in the morning. Oh, Ella, I forgot that you never got up until nine. I forgot that anybody in the world was allowed to sleep as late as that. I can't say any more than I'm sorry, can I? Oh, you will? You're going to take that subscription from me anyhow? Well, bless you, Ella, bless you, bless you, bless you.

> *Music* #11 *fades into music cue* #11-A, *dance music, and continues into next scene. Dim out lights. Music cue* #11-A.

Act I

> Scene 6
> Scene: The same.—Only R. alley lighted, with dim light.

TOM (*Enters down* R. *and stands as before, leaning against grill work, with cigarette, wearing merchant sailor coat and cap.*)
Across the alley was the Paradise Dance Hall. Evenings in spring they'd open all the doors and windows and the music would come

outside. Sometimes they'd turn out all the lights except for a large glass sphere that hung from the ceiling. It would turn slowly about and filter the dusk with delicate rainbow colors. Then the orchestra would play a waltz or a tango, something that had a slow and sensuous rhythm. The young couples would come outside, to the relative privacy of the alley. You could see them kissing behind ashpits and telephone poles. This was the compensation for lives that passed like mine, without change or adventure. Changes and adventure, however, were imminent this year. They were waiting around the corner for all these dancing kids. Suspended in the mist over Berchtesgaden, caught in the folds of Chamberlain's umbrella —— In Spain there was Guernica! Here there was only hot swing music and liquor, dance halls, bars, and movies, and sex that hung in the gloom like a chandelier and flooded the world with brief, deceptive rainbows. . . . While these unsuspecting kids danced to "Dear One, The World is Waiting for the Sunrise," all the world was really waiting for bombardments.

  Music #11-A stops. Dim in dining-room: faint glow. Amanda is seen in dining-room.

AMANDA

  Tom, where are you?

TOM (*Standing as before.*)

  I came out to smoke.

  Exit R. *into the wings, where he again changes coats and leaves hat.*

AMANDA (*Tom re-enters and stands on fire-escape landing, smoking. He opens door for Amanda, who sits on hassock on landing.*)

  Oh, you smoke too much. A pack a day at fifteen cents a pack. How much would that be in a month? Thirty times fifteen? It wouldn't be very much. Well, it would be enough to help towards a night-school course in accounting at the Washington U! Wouldn't that be lovely?

TOM

  I'd rather smoke.

AMANDA

  I know! That's the tragedy of you. This fire-escape landing is a poor excuse for the porch we used to have. What are you looking at?

TOM

  The moon.

AMANDA

  Is there a moon this evening?

TOM

  It's rising over Garfinkel's Delicatessen.

AMANDA

  Oh! So it is! Such a little silver slipper of a moon. Have you made a wish on it?

TOM

  Um-mm.

AMANDA

  What did you wish?

TOM

  That's a secret.

AMANDA

  All right, I won't tell you what I wished, either. I can keep a secret, too. I can be just as mysterious as you.

TOM

> I bet I can guess what you wished.

AMANDA

> Why, is my head transparent?

TOM

> You're not a sphinx.

AMANDA

> No, I don't have secrets. I'll tell you what I wished for on the moon. Success and happiness for my precious children. I wish for that whenever there's a moon, and when there isn't a moon, I wish for it, too.

TOM

> I thought perhaps you wished for a gentleman caller.

AMANDA

> Why do you say that?

TOM

> Don't you remember asking me to fetch one?

AMANDA

> I remember suggesting that it would be nice for your sister if you brought home some nice young man from the warehouse. I think that I've made that suggestion more than once.

TOM

> Yes, you have made it repeatedly.

AMANDA

> Well?

TOM

> We are going to have one.

AMANDA

> *What?*

TOM

> A gentleman caller!

AMANDA

> You mean you have asked some nice young man to come over? (*Rising from stool, facing Tom.*)

TOM

> I've asked him to dinner.

AMANDA

> You really did?

TOM

> I did.

AMANDA

> And did he—accept?

TOM

> He did!

AMANDA

> He did?

TOM

> He did.

AMANDA

> Well, isn't that lovely!

TOM

> I thought that you would be pleased.

AMANDA
It's definite, then?

TOM
Oh, very definite.

AMANDA
How soon?

TOM
Pretty soon.

AMANDA
How soon?

TOM
Quite soon.

AMANDA
How soon?

TOM
Very, very soon.

AMANDA
Every time I want to know anything you start going on like that.

TOM
What do you want to know?

AMANDA
Go ahead and guess. Go ahead and guess.

TOM
All right, I'll guess. You want to know when the gentleman caller's coming—he's coming tomorrow.

AMANDA
Tomorrow? Oh, no, I can't do anything about tomorrow. I can't do anything about tomorrow.

TOM
Why not?

AMANDA
That doesn't give me any time.

TOM
Time for what?

AMANDA
Time for preparations. Oh, you should have phoned me the minute you asked him—the minute he accepted!

TOM
You don't have to make any fuss.

AMANDA
Of course I have to make a fuss! I can't have a man coming into a place that's all sloppy. It's got to be thrown together properly. I certainly have to do some fast thinking by tomorrow night, too.

TOM
I don't see why you have to think at all.

AMANDA
That's because you just don't know. (*Enter living-room, crosses to* C. *Dim in living-room.*) You just don't know, that's all. We can't have a gentleman caller coming into a pig-sty! Now, let's see. Oh, I've got those three pieces of wedding silver left. I'll polish that up. I wonder how that old lace tablecloth is holding up all these years? We can't

wear anything. We haven't got it. We haven't got anything to wear.
We haven't got it. (*Goes back to door* R.)

TOM

Mother! This boy is no one to make a fuss over.

AMANDA (*Crossing to* C.)

I don't know how you can say that when this is the first gentleman
caller your little sister's ever had! I think it's pathetic that that little
girl has never had a single gentleman caller! Come on inside! Come
on inside!

TOM

What for?

AMANDA

I want to ask you a few things.

TOM (*From doorway* R.)

If you're going to make a fuss, I'll call the whole thing off. I'll call
the boy up and tell him not to come.

AMANDA

No! You mustn't ever do that. People hate broken engagements.
They have no place to go. Come on inside. Come on inside. Will you
come inside when I ask you to come inside? Sit down.

> *Tom comes into living-room.*

TOM

Any particular place you want me to sit?

AMANDA

Oh! Sit anywhere. (*Tom sits armchair* R.) Look! What am I going to do
about that? (*Looking at day-bed.*) Did you ever see anything look so
sad? I know, I'll get a bright piece of cretonne. That won't cost
much. And I made payments on a floor lamp. So I'll have that sent
out! And I can put a bright cover on the chair. I wish I had time to
paper the walls. What's his name?

TOM

His name is O'Connor.

AMANDA

O'Connor—he's Irish and tomorrow's Friday—that means fish. Well,
that's all right, I'll make a salmon loaf and some mayonnaise
dressing for it. Where did you meet him? (*Crosses to day-bed and sits.*)

TOM

At the warehouse, of course. Where else would I meet him?

AMANDA

Well, I don't know. Does he drink?

TOM

What made you ask me that?

AMANDA

Because your father did.

TOM

Now, don't get started on that!

AMANDA

He drinks, then.

TOM

No, not that I know of.

AMANDA

You have to find out. There's nothing I want less for my daughter
than a man who drinks.

TOM
   Aren't you being a little bit premature? After all, poor Mr. O'Connor hasn't even appeared on the scene yet.

AMANDA
   But he will tomorrow. To meet your sister. And what do I know about his character? (*Rises and crosses to Tom who is still in armchair, smooths his hair.*)

TOM (*Submitting grimly.*)
   Now what are you up to?

AMANDA
   I always did hate that cowlick. I never could understand why it won't sit down by itself.

TOM
   Mother, I want to tell you something and I mean it sincerely right straight from my heart. There's a lot of boys who meet girls which they don't marry!

AMANDA
   You know you always had me worried because you could never stick to a subject. (*Crosses to day-bed.*) What I want to know is what's his position at the warehouse?

TOM
   He's a shipping clerk.

AMANDA
   Oh! Shipping clerk! Well, that's fairly important. That's where you'd be if you had more get-up. How much does he earn? (*Sits on day-bed.*)

TOM
   I have no way of knowing that for sure. I judge his salary to be approximately eighty-five dollars a month.

AMANDA
   Eighty-five dollars? Well, that's not princely.

TOM
   It's twenty dollars more than I make.

AMANDA
   I know that. Oh, how well I know that! How well I know that! Eighty-five dollars a month. No. It can't be done. A family man can never get by on eighty-five dollars a month.

TOM
   Mother, Mr. O'Connor is not a family man.

AMANDA
   Well, he might be some time in the future, mightn't he?

TOM
   Oh, I see. . . . . Plans and provisions.

AMANDA
   You are the only young man that I know of who ignores the fact that the future becomes the present, the present the past, and the past turns into everlasting regret if you don't plan for it.

TOM
   I will think that over and see what I can make of it!

AMANDA
   Don't be supercilious with your mother! Tell me some more about this.—What do you call him? Mr. O'Connor, Mr. O'Connor. He must have another name besides Mr.——?

TOM

His full name is James D. O'Connor. The D. is for Delaney.

AMANDA

Delaney? Irish on both sides and he doesn't drink? ,

TOM (*Rises from armchair.*)

Shall I call him up and ask him? (*Starts toward phone.*)

AMANDA (*Crossing to phone.*)

No!

TOM

I'll call him up and tell him you want to know if he drinks. (*Picks up phone.*)

AMANDA (*Taking phone away from him.*)

No, you can't do that. You have to be discreet about that subject. When I was a girl in Blue Mountain if it was (*Tom sits on* R. *of day-bed.*) suspected that a young man was drinking and any girl was receiving his attentions—if any girl *was* receiving his attentions, she'd go to the minister of his church and ask about his character—or her father, if her father was living, then it was his duty to go to the minister of his church and ask about his character, and that's how young girls in Blue Mountain were kept from making tragic mistakes.

Picture dims in and out.

TOM

How come you made such a tragic one?

AMANDA

Oh, I don't know how he did it, but that face fooled everybody. All he had to do was grin and the world was bewitched. (*Behind day-bed, crosses to armchair.*) I don't know of anything more tragic than a young girl just putting herself at the mercy of a handsome appearance, and I hope Mr. O'Connor is *not* too good-looking.

TOM

As a matter of fact he isn't. His face is covered with freckles and he has a very large nose.

AMANDA

He's not right-down homely?

TOM

No. I wouldn't say right-down—homely—medium homely, I'd say.

AMANDA

Well, if a girl had any sense she'd look for character in a man any-how.

TOM

That's what I've always said, Mother.

AMANDA

You've always said it—you've always said it! How could you've always said it when you never even thought about it?

TOM

Aw, don't be so suspicious of me.

AMANDA

I am. I'm suspicious of every word that comes out of your mouth, when you talk to me, but I want to know about this young man. Is he up and coming?

TOM

Yes. I really do think he goes in for self-improvement.

AMANDA

What makes you think it?

TOM

He goes to night school.

AMANDA

Well, what does he do there at night school?

TOM

He's studying radio engineering and public speaking.

AMANDA

Oh! Public speaking! Oh, that shows, that shows that he intends to be an executive some day—and radio engineering. Well, that's coming . . . huh?

TOM

I think it's here.

AMANDA

Well, those are all very illuminating facts. (*Crosses to back of armchair.*) Facts that every mother should know about any young man calling on her daughter, seriously or not.

TOM

Just one little warning, Mother. I didn't tell him anything about Laura. I didn't let on we had dark ulterior motives. I just said, "How about coming home to dinner some time?" and he said, "Fine," and that was the whole conversation.

AMANDA

I bet it was, too. I tell you, sometimes you can be as eloquent as an oyster. However, when he sees how pretty and sweet that child is, he's going to be, well, he's going to be very glad he was asked over here to have some dinner. (*Sits in armchair.*)

TOM

Mother, just one thing. You won't expect too much of Laura, will you?

AMANDA

I don't know what you mean.

Tom crosses slowly to Amanda. He stands for a moment, looking at her. Then—

TOM

Well, Laura seems all those things to you and me because she's ours and we love her. We don't even notice she's crippled any more.

AMANDA

Don't use that word.

TOM

Mother, you have to face the facts; she is, and that's not all.

AMANDA

What do you mean "that's not all"?

Tom kneels by her chair.

TOM

Mother—you know that Laura is very different from other girls.

AMANDA

Yes, I do know that, and I think that difference is all in her favor, too.

TOM

Not quite all—in the eyes of others—strangers—she's terribly shy.

She lives in a world of her own and those things make her seem a little peculiar to people outside the house.

AMANDA

Don't use that word peculiar.

TOM

You have to face the facts.—She is.

AMANDA

I don't know in what way she's peculiar.

Music cue #12, till curtain. Tom pauses a moment for music, then—

TOM

Mother, Laura lives in a world of little glass animals. She plays old phonograph records—and—that's about all——

Tom rises slowly, goes quietly out the door R., leaving it open, and exits slowly up the alley. Amanda rises, goes on to fire-escape landing R., looks at moon.

AMANDA

Laura! Laura!

Laura answers from kitchen R.

LAURA

Yes, Mother.

AMANDA

Let those dishes go and come in front! (*Laura appears with dish towel. Gaily.*) Laura, come here and make a wish on the moon!

LAURA (*Entering from kitchen R. and comes down to fire-escape landing.*)

Moon—moon?

AMANDA

A little silver slipper of a moon. Look over your left shoulder, Laura, and make a wish! (*Laura looks faintly puzzled as if called out of sleep. Amanda seizes her shoulders and turns her at an angle on the fire-escape landing.*) Now! Now, darling, wish!

LAURA

What shall I wish for, Mother?

AMANDA (*Her voice trembling and her eyes suddenly filling with tears.*)

Happiness! And just a little bit of good fortune!

The stage dims out. Curtain.

Act II

Scene 7
Scene: The same.
Inner curtains closed between dining-room and living-room. Interiors of both rooms are dark as at beginning of play. Tom has on the same jacket and cap as at first. Same dance-hall music as cue #1, fading as Tom begins.

TOM (*Discovered leaning against grill on fire-escape landing, as before, and smoking.*)

And so the following evening I brought Jim home to dinner. I had known Jim slightly in high school. In high school, Jim was a hero. He had tremendous Irish good nature and vitality with the scrubbed and polished look of white chinaware. He seemed to move in a continual spotlight. He was a star in basketball, captain of the debating club, president of the senior class and the glee club, and he sang the male lead in the annual light opera. He was forever running or bounding, never just walking. He seemed always just at the point of defeating the law of gravity. He was shooting with such velocity through his adolescence that you would just logically expect him to arrive at nothing short of the White House by the time he was thirty. But Jim apparently ran into more interference after his graduation from high school because his speed had definitely slowed. And so, at this particular time in our lives he was holding a job that wasn't much better than mine. He was the only one at the warehouse with whom I was on friendly terms. I was valuable to Jim as someone who could remember his former glory, who had seen him win basketball games and the silver cup in debating. He knew of my secret practice of retiring to a cabinet of the washroom to work on poems whenever business was slack in the warehouse. He called me Shakespeare. And while the other boys in the warehouse regarded me with suspicious hostility, Jim took a humorous attitude toward me. Gradually his attitude began to affect the other boys and their hostility wore off. And so, after a time they began to smile at me too, as people smile at some oddly fashioned dog that trots across their path at some distance. I knew that Jim and Laura had known each other in high school because I had heard my sister Laura speak admiringly of Jim's voice. I didn't know if Jim would remember her or not. Because in high school Laura had been as unobtrusive as Jim had been astonishing. And, if he did remember Laura, it was not as my sister, for when I asked him home to dinner, he smiled and said, "You know, a funny thing, Shakespeare, I never thought of you as having folks!" Well, he was about to discover that I did. . . .

Music cue #13. Tom exits R. Interior living-room lights dim in. Amanda is sitting on small table R. of day-bed sewing on hem on Laura's dress. Laura stands facing the door R. Amanda has worked like a Turk in preparation for the gentleman caller. The results are astonishing. The new floor lamp with its rose-silk shade is in place, R. of living-room next to wall, a colored paper lantern conceals the broken light fixture in the ceiling, chintz covers are on chairs and sofa, a pair of new sofa pillows make their initial appearance. Laura stands in the middle of room with lifted arms while Amanda crouches before her, adjusting the hem of the new dress, devout and ritualistic. The dress is colored and designed by memory. The arrangement of Laura's hair is changed, it is softer and more becoming. A fragile, unearthly prettiness has come out in Laura, she is like a piece of translucent glass touched by light, given a momentary radiance, not actual, not lasting. Amanda, still seated, is sewing Laura's dress. Laura is standing R. of Amanda.

AMANDA
Why are you trembling so, Laura?

LAURA
Mother, you've made me so nervous!

AMANDA
Why, how have I made you nervous?

LAURA
By all this fuss! You make it seem so important.

AMANDA
I don't understand you at all, honey. Every time I try to do anything for you that's the least bit different you just seem to set yourself

against it. Now take a look at yourself. (*Laura starts for door* R.) No, wait! Wait just a minute—I forgot something. (*Picks two powder puffs from day-bed.*)

LAURA

What is it?

AMANDA

A couple of improvements. (*Business with powder puffs.*) When I was a girl we had round little lacy things like that and we called them "Gay Deceivers."

LAURA

I won't wear them!

AMANDA

Of course you'll wear them.

LAURA

Why should I?

AMANDA

Well, to tell you the truth, honey, you're just a little bit flat-chested.

LAURA

You make it seem like we were setting a trap.

AMANDA

We are. All pretty girls are a trap and men expect them to be traps. Now look at yourself in that glass. (*Laura crosses* R. *Looks at mirror, invisible to audience, which is in darkness up* R. *of* R. *door.*) See? You look just like an angel on a postcard. Isn't that lovely? Now you just wait. I'm going to dress myself up. You're going to be astonished at your mother's appearance.

> *End of music cue. End of music cue leads into dance music, which then leads in music cue #14, a few lines below, at stage direction. Amanda exits through curtains up-stage off* L. *in dining-room. Laura looks in mirror for a moment. Removes "Gay Deceivers," hides them under mattress of day-bed. Sits on small table* R. *of day-bed for a moment, goes out to fire-escape landing, listens to dance music, until Amanda's entrance. Amanda, off.*

I found an old dress in the trunk. But what do you know? I had to do a lot to it but it broke my heart when I had to let it out. Now, Laura, just look at your mother. Oh, no! Laura, come look at me now!

> *Enters dining-room* L. *door. Comes down through living-room curtain to living-room* C. *Music cue #14.*

LAURA (*Re-enters from fire-escape landing. Sits on* L. *arm of armchair.*)
Oh, Mother, how lovely!

> *Amanda wears a girlish frock. She carries a bunch of jonquils.*

AMANDA (*Standing* C., *holding flowers.*)
It used to be. It used to be. It had a lot of flowers on it, but they got awful tired so I had to take them all off. I led the cotillion in this dress years ago. I won the cakewalk twice at Sunset Hill, and I wore it to the Governor's ball in Jackson. You should have seen your mother. You should have seen your mother how she just sashayed around (*Crossing around* L. *of day-bed back to* C.) the ballroom, just like that. I had it on the day I met your father. I had malaria fever, too. The change of climate from East Tennessee to the Delta—weakened my resistance. Not enough to be dangerous, just enough to make me

restless and giddy. Oh, it was lovely. Invitations poured in from all over. My mother said, "You can't go any place because you have a fever. You have to stay in bed." I said I wouldn't and I took quinine and kept on going and going. Dances every evening and long rides in the country in the afternoon and picnics. That country—that country—so lovely—so lovely in May, all lacy with dogwood and simply flooded with jonquils. My mother said, "You can't bring any more jonquils in this house." I said, "I will," and I kept on bringing them in anyhow. Whenever I saw them I said, "Wait a minute, I see jonquils," and I'd make my gentlemen callers get out of the carriage and help me gather some. To tell you the truth, Laura, it got to be a kind of a joke. "Look out," they'd say, "here comes that girl and we'll have to spend the afternoon picking jonquils." My mother said, "You can't bring any more jonquils in the house, there aren't any more vases to hold them." "That's quite all right," I said, "I can hold some myself." Malaria fever, your father and jonquils.

> *Amanda puts jonquils in Laura's lap and goes out on to fire-escape landing. Music cue #14 stops. Thunder heard.*

I hope they get here before it starts to rain. I gave your brother a little extra change so he and Mr. O'Connor could take the service car home.

> *Laura puts flowers on armchair R., and crosses to door R.*

LAURA

Mother!

AMANDA

What's the matter now? (*Re-entering room.*)

LAURA

What did you say his name was?

AMANDA

O'Connor. Why?

LAURA

What is his first name?

AMANDA (*Crosses to armchair R.*)

I don't remember —— Oh, yes, I do too—it was—Jim! (*Picks up flowers.*)

LAURA

Oh, Mother, not Jim O'Connor!

AMANDA

Yes, that was it, it was Jim! I've never known a Jim that wasn't nice. (*Crosses L., behind day-bed, puts flowers in vase.*)

LAURA

Are you sure his name was Jim O'Connor?

AMANDA

Why, sure I'm sure. Why?

LAURA

Is he the one that Tom used to know in high school?

AMANDA

He didn't say so. I think he just got to know him—(*Sits on day-bed.*) at the warehouse.

LAURA

There was a Jim O'Connor we both knew in high school. If that is the one that Tom is bringing home to dinner —— Oh, Mother, you'd have to excuse me, I wouldn't come to the table!

AMANDA

What's this now? What sort of silly talk is this?

LAURA

You asked me once if I'd ever liked a boy. Don't you remember I showed you this boy's picture?

AMANDA

You mean the boy in the year-book?

LAURA

Yes, that boy.

AMANDA

Laura, Laura, were you in love with that boy?

LAURA (*Crosses to* R. *of armchair.*)

I don't know, Mother. All I know is that I couldn't sit at the table if it was him.

AMANDA (*Rises, crosses* L. *and works up* L. *of day-bed.*)

It won't be him! It isn't the least bit likely. But whether it is or not, you will come to the table—you will not be excused.

LAURA

I'll have to be, Mother.

AMANDA (*Behind day-bed.*)

I don't intend to humor your silliness, Laura. I've had too much from you and your brother, both. So just sit down and compose yourself till they come. Tom has forgotten his key, so you'll *have* to let them in when they arrive.

LAURA

Oh, Mother—*you* answer the door! (*Sits chair* R.)

AMANDA

How can I when I haven't even finished making the mayonnaise dressing for the salmon?

LAURA

Oh, Mother, please answer the door, don't make me do it!

Thunder heard off-stage.

AMANDA

Honey, do be reasonable! What's all this fuss about—just one gentleman caller—that's all—just one!

Exits through living-room curtains. Tom and Jim enter alley R., *climb fire-escape steps to landing and wait outside of closed door. Hearing them approach, Laura rises with a panicky gesture. She retreats to living-room curtains. The door-bell rings. Laura catches her breath and touches her throat. More thunder heard off-stage.*

AMANDA (*Off-stage.*)

Laura, sweetheart, the door!

LAURA

Mother, please, you go to the door! (*Starts for door* R., *then back.*)

AMANDA (*Off-stage, in a fierce whisper.*)

What is the matter with you, you silly thing?

Enters through living-room curtains, and stands by day-bed.

LAURA

Please you answer it, please.

AMANDA

Why have you chosen this moment to lose your mind? You go to that door.

LAURA
I can't.
AMANDA
Why can't you?
LAURA
Because I'm sick. (*Crosses to* L. *end of day-bed and sits.*)
AMANDA
You're sick! Am I sick? You and your brother have me puzzled to
death. You can never act like normal children. Will you give me one
good reason why you should be afraid to open a door? You go to
that door. Laura Wingfield, you march straight to that door!
LAURA (*Crosses to door* R.)
Yes, Mother.
AMANDA (*Stopping Laura.*)
I've got to put courage in you, honey, for living.
> *Exits through living-room curtains, and exits* R. *into kitchen. Laura*
> *opens door. Tom and Jim enter. Laura remains hidden in hall behind*
> *door.*

TOM
Laura—(*Laura crosses* C.) this is Jim. Jim, this is my sister Laura.
JIM
I didn't know that Shakespeare had a sister! How are you, Laura?
LAURA (*Retreating stiff and trembling. Shakes hands.*)
How—how do you do?
JIM
Well, I'm okay! Your hand's *cold,* Laura!
> *Tom puts hats on phone table.*
LAURA
Yes, well—I've been playing the victrola. . . .
JIM
Must have been playing classical music on it. You ought to play a lit-
tle hot swing music to warm you up.
> *Laura crosses to phonograph. Tom crosses up to Laura. Laura starts*
> *phonograph—looks at Jim. Exits through living-room curtains and goes*
> *off* L.

JIM
What's the matter?
TOM
Oh—Laura? Laura is—is terribly shy. (*Crosses and sits on day-bed.*)
JIM (*Crosses down* C.)
Shy, huh? Do you know it's unusual to meet a shy girl nowadays? I
don't believe you ever mentioned you had a sister?
TOM
Well, now you know I have one. You want a piece of the paper?
JIM (*Crosses to Tom.*)
Uh-huh.
TOM
Comics?
JIM
Comics? Sports! (*Takes paper. Crosses, sits in chair* R.) I see that Dizzy
Dean is on his bad behavior.

TOM (*Starts to door* R. *Goes out.*)
Really?
JIM
Yeah. Where are *you* going? (*As Tom reaches steps* R. *of fire-escape landing.*)
TOM (*Calling from fire-escape landing.*)
Out on the terrace to smoke.
JIM (*Rises, leaving newspaper in armchair, goes over to turn off victrola. Crosses R. Exits to fire-escape landing.*)
You know, Shakespeare—I'm going to sell you a bill of goods!
TOM
What goods?
JIM
A course I'm taking.
TOM
What course?
JIM
A course in public speaking! You know you and me, we're not the warehouse type.
TOM
Thanks—that's good news. What has public speaking got to do with it?
JIM
It fits you for—executive positions!
TOM
Oh.
JIM
I tell you it's done a helluva lot for me.
TOM
In what respect?
JIM
In all respects. Ask yourself: what's the difference between you and me and the guys in the office down front? Brains?—No!—Ability?—No! Then what? Primarily, it amounts to just one single thing ——
TOM
What is that one thing?
JIM
Social poise! The ability to square up to somebody and hold your own on any social level!
AMANDA (*Off-stage.*)
Tom?
TOM
Yes, Mother?
AMANDA
Is that you and Mr. O'Connor?
TOM
Yes, Mother.
AMANDA
Make yourselves comfortable.
TOM
We will.
AMANDA
Ask Mr. O'Connor if he would like to wash his hands?

JIM

No, thanks, ma'am—I took care of that down at the warehouse.
Tom?

TOM

Huh?

JIM

Mr. Mendoza was speaking to me about you.

TOM

Favorably?

JIM

What do you think?

TOM

Well ——

JIM

You're going to be out of a job if you don't wake up.

TOM

I'm waking up ——

JIM

Yeah, but you show no signs.

TOM

The signs are interior. I'm just about to make a change. I'm right at
the point of committing myself to a future that doesn't include the
warehouse or Mr. Mendoza, or even a night school course in public
speaking.

JIM

Now what are you gassing about?

TOM

I'm tired of the movies.

JIM

The movies!

TOM

Yes, movies! Look at them. (*He waves his hands.*) All of those glamor-
ous people—having adventures—hogging it all, gobbling the whole
thing up! You know what happens? People go to the *movies* instead
of *moving*. Hollywood characters are supposed to have all the adventures for everybody in America, while everybody in America sits in a
dark room and watches them having it! Yes, until there's a war.
That's when adventure becomes available to the masses! Everyone's
dish, not only Gable's! Then the people in the dark room come out
of the dark room to have some adventures themselves—goody—goody!
It's our turn now to go to the South Sea Island—to make a safari—to be
exotic, far off . . . ! But I'm not patient. I don't want to wait till then.
I'm tired of the movies and I'm about to move!

JIM (*Incredulously.*)

Move?

TOM

Yes.

JIM

When?

TOM

Soon!

JIM

Where? Where?

TOM

I'm starting to boil inside. I know I seem dreamy, but inside—well, I'm boiling! Whenever I pick up a shoe I shudder a little, thinking how short life is and what I am doing!—Whatever that means, I know it doesn't mean shoes—except as something to wear on a traveler's feet! (*Gets card from inside coat pocket.*) Look!

JIM

What?

TOM

I'm a member.

JIM (*Reading.*)

The Union of Merchant Seamen.

TOM

I paid my dues this month, instead of the electric light bill.

JIM

You'll regret it when they turn off the lights.

TOM

I won't be here.

JIM

Yeah, but how about your mother?

TOM

I'm like my father. The bastard son of a bastard. See how he grins? And he's been absent going on sixteen years.

JIM

You're just talking, you drip. How does your mother feel about it?

TOM

Sh! Here comes Mother! Mother's not acquainted with my plans!

AMANDA (*Off-stage.*)

Tom!

TOM

Yes, Mother?

AMANDA (*Off-stage.*)

Where are you all?

TOM

On the terrace, Mother.

AMANDA (*Enters through living-room curtain and stands* C.)

Why don't you come in?

> *They start inside. She advances to them. Tom is distinctly shocked at her appearance. Even Jim blinks a little. He is making his first contact with girlish Southern vivacity and in spite of the night-school course in public speaking is somewhat thrown off the beam by the unexpected outlay of social charm. Certain responses are attempted by Jim but are swept aside by Amanda's gay laughter and chatter. Tom is embarrassed but after the first shock Jim reacts very warmly. Grins and chuckles, is altogether won over. Tom and Jim come in, leaving door open.*

TOM

Mother, you look so pretty.

AMANDA

You know, that's the first compliment you ever paid me. I wish you'd look pleasant when you're about to say something pleasant, so I could expect it. Mr. O'Connor?

> *Jim crosses to Amanda.*

JIM

How do you do?

AMANDA

Well, well, well, so this is Mr. O'Connor? Introduction's entirely
unnecessary. I've heard so much about you from my boy. I finally
said to him, "Tom, good gracious, why don't you bring this
paragon to supper finally? I'd like to meet this nice young man at
the warehouse! Instead of just hearing you sing his praises so
much?" I don't know why my son is so stand-offish—that's not
Southern behavior. Let's sit down.

> *Tom closes door, crosses* U.R., *stands. Jim and Amanda sit on day-bed,
> Jim,* R., *Amanda* L.

Let's sit down, and I think we could stand a little more air in here.
Tom, leave the door open. I felt a nice fresh breeze a moment ago.
Where has it gone to? Mmmm, so warm already! And not quite summer, even. We're going to burn up when summer really gets started.
However, we're having—we're having a very light supper. I think
light things are better fo'—for this time of year. The same as light
clothes are. Light clothes and light food are what warm weather calls
fo'. You know our blood gets so thick during th' winter—it takes a
while fo' us to adjust ou'selves—when the season changes. . . . It's
come so quick this year. I wasn't prepared. All of a sudden—
Heavens! Already summer!—I ran to the trunk an'—pulled out this
light dress—terribly old! Historical almost! But feels so good—so
good and cool, why, y'know——

TOM

Mother, how about our supper?

AMANDA (*Rises, crosses* R. *to Tom.*)

Honey, you go ask sister if supper is ready! You know that sister is
in full charge of supper. Tell her you hungry boys are waiting for it.
(*Tom exits through curtains and off* L. *Amanda turns to Jim.*) Have you
met Laura?

JIM

Well, she came to the door.

AMANDA

She let you in?

JIM

Yes, ma'am.

AMANDA (*Crossing to armchair and sitting.*)

She's very pretty.

JIM

Oh, yes, ma'am.

AMANDA

It's rare for a girl as sweet an' pretty as Laura to be domestic! But
Laura is, thank heavens, not only pretty but also very domestic. I'm
not at all. I never was a bit. I never could make a thing but angel-
food cake. Well, in the South we had so many servants. Gone, gone,
gone. All vestige of gracious living! Gone completely! I wasn't prepared for what the future brought me. All of my gentlemen callers
were sons of planters and so of course I assumed that I would be
married to one and raise my family on a large piece of land with
plenty of servants. But man proposes—and woman accepts the

proposal!—To vary that old, old saying a little bit—I married no planter! I married a man who worked for the telephone company!—That gallantly smiling gentleman over there! (*Points to picture.*) A telephone man who—fell in love with long-distance!—Now he travels and I don't even know where!—But what am I going on for about my—tribulations? Tell me yours—I hope you don't have any! Tom?

TOM (*Re-enters through living-room curtains from off* L.)

Yes, Mother.

AMANDA

What about that supper?

TOM

Why, supper is on the table.

> *Inner curtains between living-room and dining-room open. Lights dim up in dining-room, dim out in living-room.*

AMANDA

Oh, so it is. (*Rises, crosses up to table* C. *in dining-room and chair* C.) How lovely. Where is Laura?

TOM (*Going to chair* L. *and standing.*)

Laura is not feeling too well and thinks maybe she'd better not come to the table.

AMANDA

Laura!

LAURA (*Off-stage. Faintly.*)

Yes, Mother?

> *Tom gestures re: Jim.*

AMANDA

Mr. O'Connor.

> *Jim crosses up* L. *to table and to chair* L. *and stands.*

JIM

Thank you, ma'am.

AMANDA

Laura, we can't say grace till you come to the table.

LAURA (*Enters* U.L., *obviously quite faint, lips trembling, eyes wide and staring. Moves unsteadily toward dining-room table.*)

Oh, Mother, I'm so sorry.

> *Tom catches her as she feels faint. He takes her to day-bed in living-room.*

AMANDA (*As Laura lies down.*)

Why, Laura, you are sick, darling! Laura—rest on the sofa. Well! (*To Jim.*) Standing over the hot stove made her ill!—I told her that it was just too warm this evening, but——(*To Tom.*) Is Laura all right now?

TOM

She's better, Mother. (*Sits chair* L. *in dining-room. Thunder off-stage.*)

AMANDA (*Returning to dining-room and sitting at table, as Jim does.*)

My goodness, I suppose we're going to have a little rain! Tom, you say grace.

TOM

What?

AMANDA

What do we generally do before we have something to eat? We say grace, don't we?

TOM
> For these and all Thy mercies—God's Holy Name be praised.
> *Lights dim out. Music cue #15.*

Act II

> *Scene 8*
> *Scene: The same. A half-hour later. Dinner is coming to an end in dining-room.*
> *Amanda, Tom and Jim sitting at table as at end of last scene. Lights dim up in both rooms, and music cue #15 ends.*

AMANDA (*Laughing, as Jim laughs too.*)
> You know, Mr. O'Connor, I haven't had such a pleasant evening in a very long time.

JIM (*Rises.*)
> Well, Mrs. Wingfield, let me give you a toast. Here's to the old South.

AMANDA
> The old South.
> *Blackout in both rooms.*

JIM
> Hey, Mr. Light Bulb!

AMANDA
> Where was Moses when the lights went out? Do you know the answer to that one, Mr. O'Connor?

JIM
> No, ma'am, what's the answer to that one?

AMANDA
> Well, I heard one answer, but it wasn't very nice. I thought you might know another one.

JIM
> No, ma'am.

AMANDA
> It's lucky I put those candles on the table. I just put them on for ornamentation, but it's nice when they prove useful, too.

JIM
> Yes, ma'am.

AMANDA
> Now, if one of you gentlemen can provide me with a match we can have some illumination.

JIM (*Lighting candles. Dim in glow for candles.*)
> I can, ma'am.

AMANDA
> Thank you.

JIM (*Crosses back to* R. *of dining-room table.*)
> Not at all, ma'am.

AMANDA
> I guess it must be a burnt-out fuse. Mr. O'Connor, do you know anything about a burnt-out fuse?

JIM
> I know a little about them ma'am, but where's the fuse box?

AMANDA

Must you know that, too? Well, it's in the kitchen. (*Jim exits* R. *into kitchen.*) Be careful. It's dark. Don't stumble over anything. (*Sound of crash off-stage.*) Oh, my goodness, wouldn't it be awful if we lost him! Are you all right, Mr. O'Connor?

JIM (*Off-stage.*)

Yes, ma'am, I'm all right.

AMANDA

You know, electricity is a very mysterious thing. The whole universe is mysterious to me. Wasn't it Benjamin Franklin who tied a key to a kite? I'd like to have seen that—he might have looked mighty silly. Some people say that science clears up all the mysteries for us. In my opinion they just keep on adding more. Haven't you found it yet?

JIM (*Re-enters* R.)

Yes, ma'am. I found it all right, but them fuses look okay to me. (*Sits as before.*)

AMANDA

Tom.

TOM

Yes, Mother?

AMANDA

That light bill I gave you several days ago. The one I got the notice about?

TOM

Oh—yeah. You mean last month's bill?

AMANDA

You didn't neglect it by any chance?

TOM

Well, I ——

AMANDA

You did! I might have known it!

JIM

Oh, maybe Shakespeare wrote a poem on that light bill, Mrs. Wingfield?

AMANDA

Maybe he did, too. I might have known better than to trust him with it! There's such a high price for negligence in this world today.

JIM

Maybe the poem will win a ten-dollar prize.

AMANDA

We'll just have to spend the rest of the evening in the nineteenth century, before Mr. Edison found that Mazda lamp!

JIM

Candle-light is my favorite kind of light.

AMANDA

That shows you're romantic! But that's no excuse for Tom. However, I think it was very nice of them to let us finish our dinner before they plunged us into everlasting darkness. Tom, as a penalty for your carelessness you can help me with the dishes.

JIM (*Rising. Tom rises.*)

Can I be of some help, ma'am?

AMANDA (*Rising.*)

Oh, no, I couldn't allow that.

JIM

Well, I ought to be good for *something*.

AMANDA

What did I hear?

JIM

I just said, "I ought to be good for something."

AMANDA

That's what I thought you said. Well, Laura's all by her lonesome out front. Maybe you'd like to keep her company. I can give you this lovely old candelabrum for light. (*Jim takes candles.*) It used to be on the altar at the Church of the Heavenly Rest, but it was melted a little out of shape when the church burnt down. The church was struck by lightning one spring, and Gypsy Jones who was holding a revival meeting in the village, said that the church was struck by lightning because the Episcopalians had started to have card parties right in the church.

JIM

Is that so, ma'am?

AMANDA

I never say anything that isn't so.

JIM

I beg your pardon.

AMANDA (*Pouring wine into glass—hands it to Jim.*)

I'd like Laura to have a little dandelion wine. Do you think you can hold them both?

JIM

I can try, ma'am.

AMANDA (*Exits* U.R. *into kitchen.*)

Now, Tom, you get into your apron.

TOM

Yes, Mother.

> *Follows Amanda. Jim looks around, puts wine-glass down, takes swig from wine decanter, replaces it with thud, takes wine-glass—enters living-room. Inner curtains close as dining-room dims out. Laura sits up nervously as Jim enters. Her speech at first is low and breathless from the almost intolerable strain of being alone with a stranger. In her speeches in this scene, before Jim's warmth overcomes her paralyzing shyness, Laura's voice is thin and breathless as though she has just run up a steep flight of stairs.*

JIM (*Entering holding candelabra with lighted candles in one hand and glass of wine in other, and stands.*)

How are you feeling now? Any better?

> *Jim's attitude is gently humorous. In playing this scene it should be stressed that while the incident is apparently unimportant, it is to Laura the climax of her secret life.*

LAURA

Yes, thank you.

JIM (*Gives her glass of wine.*)

Oh, here, this is for you. It's a little dandelion wine.

LAURA

Thank you.

JIM (*Crosses* c.)

Well, drink it—but don't get drunk. (*He laughs heartily.*). Say, where'll I put the candles?

LAURA

Oh, anywhere . . .

JIM

Oh, how about right here on the floor? You got any objections?

LAURA

No.

JIM

I'll just spread a newspaper under it to catch the drippings. (*Gets newspaper from armchair. Puts candelabra down on floor* c.) I like to sit on the floor. (*Sits on floor.*) Mind if I do?

LAURA

Oh, no.

JIM

Would you give me a pillow?

LAURA

What?

JIM

A pillow!

LAURA

Oh . . .

> *Puts wine-glass on telephone table, hands him pillow, sits* L. *on day-bed.*

JIM

How about you? Don't you like to sit on the floor?

LAURA

Oh, yes.

JIM

Well, why don't you?

LAURA

I—will.

JIM

Take a pillow! (*Throws pillow as she sits on floor.*) I can't see you sitting way over there. (*Sits on floor again.*)

LAURA

I can—see you.

JIM

Yeah, but that's not fair. I'm right here in the limelight. (*Laura moves a little closer to him.*) Good! Now I can see you! Are you comfortable?

LAURA

Yes. Thank you.

JIM

So am I. I'm comfortable as a cow! Say, would you care for a piece of chewing-gum? (*Offers gum.*)

LAURA

No, thank you.

JIM

I think that I will indulge. (*Musingly unwraps it and holds it up.*) Gee, think of the fortune made by the guy that invented the first piece of chewing-gum! It's amazing, huh? Do you know that the Wrigley Building is one of the sights of Chicago?—I saw it summer before last at the Century of Progress.—Did you take in the Century of Progress?

LAURA

No, I didn't.

JIM

Well, it was a wonderful exposition, believe me. You know what impressed me most? The Hall of Science. Gives you an idea of what the future will be like in America. Oh, it's more wonderful than the present time is! Say, your brother tells me you're shy. Is that right, Laura?

LAURA

I—don't know.

JIM

I judge you to be an old-fashioned type of girl. Oh, I think that's a wonderful type to be. I hope you don't think I'm being too personal—do you?

LAURA

Mr. O'Connor?

JIM

Huh?

LAURA

I believe I *will* take a piece of gum, if you don't mind.
      Jim peels gum—gets on knees, hands it to Laura. She breaks off a tiny piece. Jim looks at what remains, puts it in his mouth, and sits again.
Mr. O'Connor, have you—kept up with your singing?

JIM

Singing? Me?

LAURA

Yes. I remember what a beautiful voice you had.

JIM

You heard me sing?

LAURA

Oh, yes! Very often. . . . I—don't suppose—you remember me—at all?

JIM (*Smiling doubtfully.*)

You know, as a matter of fact I did have an idea I'd seen you before. Do you know it seemed almost like I was about to remember your name. But the name I was about to remember—wasn't a name! So I stopped myself before I said it.

LAURA

Wasn't it—Blue Roses?

JIM (*Grinning.*)

Blue Roses! Oh, my gosh, yes—Blue Roses! You know, I didn't connect you with high school somehow or other. But that's where it was, it was high school. Gosh, I didn't even know you were Shakespeare's sister! Gee, I'm sorry.

LAURA

I didn't expect you to.—You—barely knew me!

JIM

But, we did have a speaking acquaintance.

LAURA

Yes, we—spoke to each other.

JIM

Say, didn't we have a class in something together?

LAURA

Yes, we did.

JIM

What class was that?

LAURA

It was—singing—chorus!

JIM

Aw!

LAURA

I sat across the aisle from you in the auditorium. Mondays, Wednesdays and Fridays.

JIM

Oh, yeah! I remember now—you're the one who always came in late.

LAURA

Yes, it was so hard for me, getting upstairs. I had that brace on my leg then—it clumped so loud!

JIM

I never heard any clumping.

LAURA (*Wincing at recollection.*)

To me it sounded like—thunder!

JIM

I never even noticed.

LAURA

Everybody was seated before I came in. I had to walk in front of all those people. My seat was in the back row. I had to go clumping up the aisle with everyone watching!

JIM

Oh, gee, you shouldn't have been self-conscious.

LAURA

I know, but I was. It was always such a relief when the singing started.

JIM

I remember now. And I used to call you Blue Roses. How did I ever get started calling you a name like that?

LAURA

I was out of school a little while with pleurosis. When I came back you asked me what was the matter. I said I had pleurosis and you thought I said Blue Roses. So that's what you always called me after that!

JIM

I hope you didn't mind?

LAURA

Oh, no—I liked it. You see, I wasn't acquainted with many—people . . .

JIM

Yeah. I remember you sort of stuck by yourself.

LAURA

I never did have much luck at making friends.

JIM
Well, I don't see why you wouldn't.

LAURA
Well, I started out badly.

JIM
You mean being ——?

LAURA
Well, yes, it—sort of—stood between me . . .

JIM
You shouldn't have let it!

LAURA
I know, but it did, and I ——

JIM
You mean you were shy with people!

LAURA
I tried not to be but never could ——

JIM
Overcome it?

LAURA
No, I—never could!

JIM
Yeah. I guess being shy is something you have to work out of kind of gradually.

LAURA
Yes—I guess it ——

JIM
Takes time!

LAURA
Yes . . .

JIM
Say, you know something, Laura? (*Rises to sit on day-bed* R.) People are not so dreadful when you know them. That's what you have to remember! And everybody has problems, not just you but practically everybody has problems. You think of yourself as being the only one who is disappointed. But just look around you and what do you see—a lot of people just as disappointed as you are. You take me, for instance. Boy, when I left high school I thought I'd be a lot further along at this time than I am now. Say, you remember that wonderful write-up I had in "The Torch"?

LAURA
Yes, I do! (*She gets year-book from under pillow* L. *of day-bed.*)

JIM
Said I was bound to succeed in anything I went into! Holy Jeez! "The Torch"! (*She opens book, shows it to him and sits next to him on day-bed.*)

LAURA
Here you are in "The Pirates of Penzance"!

JIM
"The Pirates"! "Oh, better far to live and die under the brave black flag I fly!" I sang the lead in that operetta.

LAURA
So beautifully!

JIM
>Aw . . .

LAURA
>Yes, yes—beautifully—beautifully!

JIM
>You heard me then, huh?

LAURA
>I heard you all three times!

JIM
>No!

LAURA
>Yes.

JIM
>You mean all three performances?

LAURA
>Yes!

JIM
>What for?

LAURA
>I—wanted to ask you to—autograph my program. (*Takes program from book.*)

JIM
>Why didn't you ask me?

LAURA
>You were always surrounded by your own friends so much that I never had a chance.

JIM
>Aw, you should have just come right up and said, Here is my ——

LAURA
>Well, I—thought you might think I was ——

JIM
>Thought I might think you was—what?

LAURA
>Oh ——

JIM (*With reflective relish.*)
>Oh! Yeah, I was beleaguered by females in those days.

LAURA
>You were terribly popular!

JIM
>Yeah . . .

LAURA
>You had such a—friendly way ——

JIM
>Oh, I was spoiled in high school.

LAURA
>Everybody liked you!

JIM
>Including you?

LAURA
>I—why, yes, I—I did, too. . . . .

JIM
>Give me that program, Laura. (*She does so, and he signs it.*) There you are—better late than never!

LAURA
My—what a—surprise!

JIM
My signature's not worth very much right now. But maybe some day—it will increase in value! You know, being disappointed is one thing and being discouraged is something else. Well, I may be disappointed but I am not discouraged. Say, you finished high school?

LAURA
I made bad grades in my final examinations.

JIM
You mean you dropped out?

LAURA (*Rises.*)
I didn't go back.
> *Crosses* R. *to menagerie. Jim lights cigarette still sitting on day-bed. Laura puts year-book under menagerie. Rises, picks up unicorn—small glass object—her back to Jim. When she touches unicorn, music cue #16-A.*
How is—Emily Meisenbach getting along?

JIM
That kraut-head!

LAURA
Why do you call her that?

JIM
Because that's what she was.

LAURA
You're not still—going with her?

JIM
Oh, I never even see her.

LAURA
It said in the Personal section that you were—engaged!

JIM
Uh-huh. I know, but I wasn't impressed by that—propaganda!

LAURA
It wasn't—the truth?

JIM
It was only true in Emily's optimistic opinion!

LAURA
Oh . . .
> *Turns* R. *of Jim. Jim lights a cigarette and leans indolently back on his elbows smiling at Laura with a warmth and charm which lights her inwardly with altar candles. She remains by the glass menagerie table and turns in her hands a piece of glass to cover her tumult. Cut music #16-A.*

JIM
What have you done since high school? Huh?

LAURA
What?

JIM
I said what have you done since high school?

LAURA
Nothing much.

JIM
You must have been doing something all this time.

LAURA

Yes.

JIM

Well, then, such as what?

LAURA

I took a business course at business college . . .

JIM

You did? How did that work out?

LAURA (*Turns back to Jim.*)

Well, not very—well. . . . I had to drop out, it gave me—indigestion. . . .

JIM (*Laughs gently.*)

What are you doing now?

LAURA

I don't do anything—much. . . . Oh, please don't think I sit around doing nothing! My glass collection takes a good deal of time. Glass is something you have to take good care of.

JIM

What did you say—about glass?

LAURA (*She clears her throat and turns away again, acutely shy.*)

Collection, I said—I have one.

JIM (*Puts out cigarette. Abruptly.*)

Say! You know what I judge to be the trouble with you? (*Rises from day-bed and crosses* R.) Inferiority complex! You know what that is? That's what they call it when a fellow low-rates himself! Oh, I understand it because I had it, too. Uh-huh! Only my case was not as aggravated as yours seems to be. I had it until I took up public speaking and developed my voice, and learned that I had an aptitude for science. Do you know that until that time I never thought of myself as being outstanding in any way whatsoever!

LAURA

Oh, my!

JIM

Now I've never made a regular study of it—(*Sits in armchair* R.) mind you, but I have a friend who says I can analyze people better than doctors that make a profession of it. I don't claim that's necessarily true, but I can sure guess a person's psychology. Excuse me, Laura. (*Takes out gum.*) I always take it out when the flavor is gone. I'll just wrap it in a piece of paper. (*Tears a piece of paper off the newspaper under candelabrum, wraps gum in it, crosses to day-bed, looks to see if Laura is watching. She isn't. Crosses around day-bed.*) I know how it is when you get it stuck on a shoe. (*Throws gum under day-bed, crosses around* L. *of day-bed. Crosses* R. *to Laura.*) Yep—that's what I judge to be your principal trouble. A lack of confidence in yourself as a person. Now I'm basing that fact on a number of your remarks and on certain observations I've made. For instance, that clumping you thought was so awful in high school. You say that you dreaded to go upstairs? You see what you did? You dropped out of school, you gave up an education all because of a little clump, which as far as I can see is practically non-existent! Oh, a little physical defect is all you have. It's hardly noticeable even! Magnified a thousand times by your imagination! You know what my strong advice to you is? You've got to think of yourself as *superior* in some way! (*Crosses* L. *to small table* R. *of day-bed. Sits. Laura sits in armchair.*)

LAURA

In what way would I think?

JIM

Why, man alive, Laura! Look around you a little and what do you see? A world full of common people! All of 'em born and all of 'em going to die! Now, which of them has one-tenth of your strong points! Or mine! Or anybody else's for that matter? You see, every-body excels in some one thing. Well—some in many! You take me, for instance. My interest happens to lie in electrodynamics. I'm tak-ing a course in radio engineering at night school, on top of a fairly responsible job at the warehouse. I'm taking that course *and* studying public speaking.

LAURA

Ohhhh. My!

JIM

Because I believe in the future of television! I want to be ready to go right up along with it. (*Rises, crosses* R.) I'm planning to get in on the ground floor. Oh, I've already made the right connections. All that remains now is for the industry itself to get under way—full steam! You know, *knowledge*—ZSZZppp! *Money*—Zzzzzzpp! *POWER!* Wham! That's the cycle democracy is built on! (*Pause.*) I guess you think I think a lot of myself!

LAURA

No—o-o-o, I don't.

JIM (*Kneels at armchair* R.)

Well, now how about you? Isn't there some one thing that you take more interest in than anything else?

LAURA

Oh—yes . . .

JIM

Well, then, such as what?

LAURA

Well, I do—as I said—have my—glass collection . . .
Music cue #16-A.

JIM

Oh, you do. What kind of glass is it?

LAURA (*Takes glass ornament off shelf.*)

Little articles of it, ornaments mostly. Most of them are little animals made out of glass, the tiniest little animals in the world. Mother calls them the glass menagerie! Here's an example of one, if you'd like to see it! This is one of the oldest, it's nearly thirteen. (*Hands it to Jim.*) Oh, be careful—if you breathe, it breaks!
The bell solo should begin here. This is last part of cue #16-A and should play to end of record.

JIM

I'd better not take it. I'm pretty clumsy with things.

LAURA

Go on, I trust you with him! (*Jim takes horse.*) There—you're holding him gently! Hold him over the light, he loves the light! (*Jim holds horse up to light.*) See how the light shines through him?

JIM
> It sure does shine!

LAURA
> I shouldn't be partial, but he is my favorite one.

JIM
> Say, what kind of a thing is this one supposed to be?

LAURA
> Haven't you noticed the single horn on his forehead?

JIM
> Oh, a unicorn, huh?

LAURA
> Mmmm-hmmmm!

JIM
> Unicorns, aren't they extinct in the modern world?

LAURA
> I know!

JIM
> Poor little fellow must feel kind of lonesome.

LAURA
> Well, if he does he doesn't complain about it. He stays on a shelf with some horses that don't have horns and they all seem to get along nicely together.

JIM
> They do. Say, where will I put him?

LAURA
> Put him on the table. (*Jim crosses to small table* R. *of day-bed, puts unicorn on it.*) They all like a change of scenery once in a while!

JIM (C., *facing upstage, stretching arms.*)
> They do. (*Music cue #16-B: Dance Music.*) Hey! Look how big my shadow is when I stretch.

LAURA (*Crossing to* L. *of day-bed.*)
> Oh, oh, yes—it stretched across the ceiling!

JIM (*Crosses to door* R., *exits, leaving door open, and stands on fire-escape landing. Sings to music.* [*Popular record of day for dance-hall.*] *When Jim opens door, music swells.*)
> It's stopped raining. Where does the music come from?

LAURA
> From the Paradise Dance Hall across the alley.

JIM (*Re-entering room, closing door* R., *crosses to Laura.*)
> How about cutting the rug a little, Miss Wingfield? Or is your program filled up? Let me take a look at it. (*Crosses back* C. *Music, in dance-hall, goes into a waltz. Business here with imaginary dance-program card.*) Oh, say! Every dance is taken! I'll just scratch some of them out. Ahhhh, a waltz! (*Crosses to Laura.*)

LAURA
> I—can't dance!

JIM
> There you go with that inferiority stuff!

LAURA
> I've never danced in my life!

JIM
> Come on, try!

LAURA

Oh, but I'd step on you!

JIM

Well, I'm not made out of glass.

LAURA

How—how do we start?

JIM

You hold your arms out a little.

LAURA

Like this?

JIM

A little bit higher. (*Takes Laura in arms.*) That's right. Now don't tighten up, that's the principal thing about it—just relax.

LAURA

It's hard not to.

JIM

Okay.

LAURA

I'm afraid you can't budge me.

JIM (*Dances around* L. *of day-bed slowly.*)

What do you bet I can't?

LAURA

Goodness, yes, you can!

JIM

Let yourself go, now, Laura, just let yourself go.

LAURA

I'm ——

JIM

Come on!

LAURA

Trying!

JIM

Not so stiff now—easy does it!

LAURA

I know, but I'm ——!

JIM

Come on! Loosen your backbone a little!

> *When they get to upstage corner of day-bed—so that the audience will not see him lift her—Jim's arm tightens around her waist and he swings her around* C. *with her feet off floor about 3 complete turns before they hit the small table* R. *of day-bed. Music swells as Jim lifts her.*

There we go!

> *Jim knocks glass horse off table. Music fades.*

LAURA

Oh, it doesn't matter ——

JIM (*Picks horse up.*)

We knocked the little glass horse over.

LAURA

Yes.

JIM (*Hands unicorn to Laura.*)

Is he broken?

LAURA

Now he's just like all the other horses.

JIM

You mean he lost his ——?

LAURA

He's lost his horn. It doesn't matter. Maybe it's a blessing in disguise.

JIM

Gee, I bet you'll never forgive me. I bet that was your favorite piece of glass.

LAURA

Oh, I don't have favorites—(*Pause.*) much. It's no tragedy. Glass breaks so easily. No matter how careful you are. The traffic jars the shelves and things fall off them.

JIM

Still I'm awfully sorry that I was the cause of it.

LAURA

I'll just imagine he had an operation. The horn was removed to make him feel less—freakish! (*Crosses* L., *sits on small table.*) Now he will feel more at home with the other horses, the ones who don't have horns. . . .

JIM (*Sits on arm of armchair* R., *faces Laura.*)

I'm glad to see that you have a sense of humor. You know—you're—different than anybody else I know? (*Music cue #17.*) Do you mind me telling you that? I mean it. You make me feel sort of—I don't know how to say it! I'm usually pretty good at expressing things, but—this is something I don't know how to say! Did anybody ever tell you that you were pretty? (*Rises, crosses to Laura.*) Well, you are! And in a different way from anyone else. And all the nicer because of the difference. Oh, boy, I wish that you were my sister. I'd teach you to have confidence in yourself. Being different is nothing to be ashamed of. Because other people aren't such wonderful people. They're a hundred times one thousand. You're one times one! They walk all over the earth. You just stay here. They're as common as —weeds, but—you, well you're—*Blue Roses!*

LAURA

But blue is—wrong for—roses . . .

JIM

It's right for you!—You're pretty!

LAURA

In what respect am I pretty?

JIM

In all respects—your eyes—your hair. Your hands are pretty! You think I'm saying this because I'm invited to dinner and have to be nice. Oh, I could do that! I could say lots of things without being sincere. But I'm talking to you sincerely. I happened to notice you had this inferiority complex that keeps you from feeling comfortable with people. Somebody ought to build your confidence up—way up! and make you proud instead of shy and turning away and—blushing —— (*Jim lifts Laura up on small table on "way up."*) Somebody—ought to—(*Lifts her down.*) somebody ought to—kiss you, Laura!

> They kiss. Jim releases her and turns slowly away, crossing a little D.R. Then, quietly, to himself : (*As Jim turns away, music ends.*)

Gee, I shouldn't have done that—that was way off the beam. (*Gives way* D.R. *Turns to Laura. Laura sits on small table.*) Would you care for a cigarette? You don't smoke, do you? How about a mint? Peppermint—Life-Saver? My pocket's a regular drug-store. . . . Laura, you know, if I had a sister like you, I'd do the same thing as Tom. I'd bring fellows home to meet you. Maybe I shouldn't be saying this. That may not have been the idea in having me over. But what if it was? There's nothing wrong with that.—The only trouble is that in my case—I'm not in a position to —— I can't ask for your number and say I'll phone. I can't call up next week and—ask for a date. I thought I had better explain the situation in case you—misunderstood and I hurt your feelings . . .

LAURA (*Faintly.*)

You—won't—call again?

JIM (*Crossing to* R. *of day-bed, and sitting.*)

No, I can't. You see, I've—got strings on me. Laura, I've—been going steady! I go out all the time with a girl named Betty. Oh, she's a nice quiet home girl like you, and Catholic and Irish, and in a great many ways we—get along fine. I met her last summer on a moonlight boat trip up the river to Alton, on the *Majestic.* Well—right away from the start it was—love! Oh, boy, being in love has made a new man of me! The power of love is pretty tremendous! Love is something that—changes the whole world. It happened that Betty's aunt took sick and she got a wire and had to go to Centralia. So naturally when Tom asked me to dinner—naturally I accepted the invitation, not knowing—I mean—not knowing. I wish that you would—say something. (*Laura gives Jim unicorn.*) What are you doing that for? You mean you want me to have him? What for?

LAURA

A—souvenir. (*She crosses* R. *to menagerie. Jim rises.*)

AMANDA (*Off-stage.*)

I'm coming, children. (*She enters into dining-room from kitchen* R.) I thought you'd like some liquid refreshment. (*Puts tray on small table. Lifts a glass.*) Mr. O'Connor, have you heard that song about lemonade? It's

> "Lemonade, lemonade,
> Made in the shade and stirred with a spade—
> And then it's good enough for any old maid!"

JIM

No, ma'am, I never heard it.

AMANDA

Why are you so serious, honey? (*To Laura.*)

JIM

Well, we were having a serious conversation.

AMANDA

I don't understand modern young people. When I was a girl I was gay about everything.

JIM

You haven't changed a bit, Mrs. Wingfield.

AMANDA

I suppose it's the gaiety of the occasion that has rejuvenated me. Well, here's to the gaiety of the occasion! (*Spills lemonade on dress.*) Oooo! I baptized myself. (*Puts glass on small table* R. *of day-bed.*) I found some cherries in the kitchen, and I put one in each glass.

JIM

You shouldn't have gone to all that trouble, ma'am.

AMANDA

It was no trouble at all. Didn't you hear us cutting up in the kitchen?

I was so outdone with Tom for not bringing you over sooner, but now you've found your way I want you to come all the time—not just once in a while—but all the time. Oh, I think I'll go back in that kitchen. (*Starts to exit* U.C.)

JIM

Oh, no, ma'am, please don't go, ma'am. As a matter of fact, I've got to be going.

AMANDA

Oh, Mr. O'Connor, it's only the shank of the evening!
Jim and Amanda stand U.C.

JIM

Well, you know how it is.

AMANDA

You mean you're a young working man and have to keep working-men's hours?

JIM

Yes, ma'am.

AMANDA

Well, we'll let you off early this time, but only on the condition that you stay later next time, much later —— What's the best night for you? Saturday?

JIM

Well, as a matter of fact, I have a couple of time-clocks to punch, Mrs. Wingfield, one in the morning and another one at night!

AMANDA

Oh, isn't that nice, you're so ambitious! You work at night too?

JIM

No, ma'am, not work but—Betty!

AMANDA (*Crosses* L. *below day-bed.*)

Betty? Who's Betty?

JIM

Oh, just a girl. The girl I go steady with!

AMANDA

You mean it's serious? (*Crosses* D.L.)

JIM

Oh, yes, ma'am. We're going to be married the second Sunday in June.

AMANDA (*Sits on day-bed.*)

Tom didn't say anything at all about your going to be married?

JIM

Well, the cat's not out of the bag at the warehouse yet. (*Picks up hat from telephone table.*) You know how they are. They call you Romeo and stuff like that.—It's been a wonderful evening, Mrs. Wingfield. I guess this is what they mean by Southern hospitality.

AMANDA

It was nothing. Nothing at all.

JIM

I hope it don't seem like I'm rushing off. But I promised Betty I'd pick her up at the Wabash depot an' by the time I get my jalopy down there her train'll be in. Some women are pretty upset if you keep them waiting.

AMANDA

Yes, I know all about the tyranny of women! Well, good-bye, Mr.

O'Connor. (*Amanda puts out her hand. Jim takes it.*) I wish you happiness—and good fortune. You wish him that, too, don't you, Laura?

LAURA

Yes, I do, Mother.

JIM (*Crosses L. to Laura.*)

Good-bye, Laura. I'll always treasure that souvenir. And don't you
forget the good advice I gave you. So long, Shakespeare! (*Up C.*)
Thanks, again, ladies—Good night! (*He grins and ducks jauntily out R.*)

AMANDA (*Faintly.*)

Well, well, well. Things have a way of turning out so badly ——
(*Laura crosses to phonograph, puts on record.*) I don't believe that I
would play the victrola. Well, well—well, our gentleman caller was
engaged to be married! Tom!

TOM (*Off.*)

Yes, Mother?

AMANDA

Come out here. I want to tell you something very funny.

TOM (*Entering through R. kitchen door to dining-room and into living-room,
through curtains, D.C.*)

Has the gentleman caller gotten away already?

AMANDA

The gentleman caller made a very early departure. That was a nice
joke you played on us, too!

TOM

How do you mean?

AMANDA

You didn't mention that he was engaged to be married.

TOM

Jim? Engaged?

AMANDA

That's what he just informed us.

TOM

I'll be jiggered! I didn't know.

AMANDA

That seems very peculiar.

TOM

What's peculiar about it?

AMANDA

Didn't you tell me he was your best friend down at the warehouse?

TOM

He is, but how did I know?

AMANDA

It seems very peculiar you didn't know your best friend was engaged
to be married!

TOM

The warehouse is the place where I work, not where I know things
about people!

AMANDA

You don't know things anywhere! You live in a dream; you manu-
facture illusions! (*Tom starts for R. door.*) Where are you going? Where
are you going? Where are you going?

TOM

I'm going to the movies.

AMANDA (*Rises, crosses up to Tom.*)

That's right, now that you've had us make such fools of ourselves. The effort, the preparations, all the expense! The new floor lamp, the rug, the clothes for Laura! All for what? To entertain some other girl's fiancé! Go to the movies, go! Don't think about us, a mother deserted, an unmarried sister who's crippled and has no job! Don't let anything interfere with your selfish pleasure! Just go, go, go—to the movies!

TOM

All right, I will, and the more you shout at me about my selfish pleasures, the quicker I'll go, and I won't go to the movies either.

Gets hat from phone table, slams door R., *and exits up alley* R.

AMANDA (*Crosses up to fire-escape landing, yelling.*)

Go, then! Then go to the moon—you selfish dreamer!

Music cue #18. Interior light dims out. Re-enters living-room, slamming R. *door. Tom's closing speech is timed with the interior pantomime. The interior scene is played as though viewed through soundproof glass, behind outer scrim curtain. Amanda, standing, appears to be making a comforting speech to Laura who is huddled on* R. *side of day-bed. Now that we cannot hear the mother's speech, her silliness is gone and she has dignity and tragic beauty. Laura's hair hides her face until at the end of the speech she lifts it to smile at her mother. Amanda's gestures are slow and graceful, almost dance-like, as she comforts her daughter. Tom, who has meantime put on, as before, the jacket and cap, enters down* R. *from off stage, and again comes to the fire-escape landing, stands as he speaks. Meantime the lights are upon Amanda and Laura, but are dim.*

TOM

I didn't go to the moon. I went much farther. For time is the longest distance between two places. . . . I left St. Louis. I descended these steps of this fire escape for the last time and followed, from then on, in my father's footsteps, attempting to find in motion what was lost in space. . . . I traveled around a great deal. The cities swept about me like dead leaves, leaves that were brightly colored but torn away from the branches. I would have stopped, but I was pursued by something. It always came upon me unawares, taking me altogether by surprise. Perhaps it was a familiar bit of music. Perhaps it was only a piece of transparent glass. . . . Perhaps I am walking along a street at night, in some strange city, before I have found companions, and I pass the lighted window of a shop where perfume is sold. The window is filled with pieces of colored glass, tiny transparent bottles in delicate colors, like bits of a shattered rainbow. Then all at once my sister touches my shoulder. I turn around and look into her eyes. . . . Oh, Laura, Laura, I tried to leave you behind me, but I am more faithful than I intended to be! I reach for a cigarette, I cross the street, I run into a movie or a bar. I buy a drink, I speak to the nearest stranger—anything that can blow your candles out!—for nowadays the world is lit by lightning! Blow out your candles, Laura. . . . (*Laura blows out the candles still burning in the candelabrum and the whole interior is blacked out.*) And there my memory ends and your imagination begins. And so—goodby!

Exit up the alley to the right.

The music continues to the end.

Action analysis and performance suggestions

Each of the eight scenes of *The Glass Menagerie*, including Tom's narrative bridges, provides rich opportunities for informal performance. For in this melodrama (not the mustachioed excesses of the nineteenth century, but a serious drama neither tragic nor comic), the act of representation gives individualized depth to portraits otherwise realized in emblematic generalities. In this respect, Williams's art is supremely theatrical, and it requires great imaginative concentration on the part of a reader to avoid misinterpretation or overingenious criticism. The fully detailed descriptions in the stage directions and Production Notes guide the unwary toward a narrative rather than dramatic understanding of the play. Concentration on the actions of the characters and the superobjective of the play as a whole is needed both for reading and for informal performance.

Tom takes some part in all but one of the eight principal scenes. It is in scenes iii and iv that his struggle to flee the emotion-draining confines of his relationship with his mother is best represented. Either of these scenes sheds insight on his action throughout the play and suggests ways of understanding the actions that underlie his monologues. In those speeches, as in the choice Tom makes in presenting the "memory" at all (if we identify Tom as the artist who created the play, which need not be Tennessee Williams), Tom may be trying to flee the guilt created by his desertion of his responsibilities at home by exorcising the spirit of his sister from his consciousness.

Another particularly rich and central scene is the eighth and last, the conversation between Laura and Jim. The whole scene is rather lengthy for informal classroom performance, so the analysis below will deal with approximately half of it, from Jim's question "What have you done since high school?" (page 619) through Laura's gift of a "souvenir" (page 625).

DEFINING THE ACTIONS AND THE SUPEROBJECTIVE

Jim and Laura have talked for some time, and Laura has been drawn out of her shyness enough to re-establish their high school acquaintance. With his first line, "What have you done since high school?" Jim remembers his social graces enough to try to get Laura to talk about herself, continuing thereby his earlier action to put Laura at ease. Unfortunately his effort is unsuccessful; Laura wants to avoid talking about her failure to accomplish anything since high school just as she has earlier sought to avoid the pain of exposing her emotions, even though she wants to make Jim like her. Her answers are brief and evasive until she tries to offer a substitute for herself as the topic of conversation—her glass menagerie. The effort is too much for Laura, and her hesitation gives Jim the opportunity to offer her advice. Note that Jim's motive is the same honest generosity that marks all his relationships, but Jim has another motive that he does not understand. For six years he has been "disappointed but not discouraged" by his failure to make progress in his business career. His own device to escape the pain of failure and everyday reality is to project himself into the future or to dwell in the past. This involves more than a little egotism and hence Jim often needs to justify himself and his plans to others. Here his attempt to advise Laura quickly shifts into personal terms so that he begins to justify his own plans to Laura by way of advice. Only a recurrence of his desire to put Laura at ease, which is probably necessary in all his relationships since he craves affection, pulls him up short as he says, "I guess you think I think a lot of myself."

Laura has listened intently to Jim, at one point asking a question, because she wants Jim to like her and because, as a conversational topic, generalities about herself and specificities about Jim offer good substitutes to avoid the emotional outlay of talking more personally about herself. When Jim somewhat obtusely blunders ahead, forcing Laura to identify something special about herself, she again chooses to share with Jim what is nearest to (but not altogether) her secret emotions, her glass collection. Returning to his overall action in this scene of putting Laura at ease, Jim shows interest for as long as he can, then returns to his own egotism to demonstrate the length of his shadow on the ceiling.

The music from the Paradise Dance Hall offers another diversion, one that Jim thinks will help relax Laura. Although she tries to avoid the contact of dancing, Jim's booming, friendly insistence and her own desire to make Jim like her leads her to accept his proposal and even to offer a bit of coquetry (which Amanda would applaud highly). Fate intervenes to interrupt their dance when they knock into the table and break the horn on the glass unicorn. Their effort to ameliorate the situation in order to put each other at ease quickly smooths over the event. (Each understands the symbolism here only on a literal level—that the unicorn now is like all the other horses—while the audience must decide whether the unicorn stands for Laura on another level and if so, how.) Jim's shift to praising Laura is in part another form of advice giving, in part an effort to convince Laura of her worth, in part a genuine desire to flatter Laura in order to make her like him. (The proportions in the mixture of actions will determine much about the interpretation one gives to Jim's behavior.) After the kiss and the beginning of his recantation, Jim tries to justify himself once again, both for raising Laura's hopes falsely and for his future plans. Laura's action during this long series of monologues must be decided by the actress if the scene is to work. Does she try to hide herself? To ease Jim's embarassment? To learn to accept his admissions? Or to do something else?

The superobjective of the whole play lies buried under the social amenities and emotional power of this scene in motives that Tom understands best, Jim hardly understands, and Laura never articulates: to flee into a land of dreams. What is it that each character in the play must escape? What is the nature of each of their dreams?

OVERCOMING OBSTACLES

Laura's shyness certainly is an obstacle, but it is Jim's obstacle in this scene, not Laura's. The obstacles Laura perceives are her need to suppress the emotions she is unwilling to admit and the necessity of overcoming Jim's egotism so that he will pay attention to her. Her tools are not those of a coquette (though once she sounds a bit like a lady receiving a gentleman caller) but those of a socially immature young girl whose attitude when asked her age is not to say "twenty-three" but unconsciously to stress the horror of her aging unmarried state by admitting to "twenty-four in June." An obstacle Jim encounters late in the scene is his genuine affection—affection he knows he is not socially permitted to feel—for the fragile girl he has sought to put at ease. He overcomes this obstacle only by allowing his egotism to dominate him and his plans.

THE MAGIC IF AND THE GIVEN CIRCUMSTANCES

We are still close enough to the social circumstances of *The Glass Menagerie* to make it fairly easy to imagine the ranges of emotional desires present in the pre–World War II milieu with its lower-middle-class home in terror of penury and dependence. To understand Jim's IF, imagine the awkwardness of being invited to meet a girl who is not your fiancée, the threat of professional failure and the knowledge of disappointment, the human desire to help someone who is apparently helpless. Laura's IF involves both despair and pathos. What IF your options seemed closed because you were crippled, shy, and happy only in situations where you could avoid contact with all human beings? What IF you were then forced to meet the one man you had secretly admired and idolized under circumstances you not only found obviously contrived but also inexpressibly embarrassing? What IF he then treated you as if you were nearly normal, even special, and what IF he had even kissed you before telling you it was all a mistake? Such is Laura's situation. Imagine for both young people a world in which a kiss and a dance are personal encounters of deep sexual significance and in which convention forbids all but the most casual relationships with one to whom you are not engaged.

CLASSROOM ADAPTATIONS TO ARRIVE AT STYLE

Light and music play crucial roles in presenting even an informal performance of selections from *The Glass Menagerie*. Any seating arrangement —mock proscenium, mock thrust stage, mock in-the-round—is feasible since other conditions of production, the lighting for instance, provide some aesthetic distance. Try to darken all but the playing area. (A large candelabrum can be the only lighting.) The balance between realism and symbolism is crucial. Light and music stress symbolism; properties, costumes, and acting attitudes stress realism. Be sure to have real gum, real mints, real candles. The actor playing Jim should wear a coat and tie (to be removed, perhaps, in the course of the representation) and the actress portraying Laura should probably wear a long but relatively high-necked gown and should be made conscious, either through the use of a brace or a built-up shoe, of a physical disability in one leg. There should be something very like a small glass unicorn, and, if possible, it should break. Remember that in this scene there *is* a fourth wall. No matter what the seating arrangement, the actors do not see the audience. Strive to create a bittersweet mood using lights, music if possible, and the utmost sense of fragility encountering swaggering but basically fragile self-confidence.

More than realistic, expressionistic, or naturalistic techniques, the special modernism of *The Glass Menagerie* is better explained by a range of devices that might be called "cinematic." As with many of his plays, Williams sketched the basic material in earlier works. A short story, "Portrait of a Girl in Glass," and an unproduced film scenario titled "The Gentleman Caller" both preceded *The Glass Menagerie*. Many of the major innovations of the play can be explained as the adaptation of narrative and cinematic procedures to the drama. Consider some of those novelties: quick cuts between anecdotal episodes (for example, Amanda's telephone solicitations); integrated but discrete scenes whose chronology need not be immediately clear; specialized lighting where the reactions of a character not involved in the dramatized action may actually be made central; a theatrical set with separated playing areas; specialized unrealistic centers of attention that a camera's focus could make clear (for example, the father's occasionally illuminated portrait); intensive use of music; the use of a narrator (much like a film voice overlay); or the aborted notion of verbal scene projections (a holdover from silent films—see Williams's Production Notes, pages 570–571). Other American plays before and after *The Glass Menagerie*—for instance, Thornton Wilder's *Our Town* and Arthur Miller's *Death of a Salesman*—employ similar mixtures of realistic and nonrealistic techniques and bear less resemblance to such landmarks of American dramatic expressionism as Eugene O'Neill's *The Emperor Jones* and Elmer Rice's *The Adding Machine* than to the techniques and interests of the serious cinema. The overall effect of these procedures is to isolate us among the delicate, different creatures that are the Wingfields, to make us feel their pastoral, symbolic lives as emblematic of southern America in the 1930s. Like Tom, we find these memories hard to bear but hard to escape.

Ann Jellicoe
The Knack

TOLEN

TOLEN

I can tell you what I know intellectually, Colin, what my experience has been. But beyond that it's a question of intuition. Intuition is, to some degree, inborn, Colin. One is born with an intuition as to how to get women. But this feeling can be developed with experience and confidence, in certain people, Colin, to some degree. A man can develop the knack.

(page 654)

Egotistical, masculine Tolen directs all his energies into seducing women; sexually insecure Colin wants to learn the knack; Tom watches both with amused interest, then gives the real lesson; and Nancy is to be the victim. However, in *The Knack* (1961), Ann Jellicoe's happiest, most boisterously farcical play, nothing works out quite as the characters expect. Like *A Midsummer-Night's Dream,* the farce combines misunderstandings, disguises, mistakes, and confusion with the powerful emotions of sexual attraction between boy and girl. Like Shakespeare's play it invites the audience to move closer to enjoy the kaleidoscopic, energized interplay of four young people involved in a game where no one will be badly or permanently hurt. It reaches out to talk to us beneath the lines, to appeal to happy myths about sexual love that lurk under full consciousness. Theatrical, improvisational, serious at the base but never trying to make overt intellectual sense, it demands total imaginative involvement from the reader, from the actor, and from the critic. "The appeal in the theatre must be to the senses, emotions and instincts," writes Jellicoe. "So we have colour, movement, rhythmical and musical sounds and use of words, and we have appeals to the half conscious and the unconscious: symbols, myths and rituals" (Ann Jellicoe, *Some Unconscious Influences in the Theatre,* pp. 17–18). Communing together over a bed imaginatively turned into a piano, playing lions and tamers, seducing and resisting seduction become joyful rituals in which the three boys and the girl participate. A bed, discarded by Colin because he thinks it is too small, symbolizes insecurities over sexuality, and by the mythic cry of "rape!" this Eve gains control over an Adam tempted by a serpent's smooth advice on handling women. But in the end the serpent is cast out of the garden, leaving the happy couple to thrive in innocent mutual attraction.

The ending of *The Knack* is happy and so are the expectations developed from the beginning. We never seriously doubt that the four young people will be able to sort out their difficulties, and no matter what threats face them, we know that eventually those characters for whom we care will prosper. So far, these are the formal features of comedy.

However, *The Knack* is farce, a subspecies of comedy that magnifies the absurdities of life until they reach a dreamlike, surrealistic level. To mix and mingle his four young lovers in *A Midsummer-Night's Dream,* Shakespeare uses impossible but conventionally acceptable devices (love potions, invisibility) as farcical shorthand for complicated psychological states of mind. But dealing with more representational, individualized characters in the high comedy of *Love for Love,* Congreve is forced to avoid the improbable and the marvelous. While Jellicoe presents nothing in *The Knack* that could not actually happen in real life, she does present much that is highly unlikely to happen. Acquaintances of a few minutes rarely lead to imaginary games of piano playing or lion taming; a girl rarely accuses three young men she hardly knows of rape in order to draw their attention. Human inhibitions are too intense for such behavior. That the audience does not rebel against such psychological improbabilities is largely the result of the farcical atmosphere that permeates the play from the first appearance of the strangely painted wall to the final act of hanging a chair on it. In such situations we expect the characters, like cartoon figures squashed to a pancake, to survive all difficulties with marvelous resilience. Where Shakespeare (or Oscar Wilde in his classic farce *The Importance of Being Earnest*) relies largely on language, Jellicoe relies on the traditional nonverbal tools of farce: physical action, slapstick, and improvisation.

In the postclassical history of Western drama a major exploitation of the tools of farce took place in the commedia dell'arte of late Renaissance Italy. Using stock characters, stock costumes, and stock situations, street actors improvised performances. True ensemble theater, the companies developed routines, many of them completely nonverbal, as a group. And from their skill they immortalized certain stock characters such as Pantaloon (the foolish old man), Columbine (the delectable maiden), Harlequin (the dashing young rover), and Pierrot (the naïve, sometimes pathetic young man). Comic masterpieces as disparate as Shakespeare's *The Comedy of Errors,* Molière's *Tartuffe,* or the Marx Brothers' *Animal Crackers* are related to such farcical traditions as those developed through the commedia.

Although *The Knack* depends on farcical traditions (Jellicoe's script even directs the actors to improvise like ensemble farce troupes), it is also in part the product of a major contemporary movement in the theater: rejection of the primacy of language. Antonin Artaud, a famous French theoretician, argued in *The Theatre and Its Double* that we mistakenly assume drama grew from the "Word"; hence we underrate the theater's capacity to communicate nonverbally by assaulting the senses. Ann Jellicoe (1927–) had experimented with the implications of Artaud's theater of cruelty (the name given to his theory put into practice) in her first major play, *The Sport of My Mad Mother* (1958). Believing that the primary appeal of the theater is to the unconscious, Jellicoe put her characters through a rapid, rhythmic, mythic, mysterious, whirling, chanting ritual of bombing, street fighting, slashing, and psychic engorging on violence that predates Anthony Burgess's chilling popular vision of violence in *A Clockwork Orange* (1963). And in *The Rising Generation* (1960), a massive pageant drama commissioned but not accepted by the Girl Guides (the British Girl Scouts), she continued the exploration of mythic, ritualistic materials told in a largely nonverbal style.

Such experimentation speaks eloquently of a career spent in the theater. The daughter of marriage between a northern British lower-class mother and a southern British semiaristocratic father, Jellicoe claims to have known her future vocation from the time of her appearance as Beauty in *Sleeping Beauty* at age four. Following the training pattern common in Britain, she attended the Central School of Speech and Drama in London at the time most Americans would attend college, spent several years touring Europe and learning languages, acted and directed, established her own company, and eventually returned to the Central School as a teacher-director. A translator of Ibsen and Chekhov, her knowledge of the theater is both practical and literary. She began writing from the premise that "character and motive were shown in action not described in words; to give a simple example instead of a man saying 'I'm angry', he was angry" (Ann Jellicoe, preface to *Shelley or The Idealist*, p. 13), as well as from the premise that drama appeals on nonrational grounds.

Jellicoe's experiment with comedy and farce in *The Knack* marks a turn from very experimental forms. After *The Knack* Jellicoe wrote two major plays of a far more traditional nature: *Shelley or The Idealist* (1966), representational and realistic even when it cheerfully breaks the proscenium convention, and *The Giveaway* (1970), an address to popular taste in light, social comedy. Thus *The Knack* appears from this perspective of time to be somewhat transitional: experimental in its use of such techniques as ritualistic rhythmic chanting, traditional in its use of farcical techniques like mime, improvisation, and slapstick.

Through its varied theatrical techniques, *The Knack* addresses the audience on a nonrational, perhaps preconscious, level and tries to communicate insight on the eternal fears and insecurities adolescents face as sexual beings. Unlike the absurdist writers whose black comedies often involve us in terrifying situations, Jellicoe's farce lets us know from the outset that nothing serious will happen to Tom, Tolen, Colin, or Nancy—even though their problems are real. We are supposed to laugh at them all: at Tolen who preens himself on his sexual successes; at Colin who frenetically tries to master the art of seduction; at Tom who sublimates his sexual desires, who makes art from walls and music from noise, who saves Nancy from victimization, and who teaches by nourishing instinct; and even at Nancy who is much less innocent about the ways of love than she appears. Also we are supposed to remember how we ourselves faced the same problems in the game of sexual love. As in *Love for Love*, neither wit nor carefully contrived madness wins the contest, and natural, honest love triumphs over all.

The Knack

Characters

TOM *Smallish in size. Vigorous, balanced, strong and sensitive in his movements. He speaks with a great range of pitch, pace and volume and with immense energy and vitality.*

COLIN *Tall and uncoordinated. Explodes into speech and talks jerkily, flatly, haltingly. Basically a strong and intelligent man, but unsure of himself. Gets very angry with himself.*

TOLEN *Once an unpromising physical specimen he has developed himself by systematic physical exercise. His body is now much as he would like it to be. He appears strong, well-built, full of rippling muscle. All his movements are a conscious display of this body. He almost always speaks with a level, clipped smoothness and a very considered subtlety of tone.*

NANCY *Aged about seventeen. Potentially a beautiful girl but her personality, like her appearance, is still blurred and unformed. She wears an accordion-pleated skirt.*

The acting area should be as close to the audience as possible.

Act one

A room. The room is in the course of being painted by Tom. The distribution of the paint is determined by the way the light falls. There is a window up left in the back wall and another down right. The paint is darkest where the shadows are darkest and light where they are most light. The painting is not smooth, pretty or finished, but fierce and determined. Onstage there is a stepladder, a divan, two simple wooden chairs; a pair of chest expanders hangs from the door down left. Curtain up. Tom onstage. Enter Colin.

COLIN

Er . . . I . . . er . . .

TOM

Fabulous. It's fabulous. It's fantastic.
Pause.

COLIN

Er . . .

TOM

Is it dry yet?

COLIN

Where?

TOM

Anywhere.
Colin tries.

COLIN

Getting on.

TOM

Good.
Pause.

COLIN
> I . . . er . . .

TOM
> I hate that divan. (*Pause.*) More white there perhaps. More white.
> (*Pause.*) Here. How does the light fall?

COLIN
> Eh?

TOM
> The light. Get with it. White where it's light, black where it's dark,
> grey in between.
>> *Pause.*

COLIN
> Oh, yes . . . yes.

TOM
> Yes? Good. More white. (*He takes a brush of black paint and paints.*)
> Blast. (*He gets a rag, looks at wall, considers it and then starts working
> black paint with rag.*) Yes? Yes? (*Pause.*) Yes?

COLIN
> It's not in the system.

TOM
> Eh?

COLIN
> White where it's light, black where it's dark.

TOM
> It's nice. I like it.

COLIN
> You're so messy. Everything's messed. It's so badly done.

TOM
> I'm not, I'm not a decorator. It looks different, yes?

COLIN
> Different?

TOM
> Yes.

COLIN
> To what?

TOM
> To before I moved in. (*Pause.*) He won't like it.

COLIN
> Who won't?

TOM
> It'll annoy him. It'll annoy Tolen. It'll enrage him.

COLIN
> The house doesn't belong to Tolen.

TOM
> He'll say it's childish.

COLIN
> It's my house. I rent it, so it's mine. (*Pause.*) There's a lot of stuff in
> the passage.

TOM
> Ha ha! Because Tolen didn't think of it first.

COLIN
> The passage is all bunged up. I want to bring my bed downstairs.

TOM
> What's Tolen's first name?

COLIN
> He says he hasn't got one.

TOM
> Not got one?

COLIN
> He never uses it. I want to bring my bed . . .

TOM
> If he never uses it . . .

COLIN
> . . . My bed downstairs.

TOM
> He must have it.

COLIN
> I want to bring my bed—

TOM
> Well bring it down! What?

COLIN
> I can't get it out of the front door.

TOM
> You want to bring your bed—

COLIN
> There's too much stuff in the passage.

TOM
> I put the stuff in the passage.

COLIN
> There's a chest of drawers behind the front door. You can't get out.

TOM
> Or in. Where's Tolen?

COLIN
> Out. (*Pause.*) Seeing a girl.

TOM
> Oh.

COLIN
> There's too much stuff in the passage.

TOM
> Why do you want to bring your bed downstairs?

COLIN
> The wardrobe and the chest of drawers. We'll bring them in here.

TOM
> What!

COLIN
> Temporarily.

TOM
> No.

COLIN
> So I can get the bed through the front door.

TOM
> We'll bring the bed in here and take it out through the window.
> *Slight pause.*

COLIN
> You only put the wardrobe outside while you were painting.

TOM

I don't want it back. The room's so beautiful.

COLIN

But you must be practical—

TOM

This blasted thing—

COLIN

You've got to sit—

TOM

The bottom's falling out.

COLIN

You've got to sleep—

TOM

Chairs!

COLIN

You can't sleep on the floor. Chairs?

TOM

On the floor. Sleep on it! I think I'll put the mattress on the floor!

COLIN

What!

TOM

Yes! The mattress on the floor. An empty—an empty beautiful
room! What an angle! Look! Upwards? What an idea!

Colin sinks bewildered on to a chair.

You marvel, you! (*Seizes Colin's chair.*) On the wall! Out of the way!
Off the floor! I'll hang them on the wall!

COLIN

Oh, no!

TOM

Oh, yes! (*Throws mattress on floor.*) Help! You! Come on! Help me!
Help me! Colin! My God, what a splendid idea!

COLIN

There's too much stuff in the passage.

TOM

Put it in the basement.

COLIN

We haven't got a basement.

TOM

Give it to Tolen! Put it in Tolen's room! Yes! Come on, help me!
Oh! A beautiful empty room! Why do you want to bring your bed
downstairs?

COLIN

Getting another.

TOM

Oh?

COLIN

A bigger one. Six foot.

Pause.

TOM

Let's get this shifted.

COLIN

Hadn't we better bring mine in first?

TOM

> Into the basement. Give it to Tolen.
>> *Noise, off, of motor-bike which shudders to a stop outside the front door.*

COLIN

> We haven't got a basement.

TOM

> Tolen. That's his motor-bike.
>> *Sound of somebody trying front door.*

COLIN

> It's Tolen. He can't get in. (*Shouting.*) Be with you.
>> *Exit Tom and Colin with divan. Enter Tolen through window upstage.*
>> *Colin appears at window and disappears.*

COLIN (*Off.*)

> Not there.

TOM (*Off.*)

> What?

COLIN (*Off.*)

> He's disappeared.

TOM (*Off.*)

> That's odd.
>> *Enter Tom through door followed by Colin.*

COLIN

> Oh there you . . .

TOLEN

> Your windows are rather dirty.

TOM

> Let's wash them.

COLIN

> I—I've got some Windolene.
>> *Exit Colin.*

TOM

> What's that?

COLIN (*Off.*)

> For cleaning windows.
>> *Pause. Reenter Colin with Windolene which he hands to Tom.*

TOM (*Reading label.*)

> Wipe it on Windolene, Wipe it off window clean.
>> *Tom wipes some of the Windolene on the bottom half of the window.*

TOLEN

> Washing with clean water and then polishing with newspaper would
> have less electrostatic action.

COLIN

> Oh?

TOLEN

> Would repel dirt more efficiently.
>> *Tom starts to experiment with the various shapes he can make.*
> Now you must do the top half, Tom.
>> *Tom hoists the bottom half of the window up and crosses to window*
>> D.R. *and puts on the Windolene there.*
> You do realize, Tom, that in order to clean the window, you have to
> wipe off the Windolene? (*Pause.*) The white stuff has to be polished
> off the window.

TOM
>Let's get that bed down, shall we, Colin?

COLIN
>You can't leave that stuff on.

TOM
>Oh?

TOLEN
>You can't leave it on. "Wipe on sparingly with a damp cloth and wipe off immediately."

TOM
>It's as good as net curtains, only better.

COLIN
>Net curtains?

TOM
>You should paint your window white, Tolen. White reflects heat. You'll be O.K. when the bomb drops.

>>*Exit Tom.*

COLIN
>What? What did you say?

TOM (*Off.*)
>O.K. when the bomb drops. O.K. when the . . .

COLIN
>Net curtains?

>>*Exit Colin. Pause. Tolen is about to exit when he hears bumps, crashes and yells, off. This resolves into dialogue:*

COLIN (*Off.*)
>It won't go round.

TOM (*Off.*)
>It will.

COLIN (*Off.*)
>It won't. Take it apart.

TOM (*Off.*)
>What?

COLIN (*Off.*)
>Take it to bits.

TOM (*Off.*)
>Oh, all right.

COLIN (*Off.*)
>Can you take the head?

TOM (*Off.*)
>The what?

COLIN (*Off.*)
>The head! Hold the head! The head!

TOM (*Off.*)
>Help!

COLIN (*Off.*)
>Eh?

TOM (*Off.*)
>Help! Help!

COLIN (*Off.*)
>Mind the plaster. (*Crash, off.*) Oh!

TOM (*Off.*)
>You're so houseproud.
>>*Enter Colin with head of bed. Colin is about to lean head against wall.*
>Not where it's wet! Fool!
>>*Colin leans head against stepladder. Crash, off.*
>Help! Help! I'm stuck! (*Laughing.*) I'm stuck! The foot!

COLIN
>The what?

TOM (*Off.*)
>The foot!

COLIN
>Your foot!
>>*Exit Colin.*

TOM (*Off.*)
>Of the bed.
>>*Banging and crashing, off, with various imprecations. Enter Colin with foot of bed.*

TOLEN
>Have there been any telephone calls?

COLIN
>Eh?

TOLEN
>I'm expecting a couple of girls to telephone.

COLIN
>There was a Maureen and er—a Joan.

TOLEN
>Joan? Joan who?
>>*Colin is nonplussed.*
>Never mind, she'll telephone again. (*Pause.*) I was afraid it was the barmaid at the "Sun."

COLIN
>Alice?
>>*Enter Tom.*

TOLEN
>She took me into the little back room this morning.

TOM
>What about Jimmy?

TOLEN
>Probably at Chapel.

TOM
>On Saturday?

TOLEN
>She said he was at Chapel. Beyond that bead curtain you know, there's a room full of silver cups. Cases of them. And a large pink sofa in the middle. I never knew Jimmy was a sporting man.

COLIN
>Who was the other one?

TOLEN
>The other?

COLIN
>The one you were expecting to telephone.

TOLEN
>Girl I met in a telephone kiosk.

Exit Tolen. Small crash, off. Reenter Tolen.

TOLEN

Colin, would you mind moving that bed? I would like to get up to my room.

COLIN

Oh, the base. Sorry.

TOM

Can't you climb over?

Exit Colin. Crashing sounds, off. Reenter Colin.

COLIN (*To Tom.*)

Give me a hand, will you?

TOM

Why can't Tolen?

COLIN

Eh?

TOM

It's him that wants to get upstairs.

COLIN

Oh, er . . .

Exit Colin. Reenter dragging base.

TOM

Mind the paint.

Tom helps Colin onstage with bed.

TOLEN

Why are you bringing your bed downstairs, Colin?

COLIN

Getting a new one.

TOLEN

Oh?

COLIN

A bigger one—six foot.

TOLEN

Oh, like mine.

COLIN

I—er—I thought—I thought I'd like another one. You know—er—bigger. Just—just in case, you know. I thought I'd like a bigger—another bed—more comfortable. (*Pause.*) I could always put my married cousins up.

Long pause.

TOLEN

Have you got a girl yet, Colin?

COLIN

No.

TOLEN

Carol left six months ago, didn't she?

COLIN

Mm.

TOM

Have you got a girl yet, Colin?

COLIN

No.

TOM

Got a woman?

COLIN
> No.

TOM
> You haven't, have you.

COLIN
> No.

TOM
> You haven't!

COLIN
> No.

TOM
> You haven't! You haven't! You fool! Why d'you want another bed?

COLIN
> Mind my bed!

TOM
> His bed! Colin's bed!

COLIN
> It's not strong.

TOM (*Through the bars.*)
> Grr! Grr!

COLIN
> Hey! Stop! Stop it!

TOM
> It creaks! It runs! It spins! Watch it! Yahoo!

COLIN
> You'll—

TOM
> Poop—poop—

COLIN
> I say—

TOM
> Poop poop poop poop—

COLIN
> Stop it. Stop it.

TOM
> Poop poop, look out!

COLIN
> Stop stop—ow!
>> *Everything collapses. Tom and Colin are enmeshed in the bed and stepladder.*
> You—you—you nit.
>> *Pause.*

TOLEN
> Did you put turpentine in the white?

TOM
> Eh?

TOLEN
> The white paint. Did you put turpentine in the white?

TOM
> Yes.

TOLEN
> It'll go yellow.

COLIN
  What?
TOLEN
  The white paint will go yellow.
COLIN
  Yellow!
TOLEN
  Yes.
COLIN
  I never knew that.
TOLEN
  The turpentine thins the white lead in the paint and the linseed oil
  seeps through and turns the white yellow.
COLIN
  Oh. D'you think we should do it again?
      Tom is pulling at the chest expanders.
TOM
  Peter left these, wasn't it nice of him?
      Pause. A girl passes the window. Tolen starts to exit through window.
COLIN
  Where are you going? Where—
      Exit Tolen.
  How does he do it?
TOM
  He's beginning to wear out my window. Let's move the chest of
  drawers so he can come in through the front door. He doesn't actu-
  ally do them in the street, you know.
COLIN
  Doesn't he?
TOM
  He makes his contact and stashes them up for later. He's enlarging
  his collection.
COLIN
  How does he meet them?
TOM
  Your bed's in the way. What are we going to do with this bed? What
  you going to do with it?
COLIN
  Oh, that. Oh—what's the use?
      Tom lugs part of the bed across and leans it against Colin.
  What's Tolen got that I haven't got? Maureen says Tolen's got sexy
  ankles.
      Tom brings up another piece and leans it against Colin.
  Are my ankles sexy?
TOM
  What are you going to do with this bed?
COLIN
  Thought I'd take it round to Copp Street.
TOM
  Copp Street?
COLIN
  To the junk yard.

TOM

To sell?

COLIN

I thought so.

TOM

For money?

COLIN

Why not?

TOM

O.K. We'll take it round to Copp Street. How far is it to Copp
Street?

COLIN

Twenty minutes.

TOM

Twenty! (*Long pause.*) Put it back in your room.
Pause. Colin shakes his head. Pause. Tom opens his mouth to speak.

COLIN (*Interrupting.*)

Not in the passage.
Pause.

TOM

Can't you just stand there? You look quite nice really.
Slight pause.

COLIN

Put it together.

TOM

No.

COLIN

If we put it together it'll stand by itself.

TOM

No.

COLIN

On its own feet.

TOM

I can't bear it.
Pause.

COLIN

Take the foot.
Tom does so listlessly.
And the head.
Tom does so.

TOM

How can you sleep on this? I'd think I was at the zoo.

COLIN

How d'you get a woman? How can I get a girl?
They start to put the bed together.

TOM

Do you know why the Duck-billed Platypus can't be exported from
Australia—or do I mean platipi?

COLIN

How can I get a woman?

TOM

You think this is going to be a silly story, don't you.

COLIN
> Well?

TOM
> Because they eat their own weight in worms every day and they starve to death in one and a half hours or something. It's rather a nice object. It's not a nice bed but it's not a bad object. Yes. Look. It's rather nice.
>> *Colin picks up mattress.*
> No.

COLIN
> But—

TOM
> No.

COLIN
> But a mattress naturally goes on a bed.

TOM
> It's not a bed. It's an object. More than that, it's wheeled traffic. Mm. Not much room, is there? I must get those chairs off the floor. Put the mattress in the passage.

COLIN
> It's more comfy on the bed.

TOM
> Oh, very well.
>> *Tom experiments with the bed.*

COLIN
> Why is Tolen so sexy?
>> *Tolen passes the window and tries the front door. Enters by window.*

TOM
> You were very quick. Did she repulse you?

TOLEN
> No. I'm seeing her later.

TOM
> Next time I'll time you.

TOLEN
> Next time come and watch me.
>> *Tom takes the chest expanders and tries them a few times.*

TOM
> I'm getting pretty good. Whew! I can do ten of these. Whew! It's awful!

TOLEN
> I can do twenty—but then . . .

TOM
> Let's see you.
>> *Tolen indicates he is below bothering to use his energy.*

COLIN
> I can do twenty as well.

TOM
> Let's see you.
>> *Colin takes the chest expanders and starts.*
> He's bending his elbows, it's easier that way.

COLIN
> Four.

TOM

> Tolen.

TOLEN

> Yes, Tom?

TOM

> Do you think it's a good idea for Colin to buy a six-foot bed?

TOLEN

> Where's he buying it?

COLIN

> Nine. (*Pause.*) Catesby's.

TOM

> Plutocrat.

TOLEN

> Heal's would have been better.

COLIN

> Twelve. Eh?

TOLEN

> Heal's have more experience with beds.

COLIN

> Expensive. Fourteen.

TOLEN

> They may be more expensive, but they have more experience. You pay for their greater experience.

TOM

> Yes, but do you think it's a good idea, a sound idea, ethically, for Colin to buy a six-foot bed when he hasn't got a woman?

TOLEN

> Rory McBride has an eight-foot bed.

TOM

> Don't stop! You have to keep it up the whole time. You're not allowed to stop. How sexy is Rory McBride? Who is he anyway?

COLIN

> D'you think—?

TOM

> Don't stop!

COLIN

> D'you think—?

TOM

> What?

COLIN

> I ought to get an eight-foot bed?
>
> > *Colin stops.*

TOM

> How many?

COLIN

> Twenty-four. (*Staggering.*) Where's the bed?

TOM

> You mean the object.
>
> > *Colin collapses on the bed. A girl is seen to pass the window. Exit Tolen through window.*

COLIN

> Where's he gone?

TOM

A girl passed by and he went after her.

Pause.

COLIN

You got a cigarette?

TOM

I thought you didn't smoke.

COLIN

Have you got a cigarette?

TOM

No. (*Pause.*) Listen, Colin. I've had a new idea for you. For teaching children about music.

COLIN

Oh—

TOM

Listen! My idea about the chalk—was it a good one?

COLIN

It was all right.

TOM

Did you use it or not? Did you?

COLIN

All right. All right. Just tell me.

TOM

Tolen could help, blast him.

COLIN

How?

TOM

He's a musician. You need his advice. But don't let that bastard near the kids, he'll bully them. Now listen, I been thinking about this. You got a piano? Well, have you? Golly, the bleeding school wouldn't be furnished without a piano.

COLIN

We've got one.

TOM

Good. Listen, I been thinking about this. Teaching's so intellectual and when it's not intellectual, it's bossy, or most of it. The teachers tell the kids everything and all they get is dull little copycats, little automata; dim, limited and safe—

COLIN

Oh, get on.

TOM

You get the piano and you get the kids and you say it's a game see? "Right," you say, "You're not to look at the keys, 'cos that's cheating."

COLIN

Not look—

TOM

If they look at each other playing, they'll just copy each other. Now, don't put your own brain between them and the direct experience. Don't intellectualize. Let them come right up against it. And don't talk about music, talk about noise.

COLIN

Noi—

TOM

What else is music but an arrangement of noises? I'm serious. "Now," you say, "one of you come out here and make noises on the piano." And finally one of them will come out and sort of hit the keys, bang, bang. "Right," you say, "now someone come out and make the same noise."

COLIN

Eh?

TOM

The same noise. That's the first step. They'll have to *listen* to see they hit in the same place—and they can do it more or less 'cos they can sort of—you know—clout it in the middle bit. So next you get them all going round the piano in a circle, all making the same noise, and they'll love that. When they get a bit cheesed, you develop it. "O.K.," you say, "let's have another noise."

COLIN

I don't see the point, I mean—

TOM

Now listen, this way they'll find out for themselves, give them a direct experience and they'll discover for themselves—all the basic principles of music and they won't shy away—they won't think of it as culture, it'll be pop to them. Listen! You, goon, moron, you don't like Bartok, do you?

COLIN

No.

TOM

Don't be so pleased with yourself. You don't understand it, your ear's full of Bach, it stops at Mahler. But after a few lessons like this, you play those kids Schoenberg, you play them Bartok. They'll know what he's doing. I bet they will! It'll be rock'n roll to them. My God, I ought to be a teacher! My God, I'm a genius!

COLIN

What about Tolen?

TOM

What about him?

COLIN

You said he could help.

TOM

To borrow his gramophone records.

COLIN

He never lends them, he never lets anyone else touch them. (*Pause.*) It's a good idea.

TOM

Good.

COLIN

Thanks. (*Pause.*) Why do you say Tolen is a bastard?

TOM

Be careful. He only dazzles you for one reason. Really, Colin, sex, sex, sex: that's all we ever get from you.

COLIN

It's all right for you and Tolen.

TOM

We're all of us more or less total sexual failures.

COLIN
Tolen isn't a sexual failure.

TOM
He needs it five hours a day, he says.

COLIN
Then he can't be a sexual failure. (*Pause.*) He can't be a sexual failure. (*Pause.*) He can't be a sexual failure having it five hours a day. (*Pause.*) Can he?

> *Long pause.*

TOM
I don't like that wall. There's something wrong with that wall. It's not right.

COLIN
Can he?

> *Nancy appears outside behind the window up left and looks about her.*

TOM
Hm. Colin—

COLIN
Can he?

TOM
Colin.

> *Nancy vanishes.*

COLIN
What?

TOM
Oh nothing. What do you think about that wall?

COLIN
Blast the wall! Blast the bloody wall!

> *Nancy reappears outside the window.*

Oh . . . oh . . . oh . . .

TOM
Speak to her.

COLIN
I — I —

TOM
Ask her the time. Ask her to lend you sixpence.

COLIN
I — I — you.

TOM
Eh?

COLIN
You — please.

TOM
I can't do it for you.

COLIN
Oh —

> *Colin turns away. Pause. Nancy vanishes. Long pause.*

TOM
What do you think about that wall?

COLIN
What? Oh . . . it's . . . it's . . .

> *Colin does something violent. Pause. Enter Tolen through window.*

TOM

Someone was riding your motor-bike.

TOLEN

What?

    Exit Tolen through window.

COLIN

Who was riding his motor-bike?

    Reenter Tolen through window.

TOM

I swear someone was riding your motor-bike. (*Pause.*) Well?

TOLEN

Well?

TOM

How long did you take this time?

TOLEN

Did you time me?

TOM

Did you time yourself?

COLIN

How long did you take?

TOLEN

Not more than about ten minutes—

COLIN

Ten minutes! Only ten minutes!

TOLEN

Really, Colin, do you think I'm so clumsy, so vulgar as to do it in the
street? I'm meeting her . . .

TOM

Ten minutes! Ten minutes from door to door? From start to finish?
From hello to good-bye?

COLIN

Ten minutes.

TOM

Ten, Tolen! Ten! Ten minutes! Ten whole minutes! What! No!
You're slipping, man! You're sliding! You're letting us down! Ten.
You can do better than that. Faster, man! Faster! Faster! Faster!

COLIN

Eh?

TOM

Give him a drink of water. Listen, Tolen. Three! Three! Three!
D'you hear? Dreams I got for you, Tolen. Dreams and plans I got
for you. Four minutes! Get it down to four minutes. Four minutes
from start to finish—like the four-minute mile.

COLIN

Eh?

TOM

Heroic! Think! A new series in the Olympic Games!

COLIN

Is he joking?

TOM

And then, Tolen, by discipline, by training, by application: three
minutes fifty-nine seconds! Three minutes fifty-five! Three minutes

fifty! And then—one day—one unimaginable day: three minutes! Three minutes from start to finish!

COLIN

Is it nicer, faster?

TOM

Nice? Nice? Nice? That's not the point. My God! I'm disappointed in you, Tolen, my God I am! Yes! I am! A man with every advantage, every opportunity, every accoutrement—God's gift to woman! And think of those women, Tolen: waiting to be satisfied—their need, Tolen, their crying need—(*Weeping.*). And with the capacity, with the capacity for, with the capacity for spreading yourself around.

Pause while Tom regains control.

TOLEN

I think you're mad.

TOM

Ah, Tolen, never mind. Relax. I see what you mean. I'm a man, too. I understand. Yes, I do. Yes, yes, I do. (*Slight pause.*) You couldn't do it. (*Slight pause.*) You couldn't keep it up. You couldn't keep up the pace.

Tolen appears slightly restive.

Nobody could. It's too much. It's too fast. It's not human, it's super-human. No, no, let's forget it. Let's be generous. I understand. (*Pause.*) Wait! Here's what I propose. Here's what I suggest. One in three! One in three in your own time! Yes, Tolen, every third one as long as you like.

Tolen yawns and climbs on the bed.

He's tired. He's weary. He's overdone it. Poor chap. He's tired. Poor bloke. Quick, quick. Blankets! Brandy! Pills! Pillows! Nurses! Stretchers! Doses! Nurses! Horlicks! Nurses! Hot water bottles! Nurses! Nurses! Nurses! Nurses! Have a piece of barley sugar.

Nancy appears at window. Tolen takes notice. Nancy disappears.

Save yourself! Control yourself! Give yourself a chance!

TOLEN

A bit too provincial.

COLIN

What?

TOLEN

That girl.

Pause.

TOM (*Really wanting to know.*)

How can you tell she's provincial?

TOLEN

Of course, Tom, you will not appreciate that the whole skill, the whole science, is in the slowness: the length of time a man may take. The skill is in the slowness. Of course, Tom, I don't expect you can appreciate this. There is little skill, Tom, and no subtlety in the three-minute make. However—

COLIN

It's better slower?

TOLEN

However, if I wished, Tom, if I wanted, you do realize that I could do it in about eighty-five seconds.

TOM

> Yes.

COLIN

> Tolen.

TOLEN

> Yes, Colin?

COLIN

> Will you—I mean—will you show me—(*Pause.*) how—(*Pause.*)?

TOLEN

> You mean how I get women?

COLIN

> Yes.

TOLEN

> I can tell you what I know intellectually, Colin, what my experience has been. But beyond that it's a question of intuition. Intuition is, to some degree, inborn, Colin. One is born with an intuition as to how to get women. But this feeling can be developed with experience and confidence, in certain people, Colin, to some degree. A man can develop the knack. First you must realize that women are not individuals but types. No, not even types, just women. They want to surrender but they don't want the responsibility of surrendering. This is one reason why the man must dominate. On the other hand there are no set rules. A man must be infinitely subtle; must use his intuition, a very subtle intuition. If you feel it necessary in order to get the woman you must even be prepared to humiliate yourself, to grovel, to utterly abase yourself before the woman—I mean only in cases of extreme necessity, Colin. After all, what does it matter? It's just part of getting her. Once you've got her it's the woman that grovels. Finally, Colin, the man is the master.
>
> For you must appreciate, Colin, that people like to be dominated. They like to be mastered. They ask to be relieved of the responsibility of deciding for themselves. It's a kindness towards people to relieve them of responsibility. In this world, Colin, there are the masters and there are the servants. Very few men are real men, Colin, are real masters. Almost all women are servants. They don't want to think for themselves, they want to be dominated.
>
> First you must establish contact. Of course you won't find that as easy as I do. I'm not referring to touch, tactile communication, that comes later. I mean the feeling between you. You are aware of the girl, the girl is aware of you, a vibration between you . . .

COLIN

> Just a minute.

TOLEN

> Yes?

COLIN

> I just want to get it straight.

TOLEN

> Take your time.
>
> > *Pause.*

COLIN

> I don't see what you mean by contact.

TOLEN

> Very difficult to explain. Tom, can you explain?

TOM

No.

TOLEN

Once you feel it, Colin, you will know it next time. Having established this basis of contact, then you work to break down her resistance, to encourage surrender. Flattery is useful; if a woman is intelligent make her think she's pretty, if she's pretty make her think she's beautiful. Never let them think, never let them see you are clever or intellectual. Never be serious with a woman. Once you let a woman start thinking, the whole process takes infinitely more time. Keep her laughing, keep her talking; you can judge by her laughter, by the way she laughs, how you're getting on.

Perhaps it might be useful to consider what is the right food.

COLIN

The right food?

TOLEN

Food is of the utmost importance. Food is of the essence. One's body needs protein and energy-giving substance. I find with my perhaps unusual sexual demands that my body requires at least twice the normal daily intake of protein.

COLIN

Protein?

TOLEN

Cheese, eggs, milk, meat. I drink about four pints of milk a day—Channel Island milk. And eat about a pound of steak. It needn't be the most expensive, the cheaper cuts have the same food value. For instance, skirt.

TOM

Skirt?

TOLEN

Skirt.

COLIN

Skirt. Cheese, eggs, milk, meat, skirt. Got a pencil, Tom?

TOLEN

Skirt is meat.

COLIN

Oh.

TOM

Don't you see what you're doing to this growing lad? He hasn't got a woman, now he'll go and eat himself silly on milk and meat. Stoke up the fire and block up the chimney. Listen, Colin, suppose this was a piano.

TOLEN

A what?

COLIN

Shut up.

TOM

A piano. Plonk, plonk, plonk.

TOLEN

It's a bed.

TOM

It's not, it's a piano, listen.

COLIN
I want Tolen to tell me—

TOM
Shut up, he's told you enough. A piano, plonk. Now supposing you couldn't—

COLIN
Listen, Tolen—

TOM
Supposing you couldn't see my hand—

COLIN
Shut up.

TOM
I play—C sharp, F and A—

COLIN
Tolen—

Nancy passes window.

I want—listen to me. I want to hear what—I want to hear what Tolen has to say. Listen—listen to me. I want to hear wh-what Tolen has to say. So *what* you think it's b-bad for me to listen to Tolen. You're not in charge of me. I am and I'm sick of myself, I'm absolutely sick, and here I am stuck with myself. I want to hear what Tolen has to say—

Nancy reappears at window.

I want to hear what Tolen has to say. So *what* I want to hear, I want to hear what—

Nancy taps at window. Pause.

NANCY
Do you know where I can find the Y.W.C.A.?

Pause.

TOM
The what?

NANCY
The Y.W.C.A.

Pause.

TOM
Come on in. Come in by the front door.

Exit Tom.

NANCY
Oh, thanks. Thanks very much.

Sound of weighty object being moved. Enter Nancy carrying a holdall and a carrier bag and Tom carrying a large suitcase.

NANCY
Hullo.

TOLEN
Hullo.

NANCY
Hullo.

COLIN
Oh, hullo.

Pause.

TOM
Well, has anyone seen it?

COLIN
: Seen what?

TOM
: Seen what?

NANCY
: The Y.W.C.A.

TOM
: The Y.W.C.A.

COLIN
: Oh, the Y.W.C.A.

TOM
: Yes.

COLIN
: No.

> *Pause*

TOM
: Would you like to sit down?

NANCY
: Well, thanks, but—but well, thanks.

> *She sits.*

TOM
: Would you like a cup of tea or something?

NANCY
: Oh, well, no thanks, really.

TOM
: No trouble, it's no trouble. I'll put the kettle on.

> *Exit Tom.*

TOLEN
: Did he say he'd put a kettle on? He's not boiled a kettle since he came here.

TOM (*Off.*)
: Colin!

COLIN
: Yes?

TOM (*Off.*)
: How do you turn the gas on?

> *Pause. Tolen now pursues the intention of teasing Nancy and making her uncomfortable. He succeeds. If possible achieve this without words. But if necessary insert line:* TOLEN: *"Bit short in the neck. Nice hair, though." Enter Tom.*

How do you turn—(*Pause.*) What do you think of our piano?

NANCY
: What?

TOM
: Our piano. Do you like it? Our piano?

NANCY
: What piano?

TOM
: This piano.

NANCY
: Piano?

TOM
: Yes.

NANCY
   That's not a piano.
TOM
   Yes it is, it's a piano.
NANCY
   It's a bed.
TOM
   It's a piano, honest, listen: ping!
NANCY
   It's a bed.
TOM
   It's a piano, isn't it, Colin?
COLIN
   Eh?
TOM
   This is a piano.
COLIN
   Piano?
TOM
   Piano.
COLIN
   Oh yes, a piano. Ping.
NANCY
   It's a bed.
TOM (*Using the edge of the bed as keyboard.*) Ping (*High.*) ping (*Low.*). Ping
   (*Running his finger right down: glissando.*) pi-i-i-i-i-ng.
COLIN (*Middle.*)
   Ping.
NANCY
   It's a bed.
TOM
   Bechstein.
NANCY
   Bechstein?
TOM (*High.*)
   Ping. (*Medium high.*) Ping. (*Medium low.*) Ping. (*Low.*) Ping.
NANCY
   It's a bed.
TOM (*1st 3 bars "Blue Danube" starting low.*)
   Ping ping ping ping ping.
NANCY
   It's a bed.
COLIN
   Rosewood.
TOM (*4th and 5th bars B.D.*)
   Ping ping ping ping.
NANCY
   It's a bed.
TOM (*6th, 7th, 8th bars B.D.*)
   Ping ping ping ping ping ping ping.
COLIN (*Taking over 9th bar.*)
   Ping ping.

TOM, COLIN (*Together, playing chords in unison, 10–13th bars.*)
> Ping ping ping ping ping
> Ping ping
> Ping ping
> Ping ping ping ping ping
> Ping ping.

NANCY (*Tentative, taking over.*)
> Ping ping.

TOM, COLIN (*Gently encouraging Nancy, who joins in 17th, 18th, 19th bars B.D.*)
> Ping ping ping ping ping
> Ping ping
> Ping ping.
>> *All three letting go with great rich chords.*
> Ping ping ping ping ping
> Ping ping
> Ping ping
> Ping ping ping ping ping
> Ping ping ping
> Ping ping ping ping ping ping.

NANCY
> Ping.

COLIN
> Ping.

NANCY
> Ping.

COLIN
> Ping.

NANCY
> Ping.

COLIN
> Plong.

NANCY
> Plong.

COLIN
> Plong plong.

NANCY
> Ping plong.

COLIN
> Plong.

NANCY
> Ping.

COLIN
> Ping.

NANCY
> Plong.
>> *Pause.*

COLIN
> Plong.
>> *Pause.*

NANCY
> Plong.
>> *Pause.*

COLIN
>   Plong.

TOLEN
>   Why be so childish about a bed?

> [*Author's note: All the above could be rearranged or improvised to suit different actors and different productions provided the sequence of events is clear:*
> 1. *Tom and Colin charm Nancy into entering into the game.*
> 2. *Tom retires leaving Colin and Nancy getting on rather well, a growing relationship which Tolen interrupts.*]

>   *Long pause.*

TOM
>   Would anyone like to know how they train lions to stand on boxes? (*Pause.*) Would you like to know how they train lions to stand on boxes? First we must have a box. (*Taking bucket.*) That will do. Now this marks the limit of the cage—the edge, the bars.

TOLEN
>   Must you be so childish?

TOM
>   Childlike. The trainer takes his whip. Whip? Whip? We'll do without a whip. Now a lion. I must have a lion . . . Tolen, you'd make a good lion. No? O.K. Colin.

COLIN
>   No.

TOM
>   Come on, be a lion.

COLIN
>   No.

TOM
>   Go on, can't you roar? The trainer taking the box in his left hand, and the whip—imagine the whip—in his right, advances on the lion and drives him backward against the cage bars, yes? Now. There is a critical moment when the lion must leap at the attacker otherwise it will be too late, see? Right. The trainer can recognize the critical moment. So, at the moment when the lion rears to attack, the trainer draws back and the lion, no longer threatened, drops his forepaws and finds himself standing on the box. Do this a few times and you've trained a lion to stand on a box.
>   *Pause.*

COLIN
>   How does the box get there?

TOM
>   What?

COLIN
>   You've still got it in your hand.

TOM
>   The trainer puts it there.

COLIN
>   When?
>   *Pause.*

TOM
>   Let's try. You come and be lion.

COLIN
No.

TOM
All right, I'll be lion. (*He tries a roar or two.*) Whew! It makes you feel sexy.
> *He tries again.*

COLIN
I'd like to be lion.

TOM
All right.

COLIN
I wonder if I could roar into something.

TOM
Eh?

COLIN
It would help the resonance.
> *He roars into bucket.*

TOM
That's the lion's box.

COLIN
Sounds marvelous inside.
> *Colin sees Nancy's carrier bag. He picks it up.*

TOM
Hey, you can't touch that.

COLIN
Eh?

NANCY
Oh, that's all right.
> *Colin empties contents, including a copy of* Honey *magazine. Puts carrier bag on his head and goes round roaring.*

TOM
Yes! Yes! Yes! Yes! Yes!
> *Colin roars at Tom who roars back, then at Nancy. Nancy laughs, half scared, half excited. Colin roars at her and she runs away. Colin gropes around for her, but she evades him, laughing.*
You should wear a carrier bag more often.

COLIN
Just a minute.
> *Colin takes the bag off his head and makes holes for eyes. Replaces bag. Roars again after Nancy. Tolen takes off belt he wears and cracks it like a whip.*

TOLEN
I'll be trainer.

TOM
Eh? Very well.

TOLEN
Ready?
> *Pause. Tolen advances on Colin cracking his "whip" and getting a sweet pleasure from the identification. Colin roars, Tolen gets more excited.*

TOLEN
Back—back you—back you—back—back you beast you—beast you beast you back back!

> *Nancy gets mixed up between them. She screams and exits. Tolen picks up* Honey. *Pause.*

TOM

Just think what you could do with a real whip, Tolen. Or a sjambok. Think of that.

COLIN (*Taking off carrier bag.*)

What's happened? Has she gone?

TOM

She left her suitcases.

Act two

> *The room is very peaceful. Tom is painting gently and thinking about his paint. Colin has the carrier bag on his head and is feeling free and experimental. Anything the actor may improvise is probably best, but Colin might feel like some exotic bird: standing on one leg, hopping, crowing; possibly using the chest expanders in some unconventional way. After a long pause.*

TOM

What do you think?

> *Pause.*

COLIN

Not thinking.

> *Pause.*

TOM

Eh?

> *Pause.*

COLIN

Not thinking.

TOM

Look!

COLIN

Oh.

TOM

A . . . (*Pause.*). This place soothes me.

> *Pause.* Colin *takes off the carrier bag.*

COLIN

I remember the first time I saw this street.

TOM

Northam Street?

COLIN

These mean streets (*Pause.*)—the feeling of space in these streets— it's fantastic. (*Pause.*) When they're empty they're sort of—splendid, a sort of—crumbling splendor (*Pause.*) and a feeling of—in winter, on a hazy, winter day a—a—a—romantic! And in summer hot and— listless. And at weekends, summer and the sun shining and children dashing about and mothers talking—you know, gossiping and men cleaning motorbikes and (*Getting excited.*) they can be forbidding, threatening—I mean—you know—if the light's flat and darkish,—no sun—just flat and lowering, it's stupendous! And early morning— early autumn—I've walked through these streets all alone, you know, all by myself—so quiet so . . . so . . .

Telephone rings, off.

It'll be for him. It'll be for Tolen.

> *Colin replaces carrier bag on his head and picks up a magazine. Exit Tom. Telephone stops ringing. Pause. Nancy appears at the window, she doesn't see Colin. Nancy climbs through the window and goes towards the suitcases. Colin sees Nancy. Nancy sees Colin and is transfixed. Pause. Enter Tolen through window. Pause. Tolen whips off his belt. Nancy darts away hysterical. There is a maelstrom of movement during which the bed gets overturned, Nancy is caught behind it, and Colin and Tolen are covering all the exits. Enter Tom through door. Pause.*

TOM

Colin, take that carrier bag off your head.

COLIN

Eh?

TOM

Take it off.

> *Colin removes carrier bag.*

Shall we get the bed straight? (*Tom goes to the foot of the bed.*) Tolen?

> *Tom and Colin put bed right.*

You not found the Y.W.C.A.?

NANCY

No.

TOM

What's the address?

NANCY

I've got it here.

> *She hands him a scrap of paper.*

TOM

Martin's Grove, W.2. Where's Martin's Grove?

COLIN

I don't know. I'll get the street map.

> *Exit Colin. Pause.*

NANCY

Thanks.

TOLEN

That's all right.

NANCY

Oh, thanks.

TOLEN

Don't mention it.

> *Enter Colin with map.*

TOM

How does it work?

COLIN

Index.

TOM

Eh?

COLIN

Back.

TOM

I see.

TOLEN

Just come off the train, have you?

NANCY

Yes.

COLIN

James Park, James Square, turn over, and again. Ah. Mapperton, Marlow.

TOLEN

Is it the—

TOM

Martin's Grove, W.2. J4.73. What's that?

COLIN

Page seventy-three.

TOLEN

Is it the first time you've been here?

NANCY

Here?

TOLEN

In London?

NANCY

Oh, yes.

> *Tolen and Nancy laugh.*

COLIN

Square J above, 4 across.

TOM

What tiny print.

TOLEN

You've got Chinese eyebrows.

NANCY

Eh?

TOLEN

Chinese eyebrows. Very clear arch. Very delicate.

NANCY

Have I?

TOLEN

Have you got a mirror, I'll show you.

NANCY

Oh.

COLIN

Turn it the other way.

TOM

Eh?

COLIN

Round. That's it.

TOLEN

See? Very pretty.

NANCY

Oh.

TOM

Here. (*Pause.*) Here it is.

NANCY

Eh? Oh, thanks.

TOM

 Not far. Five minutes.
  Nancy is occupied with Tolen.
 We'll take you. We'll take you there.

NANCY

 Oh. Oh, thanks. (*Pause.*) Well, perhaps I ought to—

TOLEN

 What's your name?

NANCY

 Nancy, Nancy Jones. What's yours?

TOLEN

 Tolen.

NANCY

 Tolen? Tolen what?

TOLEN

 Tolen.

NANCY

 Tolen, oh I see, like Capucine.

TOLEN

 I beg your pardon?

NANCY

 Capucine.

TOLEN

 Capucine?

NANCY

 Like Capucine. Nothing Capucine, Capucine nothing.

TOLEN

 Please would you tell me what you mean?

NANCY

 You not seen her? She's an actress. She acts.

TOLEN

 On television?

NANCY

 In the films. Is it your Christian name or your surname? (*Pause.*)
 Well, is it? Is it your surname or your Christian name?

TOLEN

 It's my surname.

NANCY

 What's your Christian name?

TOLEN

 I never use my first name. I have no first name.

NANCY

 What is it?

TOLEN

 I prefer not to use it.

NANCY

 Why?

TOLEN

 I don't use it. I have no first name. I never use my first name.
  Tolen moves away. Pause. Tolen returns to near Nancy. Nancy shifts
  uncomfortably.
 What's the matter? Is anything wrong? Is anything the matter with
 you?

NANCY

No.

TOLEN

Why are you so nervous?

NANCY

I'm not.

TOLEN

You look nervous.

NANCY

Me nervous? Do I?

TOLEN

Yes.

NANCY

Oh—

TOLEN

Yes?

NANCY

Nothing.

TOLEN

What's the matter?

NANCY

It's—it's—

TOLEN

Well?

NANCY

It's—

TOLEN

You are nervous, aren't you? Very nervous. Why don't you take your coat off?

NANCY

I don't want to.

TOLEN

My dear, you take it off.

NANCY

I don't want to.

TOLEN

Why don't you want to?

NANCY

No.

> *Exit Colin.*

It's—it's—

TOLEN

Yes?

> *Pause.*

NANCY

You're looking at me.

TOLEN

Am I?

NANCY

Yes.

TOLEN

How am I looking?

NANCY

I don't know, I—

TOLEN

How am I looking?

NANCY

I—

TOLEN

Well?

NANCY

I feel—

TOLEN

What?

NANCY

I don't know, I—

TOLEN

You feel funny, don't you—go on, tell me—go on—tell me—tell me.
Nancy moves away. Tolen laughs.

TOM

What's the most frightening building in London?

TOLEN

It depends what you mean by frightening.

TOM

Break it up, Tolen.

TOLEN

What I do is my affair, not yours.

TOM

She doesn't know a thing.

TOLEN

She knows what she wants, or rather what she will want.

TOM

I don't think you're the right person to give a girl her first experience.

TOLEN

She's an independent human being. Why should you say what's good
for her? How old are you, Nancy?

NANCY

Seventeen.

TOLEN

There you are. (*Pause.*) Anyway, she's not really my type. I've had
sufficient for today. I'm merely amusing myself. It's more subtle.

TOM

You know what happens to young girls alone in London, don't you?

NANCY

Yes—no—I—

TOM

You'd better find a Catholic Girls' Refuge.

NANCY

I'm not a Catholic.

TOM

You'll find the address in any ladies' lavatory in any railway station.

NANCY

Oh—I—

TOLEN

How do you know?

NANCY

I think I ought to go—I—

Enter Colin with tea things including milk in a bottle.

COLIN

That damned stuff in the passage. You'll have to move it.

TOM

I'm not having it in here.

COLIN

I'm not having it in the passage.

TOM

I'm not having it in here.

COLIN

When you take a furnished room, you take the furniture as well.

TOM

Not that furniture.

COLIN

What's wrong with the furniture?

TOM

I'm not having it in here. Put it on the bed. Take it to Copp Street.

COLIN

It's my furniture, you're not selling my furniture.

TOM

You're selling your bed.

COLIN

You're not selling my furniture.

TOM

We'll put it on the top landing.

TOLEN

Outside my room? I think not.

TOM

Inside your room.

COLIN

Oh. Let's have some tea.

They start pouring out tea.

TOLEN

What's the most frightening building in London?

COLIN

Great Ormond Street Hospital for Children.

Pause.

TOM

What's that?

COLIN

Great Ormond Street Hospital for Children.

NANCY

That's nice. It's true. That's a nice thing to say.

COLIN

Oh? Do you think so?

Tolen touches Nancy.

TOM

Do you know how the elephant got the shape it is? Well, there was once a little piggy animal, see? With two great big front teeth that stuck out. However, there are certain advantages in being big—you know, you can eat off trees and things—like horses—

TOLEN

For you this is remarkably incoherent.

TOM

Thanks. So this animal got big and it grew an enormous great long jaw so it could scoop up the vegetation. An enormous jaw, seven foot long—imagine! As big as a door! Now. A seven-foot jaw involves certain difficulties in getting the food from the front of your jaw to the back . . .

TOLEN

Biscuits?

TOM

It had to use its upper lip to shovel the garbage along.

COLIN

Aren't there some chocolates?

TOM

I ate them. Well, the creature's upper lip began to grow. It grew so big it began to do all the work and the creature didn't bother to use its seven-foot jaw. Now, as you know, any organ not in constant use atrophies so the jaw began to shrivel. (*To Tolen.*) Not that you need . . .

NANCY

Tea?

TOM

But the two front teeth—

NANCY

More tea?

TOM

Remained. So you are left with an animal having an extraordinarily long upper jaw and two big front teeth. You're left with an elephant. No problem at all. Yes, I would, please.

> *Tolen touches Nancy's arm.*

NANCY

D'you like it? It's new.

TOLEN

You should paint that wall straight away or it'll patch up.

TOM

What?

TOLEN

It will dry blotchy.

TOM

Yes. That's a good idea. Yes!

TOLEN

You wanted to see me?

COLIN

Eh?

TOLEN

That's right.

COLIN

Wanted to see you?

TOLEN

You will.

COLIN
>What d'you—

TOLEN
>Watch this.

COLIN
>What do you mean?

TOM
>In cold blood, Colin. In cold blood.

TOLEN
>I'll show you how.

TOM
>Nancy! (*Angry.*) You should go when you're told.
>>*Tolen takes copy of* Honey *and lies on the bed.*

NANCY
>Would you like something behind your head?

TOLEN
>There is a pillow in the passage.
>>*Nancy exits, returns with pillow.*
>Why don't you look at me?

NANCY
>I can't.

TOLEN
>Why can't you?

NANCY
>I'll—I'll—

TOLEN
>What?

NANCY
>I'll laugh.

TOLEN
>Why?

NANCY
>You'll make me laugh.

TOLEN
>Why?

NANCY
>You will.

TOLEN
>Will I?

NANCY
>Yes.

TOLEN
>Will I?

NANCY
>Yes.

TOLEN
>Look at me, laugh! Go on! Look at me, laugh, look at me, go on, look at me, laugh, look at me, look at me.
>>*She laughs. She stops laughing. He might kiss her.*

NANCY
>No, no.

COLIN
>Ha!

TOLEN
  You idiot. Fool.
      Pause.
TOM
  Do you like my room?
NANCY
  What?
TOM
  My room.
NANCY
  What! It's not much. There's not much to sit on.
TOM
  Sit on the piano.
NANCY (*Irritated.*)
  Aw!
TOM
  They clutter up the place so I really must get them on the wall.
NANCY
  What?
TOM
  The chairs. On the wall.
NANCY
  What? Oh, it doesn't matter.
TOM
  To get them off the floor. Have I said anything to upset you, Tolen?
TOLEN
  Nothing you said could possibly upset me. (*Pause.*) Why do you try
  and find rational reasons for your childish impulses?
TOM
  Do I disturb you?
TOLEN
  You make me smile.
TOM
  Ooh! He's annoyed. Oh, yes, he's annoyed. Be careful or you might
  lose control. Ah well. Back to work. Pass me another cup of tea,
  Nancy.
NANCY
  What?
TOM
  Get me another cup of tea, there's a dear.
NANCY
  What do you think I am?
TOM
  Oh. (*Pause.*) Sorry.
NANCY
  Oh, all right.
      She pours out tea for Tom.
TOM
  Thanks.
NANCY (*To Tolen.*)
  Do you want some?
TOLEN
  No.

Nancy pours out tea for herself. Long pause.

All right. She's all yours.

COLIN

Eh?

TOLEN

You have a try.

COLIN

What? Me?

TOLEN

Yes.

> *Long pause.*

COLIN

Has Cardiff got big docks?

NANCY

What?

COLIN

Has Cardiff got big d-docks?

NANCY

Why ask me?

COLIN

Welsh. I mean—aren't you—don't you come from Wales?

NANCY

No.

COLIN

It was the name—Jones.

NANCY

Where d'you say the Y.W. was?

COLIN

Oh, it's in Martin's Grove. You have to take a 27 bus, get off at the top of Church Street and walk down on the left until—

NANCY

It far?

COLIN

Pardon?

NANCY

Is it far?

COLIN

No, not very.

NANCY

Good. I'm going.

COLIN

What?

NANCY

I'm off. I said I'm going. And as for you. As for you Mr. Mr. Mr. only one name. Mr. no name. As for you. As for you. As for you . . .

> *Tolen laughs.*

That's my *Honey.* Give me my *Honey.*

COLIN

I'll take you. I said I'll take you there.

TOLEN

You want your magazine?

*She retreats. Tolen follows her. She cannot retreat farther. She slaps
him. He kisses her.*

See? It's not difficult.

Nancy bursts into tears.

TOM

Well, that's that. I need this room, Tolen.

TOLEN

Expecting someone?

TOM

Maybe.

TOLEN

Man or woman? (*Pause.*) Are you a homosexual?

TOM

No. (*Pause.*) Thanks all the same.

Exit Tolen.

COLIN

Why do you like annoying him?

TOM

He was annoyed, wasn't he? He's softening up. Ha ha! Now he'll
play gramophone records and make telephone calls. Really, Colin,
what a mess, suppose the Queen were to come. Oh, this wall, this
sickening, everlasting wall, it's enormous, it goes on for ever. I'm fed
up with it. Here. (*Gives Colin a brush.*)

COLIN

Eh? What's this for?

Tom gives Nancy a brush.

TOM

Only the end bit, the plain bit, the uncreative bit, the bit that don't
need genius.

COLIN

You want us to paint the wall?

TOM

The white bit, the boring bit. I'm sick of it.

COLIN

You're so damned lazy.

TOM

Attack it. Attack it.

COLIN

And messy.

NANCY

Yes! Yes! you, yes! (*She attacks wall.*) You. ha ha! Yes. (*Mumbling between her teeth.*) Yes! Um hm um hm!

TOM

A dear girl. A darling girl. There. That's right.

Exit Tom.

COLIN

Here?

TOM (*Off.*)

Here?

COLIN

The end.

TOM (*Off*)
> The window end?

COLIN
> Yes.

TOM (*Entering.*)
> That's right.

> *Enter Tom with a sheet which he ties around Nancy. She takes her jacket off and gives it to him.*

> Ah, yes, that's nice. Faster, serfs! (*Pause.*) Elephants. (*Pause.*) The Indians keep elephants like we keep cows.— I was wondering how big an elephant's udder was. My God, imagine it swishing around. Do you know, in Walt Disney's early films there were cows and the censor cut the udders out so he put brassieres on them, imagine! . . . Jersey cows wear brassieres, it's true. Jersey cows wear brassieres. Something wrong here, cows shouldn't need brassieres. Human beings need them because they stand upright. They used to go on all fours, so they hung downwards — vertically — now they stand upright and it puts on this terrible strain . . .

> *Nancy is laughing.*

> All right, all right. It's true.

COLIN
> Oh —

TOM
> Eh?

COLIN
> I wish you wouldn't show off.

TOM (*To Nancy.*)
> Hi! (*To Colin.*) I don't show off.

COLIN
> You do.

TOM (*Restraining Nancy.*)
> Colin wishes I wouldn't show off.

COLIN
> Well, you do show off.

TOM
> I don't.

COLIN
> You do. Stop slapping it.

NANCY
> I like splashing.

COLIN
> It's splashing.

NANCY
> So what?

COLIN
> It's dripping.

NANCY
> I don't care. I don't care.

COLIN
> Don't get so excited.

NANCY
> You're talking. I hear you.

COLIN
Look at her. Look at her.

TOM
I see her.

NANCY
So what.

TOM (*Shepherding Nancy to a bit of wall away from his careful painting.*)
Watch it — yes — there's a — and now — that's right — more left.

NANCY
What's the difference between an elephant and a pillar box?

COLIN
They can neither of them ride a bicycle.

NANCY
You knew!

COLIN
What? What?

NANCY
I can reach higher than you.

COLIN (*Holding up his arm.*)
Heard it before.

NANCY
Yes, I can.

TOM
I don't show off.

COLIN
What? No, you can't.

NANCY
I can.

COLIN
You can't.

TOM
I do —

NANCY
I can —

TOM
— sometimes —

NANCY
— look —

COLIN
You don't — I mean —

NANCY
I can reach higher than you —

COLIN
Ouch!

NANCY
What?

COLIN
It's all run up my elbow. Oh.

TOM
You're dripping everywhere. There's a cloth in the kitchen.
    Exit Colin. Telephone rings, off. Pause. Enter Tolen.

TOLEN
It's for you.

TOM
> Man or woman?

TOLEN
> Woman.
>> *Exit Tom. Pause. Tolen moves to help Nancy off with sheet. She avoids him.*
> No one's going to rape you.

NANCY
> Oh!

TOLEN (*Laughing.*)
> Girls never get raped unless they want it.

NANCY
> Oh!

TOLEN
> I'm sorry about — what happened.

NANCY
> That's —

TOLEN
> It was clumsy — very —

NANCY
> That's all right.

TOLEN
> It was because they were here — the clumsiness I mean —

NANCY
> Was it?

TOLEN
> In a way, in a way.

NANCY
> Oh.

TOLEN
> Don't you believe me?

NANCY
> I don't know — I —

TOLEN
> Please —

NANCY
> I —

TOLEN
> Please believe me.

NANCY
> It doesn't matter.

TOLEN
> It does matter, it matters very much. (*Pause.*) It matters very much to me. (*Pause.*) How sweet you are. Such a sweet face, such sweetness. (*Pause. He kisses her.*) Ssh . . . ssh . . . Come . . . come up . . . come upstairs . . .

NANCY
> Oh . . . oh . . .

TOLEN
> Come up to my room . . .

NANCY
> Oh . . . oh . . . no . . .

TOLEN

You like music? I've got some records upstairs . . . I'll play you
some records.

Enter Colin.

COLIN

Well, let's get on — oh — . . . Where are you going? Are you going
out? To find the Y.W.? I'll come too.

TOLEN

What?

COLIN

I'll come as well.

TOLEN

Where?

COLIN

To find it.

TOLEN

What?

COLIN

The Y.W.

Pause.

TOLEN

Why don't you go?

COLIN

Eh?

TOLEN

Why don't you go look for the Y.W.?

COLIN

Well, you're coming, aren't you?

Tolen is exasperated.

Well — you —

NANCY

Oh —

COLIN

Oh, come on —

NANCY

I don't think I —

COLIN

Oh, please —

NANCY

What about the cases?

COLIN

The cases?

NANCY

I can't go without them.

COLIN

He'll look after them.

NANCY

Who will?

COLIN

He will.

TOLEN

Me?

NANCY
>Where are you going?

TOLEN
>I'm going out.

NANCY
>I'd like a walk.

COLIN
>So would I.

NANCY
>What about the cases?

COLIN
>You stay here.

TOLEN
>Why should I?

COLIN
>You could stay here.

TOLEN
>Why should I?

COLIN
>You could look after the cases.

TOLEN
>He can.

COLIN
>Who can?

TOLEN
>Tom can.

COLIN
>He's upstairs. Can't they stay here?

NANCY
>I need them at the Y.W.

>>*Tolen moves away. Nancy follows.*

COLIN
>Let's go look for the Y.W.

NANCY
>Are you coming?

TOLEN
>To the Y.W.?

COLIN
>Well, let's you and me go.

NANCY
>Well —

COLIN
>Well —

NANCY
>I don't think I really —

COLIN
>You said you did.

NANCY
>Did I?

COLIN
>Yes.

NANCY
>What about the cases?

TOLEN
  Why don't you carry them?
COLIN
  Me?
TOLEN
  If you're going to the Y.W., why don't you carry them?
COLIN
  Let's go for a walk.
NANCY
  What about the cases?
TOLEN
  You carry them.
COLIN
  She!
TOLEN
  Yes.
COLIN
  She can't carry them.
TOLEN
  She's already carried them. She carried them here.
COLIN
  She can't carry them.
TOLEN
  You carry them.
COLIN
  I want both hands free.
      Pause. Enter Tom. Tolen starts to exit.
NANCY
  Where you going?
TOLEN
  Oh, anywhere. D'you want to?
NANCY
  D'you want me to?
TOLEN
  If you want to.
COLIN
  Are you going to the Y.W.?
TOLEN
  Maybe.
COLIN
  I'll come too.
TOLEN
  What about the cases?
      Colin picks up the cases.
COLIN
  I'll come too.
      Tolen and Nancy exit.
TOM
  Stay with them, Colin.
COLIN
  Eh?
TOM
  Stick with them.

> *Exit Colin. Tolen and Nancy are seen to pass window, followed soon after by Colin. Exit Tom. Heavy dragging and banging, off. Enter Tom looking very pleased with himself, takes bed to bits and drags it off. More banging. Enter Tom exhausted. Drinks milk. Exits with tray. Reenters and resumes painting. Tolen and Nancy pass window. Door is tried, off. Tolen and Nancy enter through window. Both are laughing a good deal.*

TOLEN

That door blocked again?

TOM

Been moving a few things.

TOLEN

And if you push it under — ooops! (*Nancy laughs.*) and over ooops!
> *Nancy laughs.*
> *Enter Colin through window.*

TOM

You look very seasick.

COLIN

Shut up.
> *Colin thrusts carrier bag on his head. Nancy is pretty hysterical. Tolen works her up, kissing and laughing. Tom intensifies the atmosphere by beating a rhythm on bed or stepladder, possibly using mouth music as well.*

TOLEN

We'll go and listen to those gramophone records.
> *Exit Tolen and Nancy. Tom stops beating. Pause. Large crash, off. Enter Tolen.*

TOLEN

Who put that stuff on the stairs?

TOM

Oh, are the stairs blocked?

TOLEN

I can't get up to my room.

TOM

Oh, can't you?
> *Enter Nancy.*

NANCY

Why's the wardrobe on the stairs—and the bed—the stairs are blocked . . .
> *Tolen grabs her.*
Oh! You're hurting me!

TOM

Stop. Stop that.

NANCY

Let me go! Let me go! Let me go! (*She escapes but not before Tolen has hurt and thoroughly frightened her.*) Don't touch me!
> *Tom and Colin attempt to comfort her but they only excite her more.*
Keep off! Keep off! D'you hear? Keep away! Don't touch me! You — you — you — don't touch me! You don't touch me. All right? All right? . . . Now, now then, now . . . what's — what's up? What is it, eh? Yes? What you — what you want with me? — what you want — What you trying on, eh? What you trying to do? What is it, eh? What you want — you — you — you . . . Mr. Smart! Mr. Smartie!

You think you're — You think you're — You think you're pretty clever. You think you're all right. . . You do, don't you, Mr. Smartie! Mr. Tight Trousers! Mr. Tight Trousers! Mr. Narrow Trousers! You think you're the cat's — You think you're . . . I'll show you . . . I'll show you, Mr. Tight Trousers. Just you don't come near me, d'you hear? Just you don't come near me — come near me, d'you hear? Come near me! I'll show you, Mr. Tight Trousers! Tight Trousers! Yes! Yes! Come near me! Come near me! Come near me! Come! Come! Come! Come! Come!

> *Tolen laughs and walks away. Nancy moans and collapses. Colin somehow catches her as she falls.*

COLIN

She's fainted!

TOM

Lucky there was someone to catch her.

Act three

> *Before the curtain rises there is a loud banging and crashing, mixed with shouts and cries.*
> *Curtain up.*
> *Colin is holding Nancy like a sack of potatoes. Tom and Tolen are just finishing putting up the bed.*

TOM

Give it a bash! And so — oops! A bedmaker, that's you, Tolen, a master bedwright. O.K. Has she come round yet?

COLIN

Come round?

TOM

Is she still out?

COLIN

Out?

TOM

Oh, he's a thick one. This way.

COLIN

I'm not thick, she's heavy.

TOM

Don't drop her. Now we've got this out of the passage, Tolen, you can go upstairs to bed. We'll put her here to rest. Sling her over . . . Not like that!

COLIN

You said sling.

TOM

She's in a faint, fainted, can't defend herself.

> *They get Nancy on the bed.*

NANCY

Oh . . . oh, dear . . . oh, dear . . . I do feel . . . I think I'm going to be—

TOM

Sick?

> *Nancy nods.*

Not here.

Colin holds out bucket. Tom dashes to door and opens it.

Bathroom.

Exit Nancy followed by Tom. Pause. Tolen goes to door. Opens it and listens a moment, then closes door and bolts it.

COLIN

What are you doing?

TOLEN

I don't want to be interrupted, Colin. I have something I wish to discuss with you.

COLIN

Oh, I see . . . But this is Tom's room.

TOLEN

This is your room, Colin, your room. You are the landlord. The house belongs to you. It's for you to say whose room this is, Colin. Who lives here.

COLIN

Oh, yes — er —

TOLEN

There is something I would like to discuss with you, Colin. An idea I had.

COLIN

Oh?

TOLEN

You know that you need help, Colin. You do know that, don't you?

COLIN

Mm.

TOLEN

Now tell me, Colin, how many women have you had?

COLIN

Mm . . .

TOLEN

Two women. Only two. And you were late starting, weren't you, Colin? Very late. Not until last year. And Carol left you how many months ago?

COLIN

Mm . . .

TOLEN

Six months ago. That's right, isn't it. Two women in two years. Some of us have more women in two days. I have a suggestion to make to you, Colin. A suggestion which you will find very interesting and which will help you very much. (*Pause.*) Now as you know, Colin, I have a number of friends. *Men.* And they can help you, Colin, as I can help you. I am thinking particularly of Rory McBride.

COLIN

Oh.

TOLEN

Rory McBride is a man, Colin, a clever man, a gifted man, a man I can respect. He knows a great many things, Colin. Rory McBride was doing things at thirteen that you haven't ever done, Colin; things that you don't even know about.

COLIN

What sort of things?

TOLEN

In a moment, Colin. First I will tell you my suggestion. Now, as you know, I have a number of regular women, Colin. Women I regularly make. And Rory McBride has a number of regular women too. Perhaps not quite as many as I have, but several. Now. Quite recently, Rory and I were talking—comparing notes—and we decided it would be a good idea if we saw each other more often . . . if even we were to live near each other.

COLIN

Oh?

TOLEN

Yes, Colin . . . perhaps in the same house . . . and that we would share our women.

COLIN

Oh!

TOLEN

After I have had a woman, Rory can have her, and if I want I can have Rory's. Of course Rory realizes that it may, in a sense, be dangerous for him. He may lose a few of his women. However, Rory is well aware that, in the long run, he will profit by the arrangement; he will learn much, Colin, from the women who have been with me.

COLIN (*Agreeing.*)

Mm.

TOLEN

Now this is the suggestion I have to make. I would consider allowing you to come in on this arrangement.

COLIN

Oh!

TOLEN

Yes, Colin. I would allow you to come in with Rory and me, share our women. I think you would learn a great deal, Colin.

COLIN

Oh, yes.

TOLEN

It would be a privilege for you, a great privilege.

COLIN

Oh, yes, I see that.

TOLEN

I'm sure Rory will, he will agree. (*Pause.*) Now agree to this, Colin. I will ask him.

COLIN

Do you think he will?

TOLEN

If I ask him, Colin, he will agree. (*Pause.*) Now what I suggest, Colin, is that Rory moves into this house.

COLIN

Mm?

TOLEN

In here.

COLIN

Oh . . .

TOLEN

What's the matter, Colin?

COLIN

But there's no room. There's you and me and —

TOLEN

There is this room, Colin. The room you let to Tom. (*Pause.*) Remember this is your room. You are the landlord. Rory could have this room and . . .

Tom yells, off, and bangs door.

Rory McBride has a Chinese girl, Colin, slinky, very nice, do very well for you.

COLIN

Chinese?

TOLEN

It's only a question of experience. Of course you'll never be quite so —

COLIN

Good as —

TOLEN

Me, but —

COLIN

But still —

TOLEN

Oh, yes, I don't doubt —

COLIN

You really think —

TOLEN

Certainly!

COLIN

Chinese!

Enter Tom through window.

TOM

What the hell d'you think you're doing? Why d'you bloody lock the door, Tolen? You bloody remember this is my room.

He unbolts door.

TOLEN

Oh, no, Tom, this is Colin's room.

TOM

Eh? What's going on here?

Small crash upstairs. Yelling.

Stop that. What the hell's she up to now? Where's her bag? She wants her bleeding bag. I tell you she's gone bloody funny like a bleeding windmill.

Cry off. Tolen crosses the room.

TOLEN

Can you not control your women, Tom?

Exit Tom. Tolen crosses the room again.

And a German girl.

COLIN

German!

Colin crosses the room imitating Tolen.

TOLEN

Hold your head up, Colin. Head up! Don't stick your chin out. Keep your belly in. Bend your arms slightly at the elbows — not quite so — that's better. They should swing freely from your shoulders. . . .

Not both together! Keep your head up! Move! Move! Move! Move! Feel it coming from your shoulders, Colin, from your chest! From your gut! From your loin! More loin! More gut, man! Loin! Loin! Move! Move! Move! Move! Keep your head up! Authority, Colin! Feel it rippling through you! Authority! Keep your head up! Authority! Authority!

COLIN

Authority.

TOLEN

Authority! Move! Move! Move! Move! Authority!

TOM (*Off.*)

You can have a cup of tea and . . .

NANCY (*Off.*)

Tea!

TOM (*Off.*)

Tea.

NANCY (*Off.*)

I won't touch it.

> *Enter Nancy wrapped in a blanket.*

TOM (*Entering.*)

For God's sake make her some tea.

NANCY

I won't touch it. What's that?

TOM

What's what?

NANCY

That.

TOM

We've lugged this thing in here so you can lie down. Now lie down.

NANCY

I never asked you to bring it in.

TOM

You —

NANCY

Don't swear.

> *Colin walks about the stage.*

You're not getting me on that thing again, I tell you. Putting that thing together again to tempt a girl. Hiding it up passages. Stuffing it here and there. What d'you think I am? Eh? Eh? Don't you hear? Can't you hear what I say?

> *Nancy bares her teeth and growls at Colin. He is momentarily disconcerted then ignores her and struts up and down again.*

An open invitation if you ask me. Ask me! Go on, ask me! Well, somebody ask me . . . please . . . (*Pause.*) A nasty situation. Dear me, yes. Very nasty, a particularly vicious sense of — criminal, yes, that's it — positively criminal. They ought to be told, somebody should — I shall phone them, phone them — the police, Scotland Yard, Whitehall one two one two (*She catches sight of Colin walking up and down.*) one two one two.

> *She repeats "one two one two" as often as necessary. Colin picks up the rhythm and they begin to work each other up. Nancy starts to bang the rhythm. Colin stamps about and slaps himself until eventually he hurts himself. Nancy is temporarily assuaged.*

TOM
> That's an interesting movement you've got there, Colin.

COLIN
> Oh, d'you think so?

TOM
> Very interesting.

COLIN
> Tolen taught it me.

TOM
> Oh, yes?

COLIN
> It's got authority.

TOM
> Come again?

COLIN
> Authority.

TOM
> Ah. Let's see it again . . . ah.
> *Colin demonstrates, then Tom has a go.*

COLIN
> You've got to walk from your gut.

TOM
> Eh?

COLIN
> Your gut.

TOM
> Oh, I see. I see, I see. Bucket!

COLIN
> Eh?

TOM
> For a helmet. Bucket! Bucket! Jump to it! Don't keep me waiting. Bucket!

COLIN
> Oh.
> *Colin jumps for the bucket, offers it to Tom who puts it on Colin's head.*

TOM
> Now I'll show you what authority's really, Colin. Much more impressive than a carrier—a helmet. Dominating, brutal. (*Tom starts banging a 4/4 rhythm and singing the "Horst Wessel."* [1]) Ra ra ra ra, ra ra ra ra, march! March! March! March! Get on with it! Ra ra ra ra.
> *Nancy picks up the 4/4 rhythm and the tune.*
> March! Damn you! March! Jams, guns, guts, butter! Jams, guns, guts, butter! Boots! Boots! Boots! Boots! Boots for crushing! Boots for smashing! Sieg heil! Sieg heil! Ha!
> *Colin gets rid of the bucket.*
> What's the matter? What's up? Don't you like it? I thought you loved it. Tolen loves it, don't you, Tolen? Tolen loves it.

COLIN
> Tolen doesn't do that.

---

[1] The strongly marked emotional march that was the anthem of the young Nazi movement, the *Hitler-Jugend.* EDS.

TOM
> Not so loud maybe, but the same general idea. I think it's funnier louder, don't you, Tolen?

COLIN
> Shut up.

TOM
> Just look at Tolen's boots.
> > *Pause. Nancy jumps up and down.*

NANCY
> Grrr.

TOM (*Disregarding Nancy and speaking to Tolen.*)
> When I die I could be reincarnated as a sea anemone. It doesn't affect my attitude to death one little bit but it does affect my attitude to sea anemones. A sea anemone with a crew cut would starve to death. (*Pause.*) Your ears are going red. They're pulsating red and blue. No, I'm exaggerating. One is, anyway. The one nearest me. (*Pause.*) That white horse you see in the park could be a zebra synchronized with the railings.
> > *Tolen moves away. Tom looks very pleased.*

NANCY
> I wouldn't touch it if you made it.

TOM
> Eh?

NANCY
> I wouldn't.

TOM
> Made what?

NANCY
> Tea.

TOM (*To Colin.*)
> You'd better make some.

COLIN (*Disgruntled.*)
> Oh.

TOM
> Shall I tell you a story? (*Exit Colin.*) I know you'd like to hear about the kangaroo — the kangaroo. You heard me. Did you? Now of course you know that the baby kangaroo lives in its mother's pouch. Don't you? Go on, commit yourself.

NANCY
> Oh, all right.

TOM
> Don't be so cautious. This one is true and pure. All my stories are true unless I say so. Well, the baby kangaroo is born about two inches long and as soon as it's born it climbs into its mother's pouch — how does it climb? Never mind, it fights its way through the fur . . .
> > *Colin enters balefully and sets down a tray and exits.*
> When it gets inside the pouch the baby kangaroo finds one large, solid nipple. Just one. The baby latches on to this nipple and then it, the nipple, swells and swells and swells until it's shaped something like a door knob in the baby's mouth. And there the baby kangaroo stays for four months, four solid months. What an almighty suck! Isn't that interesting? Doesn't it interest you as a facet of animal

behavior so affecting human behaviour? Doesn't it make you marvel at the vast family of which God made us part? Oh, well . . .
>   *Pause.*

NANCY
>   What happened?

TOM
>   What happened when?

NANCY
>   You know when.

TOM
>   No, I do not.

NANCY
>   You know when.
>   *Enter Colin with teapot. Colin pours out tea in silence. Hands a cup to Tolen, goes with a cup to Nancy.*
>   What's that?

COLIN
>   Eh?

TOM
>   Tea.

NANCY
>   I'm not having any. I'm not touching it. He's put something in it.

COLIN
>   Eh?

TOM
>   Put something in it?

NANCY
>   Oh, yes, he's put something in it.

TOM
>   Don't be so daft.

NANCY
>   I'm not touching it.

TOM
>   But —

NANCY
>   I'm not.

TOM
>   What should he put in it? There's absolutely nothing in it. Nothing at all — look — ugh! — Sugar!
>   *Pause.*

NANCY
>   I like sugar.

COLIN
>   Two.

NANCY
>   What?

COLIN
>   Two lumps.

NANCY
>   I take two.

COLIN
>   I know.
>   *Pause. Nancy takes the tea and drinks. Long pause.*

NANCY

I've been raped. (*Pause.*) I have.

TOLEN

I beg your pardon.

NANCY

You heard.

COLIN

I didn't.

NANCY

I've been raped.
> *Tolen sneers audibly.*

COLIN

What!

NANCY

I have been—it was just after—when I fainted—there by the—before I went up with—when I fainted. I was raped.
> *Tolen sneers.*

COLIN

When she says—

NANCY

I have been, you did—

COLIN

Does she mean really—I mean, actually?

TOM

What else?

NANCY

Rape. Rape. I—I've been—

COLIN

But—

NANCY

Raped.

COLIN

But you haven't.

NANCY

I have.

COLIN

No one has—

NANCY

Rape.

COLIN

But we've been here all the time, all of us.

NANCY

Huh!

COLIN

You know we have.

TOLEN

A vivid imagination, that's what's the matter with her.

NANCY

Eh?

COLIN

Oh?

TOM

Watch it.

TOLEN
>Take no notice of her.

NANCY
>Eh?

TOLEN
>Ignore her.

NANCY
>What? Rape?

TOM
>You be careful, Tolen.

NANCY
>Rape! I've been—

TOLEN
>She quite simply wishes to draw attention to herself.

NANCY (*A little unsure.*)
>Oh?

TOLEN
>She has fabricated a fantasy that we have raped her. First because she wants us to take notice of her and second because she really would like to be raped.

NANCY
>Eh?

COLIN
>Would you mind saying that again?

TOLEN
>Her saying that we have raped her is a fantasy. She has fabricated this fantasy because she really does want to be raped; she wants to be the centre of attention. The two aims are, in a sense, identical. The fabrication that we have raped her satisfactorily serves both purposes.

COLIN
>Oh.

NANCY
>What's that word mean? Fabricated?

TOLEN
>Made it up.

NANCY (*A bit nonplussed.*)
>Oh, no. Oh, no. Not that. I know, oh, yes. I'm not having that sort of—I know, oh, yes. I'm the one that knows. You've had your fun and—and—there! It was there! You've had your fun and now I feel funny, queer, sick. I know, you're not coping with a—I'm not a fool, you know—I'm not a ninny. . . . No, no. I didn't make it up . . . fabricated . . . fabricated . . . fabricated . . .

TOM (*To Tolen.*)
>What'll you do if she tells everyone you raped her?

TOLEN
>What?

TOM
>There's a Methodist minister lives two doors down. Suppose she was to yell out of the window? By God, you'd look silly, you'd look right foolish. I'd give a lot to see that.

TOLEN
>Are you mad?

TOM (*To Nancy.*)
> Don't let him off so easily, love.

NANCY
> Eh?

TOM (*To Tolen.*)
> What'll you do if she yells down the street?

NANCY
> Rape! They done me! Rape! You done me! You did! Rape! Rape!
> Rape! Rape! Rape! (*At window.*) Rape! (*Etc., as necessary.*)

TOLEN
> Shut the window.
>> *Tolen goes for Nancy.*

NANCY
> Rape!
>> *Tolen gets her neatly under control and keeps his hand over her mouth.*

TOM
> Try and keep your dignity on that one.

COLIN
> Mind she doesn't bite.

TOLEN
> Shut the window.
>> *Colin shuts the window. Tolen releases Nancy.*

NANCY
> You don't want me yelling down the street, do you?

TOLEN
> We don't want the trivial inconvenience.

NANCY
> You're scared they'll hear and lock you up.

TOLEN
> I do not intend to expose myself to trivial indignities from petty of-
> ficials.

NANCY
> You're worried. You're scared. You're afraid. I'll tell. I will tell!

COLIN
> Eh?

NANCY
> The police. The Y.W. I'll report you. That's it. The lot. Them all. I'll
> tell them how you raped me—how you—I'll tell them. The coppers.
> The Y.W.

TOM
> Whew!

NANCY
> All the lurid details! All the horrid facts! *News of the World.* TV. Read
> all about it! Rape! Rape! Just you wait! You'll get ten years for this!

TOM
> She means it.

TOLEN
> She's simply drawing attention to herself.

COLIN
> Means what?

TOM
> She means to tell everyone we raped her. Right. (*Putting Tolen on the
> spot.*) In that case he must rape her.

COLIN
> Eh?

TOLEN
> I beg your pardon?

TOM
> In that case she must be raped by him.

NANCY
> I'm not having it twice.

TOM
> You want her to keep quiet.

TOLEN
> I do not propose to allow her to expose . . .

TOM (*Cutting him short.*)
> Right. You say she's made this up because she really does want to be raped.

COLIN
> Well?

TOM
> If he wants to keep her quiet he must rape her. According to what he says—and he's probably right—that's the only thing will satisfy her.

COLIN
> If she's raped she'll be the centre of attention, that's it!

TOM
> Just so. What do you say?
>
> *The men are talking about Nancy but, in a sense, have forgotten her. She is resentful.*

NANCY
> Rape!

TOM
> What do you say, Tolen?
>
> *Pause.*

TOLEN
> It's your idea. Why don't you rape her?

TOM
> I like her yelling down the street.
>
> *Pause.*

TOLEN
> Colin?

COLIN
> What, me? Oh no. I couldn't.
>
> *Pause.*

NANCY
> Rape!

TOLEN
> I never yet came to a woman under duress and certainly never because I was forced to it. Because she demanded it. Because I had to buy her silence. I shall not now.
>
> *Nancy explodes round the room.*

NANCY
> Ray! Ray! Ray! Ray! Ray!
>
> *Continue as long as necessary.*

COLIN
> Stop her!

TOLEN
> Don't let her—

TOM
> Whoops! Whoops!

TOLEN
> Near the—

COLIN
> What eh?

TOLEN
> Shut the door!

COLIN
> Ow!

TOLEN
> —door!

TOM
> Door? Door?

COLIN
> Door?
>> *A chase. Finally Nancy exits down left by mistake. Colin slams door and bolts it.*

TOLEN
> The front. The front door. She'll get out the front. Colin!
>> *Exit Colin through window. Banging, off, at front door. Reenter Colin.*

COLIN
> No, she won't. It's blocked.
>> *Pause.*

TOM
> She smashed up the bathroom. She might—
>> *Pause.*

TOLEN
> My records!
>> *Tolen throws himself on the door. Enter Nancy barefoot. She wears her pleated skirt thus: her right arm through the placket, the waist band running over her right shoulder and under her left arm. She carries her underclothes, which she scatters gaily.*

NANCY
> Shove you in jug! Put you in jail! One for the road! Long for a stretch! Just you wait! I'll tell!
>> *Pause.*

TOM
> That's not how a skirt is usually worn, still it's bigger than a bathing costume.

COLIN
> It's not a bathing costume.

NANCY
> I shall sue you for paternity.

TOM
> Now listen, Nancy.

NANCY
> All of you.

TOM

Nancy.

NANCY

Don't Nancy me.

TOM (*Nancy ad libs through speech.*)

Look, love—don't say anything for a minute. Now look, we haven't raped you—but—just a moment—Now listen, everything's happening so fast you must give us a chance to think. I mean you're a reasonable girl, Nancy, an intelligent girl, give us a chance now, just give us a chance like a reasonable, rational, intelligent girl, just let us talk for one moment. No yelling and no dashing off anywhere.

NANCY

It's a trap.

TOM

No, it isn't. I promise. It's pax for one minute.

NANCY

All right. I'll give you one minute.

TOM

That's not enough.

NANCY

Two minutes.

TOM

Five.

NANCY

Three.

TOM

Done.

NANCY

Three minutes and no more. Then I'll start yelling again. Lend me a wristwatch.

TOM

Oh, very well. Colin!

NANCY

And if you're naughty and cheat I can smash it.

COLIN

Oh, I say—

TOM

Oh, come on, Colin.

Colin hands over his watch. Nancy climbs step ladder.

[*Author's note: the following scene falls into four sections. 1st section: Introduction to the scene: The three confer.*]

TOM

Now, Tolen.

TOLEN

The situation is quite clear.

COLIN

Not to me it isn't.

TOM

You've got to rape her.

TOLEN

Please be quiet, Tom.

NANCY (*While the others confer.*)

I've been raped, I've been raped, I've been raped, raped, raped, I've been raped, I've been raped, I've been raped. I've been raped, I've been raped, I've been raped, raped, raped, I've been raped, I've been raped, I've been raped.

TOM

Oh, go on.

TOLEN

An impasse has been reached.

COLIN

She believes we've raped her.

TOM

She's convinced herself.

TOLEN

She's made it up to draw attention to herself and because she wants it.

TOM

She is prepared to report us.

COLIN

Yes, yes.

TOM

Tolen doesn't want that.

COLIN

No, no.

TOM

But he's not prepared to do the other thing.

COLIN

What are we going to do?

Pause.

TOLEN

She must be examined by a competent physician.

COLIN

What?

TOLEN

A doctor. If she's a virgin—

TOM

Not interfered with—

TOLEN

That lets us out!

COLIN

What if she's not?

Pause.

TOM

If she's not a virgin she could say we raped her and we'd have a job to prove otherwise.

TOLEN

She must be a virgin.

TOM

Why should she be?

TOLEN

Well, take a look at her.

NANCY

Two minutes gone. One minute to go.

TOLEN

Obviously a virgin.

TOM

I don't see why, it doesn't necessarily follow.

COLIN

Follow what?

NANCY

Finished?

TOM

No.

NANCY

Ninety seconds to go.

COLIN

Mind the watch.

NANCY

Rape!

TOLEN

Don't get so excited, Colin.

COLIN

It's my watch.

> [*2nd section: Tom begins to enjoy the humour of the situation, and states his attitude; so that Tolen also states his attitude.*]

TOM

Since you take this attitude, there seems no rational course other than to negotiate. Open negotiation.

TOLEN

Negotiate!

TOM

Negotiate.

TOLEN

Negotiate with a woman? Never.

TOM

Then what is your suggestion?

TOLEN

Authority.

COLIN

Oh?

TOLEN

Authority.

COLIN

Ah!

TOLEN

In all his dealings with women a man must act with promptness and authority—even, if need be, force.

COLIN

Force?

TOM

Force?

TOLEN

Force.

[*3rd section: Colin decides that Tolen's attitude is correct.*]

TOM
> I cannot agree to force and certainly not to brutality.

TOLEN
> Never negotiate.

TOM
> Calm, calmth.

NANCY
> Sixty seconds.

TOLEN
> Force.

TOM
> Negotiate. Parley, parley.

TOLEN
> Negotiate with a woman—

TOM
> Calm.

TOLEN
> Never! Force!

COLIN
> He's—

TOLEN
> Force. Force.

COLIN
> For—

TOM
> Calm, calm, calmth.

TOLEN
> Force, force. Never negotiate.

COLIN
> For—for—

TOM
> No brutality!

COLIN
> Force!

TOLEN
> Never negotiate! Eh?

COLIN
> Force! Force!

TOM
> Oh!

COLIN
> Force! Force! In dealing with a w-w-w-w—

NANCY
> Forty seconds to go!

COLIN
> —w-woman a man must act with promptness and authority.

TOLEN
> Force.

COLIN
> Force.

[4th section: Colin is precipitated into a forceful course of action.]

TOM
>Parley, negotiate.

TOLEN
>Authority.

TOM
>Parley.

TOLEN
>Force.

COLIN
>Force.

TOM
>No, no, parley, parley!

COLIN
>Force.

TOLEN
>Force.

NANCY
>Twenty.

TOM
>Parley, parley.

TOLEN
>No, no. Force.

COLIN
>For! For! For! He's right!

NANCY
>Ten seconds to go.

COLIN
>Force.

>>*The following should tumble across each other as the excitement mounts.*

TOLEN
>Force.

TOM
>Parley.

NANCY
>Eight.

COLIN
>Force.

TOLEN
>Never negotiate.

TOM
>Calm.

COLIN
>He's right, he's absolutely—

TOLEN
>Force.

NANCY
>Four.

COLIN
>A man—

NANCY
>Three.

COLIN
>Must—

NANCY
>Two.

COLIN
>Use—

NANCY
>One.

COLIN
>Force. (*Slight pause.*) Shut up! Just you shut your—d'you hear!
>You're talking through your—Firmness! A firm hand! Spanking! See
>who's—I've been here all the time, d'you hear? All the time. You've
>not been raped. You have not. I know. So stop squawking. I know.
>I've been here all the time.

NANCY
>Ah.

COLIN
>I've been here all the time. So I can prove, prove, testify. I have seen
>nothing. You've not been raped. I know. I've been here all the time.

NANCY
>Ah.

COLIN
>Come on down now and get them on. Get your clothes on. Come
>down, come down, you silly little . . . little messer. You've not been
>raped, I know. I've been here all the time.

NANCY
>You!

COLIN
>I've been here all the time!

NANCY
>You did it! It was you!

COLIN
>I been here . . . eh?

NANCY
>You! You! You! You! He's it! He did it! He raped me! He's been
>here all the time! He says so! He has! He did it! Yes, he raped me!

COLIN
>Me!

NANCY
>You.

TOM
>Him!

COLIN
>Me!

NANCY
>Yes, you. You been here all the time.

TOM
>You, she says. She says you did it.

COLIN
>Me.

NANCY
>Yes. You'll get ten years.

COLIN
Me, me? Me! Oh no. This is awful. You're making a terrible mistake.

NANCY
Oh, no, not likely.

COLIN
Oh, no, you are—tell her someone. Someone, Tolen, tell—her I didn't. No, really, I mean—

NANCY
I got a head on my shoulders.

COLIN
I can see that but—

NANCY
That's it, you. You raped me.

COLIN
But—but I assure you—I mean—

NANCY
That's him, officer, that's the one.

COLIN
No! Tolen—Tom—please. I mean I didn't, really, I didn't.

NANCY
Clothes!

COLIN
Clothes?

NANCY
Tore them off me.

COLIN
Tore the—oh, no.

NANCY
Scattered.

COLIN
No.

NANCY
There they are.

TOM
Clear evidence.

NANCY
That face. You'd never know, they'd never guess.

COLIN
Oh, wouldn't they?

NANCY
No girl would ever suspect.

COLIN
Oh?

NANCY
But underneath—

COLIN
What?

NANCY
Raving with lust.

COLIN
Oh, no, I mean—

NANCY
Fangs dripping with blood.

COLIN
Oh.
NANCY
Bones of countless victims hidden in the basement.
COLIN
We haven't got a basement. No! No! I mean I didn't, really I didn't.
I didn't rape you—I mean I wouldn't—but well—this is terrible! Me!
. . . You really think I did?
NANCY
Of course.
COLIN
I mean you really do think I did?
NANCY
Yes.
COLIN
You really do!
NANCY
Wait till next Sunday. What's your job?
COLIN
Eh? I'm a teacher.
NANCY
Schoolteacher rapes—rapes—rapes—Nancy Jones!
COLIN
Oh!
NANCY
Little did the pupils at—at—
COLIN
Tottenham Secondary Modern—
NANCY
Tottenham Secondary Modern realize that beneath the handsome
exterior of their tall, fair-haired, blue-eyed schoolteacher there
lurked the heart of a beast, lusting for the blood of innocent
virgins—little did they—You wait till you see the *Sunday Pictorial*.
COLIN
Oh, I say, me. Me. Me. Oh I say. Oh. Oh. Do you really think—?
NANCY
What?
COLIN
I've got a handsome exterior?
NANCY
Well—rugged perhaps, rather than handsome. And strong.
COLIN
Oh.
NANCY
Oh, yes, ever so. And lovely hands.
COLIN
Oh. Oh. Oh. . . . Are you—are you doing anything tonight?
NANCY
What?
COLIN
Are you doing anything tonight?
NANCY
Oh!

COLIN

Oh, please, I didn't mean that. I mean I didn't rape you, anyway, I mean, oh, well. Look, I mean let's go to the pictures or something or a walk or a drink or anything you please. I think you're simply—I mean—Oh, golly—do you really think I did? I mean I didn't rape you but I would like to—I mean, I would like to take you to the pictures or something.

NANCY

Well, I don't know, it doesn't seem quite—I mean after—

COLIN

Oh, please—

NANCY

Well—

COLIN

The pictures or anything.

NANCY

Would you?

COLIN

Oh, yes, I would.

TOLEN

This I find all very amusing.

TOM

I thought you might.

TOLEN

Hilarious.

TOM

I've always admired your sense of humour.

COLIN

Eh?

TOM

Well done. Very good. You're getting on very nicely, Colin. Much better than the great Tolen.

TOLEN

That sexual incompetent.

COLIN

Eh?

NANCY

He's not incompetent. What's incompetent?

TOM

No good.

NANCY

No good? He's marvellous, he raped me.

TOLEN

You have not been raped.

NANCY

I have.

TOLEN

You have not been raped and you know it.

NANCY

He raped me.

TOLEN

You have not.

NANCY
I have.
TOLEN
And certainly not by—
NANCY
Rape.
TOLEN
Him. He wouldn't know one end of a woman from the other.
NANCY
Rape, rape.
TOLEN
The number of times I've seen him. "Has Cardiff got big docks?"
He'll never make it, never.
COLIN
What?
TOLEN
Granted—
COLIN
What did you say?
NANCY
He raped me.
TOLEN
Granted he might do better with help—and he needs help. Bow-
legged, spavin-jointed, broken-winded, down and out. Look at him.
COLIN
Eh?
NANCY
He's rugged.
TOLEN
I ask you is it possible—?
NANCY
Handsome.
TOLEN
Or likely—?
NANCY
Marvellous, super.
TOLEN
It takes him four months' hard labour to get a girl to bed.
NANCY
He did, you did, didn't you?
TOLEN
That oaf.
NANCY
Go on, tell him.
COLIN
Hard labour?
TOLEN
You keep out of this.
NANCY
Yes, you shut up.
TOLEN
A rapist, oh, really.

NANCY
> Rape. Rape.

TOLEN
> That chicken.

NANCY
> Rape.

TOLEN
> How stupid can you get? Too ridiculous.

NANCY
> Rape. Rape.

TOLEN
> Probably impotent.
>> *Tom begins to knock a nail into the wall about nine feet above floor
>> level. His banging deliberately punctuates the following.*

COLIN
> Why not?

TOLEN
> What?

COLIN
> Why not me, pray?

NANCY
> Rape. Rape.

COLIN
> Why not me? (*To Tom.*) Be quiet. (*To Tolen.*) Sexually incompetent!
> Hard labour!
>> *Nancy starts to chirrup round the room, Colin while talking at the
>> others follows after her.*

NANCY
> Rape pape pape pape pape pape—
>> *Tom is banging.*

COLIN (*To Tom.*)
> Shut up. (*To Tolen.*) Now you listen—

TOM
> Rape!

NANCY
> R e e e e e e ep.

COLIN
> All, all I can say is out—out—outrage. Outrage. Outrage. (*To Tom.*)
> Shut up. (*To Tolen.*) Rape, rape, didn't I? Couldn't I? I did—I mean
> I could—(*To Tom.*) Shut up. (*To Tolen.*) Now you listen, now get this
> straight—(*To Tom.*) Shut up. (*To Tolen.*) I am not incapable!

NANCY
> Pay pay pay pay pay pay pee pee pee pee pee pee.

COLIN (*To Nancy.*)
> Really, I didn't, really, I wouldn't mind—(*To Tom.*) Shut up, be quiet.
> (*To Nancy.*) I'd love to—I mean. (*To Tom.*) Shut up!
>> *Nancy is now keeping up an almost permanent yelp. Tom starts on an-
>> other nail in another wall.*
> Shut up, shut up. Now get this, get this—get—get—shut up—I
> could've, yes. I could've if I'd wanted—rape her—shut up—I
> didn't—you think I couldn't—shut up—I—I—Shut! Shut! I'll show
> you!

Colin starts to chase Nancy round the room. Tom's banging covers the
chase and stops at the end of it.
Just let me—get her—I'll—I'll show you—I'll—I'll—yes I'll—just you
I'll show—oh—oh—oh—oh—oh—

NANCY
Oh—oh—oh—oh—
A chase with objects.

COLIN
Oh—oh—oh—oh—

NANCY
Oh—oh—oh—oh—

TOLEN
You can't even catch her, Colin, can you? Never mind rape her. I
think you are quite incapable of making a woman, Colin. Look, I'll
show you.

COLIN
If you touch her—I'll kill you!
Very long pause. Tolen releases Nancy who goes to Colin. A girl passes
the window. Tolen laughs gently and then exits through window. Tom
hoists chair on to the nails in the wall.

TOM
Ah, yes, beautiful. (*Tom hoists second chair on to nails.*) Ah, yes.
Exit Tom.

Action analysis and performance suggestions

To see the farcical, improvisational dimensions of *The Knack,* consider either Tolen's interrupted seduction of Nancy in act II (pp. 675–680 to
Tom's exit) or the initial section of Nancy's attack on the three boys in act
III (pp. 689–693, from "I've been raped" to her exit).
Nancy Jones has a common name and no known background, except
that she is provincial; Tom has no last name and no occupation; Colin is a
teacher, but has no last name either; Tolen has no background at all. Like
most characters in farce, these are types brought together to serve the
purposes of fun. While they have personalities—thoughts, feelings, attitudes, special skills ranging from zany artistic talent to a wide knowledge
of biological trivia—they are also archetypal figures: the girl, the boy, the
artist-teacher, and the wolf. Their actions spring in part from their ano-
nymity and universality. The girl like all girls hopes to gain love and some
measure of control; the boy like all boys wants to gain success in love and
thereby a sense of maturity; the artist-teacher wishes to create both art
and knowledge; and the wolf is the devourer, ready to consume all in his
path. When Tolen returns for another try at seducing Nancy near the
end of act II, he begins to succeed until Colin enters and naïvely tries to
thrust himself on them. His presence, and Tom's quick diagnosis of the
situation, prevent Tolen from achieving his goal, and very shortly there-
after Tolen overreaches himself and in rage brings about Nancy's faint.

DEFINING THE ACTIONS AND THE SUPEROBJECTIVE
Nancy's faint at the end of act II leads to her initial sickness and resuscita-
tion in act III. After she has drunk some tea, symbolic of agreeing to

trust the boys a little, she opens the action with an accusation: "I've been raped. (*Pause.*) I have." She seeks to draw their attention to her, to make them focus on her, to take control of the situation. Like Potiphar's wife in Genesis, the woman scorned—here ignored—cries "rape!" But her manner is more like that of the little boy in the fable who cries "wolf!" As she makes her accusations, she improvises so as to adjust her story to their reactions. (The predominant tone of the previous two acts and the manifest absurdity of the accusation assure us that we will not see the three boys dragged into court and prosecuted; they, however, have some anxiety about the situation.) "Take no notice of her," Tolen advises, first trying to shame Nancy, to embarrass her for making the accusation, perhaps even to test her will in sticking to the story. Colin, in his naïve way, believes she means what she says. He tries to confirm the story and the intention, questioning Nancy, Tom, and Tolen, stating the facts of their presence, asking for more information about the charge. At first Tom merely watches and listens, but somewhere before his first series of speeches in which he appears to take Nancy's accusation as a serious one directed at Tolen, he decides to use the accusation to separate Tolen and Nancy in order to bring Nancy and Colin together.

In pursuing her action Nancy decides that verbal violence and physical action will help to gain control over the boys, particularly after Tolen's cool exterior presents a challenge. She tries to get their attention by shouting, singing, stomping, clapping, and so on. Tom cleverly assumes that Nancy is directing her accusation at Tolen and is able to put the burden on Tolen. Tolen resorts to physical force. He must try to restrain Nancy even at the cost of dropping his controlled appearance.

And then a curious thing happens. As the stage direction signalizes, *"The men are talking about Nancy but, in a sense, have forgotten her."* In trying to put Tolen on the spot for his belief that a woman who cries rape really wants to be raped, Tom has drawn the three into a conference. He presses Tolen in order to force him to back up his words with action. Tolen replies in kind, feints away with an excuse, and Nancy, sensing that she is losing control, uses the opportunity to force them to pursue her by fleeing. She evades them in the chase, but by accident runs into a cul de sac off-stage, her eventual triumph held in abeyance.

Even in this fast and furious scene of sparring the superobjective is relatively clear. Nancy tries to find the knack of drawing all attention to herself; Tolen attempts to exercise the knack of dominating women; Colin tries to understand and to gain the knack of winning the games of sexual conquest; and Tom observes, then attacks Tolen in an effort to help Colin develop the knack of offering love freely, openly, instinctively. Appropriate coupling is everyone's object; to develop the knack is everyone's action, except that the definitions of the "knack" vary so greatly.

OVERCOMING OBSTACLES

Nancy faces dwindling interest. She has been the object of attention and care since she entered the house. Now she realizes that the boys have considered her a pawn in some game she instinctively, but not consciously, understands is to her disadvantage. Her obstacle is their mutual antagonism and self-concern, and she must find a way to neutralize these and make them refocus their concern on her. As in all his relationships with women, Tolen sees only an object to be controlled. This object—a woman who at first sounds calculating but then quickly sounds hysterical—must be controlled. That is the major obstacle he recognizes. To Tolen, Tom's taunting is another obstacle, and he can find no effective way to overcome his clever housemate. Colin is puzzled and wonders what is happening. He needs more information to judge the situation; hence, he seeks it from all quarters. His real obstacle is his ignorance of people, particularly girls. In this scene he cannot overcome that obstacle, but must continue to flail in every direction except the one Tom would advise. Tom realizes Colin's ignorance and Tolen's aggression, which he must overcome in order to place Colin in an advantageous position. Colin's intellectuality, which might prevent Tom's getting him to react with warmth and concern, and his caution against further involvement are Tom's obstacles. He makes inroads on the first and overcomes the second, and at the end of the scene Tolen is the principal obstacle still in Tom's path. Because Tolen cannot understand Nancy's real, instinctual attraction to Colin he removes himself by so angering the girl that she will offer herself to Colin.

THE MAGIC IF AND THE GIVEN CIRCUMSTANCES

Three boys to whom you are mildly attracted have badly frightened you, and although you really do not think they are malicious, you cannot be sure that they might not become so. More particularly, IF they ignore you, your object of gaining their attention and perhaps their affection will be lost. What IF you had to find a way to take control over them?

What IF, after many successful seductions, you encountered a girl whom you were sure you could seduce but whom your roommates were protecting? What IF she tried a new approach, accusing you of rape, to gain the upper hand?

What IF you wanted the reputation of a smooth, successful, masculine seducer, but didn't have the technique necessary to acquire the girls? What IF your habitual approach to most of life's problems was intellectual analysis, and something completely absurd—like a girl's accusing you of rape—happened?

What IF you wished to help your sensitive, insecure friend gain a sense of his own worth as a sexual being? What IF another friend, aggressively masculine and selfishly sexual, stood in the path of your efforts to help your first friend? How could you use a not-so-innocent girl's attempt to galvanize attention on herself by a cry of "rape!" to your advantage?

All four are young people, all four particularly British. (Most American readers will miss the significance of their backgrounds. Britain is still a class society. Nancy is provincial and quite uneducated; Tolen has no particular education, though his vocabulary suggests some intelligence and training; Tom's knowledge of things biological points to some education; Colin's position as a schoolteacher argues for a fair education. They are lower-middle-class young people, that is, "average" in a fashion quite different from that of American college youth.) The game of sexual fencing that they play is ritualized by habits unlike American college life's fraternity/sorority mixers and bounded by social horizons more tightly defined than in America, where the dream of social and economic upward mobility is still believed by many. And yet they're like young people everywhere, intensely interested in sex, intensely desirous of proving sexual competence, and far more likely to succeed if they rely on intuition rather than intellectual instruction. Tolen, believing though he does in some predatory, systematized, time-table-measured sexuality, is right when he speaks of the knack as inborn. Only he's got the wrong one.

CLASSROOM ADAPTATIONS TO ARRIVE AT STYLE

"The acting area should be as close to the audience as possible," directs Jellicoe at the beginning of the play. Play the scene with the audience on three sides if possible. The actors do not address the audience. No properties and little furniture beyond a couple of chairs and perhaps something made to look like a bed are neccessary. (A ladder is possible.) There must be physical obstacles for the actors to run around. Nancy should make use of the chairs or other objects in trying to get away from the boys when they chase her. Costuming can be informal, except that some attempt should be made to differentiate the three boys from one another. Tolen should be dressed with a great deal of attention to his sexual attractiveness ("Mr. Tight Trousers," Nancy once calls him); Tom could be garbed in an arty fashion; and Colin could wear slightly more formal clothes (white shirt, dark pants).

Farce is less time-bound than high comedy like *Love for Love.* It is less culture-bound as well. The universality of the given circumstances suggests an adaptation to whatever classroom it appears in, but the play's stylistic effect will depend in part on the sexual attitudes and inhibitions of those watching and participating. Jellicoe has written that the stylistic effect of the play will vary greatly with the experiences of the audience. In initial performances, *The Knack* seemed hilarious to its author when it appeared before a Cambridge University audience, slightly obscene before a staid, elderly Bath audience, innocent before a sophisticated London audience (Ann Jellicoe, *Shelley or The Idealist,* p. 14).

To maximize the farcical effects of the scenes, try to take the real and exaggerate it physically. Although the actors must not make an effort to be funny, they must carry their actions to extremes. In crying "rape" and trying to get the boys' attention, Nancy might stand on a chair, or pile one chair on top of another and climb to the top. She could stomp or pound the walls or pull at the boys' clothing. She could accompany her chant of "rape" with clapping and dancing. The boys might ignore her disdainfully by making a football-like huddle as far away from her as possible, which she then might try to penetrate. In running from them, Nancy could crawl under a table, thrust chairs in their path, climb up and over the imaginary bed, try to open a window, push one boy into another. Almost anything goes in "a play that should be full of joy, innocence and zest" (Ann Jellicoe, *Shelley or The Idealist,* p. 13).

Harold Pinter
A Slight Ache

EDWARD

It's quite absurd, of course. I really can't tolerate something so . . . absurd, right on my doorstep. I shall not tolerate it.

(page 722)

The British middle-aged and upper-middle-class Edward complains to his British middle-aged and upper-middle-class wife Flora about the matchseller who has been haunting the back gate of their country home for two months. The matchseller makes no attempt to sell matches, stands wordlessly through heat and storm, and is always present when the couple get up in the morning. Edward believes that the man is an impostor who must be exposed. "I intend to get to the bottom of it," he vows. "I'll soon get rid of him. He can go and ply his trade somewhere else. Instead of standing like a bullock . . . a bullock outside my back gate."

But it is Edward, not the matchseller, who is gotten rid of by the end of Pinter's one-act play, and neither Edward nor the audience ever gets "to the bottom of it" as he proposes. No realistic explanation is given either of the matchseller's appearance or of his usurping Edward's position in his household. Edward cannot tolerate anything so absurd on his doorstep, but the audience is in effect left with that absurdity on theirs.

Although Harold Pinter (1930–   ) does not align himself with any school of playwrights, he is considered the foremost English practitioner of what critic Martin Esslin has designated as the "theater of the absurd." Concerned with the dramatization of the dilemmas of post–World War II society lost in a senseless universe in which all former certainties and values have been called into question, the absurdists seem to share an experimental, antirealistic approach to the absurdities of human existence. This approach differentiates them from such playwrights as Jean Paul Sartre or Albert Camus, who also deal with the existential anguish of individuals out of harmony with their world and themselves, but who still retain the discursive, logical playwriting methods that the absurdists have given up. The technique of an absurdist play shocks our apprehension of reality, stimulates our feeling of non- or irrationality. Thus, in Eugene Ionesco's *Rhinoceros,* people turn into rhinoceroses until only one character is left with the burden of humanity. Or in Samuel Beckett's *Happy Days,* a woman, who is buried in a mound of dirt up to her waist in the first act and up to her neck in the second, counts her blessings, while we are given no explanation either for her burial or for her husband's failure to dig her out. And in *A Slight Ache,* an ugly, stinking matchseller, who never speaks a word or makes an aggressive move, wins the lady and the household of the inexplicably dying Edward.

The absurdists, who experiment with antirealistic forms to explore the anguish of a world that no longer makes sense, invariably mix the comic with the tragic in their dramatic works. The effect on our expectations often creates what Elder Olson has called "suspense of form" (*The Theory of Comedy*, p. 122). The author at first leads us to expect an essentially comic form, which he subsequently infuses with tragic or melodramatic implications; other times he may lead us to believe we are viewing the serious actions of a tragedy, only to reverse those expectations through comic techniques and devices. While the absurd is always at the doorstep, and is often invited in, the protagonists who confront it are not the heroes of ancient tragedy but the tragicomic descendants of Ibsen's and Chekhov's antiheroes. As victims of a senseless universe whose absurdity they can see derives partly from lack of a clear relationship between cause and effect, they inevitably take up their own absurd positions.

Originally produced as a radio play in 1959, *A Slight Ache* is one of Pinter's early "comedies of menace." Although Pinter has denied any significance to his offhand comment that his plays are about "the weasel under the cocktail cabinet," the remark is suggestive, since the realistic surfaces of his plays vibrate with the menace that inevitably erupts to disturb it. The menace is often the threat of dispossession: in Pinter's dramatic world, battles over the possession of a place (*The Room*, 1957; *The Caretaker*, 1960; *The Basement*, 1967) or of a woman (*The Collection*, 1963; *The Homecoming*, 1965; *Old Times*, 1971) often overlap in ways that are both terrifying and comic.

As a child of World War II who grew up in Hackney, a working class area of the East End of London, Pinter experienced much of the menace that he has made a part of his plays. Evacuated twice to the country, the young Pinter was known to open the back door and find his garden in flames. The son of Jewish parents (his father was a tailor), Pinter also suffered from Hackney's anti-Semitic atmosphere. He refused military service as a conscientious objector, studied acting briefly, and in 1949 became a repertory actor under the name of David Baron. Pinter's subsequent lonely existence as a traveling actor living in furnished rooms and seaside boarding houses, plus the endless supplementary jobs that the penurious acting life imposed, also might have contributed to the sense of menace and the theme of dispossession that dominate his plays. His actress wife, Vivien Merchant, has brought many of his heroines to life (for example, Sarah in *The Lover*, Ruth in *The Homecoming*, Anna in *Old Times*) and Pinter, who has written for radio, television, and film as well as for the theater, has continued to direct both his own works and those of others.

Pinter and such other absurdists as the Irish Samuel Beckett, the Roumanian Eugene Ionesco, the French Jean Genet, the German Günter Grass, the Spanish Fernando Arrabal, and the American Edward Albee, make new demands on the audience. Dispensing with conventional storytelling plots and with three-dimensional characters, they tend to explore states of being or reveal patterns. In *The Theatre of the Absurd* Esslin suggests that the plays demand a response similar to that given to abstract painting, sculpture, or poetry.

To a certain extent, the absurdists have been influenced by the actor-playwright-theorist-madman, Antonin Artaud (1896–1948), who felt the audience had to be shocked out of the complacency of a suicidal age. He conceived of theater as an assault on the senses that, like the plague, would bring either death or an extreme purification. Also like Artaud, the absurdists have gone beyond the problem-solving concerns of such play-wrights as Arthur Miller or John Osborne to approach the more mysteri-ous realms so readily accessible to myth and ritual and art. By employ-ing myth and ritual in their dramas and by envisaging the theatrical experience itself as a religious rite, they have attempted to approach an age that no longer has a body of belief. They have tried to restore the theatrical experience to a spiritual level.

But if the absurdists have been influenced by Artaud's theater of cruelty, they have not relegated language to the subsidiary and unimpor-tant position assigned it by Artaud and some of his followers in such per-forming groups as The Living Theater, which creates its dramas largely through improvisational techniques. While the poetry of absurdist drama emerges partly through elements of spectacle—for example, a labyrinth of blankets in Arrabal's *Labyrinth,* men emerging from musical in-struments in Grass's *The Wicked Cooks*—language is still organic. By chang-ing both speech and the pauses and silences that are an essential part of the rhythms of Beckett's and Pinter's dramas, one risks losing the life and meaning of the plays. And revolutionary as the absurdists may seem to be in their redefinition of the other elements of a play, they have drawn heavily on theatrical conventions of the past. Mime, vaudeville crosstalk, mad scenes, verbal nonsense, and all the scenic experiments used by the expressionists to create a subjective and surreal view of reality contribute to the absurdist technique.

Pinter, in fact, considers himself to be quite a traditional playwright in many ways. In *A Slight Ache,* as in the rest of his plays, the fourth-wall convention is retained, the plot is carefully structured, with a clear beginning, middle, and end, and Godot (who never arrives in Samuel Beckett's classic absurdist play *Waiting for Godot*) inevitably appears, bring-ing the irrevocable changes in character, situation, and thought that have been drama's subject matter through the ages.

A Slight Ache

A country house, with two chairs and a table laid for breakfast at the centre of the stage. These will later be removed and the action will be focused on the scullery on the right and the study on the left, both indicated with a minimum of scenery and props. A large well kept garden is suggested at the back of the stage with flower beds, trimmed hedges, etc. The garden gate, which cannot be seen by the audience, is off right. Flora and Edward are discovered sitting at the breakfast table. Edward is reading the paper.

FLORA

Have you noticed the honeysuckle this morning?

EDWARD

The what?

FLORA

The honeysuckle.

EDWARD

Honeysuckle? Where?

FLORA

By the back gate, Edward.

EDWARD

Is that honeysuckle? I thought it was . . . convolvulus, or something.

FLORA

But you know it's honeysuckle.

EDWARD

I tell you I thought it was convolvulus.

> *Pause.*

FLORA

It's in wonderful flower.

EDWARD

I must look.

FLORA

The whole garden's in flower this morning. The clematis. The convolvulus. Everything. I was out at seven. I stood by the pool.

EDWARD

Did you say—that the convolvulus was in flower?

FLORA

Yes.

EDWARD

But good God, you just denied there was any.

FLORA

I was talking about the honeysuckle.

EDWARD

About the what?

FLORA *(Calmly.)*

Edward—you know that shrub outside the toolshed . . .

EDWARD

Yes, yes.

FLORA

That's convolvulus.

EDWARD

That?

FLORA

Yes.

EDWARD

Oh.

Pause.

I thought it was japonica.

FLORA

Oh, good Lord no.

EDWARD

Pass the teapot, please.

Pause. She pours tea for him.

I don't see why I should be expected to distinguish between these plants. It's not my job.

FLORA

You know perfectly well what grows in your garden.

EDWARD

Quite the contrary. It is clear that I don't.

Pause.

FLORA (*Rising.*)

I was up at seven. I stood by the pool. The peace. And everything in flower. The sun was up. You should work in the garden this morning. We could put up the canopy.

EDWARD

The canopy? What for?

FLORA

To shade you from the sun.

EDWARD

Is there a breeze?

FLORA

A light one.

EDWARD

It's very treacherous weather, you know.

Pause.

FLORA

Do you know what today is?

EDWARD

Saturday.

FLORA

It's the longest day of the year.

EDWARD

Really?

FLORA

It's the height of summer today.

EDWARD

Cover the marmalade.

FLORA

What?

EDWARD

Cover the pot. There's a wasp. (*He puts the paper down on the table.*) Don't move. Keep still. What are you doing?

FLORA
> Covering the pot.

EDWARD
> Don't move. Leave it. Keep still.
>> *Pause.*
> Give me the 'Telegraph'.

FLORA
> Don't hit it. It'll bite.

EDWARD
> Bite? What do you mean, bite? Keep still.
>> *Pause.*
> It's landing.

FLORA
> It's going in the pot.

EDWARD
> Give me the lid.

FLORA
> It's in.

EDWARD
> Give me the lid.

FLORA
> I'll do it.

EDWARD
> Give it to me! Now . . . Slowly . . .

FLORA
> What are you doing?

EDWARD
> Be quiet. Slowly . . . carefully . . . on . . . the . . . pot! Ha-ha-ha.
> Very good.
>> *He sits on a chair to the right of the table.*

FLORA
> Now he's in the marmalade.

EDWARD
> Precisely.
>> *Pause. She sits on a chair to the left of the table and reads the 'Tele-*
>> *graph'.*

FLORA
> Can you hear him?

EDWARD
> Hear him?

FLORA
> Buzzing

EDWARD
> Nonsense. How can you hear him? It's an earthenware lid.

FLORA
> He's becoming frantic.

EDWARD
> Rubbish. Take it away from the table.

FLORA
> What shall I do with it?

EDWARD
> Put it in the sink and drown it.

FLORA
>   It'll fly out and bite me.

EDWARD
>   It will not bite you! Wasps don't bite. Anyway, it won't fly out. It's
>   stuck. It'll drown where it is, in the marmalade.

FLORA
>   What a horrible death.

EDWARD
>   On the contrary.
>   *Pause.*

FLORA
>   Have you got something in your eyes?

EDWARD
>   No. Why do you ask?

FLORA
>   You keep clenching them, blinking them.

EDWARD
>   I have a slight ache in them.

FLORA
>   Oh, dear.

EDWARD
>   Yes, a slight ache. As if I hadn't slept.

FLORA
>   Did you sleep, Edward?

EDWARD
>   Of course I slept. Uninterrupted. As always.

FLORA
>   And yet you feel tired.

EDWARD
>   I didn't say I felt tired. I merely said I had a slight ache in my eyes.

FLORA
>   Why is that, then?

EDWARD
>   I really don't know.
>   *Pause.*

FLORA
>   Oh goodness!

EDWARD
>   What is it?

FLORA
>   I can see it. It's trying to come out.

EDWARD
>   How can it?

FLORA
>   Through the hole. It's trying to crawl out, through the spoon-hole.

EDWARD
>   Mmmnn, yes. Can't do it, of course. (*Silent pause.*) Well, let's kill it,
>   for goodness' sake.

FLORA
>   Yes, let's. But how?

EDWARD
>   Bring it out on the spoon and squash it on a plate.

FLORA
    It'll fly away. It'll bite.

EDWARD
    If you don't stop saying that word I shall leave this table.

FLORA
    But wasps do bite.

EDWARD
    They don't bite. They sting. It's snakes . . . that bite.

FLORA
    What about horseflies?
        Pause.

EDWARD (*To himself.*)
    Horseflies suck.
        Pause.

FLORA (*Tentatively.*)
    If we . . . if we wait long enough, I suppose it'll choke to death. It'll
    suffocate in the marmalade.

EDWARD (*Briskly.*)
    You do know I've got work to do this morning, don't you? I can't
    spend the whole day worrying about a wasp.

FLORA
    Well, kill it.

EDWARD
    You want to kill it?

FLORA
    Yes.

EDWARD
    Very well. Pass me the hot water jug.

FLORA
    What are you going to do?

EDWARD
    Scald it. Give it to me.
        She hands him the jug. Pause.
    Now . . .

FLORA (*Whispering.*)
    Do you want me to lift the lid?

EDWARD
    No, no, no. I'll pour down the spoon-hole. Right . . . down the
    spoon-hole.

FLORA
    Listen!

EDWARD
    What?

FLORA
    It's buzzing.

EDWARD
    Vicious creatures.
        Pause.
    Curious, but I don't remember seeing any wasps at all, all summer,
    until now. I'm sure I don't know why. I mean, there must have been
    wasps.

FLORA

Please.

EDWARD

This couldn't be the first wasp, could it?

FLORA

Please.

EDWARD

The first wasp of summer? No. It's not possible.

FLORA

Edward.

EDWARD

Mmmmnnn?

FLORA

Kill it.

EDWARD

Ah, yes. Tilt the pot. Tilt. Aah . . . down here . . . right down . . . blinding him . . . that's . . . it.

FLORA

Is it?

EDWARD

Lift the lid. All right, I will. There he is! Dead. What a monster. (*He squashes it on a plate.*)

FLORA

What an awful experience.

EDWARD

What a beautiful day it is. Beautiful. I think I shall work in the garden this morning. Where's that canopy?

FLORA

It's in the shed.

EDWARD

Yes, we must get it out. My goodness, just look at that sky. Not a cloud. Did you say it was the longest day of the year today?

FLORA

Yes.

EDWARD

Ah, it's a good day. I feel it in my bones. In my muscles. I think I'll stretch my legs in a minute. Down to the pool. My God, look at that flowering shrub over there. Clematis. What a wonderful . . . (*He stops suddenly.*)

FLORA

What?

> Pause.

Edward, what is it?

> Pause.

Edward . . .

EDWARD (*Thickly.*)

He's there.

FLORA

Who?

EDWARD (*Low, murmuring.*)

Blast and damn it, he's there, he's there at the back gate.

FLORA

Let me see.

She moves over to him to look. Pause.

(*Lightly.*) Oh, it's the matchseller.

EDWARD

He's back again.

FLORA

But he's always there.

EDWARD

Why? What is he doing there?

FLORA

But he's never disturbed you, has he? The man's been standing there for weeks. You've never mentioned it.

EDWARD

What is he doing there?

FLORA

He's selling matches, of course.

EDWARD

It's ridiculous. What's the time?

FLORA

Half past nine.

EDWARD

What in God's name is he doing with a tray full of matches at half past nine in the morning?

FLORA

He arrives at seven o'clock.

EDWARD

Seven o'clock?

FLORA

He's always there at seven.

EDWARD

Yes, but you've never . . . actually seen him arrive?

FLORA

No, I . . .

EDWARD

Well, how do you know he's . . . not been standing there all night?

Pause.

FLORA

Do you find him interesting, Edward?

EDWARD (*Casually.*)

Interesting? No. No, I . . . don't find him interesting.

FLORA

He's a very nice old man, really.

EDWARD

You've spoken to him?

FLORA

No. No, I haven't spoken to him. I've nodded.

EDWARD (*Pacing up and down.*)

For two months he's been standing on that spot, do you realize that? Two months. I haven't been able to step outside the back gate.

FLORA

Why on earth not?

EDWARD (*To himself.*)

It used to give me great pleasure, such pleasure, to stroll along through the long grass, out through the back gate, pass into the lane. That pleasure is now denied me. It's my own house, isn't it? It's my own gate.

FLORA

I really can't understand this, Edward.

EDWARD

Damn. And do you know I've never seen him sell one box? Not a box. It's hardly surprising. He's on the wrong road. It's not a road at all. What is it? It's a lane, leading to the monastery. Off everybody's route. Even the monks take a short cut to the village, when they want to go . . . to the village. No one goes up it. Why doesn't he stand on the main road if he wants to sell matches, by the *front* gate? The whole thing's preposterous.

FLORA (*Going over to him.*)

I don't know why you're getting so excited about it. He's a quiet, harmless old man, going about his business. He's quite harmless.

EDWARD

I didn't say he wasn't harmless. Of course he's harmless. How could he be other than harmless?

> *Fade out and silence.*
> *Flora's voice, far in the house, drawing nearer.*

FLORA (*Off.*)

Edward, where are you? Edward? Where are you, Edward?

> *She appears.*

Edward?

Edward, what are you doing in the scullery?

EDWARD (*Looking through the scullery window.*)

Doing?

FLORA

I've been looking everywhere for you. I put up the canopy ages ago. I came back and you were nowhere to be seen. Have you been out?

EDWARD

No.

FLORA

Where have you been?

EDWARD

Here.

FLORA

I looked in your study. I even went into the attic.

EDWARD (*Tonelessly.*)

What would I be doing in the attic?

FLORA

I couldn't imagine what had happened to you. Do you know it's twelve o'clock?

EDWARD

Is it?

FLORA

I even went to the bottom of the garden, to see if you were in the toolshed.

EDWARD (*Tonelessly.*)
What would I be doing in the toolshed?
FLORA
You must have seen me in the garden. You can see through this window.
EDWARD
Only part of the garden.
FLORA
Yes.
EDWARD
Only a corner of the garden. A very small corner.
FLORA
What are you doing in here?
EDWARD
Nothing. I was digging out some notes, that's all.
FLORA
Notes?
EDWARD
For my essay.
FLORA
Which essay?
EDWARD
My essay on space and time.
FLORA
But . . . I've never . . . I don't know that one.
EDWARD
You don't know it?
FLORA
I thought you were writing one about the Belgian Congo.
EDWARD
I've been engaged on the dimensionality and continuity of space
. . . and time . . . for years.
FLORA
And the Belgian Congo?
EDWARD (*Shortly.*)
Never mind about the Belgian Congo.
    Pause.
FLORA
But you don't keep notes in the scullery.
EDWARD
You'd be surprised. You'd be highly surprised.
FLORA
Good Lord, what's that? Is that a bullock let loose? No. It's the matchseller! My goodness, you can see him . . . through the hedge. He looks bigger. Have you been watching him? He looks . . . like a bullock.
    Pause.
Edward?
    Pause.
(*Moving over to him.*) Are you coming outside? I've put up the canopy. You'll miss the best of the day. You can have an hour before lunch.

EDWARD
I've no work to do this morning.

FLORA
What about your essay? You don't intend to stay in the scullery all day, do you?

EDWARD
Get out. Leave me alone.
A slight pause.

FLORA
Really Edward. You've never spoken to me like that in all your life.

EDWARD
Yes, I have.

FLORA
Oh, Weddie. Beddie-Weddie . . .

EDWARD
Do not call me that!

FLORA
Your eyes are bloodshot.

EDWARD
Damn it.

FLORA
It's too dark in here to peer . . .

EDWARD
Damn.

FLORA
It's so bright outside.

EDWARD
Damn.

FLORA
And it's dark in here.
Pause.

EDWARD
Christ blast it!

FLORA
You're frightened of him.

EDWARD
I'm not.

FLORA
You're frightened of a poor old man. Why?

EDWARD
I am not!

FLORA
He's a poor, harmless old man.

EDWARD
Aaah my eyes.

FLORA
Let me bathe them.

EDWARD
Keep away.
Pause.
(*Slowly.*) I want to speak to that man. I want to have a word with him.

Pause.

It's quite absurd, of course. I really can't tolerate something so . . . absurd, right on my doorstep. I shall not tolerate it. He's sold nothing all morning. No one passed. Yes. A monk passed. A non-smoker. In a loose garment. It's quite obvious he was a non-smoker but still, the man made no effort. He made no effort to clinch a sale, to rid himself of one of his cursed boxes. His one chance, all morning, and he made no effort.

Pause.

I haven't wasted my time. I've hit, in fact, upon the truth. He's not a matchseller at all. The bastard isn't a matchseller at all. Curious I never realized that before. He's an impostor. I watched him very closely. He made no move towards the monk. As for the monk, the monk made no move towards him. The monk was moving along the lane. He didn't pause, or halt, or in any way alter his step. As for the matchseller—how ridiculous to go on calling him by that title. What a farce. No, there is something very false about that man. I intend to get to the bottom of it. I'll soon get rid of him. He can go and ply his trade somewhere else. Instead of standing like a bullock . . . a bullock, outside my back gate.

FLORA

But if he isn't a matchseller, what is his trade?

EDWARD

We'll soon find out.

FLORA

You're going out to speak to him?

EDWARD

Certainly not! Go out to *him?* Certainly . . . not. I'll invite him in here. Into my study. Then we'll . . . get to the bottom of it.

FLORA

Why don't you call the police and have him removed?

He laughs. Pause.

Why don't you call the police, Edward? You could say he was a public nuisance. Although I . . . I can't say I find him a nuisance.

EDWARD

Call him in.

FLORA

Me?

EDWARD

Go out and call him in.

FLORA

Are you serious?

Pause.

Edward, I could call the police. Or even the vicar.

EDWARD

Go and get him.

She goes out. Silence.

Edward waits.

FLORA (*In the garden.*)

Good morning.

Pause.

We haven't met. I live in this house here. My husband and I.
> *Pause.*

I wonder if you could . . . would you care for a cup of tea?
> *Pause.*

Or a glass of lemon? It must be so dry, standing here.
> *Pause.*

Would you like to come inside for a little while? It's much cooler. There's something we'd very much like to . . . tell you, that will benefit you. Could you spare a few moments? We won't keep you long.
> *Pause.*

Might I buy your tray of matches, do you think? We've run out, completely, and we always keep a very large stock. It happens that way, doesn't it? Well, we can discuss it inside. Do come. This way. Ah now, do come. Our house is full of curios, you know. My husband's been rather a collector. We have goose for lunch. Do you care for goose?
> *She moves to the gate.*

Come and have lunch with us. This way. That's . . . right. May I take your arm? There's a good deal of *nettle* inside the gate. (*The Matchseller appears.*) Here. This way. Mind now. Isn't it beautiful weather? It's the longest day of the year today.
> *Pause.*

That's honeysuckle. And that's convolvulus. There's clematis. And do you see that plant by the conservatory? That's japonica.
> *Silence. She enters the study.*

FLORA
> He's here.

EDWARD
> I know.

FLORA
> He's in the hall.

EDWARD
> I know he's here. I can smell him.

FLORA
> Smell him?

EDWARD
> I smelt him when he came under my window. Can't you smell the house now?

FLORA
> What are you going to do with him, Edward? You won't be rough with him in any way? He's very old. I'm not sure if he can hear, or even see. And he's wearing the oldest—

EDWARD
> I don't want to know what he's wearing.

FLORA
> But you'll see for yourself in a minute, if you speak to him.

EDWARD
> I shall.
> *Slight pause.*

FLORA

He's an old man. You won't . . . be rough with him?

EDWARD

If he's so old, why doesn't he seek shelter . . . from the storm?

FLORA

But there's no storm. It's summer, the longest day . . .

EDWARD

There was a storm, last week. A summer storm. He stood without moving, while it raged about him.

FLORA

When was this?

EDWARD

He remained quite still, while it thundered all about him.

Pause.

FLORA

Edward . . . are you sure it's wise to bother about all this?

EDWARD

Tell him to come in.

FLORA

I . . .

EDWARD

Now.

She goes and collects the Matchseller.

FLORA

Hullo. Would you like to go in? I won't be long. Up these stairs here.

Pause.

You can have some sherry before lunch.

Pause.

Shall I take your tray? No. Very well, take it with you. Just . . . up those stairs. The door at the . . .

She watches him move.

the door . . .

Pause.

the door at the top. I'll join you . . . later. (*She goes out.*)

The Matchseller stands on the threshold of the study.

EDWARD (*Cheerfully.*)

Here I am. Where are you?

Pause.

Don't stand out there, old chap. Come into my study. (*He rises.*) Come in.

The Matchseller enters.

That's right. Mind how you go. That's . . . it. Now, make yourself comfortable. Thought you might like some refreshment, on a day like this. Sit down, old man. What will you have? Sherry? Or what about a double scotch? Eh?

Pause.

I entertain the villagers annually, as a matter of fact. I'm not the squire, but they look upon me with some regard. Don't believe we've got a squire here any more, actually. Don't know what became of him. Nice old man he was. Great chess-player, as I remember. Three daughters. The pride of the county. Flaming red hair. Alice was the

eldest. Sit yourself down, old chap. Eunice I think was number two.
The youngest one was the best of the bunch. Sally. No, no, wait a
minute, no, it wasn't Sally, it was . . . Fanny. Fanny. A flower. You
must be a stranger here. Unless you lived here once, went on a long
voyage and have lately returned. Do you know the district?

Pause.

Now, now, you mustn't . . . stand about like that. Take a seat.
Which one would you prefer? We have a great variety, as you see.
Can't stand uniformity. Like different seats, different backs. Often
when I'm working, you know, I draw up one chair, scribble a few
lines, put it by, draw up another, sit back, ponder, put it by . . . (*Absently.*) . . . sit back . . . put it by . . .

Pause.

I write theological and philosophical essays . . .

Pause.

Now and again I jot down a few observations on certain tropical
phenomena—not from the same standpoint, of course. (*Silent
pause.*) Yes. Africa, now. Africa's always been my happy hunting
ground. Fascinating country. Do you know it? I get the impression
that you've . . . been around a bit. Do you by any chance know the
Membunza Mountains? Great range south of Katambaloo. French
Equatorial Africa, if my memory serves me right. Most extraordinary
diversity of flora and fauna. Especially fauna. I understand in the
Gobi Desert you can come across some very strange sights. Never
been there myself. Studied the maps though. Fascinating things,
maps.

Pause.

Do you live in the village? I don't often go down, of course. Or are
you passing through? On your way to another part of the country?
Well, I can tell you, in my opinion you won't find many prettier
parts than here. We win the first prize regularly, you know, the best
kept village in the area. Sit down.

Pause.

I say, can you hear me?

Pause.

I said, I say, can you hear me?

Pause.

You possess most extraordinary repose, for a man of your age, don't
you? Well, perhaps that's not quite the right word . . . repose. Do
you find it chilly in here? I'm sure it's chillier in here than out. I
haven't been out yet, today, though I shall probably spend the whole
afternoon working, in the garden, under my canopy, at my table, by
the pool.

Pause.

Oh, I understand you met my *wife*? Charming woman, don't you
think? Plenty of grit there, too. Stood by me through thick and thin,
that woman. In season and out of season. Fine figure of a woman
she was, too, in her youth. Wonderful carriage, flaming red hair. (*He
stops abruptly.*)

Pause.

Yes, I . . . I was in much the same position myself then as you are
now, you understand. Struggling to make my way in the world. I

was in commerce too. (*With a chuckle.*) Oh, yes, I know what it's like—the weather, the rain, beaten from pillar to post, up hill and down dale . . . the rewards were few . . . winters in hovels . . . up till all hours working at your thesis . . . yes, I've done it all. Let me advise you. Get a good woman to stick by you. Never mind what the world says. Keep at it. Keep your shoulder to the wheel. It'll pay dividends.

    Pause.

(*With a laugh.*) You must excuse my chatting away like this. We have few visitors this time of the year. All our friends summer abroad. I'm a home bird myself. Wouldn't mind taking a trip to Asia Minor, mind you, or to certain lower regions of the Congo, but Europe? Out of the question. Much too noisy. I'm sure you agree. Now look, what will you have to drink? A glass of ale? Curaçao Fockink Orange? Ginger beer? Tia Maria? A Wachenheimer Fuchsmantel Riesling Beeren Auslese? Gin and it? Chateauneuf-du-Pape? A little Asti Spumante? Or what do you say to a straightforward Piesporter Goldtropfchen Feine Auslese (Reichsgraf von Kesselstaff)? Any preference?

    Pause.

You look a trifle warm. Why don't you take off your balaclava? I'd find that a little itchy myself. But then I've always been one for freedom of movement. Even in the depth of winter I wear next to nothing.

    Pause.

I say, can I ask you a personal question? I don't want to seem inquisitive but aren't you rather on the wrong road for matchselling? Not terribly busy, is it? Of course you may not care for petrol fumes or the noise of traffic. I can quite understand that.

    Pause.

Do forgive me peering but is that a glass eye you're wearing?

    Pause.

Do take off your balaclava, there's a good chap, put your tray down and take your ease, as they say in this part of the world. (*He moves toward him.*) I must say you keep quite a good stock, don't you? Tell me, between ourselves, are those boxes full, or are there just a few half-empty ones among them? Oh yes, I used to be in commerce. Well now, before the good lady sounds the gong for petit déjeuner will you join me in an apéritif? I recommend a glass of cider. Now . . . just a minute . . . I know I've got some—Look out! Mind your tray!

    The tray falls, and the matchboxes.

Good God, what . . . ?

    Pause.

You've dropped your tray.

    Pause. He picks the matchboxes up.

(*Grunts.*) Eh, these boxes are all wet. You've no right to sell wet matches, you know. Uuuuugggh. This feels suspiciously like fungus. You won't get very far in this trade if you don't take care of your goods. (*Grunts, rising.*) Well, here you are.

    Pause.

Here's your tray.

He puts the tray into the Matchseller's hands, and sits. Pause.

Now listen, let me be quite frank with you, shall I? I really cannot understand why you don't sit down. There are four chairs at your disposal. Not to mention the hassock. I can't possibly talk to you unless you're settled. Then and only then can I speak to you. Do you follow me? You're not being terribly helpful. (*Slight pause.*) You're sweating. The sweat's pouring out of you. Take off that balaclava.

Pause.

Go into the corner then. Into the corner. Go on. Get into the shade of the corner. Back. Backward.

Pause.

Get back!

Pause.

Ah, you understand me. Forgive me for saying so, but I had decided that you had the comprehension of a bullock. I was mistaken. You understand me perfectly well. That's right. A little more. A little to the right. Aaah. Now you're there. In shade, in shadow. Good-o. Now I can get down to brass tacks. Can't I?

Pause.

No doubt you're wondering why I invited you into this house? You may think I was alarmed by the look of you. You would be quite mistaken. I was not alarmed by the look of you. I did not find you at all alarming. No, no. Nothing outside this room has ever alarmed me. You disgusted me, quite forcibly, if you want to know the truth.

Pause.

Why did you disgust me to that extent? That seems to be a pertinent question. You're no more disgusting than Fanny, the squire's daughter, after all. In apperance you differ but not in essence. There's the same . . .

Pause.

The same . . .

Pause.

(*In a low voice.*) I want to ask you a question. Why do you stand outside my back gate, from dawn till dusk, why do you pretend to sell matches, why . . . ? What is it, damn you. You're shivering. You're sagging. Come here, come here . . . mind your tray! (*Edward rises and moves behind a chair.*) Come, quick quick. There. Sit here. Sit . . . sit in this.

The Matchseller stumbles and sits. Pause.

Aaaah! You're sat. At last. What a relief. You must be tired. (*Slight pause.*) Chair comfortable? I bought it in a sale. I bought all the furniture in this house in a sale. The same sale. When I was a young man. You too, perhaps. You too, perhaps.

Pause.

At the same time, perhaps!

Pause.

(*Muttering.*) I must get some air. I must get a breath of air.

He goes to the door.

Flora!

FLORA
    Yes?
EDWARD (*With great weariness.*)
    Take me into the garden.
        Silence. They move from the study door to a chair under a canopy.
FLORA
    Come under the canopy.
EDWARD
    Ah. (*He sits.*)
        Pause.
    The peace. The peace out here.
FLORA
    Look at our trees.
EDWARD
    Yes.
FLORA
    Our own trees. Can you hear the birds?
EDWARD
    No, I can't hear them.
FLORA
    But they're singing, high up, and flapping.
EDWARD
    Good. Let them flap.
FLORA
    Shall I bring your lunch out here? You can have it in peace, and a
    quiet drink, under your canopy.
        Pause.
    How are you getting on with your old man?
EDWARD
    What do you mean?
FLORA
    What's happening? How are you getting on with him?
EDWARD
    Very well. We get on remarkably well. He's a little . . . reticent.
    Somewhat withdrawn. It's understandable. I should be the same,
    perhaps, in his place. Though, of course, I could not possibly find
    myself in his place.
FLORA
    Have you found out anything about him?
EDWARD
    A little. A little. He's had various trades, that's certain. His place of
    residence is unsure. He's . . . he's not a drinking man. As yet, I
    haven't discovered the reason for his arrival here. I shall in due
    course . . . by nightfall.
FLORA
    Is it necessary?
EDWARD
    Necessary?
FLORA (*Quickly sitting on the right arm of the chair.*)
    I could show him out now, it wouldn't matter. You've seen him, he's
    harmless, unfortunate . . . old, that's all. Edward—listen—he's not

here through any . . . design, or anything, I know it. I mean, he might just as well stand outside our back gate as anywhere else. He'll move on. I can . . . make him. I promise you. There's no point in upsetting yourself like this. He's an old man, weak in the head . . . that's all.

    Pause.

EDWARD

You're deluded.

FLORA

Edward—

EDWARD (*Rising.*)

You're deluded. And stop calling me Edward.

FLORA

You're not still frightened of him?

EDWARD

Frightened of him? Of *him?* Have you *seen* him?

    Pause.

He's like jelly. A great bullockfat of jelly. He can't see straight. I think as a matter of fact he wears a glass eye. He's almost stone deaf . . . almost . . . not quite. He's very nearly dead on his feet. Why should he frighten me? No, you're a woman, you know nothing. (*Slight pause.*) But he possesses other faculties. Cunning. The man's an imposter and he knows I know it.

FLORA

I'll tell you what. Look. Let me speak to him. I'll speak to him.

EDWARD (*Quietly.*)

And I know he knows I know it.

FLORA

I'll find out all about him, Edward. I promise you I will.

EDWARD

And he knows I know.

FLORA

Edward! Listen to me! I can find out all about him, I promise you. I shall go and have a word with him now. I shall . . . get to the bottom of it.

EDWARD

You? It's laughable.

FLORA

You'll see—he won't bargain for me. I'll surprise him. He'll . . . he'll admit everything.

EDWARD (*Softly.*)

He'll admit everything, will he?

FLORA

You wait and see, you just—

EDWARD (*Hissing.*)

What are you plotting?

FLORA

I know exactly what I shall—

EDWARD

What are you plotting?

    He seizes her arms.

FLORA

Edward, you're hurting me!

Pause.

(*With dignity.*) I shall wave from the window when I'm ready. Then you can come up. I shall get to the truth of it, I assure you. You're much too heavy-handed, in every way. You should trust your wife more, Edward. You should trust her judgment, and have a greater insight into her capabilities. A woman . . . a woman will often succeed, you know, where a man must invariably fail.

Silence. She goes into the study.

Do you mind if I come in?

The door closes.

Are you comfortable?

Pause.

Oh, the sun's shining directly on you. Wouldn't you rather sit in the shade?

She sits down.

It's the longest day of the year today, did you know that? Actually the year has flown. I can remember Christmas and that dreadful frost. And the floods! I hope you weren't here in the floods. We were out of danger up here, of course, but in the valleys whole families I remember drifted away on the current. The country was a lake. Everything stopped. We lived on our own preserves, drank elderberry wine, studied other cultures.

Pause.

Do you know, I've got a feeling I've seen you before, somewhere. Long before the flood. You were much younger. Yes, I'm really sure of it. Between ourselves, were you ever a poacher? I had an encounter with a poacher once. It was a ghastly rape, the brute. High up on a hillside cattle track. Early spring. I was out riding on my pony. And there on the verge a man lay—ostensibly injured, lying on his front, I remember, possibly the victim of a murderous assault, how was I to know? I dismounted, I went to him, he rose, I fell, my pony took off, down to the valley. I saw the sky through the trees, blue. Up to my ears in mud. It was a desperate battle.

Pause.

I lost.

Pause.

Of course, life was perilous in those days. It was my first canter unchaperoned.

Pause.

Years later, when I was a Justice of the Peace for the county, I had him in front of the bench. He was there for poaching. That's how I know he was a poacher. The evidence though was sparse, inadmissible. I acquitted him, letting him off with a caution. He'd grown a red beard, I remember. Yes. A bit of a stinker.

Pause.

I say, you are perspiring, aren't you? Shall I mop your brow? With my chiffon? Is it the heat? Or the closeness? Or confined space? Or . . . ? (*She goes over to him.*) Actually, the day is cooling. It'll soon be dusk. Perhaps it is dusk. May I? You don't mind?

Pause. She mops his brow.

Ah, there, that's better. And your cheeks. It is a woman's job, isn't it?
And I'm the only woman on hand. There.

> *Pause. She leans on the arm of chair.*

(*Intimately.*) Tell me, have you a woman? Do you like women? Do
you ever . . . think about women?

> *Pause.*

Have you ever . . . stopped a woman?

> *Pause.*

I'm sure you must have been quite attractive once. (*She sits.*) Not any
more, of course. You've got a vile smell. Vile. Quite repellent, in
fact.

> *Pause.*

Sex, I suppose, means nothing to you. Does it ever occur to you that
sex is a very vital experience for other people? Really, I think you'd
amuse me if you weren't so hideous. You're probably quite amusing
in your own way. (*Seductively.*) Tell me all about love. Speak to me of
love.

> *Pause.*

God knows what you're saying at this very moment. It's quite
disgusting. Do you know when I was a girl I loved . . . I loved . . .
I simply adored . . . what *have* you got on, for goodness sake? A jersey? It's clogged. Have you been rolling in mud? (*Slight pause.*) You
haven't been rolling in mud, have you? (*She rises and goes over to him.*)
And what have you got under your jersey? Let's see. (*Slight pause.*)
I'm not tickling you, am I? No. Good . . . Lord, is this a vest? That's
quite original. Quite original. (*She sits on the arm of his chair.*)
Hmmnn, you're a solid old boy, I must say. Not at all like a jelly. All
you need is a bath. A lovely lathery bath. And a good scrub. A lovely
lathery scrub. (*Pause.*) Don't you? It will be a pleasure. (*She throws her
arms round him.*) I'm going to keep you. I'm going to keep you, you
dreadful chap, and call you Barnabas. Isn't it dark, Barnabas? Your
eyes, your eyes, your great big eyes.

> *Pause.*

My husband would never have guessed your name. Never. (*She kneels
at his feet. Whispering.*) It's me you were waiting for, wasn't it? You've
been standing waiting for me. You've seen me in the woods, picking
daisies, in my apron, my pretty daisy apron, and you came and
stood, poor creature, at my gate, till death us do part. Poor Barnabas. I'm going to put you to bed. I'm going to put you to bed and
watch over you. But first you must have a good whacking great bath.
And I'll buy you pretty little things that will suit you. And little toys
to play with. On your deathbed. Why shouldn't you die happy?

> *A shout from the hall.*

EDWARD

Well?

> *Footsteps upstage.*

Well?

FLORA

Don't come in.

EDWARD

Well?

FLORA

He's dying

EDWARD

Dying? He's not dying.

FLORA

I tell you, he's very ill.

EDWARD

He's not dying! Nowhere near. He'll see you cremated.

FLORA

The man is desperately ill!

EDWARD

Ill? You lying slut. Get back to your trough!

FLORA

Edward . . .

EDWARD (*violently.*)

To your trough!

She goes out. Pause.

(*Coolly.*) Good evening to you. Why are you sitting in the gloom? Oh, you've begun to disrobe. Too warm? Let's open these windows, then, what?

He opens the windows.

Pull the blinds.

He pulls the blinds.

And close . . . the curtains . . . again.

He closes the curtains.

Ah. Air will enter through the side chinks. Of the blinds. And filter through the curtains. I hope. Don't want to suffocate, do we?

Pause.

More comfortable? Yes. You look different in darkness. Take off all your togs, if you like. Make yourself at home. Strip to your buff. Do as you would in your own house.

Pause.

Did you say something?

Pause.

Did you say something?

Pause.

Anything? Well then, tell me about your boyhood. Mmnn?

Pause.

What did you do with it? Run? Swim? Kick the ball? You kicked the ball? What position? Left back? Goalie? First reserve?

Pause.

I used to play myself. Country house matches, mostly. Kept wicket and batted number seven.

Pause.

Kept wicket and batted number seven. Man called—Cavendish, I think had something of your style. Bowled left arm over the wicket, always kept his cap on, quite a dab hand at solo whist, preferred a good round of prop and cop to anything else.

Pause.

On wet days when the field was swamped.

Pause.

Perhaps you don't play cricket.
Pause.
Perhaps you never met Cavendish and never played cricket. You look less and less like a cricketer the more I see of you. Where did you live in those days? God damn it, I'm entitled to know something about you! You're in my blasted house, on my territory, drinking my wine, eating my duck! Now you've had your fill you sit like a hump, a mouldering heap. In my room. My den. I can rem . . . (*He stops abruptly.*)
Pause.
You find that funny? Are you grinning?
Pause.
(*In disgust.*) Good Christ, is that a grin on your face? (*Further disgust.*) It's lopsided. It's all—down on one side. You're grinning. It amuses you, does it? When I tell you how well I remember this room, how well I remember this den. (*Muttering.*) Ha. Yesterday now, it was clear, clearly defined, so clearly.
Pause.
The garden, too, was sharp, lucid, in the rain, in the sun.
Pause.
My den, too, was sharp, arranged for my purpose . . . quite satisfactory.
Pause.
The house too, was polished, all the banisters were polished, and the stair rods, and the curtain rods.
Pause.
My desk was polished, and my cabinet.
Pause.
I was polished. (*Nostalgic.*) I could stand on the hill and look through my telescope at the sea. And follow the path of the three-masted schooner, feeling fit, well aware of my sinews, their suppleness, my arms lifted holding the telescope, steady, easily, no trembling, my aim was perfect, I could pour hot water down the spoon-hole, yes, easily, no difficulty, my grasp firm, my command established, my life was accounted for, I was ready for my excursions to the cliff, down the path to the back gate, through the long grass, no need to watch for the nettles, my progress was fluent, after my long struggling against all kinds of usurpers, disreputables, lists, literally lists of people anxious to do me down, and my reputation down, my command was established, all summer I would breakfast, survey my landscape, take my telescope, examine the overhanging of my hedges, pursue the narrow lane past the monastery, climb the hill, adjust the lens (*He mimes a telescope.*), watch the progress of the three-masted schooner, my progress was as sure, as fluent . . .
Pause. He drops his arms.
Yes, yes, you're quite right, it is funny.
Pause.
Laugh your bloody head off! Go on. Don't mind me. No need to be polite.
Pause.
That's right.

Pause.

You're quite right, it is funny. I'll laugh with you!

He laughs.

Ha-ha-ha! Yes! You're laughing with me, I'm laughing with you, we're laughing together!

He laughs and stops.

(*Brightly.*) Why did I invite you into this room? That's your next question, isn't it? Bound to be.

Pause.

Well, why not, you might say? My oldest acquaintance. My nearest and dearest. My kith and kin. But surely correspondence would have been as satisfactory . . . more satisfactory? We could have exchanged postcards, couldn't we? What? Views, couldn't we? Of sea and land, city and village, town and country, autumn and winter . . . clocktowers . . . museums . . . citadels . . . bridges . . . rivers . . .

Pause.

Seeing you stand, at the back gate, such close proximity, was not at all the same thing.

Pause.

What are you doing? You're taking off your balaclava . . . you've decided not to. No, very well then, all things considered, did I then invite you into this room with express intention of asking you to take off your balaclava, in order to determine your resemblance to—some other person? The answer is no, certainly not, I did not, for when I first saw you you wore no balaclava. No headcovering of any kind, in fact. You looked quite different without a head—I mean without a hat—I mean without a headcovering, of any kind. In fact every time I have seen you you have looked quite different to the time before.

Pause.

Even now you look different. Very different.

Pause.

Admitted that sometimes I viewed you through dark glasses, yes, and sometimes through light glasses, and on other occasions bare eyed, and on other occasions through the bars of the scullery window, or from the roof, the roof, yes in driving snow, or from the bottom of the drive in thick fog, or from the roof again in blinding sun, so blinding, so hot, that I had to skip and jump and bounce in order to remain in one place. Ah, that's good for a guffaw, is it? That's good for a belly laugh? Go on, then. Let it out. Let yourself go, for God's . . . (*He catches his breath.*) You're crying . . .

Pause.

(*Moved.*) You haven't been laughing. You're crying.

Pause.

You're weeping. You're shaking with grief. For me. I can't believe it. For my plight. I've been wrong.

Pause.

(*Briskly.*) Come, come, stop it. Be a man. Blow your nose for goodness sake. Pull yourself together.

He sneezes.

Ah.

He rises. Sneeze.

Ah. Fever. Excuse me.

He blows his nose.

I've caught a cold. A germ. In my eyes. It was this morning. In my eyes. My eyes.

Pause. He falls to the floor.

Not that I had any difficulty in seeing you, no, no, it was not so much my sight, my sight is excellent—in winter I run about with nothing on but a pair of polo shorts—no, it was not so much any deficiency in my sight as the airs between me and my object—don't weep—the change of air, the currents obtaining in the space between me and my object, the shades they make, the shapes they take, the quivering, the eternal quivering—please stop crying—nothing to do with heat-haze. Sometimes, of course, I would take shelter, shelter to compose myself. Yes, I would seek a tree, a cranny of bushes, erect my canopy and so make shelter. And rest. (*Low murmur.*) And then I no longer heard the wind or saw the sun. Nothing entered, nothing left my nook. I lay on my side in my polo shorts, my fingers lightly in contact with the blades of grass, the earthflowers, the petals of the earthflowers flaking, lying on my palm, the underside of all the great foliage dark, above me, but it is only afterwards I say the foliage was dark, the petals flaking, then I said nothing, I remarked nothing, things happened upon me, then in my times of shelter, the shades, the petals, carried themselves, carried their bodies upon me, and nothing entered my nook, nothing left it.

Pause.

But then, the time came. I saw the wind. I saw the wind, swirling, and the dust at my back gate, lifting, and the long grass, scything together . . . (*Slowly, in horror.*) You *are* laughing. You're laughing. Your face. Your body. (*Overwhelming nausea and horror.*) Rocking . . . gasping . . . rocking . . . shaking . . . rocking . . . heaving . . . rocking . . . You're laughing at me! Aaaaahhhh!

The Matchseller rises. Silence.

You look younger. You look extraordinarily . . . youthful.

Pause.

You want to examine the garden? It must be very bright, in the moonlight. (*Becoming weaker.*) I would like to join you . . . explain . . . show you . . . the garden . . . explain . . . The plants . . . where I run . . . my track . . . in training . . . I was number one sprinter at Howells . . . when a stripling . . . no more than a stripling . . . licked . . . men twice my strength . . . when a stripling . . . like yourself.

Pause.

(*Flatly.*) The pool must be glistening. In the moonlight. And the lawn. I remember it well. The cliff. The sea. The three-masted schooner.

Pause.

(*With great, final effort—a whisper.*) Who are you?

FLORA (*Off.*)

Barnabas?

Pause.

She enters.

Ah, Barnabas. Everything is ready.

> *Pause.*
I want to show you my garden, your garden. You must see my ja-
ponica, my convolvulus . . . my honeysuckle, my clematis.
> *Pause.*
The summer is coming. I've put up your canopy for you. You can
lunch in the garden, by the pool. I've polished the whole house for
you.
> *Pause.*
Take my hand.
> *Pause. The Matchseller goes over to her.*
Yes. Oh, wait a moment.
> *Pause.*
Edward. Here is your tray.
> *She crosses to Edward with the tray of matches, and puts it in his
> hands. Then she and the Matchseller start to go out as the curtain falls
> slowly.*

Action analysis and performance suggestions

The following scenes are particularly recommended for informal classroom
performance: the wasp scene—the opening of the play through Edward's
sighting of the matchseller: "He's there," on page 717 and Edward's final
confrontation with the matchseller beginning on page 732 and going to the
end of the play.

Despite the obscurity and the bizarre nature of the events and motivation in *A Slight Ache*, the absurdities have a logic that is accessible; and
the actions to be played are very specific. Pinter's own directorial approach emphasizes action, a view of the play as reality, and the text as the
main clue to that reality. Other directors of his works have found his
plays clear and have helped their actors avoid playing symbols or ideas by
encouraging them to concentrate on a naturalistic approach that allows
the deeper meanings to emerge. However, the text offers clues to the
director and actor for bringing out the play's ritual undercurrents and its
partly surreal effect as well.

DEFINING THE ACTIONS AND THE SUPEROBJECTIVE

One could easily mistake the play's opening interchange between Edward
and Flora as a typical absurdist scene of noncommunication between a
husband and wife no longer in touch with each other. Edward seeks to
hide behind the paper while Flora chatters on about her garden. But Pinter's characters are not so much unable to communicate as they are afraid
and unwilling to do so. While Edward does indeed hide behind the paper,
Flora's action is to bring him out from behind it, to make him aware of
the garden, and finally, in terms that relate to the play's superobjective, to
bring him to life. For Edward, we discover in the interchange, is a hider
by nature who does not know what is growing in his own garden. "I don't
see why I should be expected to distinguish between these plants. It's not
my job," Edward complains.

FLORA

You know perfectly well what grows in your garden.

EDWARD
> Quite the contrary. It is clear that I don't.
> *Pause*

The pause serves as a break for Flora, who has failed to achieve her action, namely, to shift to a new tack. Her action then is to urge Edward to work in the garden. Flora, as her name suggests, presides over the garden, and an awareness on the part of the actress of the seasonal focus of the play can give Flora's invitation to Edward to join her in the garden's "life" the necessary urgency. For Edward, whom Pinter associates with winter, the beautiful, sunny day is "treacherous weather," and the "first wasp of summer" poses a terrifying threat.

Where Flora fails to bring the hiding Edward out, the wasp succeeds. Edward's action in the ensuing section of the scene is, on one level, to kill the wasp, to get it with the newspaper, to trap it in the marmalade, to pour hot water down the spoon-hole in order to scald it. But the verb "kill" is not dramatically fruitful since as a function verb it is too quickly over; nor does it express the richness of the action in the scene. In the context of the entire play, the wasp is simply the first intruder to threaten Edward, a precursor of the more dangerous matchseller whom Flora names Barnabas, as the incarnation of summer. (The day of Saint Barnabas, June 11 in the Old Style calendar, was the day of the summer solstice, and Barnaby-Bright is the slang name for the longest day and the shortest night of the year.) Barnabas comes on the longest day of summer to take Edward's place. The now effete and dying Edward, more comfortable running about in his polo shorts in the winter, as he later tells the matchseller, is at a time in life when summer presents him with a real threat. A better designation for Edward's action in killing the wasp might then be to defend himself from destruction or even to sacrifice the wasp in order to stave off his own destruction. During the sacrifice of the wasp, Edward continues his bickering with Flora. They argue about whether wasps bite or sting and whether the wasp's death in the marmalade will be horrible. Part of Edward's attempts to save himself by killing the wasp, then, involve related efforts to assert his dominance over Flora.

Edward wins the action in this opening scene. After destroying the wasp, he finds the day beautiful, he is able to recognize the convolvulus, and he is ready to venture forth to work in the garden—until he spies the matchseller. In the rest of the play Edward loses in his efforts to save himself and remembers the morning of this day as if it were the morning of his life. "I could pour hot water down the spoon-hole," he brags to the matchseller as his strength fails him; "yes, easily, no difficulty, my grasp firm, my command established, my life was accounted for. . . ." Pouring hot water down a spoon-hole may seem an absurd way of expressing one's vitality, but the line makes perfect sense and serves to show the life-and-death nature of Edward's confrontation with the wasp. Flora's basic action as it is revealed in the rest of the play is to save herself. Her efforts in the wasp episode to help Edward sacrifice the wasp show her perfect willingness to find her salvation through Edward if he is able to respond. She is not eager to invite the matchseller in, and her subsequent efforts to seduce him and to keep him grow out of her realization of how weakened Edward is. She merely wants to polish the house for someone who can respond to her and give her life. Like so many of Pinter's heroines (for example, Stella in *The*

Collection, Ruth in *The Homecoming*), the woman inevitably plays the archetypal role of whore, as well as that of wife or mother, as she strives for the continuance of a vital life.

The matchseller must be out of sight in the opening scene, since the weasel should be only sensed under the cocktail cabinet at that point. His silence throughout the play and his seemingly complete passivity have led some to consider him a mere projection of Flora's and Edward's fantasy, but his presence and the action that informs his passivity may add much to the effectiveness and meaning of the rest of the play. The matchseller's action is to save himself from rebirth, to protect himself from its pain. Seasonal and human fatalities have placed him where he is, but if he tries very hard to close his senses, to hang on to his blindness, to avoid entrance into a house that can only cause him the pain of living, then he will be the perfect bizarre counterpart to Edward hiding behind his paper. The matchseller's efforts to avoid rebirth also fit in with the superobjective of the play, to fight for survival and salvation, since he identifies his safety and his salvation with the peace of noninvolvement.

OVERCOMING OBSTACLES

Flora's attempts to rejuvenate or awaken Edward are met with resistance. Her flowers—life—are not his job. Her main obstacle, then, is his resistance. Even her efforts to help him sacrifice the wasp in order to stave off his own doom are met with resistance. Edward considers her the enemy, a threat to his manhood rather than a partner who would welcome and encourage it.

The obstacles that prevent Edward from hiding are Flora, who tries to draw him out, and the wasp, whose sting presents a challenge he cannot ignore. For the silent matchseller, Flora and Edward are obstacles. Their bickering over the garden and the killing of the wasp penetrate the wall he would put up, thus forcing him to intensify his efforts to resist hearing and seeing what he wants to avoid.

THE MAGIC IF AND THE GIVEN CIRCUMSTANCES

The situation in *A Slight Ache* is of a life-and-death nature. Like Chekhov, Pinter concentrates on the trivial or the banal, the intrusion of a wasp at the breakfast table. However, the weasel lurks under the cocktail cabinet, and the threat includes not only the dispossession that is the crux of *The Cherry Orchard* but also total annihilation. Only in the later confrontations with the matchseller do Flora and Edward admit the life-and-death implications of the action, although they are present in the opening scene and account for the tragicomic effect gained by the enormous threat the trivial wasp seems to pose.

What, then, IF you sense that your time has come, that your hiding place has been discovered, and that you must not only face death but also face yourself? In the remaining scenes of the play Edward's confrontations with the silent matchseller force him into a confrontation with himself and the hollowness of his clichés and his life. What IF you were being urged to look into a mirror and were afraid that IF you looked you might see nothing? On a completely naturalistic level, too, how would you behave IF a wasp flew around your breakfast table?

For Flora the circumstances are also those of life and death. Edward continually denigrates her and refuses to share life with her. What IF your husband had nothing to say to you, had no interest in you as a woman, and found all your efforts to reach him annoying? What IF you, on the other hand, had lived with him for many years and still wanted him to respond? This last condition is important, for Flora does not choose the matchseller casually. She tries to get Edward to ignore him or have him removed as IF she senses the fatalities involved in his entrance.

For the matchseller the conditions are those of the womb versus life. What IF you were at peace and protected from all danger? What IF you wished only to hide, but some force insisted that you come out from your hiding place? While Edward is faced with the pain of having to give up his half-life, the matchseller is faced with the pain of being brought into full life.

CLASSROOM ADAPTATIONS TO ARRIVE AT STYLE

A stage area should be set off from the audience as it was with Chekhov and Ibsen, and the actors should concentrate their attention behind the imaginary fourth wall. In this instance, that may be a wall of a breakfast room, or, altering the stage directions, it could be the garden. The couple could be breakfasting on a patio or in a room that opens on that garden. The important ingredients of the scene are a sense of openness and the outdoor brightness of a summer day and a sense of elegance in the breakfast setting: a nice teapot, possibly silver, nice cups and saucers, and a tablecloth—all to indicate the way of life of the country gentleman and his wife.

In staging the scene, careful attention should be given to imagining the flight of the wasp. The actor and actress playing Flora and Edward must decide on its flight pattern and follow it with their eyes. Flora should never take her eyes from it and Edward should do so only to consider whether it's the first wasp of summer. If the wasp is not real to the couple, it will not be real to the audience and the menace in this comedy of menace will not exist. Sensory work must also be done on the weather and the garden. If the flowers are imagined as out in the audience, decisions must be made about their exact locations so that Flora can enjoy them and Edward can be properly confused.

Some suggestion of a British accent will also help bring out the style of the play, which depends on the contrast between the apparently restrained British couple and the passions that are surging below the surface of their lives. Equally important is the careful playing of the pauses, which should be filled with unspoken meanings and which are part of the rhythm of the play's language and action. In subsequent scenes where the matchseller is present, Flora and Edward should always expect an answer from him; otherwise what should be dramatic confrontation will come off as undramatic monologues.

If the director wants to bring out the ritual as well as the realistic aspects of the play, the couple should be directed to treat the killing of the wasp as a sacrifice. The hushed tones of Macbeth and Lady Macbeth plotting the murder of the king are in order as well as movement in careful, rhythmic patterns. The result should be both hilarious and frightening since the tone will seem both precise and wildly incongruous at the same time. Establishing a tone of sacrifice will also clarify the meaning of the play, which brings us right back to *Oedipus the King* and the origins of drama in the Dionysian sacrifices of a hero-king-god. The sacrifice of Oedipus brought new life to his city and the realization of self to Oedipus. The sacrifice of Edward brings new life to Flora and the matchseller and the realization of self to Edward. In its macabre, absurd fashion, *A Slight Ache* is a play of celebration.

Mary Ann Williams
Cinder, Tell-It
A dance-drama for soulful folks

CINDER
Dese shoes is pinchin' my feet.
(page 759)

The following four poems, "Keep Your Shoes On, Lady," "Cinder, Tell-It," "Willow Man," and "Legacy," were written to stand by themselves. Their content, cut up and then pasted together in the manner of a collage, forms the dance-drama *Cinder, Tell-It* (1976). The playscript offers only one example of how a play can be created from the poetry. Any variety of other combinations of the material is possible, and through improvisational techniques others can be discovered.

 Cinder, Tell-It was in part so created. Using four of her own poems, Mary Ann Williams explored possible combinations for drama with her fellow performers, Anna Bishop and J. D. Knight, working improvisationally on vocal, musical, and movement possibilities before settling on the arrangement of the material in the script. So developed, *Cinder, Tell-It* exemplifies the work of many experimental avant-garde groups of the 1960s and 1970s in Europe and America, both Black and White, who work improvisationally to create drama and only occasionally, if at all, use completely predetermined scripts. Such groups have not as yet produced a playscript of lasting literary importance, but the nature and aims of these recent experiments in creating drama are central to a major movement in theater today.

 Such primarily White groups of the 1960s and 1970s as the Becks' Living Theater, Joseph Chaikin's Open Theater, and Richard Schechner's The Performance Group in America, Peter Brook's and Charles Marowitz's Theater of Cruelty in England, and Jerzy Grotowski's Laboratory Theater in Poland have all taken inspiration from Antonin Artaud's cry for a theater with a religious mission (see page 710) that will overturn the traditional in its effort to reveal or create the truth that purifies and saves humanity. Different from one another and from their prophet, these groups tend to share Artaud's sense of the theater's communal, spiritual aims, though they sometimes combine political with religious zeal. Peter Brook envisions a holy theater, Joseph Chaikin bills his actors as priests, and Jerzy Grotowski expects his actors to sacrifice themselves for their audience.

 Also in Artaud fashion, the actor/audience relationship is invariably redefined along with the performance area to create a ritual experience. These groups have so often had to make do with lofts, churches, cafés, or the streets themselves that they have embraced enthusiastically what Brook calls the "empty space" and what Grotowski exalts as a "poor theater," doing all in their power to break down divisions between actor and audience either by inviting or demanding audience participation or by seating the spectators in the midst of the action. (Living Theater actors have been known to spit on recalcitrant audience members; Schechner's actors in *Dionysus in 69* included the audience in some of the erotic ritual activity of the drama.)

Like many of the absurdist playwrights, these experimental groups have often discarded a linear flow of events that has marked the theater since the Greeks and instead have employed antirealistic techniques to express themselves. Unlike the absurdists, however, they have given up the written script as a chart for the play's action in favor of a theater that, in Grotowski's terms, is an encounter with the self and the audience. All the dramas they have published emerge from the work of disciplined ensemble improvisation. Even if they work with an author such as the Open Theater's Jean-Claude van Italy or Megan Terry, the scripts are often developed improvisationally, for example, van Italy's *The Serpent*, 1969, or Terry's *Viet Rock*, 1967.

The efforts of many of these groups, though often vital and impressive, have sometimes foundered on the attempt to create a ritual experience in a world without religious belief in which Peter Brook suggests that "we do not know how to celebrate, because we do not know what to celebrate" (Peter Brook, *The Empty Space*, p. 42). Acting exercises that are devised to go beyond Stanislavski's attempt to help the actor make a character believable or true, and exercises that are focused on the discovery of the hidden self, the invisible, and the communication of what is discovered with the entire body, often come up against the conditioning they want to avoid, and the assaulted audience often remains essentially passive. As Brook puts it, "There is eventually a need for authorship to reach the ultimate compactness and focus that collective work is almost obliged to miss" (*The Empty Space*, p. 32). The word, it seems, is still an essential means of imitating dramatic action, and the more successful improvisationally built plays still have a central action that they imitate, such as *The Serpent's* stated aim, "to reunderstand the whole territory of shame" in its retelling of Genesis (Joseph Chaikin, *The Presence of the Actor*, p. 95).

Ironically enough, the spontaneous, improvisational quality that many White avant-garde groups often strain for are the natural heritage of the Black theater movement in America. If Jerzy Grotowski has proclaimed the rich aesthetic and moral possibilities in a poor theater that strips away all but the actor and an available space, Black theater people have been so rigidly excluded from the possibilities of Broadway and technological developments in theater practice, as well as from publication, that they have continually made a virtue of necessity. Their music has sometimes come from washboards and trash cans because that was all there was. They have worked improvisationally in theater because improvisation was often all that was available to groups that disdained producing White drama.

Although some of the most successful Black playwrights, such as Lorraine Hansbury (*Raisin in the Sun*, 1959) and Lonne Elder III (*Ceremonies in Dark Old Men*, 1969), have created plays with conventional plot structures, many Black writers since Imamu Amiri Baraka (LeRoi Jones), like Ed Bullins and Sonia Sanchez, have claimed a Black aesthetic, focusing on drama by and for Black people. In a time of civil rights movements and Black militancy, such a theater inevitably has a political thrust; its goal is the arousal of its people to action and to thought. Much of the White experimental theater also has political thrust and tends to be thematic and didactic despite its belief in the power of the gesture over the word. However, the essential aim of the Black aesthetic movement is to return to the roots of the Black experience in order to meet the felt needs of the people. Even when earlier Black playwrights of the Harlem Renaissance in the 1920s, especially Langston Hughes, tried to recapture the ability to speak to their people in "Black English," the form and plots were loose, and spaces were left for dance or improvisation. Hughes's plays are presently being revived, and Black authors and companies such as Chicago's Kuumba and Harlem's New Lafayette Theater continue in their natural tradition to communicate in loosely structured plays that involve a good deal of improvisation.

Mary Ann Williams (1945–   ) is presently teaching in the Department of Black Studies at The Ohio State University. She is producer and moderator of the "Black Studies Broadcast Journal," a one-hour weekly radio program that offers interviews, lectures, debates, and performances and is coproducer and hostess of "Afromation," a half-hour weekly television program with similar content and a similar goal: to explore aspects of the Black experience. She has often experimented with the dramatization of poetry, her own and that of others, on radio, television, and in live performances, one of which was significantly titled "Black Poetry in Action."

If *Cinder, Tell-It* lacks some of the high seriousness of the experiments of the 1960s and 1970s, it attains quite lightly and ironically the natural sense of ceremony and celebration that some of the more ambitious groups so arduously seek. In her use of Black English, and in her return to her own roots in what is clearly autobiographical content, Mary Ann Williams in her first published play invites the audience to respond and share her experience, even as she invites the actor to respond and create or reshape that experience. "Only when we begin to share the thing of ourselves," the author noted in a recent interview, "so that we will know that our experience is a common one, will we broaden our humanity. It helps to know that others go through what we do; it helps with the whole necessity to survive." The necessity to survive in a mechanized, rapidly changing, uncertain world is what most concerns experimental groups, Black or White, even as the need to seek one's roots and oneself is as old as Oedipus. *Cinder, Tell-It* is an invitation to an audience, both Black and White, not to take off their clothes (a common practice of contemporary theater groups who would throw off the shackles of hypocrisy) but merely to take off their shoes and feel the earth.

Keep Your Shoes On, Lady

Keep your shoes on, Lady
think of your department, your community
your successors

Naw, man, they pinchin'
besides, thought
the flag, mother country, and
apple pie went
out with Nixon

Yes, but they came
back in with Ford
What about that
black mark on
your record?

Umm-hunh—
that's just what I was
thinkin' bout
Don't want de Devil to
take my soul

What about your future?
Jobs are hard to come
by

Naw, man, you wrong
Jobs come by ev'ry day
Gettin' one to stop is
de problem

Well, how you gonna eat?
You know we'll have
to readjust your salary

Eat w'd my fingers like
I used to. Even
rich people sop—
only they call it dunkin'

Sister, lemme tell ya
somethin'—
The mo' I talks to you
de mo' I'm
sho—

Dese shoes is pinchin'
my feet.
Believe I'll take 'em
off—
Say—do that make me a hippy?
(10/6/74)

Cinder, Tell-It

Now I must admit that I,
    unlike some ladies of my race,
    do not approximate
    a queen of the Nile

However, I do not find that sufficient justification
    for me to be in this predicament
    for such a long while—

Some folks very dear to me have
    likened my story to Cinderella
Even though my shade comes
    nowheres near white or even high yella—

The tale of this Cinder begins somewhere
    between twenty-eight and six thousand
    years ago
And like most tales this one will
    concentrate on the years of
        unforgettable woe:

Like when I hit the earth
    my mama lit out on an
    upper birth
Now that part ain't so sad
    'Cause me, Sis, and two bro's
    had one hell'u'va Dad

Our country pad, more roost than
    nest,
With a loving Dad who made us
    do our best
Though far apart, we hung together
    And somehow managed to brave the weather.

And then we went to a cracker school
    where they didn't believe in
    loud laughter, bid whiss,* or
        even shootin' pool
(As a matter of fact those folks
    didn't believe in nothin' black)
But don't you know they could
    get down † on the Golden Rule?

Name callin', bloody noses (in that order),
    Lord knows, was no bed of roses
And Pop in his raggedy, red truck,
    kept bouncin' to the school house
    to get through all that muck

---

* soulful bid whist—a card game.   † done to the max.

Meanwhile, back at the tobacco road
    castle,
    Umm—ummh—what a hassle!
Step-mothers! one, two, three, four, five—
    Naw man, I ain't jive!
How the battles did rage
    Four clowns determined not to
      share their stage
Honey, how we did perform
    Just one, ol' Hike did we respect
      enough to mourn
The sorrow of that great lady's passing
    is a memory for us—everlasting.

Feasts and famines came and went
    Looking back we now know those years
      were well spent
As the others felt the need to be free
    Dad and I pressed together
      knowing they had to flee
My life became the endless rows of
    dusty plowed ground,
And the passing trucks with their
    lonely growling sound
Kinda like Cinderella danglin'
    her feet in a stagnant moat
Man, I was sure I had missed
    the boat

And then came the Wicked Witch
Even Cindy's story did not create
    such a perfect bitch
I could not begin to compete with
    this flaming dragon,
So I decided it was time for me
    to hitch up my wagon

Off to a higher school
    to learn some more about the
    white folks version of the
    Golden Rule   .
This time
    no name callin'
      no bloody noses,
    Instead, a diff'rent
      set of poses
They called themselves the Society of Friends
    Meaning what they said,
      but not knowing where
        friendship begins
        and friendship ends

I slowly began to realize those
    "well-meaning" Friends
    hadn't done me
        no favor
By concocting a peaceful world-vision
    which poor Black folks
    could only sporadically
        savor

No wind whistling in through
    the cracks
And soft beds for all work-study students'
    aching backs
Yet three and one-half years of non-unionized
    factory labor
    with me steady movin' to pacify
        the company Simon Legree slaver
(This is the part where ol' Cindy
    and I can really identify
And new meaning comes into
    Rap's statement that violence is
        as American as apple pie!)

About time for my fairy god-mother
    to make the scene—
The ball of life was passin' me by
    and I was about to scream

Saw a sign that said "Study Year
    Abroad—*All* Students Welcome"
Now could this be a fraud?

My fairy god-mother turned out
    to have a husky voice
But that was cool with me
    'cause I figured I didn't have
        no choice

He said, "Cinder, where you want to go?"
    "To the Mountain top, Daddyo!"
    He said, "Forward-Ho!"

Scholarships, loans, and a
    breath of Swiss air
For one year, no more auto-coated,
    odor-laden hair

The ball was on, jim,
    and I was swinging
Even had a moment when I
    thought church bells would
        be ringin'

More German than the Germans,
More Swiss than the Swiss
Wasn't too much my strange talkin'
  family
Would let me miss

They made me so strong
  at the end of the year
No fear that anything
  could go wrong.

But—back in the U.S.A.
  those crackers had begun to pay
My colored brothers and sisters
  had turned Black overnight
Begun to fight for what they
  thought was right
The cry was "Burn, Baby, Burn"
  A new lesson
I had to learn

The hour of 12:00 was near
And I began to fear that the
  fool with the sledge hammer
Would beat me so bad that I
  couldn't even stammer

It was time to wave good-bye to Dad
  who I know went up into the sky,
And to the Society of Friends
  who, unknowingly, converted
   my passivity
    to violent ends

I began a rough ride
  with Aunt Ida by my side
In our '36 Chevy Pumpkin
We looked like two country bumpkins
We hit some rocky, rocky roads
  But she kept sayin' God would
   let none of them be closed
At ninety-two and a half
  She said, "Be strong, Baby,
   I'll meet you, bye and bye
    at the pass"

Ida, you were right as usual,
Travelin' life's roads has become
  much more casual

But what happened to that shiny,
  Black Knight who would by
   me always do right?

Man, you don't need no glass slipper,
    A platform shoe will do!
'Cause, Baby, I would give my life
    for you.

I think such an Ebony Knight
    would jell-it.
But that ain't never gonna
    happen to hear this
    Cinder, Tell-It!
    (3/6/73)

Willow Man

Willow Man
    moves with ease
        Bends, bows, just far enough
            to let determined winds pass,
                But never loses leaves

Willow Man
    Shoots skyward
        with right amount of
            coddling and warmth
                from life's rains

Willow Man
    Spreads his protective limbs
        to share sunlight with all
            struggling shoots
                nearby
    While quietly performing
        kaleidoscopic miracles
        to enfold tossed lives
            just beyond his
                cooling shade

Willow Man
    An intricate complexity of
        millions of delicate branches,
            thin pointed leaves, and
                tiny veins all pulsating
                    with quick determined
                      systematic movement

Willow Man
    Soaking up all nourishment
        from grassy park, cindered
            alley, whatever soil
                his roots may touch,
    While always returning beauty
        to the hurricane-prone
            world

Willow Man
    Merely by his self-pruned
       regal upward thrust
    Assures that at least
      One
              fortress of manhood
              will stand
                  tall and firm
        in Blackness
                during
                    any storm

For Kojo Kamau
(5/24/75)

Legacy

If ostriches never raised
    their heads from
    the sand, they
    would never know
    whose eggs they were
    laying

If scarecrows never
    took off their hats,
    they would never know
    what bird had alighted
    and if he were polite
    during his stay

If man did not let his
    loved ones hold him close,
    he would never get
    all the hurt squeezed
    out
    (12/31/74)

Cinder, Tell-It

A dance-drama for soulful folks

Characters

CINDER *Cinder, like her name, is coal black. She doesn't look half bad in her black leotards with red shoes and accessories, but she doesn't know it. She would think you jivin' if you tried to hip her to the fact.*

SISTER DO-RIGHT *Sister Do-Right is any of the proud, matronly Negro ladies seen Sunday mornings in church doin' right by everybody. God is the first word she learned and integration is the last. She wears a white deaconess cap, black wrap-around reversible skirt, the underside of which is red, black, and green. Her shoes are half black, half white. Sister Do-Right can strut her stuff when she has a mind to.*

WILLOW MAN *Willow Man is a together brother who knows what's happenin'. He's ragged down in green and black tights.*

Setting: This is how it is. More shoes than the nearest factory outlet lets out. Brogans, ankle-breaker platforms, combat boots, pointy toes, you name it, honey—they there, only no glass slipper. And since we tellin' stories, they hangin' (instead of us) on ropes and chains high and low, the leftovers on the floor.

> *When you get a mind to, yank off a shoe*
> *and take a swing*
> *or climb*
> *like they say we do.*

Music: Get out your bones, spoons, pots, pans—whatever you want, man. Add some chains, and while you're steady cookin', croon a tune and whistle Dixie. Just do it, Baby.

Lights: The mood is YOU.

SISTER DO-RIGHT

> Keep your shoes on, Lady   *(Cinder begins to re-*
> think of your department, your community   *move one shoe.)*
> keep your shoes on, Lady—on!   *(Sings this.)*

CINDER

> Now I must admit that I,
>   unlike some ladies of my race,   *(Shoe off.)*
>   do not approximate
>   a queen of the Nile
> However, I do not find that sufficient justification
>   for me to be in this predicament   *(Other shoe off.)*
>   for such a long while—

SISTER DO-RIGHT

> Your successors

CINDER

> Some folks very dear to me have
>   likened my story to Cinderella
> Even though my shade comes
>   nowheres near white or even high yella—

SISTER DO-RIGHT
   Keep your shoes on, Lady   *(Yanks shoe from*
  Think of your department, your community   *chain and tags after*
    your successors   *Cinder.)*

CINDER
    Naw, man, they pinchin'
      besides, thought
  the flag, mother country, and
     apple pie went
        out with Nixon

SISTER DO-RIGHT
  Yes, but they came
    back in with Ford

WILLOW MAN
  Willow Man   *(Rattles chains.)*
    moves with ease

SISTER DO-RIGHT
  What about that
     black mark on
  your record?

CINDER
  The tale of this Cinder begins somewhere
    between twenty-eight and six thousand
     years ago
  And like most tales this one will
    concentrate on the years of
      unforgettable woe:

WILLOW MAN
  Bends, bows, just far enough   *(Rattles chains.)*
    to let determined winds pass,
      But never loses leaves

SISTER DO-RIGHT
  What about that
     black mark on
  your record?

WILLOW MAN
  Willow Man
    Shoots skyward   *(Begins to climb*
      with right amount of   *rope.)*
       coddling and warmth
        from life's rains

SISTER DO-RIGHT
  On your record?

CINDER
  Like when I hit the earth
    my mama lit out on an
    upper birth
  Now that part ain't so sad   *(Moves to Willow*
    'cause me, Sis, and two bro's   *Man.)*
    had one hell'u'va Dad.

WILLOW MAN
  Willow Man
    Spreads his protective limbs

    to share sunlight with all
     struggling shoots
      nearby

                                           (Rattles chains.)

SISTER DO-RIGHT
  What about that
    black mark on
   your record?

                                           (Steady on Cinder's case to break up action with Willow Man.)

CINDER
  umm-hunh-
    that's just what I was
    thinkin' bout
  Don't want de Devil to
   take my soul

WILLOW MAN
   Spreads his protective limbs
     to share sunlight with all
      struggling shoots
       nearby
    While quietly performing
      kaleidoscopic miracles
       to enfold tossed lives
        just beyond his
        cooling shade

SISTER DO-RIGHT
  What about your future?
   Jobs are hard to come by

CINDER
  Naw, Sister Do-Right, you wrong
   Jobs come by ev'ry day
  Gettin' one to stop is
   de problem

SISTER DO-RIGHT
  Well, how you gonna eat?
   You know we'll have
    to readjust your salary

CINDER
  Our country pad, more roost than
   nest,
  With a loving Dad who made us
   do our best
  Though far apart, we hung together
   And somehow managed to brave the weather.

                                         (Cinder and Willow Man make roost with ropes.)

  And then we went to a cracker school
   where they didn't believe in
   loud laughter, bid whiss, or
    even shootin' pool
  (As a matter of fact those folks
   didn't believe in nothin' black
  But don't you know they could
   get down on the Golden Rule?)
  Name callin', bloody noses (in that order),
   Lord knows, was no bed of roses

                                         (Willow Man whistles "Dixie" throughout verse while Sister Do-Right does her "ain't this a shame" act.)

And Pop in his raggedy, red truck
    kept bouncin' to the school house
        to get through all that muck

WILLOW MAN
    An intricate complexity of
        millions of delicate branches,
            thin pointed leaves, and
                tiny veins all pulsating
                    with quick determined
                        systematic movement

SISTER DO-RIGHT
    Well, how you gonna eat?   *(Chains rattled*
        You know we'll have   *loud.)*
            to readjust your salary

CINDER
    Eat w'd my fingers like
        I used to. Even
        rich people sop—
        only they call it dunkin'

SISTER DO-RIGHT
    Think of your department, your community,   *(Punctuate by chain*
        your successors   *rattles.)*

CINDER
    Meanwhile, back at the tobacco road
        castle,
        Umm—ummh—what a hassle!
    Step-mothers! one, two, three, four, five—   *(Cinder plucks five*
        Naw, man, I ain't jive!   *shoes, while drums*
        How the battles did rage   *beat right on time.)*
            Four clowns determined not to
            share their stage
    Honey, how we did perform
        Just one, ol' Hike did we respect
            enough to mourn.
    The sorrow of that great lady's passing
        is a memory for us—everlasting

WILLOW MAN
    Bends, bows, just far enough   *(Piano.)*
        to let determined winds pass,
            But never loses leaves

SISTER DO-RIGHT
    Well, how you gonna eat?

CINDER
    Feasts and famines came and went
        Looking back we now know those years
            were well spent
    As the others felt the need to be free
        Dad and I pressed together
            knowing they had to flee

SISTER DO-RIGHT
    Keep your shoes on, Lady

CINDER

My life became the endless rows of
    dusty plowed ground,
And the passing trucks with their
    lonely growling sound
Kinda like Cinderella danglin'   (*Does it.*)
    her feet in a stagnant moat

SISTER DO-RIGHT

Keep your shoes on, Lady   (*Sings.*)

CINDER

Man, I was sure I had missed
    the boat
And then—

SISTER DO-RIGHT

Well, how you gonna eat?

WILLOW MAN

Willow Man
    Soaking up all nourishment
        from grassy park, cindered
        alleys, whatever soil
           his roots may touch,
    While always returning beauty
        to the hurricane-prone
           world

CINDER

Eat w'd my fingers like
    I used to

SISTER DO-RIGHT

Think of your department

CINDER

And then came the Wicked Witch   (*Indicates Sister Do-*
Even Cindy's story did not create   *Right.*)
    such a perfect bitch
I could not begin to compete with
    this flaming dragon
So I decided it was time for me
    to hitch up my wagon

SISTER DO-RIGHT

Keep your shoes on, Lady   (*Sings this while she*

CINDER   *puts shoes on Cin-*

Off to a higher school   *der.*)
    to learn some more abut the
    white folks' version of the
    Golden Rule
This time
    no name callin'
        no bloody noses,
    Instead, a diff'rent
        set of poses
They called themselves the Society of Friends   (*Sister does Do-*
    Meaning what they said   *Right act.*)
        But not knowing where

> friendship begins
> and friendship ends

I slowly began to realize those
    "well-meaning" Friends
    hadn't done me
        no favor
By concocting a peaceful world-vision
    which poor Black folks
    could only sporadically
        savor

WILLOW MAN
    Shoots skyward
SISTER DO-RIGHT
What about your future?
CINDER
No wind whistling in through
    the cracks
And soft beds for all the work-study
    students' aching backs
Yet three and one-half years of non-unionized
    factory labor
    with me steady movin' to
        pacify the company Simon Legree slaver.
(This is the part where ol' Cindy
    and I can really identify
And new meaning comes into
    Rap's statement that violence
        is as American as apple pie!)

WILLOW MAN
    Shoot skyward   *(Doin' it on ropes.)*
SISTER DO-RIGHT
What about your future?
CINDER
About time for my fairy god-mother
    to make the scene
WILLOW MAN
    Shoot skyward   *(Piano run or riff.)*
CINDER
The ball of life was passin' me by
    and I was about to scream
WILLOW MAN
    Move with ease   *(To Cinder.)*
CINDER
Saw a sign that said "Study Year
    Abroad—*All* Students Welcome"
Now could this be a fraud?
SISTER DO-RIGHT
Keep your shoes on, Lady.
CINDER
My fairy god-mother turned out   *(Willow Man be-*
    to have a husky voice   *comes god-father.*

But that was cool with me
    'cause I figured I didn't have
        no choice

WILLOW MAN
Cinder, where you want to go?

CINDER
    To the mountain top, Daddyo

WILLOW MAN
Forward-Ho!

CINDER
    Scholarships, loans, and a
        breath of Swiss air
For one year, no more auto-coated,
        odor-laden hair

WILLOW MAN
    An intricate complexity of
        millions of delicate branches,
            thin pointed leaves, and
                tiny veins all pulsating
                    with quick determined
                        systematic movement

CINDER
The ball was on, jim,
    and I was swinging
Even had a moment when I
    thought church bells would
        be ringin'

SISTER DO-RIGHT
What about that
    Black mark on
    your record?

CINDER
More German than the Germans,
More Swiss than the Swiss
Wasn't too much my strange talkin'
    family
Would let me miss
They made me so strong
    at the end of the year
No fear that anything
    could go wrong.

WILLOW MAN
    Shoot skyward

SISTER DO-RIGHT
What about that
    Black mark on
    your record?

CINDER
But—back in the U.S.A.
    those crackers had begun to pay
My colored brothers and sisters
    had turned *Black*—overnight

Turns Sister Do-
Right into a table on
which he and Cinder
sit.)

(Willow Man and
Cinder on rope
together.)

(Willow Man and
Cinder get down
with the "Bump" or
some other dance;
Sister Do-Right is
still meddlin'.)

(Piano riff.)

(Whistling Dixie,
drums, chains
Cinder takes off
shoes puts on com-
bat boots.)

Begun to fight for what they
    thought was right
The cry was "Burn, Baby, Burn"
    A new lesson
I had to learn

WILLOW MAN
Bends-bows-never loses leaves   (*Same piano riff as used for this line before*)

SISTER DO-RIGHT
Keep your shoes on, Lady

CINDER
The hour of 12:00 was near   (*Cinder takes off shoes.*)

SISTER DO-RIGHT
Keep your shoes on, Lady

CINDER
And I began to fear that the
    fool with the sledge hammer
Would beat me so bad that I
    couldn't even stammer

WILLOW MAN
    While always returning beauty
        to the hurricane-prone
            world—
    Shoot skyward   (*One high piano note.*)

CINDER
It was time to wave good-bye to Dad
    who I know went up into the sky,
and to the Society of Friends
    Who, unknowingly, converted
        my passivity
            to violent ends

WILLOW MAN
    While always returning beauty
        to the hurricane-prone
            world—
    Shoot skyward   (*One higher note.*)

SISTER DO-RIGHT
    You know we'll have   (*Becoming more soulful.*)
        to readjust your salary

CINDER
I began a rough ride   (*Cinder puts shoes on, then grabs Sister Do-Right—turns her into Aunt Ida and they ride ropes. Sister Do-Right doesn't entirely dig it.*)
    with Aunt Ida by my side
In our '36 Chevy Pumpkin
We looked like two country bumpkins
We hit some rocky, rocky roads
    But she kept sayin' God would
        let none of them be closed
At ninety-two and a half
    She said,
    "Be strong, Baby,
        I'll meet you, bye and bye
            at the pass."

SISTER DO-RIGHT
Well, how you gonna eat?

CINDER
Ida, you were right as usual,
    Travelin' life's roads has become
        much more casual
WILLOW MAN
    Shoot skyward   *(To Cinder.*
                                        Two notes.)
SISTER DO-RIGHT
    Keep your shoes on, Lady?
CINDER
    Sister Do-Right, lemme tell ya
           somethin'—
        The mo' I talks to you
        de mo' I'm
        sho
        Dese shoes is pinchin'
           my feet.
           Believe I'll take 'em   *(Kicks off shoes.)*
           off—
        Say—do that make me a hippy?
WILLOW MAN
        Shoot skyward—   *(To Cinder.*
                                        Two higher notes.)
CINDER
    But what happened to that shiny,
        Black knight who would by
           me always do right?
    Man, you don't need no glass slipper,
        A platform shoe will do!
    'Cause, Baby, I would give my life
        for you.
WILLOW MAN
        Shoot skyward—   *(Two even higher*
                                        notes.)
SISTER DO-RIGHT
    I think such an Ebony Knight
        would jell-it.
    But that ain't never gonna
        happen to hear this
        Cinder, Tell-It!
    Dese shoes is pinchin'   *(Takes off shoes.*
        my feet.   *Removes skirt and*
        Believe I'll take 'em   *drapes the red,*
        off—   *black, green side*
                                        around Willow
CINDER
    Willow Man   *Man's shoulders.)*
        Merely by his self-pruned
           regal upward thrust
        Assures that at least
           One
                fortress of manhood
              will stand
                  tall and firm
          in Blackness
               during
                  any storm

CINDER, SISTER DO-RIGHT AND WILLOW MAN (*Together.*)
>If ostriches never raised
>>their heads from
>>the sand,

WILLOW MAN
>>they would never know
>>whose eggs they were
>>laying

SISTER DO-RIGHT *and* CINDER
>Amen

ALL
>If scarecrows never
>>took off their hats,

SISTER DO-RIGHT
>>they would never know
>>what bird had alighted
>>and if he were polite
>>during his stay

WILLOW MAN *and* CINDER
>Amen!

ALL
>If man did not let his
>>loved ones hold him close,
>>he would never get
>>all the hurt squeezed out.
>Amen. Aaaaaamen!

(Willow Man en-
folds them in cape.)

(Freedom and unity
dance with all toes
hangin' out.)

Action analysis and performance suggestions

The entire play may be performed either as it is or reshaped from
the poems. The following suggestions are for the performance of the
given script.

DEFINING THE ACTIONS AND THE SUPEROBJECTIVE

Sister Do-Right's action is to get Cinder to put her shoes on, with all that
putting one's shoes on implies. She is worried about Cinder's worldly success, the black mark on her record, her blackness (note the touches of
white in Sister Do-Right's costume, which suggest her concern with White
expectations). Sister is concerned not only with appearances but also with
Cinder's survival, her soul, her job possibilities, and her successors. Hence
to get her to put her shoes on involves the larger action—to save her, her
people, and hence Sister herself.

Cinder's Cinderella story should not be a story but a search through
her past for the missing glass slipper, the princess she never was and
never will be. Her action is to take her shoes off, with all that this implies
in being herself and denying White standards. If Sister wants to help
Cinder survive by giving her advice about appearance, Cinder wants to
help herself survive by finding and being herself. She uses irony to protect herself from life's disappointments and tries to lay her story on Willow Man and Sister in order to defend herself from the restrictions of the

one and from the dangers that must surround her if she is to swing (literally on the ropes suggested for setting) with the other. Cinder finds the courage to embrace Willow Man, shoeless, and hence comes to accept herself as the Black princess, without slipper, that she is.

Willow Man's action is to make music with the chains (note the opening suggestion of chains as setting and musical source) that bind the three in order to set them all free. His effort is to shoot skyward, to protect others, and to nurture their growth with his strength and his love.

The actions of the three characters unite in the superobjective, to take your shoes off with that gesture's connotations, to free oneself, to swing as self. Shoeless, Willow Man offers the rope and his protective strength for swinging; Sister Do-Right, whose own shoes have been pinching, joins Cinder and Willow Man, all shoeless at the end.

OVERCOMING OBSTACLES

Sister Do-Right must overcome her anxieties about her survival as a Black in a White world and as a Black in a possibly White hereafter. Her major obstacle is the stereotype forced on her by experience, the white gloves she wears and the shoes that pinch.

Cinder's major obstacle is Sister Do-Right, another part of herself, who imposes White standards, stereotyped religious restrictions, and admonitions of the dangers of her own experience. Willow Man's obstacles are the chains that could bind, but out of which he shakes music, the ropes that could hang, but which he uses to soar skyward, and the countless shoes that could bind and stop his growth, over which he steps.

THE MAGIC IF AND THE GIVEN CIRCUMSTANCES

The circumstances are represented in the stage decor: chains, ropes, and shoes, the circumstances of enslavement, and of a White America that is alternately viciously cruel or patronizingly kind. More specifically, the circumstances are Cinder's biography, which reflects a changing world and the growth of a Black militancy. This militancy is foreign to the survival tactics of Sister Do-Right, who still exerts an influence from within the Black community, even as that new growing militancy confronts the dangers from without.

What IF, being Black, you had to survive in a White world that deprived you of your rights and imposed its own standards and forms on you? Would you have the courage to swing with Willow Man?

CLASSROOM ADAPTATIONS TO ARRIVE AT STYLE

Obviously few classrooms will permit the hanging of ropes and chains for the swinging suggested in the script. If they do, then by all means hang them, swing, and make music with the chains. Even if not hung, chains are a valuable source of sound or music and Sister Do-Right can shake them in warning, while Willow Man shakes them away. Shoes, however, are easily available. Let everyone in the class contribute theirs and distribute them around the playing area. If ropes and chains are not available for climbing and swinging, then be sure to arrange levels—tables or chairs will do—so that the actors can jump to and from the different elevations.

Since the play is a dance-drama, movement does not have to be literal. Willow Man can move in treelike measures or in the rhythms of jazz. He can easily assume all the roles in Cinder's life, moving in and out of them with ease, just as Sister can assume the various female roles that the action requires. The taking off and putting on of shoes need not coincide with the stage directions, and improvisational work with the shoes may lead to numerous uses of them in the action. Perhaps the actors should move through the audience, taking off and putting on the shoes of its members, Sister admonishing them, Cinder laying her story on them, Willow Man inviting them to swing. Generally the actors should find their own rhythms, repeat or rearrange lines, make music with whatever is available, and interact with the audience in any way that they wish.

The costume colors should be maintained since the colors of Black Liberation are red, green, and black. These colors are so distributed among the three characters, along with the white elements that Sister should take off at the end, that only in combination under the colors of the reverse side of Sister's skirt turned cape do they come together. This skirt, converted to a cape, may be used in numerous ways in a final, shoeless dance of celebration.

Glossary

ABSURDIST DRAMA

Plays written in the 1950s and 1960s by Eugene Ionesco, Samuel Beckett, Harold Pinter, Edward Albee, Jean Genet, and others have been labelled "absurdist" by Martin Esslin in *The Theatre of the Absurd*. While the playwrights are quite individual and do not form a school of writing, they do share a concern with the suffering of post–World War II humanity—a suffering derived from a feeling of existential anguish in the face of a universe that no longer makes sense. To explore this senselessness or absurdity, the dramatists employ antirealistic techniques, which originated in part in expressionism, surrealism, and vaudeville. Absurdist playwrights blend the tragic and the comic in a fashion that seems to be at the heart of the modern perspective.

ACTION

The word "drama" is a transliteration of the Greek word for "action." According to Aristotle (*Poetics*), action is that which a play imitates with all its elements—plot, character, thought, diction, song, and spectacle. Action springs specifically from character and thought. A play's action is not the physical movement of the actors; rather it is a kind of spiritual movement or process that is the goal of the psychic life of the play. See *Aristotle's six elements of drama, central action, superobjective.*

AGON

A portion of a Greek play devoted to a debate or verbal combat between two characters.

ANAGNORISIS

A recognition or a movement from ignorance to knowledge. See *tragedy.*

ARISTOTLE'S SIX ELEMENTS OF DRAMA

In his formal definition of tragedy, Aristotle discusses and analyzes six parts that "determine its [tragedy's] quality." However, many critics consider these parts to be the elements of *all* plays. In order of the importance assigned by Aristotle, the six elements of drama are: plot, character, thought, diction, song, and spectacle.

Plot The arrangement of incidents within a drama to achieve a particular effect; the basic form of a play's action; its "soul." The plot is organic and unified, showing one complete action with a beginning, a middle, and an end. According to Aristotle, plots in the best tragedies are complex, containing at least one *peripetia* or reversal of situation; they may also contain an *anagnorisis* or recognition involving the movement from ignorance to knowledge, and a *pathos* or scene of suffering which, in tragedy, involves death, doom, or destruction. Plots have two major sections: the complication leading to the turning point, and the dénouement showing how the plot unravels from that point to the ending.

Character Along with thought, that aspect of a plot from which the action arises. The qualities of the agents of the action make up their characters; those qualities are manifest in humanity's habitual activities. Tragedy represents people as better than they are, comedy as worse.

Thought Along with character, the matter out of which a play's action and plot are formed. Thought is closely associated with language, because thought is revealed through words as well as action, and it is used to prove statements of general truths. Some modern critics equate thought with "theme."

Diction Considered with song to be the medium of imitation, as opposed to the objects or matter of imitation (plot, character, thought) or the manner of imitation (spectacle). Diction is variously defined as the poet's arrangements of words; as appropriate verbal expression of the plot, character, and thought; or as the actor's art of delivery.

Song Involves the rhythm of speeches and the rhythm and melody of choral odes; it is the chief embellishment of tragedy. Song and diction constitute the media of imitation. Some modern critics treat the "poetic qualities" of plays as song.

Spectacle The manner of imitation; those production elements of a play, such as costume, setting, and sound effects, that appeal to the senses and the emotions. The effects of spectacle are considered more the work of the stage machinist than of the poet and are least important among the identifiable parts of a play.

ASIDE

A theatrical convention that permits a character to speak his or her thoughts to the audience, unobserved and/or unheard by other characters in the scene. See *convention*.

BOX SET

A type of setting having three continuous walls and a ceiling, and employed by nineteenth- and twentieth-century realists. The window, doors, and properties in box settings are practical in order to give the illusion of reality. The actors imagine a fourth wall to the box, a convention that the audience also accepts. Most box sets were designed for proscenium stages. See *convention, illusionistic, realism*.

CATHARSIS

The purgation of the emotions of pity and fear that Aristotle suggests is experienced by the members of the audience who view a tragedy and who are thereby purified; the end or purpose of a tragedy. The exact nature of the catharsis and of Aristotle's description of it is a matter of much critical debate.

CENTRAL ACTION

Another term for Aristotle's action or Stanislavski's superobjective; that action which all the elements of the play imitate and which includes all the lesser goals or actions of the play. See *action, superobjective*.

CHARACTER

See *Aristotle's six elements of drama*.

CHORUS

A word derived from the Greek word for "dance." In Greek drama, the chorus was a group of twelve to fifteen people, wearing masks, who sang or chanted verse to a musical accompaniment while performing dancelike movements. Members of the chorus often served as commentators of the action, usually voicing the traditional moral, religious, and social attitudes that the audience itself might hold or interpreting the moral and religious wisdom of the play. The chorus usually entered chanting an opening song, the *parados*, sang and danced *stasima* between episodes (an *episode* is that which takes place, literally, "between the odes" or songs of the chorus), and exited singing an *exode*. Aristotle thought the chorus should be regarded as an integral part of the action, as in the plays of Sophocles.

COMEDY

In contrast to tragedy, comedy implies a movement from potential disaster to happy consummation; it is generally characterized by lightness of style and objectivity of viewpoint rather than intensity of emotion. Aristotle believed that comedy evolved from the phallic songs in honor of Dionysius, and that it imitated characters who were lower than the moral norm—people who were not essentially bad, but were ludicrous by moral standards. The only extant examples of Greek Old Comedy are the plays of Aristophanes (c.465–c.400 B.C.), which are licentious satires on political events and personalities, and which contain obscenity, fantasy, and great lyric beauty. The other influential model for subsequent comedic forms is Greek New Comedy as translated and adapted by the Roman playwrights, Plautus and Terence. The originals, many of them by the Greek playwright Menander, are lost. The New Comic model, involving a boy-meets-girl-overcomes-obstacles-and-gets-girl formula, has been the more influential of the two forms on comedy through the ages. In all kinds of comedy, those elements in society that have obstructed release and freedom tend to give way, and are either excluded from or included in the final festivities, which often involve a wedding. Among the kinds of comedy that have evolved from the Greek models are romantic forms like *A Midsummer-Night's Dream,* comedies of wit like *Love for Love,* and farcical forms as diverse as *The Second Shepherds' Play* or *The Knack.* See *melodrama, tragedy.*

CONCENTRATION

The actor's focusing of attention on the specific demands of the moment, whether the demands involve something on stage, someone in the stage environment, or some inner thought or state of being. Constantin Stanislavski encouraged the actor to concentrate on very specific actions. See *action, objective, relaxation.*

CONVENTION

A customary, agreed upon departure from literal reality in the interest of artistic economy. Conventions are common agreements between audiences and playwrights (or theater workers) that concern the methods of depicting the action, such as invisibility, asides, the imaginary fourth wall, or a chorus.

CYCLE PLAY

See *mystery play.*

DECORUM

Derived from the Latin word meaning "fitting"; part of a literary doctrine whose roots in classical theory (Horace, *The Art of Poetry*) demand the use of a style appropriate to the subject or situation. Decorum was particularly emphasized in the Renaissance and neoclassical periods: Critics established rules of decorum to regulate the distinctions among literary genres and to determine appropriate styles for various subjects. From the viewpoint of neoclassical critics, Shakespeare's plays lack decorum because they mingle the comic and the tragic, permit violence on the stage, and mix poetry and prose in the diction, rather than reserving verse exclusively for the nobility and prose for the lowly.

DEUS EX MACHINA

Literally, "the god from the machine." The ancient Greeks often used the device of lowering a god mechanically onto the stage in order to resolve a play's dilemmas. The term is used for any device that resolves a complex dramatic situation arbitrarily or merely by means of exterior coincidence.

DICTION

See *Aristotle's six elements of drama.*

DIKE

According to the belief of the ancient Greeks, the tendency of the world to restore itself to balance after violent outbursts.

DITHYRAMB

A Greek hymn or narrative song honoring the god, Dionysius, and presented by a chorus; conjectured by Aristotle to be the origin of tragedy. See *chorus, tragedy.*

DRAMATIC IRONY

The word "irony" comes from the Greek word "eiron," which names the dissembler character in Greek comedy who pretends to know less than he does. All irony involves a discrepancy between what is asserted and what is the truth; dramatic irony occurs when the audience is apprised of a character's real situation but the character does not possess this knowledge. For example, in *Oedipus the King* the audience knows that if Oedipus continues his search it will lead him to find the reverse of all his expectations.

EXPRESSIONISM

A movement in art, and especially drama, arising in reaction to realism and naturalism; developed in the early twentieth century under the strong influence of the Swedish playwright, August Strindberg (1849–1912). It uses distorted stage settings, dislodged time sequences, and stylized dialogue to express subjective accounts of reality; it often dramatizes psychological states of mind and radical themes. See *naturalism, realism.*

FARCE

Low comedy, usually employing extremes of physical action and exaggeration. See *comedy.*

GIVEN CIRCUMSTANCES

The situation of a play, the setting in which it takes place, its social and economic milieu, its human relationships and pressures; the physical, moral, and environmental conditions of which Stanislavski advised the actor to be aware. The actor, Stanislavski held, could avoid false effects by imagining the given circumstances of a play and what it would be like to be in them. See *Magic IF*.

HISTRIONIC SENSIBILITY

The capacity to read a playscript as potential performance and to grasp its dramatic action. Coined by Francis Fergusson, histrionic sensibility was anticipated by a related concept, Aristotle's description in the *Poetics* of man's innate capacity to imitate.

HAMARTIA

A weakness, flaw, or error of judgment in an otherwise noble hero. *Hamartia* sometimes bears no relationship to moral character, and may describe only the workings of fate on a character. See *tragedy*.

HUBRIS

Excessive pride, often the *hamartia* in a tragedy. See *hamartia, tragedy*.

ILLUSIONISTIC

Pertaining to plays whose means of presentation emphasize attempts to mirror actual life as it might appear to an unseen observer; characterized by authentic costumes, set, lighting, sound, diction, and representation; realistic. See *realism, box set, naturalism, expressionism*.

LIAISON DES SCENES

Literally, the "joining of scenes"; in French neoclassical drama, the practice of maintaining at least one actor on stage at all times throughout an act so that the stage is never vacant; intended to increase the illusion of reality.

MAGIC IF

A term employed by Stanislavski to instruct the actor to imagine what it would be like to live in the milieu and circumstances of a given play. The IF used for such an imaginative effort is magical since the actor is invited to enter into the character's life, rather than forced to be the character.

MELODRAMA

Originated in eighteenth-century France to describe dramas using song and music to heighten emotion. Melodrama, in one sense, may describe all plays, neither comic (or farcical) nor tragic, in which expectations for the fates of the characters are suspended so that the audience is not certain that the characters who arouse sympathy will eventually be happy (as in comedy and farce) or that they will be miserable (as in tragedy). Many modern plays, such as *The Wild Duck* and *The Glass Menagerie*, are melodramatic in this sense. In its pejorative sense, melodrama refers to plays that sacrifice subtle action and character development to improbable, romantic, sensational, or exciting plots. Many plays of the eighteenth and nineteenth centuries fall into this category of melodrama.

MYSTERY PLAY

A term first applied in the eighteenth century to medieval cycle plays that dramatized humanity's history as seen through its Christian tradition. The term originated either in the plays' association with the guilds performing them (guilds shared the "mystery" of a craft) or in one derivation of the word "ministry." The cycles were playlets which together formed a unity and were usually based on Biblical narratives. Now usually called "Scriptural drama."

NATURALISM

An extreme form of realism that emphasizes a sordid and/or deterministic view of life. First appeared in France in the late nineteenth century in conjunction with the scientific revolution of the time. See *expressionism, realism, verisimilitude.*

NEOCLASSICISM

A literary movement of the seventeenth and eighteenth centuries that attempted to follow what were thought to be the practices of the ancients in their drama. Essentially, neoclassical drama demanded verisimilitude, "the appearance of truth," though the playwright was not to copy life but to reveal its ideal patterns or norms. Rules of dramatic construction were codified, such as the three unities, preservation of decorum, and so forth.

OBJECTIVE

A goal; in Stanislavski's terms life is a series of goals or objectives and the actor should designate these goals with infinitive phrases. See *superobjective.*

OBSTACLE

Those elements, both interior and exterior, that must be overcome if a character's objectives are to be reached. See *objective.*

ORCHESTRA

Literally, the "dancing place" of the Greek theatrical stage. Situated before the *skene* and partially surrounded by the semicircular auditorium, the circular orchestra was the primary acting area. In the earliest days of the theater it had an altar in its center to and from which the chorus danced. See *parados, skene.*

PARADOS

The entrance on either side of the Greek orchestra through which the chorus and possibly the actors entered and through which members of the audience entered to take their seats.

PERIPETIA

An Aristotelian critical term referring to a sudden change or reversal in the fortunes of the protagonist. See *tragedy.*

PLOT

See *Aristotle's six elements of drama.*

PROSCENIUM STAGE

A theater stage framed by an arch through which the audience views the play. The box-set staging techniques are associated with the proscenium stage. Depending on its shape and location relative to the audience seating, the apron or stage area in front of the proscenium can vary greatly; it was large in the seventeenth and eighteenth centuries, but small in the nineteenth century (the era of the box set). See *box set.*

REALISM

Relative to literature and drama, a loosely defined term describing efforts to portray truth by giving the illusion of life as it is lived; verisimilitude; relative to staging practices, illusionism. As a literary movement, realism arose in the nineteenth century in reaction to romanticism and to melodrama. However, almost all drama displays some realistic aspects since drama imitates action and life consists in action. See *box set, expressionism, illusionistic, naturalism, verisimilitude, vraisemblance.*

RELAXATION

According to Stanislavski, actors can attain tension-free bodies and minds by concentrating on specific goals or actions of the characters they play as well as by performing exercises. See *concentration, objective, superobjective.*

REVERSAL

See *peripetia.*

SKENE

A term for the stage house or scene building used in performances of Greek drama. It was originally a temporary structure for costume changes and property storage. Later it became a permanent façade and could represent a temple, palace, or house. Its three doors may have been used for entrances and exits. See *orchestra, parados.*

SPECTACLE

See *Aristotle's six elements of drama.*

SOLILOQUY

Speech of a single character who shares his or her thoughts with the audience.

SONG

See *Aristotle's six elements of drama.*

STYLE

The blending of form and content to produce the distinctive quality of a play.

SUPEROBJECTIVE

Stanislavski's term to designate the goal toward which all the lesser actions and objectives of the play move, sometimes called the spine of the play and similar in meaning to Aristotle's "action." Stanislavski recommended its statement in an infinitive phrase. See *action, central action, objective.*

THOUGHT
See *Aristotle's six elements of drama.*

TRAGEDY
According to Aristotle, tragedy is an imitation of an action involving a dramatic reversal of fortune (*peripetia*) for a hero whose fall from great heights is due partly to a flaw in character or error in judgment. The best tragic plots contain a recognition (*anagnorisis*) in which the hero perceives the nature of the error committed. Tragedy evokes emotions of pity and fear in the audience, which is purged by the experience (*catharsis*) or purified. There is much controversy among the critics about the elements of Aristotle's definition. In medieval times tragedy was defined more simply as a play with an unhappy ending; in modern times plays that relate the fall of a common individual are sometimes referred to as tragedies. See *anagnorisis, catharsis, peripetia.*

TRAGIC FLAW
See *hamartia, hubris.*

TYPOLOGY
The study of symbolic representation, particularly the origin and meaning of Scriptural types; in art, especially visual art, the study of symbolic significances and treatment; symbolism.

VERISIMILITUDE
The illusion of reality created in the minds of an audience. The means for achieving verisimilitude have changed through the ages according to contemporary visions of truth. Aristotle believed it was important to represent the probable, and neoclassicists sought to achieve a generalized psychological realism representing what they considered typical of human nature, rather than photographic realism of the particular.

VRAISEMBLANCE
French neoclassic idea of psychological probability, attained by following the unities of action, place, and time and other Horatian ideas of decorum. See *decorum, neoclassicism, verisimilitude.*

Suggestions for
Further Reading

Theory of Drama

·Abel, Lionel. *Metatheatre: A New View of Dramatic Form.* Hill and Wang,
    New York, 1963.
·Aristotle. *Aristotle's Poetics.* Translated by S. H. Butcher, edited by Francis
    Fergusson. Hill and Wang, New York, 1961.
·Artaud, Antonin. *The Theater and Its Double.* Translated by Mary Caroline
    Richards. Grove Press, New York, 1958.
·Auerbach, Erich. *Mimesis: The Representation of Reality in Western Literature.*
    Translated by W. R. Trask. Princeton University Press, Princeton,
    N.J., 1953.
·Bentley, Eric. *The Life of the Drama.* Atheneum, New York, 1966.
·Fergusson, Francis. *The Idea of a Theater.* Princeton University Press,
    Princeton, N.J., 1968.
·Frye, Northrup. *Anatomy of Criticism.* Princeton University Press, Prince-
    ton, N.J., 1957.
·Olson, Elder. *Tragedy and the Theory of Drama.* Wayne State University
    Press, Detroit, 1961.
·———. *The Theory of Comedy.* Indiana University Press, Bloomington,
    1968.
·Styan, J. L. *The Dark Comedy: The Development of Modern Comic Tragedy.*
    Cambridge University Press, Cambridge, 1962.

History of theater

·Brockett, Oscar G. *The Theatre: An Introduction,* 2d ed. Holt, Rinehart and
    Winston, New York, 1969.
·Brockett, Oscar G., and Robert R. Findlay. *A Century of Innovation: A His-
    tory of European and American Theatre and Drama 1870–1970.* Prentice-
    Hall, Englewood Cliffs, N.J., 1973.
·Gassner, John, and Ralph G. Allen. *Theater and Drama in the Making.*
    Houghton Mifflin, Boston, 1964.
·Gorelik, Mordecai. *New Theatres for Old.* Samuel French, New York, 1940.
·Nagler, A. M. *A Source Book in Theatrical History.* Dover Publications, New
    York, 1952.
·Slonim, Marc. *Russian Theater: From the Empire to the Soviets.* World Publish-
    ing, Cleveland, 1961.
·Southern, Richard. *The Seven Ages of the Theatre.* Hill and Wang, New
    York, 1961.

Performance of drama

ACTING AND DIRECTING
·Chaikin, Joseph. *The Presence of the Actor.* Atheneum, New York, 1972.
·Chekhov, Michael. *To the Actor.* Harper & Brothers, New York, 1953.
·Joseph, Bertram. *Acting Shakespeare.* Routledge & Kegan Paul, London, 1960.
·———. *The Tragic Actor.* Routledge & Kegan Paul, London, 1959.
·Saint-Denis, Michael. *Theatre: The Rediscovery of Style.* Theatre Arts Books, New York, 1969.
·Seyler, Athene, and Stephen Haggard. *The Craft of Comedy.* Theatre Arts Books, New York, 1946.
·Stanislavski, Constantin. *An Actor Prepares.* Translated by Elizabeth Reynolds Hapgood. Theatre Arts Books, New York, 1936.
·———. *Building a Character.* Translated by Elizabeth Reynolds Hapgood, Introduction by Joshua Logan. Theatre Arts Books, New York, 1949.
·———. *Creating a Role.* Translated by Elizabeth Reynolds Hapgood, Foreword by Robert Lewis. Theatre Arts Books, New York, 1961.
·———. *My Life in Art.* Translated by J. J. Robbins. World Publishing, Cleveland, 1956.

DESIGN, LIGHTING, AND COSTUMING
·Jones, Robert E. *The Dramatic Imagination.* Duell, Sloan & Pearce, New York, 1941.
·Laver, James. *Drama, Its Costume and Decor.* Viking Press, New York, 1951.
·McCandless, Stanley. *A Method of Lighting the Stage,* 4th ed. Theatre Arts Books, New York, 1958.
·Oxenford, Lynn. *Design for Movement.* Theatre Arts Books, New York, 1951.
·———. *Playing Period Plays.* J. Garnet Miller, London, 1957.
·Powell, Kenneth. *Stage Design.* Reinhold Publishing, New York, 1968.
·Selden, Samuel, and Hunter P. Sellman. *Stage Scenery and Lighting,* 3d ed. Appleton Century Crofts, New York, 1959.
·Simonson, Lee. *The Stage Is Set.* Harcourt Brace Jovanovich, New York, 1932.

Criticism of drama

SOPHOCLES: OEDIPUS THE KING
·Jaeger, Werner. *Paideia: The Ideals of Greek Culture.* Translated by Gilbert Highet. 3 vols. Oxford University Press, New York, 1939–1944.
·Kitto, H. D. F. *Greek Tragedy,* 3d rev. ed. Barnes & Noble, New York, 1966.

THE WAKEFIELD MASTER: THE SECOND SHEPHERDS' PLAY
·Gardner, John. *The Construction of the Wakefield Cycle.* Southern Illinois University Press, Carbondale, 1974.
·Nelson, Alan H. "Some Configurations of Staging in Medieval English Drama." In *Medieval English Drama: Essays Critical and Contextual,* edited by Jerome Taylor and Alan H. Nelson, pp. 116–147. University of Chicago Press, Chicago, 1972.

·Rose, Martial, ed. *The Wakefield Mystery Plays.* Norton Library, New York, 1969.
·Ross, Lawrence J. "Symbol and Structure in the *Secunda Pastorum.*" In *Medieval English Drama: Essays Critical and Contextual,* edited by Jerome Taylor and Alan H. Nelson, pp. 177–211. University of Chicago Press, Chicago, 1972.
·Watt, Homer A. "The Dramatic Unity of the 'Secunda Pastorum.'" In *Essays and Studies in Honor of Carleton Brown,* pp. 158–166. New York University Press, New York, 1940.

WILLIAM SHAKESPEARE: A MIDSUMMER-NIGHT'S DREAM AND OTHELLO
·Barber, C. L. *Shakespeare's Festive Comedy.* Meridian Books, New York, 1963.
·Bradley, A. C. *Shakespearean Tragedy.* 1905. Reprint. Fawcett World, Greenwich, Conn., n.d.
·Chapman, Gerald W., ed. *Essays on Shakespeare.* Princeton University Press, Princeton, N.J., 1965.
·Fergusson, Francis. "Macbeth as the Imitation of an Action." In *The Human Image in Dramatic Literature.* Anchor Books, Doubleday & Company, Garden City, N.Y., 1957.
·———. *Shakespeare: The Pattern in His Carpet.* Delacorte Press, New York, 1949.
·Guillamet, Leon. "*A Midsummer-Night's Dream* as an Imitation of an Action." *Studies in English Literature 1500–1900,* 15, No. 2 (Spring 1975), 257–271.
·Harbage, Alfred. *William Shakespeare: A Reader's Guide.* Octagon Books, New York, 1971.
·Kernan, Alvin B. "*Othello:* An Introduction." In *The Tragedy of Othello,* edited by Alvin B. Kernan. New American Library, New York, 1963.

JEAN RACINE: PHAEDRA
·Knapp, Bettina L. *Jean Racine: Mythos and Renewal in Modern Theater.* The University of Alabama Press, University, 1971.
·Weinberg, Bernard. *The Art of Jean Racine.* University of Chicago Press, Chicago, 1963.

WILLIAM CONGREVE: LOVE FOR LOVE
·Fujimura, Thomas H. *The Restoration Comedy of Wit.* Princeton University Press, Princeton, N.J., 1952.
·Holland, Norman H. *The First Modern Comedies.* Indiana University Press, Bloomington, 1959.
·Novak, Maximillian. *William Congreve.* Twayne's English Authors Series. Twayne Publishers, New York, 1971.

HENRIK IBSEN: THE WILD DUCK
·Fjelde, Rolf, ed. *Ibsen: A Collection of Critical Essays.* Twentieth-Century Views Series. Prentice-Hall, Englewood Cliffs, N.J., 1965.
·Herberg, Hans. *Ibsen: A Portrait of the Artist.* Translated by Joan Tate. University of Miami Press, Coral Gables, Fla., n.d.
·Horton, Orley. *Mythic Patterns in Ibsen's Last Plays.* University of Minnesota Press, Minneapolis, 1970.
·Hurt, James. *Cataline's Dream: An Essay on Ibsen's Plays.* University of Illinois Press, Urbana, 1972.

·Meyer, Hans Georg. *Henrik Ibsen.* Frederick Ungar Publishing, New York, 1972.
·Meyer, Michael L. *Ibsen: A Biography.* Doubleday, Garden City, N.Y., 1971.
·Northam, John. *Ibsen: A Critical Study.* Cambridge University Press, Cambridge, 1973.

ANTON CHEKHOV: THE CHERRY ORCHARD
·Chekhov, Anton. *The Seagull and Other Plays.* Edited by Elisaveta Fen. Penguin Books, London, 1954.
·Garnett, Constance. *Letters of Anton Chekhov to His Family and Friends.* Macmillan, New York, 1970.
·Jackson, Robert Louis, ed. *Chekhov: A Collection of Critical Essays.* Twentieth-Century Views Series. Prentice-Hall, Englewood Cliffs, N.J., 1967.
·Magarshack, David. *The Real Chekhov: An Introduction to Chekhov's Last Plays.* Barnes & Noble, New York, 1972.
·Pitcher, Harvey. *The Chekhov Play: A New Interpretation.* Barnes & Noble, New York, 1973.

TENNESSEE WILLIAMS: THE GLASS MENAGERIE
·Falk, Signi Lenea. *Tennessee Williams.* Twayne's United States Authors Series. Twayne Publishers, New York, 1961.
·Weales, Gerald. *Tennessee Williams.* University of Minnesota Pamphlets on American Writers. University of Minnesota Press, Minneapolis, 1965.

ANN JELLICOE: THE KNACK
·Anderson, Michael, *et al.,* eds., *Crowell's Handbook of Contemporary Drama.* Thomas Y. Crowell Company, New York, 1971, pp. 266–268.
·Corrigan, Robert W. *The Theatre in Search of a Fix.* Dell Publishing, New York, 1973, pp. 305–308.
·Jellicoe, Ann. Preface to *Shelley or The Idealist.* Faber & Faber, London, 1966, pp. 13–20.
·———. *Some Unconscious Influences in the Theatre.* The Judith Wilson Lecture, 1967. Cambridge University Press, Cambridge, 1967.
·Taylor, John Russell. "Ann Jellicoe." In *The Angry Theatre: New British Drama.* Hill and Wang, New York, 1962.
·Wakeman, John, ed. *World Authors 1950–1970.* H. W. Wilson Company, New York, 1975, pp. 717–719.

HAROLD PINTER: A SLIGHT ACHE
·Burkman, Katherine. *The Dramatic World of Harold Pinter: Its Basis in Ritual.* The Ohio State University Press, Columbus, 1971.
·Esslin, Martin. *The Theater of the Absurd.* Doubleday & Company, Garden City, N.Y., 1961.

MARY ANN WILLIAMS: CINDER, TELL-IT
·Brockett, Oscar G. *Perspectives on Contemporary Theatre.* Louisiana State University Press, Baton Rouge, 1971.
·Brook, Peter. *The Empty Space.* Avon Books, New York, 1968.
·Croyden, Margaret. *Lunatics, Lovers and Poets: The Contemporary Experimental Theatre.* McGraw–Hill, New York, 1974.
·Gayle, Addison, Jr., ed. *The Black Aesthetic.* Anchor Books, Doubleday & Company, Garden City, N.Y., 1972.

·Grier, William H., and Price M. Cobbs. *Black Rage.* Bantam Books, New York, 1968.
·Mitchell, Loften. *Black Drama: The Story of the American Negro in the Theatre.* Hawthorn Books, New York, 1967.
·Schevill, James. *Break-Out! In Search of New Theatrical Environments.* The Swallow Press, Chicago, 1973.
·*Tulane Drama Review,* Vol. 12, No. 4. Issue devoted to Black Theater.

Teaching drama through performance

·Auburn, Mark S., Katherine H. Burkman, and Mildred B. Munday. "Classroom Performance in the Teaching of Dramatic Literature: Some Observations on an Experiment." *New Directions in Teaching,* 4, No. 3 (Summer 1974), 10–19.
·Gilbert, Miriam. "Teaching Dramatic Literature." *Educational Theatre Journal,* 25, No. 1 (March 1973), 86–94.